The Educator's Guide to Autism Spectrum Disorder

Interventions and Treatments

For Educators, By Educators

Edited by

Kaye L. Otten

Sonja R. de Boer

Leslie Ann Bross

CORWIN

FOR INFORMATION:

Corwin
A SAGE Company
2455 Teller Road
Thousand Oaks, California 91320
(800) 233-9936
www.corwin.com

SAGE Publications Ltd.
1 Oliver's Yard
55 City Road
London EC1Y 1SP
United Kingdom

SAGE Publications India Pvt. Ltd.
Unit No 323-333, Third Floor, F-Block
International Trade Tower Nehru Place
New Delhi 110 019

SAGE Publications Asia-Pacific Pte. Ltd.
18 Cross Street #10-10/11/12
China Square Central
Singapore 048423

Vice President and
  Editorial Director: Monica Eckman
Publisher: Jessica Allan
Senior Content
  Development Editor: Lucas Schleicher
Associate Content
  Development Editor: Mia Rodriguez
Editorial Assistant: Natalie Delpino
Project Editor: Amy Schroller
Copy Editor: Diane DiMura
Typesetter: C&M Digitals (P) Ltd.
Proofreader: Lawrence W. Baker
Indexer: Integra
Cover Designer: Rose Storey
Marketing Manager: Olivia Bartlett

Printed in the United States of America

ISBN 9781071838778

This book is printed on acid-free paper.

23 24 25 26 27 10 9 8 7 6 5 4 3 2 1

Contents

Introduction

Section 1: Behavioral Interventions   43

Preface

· ·

Dr. Richard L. Simpson was a leader in the evidence-based practices (EBPs) movement regarding educating students with autism spectrum disorder (ASD) from the beginning (Juane Heflin & Simpson 1998a and b; Simpson 2005). His passion for this subject and serving students with ASD led to the writing and 2005 publication of *Autism Spectrum Disorders: Interventions and Treatments for Children and Youth*–the first review and rating system employed regarding interventions for individuals with ASD. Many researchers have built on this work and the work of others to develop a much more rigorous process for identifying EBPs for use with individuals with ASD. This guide is an effort to promote the full understanding and appropriate application of this collective work in order to guide the daily decisions made by educators on the front lines of daily serving students with ASD in schools. This collaboration of authors consisted of practitioners who all are currently working or have extensive experience working in educational settings serving students with ASD. Three were also authors on the 2005 Simpson seminal publication, others have doctorate degrees in special education, are currently pursuing their doctorate in special education or a closely related field, and/or are Board Certified Behavior Analysts (BCBAs). This make-up of authors is uniquely qualified to contribute a valuable perspective that will help continue to advance the EBP movement with individuals with ASD in truly identifying not only what interventions work but for whom and under what conditions. Having such a diverse group of authors also results in various voices and styles, which is to be expected. The ultimate result of this resource will hopefully be maximizing the benefit of educational services for students with ASD, which will bode well for their quality of life and the lives of their loved ones.

About the Editors and Authors

Kaye Otten, PhD, BCBA

Kaye Otten has a doctorate from the University of Kansas in special education with an emphasis in emotional, behavioral, and autism spectrum disorders and is a board-certified behavior analyst with Summit Behavioral Services specializing in school-based services. She provides collaborative coaching to school districts in developing evidence-based multi-tiered systems of behavioral support and serves as an adjunct faculty member with The Mandt System, an international leader in crisis prevention and intervention. Kaye has over 30 years of experience in public and private schools as a general and special educator and behavioral consultant and has experience working with all ages, ability levels, and disability categories. She is the co-author of the book *How to Reach and Teach Children With Challenging Behavior: Practical Ready-to-Use Strategies That Work* and the online professional development courses *Managing Challenging Behavior: Part 1–Antecedent Strategies* and *Part 2–Consequence Strategies* provided by Exceptional Child of Vector Solutions.

Sonja de Boer, PhD, BCBA-D

Sonja R. de Boer is a Board Certified Behavior Analyst-doctoral (BCBA-D) and obtained her PhD in special education and psychology and research in education at the University of Kansas, with an emphasis on early intervention for children with autism spectrum disorders (ASD). Richard Simpson was her advisor through her doctorate program. She was one of the earliest to receive her BCBA in 2000 and has approximately 30 years of experience working in early childhood special education, early intervention services, Applied Behavior Analysis (ABA), with students with disabilities, and specifically children with ASD. For children with ASD, she has designed and supervised in-home intervention programs (ages 0 to 10), preschool programs (ages 3 to 6; both intensive ABA and inclusive preschools), as well as elementary school educational and behavioral programs (ages 5 to 12).

For more than half of her career, she has focused on serving students with ASD and their families and educators in rural communities. She is currently a faculty member for Tufts University Medical Center in Child Psychiatry and provides training and consultation around the nation regarding interventions for children with ASD. Besides the United States, she has worked with professionals, universities, nonprofit organizations and families with children with ASD and other disabilities in Australia, New Zealand, Ireland, Russia, Nigeria, China, Chile, Abu Dhabi, and Dubai. She is the author of the book *Successful Inclusion Practices for Children With Autism: Creating a Complete, Effective, ASD Inclusion Program* (currently being revised and updated for publication); *Discrete Trial Training*, 2nd edition (part of the How To Series on Autism Spectrum Disorders); and is one of the original co-authors of the first edition of *Autism Spectrum Disorders: Interventions and Treatments for Children and Youth* written with Richard Simpson in 2005.

Leslie Bross, PhD, BCBA-D

Leslie Bross is an assistant professor of special education in the Department of Special Education and Child Development at the University of North Carolina (UNC) at Charlotte. She serves as the director of the Graduate Certificate in Autism Spectrum

Disorder (ASD) program at UNC Charlotte. Leslie earned her doctoral degree from the University of Kansas in 2019 with an emphasis in evidence-based practices and ASD. Her primary research interest is examining ways to support individuals with ASD during their transition to adulthood in the areas of postsecondary education, competitive employment, and community integration. Prior to her experiences in higher education, Leslie was a special education teacher for 6 years in Lee's Summit, Missouri. She taught social skills for secondary students with ASD and established a community-based employment program. She also taught English as a second language in Nagasaki, Japan, and Barcelona, Spain.

About the Contributing Authors

Ashley Anderson, MEd

Ashley Anderson is a doctoral student at the University of North Carolina (UNC) at Charlotte. She has an MEd in special education from UNC Charlotte and a bachelor's in special education from Western Carolina University. She has 10 years of experience in the classroom serving students with extensive support needs. Her research interests include supporting students with extensive support needs, communication, early transition-based skill learning, and community-based instruction.

Mariah Chavez

Mariah Chavez is currently an elementary school special education teacher on the central coast of California. Before her time in the classroom, Ms. Chavez attended California Polytechnic State University as a Teaching for Inclusivity & Equity Residency (TIER) scholar. During her time at Cal Poly, Mariah worked as a graduate research assistant on a federally funded grant to develop technology-delivered self-monitoring tools for students with autism.

Amy Clausen, PhD

Amy Clausen earned a doctorate in special education from the University of North Carolina at Charlotte. She is an instructor of special education and the director of the Think College program at Winthrop University. Prior to earning her doctorate, Amy was a classroom teacher of 7th and 8th grade students with autism for 2 years and served as a curriculum and behavior specialist for 3 years. Amy's research interests include general curriculum access for students with extensive support needs and preparing teachers to support all students in inclusive settings.

Stephen Crutchfield, PhD

Stephen Crutchfield is currently an associate professor of special education at California Polytechnic State University in San Luis Obispo, California. Dr. Crutchfield's current research interests include technology-delivered self-management and self-monitoring supports for students with autism. He completed his doctoral program at the University of Kansas. Before his graduate work, Dr. Crutchfield worked as a classroom teacher for 5 years, primarily providing services to students with autism and their families in elementary and middle school programs.

Theresa Earles-Vollrath, PhD, BCBA

Theresa Earles-Vollrath completed her MSE and doctorate at the University of Kansas in special education with an emphasis in emotional, behavioral, and autism spectrum disorders. She is currently a professor of special education at the University of Central Missouri where she teaches courses in special education law, behavior management, severe developmental disabilities, and autism. Theresa is also a Board Certified Behavior Analyst (BCBA) and has over 30 years of experience working in public schools as a teacher of students with autism, a teacher of students with intellectual disabilities, an autism specialist, and autism/behavioral consultant. Theresa was also a director of an autism resource center at the University of Kansas. Theresa has authored numerous articles, book chapters and books including being a co-author of *Visual Supports,* second edition *(Pro-Ed Series on Autism Spectrum Disorders)* and *How to Write and Implement Social Scripts,* first edition *(Pro-Ed Series on Autism Spectrum Disorders).*

Janet Enriquez, MS, BCBA

Janet Sanchez Enriquez is a bilingual Board Certified Behavior Analyst and doctoral student at the University of North Carolina (UNC) at Charlotte. Janet has over 15 years of experience supporting families and professionals in various settings in school districts and community organizations across the United States and Latin America. Prior to being a doctoral student, she provided technical assistance and professional development to 53 public school districts across 19 counties in South Texas. She serves on the Board of Directors for World Behavior Analysis Day Alliance and is the co-chair of the International Affairs Committee. Additionally, she is a founding member and secretary of the Mexican Organization of Practitioners of Applied Behavior Analysis (OMPAC). She strives to work alongside vulnerable and diverse populations to promote applied behavior analysis for teaching and learning through research and the development of culturally and linguistically diverse verbal behavior assessments and interventions.

Melanie Harms Espeland, PhD

Melanie Harms Espeland has a doctorate from the University of Kansas in special education with an emphasis in emotional, behavioral, and autism spectrum disorders and is a Board Certified Music Therapist. After 15 years in higher education, Dr. Espeland has returned to the public schools to provide social, emotional, and behavioral programming at the elementary level. She continues her private music therapy business, CADENCE, as well as teaching research methods and music appreciation online for Waldorf University. Recent contributions on the *Virtual Reality Opportunities to Implement Social Skills, VOISS Advisor*, re-inspired her research interests to include music-mediated interventions on self-regulation, music as an antecedent-based intervention on acquisition and retention of skills, implications of memory on reinforcement effectiveness, virtual reality and executive functioning, and cross-setting coaching for peers, parents, teachers, and community.

Birdie Ganz, PhD, BCBA-D

Birdie Ganz has been a professor of special education at Texas A&M University since 2008 and has provided services for individuals with autism and their families since 1996, as a teacher, consultant, behavior analyst, and project director/principal investigator. Their research focuses on working with natural communication partners to improve communication in individuals with autism.

Trudy Georgio, BCBA

Trudy Georgio is a special education doctoral student at Texas A&M University and a board-certified behavior analyst. Trudy has over 12 years of experience providing behavior support services in the home, school, clinic, and community settings. She is the founder of Tru Behavior Development, LLC, a consultation and training service grounded in the science of behavior. Trudy specializes in teaching language to students with autism spectrum disorders and mentoring students and practitioners of applied behavior analysis.

Matthew Klein, MEd

Matthew Klein is a doctoral student in educational psychology at Texas A&M University in the special education division. He holds a bachelor's degree in collaborative special education with a minor in social welfare from the University of Alabama. He earned his master's in education from the University of La Verne in California where he completed his master's research on parents' observations of changes in literacy routines and social behaviors of their children with autism during the COVID-19 pandemic. He worked as a classroom teacher in autism transition programs and in early childhood programs, as well as an itinerant educational specialist.

Paul LaCava, PhD

Paul LaCava is an associate professor of special education at Rhode Island College (RIC) in Providence where he teaches courses in elementary/special education, autism spectrum disorder (ASD) and research methods. He also directs RIC's Certificate of Graduate Study in Autism Education and Exceptional Learning Needs Master's programs. Paul has over 30 years of experience working in the field of autism/developmental disabilities as an educator, social skills group leader, respite provider, consultant, and researcher. His research focus has been on autism history, evaluating various methods to improve social/emotional outcomes, technology, and evidence-based practices. Paul has a bachelor's degree in history from Central Connecticut State University where he received his initial training in teaching and disabilities. Paul's master's and doctorate degrees in special education are from The University of Kansas.

Lindsey Loflin, MA, BCBA

Lindsey Loflin is a doctoral student at Texas A&M University studying educational psychology with an emphasis in special education. She worked in public schools for 10 years as a classroom teacher, interventionist, and instructional coach. After earning her master's from Sam Houston State University in special education, she became a Board Certified Behavior Analyst and has since provided behavioral support services in the home, school, clinic, and community settings. Lindsey is interested in the use of applied behavior analysis in school settings and has provided paraprofessionals and teachers professional development on preventing and responding to disruptive behaviors.

Lane Maxcy, PhD

Lane Maxcy has a doctoral degree from the University of Mississippi with an emphasis in emotional and behavioral disorders. Lane is currently an assistant professor at the University of Central Missouri in the Department of Career, Technical, and Special Education. Prior to training future teachers, Lane had 5 years of elementary teaching experience. Her research interests involve technology-based interventions for students with emotional and behavioral disorders in the general education classroom.

Catherine Tobin McDermott, MSEd, MEd

Catherine (Katie) Tobin McDermott is a transition coach who supports autistic young adults with their plans after high school, primarily focusing on transition to college and college success. A proud graduate of Boston College and the University of Kansas, she has graduate degrees in special education with a focus on autism spectrum disorder. Katie has worked as a classroom teacher for 13 years, student support specialist for college students, and transition coordinator at a high school for autistic students. She participates as a practitioner in the College Autism Network and her research is published in *Teaching Exceptional Children* and the *Journal of Autism and Developmental Disorders*.

Sabrina Mitchell, PhD, BCBA

Sabrina Mitchell holds a master's degree in special education with an emphasis in violent and aggressive behaviors and a doctorate of philosophy in special education with an emphasis in autism from the University of Kansas as well as certification as a Board Certified Behavior Analyst. She has been teaching and working in the area of special education for 23 years working as a special education teacher and autism/behavior consultant serving students with various disabilities from early childhood to 21 in public schools. In addition, Dr. Mitchell is the owner and an instructor at Authentic Connections, LLC, which provides social skills instruction and support groups for neurodiverse individuals in ages middle school through young adulthood.

Mary Beth Patry, PhD, BCBA

Mary Beth Patry has a PhD in early childhood special education from the University of Kansas with a specific focus on children with autism. Prior to pursuing her doctorate, Mary Beth was an autism and behavior specialist and an educator of children with autism in Kansas and Missouri school districts. Mary Beth earned her masters of science in education (MSEd) at The University of Kansas in 2007 and her BCBA certification in 2013.

Mary Beth has extensive experience supporting the language, play, and social skills of children with developmental delays using a variety of strategies including early and intensive behavioral interventions, verbal behavior interventions, peer-mediated interventions, discrete trial teaching, naturalistic behavior interventions, functional communication training, and more. She has published multiple peer-reviewed articles related to interventions for children with autism and has provided numerous professional development trainings to educators on the implementation of these strategies.

Monique Pinczynski, MEd, BCBA

Monique Pinczynski is a first-generation doctoral student at the University of North Carolina (UNC) at Charlotte in special education. She was previously a classroom teacher in Henderson, Nevada, for 5 years where she taught students with extensive support needs, autism, and learning disabilities. Monique earned her BS and MEd in special education at the University of Nevada Las Vegas, where she also attained her Board Certified Behavior Analyst certification. Her research interests include implementing evidence-based practices with students with autism and extensive support needs with a focus on communication as well as supporting teachers in this area.

Lisa Robbins, PhD

Lisa Robbins is a professor and chair of the Department of Career, Technical and Special Education at the University of Central Missouri. She has been working in the field of special education for 40 years—22 years in higher education and 18 years in public education and has taught almost all areas of special education. She has published and presented, nationally and internationally, on various topics related to autism spectrum disorders, and has been providing autism and behavioral consulting to families and school districts for 30 years.

Jessica Rousey

Jessica Rousey is a doctoral student in special education at the University of North Carolina (UNC) at Charlotte. Her primary research interests include secondary transition and supports for young adults with intellectual and developmental disabilities. Prior to beginning her doctoral studies, Jessica was a public school special education teacher for 2 years and also taught college students with disabilities in an inclusive postsecondary education program for 3 years. Jessica is a graduate research assistant with the National Technical Assistance Center on Transition: The Collaborative (NTACT:C) and also currently serves as the editorial assistant for *Career Development and Transition for Exceptional Individuals* (CDTEI).

Paula Williams, MSEd

Paula Williams is a third-year special education doctoral student at the University of North Carolina (UNC) at Charlotte. Paula earned her bachelor's (1992) and master's (2000) degrees from Western Carolina University. Her primary research interest is in learning how schools can more effectively promote family engagement and advocacy for students with disabilities. Paula has 30 years of experience in education including as a special education teacher, school administrator, and in district leadership positions. In addition to her current job with Charlotte-Mecklenburg Schools, she also works for UNC Charlotte as an adjunct professor in the teacher education program.

About the Authors of the Practitioner Testimonials

Brooke Bailey, MS, BCBA

Brooke Bailey has a bachelor's degree in special education and a master's in behavior analysis and therapy and is a Board Certified Behavior Analyst. For the past 6 years, she has taught in an elementary special education program focusing on teaching communication, language, and social skills using applied behavior analysis. She also works for an overnight camp for kids ages 8 to 18 with ASD, Camp Encourage, as a behavior specialist. She has been on staff with Camp Encourage for 1 year and previously volunteered for 5 years.

Teri Berkgren, MS, BCBA, CCC-SLP

Teri Berkgren has 29 years of experience in education as an SLP, preschool teacher, autism and low-incidence consultant, TASN ATBS regional autism consultant, master teacher and presenter, autism specialist, and autism and behavior instructional coach. She is currently the autism and behavior instructional coach for WCKSEC/USD 489 in Hays, Kansas, and provides itinerant support in all types of classroom settings in 25 rural school districts in western Kansas. Teri received the Outstanding Educator of Students with Autism Award from the Midwest Symposium of Leadership in Behavior Disorders at the Richard L. Simpson Conference on Autism in 2021.

Tracie Betz, MEd

Tracie Betz has been a special education teacher for the past 21 years in the Quinter School District. Thirteen of those years were in a preschool setting and the last 8 have been as an elementary special education teacher. Through her experiences, she has had the opportunity to work in a variety of settings including inclusion, resource, and self-contained. Tracie is also a member of the NKESC autism team. She received her master's in early childhood special education, bachelor's in elementary education, and endorsements in early childhood and K–12 adaptive special education.

Ben Harder, MS, CCC-SLP/L

Ben Harder is a licensed speech-language pathologist who has been a practicing clinician for the last 8 years. Ben earned his bachelor's degree from the University of Nebraska-Lincoln in May 2013 and master's degree in speech-language pathology from Rockhurst University in May 2015. Ben holds a Certificate of Clinical Competence from the American Speech-Language-Hearing Association (ASHA), a Nebraska teaching certification, and licensure in the state of Nebraska. Ben earned a graduate certificate from Bowling Green State University in December 2020 specializing in assistive technology and special education. Ben currently is employed by ESU #3/Brook Valley Schools in La Vista, Nebraska, serving students with complex support needs in a self-contained Level 3 setting.

Kelli Heller, MEd

Kelli Heller has been a teacher for 23 years. She taught for 11 years in general education at the elementary level, 6 years in special education Grades 6 through 8, 6 years as an administration at the elementary level, and 1 year as a college instructor. She has a bachelor's degree in elementary education with a focus on mild/moderate special education from the University of Nebraska Omaha, and a master's degree in elementary administration from Doane College in Nebraska. She has taught special education in both inclusion and self-contained settings and is currently teaching Grades 6 to 8 at Brook Valley South, which is a self-contained Level 3 setting with Educational Service Unit #3 in La Vista, Nebraska.

Mary Ellen Hodge, MEd, BCBA, LBA

Mary Ellen Hodge has been a teacher for 23 years. She was a general education teacher for 2 years, a special education teacher for 16 years in self-contained setting, and an autism specialist for 2 years and is currently a state trainer with the Kansas Technical Assistance System Network Autism and Tertiary Behavior Supports Team (TASN-ATBS). She provides trainings on Structured Teaching, Verbal Behavior Programming and Establishing Basic Skill Sets. She has a master's degree in special education, a certification in autism, and a master's degree in behavior analysis and is a Board Certified Behavior Analyst.

Stephanie Kopecky, MEd

Stephanie Kopecky is a K–8 Essentials teacher at Brook Valley South, a Level 3 placement for special education in La Vista, Nebraska, for Educational Service Unit #3. She has taught for over 16 years in special education, including 14 years as an elementary resource teacher. Stephanie graduated in 2005 from the University of Nebraska Omaha with a bachelor's degree in special education and completed a graduate program at Concordia University in Nebraska in 2013 with a master's of science in education with an emphasis on K–12 reading instruction. Stephanie has presented at the Nebraska ASD Network State Conference with her teaching partner, Kristen McKearney. She has a passion for all things behavior and social skills while continuing to develop an innovative program supporting students with emotional and behavioral challenges.

Lindy McDaniel, MEd

Lindy has been in education for 19 years and has a master's in special education preschool through 12th grade in addition to a master's in building level leadership. She has worked as a Head Start preschool teacher, special education preschool teacher, K–5 functional life skills teacher, and behavior interventionist. She currently serves as an administrator for an alternative school and as the assistant director for a special education cooperative in Kansas.

Kristen McKearney, MEd

Kristen McKearney is a K–8 Essentials teacher at Brook Valley South, a Level 3 placement for special education in La Vista, Nebraska, for Educational Service Unit #3 and has served 3 years in her current position. She has taught for 18 years in special education, including 15 years as an elementary resource teacher. Kristen has a bachelor's degree in special education and a master's degree in curriculum and instruction.

Amy Schulte, MS, CCC-SLP

Amy Schulte graduated with a master of science degree in speech-language pathology from Fort Hays State University in 2010. She worked for one year for Eastern Colorado and has worked for Northwest Kansas Educational Service Center (NKESC) for 11 years primarily with school-age children.

Ali Sweitzer, MEd, BCBA

Ali Sweitzer taught elementary special education for Papillion-La Vista Public Schools and Westside Community schools for a combined 10 years. She continued with Westside Community schools for 3.5 years as a Behavior Facilitator and Verbal Behavior Coach. Ali is currently a Behavior Specialist for the Nebraska ASD Network. As a Behavior Specialist, Ali presents on a variety of topics related to autism and behavior and provides consultation and coaching for educators working with students with autism and challenging behavior, Birth–21. Ali holds a master's degree in special education and a special education leadership endorsement from the University of Nebraska-Omaha. She is also a Board Certified Behavior Analyst.

Dixie Teeter, MS, CCC-SLP

Dixie L. Teeter is a licensed Speech-Language Pathologist and holds a Certificate of Clinical Competence from the ASHA. She has a master's degree in speech-language pathology with a specialization in autism and a graduate certificate in autism specialist disorders. She has been working as a speech-language pathologist for 25 years working in inclusion, resource, self-contained, and functional classroom settings. She is currently a state trainer with the Kansas Technical Assistance System Network Autism and Tertiary Behavior Supports Team (TASN-ATBS).

Josh Wikler, MS, RBT

Josh Wikler is a Behavior Support Classroom teacher at Wyandotte High School in Kansas City, Kansas. He received his undergraduate degree at Southwest Baptist University in Bolivar, Missouri, and his master's degree from Emporia State University in Emporia, Kansas. He has been teaching students with behavior disorders for 20 years and cannot imagine doing anything else. He has been named teacher of the year for Wyandotte High School and also been named the Kansas City Rotary Club teacher of the year. He became a master teacher with the Midwest Symposium for Leadership in Behavior Disorders in 2018 and has presented at the symposium three times. He is currently working on using hope-based storytelling to reach his students and help them make connections to their own lives.

To Rich.

We miss you, we love you, and we are proud to continue your legacy.

Person-First Language Versus Identity-First Language

Within this book, we purposely use both identity-first and person-first language. We also use several variations of autism, including ASD and "on the spectrum." Our varied language use is purposeful in nature to represent both individuals who prefer identity-first language and those who prefer person-first language. In addition, the American Psychological Association (APA, 2020) provides specific guidance regarding disability and language. Most importantly, the language used to describe people with disabilities, including autism, should preserve their dignity and represent their preferences. If an autistic person or their family has a preference of identity-first language, then teachers and other professionals working with that individual should use identity-first language. Similarly, if the person with autism or their family has a preference for person-first language, then person-first language should be used.

What Is Person-First Language?

Person-first language is typically the default or standard language used in special education professional settings for both verbal and written language. Special education teachers and other school professionals who work with students with autism are likely to use person-first language when speaking with families and writing Individualized Education Programs (IEPs). In person-first language, the person is emphasized rather than their disability, such as "the third-grade student with autism" or "the young adult with ASD." Person-first language first emerged in the 1970s and was intended to humanize individuals with disabilities (Dunn & Andrews, 2015). Person-first language is generally viewed as polite and respectful. However, professionals who use person-first language perceived distance between themselves and individuals with disabilities (Draper, 2018). In addition, some autistic people and disability advocates note that a person's autism is an integral part of a person's identity and should not be separated from the person as in the phrasing "the person with autism."

What is Identity-First Language?

Identity-first language emerged as somewhat of a critique of person-first language by stating that autism is not a deficit that should be remedied or changed. Identity-first language does not attempt to separate the person and their disability label. Examples of identity-first language include "the autistic girl," "the autistic teenager," and "Steve is autistic." Most autistic people report a preference for identity-first language (Abel et al., 2019) and have adopted a neurodiversity paradigm (Bradshaw et al., 2021). The neurodiversity perspective views autism as a form of diversity among humans. Many autism self-advocacy groups, such as the Autistic Self-Advocacy Network, promote the concept of autism as a form of neurodiversity and, therefore, also promote identity-first language.

Other Terminology Related to Autism

Given that language preferences and language itself can change frequently, teachers and school professionals should remain up to date on the language preferences of the students with autism and families with whom they work. Teachers should also refer to the current version of the *Diagnostic and Statistical Manual of Mental Disorders* (DSM-V-TR; American Psychiatric Association [APA], 2013) for terminology updates based on the scientific literature and research. Lastly, terms such as *high-functioning* and *low-functioning* autism should be avoided but is still often used. Although autism is a spectrum disorder, these terms can be patronizing and inappropriate (APA, 2020). Another way to deliver this same information is to focus on support needs rather than a person's functioning level (e.g., "a person with mild support needs" or "a person with significant support needs"). In short, the preferred language of autistic people must be incorporated and respected, which the authors of this book strive to do.

An Overview of Autism Spectrum Disorder (ASD)

What Is Autism Spectrum Disorder?

In 1943, Leo Kanner first described autism in his article "Autistic Disturbances of Affective Contact." Previously, most of the individuals who exhibited the symptoms that Kanner described were classified under the diagnosis of schizophrenia or intellectual disabilities (ID). Kanner noted distinct differences in the subjects that he observed with autism than others in the schizophrenia and ID categories: resistance to change, insistence on sameness, echolalia, and without a desire to be social (Kanner, 1943). Unfortunately, his description of these individuals' preference for being alone, often not showing a desire for affection from their parents, led to some confusing and erroneous viewpoints that the mother's aloof interactions with their children caused the autism disorder (Kanner, 1943). Hans Asperger also published his dissertation about the disorder of autism in 1944 (but it was not found or translated until 1981) and described it as being inherited from the parents because he found that the fathers of the children seemed to demonstrate similar characteristics. Asperger's description of autism later was recognized as one that fit a distinct subgroup of individuals within the autism category and thus the label "Asperger's syndrome" was created and provided to individuals with more advanced expressive language skills and no intellectual delays.

In the 1960s and 70s several researchers, most notably Bernard Rimland and Michael Rutter, made significant gains in clarifying and describing the disorder of autism in order to develop a more accurate means of diagnosis, with the hope of developing effective interventions and treatments for individuals with autism. In 1975 when the first federal special education law was passed, Education for All Handicapped Children Act (PL 94-142) (U.S. Department of Education, 2022), children with autism, along with all other children with disabilities, were granted a right to be educated free in public schools. This also increased the need for further research regarding a consistent diagnostic criteria for autism and effective intervention methods for children with autism (Fine, 1979).

In 1978, Rutter wrote a new definition of autism and in 1980 the third revision of the *Diagnostic and Statistical Manual of Mental Disorders-III (DSM-3)* (American Psychiatric Association [APA], 1980) was published and included the first diagnostic criteria for "infantile autism" under the category of Pervasive Development Disorder. The emphasis was on early childhood characteristics and development. At that time in 1980 autism was considered to be a rare disorder with a prevalence of 3 in 10,000 (Maenner et al., 2021). Currently, the prevalence of autism is considered to be 1 in 44, and is 4 times more common in boys than girls (Maenner et al., 2021).

In 1994, the reauthorization of the federal special education law PL 94-142 occurred and "Autism" was added as one of the federal diagnoses with its own disability category and eligible to receive federal funding for services (the law's name was also changed to "Individuals with Disabilities Education Act" [IDEA] in 1994) . This disorder is characterized by difficulty in social interaction with others; speech, language, and communication impairments (e.g., delayed speech, echolalia); restrictive and repetitive behavior patterns; stereotypic and other self-stimulatory responses; and a variety of aberrant responses to sensory stimuli (Chawarska, et al., 2008). At the same time, however, it is not unusual for individuals with autism to have typical physical growth and development, and some children and youth with ASD have splinter skills and other isolated and unique skills, knowledge, and abilities (Berkell Zager, 1999). Moreover, individuals with autism have a wide range of abilities, ranging from near- or above-average intellectual and communication abilities to severe cognitive delays and an absence of spoken language (Myles & Simpson, 2003).

The most current definition and diagnostic criteria for ASD comes from the new edition of the *Diagnostic and Statistical Manual of Mental Disorders V (DSM-V)* (May, 2013) and was officially sanctioned for use by the American Psychiatric Association (APA). One of the major changes within the new edition (previous edition was DSM-IV-TR [2000]) was a complete revision of the diagnostic criteria for ASD. The Asperger syndrome diagnostic classification was eliminated along with other specific subtypes of autism and replaced with a continuum of severity. Individuals with severe forms of autism fall at Level 3; Moderate is Level 2; and Mild forms of autism are coded as Level 1. It also added the social (pragmatic) communication disorder (now referred to as SPCD) which focuses on difficulties with the use of verbal and nonverbal communication in social contexts as well as the person demonstrating challenges with the functional use of communication in social relationships in both personal and school or professional environments. It is important to note that SPCD diagnosis criteria does not include anything about the individual demonstrating sensory challenges or restrictive and repetitive behaviors. Thus, it is not the same as the previous Asperger's syndrome diagnosis.

The Autism Spectrum Disorder Diagnostic Criteria of the *DSM-V* (APA, 2013) outlines the different pertinent factors that professionals utilize to determine whether an individual manifests an ASD and then provides a table that delineates the three dimensions of severity in which an individual would be classified. In summary, the diagnosis considers the following: Deficits in at least three subcategories of social communication and social interaction and at least two subcategories of restricted and repetitive behaviors or interests *and* symptoms need to be evident at an early age, symptoms result in significant impairment in current functioning, and symptoms cannot be otherwise explained by other disabling conditions, specifically cognitive impairments. For each of the two deficit areas of social communication and interaction and restrictive and repetitive behaviors, the three classifications of severity essentially fall within the three levels of mild (requiring support), moderate (requiring substantial support), and severe (requiring very substantial support).

Table 0.1 Severity Levels for ASD

SEVERITY LEVEL	SOCIAL COMMUNICATION	RESTRICTED, REPETITIVE BEHAVIORS
Level 3 **"Requiring very substantial support"**	Severe deficits in verbal and nonverbal social communication skills cause severe impairments in functioning, very limited initiation of social interactions, and minimal response to social overtures from others. For example, a person with few words of intelligible speech who rarely initiates interaction and, when they do, makes unusual approaches to meet needs only and responds to only very direct social approaches.	Inflexibility of behavior, extreme difficulty coping with change, or other restricted/repetitive behaviors markedly interfere with functioning in all spheres. Great distress/difficulty changing focus or action.

SEVERITY LEVEL	SOCIAL COMMUNICATION	RESTRICTED, REPETITIVE BEHAVIORS
Level 2 **"Requiring substantial support"**	Marked deficits in verbal and nonverbal social communication skills; social impairments apparent even with supports in place; limited initiation of social interactions; and reduced or abnormal responses to social overtures from others. For example, a person who speaks simple sentences, whose interaction is limited to narrow special interests, and who has markedly odd nonverbal communication.	Inflexibility of behavior, difficulty coping with change, or other restricted/repetitive behaviors appear frequently enough to be obvious to the casual observer and interfere with functioning in a variety of contexts. Distress and/or difficulty changing focus or action.
Level 1 **"Requiring support"**	Without supports in place, deficits in social communication cause noticeable impairments. Difficulty initiating social interactions, and clear examples of atypical or unsuccessful response to social overtures of others. May appear to have decreased interest in social interactions. For example, a person who is able to speak in full sentences and engages in communication but whose to- and-fro conversation with others fails, and whose attempts to make friends are odd and typically unsuccessful.	Inflexibility of behavior causes significant interference with functioning in one or more contexts. Difficulty switching between activities. Problems of organization and planning hamper independence.

Source. American Psychiatric Association (2013).

It is important to note that there are many professionals, families, and individuals with autism and persons previously identified as having Asperger's syndrome who do not agree with this new diagnostic criteria (Carmack, 2014; Gamlin, 2017; Giles, 2014; Moloney, 2010; Parsloe & Babrow, 2016). These people who received a diagnosis of Asperger's syndrome prior to the change in the *DSM* diagnostic criteria and who do not want to change their diagnosis to be one that is now listed in the *DSM-V* do continue to self-label as having Asperger's syndrome, regardless of the fact that the *DSM-V* no longer includes it as a diagnostic criteria area or disability (Carmack, 2014; Smith & Jones, 2020; Soffer & Argaman-Donas, 2021). Many individuals previously diagnosed with Asperger's syndrome report feelings of concern and disappointment that Asperger's syndrome is no longer recognized as a separate disorder because of the sense of identity associated with the Asperger syndrome label (Chambers et al., 2020;

Gamlin, 2017; Giles, 2014). The American Psychiatric Association's decision to move Asperger's into the autism spectrum hinged on the issue of language development; the American Psychiatric Association argued that language impairment is not a "necessary criterion" for diagnosing autism (Adams, 2011). Several disability scholars argue for a reenvisioning of Asperger's not as a medical disorder or disability but rather as a socially constructed mental disorder, if it is a disorder at all (Allred, 2009; Molloy & Vasil, 2002). Rather than seeing Asperger's as a neurological impairment, Allred (2009) and Molloy and Vasil (2002) argued that Asperger's is a "difference." It is not that individuals with Asperger's are impaired; it is that they experience the world differently, and thus, respond differently. No matter the type and amount of disagreement regarding the diagnostic criteria and labels in past *DSM*s, it is critical that individuals with ASD of all levels of functioning receive appropriate intervention for their individual needs.

As mentioned above, SPCD is a new diagnostic criteria in the *DSM-V*. Mandy et al. (2017) expresses the views of many other researchers at this point in time when they state, "It is currently unclear whether SPCD is a valid diagnostic category, because little is known about the characteristics of those who meet its criteria" (p. 1116). There is currently no consistent and clear definition or criteria, nor are there any specific screening and assessment tools to help definitively provide a diagnosis of SPCD (Adams et al., 2020; Mandy et al., 2017; Taylor et al., 2016).

The question of whether SPCD can be meaningfully and consistently distinguished from other disorders and from typical development remains to be answered (e.g., Lord & Bishop, 2015; Norbury, 2014). In particular, a crucial consideration is how SPCD relates to, and can be differentiated from, ASD (Brukner-Wertman et al., 2016; Dolata et al., 2022; Weismer, et al., 2021). Some professionals are still not differentiating in their treatment between children who have a Level 1 (mild) ASD diagnosis and those with an SPCD diagnosis when studying effective interventions for working on social communication skills (Adams et al., 2020).

While there are several research articles published since 2013 that address the need to clarify and validate the new SPCD disorder, no research articles were found that discussed or studied how schools are handling the diagnosis of SPCD as far as eligibility for special education, how assessments are conducted, or who and how services are provided. In an online search of reputable organizations (i.e., Centers for Disease Control [CDC], American Psychological Association [publisher of the *DSM*], and Council for Exceptional Children [CEC]), only the ASHA included information about SPCD. While they do provide a clear definition with symptoms and characteristics, it is not a definition that was found anywhere else. They discuss screening and assessment and diagnosis, but no specific tools and all emphasis is placed on observation of the individual and interviewing people who live and work with the child (ASHA, n.d.). They do make it clear that social communication skills are ones that speech and language pathologists (SLPs) are trained to work with in individuals and that SLPs can provide effective treatment for such individuals in 1:1 or small group settings (ASHA, n.d.). Other psychology, psychiatry, and autism center websites all note that the most important professional to be involved in diagnosis, assessment, and treatment is a SLP.

One common characteristic among all individuals with ASD, no matter the severity of diagnosis, is their uneven pattern of skill development (Burack & Volkmar, 1992; National Research Council, 2001; Roane et al., 2016; Van Meter et al., 1997). For instance, an individual with ASD may display math skills several years beyond their age yet may be unable to use the toilet independently. In this connection individuals who teach and plan skill development programs for learners with ASD, including professionals and parents, typically consider the following skill domains: (a) cognition, (b) learning, (c) social interaction, (d) play, (e) communication, (f) adaptive behavior, (g) behavior, (h) motor, and (i) sensory sensitivities (Atwood, 1998; de Boer, 2018;

Klinger et al., 2021; Koegel et al., 1995; Mauk et al., 1997; Mazurek et al., 2012; Myles & Simpson, 2003; Roane et al., 2016).

The Individuals with Disabilities Education Act (IDEA) of 2004 is the current federal law that regulates providing services and support to children with disabilities within schools, ages 0 to 3 (Part C) and ages 3 to 22 (Part B). The IDEA refers to ASD as "a developmental disability significantly affecting verbal and nonverbal communication and social interaction, generally evident before age three, that adversely affects a child's educational performance" [Sec. 300.8 (c) (1) (i)]. This federal definition then proceeds to name traits commonly related to the condition: "Other characteristics often associated with autism are engaging in repetitive activities and stereotyped movements, resistance to environmental change or change in daily routines, and unusual responses to sensory experiences. The term autism does not apply if the child's educational performance is adversely affected primarily because the child has an emotional disturbance, as defined in IDEA" [Sec. 300.8 (c) (1) (ii)].

IDEA also notes that a child who shows the characteristics of ASD after age three could be diagnosed as having ASD if the criteria above are satisfied. This enables a child to receive special education services under this classification if they display signs of ASD after their third birthday. This does not mean that a child who is showing signs of ASD prior to age three should not be diagnosed earlier. In fact, it is important to identify children with ASD as early as possible so that early intervention can occur as soon as possible in the child's early development years (Estes et al., 2015; Howard et al., 2005; Reichow, 2012; Zwaigenbaum et al., 2021). Research over the decades has overwhelmingly indicated that young children with ASD who receive early and intensive intervention after early diagnosis make statistically significant progress (this means that the research showed that the only reason for the improvement in the child's skill development was because of the intervention that was provided) and gains in all skill areas if they receive the appropriate and individualized intervention as early as possible (Mazurek et al., 2012; Zwaigenbaum et al., 2021). Many of these children go on to be included for much of their education within the general education environment and pursue postsecondary goals such as attending college or obtaining meaningful jobs.

Cause

ASD is an extremely complicated disorder and one that has taken and is still taking researchers and professionals a long time to figure out the causes and the diagnostic process. Traditionally (1940s–1990s) ASD was noticed, observed, and diagnosed by professionals simply through the demonstration of characteristics such as repetitive and restrictive behaviors (e.g., not playing with toys or handling objects as designed, doing one thing over and over, rocking, hand flapping, lining things up), delayed communication (e.g., no speech development, echolalia [repeating others' words] or development of only a few words), and lack of desire to interact with others in typical ways (e.g., lack of eye contact, not wanting to be touched, not noticing other people in the room, not talking or playing with other children) and also challenging behaviors that came with lack of communication and wanting things to be a certain way (e.g., screaming and yelling when a person moved one of their objects, not being able to tell a parent they are thirsty). And there was little to no recognition of the sensory difficulties that most individuals on the spectrum experience (e.g., certain noises, the tactile feel of certain things, lighting, the tasted of certain foods) and how those sensitivities or lack of sensitivities (e.g., lack of pain, lack of reaction to noises, lack of reaction to touch) affect their daily ability to function.

During this time, there was no known cause for "autism." There was no medical or DNA test, or any other physical or biological "autism" test that was provided to an individual to help definitively identify and diagnose the disorder. As a result, there were unfortunately many harmful theories or myths perpetuated to explain the cause of the disorder. For example, in the 1940s through the 1960s, it was common to believe that autism was caused by having a "cold" or "refrigerator mother," meaning that she was not attentive or affectionate enough to her child during their early life and thus the child withdrew into their own world and developed "autism" (Kanner, 1943).

In 1998, a now famous article was published in the *Lancet* by a then-British medical doctor, Andrew Wakefield, that claimed there was a link between the vaccinations that young children received between 18 and 24 months and the development of autism (Wakefield, 1998). He claimed that vaccinations for diseases such as measles, mumps, and rubella were triggering something in the bodies and brains of some children and were causing autism to develop after they received these vaccinations. Immediately, this article caused much controversy and many parents began to refuse to allow their children to be vaccinated. This resulted in a rise of the occurrence of many harmful childhood diseases. Many extensive studies were done by medical professionals after this article was published and these studies proved over and over that there was no link between vaccinations and autism (Bölte et al., 2019; Miller & Reynolds, 2009; van der Linden, 2015). Finally, in February of 2010, Wakefield's study was proven fully fraudulent, his article was completely retracted from the journal, and his medical license was taken away (the Editors of the *Lancet*, 2010). It was then further proven that he was in the process of starting a business venture in which he would profit more than $40 million for developing and selling his own "safe vaccinations" for children. Unfortunately, to this day, many parents continue to believe that vaccinations can cause autism and refuse to allow their children to be vaccinated or claim that their child developed autism from vaccinations they received.

Perhaps the biggest advance in understanding autism and its origins has been the increase in genetic research and its contribution to ASD's etiology. Three types of studies show that there is clearly a genetic and heritable link in ASD: (Castellani 2020; Gaugler et al., 2014; Geschwind, 2011; National Institute of Health (NIH), 2017).

▶ twin studies, comparing monozygotic (identical) twins and dizygotic (fraternal) twins,

▶ family studies comparing the rate of autism in first-degree relatives of affected probands versus the population, and

▶ studies of rare genetic syndromes with a comorbid autism diagnosis.

In 2019, a global research project (50 centers around the world) looking into the possible genetic causes for autism was completed. They reported that there are definitively 102 genes associated with ASD (Satterstrom et al., 2020). The researchers found that the majority of these ASD risk genes are active early in brain development and play a part in controlling the expression of other genes or the communication between brain cells (synapses) (Satterstrom et al., 2020). Additionally, both "excitatory" neurons (increase the likelihood that the neuron will fire an action) and "inhibitory" neurons (decrease the likelihood that the neuron will fire an action) can express the risk genes (nerve cells). This demonstrates that autism involves "multiple abnormalities" in how brain cells work rather than only being linked to one main type of brain cell (Satterstrom et al., 2020). To fully comprehend what each of these genes does, more study is required. The implications for identifying specific genes means that it could be possible for medications or medical treatments to be developed and used with individuals with autism, in addition to or instead of behavioral interventions.

Diagnostic Process

Because there is not one known cause for autism and not one single test to determine the existence of autism within an individual, it is important for teachers and parents to understand how the autism diagnostic process occurs. Starting in the early 2000s, professionals began developing and researching assessment tools that could be used to determine if an individual could be diagnosed with an ASD. The goal was, and continues to be, to help standardize the process so that there is objectivity and consistency across and among professionals when an ASD diagnosis is provided (Pringle et al., 2012; Volkmar et al., 2014). There has also been the development of several screening tools to help professionals and parents determine if an individual is at risk for ASD. These tools are frequently used to detect characteristics in very young children (as young as 6 months up to 3 years old) so that people can be alerted and begin closer monitoring of the child's development.

The diagnostic process is neither simple nor quick. It requires that professionals who have experience working with individuals with ASD and experience using the assessment tools implement the assessment process. A positive diagnosis of ASD also requires a comprehensive assessment, using several different tools that evaluate the different aspects and characteristics that are common deficits in individuals with ASD. A parent or teacher should be wary of a diagnosis that has been provided to an individual by a professional that has only utilized their "professional expertise" to provide the diagnosis. The best process is for a team of individuals, with different expertise and experience in working with individuals with ASD such as Speech and Language Pathologists, Occupational Therapists, Psychologist or School Psychologists, and Board Certified Behavior Analysts, to work together providing assessments related to their field. Then the team discusses the results across the assessments and across their areas of expertise to determine if they reach the same conclusions regarding the diagnosis or non-diagnosis of ASD. Finally, for the purpose of providing the rationale for giving or not giving a ASD diagnosis, these professionals can either write one comprehensive report, which would combine all of the results, or individual reports with the results of the specific assessments each one administered.

To help teachers and parents understand more about the screening and assessment process that occurs regarding the diagnosis of ASD, a list with corresponding brief descriptions has been provided below regarding the most commonly used, as well as evidence-based screening and diagnostic tools used.

Developmental Screening Tools

The Modified Checklist for Autism in Toddlers—Revised with Follow-Up (M-CHAT-R/F) (Robins, et al., 2009) can be administered and scored as part of a well-child care visit, and also can be used by specialists or other professionals to assess risk for ASD. The primary goal of the M-CHAT-R is to maximize sensitivity, meaning to detect as many cases of ASD as possible. Therefore, there is a high false positive rate, meaning that not all children who score at risk will be diagnosed with ASD. To address this, the Follow-Up Questions (M-CHAT-R/F) were developed. Users should be aware that even with the follow-up, a significant number of the children who screen positive on the M-CHAT-R will not be diagnosed with ASD. However, these children are at high risk for other developmental disorders or delays, and therefore, evaluation is warranted for any child who screens positive (for ages 16 to 30 months).

The Battelle Developmental Inventory—Third Edition (BDI-3) (Newborg, 2020) is an assessment that measures global domains across the early development years of children. The BDI-3 provides examiners with a complete assessment, a screening assessment, and an early academic survey. BDI-3 is used across the country—and exclusively in 16 states—to (1) assess developmental milestones for school readiness, (2) help determine eligibility for special education services, and (3) assist in the development of IEPs (for ages Birth to 7 years, 11months).

The Ages & Stages Questionnaires—Third Edition (ASQ-3) (Squires & Bricker, 2009) is a developmental screening tool designed for use by early educators and health care professionals. Its success lies in its parent-centric approach and inherent ease of use—a combination that has made it one of the most widely used developmental screeners across the globe. It relies on parents as experts, is easy to use, is family friendly, and creates the snapshot needed to catch delays *and* celebrate milestones (for ages birth to 5 years, 6 months).

The Ages & Stages Questionnaires—Social-Emotional—Second Edition (ASQ:SE-2) (Squires et al., 2015) is modeled after the ASQ-3 and is tailored to identify and exclusively screen social and emotional behaviors. ASQ:SE-2 is an easy-to-use tool; it is parent completed, photocopiable, and culturally sensitive. With questionnaire results, professionals can quickly recognize young children at risk for social or emotional difficulties, identify behaviors of concern to caregivers, and identify any need for further assessment (for ages 1 to 72 months).

The Social Communication Questionnaire (SCQ) (Rutter et al., 2003a) brief instrument helps evaluate communication skills and social functioning in children who may have ASD. Completed by a parent, adult, or other primary caregiver in less than 10 minutes, the SCQ is a cost-effective way to determine whether an individual should be referred for a complete diagnostic evaluation. It is available in two forms—Lifetime and Current—each composed of just 40 yes/no questions. Both forms can be given directly to the parent, who can answer the questions without supervision (for ages 4 years and older—mental age of 2+).

The Social Responsiveness Scale—Second Edition (SRS-2) (Constantino, 2012) is used as both a screener and a diagnostic tool. The SRS-2 identifies social impairment associated with ASD and quantifies its severity. It's sensitive enough to detect subtle symptoms, yet specific enough to differentiate clinical groups, both within the autism spectrum and between ASD and other disorders. The SRS-2 asks teachers, parents, and others to rate symptoms that they've noticed—at home, in the classroom, or elsewhere—over time. Raters evaluate symptoms using a quantitative scale representing a range of severity. There are Preschool (ages 2.5 to 4.5 years) and School-Age forms (ages 4.0 to 18 years) with Teacher and Parent/Caregiver versions and Adult forms (ages 19 years and older) with Self-Report and Relative/Other Adult versions.

Components of Comprehensive Assessment for Diagnosis

The Autism Diagnostic Observation Schedule–Second Edition (ADOS-2) (Lord et al., 2012b), which also has a Toddler Module version (Lord et at. 2012a), is an activity-based assessment administered by trained clinicians to evaluate communication skills, social interaction, and imaginative use of materials in individuals who are suspected to have ASD. The ADOS-2 was developed to provide an opportunity to observe symptoms and behaviors associated with ASD in a consistent manner across different clients, clinicians, and locations. The ADOS-2 is currently considered the "gold standard" and a necessary component in the assessment of ASD (for ages 12 months to 90 years).

The Autism Diagnostic Interview–Revised (ADI-R) (Rutter et al., 2003b) has been used in research for decades. This comprehensive interview provides a thorough assessment of individuals suspected of having autism. The ADI-R has proven highly useful for formal diagnosis as well as treatment and educational planning. To administer the ADI-R, an experienced clinical interviewer questions a parent or caretaker who is familiar with the developmental history and current behavior of the individual being evaluated. The interview can be used to assess both children and adults, as long as their mental age is above 2 years, 0 months.

The Developmental Neuropsychological Assessment–Second Edition (NEPSY-II) (Korkman et al., 2007) combined with quantifiable behavioral observations analysis during assessment and observations analysis from home and school help clarify the nature of a child's skill deficits and provide a basis for developing appropriate intervention recommendations. It enables the evaluator to assess executive functioning/ attention, language, memory/learning, sensorimotor functioning, visuospatial processing, social perception, vary the number of subtests according to the needs of the child, obtain a comprehensive view of quantitative and qualitative patterns of neuropsychological performance, facilitate recommendations for mental health interventions, and link results to educational difficulties (for ages 3 to 16 years).

The Behavior Rating Inventory of Executive Functions–Second Edition (BRIEF-2) and *Preschool Version (BRIEF-P)* (Gioai et al., 2017) give the information needed to help children and adolescents with executive dysfunction. It digs deeper than similar measures and pinpoints exactly where and why children struggle, so therapists and schools can make informed and impactful intervention and accommodation recommendations. Three domains evaluate cognitive, behavioral, and emotional regulation, and a Global Executive Composite score provides an overall snapshot of executive functioning. It includes 10 clinical scales: Inhibit, Self-Monitor, Shift, Emotional Control, Working Memory, and Plan/Organize which are included on all forms. Initiate, Task-Monitor, and Organization of Materials are also on the Parent and Teacher forms. The Self-Report Form also includes Task Completion. The inventory includes optional ADHD and ASD scoring profiles to use if a professional is utilizing the tool as part of a diagnostic assessment (BRIEF-P for ages 3 to 5.11 years; BRIEF-2 for ages 5 to 18 years).

The Comprehensive Executive Function Inventory (CEFI) (Naglieri & Goldstein, 2017) is a comprehensive behavior rating scale of executive-functioning strengths and weaknesses. Completed in just 15 minutes, the CEFI is a versatile instrument that offers information that can be used to guide assessment, diagnosis, and intervention for children and adolescents. In addition to clinical use, it is also useful in research settings because it can effectively measure the success of intervention programs (for ages 5 to 18 years).

The Vineland Adaptive Behavior Scales–Third Edition (Sparrow et al., 2016) is an instrument used for supporting the diagnosis of intellectual and developmental disabilities (IDD), as well as for qualification for special programs, progress reporting, program and treatment planning, and research. The Vineland provides corresponding scales to the three broad domains of adaptive functioning specified by the American Association on Intellectual and Developmental Disabilities and by *DSM-5*— communication, daily living skills, and socialization (for ages birth to 90 years).

The Behavior Assessment System for Children–Third Edition (BASC-3) (Reynolds & Kamphaus, 2015) is an individually administered, norm-referenced, comprehensive set of rating scales and forms designed to inform understanding of the behaviors and emotions of children and adolescents. Forms available in this system include Parent Rating Scales (PRS), Teacher Rating Scales (TRS), the Self-Report of Personality (starting at 6 years), Student Observation System (SOS), the Structured Developmental History (SDH), and new to the BASC-3, a Parenting Relationship Questionnaire (PRQ). The TRS, PRS, and SOS measure the child's behavior patterns in home, community, and school settings. The SRP can be used to assess the child's thoughts and feelings. The SDH is useful for obtaining students' comprehensive history and background information across social, psychological, developmental, educational, and medical domains. (There are three separate versions/forms: Preschool: ages 2 to 5 years; Child: ages 6 to 11 years; Adolescent: ages 12 to 21 years.)

The Adaptive Behavior Assessment System–Third Edition (ABAS-3) (Harrison & Oakland, 2015) is a rating scale useful for assessing skills of daily living in individuals with developmental delays, ASD, intellectual disability, learning disabilities, neuropsychological disorders, and sensory or physical impairments. Rating forms are filled out by the parent and a teacher. There is also an adult self-rating form. The ABAS-3 covers three broad domains: conceptual, social, and practical, using 11 skill areas within these domains (for ages Birth to 89 years).

A Functional Behavior Assessment (FBA) is conducted if the child or adolescent is also exhibiting maladaptive behaviors that are impeding overall daily functioning for self and/or family or impeding learning and functioning within a class environment. The FBA is conducted to determine the function of the behavior through an analysis of setting events, antecedent, behavior, and consequences (ABC). This assists the diagnostic process through providing a more in-depth view of the individual's behavior and root causes.

History of Interventions and Treatments

It is helpful for educators to understand the history of interventions and treatments for individuals with ASD because it is a short history, a controversial history, and one in which we are still in the making of history. Understanding the history of interventions and treatments of individuals with ASD also helps educators understand how we have come to this current place and time in which it is still critical to do research and publish articles and books about what are and are not EBPs for working with students with ASD.

It is common knowledge that children and adults with disabilities have historically not been treated well in American society and that the rights of these individuals continually need to be advocated and fought for. As previously stated, it wasn't until 1975 that this country gave children with disabilities the right to be educated in public schools. Another right that individuals with disabilities (and also mental disorders) have not had until more recently (within the past 20 years or so) is the right to not be treated with physically aversive methods as a means of punishing their undesirable behaviors.

Even in the early stages of using ABA interventions and treatments, researchers, and clinicians used physically aversive methods to decrease stereotypical behavior (self-stimulation), self-injurious behavior (SIB), destructive behaviors, and aggressive behaviors. While reinforcement for appropriate behavior has always been a part of the intervention methods within ABA, a more preventative and proactive approach to decreasing target problem behaviors has only been emphasized since the early 2000s when Positive Behavior Intervention Supports (PBIS) were researched and found to be more effective than a reactive approach to decreasing inappropriate behaviors.

Back in the 1970s and 1980s, main techniques for decreasing problem behaviors, using the principles of ABA that were used with varying, and sometimes contradictory, reports of success, were differential reinforcement of other or incompatible behavior (DRO/DRI) (Frankel et al., 1976; Homer & Peterson, 1980; Tarpley & Schroeder, 1979), extinction (Jones et al., 1974; Lovaas & Simmons, 1969; Myers, 1975), time-out (Duker, 1975; Harris & Romanczyk, 1976; Measel & Alfieri, 1976), and sensory extinction (Rincover & Devaney, 1982). These are still effective consequence intervention methods, but now Antecedent-Based Interventions (ABI) are the focus of ABA interventions and treatments.

During the same time the only treatments that were reported to consistently have an effect in reducing SIB to clinically acceptable levels were based on the presentation of an aversive punisher contingent upon the demonstration of SIB, noncompliance, destruction, or aggression. Corte et al. (1971) found that response-contingent electric shock was more effective than DRO or extinction in suppressing SIB. Electric shock was also used to suppress the behaviors of climbing on furniture (Risley, 1968), for incorrect picture identification (Kircher et al., 1971), and failure to come when called (Lovaas et al., 1965; Sajwaj et al., 1974). Lemon juice was put on the lips of an infant as an aversive punisher to decrease life-threatening rumination (regurgitating and chewing food) and presenting an open jar of ammonia under the nose of individuals contingent upon the occurrence of SIB was found to reduce SIB (Altman et al., 1978; Tanner & Zeiler, 1975). Barrett et al. (1981) reported the overall superiority of punishment procedures to the use of differential reinforcement of appropriate behaviors in suppressing stereotypic behavior in two children with mental retardation and autism. Visual screening (putting a cloth on the face of the individual) was used as a punisher for finger sucking with one subject, and tongue depression was used to punish tongue protrusion in the other subject (Bailey et al., 1983). Many of the same aversive punishers were used by educators in special education classrooms (Barton et al., 1983; Kazdin, 1975; McGinnis et al., 1985; Zabel et al., 1985).

Despite the reported successes of these procedures, several issues and protestations by families and professionals continued to arise when the "need" and proposal for using aversive stimulation was discussed. The use of response-contingent electric shock was controversial even in the 1970s and 1980s (Lichstein & Schreibman, 1976). Excessive or improper use of lemon juice can cause permanent damage to an individual's tooth enamel and repeated applications of lemon juice to a person's mouth could result in serious irritation to the mouth and lips. Ammonia, if used excessively or improperly, can result in serious burns on the face. Proponents of using these punishers did caution that they should only be used as the proverbial last resort and then only in highly controlled situations (Bailey et al., 1983). However, the use of highly aversive techniques or the reliance upon laboratory-like environments was continually proven to not generalize to more natural environments or situations (Stokes & Baer, 1977).

In 1988, an important article was published by a group of behavior analysts/ researchers. It was titled "The Right to Effective Behavioral Treatment" (Van Houten et al., 1988). These behavior analysts provided and explained six tenements that should be rights of individuals with disabilities and the foundation of behavioral treatments and services for individuals with disabilities. An individual has a right to the following:

1. a therapeutic environment,

2. services whose overriding goal is personal welfare,

3. treatment by a competent behavior analyst,

4. programs that teach functional skills,

5. behavioral assessment and ongoing evaluation, and

6. the most effective treatment procedures available (Van Houten et al., 1988).

These rights became foundational components of the policies and procedures and ethical guidelines when the Behavior Analyst Certification Board® (BACB) was formed as a nonprofit organization in 1998 (see more information below in History of Applied Behavior Analysis).

By the 1990s and 2000s, many professionals and families were advocating for strict and ethical guidelines regarding the use of aversive punishers and consequences or reactive-based interventions over antecedent-preventative interventions. In 1999, the BACB published the first set of policies and procedures to ensure that behavior analysts implemented legal, confidential, respectful, and safe treatment for individuals with disabilities. It was titled the "Professional Disciplinary and Ethical

Standards." Over the years as new research and studies were conducted regarding intervention methods and the implementation of ABA procedures and practices, the BACB continued to modify and expand the standards and they became guidelines for behavior analysts (BACB, 2019). Eventually, and as is the case today, the guidelines became an actual code by which all applicants and certificants are required to adhere: "Ethics Code for Behavior Analysts." The current version at the date of publication of this book is 2020 which became effective in January 2022 and is available on the BACB website (BACB, 2020).

History of Applied Behavior Analysis (ABA) as Treatment

In the late 1800s and early 1900s, John Watson, a professor of psychology, presented a paper to colleagues at a conference, proposing a different viewpoint regarding human behavior. He proposed that it is possible to study behavior, take data on what a person is doing, figure out the reasons why (function or purpose of the behavior), and predict and change that person's behavior. This was the genesis of behaviorism and the science of behavior. He drew on Ivan Pavlov's research on reinforcement as a means of increasing certain behaviors that otherwise would not have increased, if not for the reinforcement occurring directly after the behavior ("John Watson and Behaviorism," 2014).

Many scientists followed Watson's research and principals and conducted their own research. The science of behavior analysis developed and experimental behavior analysis became a specific area of study—clinical research conducted within laboratory settings studying how changes made prior to and after a specific behavior can change that behavior either increasing or decreasing its future occurrence. Finally, Baer et al. (1968) published the seminal article, "Some Current Dimensions of Applied Behavior Analysis," in the first publication of the peer-reviewed *Journal of Applied Behavior Analysis* which was considered to be the official birth of ABA. ABA as a science involves changing the environment (antecedents and consequences) while working in learning settings (home, clinics, school, community) with individuals in order to make lasting and meaningful changes in their and their family's lives.

It was not until the 1980s and the publication of the article "Behavioral Treatment and Normal Educational and Intellectual Functioning in Young Autistic Children" by Ivar Lovaas (1987) that the use of ABA with individuals with ASD was studied and researched. He demonstrated that 40 hours a week of an ABA-only intervention compared to 10 hours a week of an eclectic model of intervention produces statistically significant, meaningful, and life-altering improvements in young children with ASD. McEachin et al. (1993) conducted a follow-up study on the same children who received the 40-hour-a-week ABA intervention and all but one of the children maintained their level of skills and functioning. To this day, behavior analysts continue to successfully replicate similar types of ABA-based intensive early interventions with children with ASD and continue to demonstrate its significant effectiveness.

In 1998, due to the increase in demand for behavior interventionists to create and implement ABA-intensive early intervention programs, the BACB was established as a regulatory entity "to meet professional certification needs identified by behavior analysts, governments, and consumers of behavior-analytic services. The BACB's mission is to protect consumers of behavior-analytic services by systematically establishing, promoting, and disseminating professional standards of practice" (BACB, 2022a). In 1999, the first 28 professionals became BCBAs and today (as of July 2022) there are 56,691 BCBAs (not including the Board Certified Assistant Behavior Analysts (BCaBA) and Registered Behavior Technicians (RBT) (BACB, 2022b). The certification includes the use of ABA practices in general with any population and is not specific to ASD. Of all BCBAs and BCBA-Ds (behavior analysts with doctorate degrees in behavior analysis) who responded to a survey in January 2022, 71.4 percent work in the field of ASD (BACB, 2022b).

Up until the year 2000, most parents and families across the nation had to pay all costs and expenses for implementing ABA early intervention intensive programs implemented within the home or a private clinic or school. These costs ranged around $40,000 a year. In 2001, Indiana was the first state to pass a law that mandated health insurance to cover the costs of ABA services for children with autism. As of 2019, all 50 states have mandated insurance coverage for ABA services for individuals with autism outside of the 5- to 22-year age range in which public schools are required to provide services for children with disabilities through IDEA. In 2004, with the reauthorization of IDEA, and the mandate that scientifically based interventions be used in schools for children with disabilities, many mediation and due process hearings, in which parents request ABA services be implemented in the school setting, have been upheld.

In the past decade, professional organizations that support behavior analysts and are governed by behavior analysts have produced and published documents for professionals and parents to help clarify what ABA is, the evidence base of ABA interventions, how to identify ABA interventions, EBPs for individuals with autism, how ABA interventions should be implemented with individuals with ASD, and the experience, education and certification requirements of people practicing as behavior analysts. In 2005 the first notable publication, summarizing and providing factual information regarding the majority of interventions and treatments that were available for use with individuals with ASD was a book by Simpson et al. (2005) titled *Autism Spectrum Disorder: Interventions and Treatments for Children and Youth.* The purpose of the book was to help families and professionals working with children with autism understand, from an objective point of view, what the interventions and treatment were, the risks and costs of use, what research and evidence there was or was not for the use of these interventions, what training and qualifications were needed to implement the intervention, and finally a rating that placed the intervention or treatment into a category indicating the evidence base and effectiveness of the intervention.

Since then, several other publications came out using similar rating scales to classify the different interventions and treatments that are available and being used with individuals with ASD. We provide further information about these reviews in the next chapter, Evidence-Based Practices, and incorporate the information from these reports within the different chapters on interventions and treatments.

In 2012, the first edition of "Applied Behavior Analysis Treatment of Autism Spectrum Disorder: Practice Guidelines for Healthcare Funders and Managers" was created by the BACB and revised in 2014. This set of "guidelines are intended to be a resource for healthcare funders and managers, regulatory bodies, consumers, service providers, employers, and other stakeholders" (CASP, 2020) regarding the implementation of ABA intervention with individuals with ASD. In 2016 and again with an update in 2017, the Association for Professional Behavior Analysts (APBA) issued a white paper titled *Identifying Applied Behavior Analysis Interventions* (APBA, 2017) to "dispel some of the most common misconceptions about behavior analysis and to help consumers, members of various professions, funders, and policymakers differentiate ABA interventions from others. It presents key facts about the defining features of the discipline with supporting documentation" (APBA, 2017, p. 4). In 2019, APBA, in collaboration with the BACB, posted a white paper on *Clarifications: ASD Practice Guidelines* to update the 2014 guidelines and "to assist payers and providers by clarifying and amplifying the Guidelines that pertain to the intensity of treatment, the intensity of case supervision, and caregiver training" (APBA, 2019, p.3) regarding ABA interventions for individuals with ASD. All of these documents are easy to read and are very helpful for educators to utilize as guidelines for their own practice in schools.

These documents are also helpful for educators to provide to other professionals and parents and family members with whom they work.

Co-Occurring Conditions

Comorbidity refers to the presence of two or more mental health conditions, disorders, or disabilities. Many individuals with ASD have comorbid conditions in addition to their ASD diagnosis. Many professionals, and particularly those in the medical field, use the terminology *comorbidity*. However, we will use the term *co-occurring* to represent a strengths-based, educational approach rather than a medical approach. Special education teachers and other related school professionals (e.g., general education teachers, counselors, administrators) must support the complex needs of students with ASD, including those needs that manifest as a result of a co-occurring condition. Sometimes it can be difficult to determine if a student's behavior is a manifestation of ASD or another condition or disorder. Distinguishing ASD characteristics from other characteristics is important for not only diagnostic purposes but treatment as well (Mannion, & Leader, 2013; Ung et al., 2013). Therefore, it is advantageous for school professionals to develop awareness and knowledge related to common co-occurring conditions of individuals with ASD. It is also highly likely that school professionals will work with students with ASD and co-occurring conditions.

In addition, characteristics associated with ASD are related to the mental health and overall well-being of the individual with ASD. For example, students with ASD are unfortunately vulnerable to being teased or bullied due to characteristics associated with the disorder (e.g., challenges with social and communication skills, repetitive patterns of behavior). Students with higher levels of bullying in their lives are more vulnerable to anxiety and depression (Chou et al., 2020). Teachers who work with students with ASD must support the entire student, not one discrete area of need. In the section below, we review some common co-occurring conditions with ASD.

Please note teachers do not diagnose ASD or any other mental health condition, disorder, or other disability. Rather, students and their families typically receive diagnostic information from a medical doctor, pediatrician, or assessment clinic and then bring that information to the school. The school team reviews all available medical information as part of the referral process to determine the student's eligibility for special education services. The student will then receive an educational diagnosis following one of the 13 disability categories as described by IDEA (2004). Students with ASD typically receive special education services under the "Educational Autism" disability category (IDEA, 2004). However, they may also receive services under the "Intellectual Disability," "Other Health Impairment," or other disability category determined most appropriate by the IEP team. It is the responsibility of the IEP team to determine which disability category is most appropriate for a student to receive special education services.

Mental Health

The prevalence of school-age students with ASD and co-occurring mental health conditions is high. The specific prevalence varies according to different sources but anxiety and depression are particularly prominent. A meta-analysis found approximately 40 percent of children and adolescents with ASD have at least one type of anxiety disorder such as excessive worry, the need for reassurance, the inability to unwind, and feelings of self-consciousness (van Steensel et al., 2011). The two illnesses can be distinguished from one another, however, by the pronounced social and communicative impairments present in ASD but absent in anxiety disorders, as well as the developed social insight seen in children with anxiety disorders but absent in ASD (Hollocks et al., 2019; Kim et al., 2000).

Children, adolescents, and adults with ASD are also more likely to have depression compared to individuals without ASD (Hudson et al., 2019). Specifically, individuals with ASD are four times more likely to experience depression at some point in their lifespan. There are varying reports of prevalence rates, which can be attributed to a variety of factors such as a lack of validated instruments for measuring co-occurring psychiatric disorders (DeFilippis, 2018). Areas of concern related to co-occurring ASD and depression are vast and include potentially being at risk for suicide and overall higher levels of care (Pezzimenti et al., 2019).

In addition to depression, generalized anxiety, social anxiety, specific phobias, and obsessive compulsive disorder, are also common. Youth with ASD have a higher prevalence of social anxiety than the general population (Vasa & Mazurek, 2015). Higher levels of autism-specific characteristics have been associated with higher levels of social anxiety (Hallett et al., 2010; Min Liew et al., 2015). In particular, the overall social competence of an individual affects their autistic characteristics and social anxiety (Min Liew et al., 2015). Students with co-occurring ASD and social anxiety may receive both educational and medical treatments. In regard to OCD, this disorder has a later onset than ASD, is marked by ego dystonic repetitive patterns of behavior, and is not often linked to social or communicative difficulties (APA, 2013).

Intellectual Disability

The key characteristics of intellectual disability include impairments in cognitive abilities and everyday life or adaptive functioning skills (APA, 2013). These characteristics appear during a child's developmental period, vary in severity, and last throughout an individual's lifetime. Cognitive abilities are typically measured through standardized intellectual quotient (IQ) tests such as Wechsler Intelligence Scale for Children—Fifth Edition (WISC-V; Wechsler, 2014). ID is considered two standard deviations or below the general population, which would be an IQ score of approximately 70 or below (APA, 2013).

ID is one of the most common co-occurring disorders with ASD. Prevalence rates vary from an estimated 30 to 70 percent of individuals with ASD reported as having an ID (Fombonne, 2009; Matson & Shoemaker, 2009; Schofield et al., 2019). Individuals with co-occurring ASD and ID have unique needs compared to individuals with ASD alone. For instance, youth with ASD and ID experience more psychological and social difficulties compared to youth without disabilities and youth with ID alone (Baker & Blacher, 2021). Examples of such social difficulties include internalizing behavior, problems with developing friendships, and peer acceptance. Similarly, youth with ASD and ID are at risk for overall lower quality of life in important areas such as social inclusion and well-being (Arias et al., 2018). Teachers who work with students with co-occurring ASD and ID will need to support all of their areas of needs and particularly cognitive skills and adaptive functioning.

Seizure Disorders

One of the things that can be difficult for educators working with children with ASD is that they have a higher prevalence of seizure disorder or epilepsy compared with the general population (Capal et al., 2020; Viscidi et al., 2014). Epilepsy commonly occurs in individuals with ASD with a prevalence ranging from 2.4 percent to 46 percent vs 0.4% to 0.8% in the general population (Capal, 2020; Strasser et al., 2018). Conversely, rates of comorbid ASD in individuals with epilepsy are also higher, suggesting a common neurodevelopmental pathway (Capal et al., 2020).

Epilepsy is a disorder in and of itself that is still not well understood, although a significant amount of research has been conducted to determine the causes of seizures, the neurological impact of seizures, and medications that can help prevent or help individuals recover from seizures. In about half of the people that have epilepsy, there is no known cause (Mayo Clinic Staff, 2021). Epilepsy is a serious medical disorder and the occurrence of seizures can occur at any time and without warning. Educators need training in handling seizures and remaining calm and decisive while attending to an individual during and after a seizure.

Comorbid ASD and epilepsy have been associated with worse adaptive functioning, behavior, and quality of life. In one large cross-sectional study of children with ASD, Viscidi et al. (2014) found that children with both ASD and epilepsy exhibited greater impairment when compared with children with ASD and no epilepsy. They found that this relationship was mostly explained by low IQ. In a separate study comparing children with ASD with and without epilepsy, Turk et al. (2009) found that children with both ASD and epilepsy had more impaired daily living skills, motor skills, and challenging behaviors.

Results of Capal et al.'s (2020) recent exploratory study demonstrated that individuals with ASD, who were followed before they developed a seizure disorder, were found to already be distinct in differences and severity of characteristics from their same-age and same-sex compatriots. This suggests that it is not the seizures or neural activity that are responsible for more severe symptoms. Overall, the clinical impact of seizures on the phenotype (observable characteristics and symptoms) of ASD is still not well understood and researchers continue to investigate the relationship between the two (Capal et al., 2020; El Achkar et al., 2015).

Evidence-Based Practice (EBP)

You notice that a student in your classroom is having difficulty playing with his classmates at recess. While he wants to interact with his peers, oftentimes the interactions are awkward, non-productive and end up with your student alone and upset. You want to help, but where do you start? Finding and implementing the best teaching methods to help our autistic students learn is one of our prime directives as educators. But which practices should you choose from? Where do you start? What questions do you ask?

Over the last two decades, educators have been paying increasingly more attention to the use of Evidence-Based Practice (EBP). This push has been driven by families, advocates, lawmakers, educators, and researchers alike. Although these stakeholders have been searching for the best ways to teach, support, and address the needs of autistic individuals for almost a century, the emphasis on EBP has been more recent. In fact, other fields (e.g., medicine) realized the importance of EBP some time ago and created the practice standards and guidelines to inform their communities. Education has now lifted this mantel and continues to promote the use of EBP in research, policy, and practice. Evidence-Based Practice refers to the entire process while Evidence-Based Practices (EBPs) is used when referring to the actual intervention(s) being considered. The purpose of this chapter is to answer the basic questions about EBP(s) as the foundation to this book.

- ▶ What is EBP?

- ▶ Why use EBP?

- ▶ What EBP and autism reviews have been conducted and what are their findings?

- ▶ What questions should educators ask when choosing, using, and evaluating EBPs?

- ▶ What are the supports and barriers to implementing EBP?

What Is Evidence-Based Practice?

Many terms have been used to talk about the kinds of practices teachers use and how effective they are. This has been true for typically developing students, students with disabilities, and students with ASD in particular. The vocabulary may change between organizations and authors, but often different terms are referring to similar or the same thing(s). See Table 0.2 for a list of various terminology used.

Table 0.2 Terminology

WORDS USED TO DESCRIBE PRACTICES	WORDS USED TO DESCRIBE QUALITY OF PRACTICES
Teaching	Evidence-based
Practice	Peer-reviewed
Intervention	Scientifically based
Treatment	Research-based

(Continued)

(Continued)

WORDS USED TO DESCRIBE PRACTICES	WORDS USED TO DESCRIBE QUALITY OF PRACTICES
Model	Effective
Package	Validated
Training	Established
Special education	Promising
	Emerging
	Unestablished
	Not recommended
	Harmful

At various times, different words have been more in vogue. For example, during the several years before and after the No Child Left Behind Act (NCLB; 2001) was passed, *scientifically based practice* was the preferred term. Before further examining EBP, we need to unpack the term *practice*. This will go a long way to helping us understand why there are different understandings of EBP. For some, a practice is any method, intervention, or curriculum that is used to teach a specific skill or address a behavior. For example, if a student with autism needs help understanding the perspectives of his peers at recess, you might choose a social narrative to target this need. But others may use the term *practice* as a broad approach to doing work. This would include planning, decision-making, troubleshooting, or collaboration, for example, and therefore is seen as the professional's overall actions, behavior, or interactions. For example, while the social narrative might be the intervention used to teach the above student about his peers' views, the "practice" here would be everything involved with choosing, using, and evaluating the intervention. Yes, it matters that the teacher choose an intervention that has strong research evidence to support its efficacy, but just as important is making sure that this intervention fit this student's needs, that the teacher has the capacity to implement it with fidelity, that the student's family was collaborated with, and so forth.

Based on these understandings of *practice*, EBPs have been most commonly understood in two ways and both are needed. As stated above, the most prevalent idea about EBPs is that they are practices that have been vetted rigorously and proven to be effective (Cook & Odom, 2013). For example, positive reinforcement has been studied for decades and there are over 100 research studies that have shown positive reinforcement to be an effective intervention to address a wide range of skills and behaviors for autistic students (NCAEP, Steinbrenner et al., 2020). The preponderance of the research evidence supports its use and therefore it gives educators confidence that if they use positive reinforcement with fidelity that they are likely to see desired outcomes.

In most publications, EBP is seen in this manner—using the best research evidence that we have about a method, practice, or intervention to make good decisions about what practices we use with what students to teach what skills. This definition clearly emphasizes the research evidence behind any given practice. But EBP is also understood as a process. Following the lead of the medical profession (Sacket et al., 2000), EBP can be seen as a process of integrating three main pillars: (1) the best available research; (2) the needs, values, and strengths of the student (and family); and (3) the educator's experience and clinical judgment. This coincides with the second definition of practice used above: that is, the professional's overall actions, behavior, interactions, and the like.

Prizant (2011) has respectively termed these two EBP conceptualizations as narrow and appropriate views of EBP. Prizant wisely guides the field to consider more than just the research evidence. Indeed, past the three major components of the second definition, one may also include several other important factors that can and should be considered when implementing EBP including legal aspects (e.g., IDEA), family input, educators' capacity to implement practices, data-based decision-making, and so forth (LaCava, 2018; LaCava et al., 2021; National Autism Center, 2015; NCAEP, Steinbrenner et al., 2020).

Educators, clinicians, and families have been searching for the best practices to teach and support children and youth with autism for almost a century. Depending on the time and prevailing perspectives, various methods, treatments and practices have been developed and tested. For example, during the middle of the 20th century, psychoanalysis and institutionalization was common, reflecting the zeitgeist of the time. Through the years, behavioral, developmental, cognitive, naturalistic, and other models have gone through favor, more review, and use. This leads to our next question. . . .

Why Use EBP?

There are many reasons to use EBP including (1) ethical and moral imperatives; (2) overcoming a legacy of ineffective, overvalued and nonvalidated methods; (3) time factors; (4) legal mandates; and (5) the research to practice gap. Quite simply, we need to use EBP so that we are choosing and implementing practices that have the most up-to-date research behind them that support their use. Educators choose practices for many reasons including listening to authority figures because it is what they were taught in school, what is popular, and so forth. If your administrator tells you to use a practice, you do it. If your teammate shares a new method with you, you might use it. If a school has been doing something a certain way over many years, you follow that. You see something shared on Facebook and you want to try it. Now all of these might be perfectly good reasons, but knowing what the research says about any given practice is essential for success. We have enough knowledge now about dozens of effective methods and should be using these within a practice framework.

Students with IEPs have until age 22 to receive special education services. Even with this extended time, there are only so many hours in the day. If teachers are using ineffective practices, that wastes the student's time and reduces growth and future opportunities. Sadly, in the autism field we have had a long history of using methods that have no science behind them and that are ineffective or even harmful. This reduces progress and puts even more pressure on the student to learn before exiting school at 22. Families and teachers may be bombarded by endless products that tout all kinds of positive outcomes for autistic children, but with relatively little or no evidence to back up claims. Especially now with social media impacts, discerning which practices to use can be a Herculean task.

Legal mandates also guide EBP use. Starting with the NCLB Act in 2001, several laws have included EBP obligations in general and special education (see Every Student Succeeds Act, 2016; Individuals with Disabilities Education Improvement Act, 2004). This includes the fact that educators must use methods based in science and with proven effectiveness, training teachers in EBP, and improving student outcomes with EBP. Lastly, the Autism Collaboration, Accountability, Research, Education and Support (Autism CARES) Act of 2019 provided over $3 billion of funding for research, monitoring, and training. This includes money for research on EBP to be used across the lifespan as well as training for educators and providers.

By using EBP, we know we are using practices that have been vetted and can get the biggest bang for our buck and help students consistently make progress. Finally, there exists a gap between what research knowledge is available about teaching practices and what educators know and use in their classrooms. This research to practice gap has existed for decades and we can address it by disseminating knowledge about EBP and supporting EBP implementing for students with autism. The next section addresses this knowledge.

What EBP and Autism Reviews Have Been Conducted and What Are Their Findings?

To understand what has been published on EBP, one can review the literature in three ways: (1) single practice reviews, (2) single domain views, and (3) broad systematic reviews of many practices. For example, if we were considering using a social narrative to teach our students about recess interactions, we could do a single practice review of all published studies about social narratives. Or we might review the literature for all studies completed in the social skills domain. Finally, we might look at broad reviews of EBP that have been conducted that cover a range of different practices and parameters. While doing one of the first two reviews may take significant time, broad systematic reviews have already done this work and can provide educators with research information to support their choices more quickly.

Since 2000, several of these broad reviews have taken place. Some of these reviews have been more subjective in nature (Simpson et al., 2005), others have only focused on younger children with autism (National Research Council [NRC], 2001), while other reviews took place in non-education fields such as psychology (Reichow et al., 2011) or health care (Centers for Medicare and Medicaid Services [CMMS], 2010). We will briefly summarize the findings of some of these historical reviews and then spend the majority of our time looking at the four most recent education-related works.

The NRC published its landmark text, *Educating Students With Autism*, in 2001. This work represented the best available research evidence and practice for young children with autism to age 8. The NRC laid out general guidelines for effective programs including intensity, goals, student–teacher ratio, strength of evidence of research, as well as provided evidence to support the use of 10 unique comprehensive programs in the United States for autism.

In 2005, Simpson et al. did a subjective review of 33 common autism interventions and programs representing five domains: interpersonal relationship, skill-based, cognitive, physiological/biological/neurological, and others. Practices were classified along a continuum of evidence as scientifically based practice, promising practice, limited supporting information for practice, and not recommended. The authors considered each practice's reported outcomes, risks, costs, and such and concluded that only four practices met the highest scientifically based practice classification: ABA, discrete trial teaching, pivotal response training (PRT), and the LEAP program. An additional 12 practices were deemed promising in nature (e.g., cognitive behavior modification, Social Stories, incidental teaching). There was not enough information to judge 16 practices, and two practices were not recommended due to the potential for harm (i.e., holding therapy, facilitated communication).

In 2010, the CMMS published their findings from their environmental scan of the evidence regarding autism-related psychosocial services and supports for children, transitioning youth, and adults. They reviewed literature from 1998 through 2008 and judged practices based on the rigor of the research and then deemed practices as either evidence-based interventions, emerging evidence-based interventions, or unestablished interventions. The CMMS found that for children, there were 15 practices that met the level of evidence-based interventions, 13 emerging evidence-based interventions, and three unestablished interventions. The majority of evidence-based interventions were behavioral in nature. At the transitioning youth level, only one practice met evidence-based interventions standards, while at the adult level only three did.

Past our brief explanations above, we encourage you to look at these older reviews to understand history and trends over time. We will now focus on the most recent works. Three organizations have led the push for understanding and implementing EBP in the United States: (1) the National Autism Center (NAC), (2) the National Professional Development Center on Autism Spectrum Disorder (NPDC), and (3) the National Center on Autism Evidence and Practice (NCAEP). These groups have created rigorous guidelines for reviewing the literature, judging the quality of research studies, classifying practices, and disseminating the information to all stakeholders. The NAC completed broad reviews in 2009 and 2015 and as of this writing, was in the process of conducting a literature review for Phase 3 of its National Standards Project. The NPDC completed a broad review in 2014 (NPDC, Wong et al., 2014) and the NCAEP built on this work to publish the most up-to-date study in 2020 (Steinbrenner et al., 2020), which reviewed the research literature up until 2017 for individuals with autism ages birth to 22 years. These four reviews, in addition to the seminal 2005 work by Simpson et al., will be referred to as "core reviews" throughout the rest of this resource.

An analysis of the Table 0.3 information, as well as the details of their related publications (see Appendices), leads to conclusions about review similarities and differences. All reviews concluded that there were numerous practices that met the highest level of evidence and are rated as EBP. A majority of these practices are from the behavioral literature (e.g., reinforcement, prompting, differential reinforcement, discrete trial training [DTT]) although over time more and different practices have been rated as EBP. See Table 0.4 for a list of all 28 NCAEP and 14 NAC EBPs; you'll notice that many entries are on both lists.

One caveat to all this, the NPDC and NCAEP reviewed focused interventions, which they defined as practices that address specific student skills or goals (Odom et al., 2010). Steinbrenner et al. (2020) added that "these practices are operationally defined, address specific learner outcomes, and tend to occur over a shorter time period . . ." (p. 11). While the NAC also looked at some specific focused interventions (e.g., story-based interventions), they also reviewed treatment packages or combinations of practices referred to as comprehensive treatment model. This is when several practices are combined to address core autism features and several outcomes. So whereas the NCAEP identified individual behavioral practices such as reinforcement and prompting as evidence-based, the NAC rated the broader category of behavioral behavioral interventions as an established practice. In this case, behavioral interventions include many focused interventions such as reinforcement and prompting. You'll also note that the NAC and NCAEP used different terms to rate the practices. In this case, evidence-based and established practices are at the same highest level of evidence.

There has also been a trend over time of more research articles being published, more research studies meeting criteria for these reviews and thus, ultimately, more practices reaching the EBP level as well as more practices having some support.

Table 0.3 Evidence-Based Practice

NCAEP 2020	NAC 2015
28 EVIDENCE-BASED PRACTICE	**14 ESTABLISHED PRACTICES**
Antecedent-Based Interventions	Behavioral Interventions
Augmentative and Alternative Communication	Cognitive Behavioral Intervention Package
Behavior Momentum Intervention	Modeling
Cognitive Behavioral Instructional Strategies	Naturalistic Teaching Strategies
Differential Reinforcement of Alternative, Incompatible or Other Behavior	Parenting Training
Direct Instruction	Peer Training Package
Discrete Trial Teaching	Pivotal Response
Exercise and Movement	Treatment
Extinction	Schedules
Functional Behavior Assessment	Scripting
Functional Communication Training	Self-Management
Modeling	Social Skills Package
Music-Mediated Intervention	Story-Based Intervention
Naturalistic Intervention	Language Training
Parent-Implemented Intervention	Comprehensive Behavioral Treatment for Young Children
Peer-Based Instruction and Intervention	
Prompting	
Reinforcement	
Response Interruption/Redirection	
Self-Management	
Sensory Integration	
Social Narratives	
Social Skills Training	
Task Analysis	
Technology-Aided Instruction and Intervention	
Time Delay	
Video Modeling	
Visual Supports	

So now you know what EBP is, some of the brief EBP history, why EBP should be used, and what broad reviews have revealed regarding EBP use with students with ASD. However, just because a teacher chooses an EBP does not guarantee success. This is where the "practice" comes into play as so many factors must be considered for the best implementation and outcomes. According to IDEA (2004), Every individual between the ages of 3 and 21 must be provided a free and appropriate public education (FAPE). The exact statute reads as follows:

IDEA: Free Appropriate Public Education

Section 300.101 Free appropriate public education (FAPE).

(a)　General. A free appropriate public education must be available to all children residing in the State between the ages of 3 and 21, inclusive, including children with disabilities who have been suspended or expelled from school, as provided for in §300.530(d).

(b)　FAPE for children beginning at age 3.

(1) Each State must ensure that—

(i) The obligation to make FAPE available to each eligible child residing in the State begins no later than the child's third birthday; and

(ii) An IEP or an IFSP is in effect for the child by that date, in accordance with §300.323(b).

The most recent supreme court case on the principle of FAPE was *Endrew F. v. Douglas County School District Re-1* (2017). According to this decision, in order to provide FAPE the school must offer an IEP that is reasonably calculated to enable a child to make progress appropriate in light of the child's circumstances, which includes (1) identifying present levels of academic achievement and functional performance, (2) setting measurable academic and functional annual goals, and (3) stating how progress toward meeting annual goals will be measured and reported. In cases where the student's behavior impedes their own learning and/or the learning of their peers, the Individual Education Plan (IEP) team must consider and, if necessary to provide FAPE, include appropriate behavioral goals and objectives and other appropriate services and supports. In addition, the law requires that the intervention practices that educators use to address their students' IEP goals must be evidence-based, meaning there is some empirical demonstration of their likelihood of being successful. This legal mandate poses a huge challenge for educators of students with ASD as their learning needs are complex and many engage in behavior that impedes their learning and/or the learning of others. When choosing, using, and evaluating the use of EBPs with their students, there are important questions that educators should ask.

What Questions Should Educators Ask When Choosing, Using, and Evaluating EBP?

1. What Are the Research Designs Used by the Existing Evidence?

The current body of research is the best information to date that educators have to make decisions about what intervention(s) will most likely lead to the desired outcomes for their students. The first place they should look is evidence-based reviews as researchers may have already objectively identified, evaluated, and synthesized the research relevant to a particular intervention. These reviews typically only contain experimental designs that are used to examine whether an intervention actually causes improved outcomes because the variables are highly controlled. There are three main types of experimental designs: (1) randomized controlled trials (RCTs), (2) group quasi-experimental, and (3) single case or subject. Research involving students with ASD is largely single subject due to the fact that the needs of this population are so deep, varied, and complex and each individual has a very unique set of circumstances. Single case designs (SCDs) involve one or a very small number of subjects and their performance prior to the intervention that is compared to their performance during and/or after the intervention.

For many years "evidence-based" reviews were somewhat subjective. The author collected articles on a topic, summarized them, and came to subjective conclusions. Meta-analysis was developed to make literature reviews more objective using statistics. In performing a meta-analysis, the author searches the literature, has specific criteria as to which articles are included and excluded, calculates effect size, and then calculates an estimation of the "true" effect size in the larger population. Effect size tells you how meaningful the differences are between the performance of the experimental and control groups, which indicates how likely the intervention would be to make a significant impact in the real world. There are different ways to calculate effect size, but an educator basically needs to know that in general 0.1 to 0.3 effect sizes are considered small, 0.3 to 0.5 are considered medium, and 0.5 or greater are considered large with 0.8 or greater definitely showing significance.

"Gray" or fugitive literature is "any study report outside of commercially published journal articles." (Polanin et al., 2016, p. 209). Examples are unpublished dissertations, conference presentations, and other papers either not submitted for or rejected from publication. Traditionally, even though they may have used experimental designs, unpublished studies have been excluded from evidence-based reviews because they have not been peer-reviewed. However, meta-analyses have been done that conclude that not including unpublished studies in literature reviews may skew and overestimate the true effect size of an intervention. (Gage et al., 2017). In addition, "gray" literature that uses experimental designs provides some degree of evidence that an intervention may work with certain students in certain contexts.

Another type of research is qualitative research, which includes focus groups, one-on-one interviews, case studies of an individual, questionnaires, observing individuals, audio recordings, and picture/artifact analysis. In general, this research does not involve numbers but is considered a detailed description that the researcher provides about a topic, experience, item, person, and such that cannot be "quantified" by numerical statistics. This type of research is used within sociology, anthropology, political science, psychology, social work, and education. These are fields of study in which taking into consideration the uniqueness of the human characteristics and experiences can be important when trying to glean information about specific populations.

In the past couple of decades, qualitative data computer analyses programs have been developed so that the researcher can input typed notes or audio recordings and the computer will analyze the words, phrases, and sentences for patterns that can be coded and analyzed by the researcher. Within education and special education we commonly use focus groups, case studies, questionnaires, and observations of individuals to help us better understand about things such as people's viewpoints of inclusion of children with disabilities, experiences with certain teaching or intervention methods, amount of training and education with specific academic teaching methods, and/or describe the behaviors demonstrated by a student.

No specific intervention or method of teaching and handling behaviors can be proven to be evidence-based using only qualitative research. But, individuals with autism have such different manifestations within their own ASD condition making it difficult to create large groups to study something specific across all individuals, which is what quantitative research seeks to do. Arguments against qualitative research often center around the "subjectivity" of the information gained and that it is not "objective" enough to be able to make claims of effectiveness about an intervention. This can often be true and is why we still need to use quantitative research methods to prove the actual effectiveness of interventions and strategies. Even so, educators also need qualitative research and information in order to better understand children with ASD and their individual and unique needs.

The information within this book about whether or not an intervention or teaching strategy is evidence-based is all based on quantitative research that has been published in peer-reviewed articles. It has taken 30 to 50 years to establish some of these interventions as evidence-based due to the difficulty of implementing large group and randomized control studies with individuals with ASD. There are many interventions out there that have been around for decades with no quantitative research studies that have been conducted to analyze their effectiveness. It is important for educators to do their best to remain objective about the interventions and teaching methods they use while also taking the time to subjectively understand and care about each child with ASD's well-being and experiences throughout their education.

2. Is There a Contextual Fit Between the EBP and the Specific Situation?

In addition to knowing what the best available research is, educators also need to consider characteristics and perhaps preferences of the student and family and the knowledge and skill of the implementing practitioner(s) (Sam & Hume, 2019), an approach aligned with evidence-based medicine (Sackett et al., 1996). In other words, educators need to review the best available evidence to identify and prioritize interventions with the strongest chance of resulting in positive outcomes in their particular situations, known as the contextual fit. In order to do this, teachers need to know nuanced details of the evidence they are considering, including information about the student population such as co-morbid conditions (e.g., ID, anxiety, or depression), setting (e.g., urban, rural, suburban, socioeconomic status of the school), implementers (e.g., researchers, teachers, instructional assistants, level of training and experience), and specific skills being targeted (e.g., social interaction, emotional regulation, language production, social use of language).

Educators also must consider if the expense of the resources needed is feasible enough for sustainable implementation and if the predicated outcomes are beneficial enough to justify the cost, a process called cost-effectiveness or benefit-cost analysis (Cook et al., 2020; Leko et al., 2019). Cost-effectiveness analysis is an important component of EBP as it guides "decisions about how limited financial resources should be spent to produce the best educational outcome" (Detrich, 2020, p. 423). To do this, there needs to be a summary of required training, materials, and preparation time and a comparison of those costs to the anticipated benefit based on the best available evidence. There is currently limited guidance available to decision-makers in navigating this process (Cook et al., 2020; Leko et al., 2019). A fairly recent evaluation process has been developed to assist in this process referred to as economic evaluation, which is "the evaluation of time and financial resources consumed during intervention implementation" (Scheibel et al., 2022, p. 4). This is helpful in determining feasibility, total cost of anticipated outcomes, and long-term economic benefits (Scheibel et al., 2022). The Ingredients Method (Levin et al., 2018) is an economic evaluation process that applies to emerging and promising, ineffective, and harmful interventions, which include not only the cost of the material resources needed in the moment but also the more distant resources that may be needed, educator's time spent preparing for and providing the intervention, and the time the student with ASD spent receiving the intervention. In addition, the method considers the "opportunity cost," which is other learning opportunities at risk of being lost and the overall estimated implementation cost, which can be statistically analyzed. This process is obviously outside of most teachers' job description or expertise, but it is important for them to be aware of these concepts especially when considering or being a part of a decision-making team that is considering interventions that have exorbitant costs.

3. What Should Be Done if There Is Not an EBP With a Contextual Fit?

Cook et al. state "evidence-based reviews are a trustworthy approach for identifying generally effective instructional practices—but no practices, not even EBPs, are effective for all learners" (2020, p. 7). Because of the huge variety in learning profiles and individual circumstances, each student with ASD is a single subject or "n of 1" so to speak. In these cases, teachers must make decisions using the best available evidence and potentially consider emerging or promising interventions, particularly if those interventions are not harmful and are feasible in terms of costs. Some interventions can be harmful in a number of ways, with some being more concerning than others. The most serious harm can have devastating and life-altering effects on families and children such as Facilitated Communication leading to false accusations about child abuse (Boynton, 2012); the Rapid Prompting Method (RPM) leading to prompt dependency (Lang et al., 2014); violating the personal rights of individuals with disabilities such as access to effective treatment, self-expression, communication, and self-determination (Todd, 2016; Tostanoski et al., 2014); and giving the individual, caregivers, and educators false hope through exaggerated claims and promises of the interventions, effectiveness (e.g., such as "curing autism") (Heflin & Simpson, 1998).

Others potential harms are important to consider but not as serious such as taking valuable instructional time and financial resources away from more evidence-based strategies. Obviously using Facilitated Communication or the RPM is more harmful than say, trying a Social Decision-Making Intervention. If an intervention can be quickly created and implemented and is free or has very lost costs, does it truly inhibit the use of another intervention in any way? If not and especially if it has SOME evidence that it may be beneficial to students with similar profiles in similar contexts, it may be worth considering as long as individual student data is taken that guides future decision-making about continuing or terminating the intervention which is further described later in this resource.

In terms of cost effectiveness, it is important to note that special education has been underfunded from its inception. Although using economic evaluation is very valuable and increasing, it is often classroom teachers who are making intervention decisions with extremely limited budgets. We would recommend that these decision-makers consider that if there are resources consistent with the critical elements of the EBP already freely available either through prior expenditures or via the internet that can be adapted to align with the critical features of the EBP, using them may be the best decision rather than spending scarce resources on purchasing, providing training, and supporting the appropriate implementation of something new.

4. What Are the Critical Elements of the Intervention and How Do I Ensure They Are Used With Fidelity?

"If the EBP is being implemented with fidelity and the student is still not responding, consider adapting it in ways that might make it more effective for the student, but do not alter its critical elements" (Cook et al., 2020, p. 12). For this to be possible, the "critical elements" of every intervention need to be clearly identified because they make the intervention effective and evidence-based. To ensure that the critical elements are implemented with fidelity in either the original or adapted intervention, educators should use an implementation checklist. These are sometimes provided by the creator(s) of the intervention or credible sources such as the National Professional Development Center on Autism Spectrum Disorders. Educators can also develop their own based on a detailed description of the intervention. It is also recommended that someone else observe the intervention being implemented making note of whether it was used as designed and researched. At the end of each chapter regarding an evidence-based or emerging or promising practice intervention, we have provided suggested resources that can be used to assist with understanding the critical elements of that intervention.

5. How Do I Determine if the EBP Is Working for an Individual Student?

"Because no instructional practices, not even EBPs, are guaranteed to work for every learner, teachers should engage in progress monitoring to determine whether students are making adequate progress" (Cook et al., 2020, p. 8). The target skill should be operationalized for data collection purposes. Baseline data needs to be taken prior to implementing, and data during the intervention should be collected in the same manner for comparison. The data should be graphed with a trendline. This can be done by hand or on graphing software such as Excel. If the student has met mastery criterion, the teacher should adjust the goal to focus on fluency, maintenance, or generalization. If the student is making progress (the data shows an upward trend), continue as planned. If the student is not making progress, or is making inadequate progress, the teacher should simplify the skill or improve the antecedents. Some ways to simplify skills include using chaining, breaking a task analysis into smaller steps, using assistive technology (AT), or requiring a different set of responses. To improve antecedents, the teacher can change the prompting system, use peers as a model, or use video modeling (VM). Finally, if the data is variable (the trend is up and down), the teacher should improve motivation by embedding choice, varying praise statements, or involve the student in self-graphing.

Graph Example:

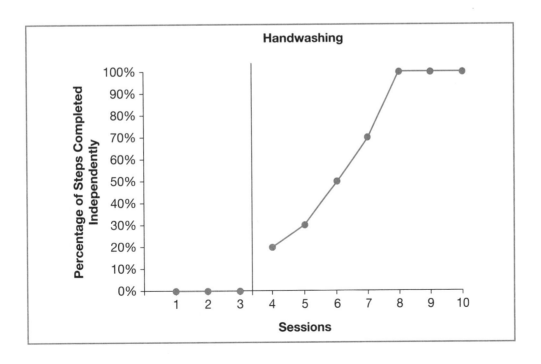

What Are the Supports and Barriers to Implementing EBP?

One effort to make evidence-based information more useable and accessible was led by Dr. Ann Sam and resulted in the online e-learning module *Autism Focused Intervention Resources and Modules (AFIRM)* (Sam et al., 2020). The NPDC investigators and staff collaborated with staff at the Ohio Center for Autism and Low Incidence Disorders (OCALI) to develop online training modules. The Nebraska ASD Network, the Kansas Technical Assistance System Network (TASN), and the Colorado Department of Education have collaborated, forming a "tri-state network" that provides many free webinars and other resources on EBPs. We have included the Uniform Resource Locator (URL) for the corresponding modules if they exist in the Recommended Readings and Resources section of each intervention.

Consumers of research in the education field need to be able to evaluate the quality of the current research literature in all fields related to the education of students with ASD and especially general and special education. Carnine (1997) identifies three elements that permit quality research to be evaluated: trustworthiness, useability, and accessibility. Trustworthiness is the extent to which practitioners have confidence in the research findings. Useability is the practicality of research-based findings relative to the daily practices of practitioners. To be useable, research must be disseminated in a clearly written way that is understandable by and must deal with topics of importance to the average practitioner. Accessibility is the extent to which research findings are available to practitioners. To be accessible, it is important that practitioners have quick and easy access to its information. Since the high standard was set by the latest Supreme Court case on what constitutes FAPE, there is increased accountability for students making meaningful progress. Because the vast majority of educators truly care about the quality of life of their students, they are typically very motivated to do what works simply for their survival in the field. If they are not using EBPs, it is potentially because there are one or more of the following: trustworthiness, useability, and/or accessibility barriers.

Lack of Replication and Publication Bias

Educators and the field of education in general have concerns about the trustworthiness of the current research base and two things in particular: (1) lack of replication studies and (2) publication bias (Cook, 2014). Since some error is unavoidable in research, replication is essential for identifying and correcting findings that may be invalid (Travers et al., 2016). However, they are seldom conducted (Makel & Plucker, 2014) and when they are, they too often fail to validate original findings (Klein et al., 2014; Open Science Collaboration, 2015). Publication bias is when the published literature is unrepresentative of the population of completed studies. This happens because studies with positive findings regarding the intervention results are more likely to be published than those that did not show results that were statistically significant because researchers are less likely to submit them and they are more likely to be rejected (Franco et al., 2014; Shadish et al., 2016). This skews the published research base leading to inaccurate or incomplete information for the consumer as they attempt to make important daily decisions about which intervention(s) to use.

"Cherry Picking" Research Subjects/Lack of Contextual Fit

The fact that no EBP is guaranteed to work for every learner is especially relevant for teachers on the front lines in a vast range of classroom situations serving a wide variety of students. Educators have the unique challenge of identifying and using the most effective interventions to support all of the students they serve, which requires making daily decisions with life-impacting consequences. However, they do not have the luxury that researchers do of not including subjects who do not fit the traditional research designs, who do not make significant progress, or who are potentially dangerous to themselves or others. Public schools are the only entity that cannot refuse to serve any student due to the FAPE for all students mandate of the IDEA. Therefore, it stands to reason that they sometimes find themselves serving students for which there are currently no EBPs that are a contextual fit to their circumstances. The most common co-occurring condition reported in the most recent core review was an ID, which, as stated in the Overview of ASD chapter, co-occurs an estimated 30 to 70 percent of the time. In a 2019 study conducted by Knight and colleagues, the majority of the 535 special educators surveyed (70%) reported teaching students with both ID and ASD and were more likely to use EBPs if they taught in self-contained settings. Since it is more likely that students with ASD with co-occurring ID are educated in self-contained settings than those with Level 1 (mild autism) and the research literature disproportionately includes subjects with co-occuring ASD and ID, this is not a surprising finding. A commonsense conclusion is that when educators have evidence-based interventions that apply to their individual situations, they use them.

Lack of Research Involving Students With Previous Diagnosis of Asperger's and/or High Functioning Autism

Dr. Simpson and colleagues contributed a great deal to the literature on individuals with Asperger's syndrome and/or "high functioning autism" (e.g. Barnhill et al., 2000; Griswold et al., 2002; Myles et al., 1994, 1995, 1999, 2001, 2002; Myles & Simpson, 1994, 2001a, 2001b, 2002a, 2002b, 2002c; Simpson & Myles, 1998; Simpson et al., 2000). At the time of his seminal writings on EBPs, ASD was defined in terms of five pervasive developmental disorders: (1) Autism, (2) Rett syndrome, (3) Childhood Disintegrative Disorder, (4) Asperger's syndrome, and (5) Pervasive Developmental Disorder Not Otherwise Specified (PDD-NOS). The major modification in the definition of ASD came in the fifth revision of the *Diagnostic Statistical Manual of Mental Disorders* (DSM) in 2013, when it dropped the five separate disorders and made ASD one encompassing category effectively removing the diagnoses of Asperger's and PDD-NOS. Smith et al. (2015) systematically reviewed 25 articles evaluating the criteria for an ASD diagnosis in both the *DSM-IV-TR* and *DSM-5*. The findings were that 25 to 50 percent of individuals did not maintain their diagnosis with the greatest decreases being among those with previous diagnoses of Asperger's disorder or PDD-NOS and/or with IQs over 70, which many referred to as "high functioning autism" (HFA) in the past. The concern with this recategorization is that in the most recent time period of the core reviews (2012–2017), only 11 percent of the studies included even one subject diagnosed with Asperger's syndrome, and only 13.9 percent included even one subject with PDD-NOS (NCAEP, 2020, p. 33). Even though they are no longer official *DSM* diagnoses, there are still many school-age individuals who are receiving special education services with those characteristics, who were given those diagnoses before 2013, or who self-identify under those "labels." Teachers desperately need guidance on what practices have an evidence base with these student populations.

Lack of Sufficient Detail

Details of the evidence being considered and, specifically, information about the student population (e.g., co-morbid conditions such as ID, anxiety, or depression), specific skills being targeted (e.g., social interaction, emotional regulation, language production, social use of language), and the critical elements of the intervention are often not described in enough detail to either be replicated or be useful in the selection process. In fact, many of the studies included none or only one subject with ASD. In fact, 64% of studies in the latest core review included at least one participant with autism, indicating no guarantee that there was more than one. There was, however, a drop of about 35% from the 1990 to 2011 period (83%) to the 2012 to 2017 period (48%); and only 5% reported co-occurring conditions (NCEAP, Steinbrenner et al., 2020). Considering the vast differences in the ASD population, simply stating that at least one subject has "autism" without any additional details about the subjects tells a practitioner very little.

Accessing EBP's Is Time-Consuming, Difficult, and Potentially Expensive

If it is time-consuming and difficult to find the needed information, teachers are less likely to put forth the effort to locate and consume it. Implementation and diffusion sciences both emphasize the need to translate scientifically based information into practical information that service providers can use in their work with children and youth with ASD and their families (Dingfelder & Mandell, 2011; Fixsen et al., 2013). As Carnine (1997) stated in his seminal article 25 years ago, "the audience for educational research is frequently assumed to be other researchers and theoreticians, rather than practitioners and families. Many reports are too difficult (for practitioners) to comprehend" (p. 516). Compounding this problem is the fact that many practitioner consumers have no training and little experience in reading and interpreting research (Carnine, 1997). Rather than categorizing these reports as too "difficult," a more appropriate conceptualization is that the two worlds are just very different. Some researchers have no or little training or experience working with learners with ASD in actual school environments. Since practitioners are the ones implementing in a real-world setting, it is imperative that research reports be written in a way that truly serves the population for which it was intended and is understandable and, therefore, useable by the average practitioner resulting in the highest possible levels of external and social validity.

Advancing the
EBP Movement

· ·

The field of educating students with ASD has come a long way since Dr. Simpson's seminal articles on EBPs (Heflin & Simpson 1998; Simpson, 2005), but it still has a long way to go. As practitioners, we are going to take the advice of Cook et al. (2018) that "Instead of simply following along, special educators could take the lead in implementing open science" (p. 112) and make some recommendations that will help close the well-documented research to practice gap that has existed for far too long.

Research the Entire ASD Spectrum and
Social Pragmatic Communication Disorder (SPCD)

There is clearly not enough research on school-based interventions for individuals on the spectrum who previously had the diagnosis of Asperger's syndrome or PDD-NOS (before the *DSM* changes in 2013) and who now would either not qualify for an ASD diagnosis or would fall within the Level 1 (mild) category. Since 2013, there is still a lack of definitive diagnostic criteria and assessment tools used to define and identify SPCD, as well as a lack of information about how SPCD relates or does not relate to ASD (Dolata et al., 2022; Mandy et al., 2017; Norbury, 2014). This results in teachers making day-to-day decisions about interventions used with many of the students they serve with little to no guidance provided by the available evidence.

Focus on Specific Skills Targeted

Every student with ASD has a unique profile regarding skill deficits. Identifying specifically what skill deficits are being targeted in individual studies and reporting the outcomes on those skills will make it easier for educators to match the intervention to the skills they are trying to teach. We took the various skill definitions from the core reviews and tried to combine and clarify.

Language Production	Skills related to expressive and receptive language including expressive language skills include the ability to functionally use spoken words (production) for communicating wants and needs; labeling items in the environment; and describing events, actions, or ideas. Receptive language skill includes the understanding of words indicated by responding to directions; selecting images, colors, or words upon request; and responding to one's name.
Social Communication	Skills related to the use of verbal and nonverbal language for social purposes including but not limited to understanding of the mental and emotional states of self and others and how this impacts how behavior is interpreted in social situations; the use of language in social contexts; and the ability to share experiences, thoughts, and emotions.

(Continued)

(Continued)

Social Skills	Skills needed to interact with one or more individuals including but not limited to social engagement, social problem solving, appropriate participation in group activities, and friendship skills.
Executive Functioning Skills	Complex skills in two subcategories: (1) metacognition and (2) behavior regulation. Metacognition skills include but are not limited to initiation, working memory, organizational skills, problem-solving, setting goals, making decisions, time management, and monitoring. Behavior regulation skills include but are not limited to inhibiting impulses, adapting to changes, and self-regulation.
Emotional Regulation	Skills needed for emotional well-being.
Joint Attention	Skills needed for sharing interests and/or experiences.
Play	Skills related to the use of toys or leisure materials that do not involve self-stimulatory behavior or require interaction with others such as functional independent play (e.g., manipulation of toys to determine how they "work").
Functional Skills	Skills related to personal care and independent living that are embedded into daily routines including but not limited to feeding, dressing, toileting, hygiene tasks, sleeping, family and community activities, health and fitness, phone skills, money management, and self-advocacy.
Learning Readiness	Skills related to task performance versus task content or curriculum areas that serve as the foundation for successful mastery of skills in other domains including but not limited to imitation, following instructions, attending to environmental sounds, and not disrupting others.
Academic/ Pre-academic	Skills that are precursors or required for success with school activities including but not limited to sequencing, color identification, letter identification, number identification, fluency, reading, writing, mathematics, and skills required to study or perform well on exams.
Sensory-related Skills	Skills related to movement or motion including both fine motor, gross motor, and skills related to sensory functioning.
Vocational Skills	Skills related to employment.

Prioritize Emerging/Promising Practices That Target Overlooked Social Communication Skills

In a 2012 memorandum, the federal Office of Management and Budget stated "Where evidence is strong, we should act on it. Where evidence is suggestive, we should consider it. Where evidence is weak, we should build the knowledge to support better decisions in the future" (Zients, 2012, p. 1). Of the core reviews, only the 2009 review by the NAC included any information on the effectiveness of interventions with students with Asperger's and only identified two as Established (Modeling and Story-Based Intervention Package) and five as Emerging (Cognitive Behavioral Intervention Package, Initiation Training,

Multi-Component Package, Social Skills Package, and Theory of Mind Training). Evidence is clearly weak on interventions that target social communication skills and "some effective practices may not yet be identified as EBPs" (Cook et al., 2020, p. 13). We believe, as did the authors of the latest core review, that "scientists should find fertile ground for further research in these areas" (NCAEP, Steinbrenner, 2020, p. 71).

Define and Describe Interventions, Subjects, and Settings in More Detail

"As behavior analysts know, definitions matter. A well-conceived definition can promote conceptual understanding and set the context for effective action. Conversely, a poor definition or confusion about definitions hinders clear understanding, communication, and action" (Slocum et al., 2014, p. 42). The heterogeneity of individuals with ASD requires interventions that are tailored to the specific needs of each person (Georgiades et al., 2013; Gwynette, 2013) and this requires detailed descriptions of not just the intervention but also the participants in the study, targeted outcomes, the setting, and contextual variables such as staff skills and the capacity of the environment overall. Currently this is not the case, especially as previously discussed when it comes to the study participants. Detailed descriptions including at the very minimum intellectual range; expressive language, receptive language, and pragmatic language functioning; and co-occurring conditions are needed for teachers to be able to make the best decision regarding which interventions to use with which students.

Conduct More Research in Educational and Less in Clinical Settings

A major limitation of the core reviews is that researchers primarily served as implementers in a majority of the studies (52%) and in an additional 10% were present in some capacity as coaches (NCAEP, Steinbrenner et al., 2020, p. 37). Actual educators and related service providers were implementers in only 20 percent of the studies (NCAEP, Steinbrenner, 2020, p. 37). A somewhat positive development is that in the most recent time period of the core reviews (2012 to 2017), 50% of the studies were conducted at least in an educational setting although a majority in individual sessions were still done by researchers (NCAEP, Steinbrenner, 2020, p. 46). As stated by the NCAEP in 2020, "Certainly, directions for the future would be to more often examine the efficacy of interventions when implemented in 'authentic' educational settings by practitioners such as teachers, speech pathologists, psychologists, and other service providers" (NCAEP, Steinbrenner, 2020, p. 46). If we are ever to truly close the research to practice gap, this should be a top priority for all, and especially government-funded, research.

Provide Detailed Cost Analyses

Economic evaluation of interventions is extremely important. However, it is unrealistic that a teacher would have the time or be able to do this for every intervention they are considering. We realize that there are variables that researchers are not privy to that would impact this analyses, but a "base analysis" such as that provided by Scheibel et al. (2022) regarding the implementation of DIR/Floor Time and the RPM are extremely helpful for practitioner decision-makers.

Disseminate More Efficiently and Effectively

We agree with Cook et al. (2018) that "open access to outcomes ensures that research findings are freely available to all who are interested rather than being accessible to only those who can afford to pay or are at institutions that can pay for subscriptions"

(p. 110). In addition, "the standard data-based method of reporting research in professional journals is not the most effective format for communicating research to teachers" (Landrum et al., 2007, p. 12). The use of other popular dissemination tools such as podcasts and social media, more publications in practitioner-friendly journals in practitioner-friendly language, presentations at conferences that are evidence-based but not statistics heavy, and developing more professional relationships between researchers and practitioners could all help with this endeavor.

Train More Practitioners to Be Research Consumers and Implementers Rather Than Producers

There has been a large increase in the number of teachers who are also receiving training in applied behavior analysis and becoming BCBAs. However, many who are getting this credential and are practicing in educational environments are not receiving the training necessary to be good practitioners. In the words of Malott, "We train them to value research highly and to value those who produce it. Then the new graduates get jobs as practitioners or as managers and administrators and find themselves poorly trained to do the job they were not taught to value. In other words, most of the people paying the pipers are calling for one set of tunes, but the graduate schools are teaching their students to play and value a different set" (Malott, 1992, p. 85). "This analysis suggests we should train fewer scientists and more practitioners. But this does not mean practitioners and managers should not empirically validate their work and the systems they manage, nor does it mean they should not make their decisions as data-based as possible. It only means applied settings need a special sort of program evaluation and systems analysis research, and this systems evaluation and research is rarely the sort that meets the standards of novelty and experimental control properly required for publication in prestigious research journals" (Malott, 1992, p. 85).

Pursue Practice-Based Research That Equally Values Internal and External Validity

Too much emphasis and value placed on internal validity or "proving" causal relationships often decreases the relevance, generalization, and application, to real world settings, known as external validity. "The most promising lines of remedy have been in bringing the research (or even better, producing the research) closer to the actual circumstances of practice" (Green, 2008, p. 123). This will not only address unique circumstances but also give the teacher immediate feedback. "The promise of this 'pull' approach has led to the suggestion that if we want more evidence-based practice, we need more practice-based evidence" (Green, 2008, p. 123).

Respect the Expertise of Practitioners

Leaders in behavior analysis recognize that when an EBP that is a perfect contextual fit is not available, clinicians need to use their expertise to determine the applicability of the scientific evidence for their unique situation (Slocum et al., 2014). This is also true of teachers. It is important for researchers to refrain from drawing conclusions about whether specifically Emerging/Promising interventions or interventions that have not yet been researched should be used as they are not privy to all the information needed to make that determination.

Structure of This Resource

This resource is an attempt to help continue to bridge the research-to-practice gap by translating the five "core views" previously identified into "understandable information that teachers or other practitioners can use" as suggested by Steinbrenner et al. (2020, p. 50). It is written for educators by educators as "Communicating research findings from the perspective of a fellow-teacher may be one way to enhance the teacher-friendliness of research, enhance teachers' perceptions of its useability, and increase the corresponding likelihood that they will implement what the research literature supports in their classrooms" (Landrum, 2007, p. 4). We limited the content to interventions for students ages 3 to 21, as that is the age range for which special education services are mandated. We made our best attempt at clarifying and being consistent with intervention definitions, and we also looked for other systematic reviews and meta-analyses that may have been missed or not have met the inclusion criteria of the core reviews but still provide front line educators with valuable information to consider when making day-to-day decisions and recommendations. Specifically, we looked for peer-reviewed articles published after 2017 as the NCAEP (2020) stated, "Because of the time required to conduct a review of a very large database and involve a national set of reviewers, there was a lag between the end date for a literature review (i.e., 2017) and the date on which the review is published. Certainly, studies have been published in the interim that could have moved some of the 'other practices' into the EBP classification" (p. 52).

Comprehensive Treatment Models (CTMs)

"Comprehensive treatment models (CTMs) are a set of practices designed to achieve a broad impact on the core features of ASD" (Odom et al., 2010). In their review of education programs for students with ASD, the National Academy of Science Committee on Educational Interventions for Children with Autism (National Research Council, 2001) identified 10 CTMs." And in a follow-up Odom et al., (2010) identified 30 CTMs. We included the following, as they were also referenced in the core reviews:

COMPREHENSIVE TREATMENT MODEL	SECTION INCLUDED IN
Treatment and Education of Autistic and related Communication-handicapped Children (TEACCH) (Panerai et al., 2002)	Visual Supports within Structured Teaching
Pivotal Response Training (PRT) (Koegel & Koegel, 2006)	Natural Developmental Behavioral Interventions (NDBI)
Responsive Teaching (RT) (Mahoney & Perales, 2005)	Developmental Relationship-Based Treatment (DRBT)
Relationship Development Intervention (RDI) (Gutstein et al., 2007)	Developmental Relationship-Based Treatment (DRBT)

(Continued)

(Continued)

COMPREHENSIVE TREATMENT MODEL	SECTION INCLUDED IN
DIRFloortime ® (Solomon et al., 2007)	Developmental Relationship-Based Treatment (DRBT)
Learning Experiences: An Alternative Program for Preschools and Parents (LEAP) (Hoyson et al., 1984)	Behavioral Interventions
The Denver Model (Rogers et al., 2006)	Behavioral Interventions

Although identified as a CTM and included in the Simpson et al. (2005) review, which gave it the rating of Limited Supporting Information for Practice, we did not include Son-Rise (Kaufman, 1981). The reason for this decision is Son-Rise is a novel type book and no additional peer reviewed empirical evidence has been provided since 2005.

Manualized Interventions Meeting Criteria (MIMCs)

Included in the NCAEP 2020 review were interventions that clearly fit the EBP categorical definitions but also had enough evidence to be classified as an EBP individually and had clearly established manualized procedures. We have included each of them.

MANUALIZED INTERVENTIONS MEETING CRITERIA (MIMCS)	SECTION INCLUDED IN
Joint Attention Symbolic Play and Emotion Regulation (JASPER) (Kasari et al., 2014)	Natural Developmental Behavioral Interventions (NDBI) under Joint Attention Interventions
Picture Exchange Communication System (PECS)® (Frost & Bondy, 2002)	Augmentative and Alternative Communication
Pivotal Response Training® (PRT) (Koegel & Koegel, 2006)	Natural Developmental Behavioral Interventions (NDBI)
Milieu Training (Kaiser & Roberts, 2013)	Natural Developmental Behavioral Interventions (NDBI)
Project ImPACT (Ingersoll & Dvortcsak, 2019)	Miscellaneous in Parent-Mediated Interventions
Stepping Stones Triple P (Turner et al., 2010)	Miscellaneous in Parent-Mediated Interventions
Social Stories™ (Gray, 2000)	Social, Emotional, and/or Behavioral Skills Training

MANUALIZED INTERVENTIONS MEETING CRITERIA (MIMCS)	SECTION INCLUDED IN
The Program for the Education and Enrichment of Relational Skills ® (PEERS) (Laugeson & Frankel, 2010)	Social, Emotional, and/or Behavioral Skills Training
FaceSay® (Hopkins et al, 2011)	Social, Emotional, and/or Behavioral Skills Training
Mindreading (Golan & Baron-Cohen, 2006)	Social, Emotional, and/or Behavioral Skills Training

Additional Interventions

We included thirteen educational interventions that were not included in the core reviews but based on our collective experiences are commonly used by educators.

INTERVENTION	SECTION
The Ziggurat Model/Comprehensive Autism Planning System (CAPS)	Behavioral Interventions
Verbal Behavior Intervention	Language Training
Behavioral Skills Training	Social, Emotional, and/or Behavioral Skills Training
Teaching Interaction Procedure	
Cool Versus Not Cool	
Social Thinking®	
Mindfulness-Based Interventions	Cognitive Behavioral Instructional Strategies
Zones of Regulation	
The Incredible Five Point Scale	
Responsive Teaching (RT)	Developmental Relationship-Based Treatment
Matrix Training	Relational Frame Theory (RFT)-Based Interventions
Promoting Emergence of Advanced Knowledge (PEAK)	
Acceptance and Commitment Training (ACT)	

We also included seven biomedical and nutritional treatments, some of which have the potential of causing significant harm, and four additional interventions which also have the potential of causing significant harm.

Excluded Interventions

There were interventions that were included in at least one of the core reviews but excluded from this resource due to clearly insufficient evidence in the empirical literature. We excluded the following:

▶ Exposure Therapy

▶ Massage

▶ Auditory Integration Training

▶ Perceptual Motor

▶ Sensory Diet

▶ Exploring Feelings

▶ Irlen Lenses

▶ Fast Forward

▶ Van Dijk Curricular Approach

We also excluded pharmacology and interventions that were solely academic and did not address the defining characteristics of ASD as it was outside of the scope of this resource. A great article that provides a review of pharmacology therapies for individuals with ASD is included in the references (LeClerc & Easley, 2015).

Rating System

To further guide educators in making these daily and possibly moment-by-moment decisions, we also developed a more detailed rating system. Cook et al. (2020) considered making the distinction between interventions with evidence of neutral or negative effects from interventions with positive effects but not supported by a sufficient number of high-quality empirical research designs to be of specific significance because the latter holds of the promise of positive effects and so could be considered "emerging." "Emerging interventions are interventions that have some evidence of positive outcomes, although the consistency or magnitude of these outcomes is indeterminate and caution is warranted" (Scheibel et al., 2022, p. 3). We used both the terms *promising* and *emerging* as we felt both were necessary to give the most accurate description of interventions included in this crucial category.

Ineffective or harmful interventions have evidence of neutral, contra-therapeutic, or harmful interventions (Knight et al., 2019). We separated ineffective and harmful to create and more clearly define two separate categories: (1) Ineffective in which interventions that have evidence of neutral effects would be included and (2) Potential for Causing Harm to clearly identify interventions that have contra-therapeutic or harmful effects.

	1. EBP	The interventions and treatments with this rating have undergone a substantial amount of rigorous research. The evidence repeatedly and consistently provides similar results that prove children and youth with ASD display a significant increase in skill acquisition as a result of the intervention.
	2. Promising/ Emerging Practice	Interventions and treatments in this category have (1) been widely used by educators for several years without any significant adverse anecdotally reported outcomes and/or (2) undergone research that suggests that children and youth with ASD respond favorably and display skill acquisition as a result of the intervention. However, these practices require additional scientific evidence to be considered truly evidence-based.

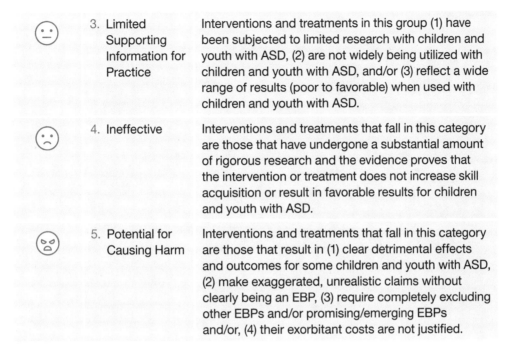

	3. Limited Supporting Information for Practice	Interventions and treatments in this group (1) have been subjected to limited research with children and youth with ASD, (2) are not widely being utilized with children and youth with ASD, and/or (3) reflect a wide range of results (poor to favorable) when used with children and youth with ASD.
	4. Ineffective	Interventions and treatments that fall in this category are those that have undergone a substantial amount of rigorous research and the evidence proves that the intervention or treatment does not increase skill acquisition or result in favorable results for children and youth with ASD.
	5. Potential for Causing Harm	Interventions and treatments that fall in this category are those that result in (1) clear detrimental effects and outcomes for some children and youth with ASD, (2) make exaggerated, unrealistic claims without clearly being an EBP, (3) require completely excluding other EBPs and/or promising/emerging EBPs and/or, (4) their exorbitant costs are not justified.

Teacher Testimonials

As stated by Landrum et al. (2007), "One important type of validation regarding the useability of an instructional technique is the endorsement of another teacher, and perhaps especially an experienced teacher. A teaching technique that is positively presented by one teacher to another may carry the implicit endorsement of being "battle tested" because it comes from someone who has intrinsic credibility due to their shared experiences and perspectives of being classroom teachers" (p. 10). For this very reason, we included testimonials on many of the interventions from experienced teachers who are either still teaching or are directly supporting teachers on a daily basis.

Behavioral Interventions

SECTION

1

Introduction

Applied behavior analysis (ABA) "is a scientific approach for discovering environmental variables that reliability influence socially significant behavior and for developing a technology of behavior change that takes practical advantage of those discoveries" (Cooper et al., 2020, p. 2). Accordingly, an instructor *applies* behavior principles in order to change an individual's *behavior* and then *analyzes* whether the actions taken caused a behavior to change. A crucial component of ABA is the process of *improving the social significance* of the individual's behavior. That is, it is important that the change in behavior be observable, meaningful, and important, such as teaching an individual to read, add and subtract numbers, not hit other people, follow a teacher's instructions, or improve their social acceptance within their community. In order for a change in behavior to be socially significant, the individual must also demonstrate *independence* and *generalization* with the skills and behaviors they have learned. If a student participates in an intensive ABA educational and behavioral intervention program for 25 to 40 hours a week, but cannot perform any skills independently in different environments in which they need to use those skills, that ABA program has not been a successful intervention program and has not benefited them. The process of implementing a successful ABA program is achieved when learners with ASD who receive ABA interventions and supports are trained in flexible and dynamic environments for independence and generalization.

As outlined in the Overview of Autism Spectrum Disorder chapter, a significant amount of research on ABA has been conducted (starting in the 1960s) demonstrating that using ABA intervention methods with individuals with ASD can produce comprehensive and lasting improvements in many important skill areas, including language, academics, behavior, and social interaction.

For over two decades there have been calls for use of evidence-based and scientifically supported methods with children and youth with ASD and other disabilities. In 2001, the U.S. Department of Education's Office of Special Education Programs requested that the National Research Council (a part of the National Academy of Science) establish the Committee on Education Interventions for Children with Autism to investigate and "integrate the scientific, theoretical, and policy literature and create a framework for evaluating the scientific evidence concerning the effects and features of educational interventions for young children with autism (ages 0-8)" (National Research Council [NRC], 2001, p. 2). In 2001, the NRC published a book titled *Educating Children with Autism* in which it recommended that "educational services [for children with autism] begin as soon as a child is suspected of having an autistic spectrum disorder" and "those services should include a minimum of 25 hours a week, 12 months a year, in which the child is engaged in systematically planned, and developmentally appropriate educational activities aimed toward identified objectives. It is critical to recognize that *early and intensive intervention* is the most important aspect of the research in regards to treatment of individuals with autism" (Matson & Jang, 2013; NRC, 2001; Smith, 2001). The second most important factor in early intervention for individuals with ASD is that the intervention be based on principles of ABA (Estes et al., 2015; Matson & Jang, 2013; NRC, 2001; Smith, 2001).

Within the last 25 years various researchers comprehensively reviewed published studies using evidence-based ABA intervention methods with children with autism. The studies had to be intensive (over 20 hours of intervention per week), provided 1:1 staff to student ratio services, and had to be comprehensive intervention programs that addressed the whole of autism (communication, adaptive skills, academic, self-help, behavior, etc.). They found a total of 21 studies published from 1998 to 2014 that utilized the following methods and procedures: (a) DTT, (b) modeling/imitation, (c) prompting, (d) reinforcement (primary and secondary), (e) fading, and (f) shaping. In sum, within the umbrella of ABA-supported interventions, these specific methods and procedures were the most effective means of achieving socially valid outcomes with children and youth (Estes et al., 2015; Matson & Jang, 2013).

Most recently, in 2016, Leaf et al. (all pioneers in the field of ABA) identified the four main components of effective early intensive behavior intervention (EIBI; Leaf et al., 2016):

- Hours of treatment—intensity (sometimes referred to as dosage): 25 to 40 hours per week;
- A comprehensive approach: language development, social skills, self-help skills, academics, play and leisure skills;
- Highly trained staff implementing the program with a focus on treatment integrity (fidelity of implementation); and
- ABA training received by staff is specific to the population being served.

Another recent study (Dixon et al., 2016) examined how a student's learning (mastery of specific skills and behavior objectives) aligned with the skill and training of program supervisors. Variables considered were (a) supervision hours for each student/case, (b) credentials, (c) years of experience, and (d) caseload (638 different students/cases were included in the study). Two of these elements were found to have a significant impact on student learning and mastery of skills. First, those students with ASD who had a BCBA supervising their program mastered significantly more learning objectives. Specifically, "supervisors with BCBA certifications produced 73.7% greater mastery of learning objectives per [treatment] hour as compared to supervisors without a BCBA" (Dixon et al., 2016, p. 345). Second, the years of experience of a program supervisor showed a significant impact on student learning. Specifically, the study revealed that "for every year of experience that a supervisor had, the number of mastered learning objectives increased by 4%. This may be trivial when considering the impact of a single year, but would indicate that cases [students] that are supervised by practitioners with 10 years of supervisory experience are mastering 40% more per [treatment] hour" (Dixon et al., 2016, p. 345).

In summary, ABA intervention methods offer families and professionals an evidence-based and systematic process for teaching skills in a way that allows individuals with ASD to most efficiently and effectively understand and learn. It is imperative that ABA intervention programs for children with ASD involve highly trained and competent professionals such as behavior analysts who hold BCBA certification.

In order to understand many of the different behavioral interventions listed in this section, the reader needs to understand the antecedent, behavior, consequences (ABC) paradigm that is the foundation of ABA principles and practices (Cooper et al., 2007). All ABA procedures involve the manipulation of one or more components of this three-term contingency:

This ABC paradigm allows analysis of behavior that is occurring in any environment. By recording the occurrence of a behavior and the events that occurred immediately before and after the behavior, one is able to evaluate the cause (antecedent)

A ANTECEDENT	B BEHAVIOR	C CONSEQUENCE
The stimulus under which a behavior occurs	An action that occurs in response to an antecedent	A response that follows a behavior that will either increase or decrease that behavior

and effect (consequence) of a behavior. By using a data collection system to maintain a record of the behavior, along with the antecedents and consequences of each occurrence, one is able to track and analyze patterns that occur and thus more accurately instruct a learner in a new skill and otherwise intervene to increase or decrease the occurrence of the behavior. Very simplistic examples of the ABC paradigm follow:

Reinforcement of Appropriate Behavior

A: Adult is holding a cookie within view of a child.

B: Child asks the adult, "Cookie, please?"

C: Adult gives the child the cookie.

Reinforcement of Inappropriate Behavior

A: Adult is holding a cookie within view of a child.

B: Child throws a tantrum and tries to take the cookie from the adult.

C: Adult gives the child the cookie.

These two examples include the same antecedent and the same consequence, but the child is displaying and being reinforced for different behaviors. In the first example, the child asks for the cookie appropriately, and the adult gives it to them; in the second, the child inappropriately throws a tantrum and tries to take the cookie from the adult, and the adult gives it to them. An instructor can view these data and see that in the future, the first child will most likely continue to appropriately ask for things that they want, and the second child will continue to try to grab things from people or throw a tantrum when they want something.

Important information can be gained by using the ABC paradigm to analyze behaviors. ABC data are very useful in revealing why a behavior occurs and in what situations it is most likely to occur again. These data can also reveal what consequences are causing a behavior to increase or decrease and, therefore, help instructors determine appropriate teaching procedures and consequences to use in the future.

Core Reviews

All of the reviews (Simpson et al., 2005; NAC, 2009 & 2015; NCAEP, Steinbrenner et al., 2020; NPDC, Wong et al., 2014); included behavioral interventions in their reviews, most of which were rated as EBPs. Some reviews also included "behavioral package" as one entity, which includes several different behavioral interventions that are all implemented together and researched as a package for use with individuals with ASD. We have included reviews of individual behavioral interventions, as well as three common behavioral intervention packages, in this section.

Interventions Included in This Section

- Antecedent-Based Interventions (ABI)
- Discrete Trial Teaching (DTT)
- Errorless Learning
- Task Analysis
- Prompting and Fading
- Time Delay
- Behavioral Momentum
- Response Interruption and Redirection (RIR)
- Reinforcement
- Differential Reinforcement
- Modeling
- Functional Behavioral Assessment (FBA) and Functional Analysis (FA)
- Functional Communication Training (FCT)
- Extinction
- Punishment Procedures
- Early Intensive Behavioral Intervention
  - UCLA Young Autism Project
  - Early Start Denver Model (ESDM)
  - Learning Experiences: An Alternative Program for Preschoolers and Parents (LEAP)
- The Ziggurate Model/Comprehensive Autism Planning System (CAPS)

Antecedent-Based Interventions (ABI)

Description

ABIs are strategies that modify the environment to reduce interfering behaviors among individuals with ASD and other developmental disorders. ABIs are built on the concept that because behaviors are often influenced by the environment, what's happening in the environment, and what other people are doing, modifying these things can eliminate many of the factors that are causing the undesirable behavior. One the main goals of using ABIs is to reduce of punishment consequences that need to be used after the undesirable behavior occurs and, instead, set the individual up for success in displaying an appropriate behavior.

To fully understand ABIs, it's important to first understand the concept of antecedent-behavior-consequence, or the ABCs of ABA. As previously explained in the Behavioral Interventions Introduction, the antecedent occurs directly before the behavior, then the individual's behavior is the response to the antecedent, and then the consequence occurs directly after the behavior. There is also the setting event and the setting that occur before the antecedent. The setting is the overall location of where the sequence of events is occurring, such as math time or bedtime or the playground. The setting event is slow triggers or situations that "sets up" the antecedent to cause the behavior. Examples of setting events are missed medication, lack of sleep, or and sitting on the bus for more than an hour.

Through ABIs, the teacher is looking to prevent the undesirable behavior from occurring by changing what they can regarding the setting, the setting event, and the antecedent. ABIs are a positive behavior support intervention strategy and are most effective when used as a part of a comprehensive behavior intervention plan, which addresses improving, teaching, and reinforcing desirable skills and behaviors, while decreasing undesirable behaviors (Conroy et al., 2005; Kern et al., 2002). Common ABIs used in the classroom include the following:

1) using highly favored activities or items to increase interest level,

2) changing the schedule or routine to meet the needs of the learner,

3) implementing pre-activity interventions (e.g., warnings),

4) offering choices,

5) increasing student engagement in activities,

6) altering the way instruction is provided, and

7) enhancing the environment so that individuals have access to sensory stimuli that serve the same function as the interfering behavior (Alberto & Troutman, 2008; Pokorski, et al., 2019).

Brief Overview of the Literature

When implemented correctly, ABIs have been shown to be effective across a wide range of abilities, behaviors, and ages of students with ASD (NPDC, Wong et al., 2015). Even with positive outcomes, antecedent-based strategies are not being used consistently in classrooms today (Conroy & Stichter, 2003). ABIs, can address social, behavior, and communication domains as well as increase academic outcomes of students with ASD.

Core Reviews

Simpson et al. (2005) did not include ABIs as a stand-alone reviewed intervention. Rather, they included Applied Behavior Analysis as one intervention under their Skill-Based Interventions and Treatments Category. The NAC used the term *Antecedent Package* in 2009 and gave a rating of Established based on 99 studies. In 2015, they included it under the broader category of Behavioral Interventions, which was rated as Established. Both the NPDC (NPDC, Wong et al., 2014) in 2014 and the NCAEP in 2020 used the term ABIs and gave the ratings of EBP based on a total of almost 50 studies.

Age and Diagnostic Considerations/ Prerequisite Skills and Abilities

According to evidence-based studies that have been conducted, this intervention has been effective for learners with ASD of all ages.

Reported Outcomes

ABIs have been shown to help prevent or reduce interfering behaviors *AND* increase engagement and on-task behaviors in learners with ASD.

Qualifications Needed

Utilizing ABIs procedures as part of an overall teaching or behavior intervention program for an individual with ASD requires training from a professional who is experienced in working with individuals with ASD and developing and implementing such programs. This would typically be a BCBA. Because Antecedent-Based Intervention procedures need to be adjusted and changed as the individual with ASD progresses with their skills and behaviors, it is also best for teachers and parents to receive ongoing supervision and feedback on the ABIs used.

How, Where, and When Typically Implemented

ABIs can be implemented in all settings including schools, clinics, homes, and communities.

Costs

ABIs are cost-effective in terms of time and other resources. There are minimal costs associated with training. It does take extra planning time to build the intervention procedures into the daily routine and to make the visual materials that are often needed. Many of the materials needed for ABIs can be found in the classroom.

Potential Risks

There are no known risks associated with the using ABIs.

Rating

 Evidence-Based Practice

Resources and Suggested Readings

AFIRM Modules through UNC Chapel Hill offers a free online course on Antecedent-Based Interventions that can be accessed at https://afirm.fpg.unc.edu/antecedent-based -intervention

Kansas Technical Assistance System Network (TASN) offers several free online webinars on topics related to Antecedent-Based Interventions that can be accessed at https://www .ksdetasn.org/resources/1957 and https://www.ksdetasn.org/resources/2138

The Ohio Center for Autism and Low Incidence (OCALI) offers a free online course on Antecedent-Based Interventions. After creating an account, it can be accessed at https:// autisminternetmodules.org/m/503

Discrete Trial Teaching (DTT)

Description

Discrete trial training (DTT) method of teaching involves the following:

- breaking a skill into smaller parts,
- teaching each part to mastery,
- providing concentrated teaching,
- providing prompting and fading as necessary, and
- using reinforcement procedures.

Each DTT teaching session involves a number of trials, each of which has a distinct beginning and end, hence the term *discrete*. The DTT method is distinguishable from traditional teaching methods because it prescribes presenting a very small unit of information and immediately seeking the student's response. Active instructor and student involvement is an element of DTT.

The DTT method mirrors the ABC paradigm as follows:

S^D DISCRIMINATIVE STIMULUS	R RESPONSE	S^R CONSEQUENCE
The instruction, question, or relevant materials presented to the student (the antecedent)	The student's reaction to the S^D (the behavior)	The reaction provided by the instructor to the student in response to the student's behavior (the consequence)

Just as the ABC paradigm is used to analyze a behavior that a student is demonstrating, the DTT method is a more narrowly focused paradigm for analyzing the learning behavior of a student. Each DTT element is recorded: the instruction provided (antecedent), the student's response (behavior), and the instructor's response to the student (consequence). This basic DTT process enables one to evaluate the cause (antecedent) and effect (consequence) of a student's learning. Using a data collection system that assists in maintaining a record of a student's responses to specific instructions and the consequences that follow those responses, an instructor can track and analyze the effects of instruction (and specific materials) and consequences and thus ultimately increase or decrease the occurrence of specific responses of the student with greater accuracy. Three examples of different ways, both appropriate and inappropriate, to increase or decrease the occurrence of a specific response follow:

Reinforcement of Appropriate Response (increases response):

S^D: Instructor says, "Give me sock." [A sock is lying on the floor in front of the student.]

R: Student picks up the sock and hands it to the instructor.

S^R: Instructor says, "All right! Good job," and tickles the student, who laughs in response.

No Reinforcement of Inappropriate Response (decreases response):

S^D: Instructor says, "Give me sock."

R: Student looks around the room and does nothing.

S^R: Instructor says, "Let's try again."

Reinforcement of Inappropriate Response (increases response):

S^D: Instructor says, "Give me sock."

R: Student looks around the room and does nothing.

S^R: Instructor says, "Come on, Johnny. Here is the sock—see it?" and tickles the student, who laughs in response.

The first example presents an instructor appropriately reinforcing a student for a correct response. Accordingly, in the future, the student is more likely to correctly identify a sock. The second example presents an instructor appropriately not reinforcing the student's failure to respond to the instruction. Therefore, the instructor has decreased the likelihood of the student not responding in the future. The third example presents an instructor *in*appropriately reinforcing the student for not responding to the instruction. Even though the student did not respond correctly to the instruction, the instructor reinforced him. Therefore, in the future, the student is more likely not to respond to an instruction, because he has learned that he may still receive reinforcement.

There are two important reasons to use DTT with students with ASD. First, because a lot of students with ASD do not naturally gain information from their environment by observing and listening to others or modeling others' behavior, the DTT method enables instructors to systematically analyze tasks that a student needs to learn, break them down into small, defined steps, and systematically teach them to a student in incremental elements that they can more easily learn. This method also enables different teachers to be consistent in their instruction by clearly writing out the procedures for implementing a discrete trial (S^D—R—S^R). This strategy assists teaching consistency—in instructional language, presentation of the S^D, and application of consequences—thereby facilitating student learning. It also allows instructors to more easily and more accurately collect data, because the trial is clearly and simply defined and easily recognized. For each component of the discrete trial, there are important factors to remember that will enable an instructor to more successfully teach students with ASD.

Delivery of Instruction: Discriminative Stimulus

Delivery of the S^D (instruction) involves several critical steps. First, it should be presented in a simple, straightforward, and concise manner to ensure student understanding. For instance, a teacher's instruction to a student might be "Find circle" rather than "Can you find where the circle is?" This allows the student to hear only the two most important words—they are supposed to *find* something and that something is a *circle*. Extraneous language can confuse the student or cause them to attend more to the other words or lose their attention altogether. Later, when attempting to help the student generalize their skills, the teacher should add more words to the instructional commands and statements.

 Second, all instructors need to be consistent in the way they present the S^D, including how they present stimulus materials, the language they use, and so forth. This is especially important during the initial teaching phase of each skill. Later, as the student advances with their skills, instructors need to add words to the instructional phrase, add different instructional phrases and sentences, and otherwise present commands and directions in a fashion that is more typical of routine instruction.

Third, only when the student is paying attention and motivated to respond should the instructor provide an S^D. This step is an important and crucial part of the student's learning and is foundational for the success of future learning. If students fail to learn to attend to someone who is speaking to them, they will have significant difficulty acquiring skills. This is a skill that will be displayed differently by each student which does not necessarily include maintaining eye contact with the instructor. Attending means that the student is ready to receive the S^D and is motivated to provide a response. A student shows that they are ready when they

- are not preoccupied with any other activity, object, or person and
- are stationary in the appropriate location designated by the instructor.

It is evident that a student is motivated when they indicate that they want to obtain a specific reinforcer that the instructor has made available contingent on a correct response. Teachers must continuously evaluate the effect of the reinforcers they are using to find out what the student wants and, therefore, what will help motivate the student to respond to the S^D and acquire skills.

While it is most desirable for a student to attend by looking directly at the instructor when they are providing an S^D, that should not be initially expected or required due to the difficulty that students with ASD often display in acquiring that skill. It is not realistic to believe that by forcing a student to look at the instructor's face or eyes the student can be made to attend to the instructor. An instructor can help the student learn how to be ready for instruction by taking a known tangible reinforcer, bringing it up in front of their own face to direct the student's eyes toward their face, and simultaneously orienting the student toward the source of instruction and reinforcement. It also is beneficial for the first S^D of a session or series of trials to require an easy or already acquired response—something the student knows and will be successful with. Beginning a session on a successful note will often help to ensure that the student will attend to future S^Ds.

Fourth, the instructor generally should present an S^D only once. Only if it is apparent that the student did not hear the instructor, or was not attending, should the instructor provide the S^D again. If a student is accustomed to an instructor providing an instruction an indeterminate number of times, the student will learn that they may respond whenever they want to. This can lead to difficulties with compliance with other instructors, as well as difficulty with learning appropriate social interaction skills. For example, if a typical peer has to ask the student a question more than two times, the peer may lose interest in pursuing further interaction. If the student learns that the instructor will provide the instruction only once and, if no response is provided, no reinforcement will be received (the instructor instead commences with the correction procedure, which will be discussed later), and the student is more likely to learn to respond the first time an instruction is provided.

Fifth, the student's name should not be used within the S^D. It may seem beneficial to use a student's name (e.g., "Johnny, give me sock") because it is a way of obtaining the student's attention. Yet there are a couple of possible adverse effects that may hinder the student's future learning. First, by using a student's name, the instructor may inadvertently teach the student that they need to pay attention only when their name is used in the S^D. Therefore, even when they are the only one present with the instructor and the instructor says, "Give me sock," the student may not respond. Second, if a student hears their name within each S^D throughout the day, their name may become aversive. They may run away or purposely not attend to the instructor when they hear their name, because they have learned to associate an instruction with it.

Obtaining the Correct Response

The second part of the DTT method, response (R), is composed of three elements that are connected to a student's ability to provide a correct response. First, it is important for all instructors to agree upon and consistently use correct response criteria. An example of two instructors accepting different responses follows:

- Instructor 1 says, "Where is your nose?" Student points in the general direction of their nose without actually touching it.

- Instructor 2 says, "Where is your nose?" Student actually touches their nose.

Adverse effects can result if different instructors accept different responses from a student as being correct. The student may become confused and give a different response to each instructor each time they are asked to respond to an S^D. Inconsistent standards may result in students learning different sets of skills for different instructors and responding in a certain way based on who is providing the S^D.

Second, instructors need to ensure that the response a student provides is not chained to another response. It is important that a student provide only one response to an S^D. When a student is unsure of what response to provide, they may attempt many different responses in the hope that one of them is correct. An example follows:

S^D: "Show me jumping."

R: Pats head, waves, jumps up and down.

If the instructor reinforces the student after they have provided the correct response along with other responses, the student may learn that all three behaviors are "jumping" and will then be confused when they are requested to "show waving" or "show patting head."

Third, the instructor needs to wait approximately 1 to 7 seconds after the S^D is delivered for the student to provide their response. It is important for the student to have enough time to recall the correct response, while also maintaining attention to the task at hand. The amount of delay time between the S^D and the response will vary for different students and skills. Accordingly, instructors need to collaborate to decide on an acceptable delay time.

Providing Immediate Consequences

The third part of the DTT method involves consequences for students' responses. In this connection, two matters are particularly important. First, an instructor needs to provide feedback (consequences) to the student after they provide a response to an S^D. Because students with ASD have difficulty learning, it is crucial that the instructor present the appropriate consequence immediately following the response. Here is an example of an instructor providing inappropriate feedback (consequences):

S^D: Instructor says, "Show me clapping."

R: Student claps their hands appropriately.

S^R: Instructor rummages through a box next to them looking for a specific toy to give to the student as a reinforcer for making the correct response; several seconds later they hand the toy to the student and say, "Good clapping."

In the meantime, the student sat and watched another student play with a music toy and then looked out the window. When they finally receive the toy and hear "Good clapping," they may not remember that they just did clapping or may not pay attention to the "Good clapping" and think they got the toy for appropriate sitting. Providing *immediate* reinforcement for a correct response will increase the likelihood that the correct response will occur the next time the same S[D] is provided. Here is an example of an instructor providing appropriate feedback (consequences):

S[D]: Instructor says, "Show me clapping."

R: Student claps their hands appropriately.

S[R]: Instructor immediately says, "Good clapping," and hands the student a ball.

Second, it is important for instructors not to *inadvertently* reinforce an incorrect response. Instructors may not realize that they are accepting a response as correct when other instructors are not accepting it. For instance, some instructors may say, "Good job," before they proceed with a correction procedure because they want to reinforce the student for trying to provide the correct response. By saying that, however, they may be communicating to a student that an incorrect response was correct. As previously indicated, some instructors may also reinforce a student for providing a correct response within a chain of other responses. It is essential that all instructors provide clear and consistent reinforcement and feedback. If a student provides an incorrect response, the instructor's immediate response should be to initiate a correction procedure that teaches the student the correct response. If a student's response is correct, the immediate result should be reinforcement that further strengthens the behavior.

Brief Overview of the Literature

The research evidence base for Discrete Trial Teaching with individuals with ASD goes back to the 1980s when Lovaas implemented a 2-year longitudinal research project with young children with ASD (Lovaas, 1981, 1987). This study demonstrated the difference between a 40-hour-a-week ABA only teaching intervention and a typical eclectic teaching intervention (average of 10 hours a week). The gains made by the children receiving the intensive ABA early intervention program were significantly greater than the children in the eclectic teaching program, and the children maintained this growth over time (Leaf & Cihon, 2016; Lovaas, 1987; McEachin et al., 1993). Over the years all studies that were conducted regarding intensive early intervention for children with autism that included DTT as a critical component determined that a minimum 20 to 25 hours a week of DTT is required in order to make a significant difference in skill acquisition (Downs et al., 2008; Fingerhut & Moeyaert, 2022; Howard et al., 2005; Leaf & Cihon, 2016; Matson et al., 2012).

Core Reviews

Simpson et al. (2005) included Discrete Trial Teaching as a part of their review and gave the rating of Scientifically Based Practice based on four studies. In 2009, the NAC referenced Discrete Trial under the broader categories of Behavioral Package and Comprehensive Behavior Treatment for Young Children, which were both rated as Established. In 2015, they included it under the broader category of Behavioral Interventions, which was rated as Established. The NPDC (NPDC, Wong et al., 2014) included Discrete Trial Teaching and the NCAEP (NCAEP, Steinbrenner et al., 2020) included DTT in its reviews and both gave a rating of Evidence-Based Practice based on a total of 38 studies.

Age and Diagnostic Considerations/ Prerequisite Skills and Abilities

DTT can be used with all ages and skill levels of individuals with ASD but is typically used within early intervention programs (ages 2 to 10) and with those who have moderate to severe learning difficulties.

Reported Outcomes

Discrete Trial Teaching is a significant component of ABA intervention programs, specifically early intervention programs, and is effective in teaching a variety of new skills to individuals with ASD, when it is implemented a minimum of 20 to 25 hours a week.

Qualifications Needed

Utilizing DTT with individuals with ASD requires a significant amount of training from a professional who is experienced in working with individuals with ASD and developing and implementing DTT programs (Fingerhut & Moeyaert, 2022). This would typically be a BCBA. RBTs, who are certified by the BACB, are the professionals who typically implement DTT procedures directly with the child with ASD on a daily basis.

Because DTT procedures need to be adjusted and changed as the individual with ASD progresses with their skills, it is also necessary for RBTs, teachers, and parents to receive ongoing supervision and feedback on the procedures used (Fingerhut & Moeyaert, 2022).

How, Where, and When Typically Implemented

DTT can be implemented as a formal teaching program in the home, in a classroom, in a special center or clinic, or in a school. Research has shown that DTT can be used as a part of Incidental Teaching (see the chapter on Incidental Teaching) and thus can also be utilized and generalized within common daily routines or such as shopping in a grocery store, playing on a playground, or driving in the car, for example.

Costs

Due to the fact that a minimum of 20 to 25 hours of DTT are required to be considered an evidence-based intervention program, this intervention method is extremely costly. The costs associated with implementing DTT intervention programs are the fees for initial training and ongoing supervision by a trained and experienced professional (BCBA), the fees for paying the RBT to work with and teach the child, as well as the cost of the time to prepare the materials and teaching procedures, and finally the costs of purchasing the materials needed when teaching the individual new skills.

Potential Risks

If a professional or parent attempts to develop and implement DTT without any initial training or ongoing supervision, it is highly probable that the instructor will not be successful in teaching new skills and the individual with ASD will not learn new skills and, as a result, may also develop challenging behaviors, be unsuccessful in their learning environment, and not acquire important and critical skills as they develop and grow older.

Rating

 Evidence-Based Practice

Resources and Suggested Readings

Autism Focused Intervention Resources & Module (AFIRM) modules through UNC Chapel Hill offers a free online course on Discrete Trial Teaching that can be accessed at https://afirm .fpg.unc.edu/discrete-trial-training

de Boer, S. R. (2018). *Pro-Ed Series on Autism Spectrum Disorders: Discrete Trial Training* (2nd ed.). Pro-Ed.

Kansas Technical Assistance System Network (TASN) offers a free online webinar on Discrete Trial Teaching that can be accessed at https://www.ksdetasn.org/resources/782

The Ohio Center for Autism and Low Incidence (OCALI) offers a free online course on Discrete Trial Teaching. After creating an account, it can be accessed at https://autisminternetmod ules.org/m/518

Errorless Learning

Description

Errorless Learning or Errorless Teaching (typically used interchangeably) involves teaching a new skill in a manner that minimizes the possibility of errors and thus increases the possibility that the student will be a successful learner. Errorless Learning:

> ▶ minimizes the number of errors a student will make,

> ▶ increases the time available to the instructor to engage in teaching rather than correcting the student,

> ▶ reduces the likelihood that errors will be repeated in the future, and

> ▶ reduces a student's frustration and inappropriate behaviors by increasing opportunities for the student to be reinforced for correct responses.

Everyone has memories of having difficulty learning a new skill. For all learners, including those with ASD, there are typically three reasons that people cannot successfully acquire a skill:

> ▶ they do not have the abilities required to perform the skill,

> ▶ they do not have the desire to learn the skill, or

> ▶ they are not appropriately taught how to perform the skill.

If instructors ensure that they are correctly and appropriately teaching skills to students with ASD, they can then concentrate on whether the student has the ability to acquire and perform the skill and is motivated to learn the skill. Thus, Errorless Learning is a teaching method in which an instructor ensures that they are assisting a student to successfully learn a skill if the student is motivated and capable.

A practical example of Errorless Learning can be found in sports. Athletes on a sports team routinely learn new skills and work to improve acquired skills. Their coaches are responsible for teaching them the skills they need to compete. When a new player joins a team, the coach typically does not expect that individual to already have all the skills they need to compete and be a successful and proficient team member. When coaches teach their athletes a new skill, they must

> ▶ ensure that the athletes are motivated to learn,

> ▶ break the skill into smaller steps,

> ▶ explain the function and use of the skill,

> ▶ demonstrate the skill,

> ▶ provide prompts needed to perform the skill initially,

> ▶ shape performance of the skill,

> ▶ provide immediate and relevant feedback regarding performance of the skill, and

> ▶ require that the athlete practice the new skill so that they become fluent in its execution and can use it at any appropriate time or place.

If coaches merely tell athletes to perform a skill that they have not yet acquired and have no prior knowledge of, they will begin the learning process by making mistakes. Those mistakes may hinder the athletes from being successful in the future and increase their frustration, thereby decreasing their motivation to learn the skill. This same pattern applies to teaching students with ASD. The two most important times to use Errorless Learning with a student are

- each time a new skill is taught, and

- when a student is demonstrating difficulty with an acquired skill.

An instructor needs to break each new skill into small, acquirable steps; model and otherwise demonstrate the skill; and then initially provide a high level of prompting, thereby ensuring motivation while decreasing frustration and increasing the likelihood that a student will be able to provide a correct response. This will increase the probability that the student will be successful in the future, as the instructor begins to fade the prompts.

When a student is demonstrating difficulty with learning a new skill or is consistently demonstrating incorrect responses for a previously acquired skill, an instructor needs to immediately stop requiring independent responses. The instructor should begin a process of "backing up" in order to diagnose the learning difficulty and find out where the student is able to provide an independent successful response. Once this is achieved, the instructor employs the errorless learning approach and begins to proceed by breaking down a given skill into small steps, demonstrating the skill, and providing a high level of prompting when presenting the instruction (S^D). Providing a high level of prompting along with an instruction (S^D) is an integral part of the errorless learning process. This allows the instructor to minimize mistakes and incorrect responses, maintain the student's motivation, decrease frustration, and increase the likelihood of future correct responses or appropriate behaviors.

Brief Overview of the Literature

The majority of research surrounding Errorless Learning or Errorless Teaching focuses on whether it is the "best" or "most effective" procedure as opposed to various error correction procedures to use when attempting to limit the number of mistakes and correcting mistakes that individuals with ASD make when they are learning new skills or behaviors (Mueller et al., 2007; Wilkinson, 2008). Both Errorless Learning and Error Correction procedures are seen as necessary components of Evidence-Based Intervention Practices. It is what should be used for different skills, different behaviors, and different environments for individuals with different needs that is studied and researched (Mueller et al., 2007).

Core Reviews

Errorless Learning and Errorless Teaching strategies were not included within any of the core reviews. The table provided below contains an overview of several of the research studies conducted on this teaching strategy.

Other Peer Reviewed Research

A list of several of the research projects that have been published specifically regarding Errorless Learning or Errorless Teaching over the past 20 years is provided below to demonstrate the variety of research conducted in this particular area. Both studies that looked at teaching instructors to use Errorless Learning/Teaching procedures effectively with students with ASD and studies that looked at how well children with ASD themselves learned concepts with Errorless Learning/Teaching are included.

AUTHOR(S) YEAR	N	SETTING	AGE/GENDER	DIAGNOSES	RESEARCH DESIGN	OUTCOMES/ FINDINGS	COMMENTS
Braga-Kenyon et al. (2017)	9	1:1 separate room with computer	Typical kids ages 6–9; ASD kids 7–13	6 typical kids & 3 kids with ASD	An ABAB reversal experimental design was used for each participant. Two conditions with prompts requiring SD versus CD control were alternated, with order of the condition presentation counterbalanced across participants	The data on the number of trials to meet the learning criteria (Table 2) do not support the general superiority of one prompt-type over another (simple discrimination [SD] vs. conditional discrimination [CD]).	Both groups did intervention with computer and adult standing behind.
Flora, et al. (2020)	3	1:1 sessions in bathroom of classroom at Autism Center	Boys, 6, 8, 9 years old	ASD	Non-concurrent AB phase design with maintenance probe (Errorless method of toilet training)	Intervention was successful in both increasing all participants' in-toilet urinations and in decreasing the number of accidents	Potty Party intervention (child is highly reinforced while sitting on toilet until voiding)
Foran-conn et al. (2021)	3	1:1 teaching sessions in hallway at school	1 girl (8 years), 2 boys (7 and 9 years)	ASD	Multiple baseline across subjects with follow-up probes	The study found that responsive prompt delay procedure was at least as effective as most to least prompting and no-no prompting procedures.	This study compared the responsive prompt delay procedure added to the literature to two well-documented prompting strategies: most to least prompting and no-no prompting.
Gerencser et al. (2018)	6 para-professionals	Special education preschool: side room for 1:1 teaching sessions	Female paraprofessionals ages 38 to 57	Students had either ASD or developmental disability or Down's syndrome	Non-concurrent multiple-baseline design across classrooms (two participant–student dyads per classroom) to evaluate the effects of the Interactive Computerized Training (ICT) program on paraprofessionals' implementation of Discrete Trial Instruction with students with developmental disabilities	Study found that ICT alone and ICT plus additional remote training components can increase paraprofessional's implementation DTI with errorless learning procedures for teaching individuals with developmental disabilities	Study evaluated the feasibility of ICT program to train para-professionals to implement DTI with an errorless learning procedure.

(Continued)

(Continued)

AUTHOR(S) YEAR	N	SETTING	AGE/GENDER	DIAGNOSES	RESEARCH DESIGN	OUTCOMES/ FINDINGS	COMMENTS
Leaf et al. (2020)	28	No gender data, age ranges of children were 3 yrs., 8 mos. to 9 years 9 mos.)	1:1 sessions in private room at autism center	ASD	Alternating treatment design with two interventions with random assignment to each intervention group (1) Error Correction and (2) Errorless Learning (1) Pre-test and post-test responding comparison (2) Mastery of skill set met comparison (3) Independent responding comparison	(1) Pretest: 0% responding in for all participants Posttests: 85.7% responding for error correction group and 77.1% for errorless learning group *Statistically significant* (2) 97.6% reached the mastery criterion in the error correction group; 95.2% reached mastery criterion in the errorless teaching group *Not statistically significant* (3) 90.8% independent responding for the error correction group and 75.3% for errorless learning group *Statistically significant*	Study contributes to the existing limited literature on error correction and errorless learning procedures through the *use of a group design.* First study to evaluate error correction and errorless learning procedures using random assignment.
Severtson et al. (2017)	6 new instructors	4 females and 2 males; ages 22 to 36	Separate room at autism clinic	New instructors at autism clinic working with students with ASD	A nonconcurrent multiple-baseline design across participants was used to evaluate the effects of two interventions (1) self-instruction only with manual (2) self-instruction, video instruction and follow-up feedback Both had generalization and follow up probes	(1) The results indicate that the self-instruction manual alone was sufficient for half of the participants to correctly implement the DTT protocol with errorless teaching procedures with a confederate student. (2) Demonstrated a method for teaching novice instructors to implement an Most-To-Least (MTL) prompt fading strategy as a part of DTT.	This study may be used as a guide for practitioners who have little background in the implementation of MTL strategies and/ or who are responsible for training new staff to implement these procedures.

Age and Diagnostic Considerations/ Prerequisite Skills and Abilities

Errorless Learning and Errorless Teaching can be used with all ages and skill levels of individuals with ASD but is typically used extensively with those who have moderate to severe learning difficulties.

Reported Outcomes

Errorless Learning and Errorless Teaching is a strategy that is combined with prompting and fading and thus not a stand-alone intervention. It is considered to be a part of all ABA intervention programs and is considered an important component of ABIs as a part of ensuring that an individual with ASD can learn a skill more quickly and without many mistakes (which slow down the skill acquisition process).

Qualifications Needed

Utilizing Errorless Learning and Errorless Teaching as part of an overall Teaching or Behavior Intervention Program for an individual with ASD requires training from a professional who is experienced in working with individuals with ASD and developing and implementing such programs. This would typically be a BCBA. Because Errorless Learning procedures need to be adjusted and changed as the individual with ASD progresses with their skills and behaviors, it is also best for teachers and parents to receive ongoing supervision and feedback on the procedures used.

How, Where, and When Typically Implemented

Errorless Learning/Teaching can be implemented by the educator during the teaching of any skill or behavior in any location.

Costs

The costs for training and ongoing supervision are the only associated costs with this Teaching Strategy and are not separate from the overall costs and process of being trained in DTT, prompting, and fading procedures.

Potential Risks

There are no inherent potential risks associated with Errorless Learning procedures. If a professional or parent attempts to develop and implement Reinforcement procedures without any initial training and supervision, there is the risk that the individual may become prompt dependent if the prompts are not faded quickly enough or that the student will continue to provide incorrect responses over a period of time and not progress with learning a skill because incorrect prompts are used or inadequate prompting is provided for the individual while learning the skill.

Practitioner Testimonial(s)

Errorless Learning is an EBP I first learned about in 2018. When I first began using it, I used it through Verbal Behavior (VB) Programming. However, as I began to get more comfortable with it, I quickly realized how I could use it in all areas of my teaching, not just during VB Programming! I realized that as an educator, I was spending more time assessing my students rather than specifically teaching them a skill, concept, or vocabulary. I began by ensuring that every day, my first encounter with the student was an assessment time. I would do a cold probe on the specific skills, concepts, or vocabulary I was teaching. After I was done assessing, I would use Errorless Learning to target what we were working on. I use Errorless Learning with a variety of students ranging from students with Level 1 autism to specific learning disabilities. I also use it in a self-contained classroom, resource room, and even during inclusion.

I have used Errorless Learning for basic skills such as learning how to point upon request and early vocabulary. I have carried Errorless Learning over into many types of skills such as letter and number identification, matching, letter sounds, shapes and colors, state capitals, and basic math facts. I love how Errorless Learning has helped me shift my focus from assessing students each time I work with them, to teaching them specific skills intentionally!

—Tracie Betz

Rating

Evidence-Based Practice

Resources and Suggested Readings

Kansas Technical Assistance System Network (TASN) offers a free online webinar on Errorless Learning that can be accessed at https://www.ksdetasn.org/resources/1052 (TASN also includes individual training modules for errorless teaching procedures for teaching specific skills, (i.e., motor imitation, intraverbals.)

The Nebraska Autism Spectrum Disorders Network offers a free online webinar on Errorless Learning that can be accessed at https://www.unl.edu/asdnetwork/errorless-teaching

Task Analysis

Description

In the chapter on Discrete Trial Teaching, as well as in the section on Errorless Learning, "breaking a skill into smaller parts" was listed as one of the basic and often essential strategies for teaching skills to students with ASD. Breaking a skill down into individual steps involves task analysis. This process may at first be difficult, because a typical learner does not usually think about or see all the small individual steps that they go through in learning to do a task, such as tying their shoe, making popcorn in the microwave, or riding a city bus.

Task analysis is a component of errorless learning because it is completed in order for the instructor to know how to errorlessly teach a skill or an overall larger task (e.g., making cookies or taking a shower). The result of a task analysis will give an instructor the sequence of steps to follow to teach a student a particular skill. Overall, there are three task analysis procedures:

- forward chaining (i.e., teaching a skill in sequence, beginning with the first steps and moving forward),

- backward chaining (i.e., teaching a skill in reverse sequence, beginning with the final steps and moving backward),

- whole task presentation (i.e., teaching a skill that one needs to generalize and use in many different contexts, such as colors or numbers).

As you approach a skill or task in order to do a task analysis, you need to first do three things:

1. define the target skill or behavior,

2. collect data on the current occurrence (or lack of) the behavior—this is the baseline data process, and

3. write out a clear goal for the student to achieve in order to demonstrate mastery in learning that skill or behavior.

Once an instructor has completed this process, they can now analyze the skill or behavior that they will be teaching. First, the instructor needs to determine if the student has the prerequisite skills to learn the new target skill. If not, this needs to be the first thing taught and is essentially the beginning of the sequence of steps in the overall task analysis. Second, the instructor needs to watch someone perform the skill or perform the skill themself in order to determine all the smaller sequential components of the skill. As the instructor is watching or performing the skill, they need to be writing down, in the actual sequence, the steps that occur. The first time an instructor completes a task analysis for a specific task, skill, or behavior, it is important to ask a couple of people to follow that exact sequence of steps in order to evaluate if a step has been omitted and if they reach the same, planned end result. The instructor also needs to clearly describe and create (if needed) the materials (e.g., pictures or written checklist) that will be used when teaching the skill.

The overall task analysis should result in a set of steps that are:

⬤ discrete (isolated and distinct from each other),

⬤ manageable and logical for the student to perform once they have learned the previous step, and

⬤ clearly described so that every instructor teaches it the same way and knows what to expect the student to do.

Brief Overview of the Literature

When looking at task analysis as a procedure or strategy that is used within an overall intervention, it is not typically researched in the sense of "does task analysis work effectively," but instead of how do we best teach (task) or (skill) to individuals with ASD, and then task analysis is used and researched in the context of teaching that task or skill, for instance, reading, making a bed, or doing laundry (Browder et al., 2007; Szidon & Franzone, 2009).

Research regarding task analysis has also been conducted surrounding its use for teachers to be able to monitor their own lesson delivery in order to make sure that they have included all the critical components that they need to address when teaching a concept, skill, or task to students (Allinder et al., 2000; Browder et al., 2007; Moats & Lyon, 1996).

Core Reviews

Simpson et al. (2005) did not include Task Analysis as a stand-alone reviewed intervention. Rather, they included Applied Behavior Analysis as one intervention under their Skill-Based Interventions and Treatments Category. The NAC included Task Analysis in its 2009 and 2014 reviews as a part of the broader categories of Behavioral Package and Behavioral Interventions, which were both rated as Established. The NPDC (NPDC, Wong et al., 2014) and the NCAEP (NCAEP, Steinbrenner et al., 2020) both included Task Analysis as a reviewed intervention giving the rating of EBP based on a total of 13 studies.

Age and Diagnostic Considerations/ Prerequisite Skills and Abilities

Task analysis can be used with all ages and skill levels of individuals with ASD.

Reported Outcomes

Task analysis is effective in increasing the skill acquisition of individuals with ASD of all ages when teaching them to complete larger tasks or skills, specifically in the areas of self-help and adaptive skills (Szidon & Franzone, 2009).

Qualifications Needed

A professional or parent who wants to use task analysis as a teaching strategy within a larger intervention context needs initial training by a professional who has experience using it with individuals with disabilities. It takes time and practice to become adept at completing task analyses. Many teachers receive training on task analysis within their teaching credential programs, but additional training is needed regarding the extent of breakdown in steps often needed for individuals with ASD.

How, Where, and When Typically Implemented

Task analysis can be used to teach any task that has more than one step in order to complete a larger task (e.g., washing hands) and within any environment that the individual needs to learn and use that skill.

Costs

There are no associated costs with using task analysis interventions, other than the time to break down and write out the steps of the task and create or purchase the materials needed to teach the skill, behavior, or task to the individual.

Potential Risks

There are no potential risks associated with task analysis interventions.

Practitioner Testimonial(s)

I wanted my students to learn what they should do when they enter the classroom so I used task analysis taught through gradual release. I started with an activity they all knew how to do, making a peanut butter and jelly sandwich. I wrote the steps on the board and then I performed the activity. For our next activity, we were each given a Lego set and the students took turns telling us what to do at each step. Next the students taught me how to do something like tie my shoes. Finally, the students had to teach me the task analysis for coming in, in the morning: (1) hang up jacket, (2) hang up bag, (3) plug in computer, (4) grab breakfast, (5) sit at seat. By giving them control in the previous examples, they were more likely to transfer those skills to a non-preferred activity.

—Josh Winkler

Rating

Evidence-Based Practice

Resources and Suggested Readings

AFIRM Modules through UNC Chapel Hill offer a free online course on Task Analysis that can be accessed at https://afirm.fpg.unc.edu/task-analysis

Kansas Technical Assistance System Network (TASN) video tutorial can be accessed at https://www.ksdetasn.org/resources/2035

The Ohio Center for Autism and Low Incidence (OCALI) offers a free online course on Task Analysis. After creating an account, it can be accessed at https://autisminternetmodules.org/m/496

Regis College Master's Program in Applied Behavior Analysis maintains a blog with many helpful task analyses that have been completed. The blog can be accessed at https://online.regiscollege.edu/blog/task-analysis/

Prompting and Fading

Description

Prompting and fading of prompts are integral elements in the process of teaching new skills to students with ASD. Without prompting and the fading of prompts, a student will neither learn a skill nor be able to independently display the skill. A *prompt* is a stimulus, provided along with an S^D, which aids the student in making a correct response. *Fading* is the systematic withdrawal of prompts. In order to effectively teach new skills and amend incorrect responses, instructors need to use a variety of prompts and fade them when appropriate. As indicated, a prompt is used when (a) teaching a new response or skill and (b) correcting a student's incorrect response. Prompting and fading of prompts is not an intervention method in and of itself, but a procedure that an educator or behavior interventionist would use within an overall teaching and behavior intervention program.

Prompting and then slowly fading the prompts are two of the most difficult skills for an instructor to master. It often involves a split-second decision about what type of prompt to use or when to use a prompt to ensure a correct response without making a student prompt dependent. It is recommended that whenever a new prompt is introduced, the instructor immediately begins to plan how it will be faded.

There are many different types of prompts that an instructor can choose to use in order to assist a student in learning a skill. A list of these prompts follows, with a very simple skill example for each:

⬧ *Full physical prompt.* The instructor physically manipulates a part of the student's body in order to assist them with *completing* a particular action.

S^D: Instructor says, "Do this." Instructor demonstrates clapping by clapping their hands, then gently puts their hands around the student's wrists and picks up their arms and hands.

R: Instructor makes the student's hands clap a couple of times.

S^R: Instructor lets go of the student's wrists and says, "Good clapping, [student's name]."

⬧ *Partial physical prompt.* The instructor physically manipulates a part of the student's body in order to assist them with *starting* an action.

S^D: A pair of scissors and a piece of paper are sitting on the table in front of the student. Instructor says, "Cut the paper" and takes the student's hand and gently places the student's fingers in and around the scissor handles and then lets go.

R: Student independently completes the action of cutting the paper.

S^R: Instructor says, "Great cutting, [student's name]."

⬧ *Model/Imitative prompt.* The instructor physically demonstrates the action (the correct response) while the student watches.

S^D: Instructor says, "Clap hands" and claps their own hands as student watches.

R: Student claps their hands.

S^R: Instructor says, "Yes, good clapping."

▶ *Gestural prompt.* The instructor provides a physical cue to indicate the correct response.

S^D: There are pictures of different animals on the table in front of the student and instructor. Instructor says, "Give me the dog," and points to the picture of the dog.

R: Student picks up the picture of the dog and hands it to the instructor.

S^R: Instructor says, "That's right. This is the dog."

▶ *Full echoic prompt.* The instructor verbalizes the *entire* correct response.

S^D: The instructor holds up a picture of a book in front of the student. Instructor says, "What is it?" and then immediately says, "Book."

R: Student says, "Book."

S^R: Instructor says, "Yes! It is a book."

▶ *Partial echoic prompt.* The instructor verbalizes the *beginning* sound of the correct response.

S^D: The instructor holds a picture of the student's mom in front of the student. Instructor says, "Who is it?" and then immediately says, "Mmmm."

R: Student says, "Mommy."

S^R: Instructor says, "Yes, that is Mommy. Good job, [student's name]."

▶ *Position prompt.* The instructor places the materials in certain positions (in relationship to the student) in order to increase the likelihood of the student locating the correct item.

S^D: The instructor has placed a red shoe closer to the student than a yellow shoe and a green shoe. Instructor says, "Go get the red shoe."

R: Student picks up the red shoe and hands it to the instructor.

S^R: Instructor says, "Good job. You found the red shoe!"

▶ *Direct verbal prompt.* The instructor provides a verbal instruction to tell the student how to complete one step of a multistep task.

S^D: Instructor says, "Go wash your hands," and then says, "First, go to the sink."

R: Student goes to the sink, turns on the water, and washes their hands with soap and water.

S^R: Instructor says, "Great job washing your hands, [student's name]."

▶ *Indirect verbal prompt.* The instructor states a question that leads the student to determine the correct response.

S^D: Instructor says, "Go wash your hands," and then says, "What do you need to do first?"

R: Student gets up and goes to the sink. They then turn on the water and wash their hands with soap and water.

S^R: Instructor says, "Nice job washing your hands, [student's name]."

▶ *Time Delay (delay of prompt).* This is another important type of prompt used in teaching skills that involves the instructor waiting several seconds after providing the instruction and before providing the prompt, to allow the child the opportunity to respond independently. Time delay will be explained in detail within this section in the chapter titled Time Delay.

Deciding on the type of prompt to use will often depend on the type of response being sought. For instance, if a student is being asked to *say* something, the instructor will use a type of *echoic* prompt; if the student is being asked to *do* something, the instructor will use a type of *physical* prompt.

It is also important for an instructor to decide when to use the least intrusive prompt and when to use the most intrusive prompt. The least intrusive prompt is the most subtle prompt from which the student will be able to give the correct response. This is used when (a) the instructor is attempting to fade prompts or (b) the student has already acquired the skill but just made an incorrect response. The most intrusive prompt is the most obvious prompt from which the student will give a correct response. This is used when (a) initially teaching a new skill or (b) engaging the errorless learning approach. The following are examples of providing a most intrusive prompt and a least intrusive prompt:

Most intrusive prompt

S^D: "Give me the red shoe." Instructor takes the student's hand and puts it on the red shoe and helps them pick it up.

R: Student puts the red shoe in the instructor's hands.

S^R: Instructor says, "Yes! You found the red shoe!"

Least intrusive prompt

S^D: "Give me the red shoe." Instructor turns their head and looks at the red shoe.

R: Student picks up the red shoe and hands it to the instructor.

S^R: Instructor says, "Great! That is the red shoe!"

As stated previously, fading prompts are extremely important. A careful plan needs to be established regarding how a student will be prompted and how the prompts will be faded. Fading prompts ensure that students will not become dependent on the instructor's assistance to complete a task or provide a correct response. The final goal is for students to be able to independently provide a correct response or complete a task within a naturally occurring situation in a typical environment. In the process of fading prompts, the instructor provides higher levels of reinforcement for each correct response that the student provides with less prompting; a less prompted response receives more reinforcement than a more prompted response. This will increase the student's motivation to provide better and more independent responses and guard against prompt dependency. Another method of decreasing prompt dependency is to use a variety of prompt styles (decreasing the predictability of certain prompts) with a student. This also makes the learning process more realistic for the student.

It is crucial for instructors to avoid providing inadvertent prompts—unintentionally helping students to make correct responses. Inadvertent prompts can be very subtle and sometimes indistinguishable to the instructor, but not to students. For example, when giving the instruction, "Get the red shoe," an instructor may inadvertently direct their gaze toward the red shoe on the floor by the door. The student notices that the instructor does this every time they ask for something (looks at the item). As a result, the student learns to wait and watch where the instructor is looking before making a response. It is a good idea for every instructor to be periodically observed by another instructor for inadvertent prompting while working with a student.

It is important to remember that a prompt is part of the instruction given and should be provided simultaneously with or immediately following the instruction. Furthermore, after a student has given an incorrect response, it is important to restate the original instruction, then provide the prompt (not just continue to provide prompting until the student makes the correct response), so that the response will be given under the control of the instruction and not the prompt.

Brief Overview of the Literature

Prompting and fading have long been an effective and evidence-based component of Discrete Trial Teaching procedures, when using task analysis to teach self-help and adaptive skills, and when teaching replacement behaviors within a BIP. At this point in time, several different prompt-fading systems have been developed and proven effective with individuals with ASD. These procedures include, but are not limited to, constant time delay (e.g., Walker, 2008), progressive time delay (PTD) (e.g., MacDuff et al., 2001; Walker, 2008), simultaneous prompting (e.g., Leaf et al., 2010), no-no prompting (e.g., Leaf et al., 2010), flexible prompt fading (e.g., Soluaga et al., 2008), and least-to-most prompting and most-to-least prompting (e.g., Libby et al., 2008).

Core Reviews

Simpson et al. (2005) did not include Prompting and Fading as a stand-alone reviewed intervention. Rather, they included Applied Behavior Analysis as one intervention under their Skill-Based Interventions and Treatments Category. The NAC included Prompting in its 2009 and 2014 reviews as a part of the broader categories of Behavioral Package and Behavioral Interventions, which were both rated as Established. The NPDC (NPDC, Wong et al., 2014) and the NCAEP (NCAEP, Steinbrenner et al., 2020) both included Prompting as a reviewed intervention with both giving the rating of Evidence-Based Practice based on a total of 140 studies.

Age and Diagnostic Considerations/ Prerequisite Skills and Abilities

Prompting and Fading procedures can be used with all ages and skills levels of individuals with ASD.

Reported Outcomes

Prompting and Fading procedures are established, effective, and evidence-based components of DTT when teaching new skills (e.g., reading, colors, numbers), when using task analysis to teach self-help and adaptive skills, and when teaching replacement behaviors within a BIP.

Qualifications Needed

Utilizing prompting and fading procedures as part of an overall teaching or behavior intervention program for an individual with ASD requires training from a professional who is experienced in working with individuals with ASD and developing and implementing such programs. This would typically be a BCBA. Because prompting and fading procedures need to be adjusted and changed as the individual with ASD progresses with their skills and behaviors, it is also best for teachers and parents to receive ongoing supervision and feedback on the prompting and fading procedures used.

How, Where, and When Typically Implemented

Prompting and Fading procedures can be utilized wherever and whenever an educator is teaching skills or behaviors.

Costs

There are no associated costs with using Prompting and Fading procedures within interventions.

Potential Risks

While there are no inherently potential risks associated with prompting and fading procedures within an intervention, people need to be careful about the use of physical prompting, especially in school settings in which many forms of physical prompting have become identified as physical restraint and forcing the individual to do something they may not want to do. In private schools and homes, many interventionists have clear guidelines written out to explain in detail how physical prompting is used for teaching new skills (i.e., "give me the red one" and physically guiding the child's hand to pick up the red item) and how physical prompting or physical restraint is used for managing inappropriate behaviors (i.e., the child is running around throwing objects at people and an adult will physically block access to locations or items and may put their hands on the shoulders of the child and physically guide them to a safe place) displayed by the individual. Regardless, it is very important that any time educators or behavior interventionists are working with an individual with ASD, they have agreed upon (and possibly legally approved) physical prompting processes and procedures that are in writing and signed by parents or guardians.

Practitioner Testimonial(s)

We use prompting in a variety of ways daily in our classroom. Visual, verbal, hand-over-hand, and gestural prompting promotes scaffolded learning, gives students differentiated support, and allows for regular practice learning new skills. We have seen positive benefits with prompting in our classroom with an increase of student engagement and independence. All students learn at their own pace and giving prompts while they are getting used to a new skill or practicing everyday skills supports where they are at as learners.

—Kristen McKearney and Stephanie Kopecky

Rating

Evidence-Based Practice

Resources and Suggested Readings

AFIRM training modules through UNC Chapel Hill offers a free online course on Prompting that can be accessed at https://afirm.fpg.unc.edu/prompting

Kansas Technical Assistance System Network (TASN) offers a free online webinar on Fading that can be accessed at https://www.ksdetasn.org/resources/929

Kansas Technical Assistance System Network (TASN) offers a free online webinar on Prompting that can be accessed at https://www.ksdetasn.org/resources/932

The Ohio Center for Autism and Low Incidence (OCALI) offers a free online course on prompting. After creating an account, it can be accessed at https://autisminternetmodules.org/m/493

Time Delay

Description

Systematic instruction is based on the principles of ABA and dates back to the 1970s in the first research on instructional strategies for individuals with extensive support needs, including those with ASD (Browder et al., 2020). It entails (a) identifying and defining the skill, (b) designing a data sheet for progress monitoring, (c) selecting a response prompting system, (d) making a plan to fade prompts, and (e) providing reinforcement and error correction (Browder et al., 2014). The step in which most research has been conducted is (c) selecting a response prompting system (Shepley et al., 2019). Response prompts refer to the presentation of some cue (e.g., verbal, model, physical) that results in the student selecting the correct response (Cooper et al., 2020). Over time these prompts are faded systematically so that stimulus control is transferred with minimal errors (i.e., errorless learning; Cooper et al., 2020). Response prompting systems include Graduated Guidance, Most-To-Least Prompts, Simultaneous Prompting, System of Least Prompts, and Time Delay (Browder et al., 2014).

Time Delay is an EBP that has been found to be an efficient way to teach many skills, including academic skills (Browder et al., 2009; Courtade et al., 2014). In Time Delay, the instructor begins by presenting the instructional stimulus and then immediately provides the answer (i.e., 0-s delay). The instructor then inserts a delay allowing the student to respond independently before providing the response prompt (Collins, 2022).

Put more plainly, Time Delay involves a no-delay "teaching" round and a delay "testing" round. There are two forms of Time Delay, constant and progressive. In each, the instructor begins with the no-delay teaching round. Take for example, learning vocabulary words. The teacher would present the vocabulary definition to the student and then immediately, with no delay, prompt the student to answer correctly. This prompt may be a verbal one (e.g., telling the student the vocabulary word), a model prompt (e.g., showing the student the vocabulary word, perhaps by pointing a card), or a physical prompt (e.g., physically guiding the student [hand-over-hand] to select the correct vocabulary word, perhaps on an AAC device). This 0-second, no-delay round continues either for a set number of days (e.g., 3 to 5 days), or until the student begins to anticipate the teacher's prompts (i.e., once the student starts to provide the correct response before the instructor has an opportunity to prompt).

Next, the instructor begins the delay or "testing" round. In constant time delay (CTD), the delay remains constant—the instructor always waits the same amount of time before prompting. In progressive time delay (PDT), the length of the delay increases over time. In CTD, a commonly used delay time is 3 seconds. The instructor presents the instructional stimuli (e.g., vocabulary definition) and waits for the student to respond. If the student responds correctly, the instructor should reinforce the student and move on to the next stimulus. If the student does not respond within the set time (e.g., 3 s), the instructor should prompt the student to respond correctly. Ideally, time delay is an errorless procedure, meaning the student has minimal opportunities to make errors. If the student begins to answer incorrectly, or appears to be guessing, the instructor should tell the student "If you don't know the answer, wait and I will help you." This delay round continues until the student has reached mastery.

In PTD, the delay required before prompting increases over time. This is particularly helpful for students who have a history of prompt dependency, or for relatively difficult tasks. For example, in the first phase, the instructor would wait only 1 second before prompting the student. After a set period of time, the delay would progress to 2 seconds, 3 seconds, 5 seconds, 10 seconds, and so on.

Brief Overview of the Literature

Time Delay was first evaluated in 1971 when a researcher taught three adolescent boys with severe ID to discriminate the color red (Touchette, 1971). It was found to be an EBP for students with severe developmental disabilities in 2009 (Browder et al., 2009). In 2014, the National Clearinghouse on Autism Evidence and Practice (NCAEP) Review Team reviewed Time Delay and found it to be an EBP for individuals with ASD for students ages 3 to 22 across the domains of social, communication, behavior, joint attention, play, cognitive, school-readiness, academic, motor, and adaptive skills (NPDC, Wong et al., 2014). Steinbrenner et al. (2020) updated the National Clearinghouse EBP manual and reviewed 31 additional articles. They widened the participants for whom time delay was effective to include toddlers ages 0 to 2 and added the domains of challenging/interfering behavior, vocational, and motor skills. It is important to note, however, that Steinbrenner and Wong included studies in which delays before prompting were assessed, but it was not truly constant or PTD, as there was no 0-s "teaching" session prior to the delay sessions. Therefore, we have decided to provide a brief description of studies specifically evaluating either constant or PTD with students with autism in school-based settings in the last 10 years (2012–2022).

We found 14 studies published between 2012 and 2022 that included the use of Time Delay with 50 students with autism in school settings. Participants ranged in age from 3 years to 20 years. Most of the studies took place in self-contained special education classrooms in public schools, although one study took place in a community setting (i.e., community-based instruction; Horn et al., 2020) and another throughout settings at the public high school (Smith et al., 2016). In the 14 studies we located, the researcher served as the interventionist in seven studies, a teacher served as the interventionist in two studies, and in five studies, the teacher was both the researcher and the interventionist.

CTD was used in 10 studies and PTD, in the remaining four. Time Delay was used to teach vocational skills in two studies (e.g., sorting task, following video models; Horn et al., 2020; Smith et al., 2016), to teach self-help skills in one study (e.g., following an activity schedule; Carlile et al., 2013), to teach verbal behavior in one study (e.g., tacting; Shelpley et al., 2016b), and to teach academic skills in the remaining 10 studies. More specifically, Time Delay was used to teach students to read sight words or environmental print (Coleman et al., 2012; Shepley et al., 2016a; Swain et al., 2015; Winstead et al., 2019), to teach identification of story elements (Browder et al., 2017), to teach listening comprehension (Spooner et al., 2015), to teach mathematics vocabulary (Root & Browder, 2019), to teach numeral identification (Jimenez & Kemmery, 2013), to teach science vocabulary (Knight et al., 2013), and to teach general academic vocabulary (Alison et al., 2017).

Core Reviews

Simpson et al. (2005) did not include Time Delay as a stand-alone reviewed intervention. Rather, they included Applied Behavior Analysis as one intervention under their Skill-Based Interventions and Treatments Category. The NAC included Time Delay in its 2009 as a part of the broader categories of Antecedent Package, which was rated as Established. It was not included in its 2015 review. The NPDC (NPDC, Wong et al., 2014) and the NCAEP (NCAEP, Steinbrenner et al., 2020) both included Time Delay as a reviewed intervention with both giving the rating of EBP based on a total of 31 studies.

Age and Diagnostic Considerations/ Prerequisite Skills and Abilities

According to the most recent EBP review conducted by Steinbrenner and colleagues in 2020, Time Delay has been evaluated with school-age children (ages 3 to 21) with ASD. There was no analysis of any prerequisite skills or abilities in the Steinbrenner review. However, Snell and Gast (1981) suggested that time delay is most effective when students can demonstrate a "waiting" behavior, in which they wait for prompting prior to responding if they do not know the answer.

Reported Outcomes

Steinbrenner et al. (2020) reported that Time Delay is appropriate for academic and pre-academic skills, adaptive and self-help skills, challenging or interfering behaviors, cognitive skills, communication skills, joint attention, play skills, school readiness, social skills, and vocational skills.

Qualifications Needed

Time Delay has been implemented by teachers, paraeducators, peers, and parents. No specific training program is required to implement Time Delay. Many special education teachers receive training in their educator preparation programs through coursework in systematic instruction. Other instructors have received training through Behavioral Skills Training (DiGenarro Reed et al., 2018) in which someone who is an expert in Time Delay provides a description, modeling, coaching, and feedback to the instructor. If potential instructors do not have access to Behavioral Skills Training, free online trainings are available through AFIRM (see resource list).

How, Where, and When Typically Implemented

Time Delay is effective on its own and as part of other instructional packages (e.g., eCoaching, VM, modified schema-based instruction, computer-assisted instruction, graphic organizers, activity schedules). Time Delay can be implemented in any setting such as clinical, community, home, and school settings.

Costs

There are no costs associated with time delay.

Potential Risks

In general, there are no potential risks to using Time Delay. If a physical prompt (e.g., hand-over-hand support) is determined to be the controlling prompt, however, it is crucial to ensure no physical harm is caused and that the student's dignity is preserved (Wolery et al., 1992).

Rating

 Evidence-Based Practice

Resources and Suggested Readings

AFIRM modules through UNC Chapel Hill offers two free online modules for learning to implement time delay (one for Paraeducators and one for Teachers). These can be accessed at https://afirm.fpg.unc.edu/node/2636 (paraeducators) and https://afirm.fpg.unc.edu/time-delay (teachers)

Kansas Technical Assistance System Network (TASN) offers a free online webinar on Time Delay (including data sheets). It can be accessed at https://www.ksdetasn.org/resources/2046

The Ohio Center for Autism and Low Incidence (OCALI) offers a free online course on Time Delay. After creating a free account, it can be accessed through the Autism Internet Modules tab at htttps://autisminternetmodules.org/m/497

Behavioral Momentum

Description

Behavioral Momentum is a concept and method used in ABA when teaching new behaviors and skills. Learning something new is always more difficult than performing already mastered skills. Thus, behavior analysts drew on the theory from physics that once something is already moving it is easier to keep it moving. Behavioral Momentum basically means to build up momentum to what you really want the student to do, by tossing out easy, or "throw away," demands that they are likely to do first. Or to put it another way, you approach the student, not with what YOU have in mind for them to do, but with what they are most likely to want to do.

Within the ABA practice, Behavioral Momentum is used as an Antecedent Management or Proactive Strategy for increasing the likelihood that the student will comply with an instruction and respond appropriately to do something. Often, that instruction is to do something that is at a higher difficulty level than what the student has had to do previously. One of the benefits and goals of using Behavioral Momentum is to decrease the likelihood of the student demonstrating challenging behaviors to escape the demand to perform a difficult task, but instead will respond appropriately and correctly.

Thus, the instructor first presents the student with several easy and mastered tasks at a high pace before presenting the more difficult task. By providing praise and small amounts of reinforcement for the easier previously learned tasks and by helping the student be successful several times in a row, the instructor is increasing the likelihood that the student will be amenable to performing the more difficult task that is presented after the successive easy tasks. Then a high level of reinforcement is provided to the student after they comply with and correctly respond to the instruction to perform the more difficult task.

Motivation and compliance are crucial components of skill acquisition; when they are lacking, learning is impeded. Using behavioral momentum not only boosts motivation and compliance, but it also gives the student the confidence they need to complete tasks and shapes their overall success with skill performance and compliance with instructions in general.

It helps to think of Behavior Momentum as a chain. You are trying to make a long chain and each correct response is a link in the chain. If you do not make it easy to get the chain started, then you will never be able to build the chain. If you get the chain started but then lose momentum, you lose links, or do not add links to the chain, either because the task is too difficult or the student is not motivated.

One way to ensure that tasks are not too difficult when teaching a new skill, and thus to help make certain that the instructor can build and maintain Behavioral Momentum, is to engage in task analysis of skills before teaching them. It has been determined through extensive research that children with ASD, in particular, have great difficulty learning through observation and learning multiple components or multiple steps of an overall skill simultaneously. This comes back to the point that, when deciding what and how to teach a new skill, instructors need to make sure they break down skills or tasks into manageable segments thus making it not too difficult for the student to learn and, therefore, enable instructors to build and maintain Behavioral Momentum throughout the many teaching sessions they will encounter with a particular student.

It is also imperative that instructors guard against the loss of Behavioral Momentum during a teaching session. Building and gaining Behavioral Momentum with a student during a teaching session provides the instructor with their own teaching momentum. The more the student's behavioral momentum is built and maintained, the easier it is to teach the student due to having *less* noncompliant behaviors and *less* incorrect responding while acquiring more appropriate skills. This increases the instructor's motivation to continue engaging in learning activities (both easy and difficult) and thus builds and maintains the overall instructional control and the success of being a competent instructor for students with ASD.

Brief Overview of the Literature

The original research and concept of Behavioral Momentum as a strategy to use when teaching individuals with ASD was conducted and published by Nevin et al. (1983). This article discusses the physics theory that momentum is defined by mass and velocity and that the relationship between the two determines whether an object in movement is less or more resistant to change. These authors said, "It is now well established that learned behavior varies in its resistance to change and that resistance to change depends lawfully on the rate of reinforcement across a wide variety of procedures" (p. 49) and that "the persistence of behavior in the face of altered conditions suggests that it may be profitable to consider learned behavior as possessing momentum" (p. 49). They proposed that the amount of reinforcement (meaning the use of differential reinforcement) used creates the velocity (how fast something moves) on the mass (task being required to perform) and if more reinforcement is provided at a higher rate (velocity) to the greater difficulty tasks (mass) there is less resistance to change.

Further research and articles have been published over the years reviewing behavioral momentum as a strategy to use within behavioral and teaching interventions with individuals with ASD to increase the probability of compliance and on-task performance and thus increasing the rate and occurrence of correct responding (Fisher et al., 2018; Nevin & Shahan, 2011; Rosales et al., 2021). Specifically two types of Behavioral Momentum procedures have been researched and are currently commonly utilized: high-probability instruction or high-probability command sequence also known as "high-p" and task interspersal (Cowan, 2017; Rosales et al., 2021). In 2017, Cowan et al., conducted a meta-analysis on these Behavioral Momentum procedures. One hundred and twenty-four articles were reviewed and based on the inclusion criteria, 16 met criteria and were analyzed for the study (69% high-p and 31% task-interspersal). Across the studies, 80 percent of the research results demonstrated improvements from baseline to maintenance stages, indicating large to very large effect sizes.

Core Reviews

Neither Simpson et al. (2005) nor the NAC (2009, 2015) included Behavioral Momentum as a reviewed intervention. The NPDC (NPDC, Wong et al., 2014) and the NCAEP (Steinbrenner et al., 2020) both included Behavior Momentum in their reports. The NPDC gave a rating of Some but Insufficient Support based on eight studies and the NCAEP gave a rating of EBP.

Age and Diagnostic Considerations/ Prerequisite Skills and Abilities

Behavioral Momentum strategies can be used with all ages and skill levels for individuals with ASD.

Reported Outcomes

Behavioral Momentum is an effective strategy to use within behavioral and teaching interventions with individuals with ASD to increase the probability of compliance with instructions and on-task performance and resulting in increasing the rate and occurrence of correct responding.

Qualifications Needed

Utilizing Behavioral Momentum strategies with individuals with ASD requires a significant amount of training from a professional who is experienced in working with individuals with ASD and developing and implementing teaching and behavioral intervention programs. This would typically be a BCBA. Because Behavioral Momentum procedures need to be adjusted and changed as the individual with ASD progresses with their skills, it is also necessary for teachers and parents to receive ongoing supervision and feedback on the procedures used.

How, Where, and When Typically Implemented

Behavioral Momentum procedures can be utilized wherever and whenever an educator is teaching skills or behaviors.

Costs

The costs associated with implementing Behavioral Momentum Intervention programs are the fees for initial training and ongoing supervision by a trained and experienced professional (BCBA).

Potential Risks

If a professional or parent attempts to develop and implement a Behavioral Momentum program and strategies without any initial training or ongoing supervision, it is highly probable that the instructor will not be successful in using the strategy. If the individual with ASD already has challenging behaviors or is in the moderate to severe range of ASD, they may not learn new skills and, as a result, may also develop more challenging behaviors as a result of being unsuccessful in their learning environment and not acquiring important and critical skills as they develop and grow older.

Rating

 Evidence-Based Practice

Resources and Suggested Readings

AFIRM modules through UNC Chapel Hill offer a free online course on Behavior Momentum that can be accessed at https://afirm.fpg.unc.edu/behavioral-momentum-intervention

Kansas Technical Assistance System Network (TASN) offers a free online webinar on Behavioral Momentum that can be accessed at https://www.ksdetasn.org/resources/964

The Nebraska Autism Spectrum Disorders Network offers a video demonstration of Behavior Momentum that can be accessed at https://www.unl.edu/asdnetwork/virtual-strategies

Response Interruption and Redirection (RIR)

Description

RIR involves introducing a prompt, comment, or other distractor when an interfering behavior is occurring, so that interfering behaviors will decrease. RIR is often used after the completion of a FBA and along with other EBP including Prompting, Reinforcement, and Differential Reinforcement. RIR is used predominantly to address behaviors that are repetitive, stereotypical, and/or self-injurious. It is specifically useful for interfering behaviors that occur when the individual is alone, in multiple settings, and during a variety of tasks which are not likely to be maintained by attention or escape. Behaviors that are most likely maintained by sensory reinforcement and resistant to intervention attempts have been effectively decreased using RIR (NCAEP, Steinbrenner et al., 2020).

Research suggests that RIR may be most effective if the form of the directed response matches the type of stereotypy targeted (Ollendick et al., 1978). Therefore, RIR that requires a vocal response may be more effective for vocal stereotypy and motor RIR to interrupt and reduce motor stereotypy. Vocal stereotypy that one might target as a behavior to decrease could include delayed echolalia (repeating exactly the same words someone else is saying), scripting (reciting the exact same words, phrase and sentences heard in a book or movie), repetitive vocal noises or sounds and non-communicative vocalizations that interfere with engagement in ongoing activities. Motor stereotypy that one might target as a behavior to decrease could include SIB, finger-flicking, or arm movements that interfere with ongoing activities. Practitioners should take special care to ensure social validity surrounding reduction of vocal and motoric stereotypy and consider whether or not the reduction of these behaviors improves quality of life or safety for the person. Stereotypy should not be targeted for reduction simply for the sake of reduction or because it is annoying for another person. Reduction of this behavior should in turn allow for an increase in prosocial behaviors that improves engagement with the learner's environment and quality of life.

Brief Overview of the Literature

RIR was initially described by Ahearn et al. (2007) as an effective treatment for vocal stereotypy. It was described as a variation of response blocking because the response was interrupted by delivering demands contingent on the occurrence of stereotypy and redirected the individual to admit a more appropriate response (e.g., asking the social question, "What is your name?" when the individual emits a noncommunicative vocalization). RIR is most effective for sensory-maintained behaviors because learners are interrupted from engaging in the interfering behaviors, blocking access to reinforcement for that behavior, and redirected to more appropriate, alternative behaviors.

Core Reviews

The NCAEP Review Team has included 10 articles in their review from 1990 to 2011 (NPDC, Wong et al., 2014) and 29 articles in their review from 2012 to 2017. In both the 2014 and 2020 reviews, RIR met criteria to be considered an Evidence-Based Practice (NCAEP, Steinbrenner et al., 2020; NPDC, Wong et al., 2014).

Age and Diagnostic Considerations/ Prerequisite Skills and Abilities

The use of RIR to mitigate challenging or interfering behavior in individuals with autism has been researched with individuals from 3 to 22. Additionally, RIR has been researched in preschoolers and elementary-age individuals with ASD for outcome areas such as communication, social play, school readiness, academic/preacademic, and adaptive/self-help (NCAEP, Steinbrenner et al., 2020). While RIR can be effective within any diagnostic category, the majority of research establishing evidence base was with individuals with autism and one participant with a diagnosis of Down syndrome (Athens et al., 2008). Prerequisite skills and abilities may include established echoic and motor imitation repertoires depending on the stereotypy targeted. Additionally, Aherns et al. (2011) suggests that RIR may not be a viable treatment option for individuals with limited vocal repertoire or who are generally noncompliant with questions or requests.

Reported Outcomes

RIR has been found to be effective in reducing challenging and interfering behaviors in age groups from 3 to 22. RIR has been reported to have favorable outcomes in the area of communication for individuals ages 3 to 14 (NCAEP, Steinbrenner et al., 2020). Additionally, outcome areas reported for ages 3 to 11 include social, play, school readiness, academic/preacademic, and adaptive/self-help (NCAEP, Steinbrenner et al., 2020).

Qualifications Needed

No formal training in RIR as a stand-alone intervention is required. Nonetheless, individuals who use this intervention should be familiar with and trained in its application through consultation with an experienced implementer or other training formats.

How, Where, and When Typically Implemented

RIR can be implemented in any environment in which the interfering behaviors are occurring. In order to maintain treatment fidelity and achieve maximum effectiveness when using RIR, individuals must be consistently monitored in order to interrupt and redirect each occurrence of the targeted stereotypy. For this reason, there may be some environments or activities where implementation may be more difficult.

Costs

RIR is cost-effective in terms of time and other resources. There are no costs associated with training and no additional teaching time is required or materials need to be purchased other than those typically found in natural settings.

Potential Risks

There are no known risks associated with the use of RIR.

Rating

   Evidence-Based Practice

Resources and Suggested Readings

AFIRM modules through UNC Chapel Hill offers a free online training on Response Interruption/Redirection that can be accessed at https://afirm.fpg.unc.edu/response-interruption-and-redirection

Kansas Technical Assistance System Network (TASN) offers a free online webinar on Response Interruption/Redirection that can be accessed at https://www.ksdetasn.org/resources/2962

The Ohio Center for Autism and Low Incidence (OCALI) offers a free online course on Response Interruption/Redirection After creating an account, it can be accessed at https://autisminternetmodules.org/m/495

Reinforcement

Description

The assertion that a student needs to be motivated in order to learn is well documented. Instructors employ Reinforcement and Prompting to motivate students to learn. Prompting is explained in detail in a different chapter. Reinforcement involves providing a consequence following a student's response that increases the likelihood that the response (behavior) will occur again in the future. A reinforcer is anything that the student wants to gain (e.g., food, attention, toys).

Food and drink are primary reinforcers because they are biological and something that all humans need and want (though how much and how often may vary). Other reinforcers, such as praise, getting a toy, or tokens, are secondary reinforcers; they require conditioning in order to actually be reinforcing. In other words, a history of association with primary reinforcers has to be established and to make those things reinforcing (in and of themselves they may initially not have any reinforcing value). Teaching the value of secondary reinforcers can be very effectively done through the use of token economy systems.

It is important for instructors to understand that any behavior or response—inappropriate (incorrect) or appropriate (correct)—can be reinforced. It is, therefore, important for instructors to closely monitor the type of consequences that follow a student's responses. Four examples are provided to demonstrate appropriate use or withholding of Reinforcement and inappropriate use or withholding of Reinforcement after a behavior.

Reinforcement of Appropriate Behavior

A: Adult is holding a cookie within view of a child.

B: Child asks adult, "Cookie, please?"

C: Adult gives the child the cookie and says, "Good asking."

No Reinforcement of Inappropriate Behavior

A: Adult is holding a cookie within view of a child.

B: Child throws a tantrum and tries to take the cookie from the adult.

C: Adult ignores the child, walks away, and hides cookies.

Reinforcement of Inappropriate Behavior

A: Adult is holding a cookie within view of a child.

B: Child throws a tantrum and tries to take the cookie from the adult.

C: Adult gives the child the cookie.

No Reinforcement of Appropriate Behavior

A: Adult is holding a cookie within view of a child.

B: Child asks adult, "Cookie, please?"

C: Adult ignores the child and does not give the child the cookie.

The first and second examples illustrate an instructor who is *appropriately reinforcing* a student for a correct response and not reinforcing a student for an incorrect response. This instructor is appropriately using Reinforcement to increase appropriate responses or behaviors and decrease inappropriate responses or behaviors. The third and fourth examples present an instructor who is *inappropriately reinforcing* a student for an incorrect response and not reinforcing a student for a correct response. This instructor is inappropriately using Reinforcement and will likely increase inappropriate responses or behaviors and decrease appropriate responses or behaviors.

There are two primary purposes for using Reinforcement when teaching new skills and managing appropriate and inappropriate behaviors with students with ASD. First, Reinforcement is a critical factor in teaching a student new skills or behaviors. By tying reinforcers directly to the target behavior that the instructor wishes to increase, the student is taught the correct response. Second, reinforcers can provide the motivation a student needs to learn a skill or behavior that they may not necessarily care about or whose importance they do not yet understand. A student needs to see a reason (a "payoff") for providing a response, specifically a correct response, to an instruction. If the instructor makes it clear that they have something the student wants to obtain, the student will be more apt to be motivated to do what the instructor requests in order to obtain that item or activity (the reinforcer).

It is imperative that instructors use reinforcers that the *student* prefers and not reinforcers that the *instructor* chooses and thinks the student prefers. Consistently employing the use of a *reinforcer assessment* (a checklist of items and activities the student has preferred in the past and novel, age-appropriate items the student may prefer) will allow an instructor to find out what the student wants to gain and will provide ideas for new items and activities that the student may like. Because the strength of a reinforcer (the amount of motivation that the reinforcer elicits) can vary from moment to moment, instructors need to implement this quick reinforcement survey at the beginning of each day or learning session. This will ensure that the student is highly motivated and decrease the likelihood of incorrect responses or inappropriate behaviors due to lack of motivation.

Whenever possible, it is appropriate and beneficial to allow the student to choose (prior to a learning session) what they would like to earn as a reinforcer after successfully completing a particular learning session or activity. Choice, in and of itself, can be a motivating factor that leads to successful learning, as it can make a student feel that they have some control over their environment and learning. For example, an instructor knows that a particular student enjoys looking at books, playing on the computer, and playing with trains, so they pull out a choice board with some pictures on it when they and the student sit down to begin working together. One picture shows a student working appropriately with an instructor, and there is an arrow to a blank spot. There are three pictures at the bottom of the board of the student reading books, playing on the computer, and playing with trains. The instructor asks the student to pick what activity they would like to do after "completing [task/activity]." The student picks a picture and puts it next to the arrow, establishing their choice to play with trains when they finish working. The board remains visible throughout the session.

There are four crucial factors that an instructor needs to take into consideration regarding the use of reinforcers. First, in order for a reinforcer to be effective, it needs to reinforce the actual skill or behavior that is appropriate and desirable or that the instructor is trying to teach. Effective Reinforcement means that a reinforcer is provided to the student *immediately* after the appropriate behavior or correct target response occurs. There cannot be a long space of time, nor can other skills or behaviors be performed or demonstrated in between the occurrence of the target skill or behavior and the delivery of Reinforcement. This may sound logical and simple, but once this is pointed out to instructors, many are surprised at how often they inadvertently provide reinforcement to a student after they have engaged in other behaviors after performing the target behavior. This often happens with self-stimulation (i.e., stimming). For example, during a session, there is a discrete trial in which a student correctly identifies the blue ball and then starts flicking his fingers in front of his eyes and then the instructor hands him a piece of a cookie, saying "You're right! That's the blue ball." In this scenario, the student was just reinforced for engaging in the self-stimulation behavior of flicking his hands in front of his eyes, a behavior that the instructor does not want to reinforce and increase.

Second, there should be reinforcers that the student has access to only during learning sessions or while completing a specific task or demonstrating a particular skill and not during the rest of the day, either at home or at school. This ensures that the reinforcers maintain their strength and that the student does not become satiated. These items may be kept in special containers in locations that the student cannot access. Special reinforcers may also be used for some specific, very difficult learning activities. For example, if a student loves looking at books about trains and particularly dislikes writing activities, a teacher might allow the student to read or look at a page in the child's favorite train book for 1 minute for every sentence they write without protesting. This particular book would not be used during other learning sessions nor during play time.

Third, the amount or level of reinforcement provided to the student needs to match the level of difficulty or desirability of the task or skill they are being asked to perform. This is called *differential reinforcement* and explained in more detail in the chapter titled Differential Reinforcement. If the student enjoys the task or the task is fairly easy for the student, they require smaller amounts of reinforcement or reinforcement at less frequent intervals. If the student dislikes the task or the task is difficult, they will likely need a larger amount of reinforcement or reinforcement at more frequent intervals.

Fourth, the student needs to be provided access to reinforcers *only* when they have earned them. That is, to receive a reinforcer, students must comply with a request or respond correctly to an instruction. Inappropriate behavior, noncompliance, and incorrect responses do not earn reinforcement. In order for the student to learn, they must understand that they must do or give something in exchange for something that they want to gain.

There are also two different schedules of Reinforcement that instructors utilize when teaching students: Continuous Reinforcement and Intermittent Reinforcement. Continuous Reinforcement means that you reinforce the student every time they perform the correct skill or behavior. Intermittent reinforcement means that sometimes you reinforce the student for performing the correct skill or behavior. Continuous reinforcement is used when teaching a new skill or behavior. Every time the student responds correctly or behaves appropriately, you reinforce them because you want them to know that response or behavior is correct and to do it again in the same way next time. But after a while, the student may become satiated (have all that they want) if they are reinforced every single time they perform the skill. The student's motivation to continue to perform that skill typically decreases if the same thing continues to happen over and over. But if they don't know when they will be reinforced for responding correctly, then they will typically try harder and be more motivated to continue to do the correct response or behave appropriately with the hope that THIS time they will get that reinforcer—this is intermittent reinforcement. Therefore, as a skill or behavior becomes acquired, the instructor will decrease the frequency of Reinforcement in order to maintain the motivation to continue to perform that skill and to perform it correctly.

Brief Overview of the Literature

Reinforcement of behavior and its causal relationship with increasing the behavior that immediately preceded it is one of the foundations of the science of behavior and thus the science of ABA (Nevin, 1988). Within the A-B-C paradigm that behavior analysts utilize to study and implement changes on behavior, Reinforcement is the most powerful of the two consequences that can occur after a behavior. Thus, all of the research that is conducted regarding Reinforcement surrounds the different ways of using Reinforcement to increase desirable behaviors and withhold reinforcement to decrease undesirable behaviors (Fiske et al., 2019; Nevin, 1988; Rey et al., 2020; Slocum & Vollmer, 2015). Research has proven that the following strategies (not an exhaustive list) are proven effective and need to be considered within different teaching and BIP:

▶ Amount of reinforcement

▶ Rate of reinforcement

▶ Quality of reinforcement

▶ Differential reinforcement

▶ Schedules of reinforcement

▶ Use of primary versus secondary reinforcers

▶ Satiation

▶ Reinforcer assessments

▶ Non-contingent versus contingent reinforcement

▶ Natural/functional versus non-functional reinforcement

▶ Positive versus negative reinforcement (Camponaro et al., 2020; Cividini-Motta et al., 2013; Delmolino et al., 2014; Fiske et al., 2019; Nevin, 1988; Rey et al., 2020; Richman et al., 2015; Slocum & Vollmer, 2015; Weston et al., 2018; Whitaker et al., 1996)

Core Reviews

Simpson et al. (2005) did not include Reinforcement as a stand-alone intervention. It was discussed as a part of the overall review of ABA that was determined to be Evidence-Based. The NAC included Reinforcement in both its 2009 and 2015 reviews as a part of behavioral interventions for individuals with ASD, which was determined to be an Established Practice with 231 articles reviewed in 2009 and 155 articles reviewed in 2015. Reinforcement was reviewed by the NDCP (NPDC, Wong et al., 2014) and the NCEAP (Steinbrenner et al., 2020) as one procedure or strategy utilized within a comprehensive behavioral intervention or package that is implemented with individuals with ASD in teaching skills and tasks, which was determined to be Evidence-Based with 43 articles reviewed in 2014 and 106 articles reviewed in 2020. Overall, all the reviews considered Reinforcement to be an important component of any comprehensive behavior intervention and contributed to that intervention being Evidence-Based.

Age and Diagnostic Considerations/ Prerequisite Skills and Abilities

Reinforcement procedures can be used with all ages and skill levels of individuals with ASD.

Reported Outcomes

Reinforcement has been found to be effective in reducing challenging behaviors, increasing desirable behaviors, and in teaching new skills to individuals with ASD.

Qualifications Needed

Utilizing Reinforcement as part of an overall teaching or behavior intervention program for an individual with ASD requires training from a professional who is experienced in working with individuals with ASD and developing and implementing such programs. This would typically be a BCBA. Because Reinforcement procedures need to be adjusted and changed as the individual with ASD progresses with their skills and behaviors, it is also best for teachers and parents to receive ongoing supervision and feedback on the Reinforcement procedures used.

How, Where, and When Typically Implemented

Reinforcement procedures can be used whenever and wherever an educator is implementing teaching and behavioral interventions.

Costs

There costs associated with implementing Reinforcement procedures are the fees for initial training, ongoing supervision by a trained and experienced professional, and the costs of purchasing the reinforcers the individual wants to earn.

Potential Risks

There are no inherent potential risks associated with Reinforcement interventions. If a professional or parent attempts to develop and implement Reinforcement procedures without any initial training and supervision (i.e., from a BCBA), there is the risk that an individual will not learn new skills at an acceptable rate, and inappropriate and undesired behaviors may inadvertently be reinforced. If this occurs, then, appropriate and desired behaviors may inadvertently be decreased.

Rating

  Evidence-Based Practice

Resources and Suggested Readings

AFIRM modules through UNC Chapel Hill offer a free online course on Reinforcement that can be accessed at https://afirm.fpg.unc.edu/reinforcement

Kansas Technical Assistance System Network (TASN) offers a free online webinar on Reinforcement. It can be accessed at https://www.ksdetasn.org/resources/1889

The Ohio Center for Autism and Low Incidence (OCALI) offers a free online course on Reinforcement. After creating an account, it can be accessed at https://autisminternetmodules.org/m/521

Differential Reinforcement

Description

Reinforcement is the process of providing a consequence immediately after a behavior in order to try to increase the occurrence of that behavior in the future. This was fully described in a previous chapter, Reinforcement.

The amount or level of reinforcement provided to the student needs to match the level of difficulty or desirability of the task they are being asked to perform. This is called Differential Reinforcement. If the student enjoys the task or the task is fairly easy for the student, they require smaller amounts of reinforcement or reinforcement at less frequent intervals. If the student dislikes the task or the task is difficult, they will likely need a larger amount of reinforcement or reinforcement at more frequent intervals.

Instructors need to pay attention to the amount of motivation that the student displays to perform various tasks and provide enough reinforcement to ensure that the student maintains a high enough level of motivation to perform a particular task. Generally speaking, difficult tasks need more reinforcement and easy tasks need less reinforcement. High motivation needs low reinforcement; low motivation needs high reinforcement.

There are several types of Differential Reinforcement:

- Differential Reinforcement of Alternative Behavior (DRA)

- Differential Reinforcement of Incompatible Behavior (DRI)

- Differential Reinforcement of Other Behavior (DRO)

- Differential Reinforcement of Higher Rate of Behavior (DRH)

- Differential Reinforcement of Lower Rate of Behavior (DRL)

TYPE OF DIFFERENTIAL REINFORCEMENT	WHAT TO REINFORCE	APPLICATIONS
Differential Reinforcement of Alternative Behavior (DRA)	A functionally equivalent alternative behavior	Widely applicable for reducing maladaptive behavior (e.g., raising hand to obtain permission to talk rather than shouting out)
Differential Reinforcement of Incompatible Behavior (DRI)	A functionally equivalent incompatible behavior	Widely applicable for reducing maladaptive behavior and used to differentially reinforce independent responding (e.g., squeezing a toy rather than squeezing someone's arm)

TYPE OF DIFFERENTIAL REINFORCEMENT	WHAT TO REINFORCE	APPLICATIONS
Differential Reinforcement of Other Behavior (DRO)	The absence of the target behavior	Useful in reducing potentially dangerous behavior (e.g., head banging)
Differential Reinforcement of Higher Rates of Behavior (DRH)	Behavior occurring at a rate above (higher) a predetermined minimum rate	Useful in increasing the rate of desired behaviors that are in a learner's repertoire but occur too infrequently (e.g., initiating social interaction)
Differential Reinforcement of Lower Rates of Behavior (DRL)	Behavior occurring at a rate below (lower) a predetermined maximum behavior	Useful for decreasing the rate of appropriate behavior that occurs too frequently (e.g., talking to peers)

Differential Reinforcement is used to increase very specific behaviors or skills that an individual needs to gain or needs to increase how often or how much they display or use a particular skill or behavior. If a student does not show internal motivation to perform a skill or display an appropriate behavior, a higher amount of reinforcement is needed to externally motivate them to do it. If a student is internally motivated to perform a skill or display an appropriate behavior, then a lower amount of reinforcement is needed to externally motivate them to do it. For example, a child who enjoys reading books and is presented with a new book and instructed to read it is probably going to need less reinforcement provided by a parent or teacher to be motivated to read that new book. If that child does not like doing addition problems as a part of their math work, they will probably need more reinforcement to be motivated to complete those math problems.

Brief Overview of the Literature

The application of differential reinforcement on challenging behavior to serve as a behavior reduction tool has been utilized for decades (Homer & Peterson, 1980; Jessel & Ingvarsson, 2016; Poling & Ryan, 1982; Weston et al., 2018; Whitaker, 1996). DRA is the most common form of differential reinforcement used to treat problem behavior (Cooper et al., 2007). More recently differential reinforcement in relation to skill acquisition has been researched and found to be effective when the procedure consists of arranging higher quality and denser schedules of reinforcement for unprompted correct responses, while also delivering lower quality and thinner schedules of reinforcement for prompted correct responses (Cividini-Motta & Ahearn, 2013; Weston et al., 2018).

Core Reviews

Simpson et al. (2005) did not include Differential Reinforcement as a stand-alone reviewed intervention. Rather, they included it as a component of Applied Behavior

Analysis, which was considered an Evidence-Based Intervention. The NAC (2009, 2015) included Differential Reinforcement in its 2009 and 2015 reviews as a part of the broader categories of Behavior Package and Behavior Interventions with 231 articles reviewed in 2009 and 155 articles reviewed in 2015. Both reviews rated the Behavior Package/Interventions as Established Interventions. The NPDC (NPDC, Wong et al., 2014) did not include Differential Reinforcement in its review. The NCAEP (Steinbrenner et al., 2020) reviewed 58 articles and gave a rating of EBP.

Age and Diagnostic Considerations/ Prerequisite Skills and Abilities

Differential Reinforcement procedures can be used with any age and skill level for individuals with ASD.

Reported Outcomes

Differential Reinforcement has been found to be effective in reducing challenging behaviors and in teaching new skills to individuals with ASD.

Qualifications Needed

Utilizing Differential Reinforcement as part of an overall teaching or Behavior Intervention program for an individual with ASD requires training from a professional who is experienced in working with individuals with ASD and developing and implementing such programs. This would typically be a BCBA. Because Reinforcement procedures need to be adjusted and changed as the individual with ASD progresses with their skills and behaviors, it is also best for teachers and parents to receive ongoing supervision and feedback on the Reinforcement procedures used.

How, Where, and When Typically Implemented

Differential Reinforcement procedures can be used whenever and wherever an educator is implementing teaching and behavior intervention procedures.

Costs

The costs associated with implementing Differential Reinforcement procedures are the fees for initial training, and some ongoing supervision by a trained and experienced professional (i.e. BCBA), as well as the costs of purchasing the reinforcers the individual wants to earn.

Potential Risks

There are no inherent potential risks associated with Differential Reinforcement procedures. If a professional or parent attempts to develop and implement Reinforcement procedures without any initial training and supervision, there is the risk that inappropriate and undesired behaviors may inadvertently be reinforced and thus increased in occurrence and the appropriate and desired behaviors may inadvertently be decreased.

Practitioner Testimonial(s)

I have used some form of Reinforcement throughout my 28 years in education. It has become the driving force in motivating students in compliance and task completion. It is most successful when the student/students are included in choosing the type of Reinforcement as well as personalizing the system. When a student determines what they want to work for or what motivates them, such as earning 5 minutes of coloring with favorite markers, the whole purpose changes. In order for it to work, the reinforcement must be highly motivating to the individual. Using the student's interests to aid in the reinforcement process adds another layer of motivation. For example, my student loves dinosaurs so we used pieces of a dinosaur puzzle to help him recognize that he was getting closer to earning his reinforcement as he was constructing the dinosaur puzzle. Once the puzzle was complete, his reinforcement was earned.

—Teri Berkgren

Rating

 Evidence-Based Practice

Resources and Suggested Readings

AFIRM modules through UNC Chapel Hill offer a free online course on Differential Reinforcement that can be accessed at https://afirm.fpg.unc.edu/node/1591

Kansas Technical Assistance System Network (TASN) offers a two free online webinars on Differential Reinforcement. It can be accessed at https://www.ksdetasn.org/resources/2968 and https://www.ksdetasn.org/resources/2524

The Ohio Center for Autism and Low Incidence (OCALI) offers a free online course on Differential Reinforcement. After creating an account, it can be accessed at https://autisminternetmodules.org/m/488

Modeling

Description

Modeling is the "demonstration of a desired target behavior that results in the use of the behavior by the learner and that leads to the acquisition of the target behavior" (NCAEP, Steinbrenner et al., 2020). Demonstrating to another person how to perform a skill or task is one of the most basic teaching strategies. Any individual (e.g., teacher, other school professional, parent, peer) can demonstrate the target behavior for the student with ASD and then the student imitates the same behavior. However, many students with ASD lack the necessary prerequisite skills for Modeling such as attending to the target behavior and imitation skills (DeQuinzio & Taylor, 2015). Therefore, Modeling is often combined with other teaching strategies, such as prompting and reinforcement, to teach the student which behavior to attend and imitate.

Modeling is closely related to observational learning. Plavnick and Hume (2014) describe Modeling as a teaching strategy within the broader category of observational learning. To effectively learn through observing others, students with ASD must observe both a behavior and consequence associated with that behavior. For example, students with ASD may observe peers in classroom settings demonstrating a variety of prosocial behaviors (e.g., hand raising, lining up) and imitate those behaviors. Indeed, observational learning has been described as important for success in general education settings and K–12 education and learning broadly (Plavnick & Hume, 2014; Taylor & DeQuinzio, 2012; Townley-Cochran et al., 2015). Although students with ASD can learn tasks by naturally observing others (e.g., peers, siblings, teachers), they will likely need assistance to determine which tasks should be imitated (National Autism Center, 2015). In addition, effective Modeling requires both attention and imitation skills (DeQuinzio & Taylor, 2015).

It is important to note video modeling (VM) is a type of Modeling and is further described in Section 4. Similarly, peer-mediated instruction and intervention (PMI) uses peers to model target behavior and is further described in Section 9.

Brief Overview of the Literature

Observational learning was first proposed and researched by Albert Bandura through his social learning theory. This theory proposes that children learn by observing and then imitating the behavior of others. In the seminal study by Bandura et al. (1961), children demonstrated aggressive behavior toward toys and dolls (i.e., "Bobo doll") after observing an adult demonstrating similarly aggressive behavior. Other Bandura studies during this time period indicated similar findings (e.g., Bandura et al., 1963) and the means of learning by observing the behavior of others.

Modeling, imitation, and observational learning have been used to teach children with ASD. For example, an early study conducted by Rigsby-Eldredge and McLaughlin (1992) found modeling and verbal praise effectively increased the pro-social work behaviors of two high school students with ASD. The students observed staff members modeling appropriate work behaviors (e.g., social greetings, work task completion) and then had the opportunity to demonstrate the target behaviors. Modeling and verbal praise were found to be effective for the two participants across three of the four target behaviors. This study also demonstrates how Modeling can be combined with other teaching strategies such as reinforcement.

Modeling has a large literature base supporting its efficacy and was classified as an established treatment in both of the National Standards Project (National Autism Center [NAC], 2009, 2015) reviews. VM was included as a type of Modeling in the National Standards Project reviews. However, the NCAEP Review Team classified Modeling and

VM as two different types of interventions. Modeling was found to be an EBP for both the NCAEP reviews (2014, 2020). McDowell et al. (2015) examined the effects of Live Modeling and VM to teach imitation skills to four young children with ASD and found Live Modeling combined with a prompting procedure to be more effective. However, other studies have found VM to be more effective (e.g., Charlop-Christy et al., 2000).

Finally, several reviews have been conducted on Modeling. Townley-Cochran et al. (2015) conducted a systematic review focused on observational learning procedures for children with ASD with 20 articles included in their review. Eighty percent of the included studies used peers to model the target behavior, which represents the related nature of modeling and peer-mediated intervention and instruction. Matson et al. (2007) conducted a review to evaluate trends in social skills instruction for children with ASD and found that Modeling and Reinforcement were particularly prominent. This review included 79 articles, of which 33 articles used Modeling and Reinforcement. The majority of studies were conducted in school settings by teachers or other professionals.

Core Reviews

Simpson et al. (2005) did not include Modeling as a stand-alone reviewed intervention. Rather, they included Applied Behavior Analysis as one intervention under their Skill-Based Interventions and Treatments Category. The NAC gave Modeling the rating of Established in both 2009 and 2015 based on over 75 studies. Both the National Professional Development Center (NPDC; Wong et al., 2014) and the NCAEP (Steinbrenner et al., 2020) used the term Modeling and gave the ratings of EBP based on a total of 28 studies.

Age and Diagnostic Considerations/ Prerequisite Skills and Abilities

Modeling is effective for all age ranges as young as toddlers (0 to 2) through young adults (19 to 22). Individuals with ASD must demonstrate attention, discrimination, and imitation skills to effectively model the behavior of another person.

Reported Outcomes

Modeling has been used to teach nearly all outcome areas including, but not limited to, communication, social, joint attention, school readiness, vocational, and motor skills.

Qualifications Needed

The implementer does not need specific training to model a target behavior. Rather, the implementer must simply know how to do the target behavior themselves.

How, Where, and When Typically Implemented

Modeling can be implemented in any setting (e.g., clinical, community, home, school). Modeling is typically implemented in conjunction with other teaching strategies and interventions (e.g., reinforcement, social skills training, PMI). Modeling can be implemented one-on-one, in small groups, or in large groups. In addition, Modeling can be used with both simple and complex behaviors.

Costs

There are no costs associated with Modeling.

Potential Risks

There are no potential risks associated with Modeling.

Rating

  Evidence-Based Practice

Resources and Suggested Readings

Cox, A. W. (2013). *Modeling fact sheet.* The University of North Carolina, Frank Porter Graham Child Development Institute, The National Professional Development Center on Autism Spectrum Disorders.

Sam, A., & AFIRM Team. (2016). *Modeling.* National Professional Development Center on Autism Spectrum Disorder, FPG Child Development Center, University of North Carolina. It can be accessed at https://afirm.fpg.unc.edu/modeling

Functional Behavior Assessment (FBA)

Description

An FBA is a process by which a professional uses tools like interviews, ratings scales, and direct observations of individuals to collect data on behavior and make a hypothesis about what is motivating a target problem behavior (e.g., the function) that an individual is displaying. The development of an FBA is typically a three-step process: (1) defining the target problem behavior(s), (2) collecting data about the antecedents and consequences of the behavior (direct observation of behavior, interviews, questionnaires), and (3) developing a hypothesis about the function of the behavior.

Behavior analysts observe the student within different and contrived situations that will or will not elicit the target problem behavior and then take data on what reinforces that behavior. Once it is determined what behaviors increase when reinforced in certain situations with certain reinforcers, the behavior analysts can determine why the student engages in the behavior and decide on the main function(s) of the behavior. For example, if a student is playing with a toy and the teacher says it's time to go to the desk and takes the toy, the behavior analyst may observe that the student cries and screams and tries to get that toy back, or maybe they run away and refuse to go to their desk. Through these methods we can typically come to a conclusion about what the function (or purpose) of the behavior is and what interventions we can use to decrease it. But how do we know for sure? Or what if our hypothesis is wrong?

Determining the *function of the target problem behavior* in order to understand what is maintaining the target problem behavior involves categorizing the behavior into one of four main functions. All behaviors can be categorized into one of these four concepts or functions:

 ▶ Tangible: to gain or maintain access to something

 ▶ Attention: to gain or maintain attention from someone

 ▶ Escape: to escape or avoid something

 ▶ Automatic Reinforcement: for own self-pleasure or enjoyment

Once the function of the target problem behavior has been determined through a FBA, a *replacement behavior* (appropriate and desirable) is selected to teach the student and to be reinforced when it is displayed. The replacement behavior is often a functional communication phrase, such as "one more minute" (function of tangible), "I need a break" (function of escaping something), or "let's play" (function of gaining someone's attention) that can be taught to the child to do instead of engaging in the target problem behavior. The replacement behavior needs to be able to be generalized across a variety of environments, people, and formats including verbal requests, picture exchange, and speech-generating devices (SGDs), depending on each student's individual communication needs. The replacement behavior must be one that is functionally equivalent: meaning the student will continue to gain the same outcome with this new response as they did with the target problem behavior. The goal is that over time this replacement behavior will increase and replace the target problem behavior that will, in turn, decrease in occurrence. For example, instead of the student screaming and crying and trying to grab an item, or run away with an item that the teacher tries to take or say it's time to put away, the student will calmly say "one more minute" and then the teacher will grant the student more time to play with the item as reinforcement for using the communication phrase instead of screaming and crying and grabbing the item.

Once the function of the target (inappropriate) behavior and the replacement (appropriate) behavior have been identified, the intervention team develops a behavior intervention plan (BIP) that provides all the teaching procedures for the replacement behavior, the ABIs, the consequence interventions (including reinforcement procedures for the replacement behavior and the punishment procedures for the target problem behavior), and the method of data collection to determine progress or lack of progress that the student makes with the changes and improvements in their behavior. It is also important that there are checks on the fidelity of implementation of the BIP so that the team ensures it is being implemented as it was designed and that the progress or lack of progress is due to the effective implementation of the plan.

Another form of analyzing the function of a behavior that is used by some behavior analysts is called a functional analysis (FA). It is not the same thing as an FBA. When behavior analysts utilize FA to determine the function(s) of a behavior, they set up conditions in a very controlled environment, which will cause the target problem behavior to occur (for a short time) and allow them to systematically manipulate and analyze the setting events, settings, antecedents, triggers, precursors, and consequences that are maintaining the target problem behavior. The conditions are based on the functions discussed previously and by determining which condition produces the highest frequency of behavior. Then, behavior analysts and the intervention team state that they find more confidence regarding the function(s) of the behavior and its causes.

There are five conditions that behavior analysts set up when conducting an FA with an individual with ASD. Each condition allows the behavior analyst to take data that they can later analyze to determine the function of the target problem behavior. Below is an outline of these conditions:

- Play/Control Condition: The individual is provided with access to all known reinforcers at once and no demands are placed. This is the baseline or control condition against which all the other conditions are measured.

- Alone Condition: The individual is left alone, and no consequences are provided for the target behavior. (Changes are made to the procedure for behaviors that have the potential to become dangerous to self or others.)

- Attention Condition: Every time the target behavior occurs, attention is provided to the individual. Could be desirable attention (e.g., smiles, tickles, "nice work") or undesirable (e.g., "stop it"!).

- Demand Condition: Every time the target behavior occurs, escape from demands is provided for a short time.

- Tangible Condition: Every time the target behavior occurs, access to a preferred tangible item or activity is provided.

FA procedures are very controversial in the field of ABA because the behavior analysts are causing and reinforcing the target problem behavior to occur for a short time, and this is viewed as inappropriate and possibly dangerous (e.g., reinforcing self-injurious or aggressive behavior) by many behavior analysts. Conducting a full FA may not be necessary to determine and understand the function of the behavior when a thorough FBA can be implemented instead.

Due to the controversial and inconclusive nature of implementing FAs with students with ASD, the fact that FAs need very experienced behavior analysts to implement within a controlled setting, and the fact that none of the core reviews included FA within their reports, we will also not be including it in this review. We provided this brief explanation and description so that teachers and other educators who hear about FA as another way to determine the function of a behavior can gain objective information about it and understand why it is not commonly used within a school or classroom setting.

Brief Overview of the Literature

The use of Function-Based Interventions has been supported by research for several decades and several studies have directly compared the effects of Function-Based and Nonfunction-Based Interventions, concluding that Function-Based Interventions are, on average, more successful (Edwards et al., 2002; Filter & Horner, 2009; Ingram et al., 2005; McIntosh et al., 2008). Treatment effectiveness is also influenced by the method used to evaluate function, with more stringent methods being linked to better results (Alter et al., 2008; Campbell, 2003;).

The U.S. Department of Education acknowledges functional behavior evaluation as a crucial element of behavioral interventions in schools in the IDEA (Office of Special Education Programs, 2004). This change has been reflected in the school-based intervention literature, where more intervention studies now include an FBA as a step in the intervention selection process. In 1999, only 23 percent of school-based studies had FBAs (Nelson et al., 1999); by the time IDEA was reauthorized in 2004, which requires FBAs for students in specific instances such as discipline and suspensions, the percentage had increased to 44 percent (Beavers et al., 2013).

Core Reviews

Simpson et al. (2005) did not include FBA or FA as reviewed interventions. The NAC did not review any studies regarding FBA or FA in 2009. In 2015, the NAC included Function-Based Interventions as part of the broader category of Behavioral Interventions, which was rated as an Established Intervention. The NPDC (NPDC, Wong et al., 2014) and NCAEP (Steinbrenner et al., 2020) both included FBA, but not FA, within their reports in 2014 and 2020. They both gave the rating of EBP based on a total of 21 studies.

Age and Diagnostic Considerations/ Prerequisite Skills and Abilities

FBAs can be used with all ages and skill levels of individuals with ASD but are typically used when professionals and parents are having difficulty determining the function of a challenging behavior or have been unsuccessful in decreasing the occurrence of a challenging behavior and teaching an appropriate replacement behavior.

Reported Outcomes

FBAs are Evidenced-Based Practices that are found to be effective in analyzing behaviors exhibited by individuals with ASD, determining the function(s) of target problem behaviors, identifying the causal setting events and antecedents, as well as the maintaining consequences for problem behaviors, and identifying appropriate and functionally equivalent replacement behaviors and reinforcers that will be needed to increase the replacement behaviors.

Qualifications Needed

Conducting FBAs with individuals with ASD requires a significant amount of experience and training in ABA and, specifically these procedures, from a professional who is experienced in working with individuals with ASD and developing and implementing behavior intervention programs, such as a BCBA. Because the resulting teaching and BIP and procedures constantly need to be adjusted and changed as the individual with ASD progresses with their behaviors and skills, it is also necessary for teachers and parents to receive ongoing supervision and feedback on the procedures used. Data collection is particularly important when implementing the BIP in order to determine if it is effective and if the FBA identifies the correct functions of behavior and intervention procedures.

How, Where, and When Typically Implemented

FBAs are specifically designed to be conducted within the environment in which the target problem behavior is most likely to occur the most and the least.

Costs

The costs associated with implementing FBA procedures are the fees for initial training and ongoing supervision by a trained and experienced professional (e.g., BCBA) or the cost of contracting with someone to complete the FBA and provide a report to the intervention team, as well as the cost of the curriculum and materials needed when teaching the individual new skills.

Potential Risks

If a professional or parent attempts to develop and conduct an FBA without any initial training or ongoing supervision by a BCBA, it is highly probable that the instructor will not be successful in identifying the correct functions of the challenging behavior or the appropriate replacement behaviors to teach and reinforce. The challenging behaviors will most likely increase in occurrence and, as a result, the student with ASD may also be unsuccessful in their learning environment and not acquire important and critical skills as they develop and grow older.

Rating

 Evidence-Based Practice

Resources and Suggested Readings

AFIRM modules through UNC Chapel Hill offer a free training module for Functional Behavior Assessment that can be accessed at https://afirm.fpg.unc.edu/node/783

Kansas Technical Assistance System Network (TASN) offers a free training module for Functional Behavior Assessment that can be accessed at https://www.ksdetasn.org/resources/1809

The Office of Special Education Programs (OSEP) Resources for Teachers on Discipline and Behavior Supports in Classrooms offers resources at https://osepideasthatwork.org/supporting-and-responding-behavior-evidence-based-classroom-strategies-teachers

The Office of Special Education Programs (OSEP) Resources for Teachers on Positive and Proactive Approaches for Supporting Students with Disabilities and Behavior Challenges offers resources at https://sites.ed.gov/idea/idea-files/guide-positive-proactive-approaches-to-supporting-children-with-disabilities/

The Ohio Center for Autism and Low Incidence (OCALI) offers a free online course on Functional Behavior Assessment. After creating an account, it can be accessed at https://autisminternetmodules.org/m/491

Functional Communication Training (FCT)

Description

FCT is built on the theory that challenging behavior (e.g., yelling, hitting, screaming, throwing objects) is an inappropriate means of communicating. The aim for this intervention is to replace those behaviors with a more appropriate communicative response.

Overall, there are three main steps in implementing an FCT regime:

1. *Determine the function of the target behavior.* Why does the individual do it? What are they trying to gain access to or avoid? Both FBA and Analog Functional Assessment (AFA) are used to determine what is happening, when, and why.

2. *Select a replacement behavior.* Once the function of the behavior has been determined, an appropriate alternative behavior can be selected. The replacement behavior must give the individual access to the same things as the challenging behavior. The alternative must also be individualized based on the student's needs.

3. *Create a plan for using FCT with the student* (generally included within a BIP). Important components of the plan will include setting up both naturally occurring and contrived situations to practice the communication request and then generalize that behavior to other locations, people, and settings.

Determining the *function of the target behavior* in order to understand what is maintaining the behavior involves categorizing the behavior into one of four main functions. All behaviors can be categorized into one of these four concepts:

▶ Tangible: to gain access to something

▶ Attention: to gain attention from someone

▶ Escape: to escape or avoid something

▶ Automatic Reinforcement: for own self pleasure or enjoyment

Behavior analysts observe the student within different and contrived situations that will or will not elicit the target inappropriate behavior and then take data on what reinforces that inappropriate behavior. Once it is determined what behaviors increase when reinforced in certain situations with certain reinforcers, the behavior analysts can determine why the student engages in the behavior and decide on the main function(s) of the behavior. For example, if a student is playing with a toy and the teacher says it's time to go to the desk and takes the toy, the behavior analyst might take data on whether the student cries and screams and tried to get that toy back (tangible) or if he runs away and refuses to go to the desk (escape).

Once the function has been determined, a *replacement behavior*—a new communications phrase, such as "one more minute" (function of maintain access to something), "I need a break" (function of escaping something) or "let's play" (function of gaining someone's attention)—is to be selected as a teaching aim. The communication phrase can be taught across a variety of formats including verbal requests, picture exchange, and SGDs, depending on each student's individual communication needs. The response must be one that is functionally equivalent, meaning the student will continue to gain the same outcome with this new response as they did with the challenging behavior. The goal is that over time this communication response will replace the challenging behavior. For example, instead of the student screaming and crying and trying to grab an item, or run away with an item that the teacher tries to take or say it's time to put away, the student will calmly say "one more minute" and then the teacher will grant the student more time to play with the item as reinforcement for using the communication phrase instead of screaming and crying and grabbing the item.

Once the function of the target (inappropriate) behavior and the replacement (appropriate) behavior have been identified, the intervention team *creates a plan* for implementing FCT in general across the school day and at home if possible.

Brief Overview of the Literature

FCT was one of the first proactive and preventative approaches researched in relation to decreasing challenging behavior. To address both communication and behavioral needs of children with autism, several researchers developed the intervention of FCT (Carr & Durand, 1985; Ghaemmaghami, et al., 2021; Mancil et al., 2006; Wacker et al., 1990). Developed in the mid-1980s, FCT involves assessing the function (i.e., outcome and consequence) of a behavior (e.g., attention, escape, tangible, sensory) through analogue assessment methodology, referred to as "functional analysis," and then replacing the challenging behavior by teaching a communicative response that serves the same function (Durand & Carr, 1987).

Previously, the focus had been on reactive measures and punishment procedures utilized to decrease challenging behavior. While these types of procedures may be effective in decreasing challenging behaviors, they do not teach an appropriate alternative. The focus of ABA is to make socially significant changes. This can only be achieved by decreasing challenging behaviors *while simultaneously* increasing appropriate alternative behaviors (Landa et al., 2022).

As researchers first developed the methods and procedures for FCT, they provided interventions in clinical settings removed from natural environments (e.g., children's classrooms, homes), which is typical for the initial stages of procedural development (Mancil et al., 2006; Reichle & Wacker, 2017). When implementing these procedures during initial development stages, researchers and practitioners can produce positive behavioral and communication results across the age ranges of toddlers to adults (Gregori et al., 2020). For example, Durand and Carr (1987) indicated an increase in communication with a simultaneous decrease in challenging behaviors. Researchers today have consistently shown the effectiveness of FCT with individuals on the autism spectrum across environments (home, school, and community) (Lambert et al., 2012; Lindgren et al., 2020; Reichle & Wacker, 2017; Tiger et al., 2008)

These positive results have continued to be shown across behavioral topographies and language levels for the past 40 years (Ghaemmaghami et al., 2021; Reichle & Wacker, 2017). The behavioral categories FCT has helped ameliorate include aggression (e.g., hitting, hair pulling), SIB (e.g., hand biting, head banging), property destruction, tantrums (e.g., yelling), body rocking, hand flapping, oppositional behavior (e.g., refusing to do work), and walking away (Landa et al., 2022; Lindgren et al., 2020; Mancil et al., 2006; O'Neill & Sweetland-Baker, 2001).

FCT, built on the theory that challenging behavior (hitting, screaming, throwing objects, etc.) is an inappropriate means of communicating, is also an evidence-based Positive Behavior Support practice. All behaviors happen for a reason, either to gain access to something, to gain attention from someone, to escape or avoid something, or for one's own self pleasure or enjoyment. Challenging behavior is often used as a way of achieving one or more of these outcomes. By teaching an appropriate alternative behavior, the individual can gain access to the same outcome without engaging in the challenging behavior, therefore making the challenging behavior redundant and ineffective.

Core Reviews

Simpson et al. (2005) did not include FCT as a reviewed intervention. In 2009, the NAC did not review FCT as a stand-alone intervention but included it under the broader category of Behavioral Package, which was given the rating of Established. In 2015, NAC included FCT as a stand-alone intervention and gave it the rating of Emerging Intervention based on an unspecified number of studies. The NPDC (Wong et al., 2014) and NCAEP (Steinbrenner et al., 2020) both included FCT as a stand-alone intervention and gave the rating of EBP based on a total of 31 studies.

Age and Diagnostic Considerations/ Prerequisite Skills and Abilities

FCT can and has been utilized with all ages of individuals with ASD and other disabilities. There are no prerequisite skills that the individual needs to implement this intervention. FCT is, in fact, often one of the first interventions used with individuals with ASD who have challenging behaviors in order to decrease the occurrence of those challenging behaviors and be able to engage in learning activities.

Reported Outcomes

A meta-analytic review of FCT across modes of communication, age, and disability was conducted on all FCT research published since 1985. The review established that FCT is absolutely effective in decreasing challenging behavior, including SIB; studies show a direct correlation between increased appropriate communication and decreased challenging behavior (Heath et al., 2015; Landa et al., 2022). Interestingly and encouragingly, the age of the individual has shown limited impact on FCT's outcome. Research shows individuals of all ages can successfully learn to use FCT. The research suggests some limitations to success linked to cognitive abilities. Those with more severe cognitive delays were less effective in learning FCT; however, they did still show a statistically significant improvement (Heath et al., 2015; Mancil & Boman, 2010).

Qualifications Needed

Initially, as discussed above, there are several procedures that need to be completed prior to implementing an FCT intervention with any individual with ASD. These procedures all need to be conducted by a BCBA:

1. An initial FA or FBA needs to be conducted in order to determine the function of the challenging behavior and also to determine the appropriate replacement/alternative behavior that will be taught (and reinforced);

2. The subsequent FCT intervention plan and teaching procedures to be used with the individual need to be written; and

3. Training needs to be provided for the professionals and/or parents who will be implementing the FCT procedures with the individual.

Once the initial procedures are completed, educational or other behavioral professionals and parents are able to implement this intervention while continuing to receive ongoing supervision while implementing FCT with an individual with ASD.

How, Where, and When Typically Implemented

FCT can be implemented in any environment and is typically implemented in the same setting, during the same activities in which the challenging behavior(s) is most likely to occur.

Costs

There are no associated costs specific to using FCT interventions as an intervention in and of itself. However, there are the costs of paying the BCBA to conduct the initial FBA or FA, develop the teaching procedures, and provide the ongoing supervision for the intervention.

Potential Risks

There are no potential physical harmful risks from implementing FCT. But, if the initial procedures listed above are not conducted by a BCBA and ongoing supervision by a BCBA is not provided, the FCT intervention has a very limited chance of being successful or effective. It is then possible that the occurrence of the individual's challenging behaviors may increase instead of decrease.

Rating

  Evidence-Based Practice

Resources and Suggested Readings

AFIRM modules through UNC Chapel Hill offers a free online course on Functional Communication Training that can be accessed at https://afirm.fpg.unc.edu/functional -communication-training

Kansas Technical Assistance System Network (TASN) offers a free online webinar on Functional Communication Training that can be accessed at https://www.ksdetasn.org/resources/3014

The Ohio Center for Autism and Low Incidence (OCALI) offers a free online course on Functional Communication Training. After creating an account, it can be accessed at https://autis minternetmodules.org/m/486

Tiger, Hanley, & Bruzek. (2008). Functional communication training: A review and practical guide. It can be accessed at https://www.ncbi.nlm.nih.gov/pmc/articles/PMC2846575/

Extinction

Description

One strategy that is used in ABA is Extinction. When implementing Extinction, reinforcement is no longer provided (withheld) for any behavior that had previously been reinforced. Extinction occurs when reinforcement of a previously reinforced behavior is discontinued and occurrence of that behavior decreases in the future (Cooper et al., 2020). It is only considered to be effective if the target problem behavior actually decreases.

An important and common component of using Extinction with a target problem behavior is that there can be what is called an "extinction burst." When an educator begins to implement a BIP that involves extinction procedures, it is expected that initially there will be an extinction burst with the target problem behavior. This is when a behavior that used to occur at a certain rate or frequency increases in rate or frequency or even intensity because now that reinforcement is being withheld for that target problem behavior. The individual used to be able to engage in the problem behavior and gain or avoid what they were trying to, but now they are not receiving the reinforcement so they will try harder, and thus increase of occurrence of the behavior is observed and seen within the data collection. This is a period of time during the Behavior Intervention that is called the extinction burst. Only if the procedure continues to be implemented correctly and the reinforcement for that behavior is consistently withheld, will the burst discontinue and then a decrease in the occurrence of the behavior will be observed. It is important that along with extinguishing a target problem behavior, the intervention plan outlines and educators implement reinforcement procedures for reinforcing an alternative appropriate replacement behavior that serves the same function as what the target problem behavior served.

An example is implementing Extinction of a child's cries and stands near the refrigerator when they want milk. The BIP explains that the child will no longer be provided any milk or anything at all while they are crying and standing next to the refrigerator. Alternately the intervention team will be teaching the child how to do the sign language word for "milk" and produce that sign when they want milk. The child will immediately receive some milk differential reinforcement of alternative behavior (DRA) upon demonstrating that sign (this is a simplified explanation and the plan would also include all kinds of prompting, fading, and shaping procedures to occur as part of the teaching and reinforcement that are not explained here). Once the team has started to implement the plan in all environments, the child starts to cry louder and also bang their fist on the refrigerator and this goes on much longer than it did before (because it used to end when they were given the milk). The team continues to work on teaching the child the sign for milk during all other times that they are not engaging in the problem behavior, and at the beginning, even when they are prompted to sign milk and do so without resistance, they are given milk immediately. After a while, the crying and banging start to decrease and the child is more and more using the sign for milk when they want it.

Brief Overview of the Literature

Extinction has been shown to be effective in a wide variety of settings and with many different types of behaviors (e.g., Cuvo et al., 2010; Devlin et al., 2011; Waters et al., 2009). Extinction has been studied over many areas including these:

- ▶ Functional Communication Training (FCT) (Kelley et al., 2002)
- ▶ Self-injurious behavior (SIB) (Kahng et al., 2002; Matson & Lovullo, 2008)

 ⏵ Eliminating low-intensity challenging behavior during classroom instruction (O'Reilly et al., 2007)

Core Reviews

Simpson et al. (2005) and the NAC (2009, 2015) did not include, nor discuss, Extinction as a reviewed intervention. The NPDC (NPDC, Wong et al., 2014) and NCAEP (NCAEP, Steinbrenner et al., 2020) both included Extinction and gave a rating of EBP based on a total of 25 studies.

Age and Diagnostic Considerations/ Prerequisite Skills and Abilities

According to research, Extinction can be used effectively with children and youth in early childhood, elementary, middle, and high school settings. Extinction should not be used in the following circumstances:

1. The behavior is harmful.

2. All sources of reinforcement cannot be withheld.

3. A rapid reduction in response rate is required.

4. Others are likely to imitate the problem behavior.

Reported Outcomes

Studies have shown effectiveness of Extinction procedures to reduce all types of challenging behaviors with individuals with ASD in preschool through high school learners (Waters et al., 2009). Extinction's effectiveness is usually amplified and its negative effects can be reduced when it is combined with other procedures, such as ABIs and DRA (MacNaul & Neely, 2018; Sullivan & Bogin, 2010; Waters et al., 2009).

Qualifications Needed

Due to some of the possible harmful effects (due to extinction bursts, as mentioned above) of implementing Extinction procedures with target problem behaviors, any extinction procedure that is implemented with an individual with ASD should be supervised by a BCBA. It is important that a FBA has first been completed so that those implementing the procedure understand the function of the behavior and what is actually reinforcing the problem behavior. A BIP needs to then clearly explain the extinction procedures that will be used by all people working with the individual. Data collection is imperative to track and analyze the extinction burst and subsequent decrease or possible increase of the problem behavior. It is also important that the replacement behavior (the target appropriate behavior that the intervention team has identified for the individual to perform instead of the problem behavior) is clearly defined and taught and highly reinforced while the reinforcement for the target problem behavior is withheld. Secondly, extinction procedures should only be used after other more positive interventions have been tried with the child and the child has shown that these positive interventions were unsuccessful without also including punisher procedures, such as Extinction. When extinction procedures are implemented, it is very important that a lot of reinforcement is provided for the demonstration of appropriate behaviors, as well as for not demonstrating the target problem behavior when the child would typically have engaged in it in the past.

How, Where, and When Typically Implemented

Extinction procedures can be implemented in any environment and is typically implemented in the same setting, during the same activities in which the challenging behavior(s) is most likely to occur.

Costs

Extinction procedures are cost-effective in terms of time and other resources. There are some costs associated with training and it does take some planning and preparation to create the data sheets and set up the daily routines that will allow for time to follow through with extinction procedures; initially it make take additional staff to safely and effectively implement the extinction/punishment and reinforcement procedures. Ongoing supervision by a qualified person is also needed to ensure the safe and appropriate implementation of the BIP.

Potential Risks

As mentioned previously, placing a behavior on extinction may evoke an extinction burst, which can result in some extreme and intense emotional or aggressive behaviors in the student. Some extinction procedures cannot be implemented because of the possible harmful or dangerous behaviors that can occur during that time period. Thus, implementing extinction procedures should only be implemented by people with extensive training in ABA and experience or are supervised by a BCBA. A second risk of Extinction is Spontaneous Recovery. What this means is that the behavior that was stopped or reduced now comes back for a short time even though that behavior is still not producing reinforcement. Typically, if parents and professionals maintain the effective behavior interventions originally used to extinguish the behavior, it will again quickly decrease in occurrence. Relatively recent work on developing alternatives to Extinction based on practical functional assessment methods, establishing instructional control, and creating contexts where the learner is happy, relaxed, and engaged is building a research base on interventions that will allow educators to prevent escape-motivated behavior and avoid some of these risks (MacNaul & Neely, 2018).

Rating

   Evidence-Based Practice

*To be used with EXTREME caution under the close supervision of a BCBA

Resources and Suggested Readings

AFIRM modules through UNC Chapel Hill offer a free online course on extinction that can be accessed at https://afirm.fpg.unc.edu/extinction/

Kansas Technical Assistance System Network (TASN) offers a free online webinar on Extinction that can be accessed at https://www.ksdetasn.org/resources/3140

The Ohio Center for Autism and Low Incidence (OCALI) offers a free online course on Extinction. After creating an account, it can be accessed at https://autisminternetmodules.org/m/490

Punishment Procedures

Description

Punishers are a type of consequence that is delivered immediately after a behavior. A consequence is only a punishment consequence if it actually decreases the occurrence of the behavior in the future (Cooper et al., 2007). There are only two types of consequences for behaviors—Punishers and Reinforcers. All behavior has one of these consequences that occur after it, whether it is naturally occurring in the environment (i.e., you drink a glass of water when you feel thirsty and no longer feel thirsty—that was a reinforcer for the behavior of drinking water because it increases the behavior of drinking water in the future when you feel thirsty *or* you accidentally walk into something because you had your head turned and didn't see it—that was a punisher for the behavior of not looking in front of you as you walk because it decreases the likelihood of not looking where you are walking in the future) or it is contrived (i.e., you mow the lawn for someone and they give you $20—a contrived reinforcer for the behavior of mowing the lawn that increases the behavior of mowing lawns in the future *or* you do not pay your electricity bill and the electric company turns off the electricity to your house—a contrived punisher for the behavior of not paying money to the electric company that decreases the likelihood of not paying the electricity bill in the future).

Punishers are only effective if simultaneously, the Reinforcers that were previously provided for the target problem behavior are no longer provided. Punishment, as an intervention procedure, needs to also always be utilized as a part of a comprehensive behavior intervention plan (BIP) to decrease the occurrence of target problem behaviors, which is simultaneously using reinforcement procedures for increasing appropriate replacement behaviors that the individual can do instead of the problem behavior to get what they want or need. Punishment should never be used as a stand-alone intervention.

When a team is planning to decrease a target problem behavior, a functional behavior assessment (FBA) (*see chapter on FBA*) and subsequent BIP is conducted in order to understand the function of the target problem behavior *and* in order to understand what appropriate alternative behavior will be taught and reinforced in order to replace the target problem behavior.

Within the practice of ABA, punishment procedures are used as the last resort intervention practices to decrease a target problem behavior after implementing antecedent-based interventions (ABI) (*see chapter on ABI*) and teaching and reinforcing desirable or appropriate replacement behaviors. These proactive and preventative procedures can be used to greatly decrease the occurrence of the target problem behavior, while allowing for more data collection and understanding of the function of the problem behavior and what punishers (if any) will be needed.

In general, two forms of Punishment are defined within ABA procedures relating to behavior reduction: positive punishment and negative punishment. Positive punishment is described as the addition of something that acts to decrease the likelihood of a behavior happening in the future. Negative punishment involves the removal of a reinforcing stimulus such as attention or tokens, contingent on the occurrence of the target behavior (Cooper et al., 2007). This can be directly related to how positive reinforcement and negative reinforcement work to increase desirable behaviors. See the chart below describing the differences and relationships between positive and negative punishment and reinforcement:

	ADD SOMETHING TO ENVIRONMENT	REMOVE SOMETHING FROM ENVIRONMENT
Behavior Increase	Positive/Additive Reinforcement	Subtractive/Negative Reinforcement
Behavior Decrease	Positive/Additive Punishment	Subtractive/Negative Punishment

An example of utilizing positive punishment is requiring an individual to clean up their toys when they picked up the box of toys and threw them across the room. The interventionist is *adding* something to the environment that is a consequence they are using to decrease the behavior of throwing toys in the future. An example of utilizing negative punishment is when a parent walks out of the room and closes the door when their child starts hitting the parent's arm in order to get the parent's attention. They are removing attention from the environment as a result of the hitting and doing it to decrease the occurrence of hitting to get attention in the future.

Brief Overview of the Literature

Punishment is a recognized and Evidence-Based Procedure used by behavior analysts (Cooper et al., 2007; Westling, 2010), teachers (Westling, 2010), and parents (Regalado et al., 2004; Vittrup et al., 2006). While Punishment is a widely debated topic, all parties listed above agree that guidelines must be provided and used by all who implement in as a part of a BIP (Cooper et al., 2007; Favell & Lovaas, 1987; Van Houten et al., 1988). Many organizations have released statements on punishment and have even created standards around the area of punishment, and they recommend that punishment procedures not be used without reinforcement of alternative appropriate behaviors (e.g., Behavior Analyst Certification Board, 2020; Hanley et al., 2005).

Core Reviews

Simpson et al. (2005) did not include Punishment in their review of interventions. The NAC (2009) included Punishment Procedures under the broader category of a Reductive Package in 2009, which was rated as Emerging. The NCAEP (Steinbrenner et al., 2020) included Punishment Procedures in its 2020 review giving a rating of Insufficient Evidence. It should be noted that the Insufficient Evidence and Emerging Practice ratings are a result of viewing Punishment Procedures as a stand-alone intervention that was occurring and not alongside the consequence of differential reinforcement of an alternative and appropriate behavior that was being taught to replace the target problem behavior.

Age and Diagnostic Considerations/ Prerequisite Skills and Abilities

According to research, Punishment Procedures have been used with children and youth in early childhood; elementary and middle, high school settings; and adulthood.

Reported Outcomes

The utility of punishment-based approaches in the treatment of ASD, and ABA in general, is still debatable despite the recorded evidence of their efficacy. As a result, numerous experts have argued in favor of or against the employment of punishment-based methods (Leaf et al., 2019; Lerman et al., 2002). Some researchers believe that the controversy surrounding the use of less acceptable forms of punishment (such as shock, water misting, taste aversion, and loud reprimands) has led to professionals avoiding all forms of punishment, even less drastic ones like verbal feedback, token removal, or loss of a toy or activity (Leaf et al., 2019). Most importantly there is support for Punishment Procedures being used alongside reinforcement procedures by the Behavior Analysis Certification Board (BACB), within the *Ethics Code for Behavior Analysts*; Section 2: Responsibility in Practice (2020) advises that Punishment Procedures only be employed as part of a comprehensive program that also uses reinforcement-based methods.

Qualifications Needed

Due to some of the possible harmful effects of some Punishment Procedures (e.g., physical restraint, extinction bursts) with target problem behaviors, any punishment procedure that is implemented with an individual with ASD should be supervised by a BCBA. As stated previously, it is important that an FBA has first been completed so that those implementing the procedure understand the function of the behavior and what is actually reinforcing the problem behavior. A BIP needs to then clearly explain the punishment procedures that will be used by all people working with the individual. Data collection is imperative to track and analyze any extinction bursts and subsequent decrease or possible increase of the problem behavior. It is also important that the replacement behavior, the target-appropriate behavior that the intervention team has identified for the individual to perform instead of the problem behavior, is clearly defined and simultaneously taught and highly reinforced while the reinforcement for the target problem behavior is withheld. Also, as stated previously, Punishment Procedures should only be used after ABIs, Positive Reinforcement, or interventions have been tried with the child and the child has shown that these interventions were unsuccessful without also using punishment procedures.

How, Where, and When Typically Implemented

Just like gravity, natural reinforcement and Punishment always exist in some form within our naturally occurring environment and in the classroom environment every day. Contrived and manipulated punishment procedures, implemented alone, without implementation alongside reinforcement of appropriate replacement behaviors are not supported and have the potential to be harmful. Contrived and manipulated Punishment Procedures, alongside reinforcement procedures of appropriate replacement behaviors, can and are regularly implemented in any environment and are typically implemented in the same setting, during the same activities in which the challenging behavior(s) is occurring.

Costs

Punishment procedures are cost-effective in terms of time and other resources. There are some costs associated with training and it does take some planning and preparation to create the data sheets and set up the daily routines that will allow for time to follow through with punishment procedures, and initially it may take additional staff to safely and effectively implement the punishment and reinforcement procedures.

Ongoing supervision by a qualified person is also needed to ensure the safe and appropriate implementation of the BIP.

Potential Risks

Punishment is a controversial topic in many educational avenues because there are concerns that it is too aversive or restrictive of an intervention. As discussed previously, the controversy exists around "punishment alone" interventions and also "what type of punishment" procedures (e.g., electric shock or spraying lemon juice; Tanner & Zeiler, 1975) are used and "how is the punishment delivered" (e.g., is it explained to the individual before implementation) procedures that create the controversy.

Educators also need to remember that when Punishment Procedures (as a part of a comprehensive behavioral package) are first implemented, a temporary increase in the undesired behavior can be seen (otherwise known as an extinction burst). The team of people working with the student need to take into consideration what the extinction burst could look like and, if there is potential for harmful behaviors to occur, decide if they can implement the procedures they are considering.

Rating

    Evidence-Based Practice

*ONLY IF used with EXTREME caution under the close supervision of a BCBA AND only in conjunction with instruction of replacement behaviors and high levels of reinforcement for those competing behaviors.

Resources and Suggested Readings

As explained previously, Punishment Procedures are not a stand-alone intervention. The resources provided by AFIRM, TASN, and others regarding punishment procedures are included in the resources and training modules of Extinction and Reinforcement and Differential Reinforcement.

The Ziggurat Model and Comprehensive Autism Planning System (CAPS)

Description

The Ziggurat Model is a comprehensive planning system designed to address the underlying needs and characteristics in autistic individuals (Aspy & Grossman, 2007). It is named for the physical structure of a ziggurat, an ancient stepped tower similar in shape to a pyramid but with rectangular levels. The five levels of the Ziggurat Model comprise a hierarchical system and include Sensory Differences and Biological Needs, Reinforcement, Structure and Visual/Tactile Supports, Task Demands, and Skills to Teach (Aspy & Grossman, 2007; Myles et al., 2009). Teachers, parents, and other support professionals use assessment components including the Underlying Characteristics Checklist (UCC) and the Individual Strengths and Skills Inventory (ISSI) to gather information on the student's individual strengths and attributes as related to autism. Upon completion of the UCC and ISSI, the team uses the Intervention Ziggurat as the framework for comprehensive interventions. The five levels comprise a hierarchical system: Sensory Differences and Biological Needs, Reinforcement, Structure and Visual/Tactile Supports, Task Demands, and Skills to Teach (Aspy & Grossman, 2007; Myles et al., 2009). A student's team uses a Ziggurat worksheet to create a plan that incorporates strengths and skills as well as areas of need. This worksheet ensures that all interventions suggested address the student's underlying needs noted in the UCC. The Ziggurat worksheet also supports collaboration among team members to identify their role in the intervention (Myles et al., 2007).

Upon completion of the Ziggurat worksheet, a student's team is ready to implement the CAPS (Henry & Myles, 2007). CAPS organizes a student's day by time and activity and allows for the team to plan the specific supports needed for each activity (Myles et al., 2007). CAPS is individualized, comprehensive, universal, and promotes consistent use of supports for the student. Henry and Myles (2007) suggest CAPS aligns with educational mandates and best practices.

Brief Overview of the Literature

The Ziggurat Model provides an intervention that promotes team collaboration when designing a student's programming. Webster et al. (2017) noted that by using the Ziggurat Model, parents can take an active role in decision-making and educational planning. These are comprehensive planning systems that use the characteristics of ASD along with Evidence-Based Interventions in a user-friendly format (Myles et al., 2007). CAPS addresses areas including structure/modification, reinforcement, sensory, and communication/social skills.

Core Reviews

The Ziggurat Model and CAPS were not included in any of the core reviews. They were included in this resource because they are increasingly being used by many professionals in the educational setting including general and special educators, OTs, SLPs, school psychologists, and counselors.

Age and Diagnostic Considerations/ Prerequisite Skills and Abilities

The Ziggurat Model and CAPS are designed to be used with autistic individuals from preschool to college age. The UCC checklists are available for ages 3 months to 72 months, 6+, and 18+. There is also a Self-Report Checklist for adults 18+. These comprehensive planning models can be used across locations including home, school, and community and target a wide range of student needs and abilities.

Reported Outcomes

Smith et al. (2010) report the Ziggurat Model can be implemented as a global planning tool or as an FBA. This model is effective because it targets student strengths, skills, interests, and individual needs. The intervention is unique to each student and strategies are systematically and comprehensively included throughout the day (Smith et al., 2010).

Qualifications Needed

Anyone who supports students with ASD including parents, teachers, clinicians, support staff, and other stakeholders can use the Ziggurat Model and CAPS.

How, Where, and When Typically Implemented

The Ziggurat Model and CAPS can be implemented in any setting that is related to the student's goals including school, home, community, and place of employment. These two models can be implemented in conjunction with other Evidence-Based Interventions throughout a student's day.

Costs

The Ziggurat Model manual is offered at texasautism.com and costs $54.95. The Ziggurat Group offers a variety of packages of materials that run $24.95–$69.95. Workshops and web-based training are also offered. Contact information is available at https://texasautism.com/blog/contact-us/. CAPS can be found at book sellers for a range of prices.

Potential Risks

There are no reported risks for implementing the Ziggurat Model and CAPS.

Practitioner Testimonial(s)

Throughout my career in special education, it has always been difficult to systematically decide where to begin when identifying goals for students who have more needs beyond just social and academic. The Ziggurat Model was my answer to this difficult task. It provides educators a systematic approach to assessing students, identifying IEP goals, and a framework for designing meaningful daily programming. The Ziggurat framework paired with a CAPS form is truly a game changer for all students. The CAPS form outlines all the child's identified needs based on the assessments from the Ziggurat and shows how to imbed the goals and supports the student needs throughout their entire day. It is a wonderful supporting document for adults to refer to for consistency when working with students.

—Ali Sweitzer

Rating

🙂   Promising/Emerging Practice

Resources and Suggested Readings

Grossman, B. G., & Aspy, R. (2011). *The Ziggurat Model: A framework for designing comprehensive interventions for high-functioning individuals with autism spectrum disorders.* AAPC Publishing.

Henry, S. A., & Myles, B. S. (2007). *The Comprehensive Autism Planning System (CAPS) for individuals with Asperger syndrome, autism, and related disabilities: Integrating best practices throughout the student's day.* AAPC Publishing.

Smith Myles, B., Smith, S. M., Aspy, R., Grossman, B. G., & Henry, S. (2012). Evidence-based practices: The Ziggurat Model and a comprehensive autism planning system. In D. Zager, M. L. Wehmeyer, & R. L. Simpson (Eds.), *Educating students with autism spectrum disorders: Research-based principles and practices* (pp. 126–148). Routledge/Taylor & Francis.

The Ziggurat Group can be accessed at http://texasautism.com

Early Intensive Behavioral Interventions

Early Intensive Behavioral Interventions involve comprehensive intervention programs that target a range of skills that define or are associated with ASD such as communication, social, and pre-academic and academic skills.

Interventions Included in This Section

▶ UCLA-Young Autism Project (UCLA-YAP)

▶ Early Start Denver Model (ESDM)

▶ Learning Experiences: An Alternative Program for Preschoolers and Parents (LEAP)

UCLA Young Autism Project

Description

The University of California at Los Angeles-Young Autism Project (UCLA-YAP) is a comprehensive intervention model for young children with ASD to receive intensive ABA therapy and services. UCLA-YAP is one of the most well-researched intervention models for young children with ASD. It is based on the seminal Lovaas (1987, 1993) studies in which children received ABA for 40 hours per week for 2 to 3 years and made significant positive gains in their intellectual and educational functioning. The UCLA-YAP is grounded in principles of ABA and, therefore, interventions and teaching procedures used are ABA based. For example, token economy systems and discrete trial teaching methods are commonly used.

Brief Overview of the Literature

The Lovaas studies (1987, 1993) were seminal for the field of autism because no prior study had demonstrated such positive gains for children with ASD. In the original Lovaas (1987) study, children received 40 hours of ABA intervention and therapy for 2 to 3 years. The first year focused on discrete trial-teaching methods conducted in the family's home. The second year focused on the child with ASD spending increasing amounts of time with children without disabilities in more natural environments. The interactions with children without disabilities were meant to provide opportunities for peer interaction and increased social/communication. Finally, the third year focused on reducing discrete trial-teaching or other one-on-one methods and increasing inclusive practices with children without disabilities.

A considerable amount of research has been conducted since the Lovaas studies in a variety of settings including home, community, and school (e.g., Cohen et al., 2006; Eikeseth et al., 2007; Sheinkopf & Siegel, 1998). In addition, Nicolosi and Dillenburger (2022) conducted a systematic review to evaluate research conducted during the last 30 years on the UCLA-YAP and included 19 data-based studies in their review. The studies primarily examined the effectiveness of the UCLA-YAP compared to control groups (i.e., children receiving typical teaching methods). Across all 19 included studies, the UCLA-YAP intervention group received intervention for an average of 28 hours per week and increased their cognitive functioning and adaptive behavior, among other gains. Findings across the UCLA-YAP literature base indicate it is an overall effective treatment for children with ASD (Reichow & Wolery, 2009).

Core Reviews

The only core review that mentions the UCLA-Young Autism Project is the NPDC (Wong et al., 2014) in 2014, which referenced it as an example of a CTM.

Age and Diagnostic Considerations/ Prerequisite Skills and Abilities

The UCLA-YAP is a comprehensive intervention program for young children with ASD typically before age 4.

Reported Outcomes

The UCLA-YAP is used for young children with ASD to learn nearly any educational skill including play skills, self-help skills (e.g., toilet use, dressing, brushing teeth), academics, and social/communication skills. Children can learn skills such as identifying objects, learning time, increasing language, and taking turns.

Qualifications Needed

Teachers and other related professionals who work in settings in which the UCLA-YAP is used must have knowledge of ABA and discrete trial teaching methods.

How, Where, and When Typically Implemented

The UCLA-YAP is typically implemented in preschool settings or other school settings serving young children but can also be implemented in clinic, home, and community settings.

Costs

The cost for a child to attend a preschool setting in which UCLA-YAP depends on a variety of factors as some of these services may be covered by insurance.

Potential Risks

There are no documented or obvious risks associated with the UCLA-YAP.

Rating

    Evidence-Based Practice

Resources and Suggested Readings

The Lovaas Center, Applied Behavior Analysis (ABA) can be accessed at https://thelovaascenter .com/aba-treatment/

Early Start Denver Model (ESDM)

Description

The ESDM is a framework for intervention focusing on six critical components: (1) developmental curriculum implemented by an interdisciplinary team; (2) interpersonal engagement; (3) fluent, reciprocal, and spontaneous imitation; (4) nonverbal and verbal communication; (5) play that imparts skills and knowledge; and (6) parent partnerships (Rogers & Dawson, 2010). It is based on Piaget's theory of cognitive development (Piaget, 1954, 1962, 1966), Weiss's pragmatic theory of language development (Weiss, 1981), and Mahler et al.'s theory of interpersonal development via the attachment-separation individuation process (Mahler et al., 1975).

Brief Overview of the Literature

EDSM was first developed in 1981 by an interdisciplinary team led by Sally Rogers, including developmental and clinical psychologists, behavior analysts, special educators, SLPs, and OTs. It is described in various peer-reviewed studies published throughout the 1980s (Rogers et al., 1986; Rogers & Lewis, 1989; Rogers et al., 1987). Rogers et al. (2006) conducted a pilot study of the Denver model and prompts for restructuring oral muscular phonetic targets (PROMPT) interventions and Dawson et al. conducted an randomized control trial (RCT) ESDM with 48 children with ASD ages 18 to 30 months (Dawson et al., 2010). The ESDM is considered a comprehensive treatment model (CTM) (Odom et al., 2010).

Core Reviews

The NAC references the Denver Model in Developmental Relationship-Based Intervention (DRBI) in 2009, which was given the rating of Emerging. The NPDC (Wong et al., 2014) and NCAEP (Steinbrenner et al., 2020) identified the Denver Model (Rogers et al., 2000) as a CTM.

Age and Diagnostic Considerations/ Prerequisite Skills and Abilities

Research conducted on ESDM has included subjects under the age of 5.

Reported Outcomes

Research conducted on ESDM report significant improvement in IQ scores and adaptive behaviors and a decrease of ASD characteristics.

Qualifications Needed

A critical feature of ESDM is that it is implemented by an interdisciplinary team including behavior analysts, special educators, SLPs, and occupational therapists. All of these roles require at least a bachelor's if not a master's degree in their respective fields.

How, Where, and When Typically Implemented

ESDM has primarily been implemented in schools, clinics, early intervention centers, and home-based provided therapy.

Costs

The range in annual costs can start from $40,000 to $80,000, which, according to Cidav et al. (2017), is $14,000 higher than other community-based treatment. However, this cost is partially offset by the fact that it involves fewer hours than other treatments and research has demonstrated that costs associated with early intensive ESDM treatment were fully offset within a few years after the intervention because of the reductions in other service use and associated costs.

Potential Risks

There are no documented or obvious risks associated with the ESDM.

Rating

   Evidence-Based Practice

Resources and Suggested Readings

Applied Behavior Analysis Program Guide. *What is the Early Start Denver Model?* can be accessed at https://www.appliedbehavioranalysisprograms.com/faq/what-is-the-early-start-denver-model/

Learning Experiences: An Alternative Program for Preschoolers and Parents (LEAP)

Description

LEAP is a behavioral, developmental approach to teaching preschool children in a full-time inclusive environment. Learning activities are designed to promote skills development across all domains based on the student's interests and needs through active exploration providing multiple, meaningful opportunities to respond with concrete materials and interactions with others. Typically developing children serve as facilitators of peers with ASD after they are provided comprehensive social skills training. Learning objectives consider prompting hierarches, daily data is taken reviewed daily, and intervention is adjusted according to strict decision-making rules until independent, generalized performance is achieved. LEAP also provides skills training for adult family members in behavioral teaching strategies to use during daily routines in the home environment.

Kohler and Strain (1999) noted four features related to LEAP program implementation that enhance the effectiveness of peer-mediated interventions used in integrated preschools: (1) programs should be *comprehensive,* meaning that the interventions should occur across all environments and include functional skills such as language, appropriate use of toys, sharing, and self-help; (2) programs should be *intensive,* referring to implementation of the intervention for suitable periods of time, with the student highly engaged in the activity; (3) programs should be *practical,* meaning that the method should be easily employed with any child; and (4) programs must be *effective,* requiring that the goal of peer-mediated techniques should be to improve the quality of life for students and families.

Brief Overview of the Literature

LEAP was developed by Dr. Philip Strain in 1981. It is described in various literature published throughout the next two decades (Hoyson et al., 1984; Kohler & Strain, 1999; Strain & Cordisco, 1993; Strain & Hoyson, 2000; Strain & Kohler, 1998). In 2011, Strain and Bovey conducted an randomized control trial (RCT) in 28 inclusive preschool classrooms with 118 children receiving the intervention. LEAP is considered a comprehensive treatment model (CTM) (Odom et al., 2010).

Core Reviews

Simpson et al. (2005) gave LEAP the rating of Scientifically Based Practice based on three articles (Kohler & Strain, 1999; Strain & Hoyson, 2000; Strain & Kohner, 1998) and one book (Strain & Cordisco, 1993). The NAC includes one article on LEAP under Comprehensive Behavioral Treatment of Young Children in 2009 (Hoyson et al., 1984) and makes a reference to LEAP under Peer Training Package in 2015, which was given the rating of Established includes one article under Comprehensive Behavioral Treatment of Young Children in 2009 (Hoyson et al., 1984). The NPDC (Wong et al., 2014) and NCAEP (Steinbrenner et al., 2020) considered LEAP to be a CTM and reference two studies (Strain & Bovey, 2011; Strain & Hoyson, 2000).

Age and Diagnostic Considerations/ Prerequisite Skills and Abilities

Research conducted on ESDM has included subjects under the age of 6 across the entire ASD spectrum.

Reported Outcomes

Improvements in functional, social interaction, language, cognitive function, and behavior skills, as well as reduction in autistic characteristics, were reported in a follow-up study of children with autism who participated in the LEAP program (Strain & Cordisco, 1993; Strain & Hoyson, 2000) to the degree that subjects no longer scored in the range for autism on the Childhood Autism Rating Scale (CARS) (Schopler et al., 1998). Developmental gains were raised 1.41 months per month of participation in LEAP. Further, appropriate behavior in interactions with parents and other caregivers improved to 98 percent from 51 percent, and the rate of positive social interactions increased from 3 percent to 25 percent at age 10.

Qualifications Needed

LEAP staff includes well-trained teachers, SLPs, and paraeducators. Ideally, a specialist in assessment gathers data about and from students and families; coordinators help families in obtaining community resources, including behavior management training; and clinical supervisors, directors, and office managers contribute to support and supervise of the program.

How, Where, and When Typically Implemented

LEAP is implemented in public school settings in classrooms using a variety of models and curricula, including the *Creative Curriculum for Preschool* (4th ed.) (Dodge et al., 2002), High Scope, and Head Start programs, and utilizes a variety of interventions, including errorless learning, time delay, incidental teaching, pivotal response training (PRT), and the Picture Exchange Communication System (PECS).

Costs

No information is available regarding per-pupil cost for LEAP participation. Strain and Cordisco (1993) anticipated a savings of about $51,000 for each student who remains in regular education over a 12-year school experience related to the anticipated benefits of LEAP training.

Potential Risks

There are no documented or obvious risks associated with LEAP.

Rating

  Evidence-Based Practice

Resources and Suggested Readings

LEAP Preschool Model can be accessed at https://morgridge.du.edu/pele-center/leap

Visual Supports

Introduction

Visual Supports is a broad category of interventions that provides cues and specific information to students with ASD in a visual manner. The NCAEP (Steinbrenner et al., 2020) review team defined *Visuals Supports* as "concrete cues that provide information about an activity, routine, or expectation and/or support skills demonstration" (p. 139). The concrete cues can include pictures, text, labels, objects, or other aspects of the student's environment.

There are many different types of Visual Supports that teachers can use to support students to transition between tasks, navigate their school environment, and increase engagement, among other target skills. Visual Supports vary greatly and present in different forms and functions (e.g., rule reminder cards, activity schedules, graphic organizers). Regardless of the type of visual support, students can typically refer to them as many times as needed. This contrasts with information delivered verbally in which students have no record of that information. Students with ASD are likely to struggle when information is presented in verbal modes only. Therefore, teachers and other related educational professionals may consider visual supports to supplement verbal information. Note that not every type of visual support has the same level of empirical evidence demonstrating its efficacy. For example, there is a larger literature base for visual schedules than graphic organizers (NCAEP, Steinbrenner et al., 2020).

Visual Supports can be used to teach students a variety of skills and deliver information. Specifically, Visual Supports can be used to tell students what is expected of them, how to communicate their wants and needs, and how to cope with changes in schedules. Visual Supports are commonly combined with other practices such as Prompting and Reinforcement. They can also be embedded into more complex intervention packages. Visual Supports are used to organize the learning environment and establish routines and expectations (NPDC, Wong et al., 2014). They can also assist to provide structure and routine, as well as encourage independence.

Visual Supports can use "high technology" or "low technology." For example, visual pictures and images are commonly included as a key component of a student's Augmentative and Alternative Communication (AAC) device, which is a type of technology. In addition, Visual Supports can be presented on different types of technology used by students. If teachers are making Visual Supports with paper (i.e., low technology), the Visual Supports should be portable, durable, and easy for students to use. Teachers can laminate paper or use poster board or cardboard to make the visual supports durable.

Examples of different types of Visual Supports include, but are not limited to, the following:

- Choice boards
- "Finished" boxes
- Instructional cues

- ▶ Labels or environmental visuals
- ▶ Maps
- ▶ Organization systems
- ▶ Power card strategy
- ▶ Scripts
- ▶ Technology-based visual supports
- ▶ Timelines
- ▶ Timers
- ▶ Visual activity schedule
- ▶ Visual boundaries
- ▶ Visual cues
- ▶ Visual rule reminder cards
- ▶ Visual task analysis
- ▶ Work systems
- ▶ Written words

Core Reviews

Simpson et al. (2005) did not review Visual Supports as an overall intervention category but did review Structure Teaching (TEACCH) giving the rating of Promising Practice and referenced visual schedules and work systems under that intervention. The NAC also did not review Visual Supports as an overall intervention category but did review Schedules giving the rating of Established Treatment in both 2009 and 2015 based on 11 or 12 (there was a slight discrepancy in the two reports) and two studies respectively. The NPDC (Wong et al., 2014) and NCAEP (Steinbrenner et al., 2020) both reviewed Visual Supports as an overall intervention category and gave the rating of EBP in both of their reports based on a total of 65 studies. The NCAEP included articles on Schedules, Scripting, Independent Work Systems, Structured Teaching, and Power Cards under Visual Supports.

Interventions Included in This Section

- • Schedules
- • Independent Work Systems
- • Scripting
- • Power Cards

Resources and Suggested Readings

Boardmaker can be accessed at https://get.myboardmaker.com/

Fleury, V. P. (2013). *Scripting (SC) fact sheet*. The University of North Carolina, Frank Porter Graham Child Development Institute, The National Professional Development Center on Autism Spectrum Disorders.

Hume, K. (2008). *Overview of visual supports*. National Professional Development Center on Autism Spectrum Disorders, Frank Porter Graham Child Development Institute, The University of North Carolina.

Hume, K. (2013). *Visual supports (VS) fact sheet*. The University of North Carolina, Frank Porter Graham Child Development Institute, The National Professional Development Center on Autism Spectrum Disorders.

Kansas Technical Assistance System Network (TASN) offers several free online webinars on Visual Supports. They can be accessed at ksdetasn.org by searching Visual Supports and Boardmaker in their resource library.

McClannahan, L. E., & Krantz, P. J. (2010). *Activity schedules for children with autism: Teaching independent behavior* (2nd ed.). Woodbine House. (Listed in the NSP, 2015 as a resource)

The Nebraska Autism Spectrum Disorders Network offers several free online webinar on Visual Supports. They can be accessed at https://www.unl.edu/asdnetwork/webinars?combine=visual+supports&tid=All

The Ohio Center for Autism and Low Incidence (OCALI) offers a free online course on Visual Supports. After creating an account, it can be accessed at https://autisminternetmodules.org/search?qtitle=visual+supports

Sam, A., & AFIRM Team. (2015). *Visual supports*. National Professional Development Center on Autism Spectrum Disorder, FPG Child Development Center, University of North Carolina. This site can be accessed at http://afirm.fpg.unc.edu/visual-supports

Sam, A., Steinbrenner, J., Morgan, W., Chin, J., & AFIRM for Paras Team. (2019). *Visual cues*. FPG Child Development Institute, University of North Carolina. This site can be accessed at https://afirm.fpg.unc.edu/visual-cues-introduction-practice

"Visual supports" website from National Autistic Society can be accessed at https://www.autism.org.uk/advice-and-guidance/topics/communication/communication-tools/visual-supports

Schedules

Description

Schedules identify the activities that a student must complete during a specific time period and the order in which those activities will be completed (NAC, 2015). Schedules could include written words, pictures, or graphics. There are many different forms of Schedules, perhaps the most common being a Visual Activity Schedule. These types of Schedules use videos, photographs, or drawings to provide information related to a sequence of activities or events (NCAEP, Steinbrenner et al., 2020; NPDC, Wong et al., 2014). Visual Activity Schedules can be paper or technology based. Images used in Visual Activity Schedules can be created from real photos, images created by Boardmaker, or illustrations created by hand.

Brief Overview of the Literature

Early studies on the use of schedules with learners with ASD were conducted in the 1990s (Arntzen et al., 1998; Hall et al., 1995; Krantz et al., 1993; MacDuff et al., 1993) and early 2000s (Bryan & Gast, 2000; Dettmer et al., 2000; Massey & Wheeler, 2000; Morrison et al., 2002; O'Reilly et al., 2005; Schmit et al., 2000). For example, Cihak (2011) compared static-picture and video-based activity schedules to teach independent transition skills to four adolescents with ASD, ages 11 to 13. Both types of schedules were found to be effective. Similarly, Giles and Markham (2017) compared book and tablet-based activity schedules because schedules in books are not always portable for students with ASD and can be stigmatizing. Conversely, students can carry mobile technological devices (e.g., iPod, iPad) with them. Three young children with ASD, ages 3 to 5, used both book-and tablet-based activity schedules to participate in leisure activities (Giles & Markham, 2017). Both types of schedules were effective, but preferences varied across the different participants. Teachers should consider the social validity of picture activity schedules and how students will engage with the materials used to make the schedule.

Core Reviews

Simpson et al. (2005) describe schedules as part of Structured Teaching (TEACCH), which is rated as a Promising Practice. The NAC rated Schedules as Established in 2009 based on 12 articles and again in 2015 based on two additional articles. The NPDC (Wong et al., 2014) and NCAEP (Steinbrenner et al., 2020) did not review schedules as stand-alone intervention but did include articles on schedules under Visual Supports, which was given the rating of EBP in both 2014 and 2020.

Age and Diagnostic Considerations/ Prerequisite Skills and Abilities

Most of the research on schedules has subjects from ages 3 to 14 but it has been studied with subjects up to the age of 18 (Lequia et al., 2012) and could potentially be effective with young adults as well.

Reported Outcomes

Schedules promote independence and self-regulation skills of students with ASD (NSP, 2009, 2015). Visual supports were found to be overall effective for decreasing challenging behavior and increasing desired behavior (Lequia et al., 2012). Both video-based and picture schedules have been found to be effective in teaching transition skills (Cihak, 2011) and facilitate participation in leisure activities (Giles & Markham, 2017).

Qualifications Needed

No formal training is required to implement activity schedules.

How, Where, and When Typically Implemented

Paper visual activity schedules can be posted anywhere, such as within a home, classroom, or community setting. Technology-based visual activity schedules can be used in conjunction with devices that students use throughout their school day for learning such as iPads and other similar devices (Brodhead et al., 2018; Giles & Markham, 2017). Students can refer to paper or technology-based visual activity schedules throughout their school day as needed.

Costs

The use of Schedules is cost-effective in terms of time and other resources. There are no costs associated with training and no additional teaching time is required.

Potential Risks

There are no documented or obvious risks associated with Schedules.

Practitioner Testimonial(s)

Schedules give children the control and sense of comfort they need in a classroom. Schedules are an easy intervention to implement and can be used and displayed in a variety of different ways. We find that students who rely on a Visual Schedule or "to-do list" benefit from having their own schedule and a say in what that schedule looks like for them. We let students help develop their schedule, whether we are using pictures, words, Velcro checks, or a marker to check off after something is complete. The great thing about using schedules is they can be easily modified to work in a small group or for the whole day. This helps students become more at ease knowing what we have accomplished, as well as what is to come. Having a classroom schedule in a central location is necessary, but it isn't always enough for all your students. Individualized schedules at their desks, on their lockers, or at their cubbies can give them the opportunity to have control and calmness throughout their day.

—Kristen McKearney and Stephanie Kopecky

Rating

     Evidence-Based Practice

Resources and Suggested Readings

Kansas Technical Assistance System Network (TASN) offers several free online webinars related to Schedules that can be accessed at ksdetasn.org by searching Schedules in their resource library.

Independent Work Systems

Description

Independent Work Systems, also called structured work systems, are an "instructional process that includes visually and spatial organized location, previously mastered work, clear specification of task(s), signal when work is finished, [and] instructions for the next activity" (NPDC, Wong et al., 2014, p. 25). As described by Hume and Reynolds (2010), students must know the following information for Independent Work Systems:

- What task or activity am I supposed to do?
- How much work is required and how long will the activity last?
- How will I know that I am progressing?
- What happens when I finish?

Independent Work Systems are key components of Structured Teaching, which is based on the Treatment and Education of Autistic and Related Communication Handicapped Children (TEACCH) program. The TEACCH Program was developed at the University of North Carolina-Chapel Hill in the 1960s (Schopler, 1994) and is a model program for students with ASD. The TEACCH program takes into account the primary characteristics of students with ASD and supports them by modifying and structuring the environment in a clear manner. Assessment and on-going collaboration with parents are defining features of TEACCH.

Four other critical components of the TEACCH program include the following:

- Physical organization or how the learning environment is arranged
- Visual schedules to clearly display what the student will do next
- Work systems so students know how many activities they must do
- Tasks and activities are organized in a visual manner

Brief Overview of the Literature

An initial peer-reviewed study on TEACCH was published in the early 1990s (Schopler, 1994). Studies continued throughout the next two decades both on the official TEACCH Independent Work Systems (Panerai et al., 2002, 2009; Virues-Ortega, 2013) and other similar systems that are used outside of the TEACCH program (Hume & Odom, 2007; Hume & Reynolds, 2010; O'Hara & Hall, 2014). TEACCH is considered a CTM (Odom et al., 2010).

Core Reviews

Simpson et al. (2005) did not include Independent Work Systems as a reviewed intervention but referenced work systems in Structured Teaching (TEACCH), which was given a rating of Promising Practice based on two studies. The NAC did not include Independent Work Systems as a reviewed intervention. The NPDC (Wong et al., 2014) used the term *Independent Work Systems* in 2014 giving the rating of Some but Insufficient Evidence-based on three articles. In 2020, the NCAEP (Steinbrenner et al., 2020) included Independent Work Systems under the broader category of Visual Supports, which was rated as an EBP.

Age and Diagnostic Considerations/ Prerequisite Skills and Abilities

Most of the research on independent work systems included school-age subjects, and several have also had young adult subjects (Hume & Odom, 2007).

Reported Outcomes

Children who participated in the TEACCH program demonstrated better outcomes compared to students in nonstructured programs in terms of increasing social communication skills on task behavior and task completion and decreasing maladaptive behavior (Hume & Odom, 2007; Panerai et al., 2009; Virues-Ortega et al., 2013).

Qualifications Needed

No formal training is required to implement Independent Work Systems.

How, Where, and When Typically Implemented

Students using Independent Work Systems are commonly seated in a specific area with work tasks and activities clearly organized.

Costs

Setting up Independent Work Systems requires an upfront investment in terms of time and materials. Materials can be purchased at stores such as Walmart, Target, or Office Depot.

Potential Risks

There are no documented or obvious risks associated with Independent Work Systems.

Practitioner Testimonial(s)

I have used Independent Work Systems for the past 9 years. I have mainly used work systems in a self-contained classroom but have also seen them used in a general education classroom with students during inclusion. What I like most about work systems is the independence it builds within my students. My students are able to sit down and complete an independent work time completely independently or with minimal assistance. My students understand what work they need to complete, how much work they have, when the work is finished, and what is next. I have had the pleasure of working with one student in preschool who began by having all of his work in separate tubs and the teacher handed him the tubs to complete the work. He has worked through various types of work systems and his most recent one involves using a file folder with his work inside. What an amazing practice to use to help build independence and confidence, especially in those students who have more challenges.

—Tracie Betz

Rating

☺　Promising/Emerging Practice

Resources and Suggested Readings

Kansas Technical Assistance System Network (TASN) offers several free online webinar on several topics related to Structured Teaching that can be accessed at ksde tasn.org by searching Structured Teaching in their resource library.

The Nebraska Autism Spectrum Disorders Network offers several free online webinars on Structured Teaching that can be accessed at https://www.unl.edu/asdnetwork/webinars?combine=schedule&tid=All

The Ohio Center for Autism and Low Incidence (OCALI) offers a free online course on Structured Teaching. After creating an account, it can be accessed at https://autisminternetmodules.org/search?qtitle=structured

TEACCH® Autism Program can be accessed at https://teacch.com

Scripting

Description

Scripting involves presenting the learner with a written text of specifically what to say in a situation. The NCAEP defines *Scripting* as "A verbal and/or written description about a specific skill or situation that serves as a model for the learner" (NPDC, Wong et al., 2014, 21). Scripts are usually practiced repeatedly before the skill is used in the actual situation. Scripting may be textually based (written) or audio based.

Brief Overview of the Literature

The earliest studies on Scripting were published in the early 1990s (Goldstein et al., 1992; Krantz & McClannahan, 1993), continuing throughout the next 25 years and culminating with a systematic review in 2016 (Akers et al., 2016). Topics of the scripts varied considerably and focused on statements related to requesting help, snacks, play time, toys, and bids for joint attention (Akers et al., 2016).

Core Reviews

Simpson et al. (2005) did not include Scripting as a reviewed intervention. The NAC gave Scripting the rating of Emerging in 2009 based on six articles and Established in 2015 based on an additional five articles. The NPDC (Wong et al., 2014) rated scripting as an EBP in 2014 based on nine articles. The NCAEP (Steinbrenner et al., 2020) included it under the broader category of Visual Supports in 2020, which was rated an EBP.

Other Systematic Reviews/Meta-Analyses

In 2020, Leaf classified Social Scripts as a Social Narrative and reviewed four articles concluding that three had partially convincing evidence (Hundert et al., 2014; Loveland & Tunali, 1991; Parker & Kamps, 2011) and one had not convincing evidence (Ganz et al., 2008).

Age and Diagnostic Considerations/ Prerequisite Skills and Abilities

Research supports the use of Scripts with all school-age individuals with ASD (NPDC, Wong et al., 2014).

Reported Outcomes

Scripts have overwhelmingly been studied on teaching social interaction skills (Brown et al., 2008; Charlop-Christy & Kelso, 2003; Ganz et al., 2008; Krantz & McClannahan, 1998; Ledbetter-Cho et al., 2015; Sarokoff et al., 2015; Stevenson et al., 2000; Wichnick-Gillis, 2016).

Qualifications Needed

No formal training is required to implement Scripting.

How, Where, and When Typically Implemented

Scripting is commonly used with other interventions such as reinforcement, modeling, and prompting. The script is generally recommended to be faded to promote as much independence as possible. However, as with other Visual Supports, students with ASD can refer to scripts as often as needed. The length of the script can vary according to the student's age and reading level. To systematically fade a script, the last word of the script is typically removed as the student begins saying the script independently. Words continue to be removed until the student no longer needs to refer to the script. A majority of studies on Scripting took place in clinical settings (Akers et al., 2016), but this intervention could easily be implemented in school, home, and community settings.

Costs

Scripting is cost-effective in terms of time and other resources. There are no costs associated with training and no additional teaching time is required or materials to be purchased other than those typically found in school settings, such as paper and writing utensils.

Potential Risks

There are no documented or obvious risks associated with Scripting.

Practitioner Testimonial(s)

I had a student who was interviewing for a job. Before the interview we looked for commonly asked interview questions and then the student helped us write a script for his answers. The challenge in this activity is helping the student match the script to the situation. For instance, a question like, "Tell us a little bit about yourself": His answer is that he has three sisters and that he is a survivalist and can defend himself with a slingshot. Obviously, this is not what an employer is looking for if you are interviewing to be a cashier at Walmart. No matter where a student is on the spectrum, matching the script to the situation is key but also will be a challenge. For my student, what worked is for every question, we asked ourselves what is the job we are interviewing for and what is the employer's motto. The student wrote the job down and then took a screenshot with his phone. Throughout the days until his interview, special education staff would ask him questions he might be asked in his interview. If the answer was not appropriate, he would be asked to tell us the job he is interviewing for and what is the store's motto. The student did not get this job, but he has gotten jobs on his own and even though he has graduated, tells us about how he still uses the script we developed together.

—Josh Wikler

Rating

⭐ Evidence-Based Practice

Resources and Suggested Readings

AFIRM modules through UNC Chapel Hill offers a free online course on Scripting that can be accessed at https://afirm.fpg.unc.edu/scripting

Power Cards

Description

A Power Card is a small, personalized card that includes text and image of a student's favorite hero, character, or special interest area (Angell et al., 2011; Gagnon, 2011). Students with ASD can have highly specialized interests, and utilizing those interests in interventions represents a strengths-based approach. Special interest areas can be highly motivating to students with ASD, and examples of such interests include animals, movie or TV characters, toys, music, machines, transportation, and objects.

The Power Card Strategy is meant to increase desired prosocial behavior such as taking turns, using greetings, raising hand during instruction, staying organized, or asking for help. The Power Card describes how the hero or character demonstrates appropriate behavior or solves a problem (Campbell & Tincani, 2011). Then, the Power Card gives encouragement for the student with ASD to display the same target behavior. Power Cards are typically shorter in length and smaller in size than social stories. For instance, students can carry their Power Cards to different places because it is typically the same size as a playing card.

Brief Overview of the Literature

Power cards were first developed by Elisa Gagnon in 2001 and first appears in the peer-reviewed literature in 2003 (Keeling et al., 2003) with a few others following about a decade later (Angell et al., 2011; Campbell & Tincani, 2011; Daubert et al., 2015; Davis et al., 2010). Studies implementing Power Cards were included within the social narrative and visual supports category for both the NPDC/NCAEP reviews (NCAEP, Steinbrenner et al., 2020; NPDC, Wong et al., 2014). For example, Angell et al. (2011) used Power Cards to decrease the latency of three students with ID or ASD in following directions to transition to the next activity in a classroom setting. Researchers interviewed teachers and family members to identify students' special interest to include on the power card. The students were ages 10 to 11 years old and their special interests were a student's father, the SpongeBob SquarePants character, and a doll (Angell et al., 2011). Results of this study indicated the Power Card was effective in reducing latency in following directions for all three students. Similarly, Daubert et al. (2015) used a Power Card to teach two elementary-age students turn-taking skills and appropriate comments while playing board games. The students' special interest characters in this study were different Teenage Mutant Ninja Turtle characters.

Core Reviews

Simpson et al. (2005) included Power Cards giving it a rating of Limited Supporting Information for Practice based on some peer-reviewed studies on using the repetitive patterns of behaviors and special interests of children with ASD as visual cues and reinforcers (Baker et al., 1998; Charlop-Christy & Haymes, 1998; Dettmer et al., 2000; Hinton & Kern, 1999; Kuttler et al., 1998; Quill, 1992, 1995). The NAC did not include Power Cards as a reviewed intervention but did include one article (Keeling et al., 2003) under Antecedent Strategies in 2009. The NPDC (Wong et al., 2014) and

NCAEP (Steinbrenner et al., 2020) did not include Power Cards as a reviewed intervention but did include articles on the intervention under Social Narratives (Campbell & Tincani, 2011; Daubert et al., 2015) and Visual Supports (Angell et al., 2011) in both of their reports, which were both rated as EBPs.

Other Systematic Reviews/Meta-Analyses

In 2020, Leaf classified Power Cards as a Social Narrative and reviewed four articles concluding that one had convincing evidence (Davis et al., 2010), two had partially convincing evidence (Campbell & Tincani, 2011; Daubert et al., 2015), and one had not convincing evidence (Angell et al., 2011).

Age and Diagnostic Considerations/ Prerequisite Skills and Abilities

Power Cards have mostly been used with elementary students but are widely applicable and can be used for all school-age learners with ASD with mild to severe support needs.

Reported Outcomes

Power Cards have been used to teach skills such as taking turns, using greetings, raising hand during instruction, staying organized, asking for help, solving problems, and making appropriate comments.

Qualifications Needed

No formal training is required to implement Power Cards. The teacher may consider implementing preference assessments to determine the student's special interest area if unknown.

How, Where, and When Typically Implemented

Power Cards can be implemented in school, clinical, home, and community settings.

Costs

Using Power Cards is cost-effective in terms of time and other resources. There are no costs associated with training and no additional teaching time is required. Materials commonly found in classroom and school settings (e.g., paper, colored markers, printer, ink) can be used to create Power Cards.

Potential Risks

There are no documented or obvious risks associated with Power Cards.

Practitioner Testimonial(s)

Many times throughout my career, Power Cards were just the hook I needed to get students' attention to engage in instruction on skills in many areas, including behavior, regulation skills, social skills, language, academics, and even organizational skills. Using students' special interests embedded in simple stories along with visuals seemed to encourage them to improve situations by decreasing challenging behaviors and increasing replacement behaviors. I have used many different characters with my students, including princesses, the Hulk, Power Rangers, Dora, Bob the Builder, SpongeBob, Blues Clue, Barney, Mickey Mouse, a dinosaur trainer, and even a train conductor. Writing a simple story about what Dora says to her friends, how Mickey can use calming strategies, or how SpongeBob completes his work was just the catch I needed to support my students in applying the appropriate skill in a variety of situations. Some of my favorite all-time Power Cards were how Hulk could use his soft hands when playing with peers and how the Red Power Ranger could use his calming strategies when he gets upset. There is POWER in the Power Card strategy.

—Dixie Teeter

Rating

😊   Promising/Emerging Practice

Resources and Suggested Readings

Kansas Technical Assistance System Network (TASN) offers several free online webinars on topics related to Power Cards that can be accessed at ksdetasn.org by searching Power in their resource library.

Language Training

Introduction

Language Training aims to improve the expressive and receptive language skills of individuals with ASD. Expressive Language Training targets a variety of skills such as an individual's ability to functionally use spoken words for communicating wants and needs; labeling items in the environment; and describing events, actions, or ideas. Receptive Language Training focuses on the individual's understanding of words. Age-appropriate receptive language skills are crucial for responding to directions; selecting images, colors, or words upon request; and responding to one's name (Grow & LeBlanc, 2013). Both expressive and receptive language targets should be developmentally appropriate and based on individualized assessment methods and tools.

Interventions Included in This Section

- Verbal Behavior-Based Intervention

- Augmentative and Alternative Communication (AAC)

- Aided Language Modeling

- Assisted Technology (AT)

- Picture Exchange Communication System (PECS®) (MIMC)

Verbal Behavior (VB)-Based Intervention

Description

VB is behavior mediated by another person's behavior. The analysis of VB is a subfield of ABA with a focus on teaching learners with communication deficits to develop functional verbal skills so they can communicate their wants and needs and interact with others. Within a Verbal Behavior-Based Intervention, teachers should emphasize teaching all functions of a word. For example, the word *truck* may be used for various purposes such as labeling (tact—"I see a truck"), requesting (mand—"I want my toy truck") answering a question (intraverbal—"What is something that has wheels?"), or repeating (echoic—"Say truck") what has been said by another individual. It is important to note that *verbal* does not just apply to vocal communication but includes all response topographies of communication. For example VB can include speaking, using sign language, gesturing, writing, and using pictures and speech-generating devices (SGDs). VB consists of both speaker and listener skills, as both are important skill sets to develop in order for social communication interactions to be effective.

Speaker Skills

Mand	Request (You say it because you want it.)
Echoic	Repeating what someone else says (You say it because someone else said it.)
Tact	Label (You say it because you see, hear, smell, taste, or feel something.)
Intraverbal	Answering questions, conversations, responding to someone when they talk (You say it because someone else asked a question or made a comment.)

Listener Skills

Imitation	Doing what someone else does (You do it because they do it.)
Listener Response	Following directions (You do something because someone else asks you to.)

Brief Overview of the Literature

The key concepts of teaching VB are based on Skinner's (1957) seminal book *Verbal Behavior*. There is a wide literature base supporting teaching VB skills to students with ASD. In one of the earliest studies, Williams and Greer (1993) compared the effectiveness of ABA in a linguistic-based curriculum (Guess et al., 1976) to a Verbal Behavior-Based Intervention to teach functional communication. This study demonstrated that when learners were taught using a Verbal Behavior-Based Intervention, they acquired more functional and spontaneous verbal skills and were able to generalize and maintain these skills better than when they were taught using the linguistic-based curriculum. Subsequent research continues to provide empirical support for Verbal Behavior-Based Intervention (Dymond et al., 2006; Eshleman, 1991; Petursdottir, 2018).

Core Reviews

Verbal Behavior-Based Interventions were not included in any of the core reviews but are included in this resource due to their increasing use by educators.

Other Peer-Reviewed Research

In the two most recent reviews, findings revealed a stable increase in VB skills after employing Skinner's analysis of VB and the implementation of VB programs by service providers and caregivers of individuals with disabilities (DeSouza et al., 2017; Petursdottir & Devine, 2017).

Age and Diagnostic Considerations/ Prerequisite Skills and Abilities

VB skills can be taught to learners with ASD from ages preschool to adulthood and there are no prerequisite skills needed. The educator should assess the current language skills and begin instruction aligned to the individual needs of the learner. Several VB language assessments and curriculum resources with a function-based approach are readily available including (1) *Assessment of Basic Language and Learning Skills—Revised* (ABLLS-R, Partington, 2006), (2) *Verbal Behavior Milestones Assessment and Placement Program* (VB-MAPP, Sundberg, 2008), (3) PEAK Direct Training Module (PEAKDT, Dixon, 2014), and (4) Stimulus Control Ratio Equation (Mason & Andrews, 2019).

Reported Outcomes

Subjects in research on Verbal Behavior-Based Interventions acquired functional and spontaneous verbal skills and were able to generalize and maintain these skills.

Qualifications Needed

No formal training is required to implement Verbal Behavior-Based Interventions. Individuals who use these practices should consider training in its application through consultation with an experienced implementer or other training formats.

How, Where, and When Typically Implemented

Verbal Behavior-Based Interventions can be implemented in any setting (e.g., home, clinical, community) but is commonly implemented in school settings. For example, there are over 600 public school classrooms successfully serving students with ASD using the VB-MAPP as a primary assessment and curriculum guide, closely following the principles of ABA and Skinner's functional analysis of verbal behavior in Pennsylvania under the Autism Initiative (Dipuglia & Miklos, 2014). Verbal Behavior-Based Interventions incorporates many evidence-based instructional strategies such as fast-paced instruction and mixing and varying learning targets for maximum student engagement and errorless learning.

Costs

Verbal Behavior-Based Interventions are cost-effective in terms of time and other resources. Training costs vary, with readily available training for any budget. Additionally, curriculum and other tangible resources are reasonably priced for implementation and can be used immediately upon purchase.

Potential Risks

There are no documented or obvious risks associated with teaching VB skills to students with ASD.

Practitioner Testimonial(s)

I started implementing Verbal Behavior-Based Interventions in my Structured Learning classroom in 2017. I had students who went from tolerating learning to loving it! The fast-paced instruction, mixing and varying of operants, and teaching errorlessly allowed my students to gain skills at a much faster rate and enjoy learning. As a teacher, I liked taking data one time a day and being able to teach the rest of the day. I could also easily pull out my graph to show progress and data for IEP goals at any time. I now help train teachers on how to implement this type of program. Through coaching, I get to see the positive change this programming makes in the lives of many students with autism and complex needs.

—Mary Beth Hodge

Rating

☺ Promising/Emerging Practice

Resources and Suggested Readings

Barbera, M. L., & Rasmussen, T. (2007). *The Verbal Behavior approach: How to teach children with autism and related disorders.* Jessica Kingsley.

Ingvarsson, E. T. (2016). Tutorial: Teaching Verbal Behavior to children with ASD. *International Electronic Journal of Elementary Education, 9*(2), 433–450.

Kansas Technical Assistance System Network (TASN) offers several free online webinar on Verbal Behavior Programming. They can be accessed at ksdetasn .org by searching Verbal Behavior in their resource library.

The Nebraska Autism Spectrum Disorders Network offers several free online webinars on Verbal Behavior Programming. They can be accessed at https://www .unl.edu/asdnetwork/webinars?combine=Verbal+Behavior&tid=All

The Pennsylvania Training and Technical Assistance Network (PaTTAN) has many free training videos and resources available related to Verbal Behavior programming and can be access at https://www.pattan.net/Disabilities/Autism/Autism-Initiative-ABA-Supports-1

Sundberg, M. L., & Michael, J. (2001). The benefits of Skinner's analysis of Verbal Behavior for children with autism. *Behavior Modification, 25*(5), 698–724.

Sundberg, M. L., & Partington, J. W. (1998). *Teaching language to children with autism and other developmental disabilities.* Behavior Analysts.

Augmentative and Alternative Communication (AAC)

Description

Communication plays an important role in our daily lives. It is critical in conveying information, like our wants and needs, to others. When we go to a doctor's appointment, we describe the state of our health, if we have pain, and its location. When we are hungry, we might tell someone how we like our hamburger cooked. If we feel upset about something that happened at work, we might call a friend to vent our frustrations or ask for advice. One of the core diagnostic features of ASD is a deficit or qualitative difference in social communication (Hume et al., 2021).

AAC is a nonverbal mode of communication that provides a substitute or replacement for speech in individuals with complex communication needs (CCN) such as people with disabilities who are unable to use speech at age-appropriate levels to meet their needs. The NCAEP defines AAC as an intervention that uses and/or teaches "the use of a system of communication that is not verbal/vocal including aided and unaided communication systems" (NCAEP, Steinbrenner et al., 2020, p. 66). Aided communication systems require additional materials, such as picture icons that can be exchanged or pointed to for preferred items or activities. High-tech aided options include electronic speech-generating devices (SGDs) or apps that can be downloaded to other devices like electronic tablets. Low-tech aided options involve exchanging or pointing to objects, pictures, or icons. Unaided communication systems such as sign language, gestures, vocalizations, and facial expressions do not require additional materials.

Approximately 30 percent of persons with ASD are nonverbal and need an alternative form of communication. Features of AAC can support communication deficits and complement learner strengths. Aided AAC simplifies the process of communication because it is less complex than speech. Pointing at a picture or pressing a button to request a desired object requires minimal fine motor skills, although sign languages may require strengths in this area (Ganz & Simpson, 2018). AAC forms that incorporate picture representations such as exchange-based AAC or SGDs with pictures or icons require the use of recognition rather than recall, which are both are cognitive processes involving memory. However, recognition uses less cognitive resources, making it easier to perform. Many learners with ASD possess strong visual-spatial abilities. Because AAC incorporates pictures, icons, or gestures, it provides a visual signifier for communication, allowing learners with ASD to capitalize on their strengths.

Brief Overview of the Literature

Unaided forms of AAC have been studied with students with disabilities including AAC since the mid-1980s (Bryen & Joyce, 1986). Within the past 10 years, there has been a significant increase in the amount of research examining the effects of AAC as a communication intervention for persons with autism. The number of AAC studies quadrupled between the NCAEP report in 2014 and its report in 2020. There have been nine systematic reviews and/or meta-analyses conducted on AAC since 2017 (Aydin & Diken, 2020; Biggs et al., 2018; Ganz et al., in press[a], 2022, in press[b]; Gevarter & Zamoa, 2018; Holyfield et al., 2017; Morin et al., 2018; White et al., 2021) further adding to the evidence base.

Core Reviews

Simpson et al. (2005) used the term *Augmentative and Alternative Communication* and gave a rating of Promising Practice based on one study (Bryen & Joyce, 1986). The NAC used the term *Augmentative and Alternative Communication Device* and gave a rating of Emerging in both 2009, based on 14 studies, and 2015, based on an unspecified number of studies. The NPDC (Wong et al., 2014) used the term Aided Language Modeling in 2014 and gave a rating of Some but Insufficient Evidence-based on one study. The NCAEP (Steinbrenner et al., 2020) used the term Augmentative and Alternative Communication in 2020 and gave the rating of EBP based on a total of 44 studies.

Age and Diagnostic Considerations/ Prerequisite Skills and Abilities

AAC has been found to be effective with diverse learners with ASD of all ages with and without ID (Ganz et al., in press[b]) and regardless of amount of symbolic language used prior to implementation of AAC interventions (Crowe et al., 2021; Ganz et al., 2011; Ganz et al., 2022; Holyfield et al., 2017; White et al., 2021). It is important to note that since no statistical difference was found in effects of AAC interventions between individuals with ASD with or without co-occurring ID, nor when comparing across age groups, age, and presence of ID should not be a factor in providing or denying access to AAC (Ganz et al., in press[b]). Individual responding is highly variable so individualization of AAC implementation is critical. Imitation skills prior to intervention were not found to be a factor, possibly because such skills are not often measured or reported. However, learners who used a formalized symbolic mode of AAC prior to study implementation had better effects than those who relied on verbal/vocal or gestural communication (Ganz et al., in press[b]). This suggests that more intensive intervention may be necessary with learners who have CCN and who do not have prior aided AAC or manual sign language experience. Although the U.S. population is becoming more diverse, research on AAC use with minoritized populations is sparse (Ganz et al., in press[b]), which indicates a need to incorporate culturally and linguistically responsive practices (Bridges, 2004; Huer et al., 2001; Kulkarni & Parmar, 2017), particularly because AAC is inherently social. Further, English learners may need more intensive instruction in both their home language and in English.

Reported Outcomes

Published studies have reported a range of positive outcomes for individuals with ASD who use AAC (Ganz et al., in press[a]). AAC interventions result in positive communication outcomes (Aydin & Diken, 2020; Logan et al., 2016; Morin et al., 2018; White et al., 2021). However, almost all of the research involves improvement in communication production such as producing a sentence and little involves communication comprehension (Ganz et al., in press[a]). In addition, most of the research focused on behavioral regulation functions of communication such as requesting or protesting. However, there is increasing interest in social functions such as sharing attention and having a conversation. There are positive outcomes associated with all of these communicative functions, which suggests that learners should be taught multiple functions and that instructions should be individualized based on learner needs.

Studies comparing the effects of AAC modes have reported inconsistent results regarding which mode produces the best outcomes for persons with ASD, although aided AAC has had generally higher effects than unaided AAC (Aydin & Diken, 2020; Ganz et al., in press[a]; White et al., 2021). That said, there has been substantially more research on use of aided AAC than unaided, such as sign language. Of the few studies that applied the use of preference assessments, a majority revealed that SGD was preferred by most participants, followed by picture exchange, then manual sign (Aydin & Diken, 2020; Lorah et al., 2022), while other reviews have found preferences were highly individual. Comparing AAC modes is an area of research that needs further study so that educators and practitioners can make evidence-based recommendations that meet each learner's specific needs (Crowe et al., 2021; Lorah et al., 2022). The takeaway message is that we know AAC works, but the type of AAC system or device is largely dependent upon the learner, their preferences, strengths, and feasibility.

Qualifications Needed

There are no specific requirements that permit or prohibit someone from teaching a learner to use AAC. However, certain professionals, such as an SLP or behavior analyst, have undergone training and are familiar with implementing AAC interventions in addition to naturalistic and behavioral instructional strategies.

How, Where, and When Typically Implemented

Instructional Context and Setting

Persons with ASD might receive AAC intervention in a public or private school, a clinic, at home, or in other places like the community. Because AAC interventions can be implemented in more than one setting, it is important for researchers and practitioners to understand the effect that instructional context or setting could have on communicative outcomes. Much of the research on AAC and ASD has been conducted in highly structured contexts versus community settings (Biggs et al., 2018; Gevarter & Zamora, 2018; Holyfield et al., 2017). Most studies involving AAC were implemented in the classroom setting, followed by the clinical setting, then multiple settings, then homes (Ganz et al., 2022). That said, effects are not dramatically different when outcomes of AAC interventions were compared across clinical, home, classroom, other, or multiple settings. This is important to note, as it highlights the need to ensure that AAC skills generalize to home and across all settings and to ensure that parents, caregivers, and other natural communication partners know how to encourage use of AAC. Much of the research on AAC with learners with ASD has been conducted in highly structured contexts versus community settings (Biggs et al., 2018; Gevarter & Zamora, 2018; Holyfield et al., 2017) starting in classrooms, followed by the clinics, multiple settings, and finally homes using both structured behavioral instructional approaches such as one-on-one sessions involving mass teaching trials and learner-led approaches in natural contexts. There were no significant differences in outcomes across settings or approaches (Ganz et al., 2022).

Considering behavioral versus more naturalistic instructional format, AAC was implemented most often in more structured approaches, including one-on-one instruction, with the interventionist (e.g., educator/practitioner) working with only the target learner, with instructor versus child-led instruction, involving massed trials of teaching limited skills, and contrived versus more authentic contexts (Ganz et al., 2022). However, studies did tend to use a range of teaching stimuli and implement in settings located within natural contexts about half of the time. There were not substantial differences in effects between more didactic behavioral approaches versus naturalistic approaches.

Given the pervasiveness of communication, in order to plan for and promote generalization as early as possible, instruction in natural contexts that is ongoing and continuous should be prioritized to ensure that the communication skills developed are functional and to ensure that parents/caregivers and other natural communication partners know how to encourage the use of AAC. See the Natural Developmental Behavioral Interventions section of this resource for more guidance.

Instructional Strategies

Simply handing an individual an AAC device or icon does not teach them how to use it with communicative intent. If a teenager gets a car for their 16th birthday, they would not necessarily know how to drive it properly. They would need to learn things like which side of the road to drive on, how to use the blinker, understanding the meaning of road signs, and so on. Similarly, the use of an AAC device or method must be taught with individual learning differences taken into consideration.

Instructional strategies can be used to teach appropriate AAC use and reinforce communication, increase learner motivation, provide useful feedback to the learner, and prevent mistakes from becoming a habit (Feeley & Jones, 2012; Gevarter et al., 2018). Prompts are a type of support that helps the learner perform a behavior or action correctly (Pennington, 2019). Learners who are new to using AAC may need physical guidance to learn the actions involved in communicating with their device (Ganz & Simpson, 2018). Prompt Fading can be used to gradually decrease support so that the learner uses their device to communicate independently. To ensure that the learner stays motivated and engaged in the learning process, educators can incorporate reinforcement and preference assessments into their instruction. These strategies are covered in more depth elsewhere in this volume.

Behavioral strategies have been used to implement AAC interventions; in particular, Reinforcement, Prompts and Prompt Fading, and Systematic Arrangement were used in almost all studies involving ASD and AAC interventions (Ganz et al., 2022). Further, although modeling was used frequently, individuals with ASD generally performed better in studies that did not specify they were implementing modeling, compared to those studies in which they did specifically implement modeling. Moreover, with one metric, people with ASD had stronger outcomes with studies that implemented physical prompting than those that did not. Considering that aided AAC is frequently implemented with this population, and that people with ASD tend to have relative weaknesses in imitation, it makes sense that more direct prompting may be more effective than modeling AAC use alone; however, modeling of language use, both verbally and via AAC, is highly recommended, paired with prompting.

Implications for Practitioners and Parents

There are many factors to consider when selecting an AAC mode and specific communication outcomes for a person with ASD. Age, assessment results, individual strengths, learner preference, cultural background, and language should also be incorporated into the decision-making process.

Naturalistic Strategies and Generalization Across Contexts

Communication happens everywhere. It happens at a desk, in the cafeteria, in learning centers, in the parent pick-up line, and so on. We need to embed communication throughout the day. Naturalistic instruction is a way to teach communicative interactions in the learner's natural environment in a way that is ongoing and continuous. When communication is taught to the learner in the context that it will need to be used, it ensures that the language is functional.

Incorporating Motivation

One way that educators or parents can incorporate naturalistic communication is to follow the lead of the learner and respond to what the learner is interested in in their environment. Not only is this a way to teach language in context, this strategy also takes into account learner motivation. By following the child's lead, the adult is responding to items or activities the learner most likely enjoys, increasing the likelihood that they will interact with the items or activity and the communicative interaction with the adult. Learner motivation plays a key role in intervention because it affects the learner's level of engagement. We never want communication or interacting with others to become aversive or something the learner avoids. Using a child's interests to facilitate communication will keep engagement high, leading to an increase in communicative outcomes.

Selection of Communication Mode and Multimodal Communication

Another consideration is whether the learner will be understood by their communication partner. For example, the average person the learner might approach may not know sign language. This means that the learner's communication partner would not be able to understand them. Most communication partners will be able to understand the meaning of a picture or spoken word, making it more likely for them to understand the learner's message.

While sign language is not used as often, compared to exchange-based communication or SGDs, by persons with ASD, there are benefits to its use. There are no additional materials that need to be purchased or for the learner to keep track of or transport. This makes sign language a relatively inexpensive mode of communication and easy to implement. Some things to consider with using sign language are the learner's skill sets. For example, does the learner have deficits in fine motor skills or in imitation? It might be necessary to address prerequisite skills before the learner could benefit from using sign language as a mode of communication. While the student may use PECS or SGDs for a majority of the time, it is acceptable to incorporate specific signs and gestures into their repertoire when it is useful and for a specific purpose.

Consideration of Key Stakeholder Needs and Preferences, Including Minoritized Populations

Before selecting or teaching an AAC method to the learner, it is important to consider the cultural practices of the family. Involving the parents or caregivers and seeking their input throughout the intervention process is one way to ensure that the family's culture is respected. Family can provide valuable insight that guides device and vocabulary selection (Huer et al., 2001). Some devices have multilanguage capabilities making it possible for the learner to communicate in the language spoken at home and at school.

If the learner uses signs or gestures to communicate, it is important to consider that gestures vary across languages, dialects, and cultures (Ganz & Simpson, 2018). One might consider the "thumbs up" to mean "good," but within another culture, it could have a different meaning. Similarly, studies have demonstrated that graphics and pictures have various meanings across cultural groups (Johnston et al., 2020). Consulting with the family and requesting feedback on target vocabulary in conjunction with demonstrating how the communicative act will look is a way to avoid selecting words that could be misinterpreted or seen as offensive in another setting.

Practitioners and educators can gather meaningful information from family members by asking them questions about their wants and needs in the home or community setting. Not only does this help the practitioner in creating an individualized program for the learner, but family input also ensures that what we implement is useful to the learner and feasible for the family to implement.

Costs

The cost of AAC will depend on the type of technology selected. Unaided and low-tech aided forms may have little to no cost whereas hi-tech aided devices could cost several thousand dollars.

Potential Risks

There are no documented or obvious risks associated with the use of AAC.

Practitioner Testimonial(s)

One of my objectives for individuals with complex support needs is to provide them a voice. These students are able to do this through the use of AAC. These can range from low-tech systems, such as pictures, to high-tech systems, such as iPads or personalized SGDs. In my practice as an SLP, I utilize varied interventions dependent on the student's individual needs as a learner. Some interventions I utilize include the following:

- Aided Language Stimulation/Modeling—This intervention is when the communication partner models language on the system for the student. Also, it does not require the student to respond. Modeling provides increased input of language for a student and provides several opportunities for a student to learn language before output is expected. One example can include modeling a request—"Can I have bubbles?"—when an individual is motivated to engage with the item.

- Core Vocabulary—This intervention entails the use of core vocabulary, which is a word that is not a noun, such as using the word *go*. Core vocabulary allows an individual to functionally communicate for a variety of functions (e.g., requesting, commenting, directing, greeting, choice making, asking/answering questions). Core vocabulary allows for an individual for increased flexibility of vocabulary rather than situation-specific situations.

- Communication Opportunities—This intervention is when opportunities are strategically created for an individual to communicate, for example, giving an individual an item they cannot open to request help. This could also include setting up situations with peer–peer interactions for increasing social use of language.

- Least to Most Prompting—This strategy is using prompts that are least invasive to most invasive. The least restrictive kinds of prompts include giving adequate wait time, indirect verbal prompts, or gestural prompts. Physical prompts are the most obtrusive and should be utilized with absolute caution, as they entail what the communication partner wants the individual to say.

- Motor Planning—This specific strategy is utilized for students who are dependent on motor planning within a communication system. Icons are kept in the same location within the system for the individual to develop a motor planning. This is the same as typing on a keyboard or text messaging.

With the use of these interventions, individuals are able to develop the communication systems needed to build autonomy within their lives.

—Ben Harder

Rating

 Evidence-Based Practice

*The type of AAC system or device is largely dependent upon the learner, their preferences, strengths, and feasibility.

Resources and Suggested Readings

The Nebraska Autism Spectrum Disorders Network offers several free online webinars related to AAC. They can be accessed at https://www.unl.edu/asdnetwork/webinars?combine=AAC&tid=All

Aided Language Modeling

Description

Aided Language Modeling is the use of several augmentative and alternative communication (AAC) strategies together, such as the simultaneous use of pointing, a communication symbol, and/or vocalization (NPDC, Wong et al., 2014, p. 25). This models communication while simultaneously developing receptive language. Aided Language Modeling is also referred to as Aided Language Stimulation, Augmented Input, and AAC Modeling. During Aided Language Modeling, the communicative partner uses a student's communication system or language boards, selects a symbol, and simultaneously provides the verbal model to show students that symbols can be combined with other forms of communication to exchange information (Drager et al., 2006).

Brief Overview of the Literature

There is very little research literature specifically on Aided Language Modeling. Drager et al. were the first to use that term in 2006.

Core Reviews

Only the NCAEP (Steinbrenner et al., 2020) included Aided Language Modeling in its review in 2014 and gave it the rating of Some but Insufficient Evidence-based on one article (Drager et al., 2006).

Other Peer-Reviewed Research

An experimental peer-reviewed study that the author of this text was able to locate that was not included in the core reviews as it was published after 2017 is summarized here.

AUTHOR(S)	N	SETTING	AGE/ GENDER	DIAGNOSES	OUTCOMES/ FINDINGS	COMMENTS
Dorney and Erickson (2019)	13	Preschool classrooms	3–6 years 9 Male 4 Female	Autism	Made overall gains in communication complexity as determined by growth on the communication matrix	This study was combined with an examination of interaction patterns between teachers and students.

Gray Literature

Gray literature such as unpublished dissertations have not been peer reviewed, therefore they are not considered to be the same level of evidence as peer-reviewed studies. However, for interventions that have no or very little peer-reviewed evidence, they should be considered as they do provide at least some level of evidence. The gray literature that the author of this text was able to locate on Aided Language Modeling is summarized here.

AUTHOR(S)	N	SETTING	AGE/ GENDER	DIAGNOSES	OUTCOMES/ FINDINGS	COMMENTS
Biggs (2017)	4	Inclusive, nonacademic setting selected by each student's special education teacher	9–10 years 1 Male 3 Female	1 ID 3 Autism	Peers' implementation of aided AAC modeling within a peer network increased students' nonprompted, symbolic communication	Dissertation
Chipinka (2016)	1		12 yrs., 9 mos. Female	Autism	Average number of initiations during shared storybook readings increased from 4.67 initiations during baseline to 7.00 initiations during intervention using familiar books. Average number of initiations during generalization probes using new books increased to 13 initiations. The average number of responses to questions increased from 5.67 responses in baseline to 10.00 responses in intervention using familiar books. Average number of responses during generalization probes using new books increased to 9.30 responses. Small gains were noted in the student's main length of utterances (MLU). The child produced 3 total multi-button messages during baseline, which increased to 8 multi-button messages during intervention. The child produced 4 multi-button messages during generalization probes using new books.	Dissertation

(Continued)

(Continued)

AUTHOR(S)	N	SETTING	AGE/ GENDER	DIAGNOSES	OUTCOMES/ FINDINGS	COMMENTS
					During baseline sessions, the student averaged 30% in accuracy for answering comprehension questions. The student demonstrated the highest accuracy (average of 68%) in answering comprehension during sessions in which the intervention was implemented.	
Hall (2014)	1	Treatment room at a university speech-language-hearing clinic	7-year-old female	Autism and receptive-expressive language delay	Increase in single spoken words, single picture symbol production, spoken word + picture symbol combinations, and production of picture symbol combinations	Dissertation
Novak (2016)	2	Self-contained classroom in a private school for students with autism	14 yrs. 6 mos.–16 yrs. 11 mos. 2 Male	Autism	Participant #1 gained 1 of 3 social game-playing language Participant #2 gained 0 of 3 social game-playing language Minimal evidence to support the effectiveness of Aided Language Modeling on the acquisition of social game-playing language for 2 students with autism using AAC.	Dissertation

Age and Diagnostic Considerations/ Prerequisite Skills and Abilities

Aided Language Modeling has been used with preschool (Drager et al., 2006), elementary (Hall, 2014) and secondary students (Chipinka, 2016; Novak, 2016) with ASD who do not have functional communication skills and are ready to use or are currently using AAC devices.

Reported Outcomes

Aided Language Modeling has been used to address a variety of communication-based skills such as receptive and expressive vocabulary (Cafiero, 2001; Drager et al., 2006), communication complexity (Dorney & Erikson, 2019), initiations and responses to questions during story-book reading (Chipinka, 2016), comprehension of story grammar during storybook reading (Chipinka, 2016), and nonprompted, symbolic communication during peer network meetings (Biggs, 2017). Aided Language Modeling can also be implemented during a variety of activities, such as book shares, facilitated play, sequenced procedures, and peer network meetings.

Qualifications Needed

No formal training is required to implement Aided Language Modeling. However, individuals should be familiar with its application through consultation with an SLP or other experienced implementer.

How, Where, and When Typically Implemented

Assisted Language Stimulation can easily be integrated into daily activities with other teaching objectives.

Costs

Aided Language Modeling is cost-effective in terms of time and other resources. Required materials include icons or other symbols for language boards or other AAC devices. Other materials such as books, games, and toys can be found in the natural environment.

Potential Risks

There are no documented or obvious risks associated with Aided Language Modeling.

Practitioner Testimonial(s)

Using Aided Language Modeling was a game changer for our classrooms. Before using Aided Language Modeling, many of our communication supports were only brought out at certain times of day (usually snack time). Teaching all adults in the room how to use this modeling intervention gave purpose to the communication support and provided language input to the AAC users across the day. We modeled verbal language for our speaking students and realized we should be modeling for our AAC speakers as well. Some examples used in our classroom included modeling how to initiate asking a peer to play at recess, giving a peer a compliment, how to comment on the show-and-tell activity, how to ask for a break, and even how to request whom they sit by at lunch. By providing communication support at all times and showing them how and when to use it with Aided Language Modeling techniques, the communication partners in the room could model meaningful communication opportunities that happened in real time.

—Dixie Teeter

Rating

☺ Limited Supporting Information for Practice

Resources and Suggested Readings

Communication Community. (2022). *What is aided language stimulation?* Author. https://www.communicationcommunity.com/what-is-aided-language-stimulation/

ICAN™ Talk Clinics. (2011). *AACtion point: Aided language stimulation.* https://communicationaactualized.com

Tamrasimmons. (2008, February 29). *Supporting language development* [video] YouTube. http://www.youtube.com/watch?v=w7jUIhNixK8

Assistive Technology (AT)

Description

According to the Individuals with Disabilities Education Improvement Act (IDEIA, 2004), AT is defined as "... any item, piece of equipment, or product system, whether acquired commercially off the shelf, modified, or customized, that is used to increase, maintain, or improve functional capabilities of a child with a disability." Thus, essentially, AT refers to any item or technology that allows an individual with a disability to perform tasks that would otherwise be extremely difficult or impossible without such a tool. Providing AT in schools and public places helps level the playing field of accessibility for people with disabilities, allowing them access to education, employment opportunities, and other services they may not otherwise have (Ennis-Cole & Smith, 2011). According to this definition, AT can include a wide range of aids, including low-tech technology such as wait cards, turn-taking cards, pencil grips, and graphic organizers; mid-tech items such as adapted keyboards and word prediction software; and hi-tech items such as tablets, video modeling software, augmented, and virtual reality, and robots.

AT can serve many functions. During their review of the literature, Odom et al. (2015) identified seven types of technology-based interventions or instruction commonly researched. These purposes included using AT for VM, visual prompts (VP), delivery of specific training on social skills or academic content, covert audio coaching (CAC), speech-generating devices (SGDs), performance feedback (PF), and self-management (SM).

AT is referred to by a variety of terms. These terms may include *computer-based interventions, technology-aided interventions, digital interventions*, and *computer-assisted interventions* (Sandgreen et al., 2021).

Brief Overview of the Literature

Chen and Bernard-Opitz (1993) first studied the use of AT with students with ASD in 1993 followed by Dyches (1998), Schlosser et al. (1998), and Hagiwara and Myles (1999). Two studies were published in 2001 (Bernard-Opitz et al., 2001; Tjus et al., 2001).

Core Reviews

Of the five core reviews, only Simpson et al. (2005) included AT as a reviewed intervention giving a rating of Promising Practice based on nine studies.

Other Peer-Reviewed Research

The author of this text was able to locate four experimental peer-reviewed studies that were not included in the core reviews and five published after 2017, which are summarized here.

AUTHOR(S)	N	SETTING	AGE/ GENDER	DIAGNOSES	FINDINGS
David et al. (2020)	5	Back part of a room of a private organization that provides services for students with ASD.	3–5 years 3 Males 2 Females	ASD	Results indicated that robot-enhanced treatment did not produce a significant difference from standard human treatment on teaching turn-taking skills. However, students tended to make better eye contact with the robot-enhanced technology condition than the standard human treatment condition.
Eden and Oren (2020)	13 high-functioning autism noncomputer-mediated interventions 15 high-functioning autism computer-mediated interventions 30 typically developing (control group)	Preschool classroom	5–6 years old 55 Males 3 Females 30 of the participants were "typically developing" and served as the control group	High-functioning autism Typically developing (control group)	The social intervention decreased the gap in prosocial abilities between students with high-function autism and the typically developing control group. In addition, when the 2 groups of students with high-functioning autism (noncomputer-mediated intervention vs. computer-mediated intervention) were compared, the students who received computer-mediated intervention made more progress than the noncomputer-mediated group.
Flores et al. (2014)	7 total 5 with ASD 2 with DD	3 Preschool classroom	4–8 years 5 Males 2 Females	ASD DD	The use of an Apple iPad as AT for story-based interventions resulted in desirable changes in student behavior across classrooms.

AUTHOR(S)	N	SETTING	AGE/ GENDER	DIAGNOSES	FINDINGS
Ganz et al. (2014)	3	Classroom used for individual testing in a school setting for 2 students and in the home for 1 student	8–14 years	Autism	The use of handheld electronic visual supports was effective in increasing verb and noun use for all participants. For 2 of 3 students, less intrusive prompts were required over time. In regard to independent communication, 1 student demonstrated independent communication during the iPad condition as compared to nontreatment conditions.
Gentry et al. (2015)	50 total 28 in Now group received intervention upon starting their job placement. 27 in Delayed group received intervention 12 weeks after beginning their job placement.	Job site	16–60 years 42 Males 8 Females	ASD	Training in the use of a PDA as an AT significantly reduced the need for job coaching support by workers with ASD, without reducing functional performance on the job. Workers who received PDA training at the beginning of their job placement required significantly fewer hours of job coaching support during their first 12 weeks on the job than those who had not yet received the intervention.

(Continued)

(Continued)

AUTHOR(S)	N	SETTING	AGE/ GENDER	DIAGNOSES	FINDINGS
Hopkins et al. (2011)	49 Total 11 in LFA (low-functioning autism) training group 14 in LFA control group 13 in HFA (high-functioning autism) training group 11 in HFA control group	School	6–15 years of age with a mental age between 6–10 years 44 Males 5 Females	ASD	Computer-based interaction simulations using *FaceSay* resulted in students with LFA demonstrating improvement in two areas of the intervention: emotion recognition and social interactions. Computer-based interaction simulations using *FaceSay* resulted in students with HFA demonstrating improvements in all three areas of the intervention: facial recognition, emotion recognition, and social interaction.
McKissick et al. (2018)	3	Special education classroom	13 yrs. 6 mos.–14 yrs. 11 mos. 2 Male 1 Female	ASD and ID	A computer-assisted instruction package assisted students in learning science terms and their functions.
Pellegrino et al. (2020)	3	Individual student cubicles in a university-based preschool	4–5 years 3 Male	ASD	There was little clinical difference in the number of teaching sessions required to acquire specific receptive labeling skills taught using stimuli delivered via flashcards versus a tablet for two of three participants.

AUTHOR(S)	N	SETTING	AGE/ GENDER	DIAGNOSES	FINDINGS
Van Laarhoven et al. (2018)	4	Faculty conference room in a large high school	15–18 years 3 Males 1 Female	ASD, ID ASD, ADD, bipolar, OCD ID, seizure disorder ASD, ID	Both devices resulted in immediate and substantial increases in independent responding for 3 of the 4 participants. All participants performed better with their preferred device and all self-faded reliance on instructional prompts as skill acquisition increased.

Age and Diagnostic Considerations/ Prerequisite Skills and Abilities

AT can be used by individuals of any age. Prerequisite skills and abilities will depend on the complexity of the aid.

Reported Outcomes

Despite mixed results in some studies (David et al., 2020; Pellecchia et al., 2020; Whalen et al., 2010), AT appears to be gaining support in its use with individuals with ASD. Recent literature reviews (Fletcher-Watson, 2014; Odom et al., 2015) support the use of AT for individuals with ASD addressing a variety of skills such as emotional regulation (Fagea et al., 2019), turn-taking (David et al., 2020), word–object relationships (Lee et al., 2021), sight word recognition (Saadatzi et al., 2018), and vocabulary development (Ganz et al., 2014). Other skills include increased independent performance during job-related tasks (Gentry et al., 2015; Van Laarhoven et al., 2018) and use of science terms and their functions (McKissick et al., 2018). The expanding and varied technology, in conjunction with the broad spectrum of characteristics and learning abilities of students with ASD, may ultimately impact the success of the AT intervention. Odom et al. (2015) suggest that an important key to using AT for students with ASD is matching individualized goals with activities that help them accomplish the goals.

Qualifications Needed

The type and amount of training will depend on the selected AT. Low-tech systems such as graphic organizers, visual schedules, or adapted paper will require little to no formal training. In contrast, high-tech technologies such as iPads, robots, and AI may require training to ensure students are taught to use them correctly. Many school districts employ SLPs and/or OTs who can assist with training and implementation. Teachers, related service personnel, paraprofessionals, families, and employers can implement AT.

How, Where, and When Typically Implemented

AT can be used in almost any setting, including schools, homes, communities, and job sites.

Costs

The cost of AT will depend on the type of technology selected. Low-tech aids may have little to no cost, whereas hi-tech devices could cost several thousand dollars.

Potential Risks

To date, little is known about the risks of using AT. Potential risks could include a strong preference for the device that interferes with engagement in other activities, social stigma, and cyberbulling (Odom et al., 2015).

Rating

   Promising/Emerging Practice

Resources/Recommended Readings

World Health Organization. Assistive Technology: https://www.who.int/health-topics/assistive-technology#tab=tab_1

Picture Exchange Communication System (PECS®)

Description

The PECS® is an alternative augmentative communication (AAC) system, which uses principles of ABA to systematically teach learners how to independently communicate. PECS® is largely based on B. F. Skinner's principles of verbal behavior (VB) (Bondy & Frost, 1994). With the use of specific prompting strategies, reinforcement, and error correction, students learn to use pictures and symbols to communicate functionally in their environment. PECS teaches students to communicate beginning with exchanging a picture for a desired item and advancing to more complex skills such as commenting during a conversation.

PECS was developed by Andy Bondy, PhD, and Lori Frost, MS, CCC-SLP in 1985. The teaching protocol consists of six phases: (1) how to communicate, (2) distance and persistence, (3) picture discrimination, (4) sentence structure, (5) responsive requesting, and (6) commenting. Two instructors are needed during the beginning phases: one to function as the listener and one to function as the prompter to assist the student in learning the system. As a student progresses through each phase, the prompter is faded to focus on the student independently communicating in their environment.

The goal of each phase is outlined below:

1. *How to communicate:* The learner will be prompted to communicate by exchanging one picture of an item for the item itself.

2. *Distance and persistence:* The learner will be able to communicate across multiple people and across different and extended distances.

3. *Picture discrimination:* The learner is using two or more pictures in their communication book to communicate items they want.

4. *Sentence structure:* The learner can construct simple sentences such as "I want the ball."

5. *Responsive requesting:* The learner can respond to the question, "What do you want?"

6. *Commenting:* The learner expands their vocabulary by responding to questions such as "What do you see?" with "I see a blue dog."

Brief Overview of the Literature

The literature base for PECS has been emerging since the 1990s. As of 2008, there were 34 published articles that investigated the use of PECS (Sulzer-Azaroff et al., 2009). Early publications on PECS were predominantly reports or program evaluations, with experimental studies evolving later. In 1993, one of the first reports published shared the effects of training school staff in Peru on PECS, which resulted in increased communication across students who attended the program (Bondy & Frost, 1993). In 1994, Bondy and Frost shared results from a five-year PECS implementation study with 85 children at the Delaware Autistic Program where 95 percent of students learned to use two or more pictures to communicate and 76 percent developed speech as their primary language or were supported by a picture-based system. The majority of the literature on PECS investigates whether it can provide a functional communication system to nonspeaking individuals (Charlop-Christy et al., 2002; Lerna et al., 2012). However, other impacts studied frequently include increased speech as a result of using PECS (Carr & Felce, 2007; Ganz et al., 2008), generalization of language (Dogoe et al., 2010; Greenberg et al., 2012), and changes in behavior as a result of using PECS (Hu & Lee, 2019; Sulzer-Azaroff et al., 2009).

Core Reviews

Simpson et al. (2005) gave PECS the rating of Promising Practice based on nine studies. The NAC gave PECS a rating of Emerging in both 2009 and 2015 based on at least 13 studies (the total number in 2015 was not specified). The NPDC (Wong et al., 2014) gave a rating of EBP in 2014 based on six studies. The NCAEP (Steinbrenner et al., 2020) identified PECS as a Manualized Intervention Meeting Criteria (MIMC) and included it under the broader category of AAC, which was rated as an EBP.

Age and Diagnostic Considerations/ Prerequisite Skills and Abilities

PECS is often used with students with ASD who have little or no spoken language and has been found to be effective for students ages 0 to 18. The only prerequisite required for PECS implementation is identification of reinforcement for students.

Reported Outcomes

The most frequently cited outcome of PECS implementation is increased communication across learners. Other outcome areas include social, joint attention, play, academic, reducing challenging behavior, and motor (NCAEP, Steinbrenner et al., 2020).

Qualifications Needed

Teachers must be appropriately trained in implementing PECS prior to using it with students. Individuals may decide to be trained by Pyramid Educational Consultants, which is the official PECS trainer. However, the majority of teachers receive training through trained researchers or other professionals (McCoy & McNaughton, 2018). Most training is delivered in a professional development format using Behavioral Skills Training consisting of direct instruction, modeling, rehearsal, and feedback.

How, Where, and When Typically Implemented

PECS training can be conducted in any setting (e.g., home, clinical, community) but is typically implemented in classroom settings. PECS is most often implemented for young children with ASD with language support needs or children who have no formal communication system yet. However, it can be implemented at any age or time in a student's life.

Costs

There are several different trainings and levels of certification offered when being trained in PECS. Teachers may have options available at their local school district or may seek some of the options outlined below.

Pyramid Educational Consultants® offer multiple types of PECS training as well as certification. Currently, the training options include: Level 1, Level 2, and Transitioning from PECS to SGDs. These trainings range from single-day to multiple trainings and cost between $219 and $429. The Level 1 training introduces individuals to PECS to gain mastery. The Level 2 training extends learning from Level 1, focusing on promoting communication throughout the day and providing solutions to everyday challenges.

AFIRM modules through UNC Chapel Hill also offer a free online course on PECS. Please note this is not in place of PECS training from Pyramid Educational Consultants. The online module can be accessed at https://afirm.fpg.unc.edu/picture-exchange-communication-system and is three hours long. This learning module covers PECS basics, using PECS, and monitoring PECS.

Potential Risks

There are no documented or obvious risks associated with PECS.

Rating

   Evidence-Based Practice

Resources and Suggested Readings

AFRIM (Autism Focused Intervention Resources & Modules) modules from UNC Chapel Hill are free, self-paced online learning modules that cover a variety of evidence-based practices for students with autism. Currently they offer a module on PECS that provides practitioners with the basis and aides in implementing PECS. It can be accessed at https://afirm.fpg.unc.edu/picture-exchange-communication-system

The Ohio Center for Autism and Low Incidence (OCALI) offers a free online course on PECS®. It can be accessed at https://autisminternetmodules.org/search?qtitle=pecs

Pyramid Educational Consultants® website offers a variety of free and paid resources. Free materials include general information on PECS®, worksheets and checklists, teaching resources, etc. Trainings and consultations can also be found here at https://pecsusa.com/

Social, Emotional, and Behavioral Skills Training

SECTION 4

Introduction

Social, Emotional, and Behavioral Skills Training takes the form of group or individual interventions designed to teach learners ways to appropriately and successfully participate in their home, school, or communities that increase their quality of life. *Social* is the most common term used in the research literature to describe interventions targeting these skills. However we included emotional and behavioral in the title of this section as not all of the skills commonly targeted in students with ASD are social meaning involving other people. Some interventions focus on understanding and regulating emotions such as anger, anxiety, and depression. Some interventions focus on executive functioning skills such as staying on task and improving working memory.

Many individuals with ASD have difficulty developing age-appropriate social, emotional, and/or behavioral skills due to challenges with the social or pragmatic use of language, especially those who would have met the diagnostic criteria for Asperger's syndrome (Faherty, 2000; McAfee, 2002; Moore, 2002; Myles & Adreon, 2001; Myles & Simpson, 2003; Myles & Southwick, 1999; Winner, 2000) which was removed from the American Psychiatric Association's DSM-5 in 2013. The American Speech and Hearing Association provides social communication benchmarks to guide practitioners in identifying potential delays in these skills and their URL is included in Resources and Suggested Readings below.

Core Reviews

Although much of the research on Social, Emotional, and/or Behavioral Skills Training has been done in clinics and via community-based individual sessions and groups, it is educators that are charged with the daily task of providing these interventions. In order to provide some clarity on the evidence base of interventions commonly used by educators, we are combining three intervention categories included in the core reviews in this section as they have considerable overlapping content: (1) Social Skills Training/Package, (2) Social Communication Intervention, and (3) Cognitive Behavioral Instructional Strategies (CBIS).

Social Skills Training/Package

The NAC used the term Social Skills Package and reviewed 16 articles in 2009 giving the category a rating of Emerging and one additional article in 2015 giving the category a rating of Established. The NPDC used the term Social Skills Training and reviewed 15 articles in 2014 and the NCAEP included 56 studies in 2020, both giving a rating of EBP.

Social Communication Intervention

The NAC included Social Communication Intervention as a separate category defined as interventions targeting "some combination of social communication impairments such as pragmatic communication skills, and the inability to successfully read social situations. These treatments may also be referred to as social pragmatic interventions" (NAC, 2009, p. 67). Both the 2009 and 2015 reviews gave Social Communication Intervention an Emerging rating. It is important for educators to note that although the NAC used the term Social Communication Intervention IT only identified five articles (Aldred et al., 2004; Ingersoll et al., 2005; Keen et al., 2007; Loncola & Craig-Unkefer, 2005; Salt et al., 2002) with only one published in the last 15 years and that study (Salt et al., 2002) focused on only preschool subjects. The other four studies had no subjects over the age of 8. However, interventions that target social communication are appropriate to use with all ages, specifically with those who may appear to need minimal support based on their more obvious cognitive functioning but upon deeper assessment have missing or weak skills in the social use of language such as those who would have met the diagnostic criteria for Asperger's which has been previously discussed or who fit the definition of social pragmatic communication disorder (SPCD) as defined by the ASHA. Interventions in these areas are particularly important to maximize the quality of life of individuals in preadolescence to adulthood as the importance of social relationships becomes more developmentally prominent. Therefore, we included the category of CBIS in this section as their research base includes many studies after 2007 on interventions that target social communication skills and involved subjects over the age of 8.

Cognitive Behavioral Instructional Strategies

Simpson et al. (2005) reviewed articles solely on self-management interventions (SMI) under their Cognitive Interventions and Treatments section, which they gave the rating of Promising Practice. All of the reviews conducted by the NAC, NPDC, and NCAEP gave CBIS their highest rating of either Established or EBP with the latest review including 43 studies. It is worth noting that many of the peer reviewed studies included under the CBIS category included subjects with Asperger's or "HFA" and targeted social communication, executive functioning skills, and the common comorbid conditions of anxiety and depression (Reaven et al., 2012; Rodgers et al., 2015; Sofronoff et al., 2005; Sofronoff et al., 2007).

CBIS are "instruction on management or control of cognitive processes that lead to changes in behavioral, social, or academic behavior" (NCAEP, Steinbrenner et al., 2020, p. 28). Learners are taught to examine their own thoughts, perceptions, emotions, and beliefs and then use strategies to change their thinking, self-awareness, and ultimately their behavior. These interventions include several commonly used strategies: (1) describing emotions and physical responses to emotions, (2) cognitive restructuring in which the teacher helps the learner modify cognitive distortions such as "all or nothing" or "catastrophizing" thinking, and (3) development of a visual scale to identify levels of anxiety and distress. (NAC, 2015).

Intervention or instructional strategies that fall within the cognitive domain actively involve the learner in the process of managing their own behavior thus shifting the focus of control from the educator to the individual themselves. Individuals are assisted in developing coping skills so they can learn to alter their own thinking, problematic emotions, and behavior through activities done both during and outside of sessions. Cognitive methods generally assume that when individuals are actively involved in their own treatment long term, generalized and sustainable outcomes are most likely to occur. Many CBT-based social skills interventions have been evaluated for children with ASD (Bauminger, 2002, 2007a, 2007b; Crooke et al., 2008; Laugeson et al., 2012; Lopata et al., 2006; Lopata, et al., 2020; Wood et al., 2009) regarding the influence of teaching emotion recognition, interpretation, social problem-solving on behavior, and the relationship of social problem-solving to later social adjustment (Koning et al., 2011).

Cognitive approaches are not appropriate for every person with ASD. These methods require that students have the capacity for self-understanding and are internally motivated to behave and perform in accordance with accepted expectations. Thus, these strategies are often most effective with learners with the cognitive and language skills needed for engaging in these interventions and who are motivated for internal, as opposed to external, controls such as individuals who resist interventions highly directed by others. CBIS are often used with other interventions such as visual supports, modeling, prompting, reinforcement, and social narratives. They have been implemented by educators, parents, and peers with the guidance of mental health professionals trained in cognitive behavioral approaches.

Interventions Included in This Section

We divided the interventions included in this section into two sub-categories: (1) Skills Training Interventions (STI) and (2) CBIS. STI are those that do not have a significant cognitive component but rather follow a more traditional lesson plan format that minimally includes explicit instruction on the steps of the targeted skill, modeling, rehearsal or practice, and feedback and may include rationale for the skill and discrimination of examples and non-examples. CBIS are more than teaching "skills" because they focus on the meta-cognitive processes of thinking and problem-solving about why and how we interact with others in different situations; that we need to be paying attention to other people's behavior and adjust our behavior accordingly; while also thinking about how others' feeling are affected by our behavior. The emphasis is on making abstract concepts more concrete by breaking them down into manageable portions, followed by interpretation of the meaning of each component, and finally reintegration of all relevant sources of information into a meaningful entity.

Skills Training Intervention

- Behavioral Skills Training (BST)
- Teaching Interaction Procedure (TIP)
- Video Modeling (VM)
- Cool Versus Not Cool
- The Program for Education and Enrichment of Relationship Skills (PEERS®) (MIMC)

Cognitive Behavioral Intervention Strategies

- Theory of Mind (ToM) Training
- Social Decision-Making Strategies
- Cartooning

(Continued)

(Continued)

- Self-Management

- The Coping Cat Program

- Mindfulness-Based Interventions

- Social Thinking™

- The Zones of Regulation™)

- The Incredible Five Point Scale

- Social Narratives/Story-Based Interventions (*Includes MIMC Social Stories*™

- FaceSay™ (MIMC)

- Mindreading: The Interactive Guide to Emotions

Resources and Suggested Readings

American Speech-Language-Hearing Association. (n.d.). *Social communication benchmarks.* https://www.asha.org/practice-portal/clinical-topics/social-communication-disorder/social-communication-benchmarks/

Brock, M. E. (2013). *Cognitive behavioral intervention (CBI) fact sheet.* The University of North Carolina, Frank Porter Graham Child Development Institute, The National Professional Development Center on Autism Spectrum Disorders.

Collet-Klingenberg, L. (2009). *Overview of social skills groups.* University of Wisconsin, Waisman Center, The National Professional Development Center on Autism Spectrum Disorders.

Fettig, A. (2013). *Social skills training (SST) fact sheet.* The University of North Carolina, Frank Porter Graham Child Development Institute, The National Professional Development Center on Autism Spectrum Disorders.

Mayer, M. J., Acker, R. V., Lockman, J. E., & Gresham, F. M. (2009). *Cognitive-behavioral interventions for emotional and behavioral disorders: School-based practice.* Guilford Press.

Suhrheinrich, J., Chan, J., Melgarejo, M. Reith, S., Stahmer, A., & AFIRM Team. (2018). *Cognitive Behavioral Intervention.* National Professional Development Center on Autism Spectrum Disorder, FPG Child Development Center, University of North Carolina. https://afirm.fpg.unc.edu/cognitive-behavioral-intervention

Suhrheinrich, J., Chan, J., Melgarejo, M., Reith, S., Stahmer, A., & AFIRM Team. (2018). *Social Skills Training.* National Professional Development Center on Autism Spectrum Disorder, FPG Child Development Center, University of North Carolina. https://afirm.fpg.unc.edu/social-skills-training

Behavioral Skills Training (BST)

Description

Four components define Behavioral Skills Training (BST): (1) instruction, (2) modeling, (3) rehearsal, and (4) feedback (Miltenberger, 2012). Instruction involves providing the learner with a written and/or verbal outline of the relevant components of the skill. The teacher then models the skill live or using video modeling (VM). During rehearsal, the learner practices the skill by role playing in a contrived situation or in a naturalistic setting and is provided feedback by the teacher regarding the accuracy of their performance, the final component of the intervention. If the student correctly demonstrated the skill being targeted, they are reinforced, and if they did not, they get additional instruction and practice until they meet the set mastery criteria.

Brief Overview of the Literature

The four components of BST have been used within various social skills training programs with various student populations (Bornstein et al., 1977; Brady, 1984; Turner et al., 1978; Whitehill et al., 1980) before they were defined by Breidenbach (1984) as Behavioral Skills Training. The four components of BST were first used to teach children with ASD social skills in a study by Taras et al. in 1988.

Core Reviews

None of the core reviews included Behavioral Skills Training as a reviewed intervention. However, the NPDC (Wong et al., 2014) included one article in 2014 with Behavioral Skills Training in the title under Naturalistic Interventions (Seiverling et al., 2010), which was rated an EBP. In 2020, the NCAEP (Steinbrenner et al., 2020) included four articles with Behavioral Skills Training in the title. There was one under Naturalistic Interventions (Gianoumis et al., 2012), one under Social Skills Training (Ryan et al., 2017), one under VM (Ledbetter-Cho et al., 2016), and one under Extinction (Seiverling et al., 2012), which were all rated EBPs.

Other Systematic Reviews/Meta-Analyses

Leaf et al. (2015) conducted a systematic review of the peer-reviewed research literature published between 1960 and 2013 that had at least one subject with an official diagnosis or characteristics of autistic disorder, ASD, Asperger's syndrome, PDD-NOS, or Retts disorder. They identified six articles and concluded that three were effective at teaching the targeted skill (Burke et al., 2010; Gunby et al., 2010; Nuernberger et al., 2013), one was somewhat effective (Taras et al., 1988), and two were ineffective (Kornacki et al., 2013; Palmen & Diden, 2012).

Age and Diagnostic Considerations/ Prerequisite Skills and Abilities

Currently, Behavioral Skills Training has mostly been studied with adolescents or adults with ASD who have mild support needs but could be more widely applicable for learners with ASD across the entire spectrum.

Reported Outcomes

Behavioral Skills Training has been used to teach a wide variety of skills, including job skills, conversational skills, and abduction prevention. It has the potential of being effective for teaching a wide variety of skills across all domains.

Qualifications Needed

No formal training in Behavioral Skills Training is needed. The components are simple, easy to understand, and are similar to how teachers have traditionally structured lesson plans.

How, Where, and When Typically Implemented

Behavioral Skills Training can be implemented in any setting (e.g., clinical, community, home, and school settings). It can serve as a stand-alone intervention, often involves VM, or could be combined with other interventions such as Visual Supports.

Costs

Behavioral Skills Training is cost-effective in terms of time and other resources. There are no costs associated with training, no additional teaching time is required and no materials need to be purchased other than those typically found in natural settings.

Potential Risks

There are no documented or obvious risks associated with Behavioral Skills Training.

Practitioner Testimonial(s)

I started using Behavior Skills Training (BST) while training staff on the components of a BIP for a student. I created a fidelity checklist that had the skill we were teaching broken down into steps (like a task analysis). I used the fidelity checklist for staff to review as instruction was given on the steps to the procedure. The teacher and I modeled the procedure with one of us acting as the student and the other acting as the teacher. We then had two staff people rehearse the procedure while any staff not rehearsing reviewed the fidelity checklist to ensure all the steps were being followed. All staff being trained gave feedback based on the fidelity checklist and skills were rehearsed again as necessary. Staff commented on how valuable it was to practice the procedure before implementing it. As a result, staff were able to implement with much more fidelity than receiving instructions alone. The teacher saw the value in BST and is using the BST model to train staff in her classroom.

—Mary Ellen Hodge

Rating

 Promising/Emerging Practice

Resources and Suggested Readings

How to ABA: The BX Resource. (2021). *What is behavioral skills training (BST)?* https://howtoaba.com/behavioural-skills-training/

Kansas Technical Assistance System Network (TASN). (2022). *Behavior skills training.* https://www.ksdetasn.org/resources/2966

Kansas Technical Assistance System Network (TASN). (2021). *Behavior skills training planning form.* https://www.ksdetasn.org/resources/2721

Navigating Behavior Change. (nd). *Behavior skills training: Your model for teaching ANY SKILL!* https://www.navigatingbehaviorchange.com/blog/behavior-skills-training-your-model-for-teaching-any-skill

The Teaching Interaction Procedure (TIP)

Description

The TIP is made up of six critical components: (1) identifying the skill to be taught, (2) providing a rationale as to why the student should learn the skill that is meaningful to them based on their experiences, (3) breaking the skill into steps and having the learner verbally state them, (4) providing an example and non-example via teacher demonstration with the learner correctly identifying which is which and why, (5) role playing the skill until the learner exhibits 100% of the steps correctly, and (6) positive reinforcement for correctly responding and corrective feedback for incorrect responding. Leaf et al. (2015) made two distinctions between Behavioral Skills Training (BST) and the TIP. The TIP always includes a meaningful rationale regarding why the student should demonstrate the skill targeted in their daily life and both an example and non-example of the targeted skill while BST does not always include either the rationale or the non-example.

Core Reviews

None of the core reviews included TIP. However the NCAEP (Steinbrenner et al., 2020) included four articles with TIP in their titles under Social Skills Training (Hui Shyuan et al., 2016; Kassardjian et al., 2014; Leaf et al., 2012; Peters et al., 2016), which was given the rating of EBP.

Other Systematic Reviews/Meta-Analyses

Leaf et al. (2015) conducted a systematic review of the peer-reviewed research literature published between 1960 and 2013 that had at least one subject that had an official diagnosis or characteristics of autistic disorder, ASD, Asperger's syndrome, PDD-NOS, or Retts Disorder. They identified eight articles and concluded that six were effective at teaching the targeted skill (Dotson et al., 2013; Kassardjian et al., 2013; Leaf et al., 2009; Leaf et al., 2010; Leaf, Oppenheim-Leaf et al., 2012; Leaf, Tsuji et al., 2012; Oppenheim-Leaf, Leaf, Call et al., 2012a; Oppenheim-Leaf, Leaf, Dozier et al., 2012b), one was somewhat effective (Ferguson et al., 2013), and one was ineffective (Dotson et al., 2010).

Age and Diagnostic Considerations/ Prerequisite Skills and Abilities

The TIP has been studied primarily with students in early elementary school who are "higher functioning" but could be more widely applicable for learners with ASD with mild support needs to more severe forms of autism.

Reported Outcomes

The TIP has been effective in teaching a variety of social skills including sportsmanship, playing board games, and social play. It has the potential of being effective for teaching a wide variety of skills across all domains.

Qualifications Needed

No formal training in the TIP is needed. The components are simple, easy to understand, and are similar to how teachers have traditionally structured lesson plans.

How, Where, and When Typically Implemented

The TIP can be implemented in any setting (e.g., clinical, community, home, and school settings). It can serve as a stand-alone intervention or could be combined with other interventions or teaching principles such as Cool versus Not Cool or Visual Supports.

Costs

The TIP is cost-effective in terms of time and other resources. There are no costs associated with training, no additional teaching time is required, and no materials need to be purchased other than those typically found in natural settings.

Potential Risks

There are no documented or obvious risks associated with the TIP.

Rating

 Promising/Emerging Practice

Resources and Suggested Readings

Learning Ready Behavior Services. (2021). *What is a teaching interaction procedure?* https://learningready.com.au/blog/f/what-is-a-teaching-interaction-procedure

SW/WC Service Cooperative. *Teaching interaction procedure.* https://www.swsc.org/cms/lib/MN01000693/Centricity/Domain/130/Marissa-Teaching Protocol for Teaching Interaction Procedure.pdf

Video Modeling (VM)

Description

VM is an intervention in which the student with ASD watches a video demonstrating a target skill, behavior, or task and then has the opportunity to imitate the same skill, behavior, or task. VM is based on Albert Bandura's social learning theory that individuals can learn by watching and imitating the behavior of another person (Bandura, 1969). The type of VM depends on how the video is filmed and who is featured in the video as the person demonstrating the skill. See below for descriptions of the different types of VM. In addition, a variety of technological devices can be used to film and edit the videos. Students with ASD can watch the videos on handheld devices (e.g., smartphones or tablets) or laptop or desktop computers. VM is commonly used with other interventions and strategies, such as visual supports, self-monitoring, prompting, and reinforcement. VM can also be used as part of an intervention package.

Different Types of Video Modeling

Traditional VM: Another person different from the student with ASD serves as a model and is filmed performing the task in its entirety. The person can be a peer, paraprofessional, teacher, or any other person who can perform the task. The student watches the video and then performs the task after viewing the video.

Video Prompting: The student watches one step of the task at a time and then performs that step. Short videos can be filmed for each step, or the student can pause a full video after viewing each step.

Video Self-Modeling: The student is filmed performing the task and then watches the video with themselves serving as the model. If the student cannot perform the task in its entirety, then the student can perform individual steps and then the video clips can be edited together to form one full video.

Video Feedback: The student is filmed performing the task and then watches the video and receives feedback on their performance. The person giving feedback can be a job coach, parent, paraprofessional, teacher, or any other instructor. The student could also watch a traditional video model before performing the task if needed.

Point-of-View: Only the necessary information and images are filmed for the student to watch and perform the task. For example, a point-of-view video of making a sandwich may include only images of hands moving to use the necessary items to perform the task (e.g., bread, knife, peanut butter, jelly to make a sandwich).

Brief Overview of the Literature

Effects of VM have also been examined for specific outcome areas. For example, Qi et al. (2018) conducted a systematic review to examine VM to teach social and communication skills to students with ASD. Twenty-four articles met inclusion criteria for the review, and 18 of those articles met *What Works Clearinghouse* design standards with or without reservations. Results indicated VM was effective for increasing social and communication skills of students with ASD and that VM can be considered an EBP according to the *What Works Clearinghouse* single-case research design standards (Qi et al., 2018). Similarly, Fragale (2014) conducted a systematic literature review to examine the effects of VM on teaching play skills to children with ASD. The average age of children included in the review was 6 years old (range 2.5 to 15 years of age). Of the 22 studies included, 12 studies focused on teaching solitary play skills and 10 studies focused on teaching social play skills with other children. VM was effective for 82% of participants and specifically increased their play actions and vocalizations (Fragale, 2014).

There are several VM studies implemented by teachers in school settings for younger and older learners. For example, Yakubova et al. (2016) used point-of-view VM to teach addition, subtraction, and number comparison skills for four elementary students with ASD (ages 5 to 6 years). The students received instruction at a private educational center that served students with ASD. The videos used point-of-view clips demonstrating hands of an adult model demonstrating the use of manipulatives and a worksheet. Results indicated all students improved in their mathematical skills but individual differences were present. For older learners, Ledoux Galligan et al. (2022) taught three educators how to use VM with three high school students with ASD to meet their individualized social goals. The educators chose the type of VM (e.g., self-modeling, traditional VM with a peer serving as the model), according to students' needs and technology available in the classroom. Social skills targeted in the videos included shaking hands, interjecting appropriately, and asking for help. Results indicated all students met their goals and demonstrated increases in the target behavior from baseline to intervention.

Core Reviews

The NAC described VM within the Modeling category and gave the rating of Established in both of their reports based on more than 50 studies. The NPDC (Wong et al., 2014) and NCAEP (Steinbrenner et al., 2020) both used the term VM and gave the rating of EBP based on more than 60 studies.

Age and Diagnostic Considerations/ Prerequisite Skills and Abilities

The NCAEP (2020) review indicates there is sufficient research supporting the efficacy of VM for learners with ASD ages 0 to 22. Some research indicates imitation skills should be considered a prerequisite for children with ASD to use VM (Rayner et al., 2009) because they watch the video and then imitate the skill demonstrated in the video. However, other research indicates children with ASD can learn imitation skills through VM (Rayner et al., 2009). Regardless of the learner's imitation skill level, the learner does need to demonstrate the ability to attend to the video. A learner can watch the video multiple times and engage with the video in different ways according to their preferences and learning needs.

Reported Outcomes

VM can be used to teach a variety of outcome areas including academic, adaptive/ self-help, cognitive, communication, joint attention, motor, play, school readiness, and vocational (NCAEP, Steinbrenner et al., 2020).

Qualifications Needed

The person implementing the VM intervention should have some knowledge of the student with ASD to select the target skill. The person will most likely be a special education teacher but could also be a parent, general education teacher, job coach, counselor, SLP, or other member of the student's Individual Education Program (IEP) team. The person should have knowledge regarding the different types of technology to film, edit, and play back videos. However, the person does not need to have advanced videography skills as the videos should be simple and straightforward. The person should have knowledge regarding how to provide error correction and feedback to the student as needed.

How, Where, and When Typically Implemented

VM can be implemented in clinical, community, home, and school settings. Prior to filming the video, the person should obtain consent from the student's parent or guardian to film the student if the student will be featured in the video. The student with ASD typically watches the video *before* performing the target skill as an antecedent strategy. However, the student can choose to engage with the video in different ways according to their learning needs. Teachers can also adapt the VM intervention as needed. For example, a student may pause after each step of a traditional VM to perform the discrete steps, which becomes video prompting. Where the student watches the video depends on the target skills. For instance, a student may watch a video focused on teaching social initiations immediately before recess and then join their same-age peers on the playground.

Costs

Costs of a VM intervention depends on the type of technology used to film, edit, and view the videos. The cost also depends if the teacher or other person making the video already has access to this technology. For example, many people have smartphones and tablets that can be used for filming purposes at no extra cost. The majority of editing programs available on smartphones and tablets are free. Librarians and other staff in school settings may also be able to assist with access to technology. It is not necessary to purchase new devices for purposes of implementing a VM intervention. However, access to technology is required.

Potential Risks

One potential risk to VM relates to video self-monitoring and if the child is filmed in the video. If a child under the age of 17 is filmed in a video, their parent or guardian should provide consent before a teacher or other professional films the child. In addition, the child should provide assent to indicate they feel comfortable being filmed. Videos should not be distributed on social media or other public platforms. Rather, the teacher should keep videos stored on a confidential platform and device and use for instructional purposes only.

Example devices that can be used to film videos:

iPhones

iPads

Video camcorders

Zoom

Example software and other platforms that can be used to edit videos:

Apple iMovie Maker

Lumen5

Nero Video

OpenShot

Example devices that can be used to watch videos:

iPhone

iPad

iPod

Laptop computer

Desktop computer

Rating

   Evidence-Based Practice

Resources and Suggested Readings

Cox, A., & AFIRM Team. (2018). *Video modeling.* National Professional Development Center on Autism Spectrum Disorder, FPG Child Development Center, University of North Carolina. http://afirm.fpg.unc.edu/video-modeling

Kellems, R. (2020). *Video modeling implementation guide for educators.* Texas Education Agency. https://www.texastransition.org/upload/page/0245/docs/Video Modeling Promption ImplementationGuide2020Final.pdf

Model Me Kids®. Videos for modeling social skills. https://www.modelmekids.com/video-modeling.html

National Autism Center. *National Autism Center free digital publications.* https://www.national autismcenter.org/resources/

The Ohio Center for Autism and Low Incidence (OCALI) offers a free online webinar on Video Modeling. https://autisminternetmodules.org/search?qtitle=video+modeling

Cool Versus Not Cool

Description

Cool Versus Not Cool is a procedure for teaching social communication skills to students with ASD. Specifically, students are taught to discriminate between "cool" (appropriate) social behaviors and "not cool" (inappropriate) social behaviors. In the research, steps for the Cool Versus Not Cool procedure varied slightly. Some of the most common steps include the following:

1. Teacher labels the skill to be practiced.

2. Teacher performs several randomized trials of the behavior shown correctly (cool) and incorrectly (not cool).

3. Student(s) indicates whether the modeled behavior is "cool" (appropriate) or "not cool" (inappropriate).

4. Teacher provides feedback regarding student(s)' response.

5. Student(s) explain why the behavior is "cool" or "not cool."

6. Student(s) are provided the opportunity to role-play the social behavior with the second teacher.

7. Teacher asks student(s) if the skill was role-played as "cool" or "not cool."

8. Teacher provides feedback on the student(s)' demonstration of the social behavior.

9. Student(s) continue with the role-play until the steps of the skill are demonstrated correctly (Cihon et al., 2022; Leaf et al., 2012; Leaf et al., 2015).

Brief Overview of the Literature

Cool Versus Not Cool first appears in the peer-reviewed literature about 10 years before the publication of this resource (Leaf et al., 2012) followed by several peer reviewed studies involving the same author (Au et al., 2016; Cihon et al., 2021; Leaf et al., 2015; Leaf, Leaf et al., 2016; Leaf, Taubman et al., 2016).

Core Reviews

Cool Versus Not Cool was not included in any of the core reviews. It was included in this resource because it is increasingly being used by many professionals in the educational setting, including general and special educators, OTs, SLPs, school psychologists, and counselors.

Other Peer-Reviewed Research

The author of this text identified six peer-reviewed studies on Cool Versus Not Cool, which are summarized here.

AUTHOR(S)	N	SETTING	AGE/ GENDER	DIAGNOSES	TARGET SKILLS	OUTCOMES/ FINDINGS
Au et al. (2016)	2	Private behavioral agency	2 males Ages 3–6 yrs.	Autistic disorder	Initiation of game play with a peer, commenting on an item shown to them by a peer, gaining peer attention	Both participants met mastery criterion on 67% of target skills with the Cool Versus Not Cool procedure with teacher demonstration only. Participants were able to meet criteria on the remaining 33% of skills when feedback was added to the intervention.
Cihon et al. (2021)	3	Setting depended on the child (home, private clinic)	3 Males Ages 4–5 yrs.	ASD	Changing a conversation when someone looks bored	The Cool Versus Not Cool procedure was delivered via Zoom conference sessions with one adult in the same setting as the child. All 3 children reached the mastery criterion.
Leaf et al. (2012)	3	Private behavioral agency	3 males Ages 4–8 yrs.	Autistic disorder	Interrupting, changing the game, appropriate greetings, interrupting, joint attention, changing the conversation, abduction prevention, eye contact	50% of social skills met criteria when only teacher demonstration was used. An additional 37.5% of the social skills met criteria when opportunities for role-playing were added to the procedure.

(Continued)

(Continued)

AUTHOR(S)	N	SETTING	AGE/ GENDER	DIAGNOSES	TARGET SKILLS	OUTCOMES/ FINDINGS
Leaf et al. (2015)	3	Private behavioral agency	1 Male 2 Female Ages 3–7 yrs.	Autistic disorder	Compromise on which game to play with a peer, sharing a snack, being assertive when a peer takes a play item without asking	All 3 children met mastery criterion and displayed 100% of steps of the target skill throughout maintenance.
Leaf, Leaf, et al. (2016)	8	Private behavioral agency	7 males 1 female Ages 3–5 yrs.	ASD	Steps in 3 different games	7 of 8 participants met mastery criteria for the sleeping game and fruit salad game. All 8 students reached mastery criteria for the mouse trap game; however, 3 students performed at least 1 step of the game correctly during baseline and another student reached mastery criterion during the baseline condition. Data indicated that it required a range of 3 to 13 sessions to perform the steps in the games correctly.
Leaf, Taubman, et al. (2016)	3	Private behavioral agency	2 males 1 female Ages 3–6 yrs.	Autistic disorder	Providing verbal support to a friend, chatting, interrupting a conversation appropriately	All 3 children reached mastery criterion on the steps of their selected skill, although 2 students required "booster sessions" to ensure continued performance during maintenance.

Age and Diagnostic Considerations/ Prerequisite Skills and Abilities

The Cool Versus Not Cool procedure appears to be applicable to students of varying ages, but, the studies conducted focused on children between 3 and 8 years of age. Additionally, children in the studies were reported to have full scale IQ scores between 80 and 127.

Reported Outcomes

Cool Versus Not Cool has been used to teach a variety of social communication skills such as providing verbal support to a peer, chatting (making comments about a YouTube video), interrupting a conversation appropriately compromising in the selection of a game, sharing snacks, being assertive when a toy is taken without asking (Leaf et al., 2015), and initiation of game play with a peer, commenting on an item shown to them by a peer, and gaining a peer's attention (Au et al., 2016; Leaf et al., 2015; Leaf, Leaf et al., 2016; Leaf, Taubman et al., 2016). Other skills taught using this strategy include changing a game when a peer looks bored, making appropriate greetings, making eye contact, establishing joint attention (Leaf et al., 2012), and changing the conversation when someone is bored (Cihon et al., 2021). Although not mentioned in the research, other skills that may increase the effectiveness of the intervention could include social awareness of others in the environment, ability to follow directions (visual or verbal), imitating actions and verbalizations, sustained attention, and an understanding of negation.

Qualifications Needed

No formal training qualifications were documented in the research. However, knowledge of the procedure and basic behavioral skills such as how to give positive and corrective feedback, an understanding of the functions of behavior to not inadvertently reinforce problem behaviors, and the ability to establish attending behavior is needed.

How, Where, and When Typically Implemented

The number of sessions required for students to reach the mastery criterion ranged from approximately 4 to 21 sessions with session duration ranging from approximately 7 to 30 minutes. Finally, the intervention can be implemented in a one-on-one or small group format.

Costs

The cost of the Cool Versus Not Cool procedure will depend on the setting in which the services are provided. If services are provided in a school setting, no cost should be incurred. If the program is provided by a private therapist, social worker, or psychologist, the cost will align with their fee schedule.

Potential Risks

There are no documented or obvious risks associated with Cool Versus Not Cool.

Practitioner Testimonial(s)

I started using the Cool Versus Not Cool intervention with my secondary students. Finding ways to get older students engaged in social skills is difficult. They are beyond cute characters and often will not allow themselves to be vulnerable. However, I have found that they respond well to social autopsies followed by a Cool Versus Not Cool discussion. The verbage is more like their slang and they often don't realize they are getting social skills instruction when I use this wording. Another great piece of this is that older kids love to tell you what you did wrong! Looking through both the cool and not cool lens draws them in and they become more engaged. One of my favorite ways to break this down is finding TikToks or quick YouTube videos and have students identify what was not cool and how it should have been handled differently to make it cool. These media components are already part of their social media platform so are relevant to them.

—Kelli Heller

Rating

🙂   Promising/Emerging Practice

Resources/Recommended Readings

Autism Partnership Cool Not Cool. https://howtoaba.com/wp-content/uploads/2019/08/Cool-Not-Cool.pdf.

The Program for the Education and Enrichment of Relational Skills (PEERS®)

Description

The Program for the Education and Enrichment of Relational Skills (PEERS®) is a social skills intervention developed by Dr. Elizabeth Laugenson at the University of California in Los Angeles. The core intervention involves small-group concrete instructional lessons, role-play demonstration, behavioral rehearsal, and generalization assignments outside the sessions. The preschool intervention also includes puppet shows. Parents, caregivers, or social coaches of the participants are required to attend separate sessions where they learn how to assist their learner to generalize the skills to various settings. PEERS also offers separate courses for assistance with social skills involved in successful careers, dating relationships, communicating effectively, making friends, and handling bullying.

Brief Overview of the Literature

The PEERS website lists 53 peer-reviewed research studies conducted on the intervention with live links to the actual articles (semel.ucla.edu). The earliest study was published in 2009 on a parent-assisted version to improve the friendships of teenagers (Laugeson et al., 2009). The majority of evidence from randomized control trials (RCTs) has taken place in controlled environments, so there is a need for research of implementation within the community setting. A pilot study conducted in 2017 explored the effects of PEERS on the social skills and anxiety of five adolescents with ASD in a community setting (Hill et al., 2017). Hill et al. (2017) extended upon findings from Schohl et al. (2014) relative to the decrease in social anxiety. However, this study utilized a more complex measure allowing for other types of anxiety to be evaluated. The most recent study investigated the effects of a parent-mediated model of the PEERS program on preschoolers (Tripathi et al., 2022), premised on literature highlighting the integral role of parents in the social rehearsal and network development of those with autism in early childhood. Parents reported outcomes 1 to 5 years following treatment.

Core Reviews

The NCAEP (Steinbrenner et al., 2020) included PEERS as an MIMC in 2020. Although they did not specify how many articles were reviewed or give a specific rating in the body of the document, six articles with PEERS in the title were included in the references (Laugeson et al., 2014; Laugeson & Frankel, 2010; McVey et al., 2016; Schiltz et al., 2017; Schohl et al., 2014; Yoo et al., 2014). The other four core reviews did not include PEERS as a reviewed intervention.

Age and Diagnostic Considerations/ Prerequisite Skills and Abilities

Of the 53 peer-reviewed research articles listed on the PEERS website, 41 of the articles involved adolescents, 10 involved young adults, and two involved preschoolers— all with ASD. Therefore, implementation of the PEERS for adolescents and young adults is clearly supported in the literature. As the fidelity of the parent-mediated model of PEERS continues to improve, the implementation with children is growing. Although the prerequisites were not stated overtly, Hill et al. (2017) addressed that when implementing in the community-based program, the team questioned if participants would follow through with the "homework" necessary to benefit from the program. Therefore, it should be noted that a responsiveness to cognitive-behavioral methods and ability to engage in the intervention components beyond the structured sessions is imperative for effectiveness. The PEERS program also involves the family, thus a consistent support system is crucial.

Reported Outcomes

Reported outcomes of previous studies include improvements in general social skills, assertion, cooperation, and responsibility within the social setting. Improvements in the community-based setting were reported by Hill et al. (2017) for social engagement, cognition, communication, and motivation. Participants demonstrated increased knowledge of specific PEERS skills and concepts as well as improved internalizing behavior and autistic symptoms. Therefore, authors support the effectiveness of the PEERS program in community-based settings. Perhaps even more meaningful are the reported increase in "get-together" invites and hostings. These findings reinforce those of Laugeson et al. (2009) and Schohl et al. (2014). Continued research on the PEERS effect on anxiety is warranted as there is no significance present in the data. However four of the five participants in the community-based pilot study (Hill et al., 2017) presented decreased scores of social and separation anxiety. Panic symptoms and school avoidance reduced in two of these four and one participant presented lower generalized anxiety. Authors noted that one participant presented increased anxiety from pre-to posttest but no causation was implied. Overall, families indicated high satisfaction with the PEERS program. In this connection, the 2022 publication of a parent-mediated model of PEERS for preschoolers indicate maintained treatment gains in the areas of social communication, responsiveness, motivation, and peer engagement over a 1-to-5-year follow-up (Tripathi et al., 2022). Areas that did not sustain the outcomes included problem behaviors and the subsequent parent stress.

Qualifications Needed

Given that the majority of the studies conducted on the efficacy of PEERS have been held in university-based clinical settings, the facilitators have been primarily students in higher education (undergraduate, masters and doctoral candidates), postdoctoral fellows, and licensed clinical psychologists with concentrated training (some by PEERS-certified trainers) on the procedures, scripts, and otherwise. That being said, the program is premised on empowering the participants, individual with autism and their parents, with tools to extend their application across settings with sustainable practices among social situations.

How, Where, and When Typically Implemented

The PEERS is what they term a "manualized treatment" that provides the facilitators with structured session plans to include scripts and suggested wordings and guidelines. The program is 14-weeks long and utilizes parent-mediated components to include individual sessions for parents and child or adolescent as well as homework to be completed by all participants, parents included. It is through these homework practices that the social competence is built and generalized for sustainable outcomes.

Costs

The cost of implementation for PEERS is dependent upon available certified which between such and are trainers. School-based certified trainings, teleconferences, off-site trainings, and such which are provided through the UCLA PEERS Clinic.

Potential Risks

There are no documented or obvious risks associated with PEERS.

Rating

  Promising/Emerging Practice

Resources and Suggested Readings

Nebraska Autism Spectrum Disorders Network. (2018). *PEERS® Part 1: An overview of the program for the education and enrichment of relational skills.* https://www.unl.edu/asdnetwork/overview-program-education-and-enrichment-relational-skills-peers®-part-1

Nebraska Autism Spectrum Disorders Network. (2018). *PEERS® Part 2: Strategies for handling teaching/bullying.* https://www.unl.edu/asdnetwork/peers®-part-2-strategies-handling-teasingbullying

Nebraska Autism Spectrum Disorders Network. (2020). *Getting started with peers for adolescents: Social skills training for adolescents with autism spectrum disorder.* https://www.unl.edu/asdnetwork/getting-started-peers-adolescents-social-skills-training-adolescents-autism-spectrum-disorder

Nebraska Autism Spectrum Disorders Network. (2020). *Getting started with peers for adults: Social skills training for adults with autism spectrum disorder.*https://www.unl.edu/asdnetwork/getting-started-peers-adults-social-skills-training-adults-autism-spectrum-disorder

UCLA PEERS Clinic. https://www.semel.ucla.edu/peers

Theory of Mind (ToM) Interventions

Description

The NAC defined ToM Interventions as designed "to teach individuals with ASD to recognize and identify mental states (i.e., a person's thoughts, beliefs, intentions, desires and emotions) in oneself or in others and to be able to take the perspective of another person in order to predict their actions" (NAC, 2009, p. 69). ToM Interventions are a type of social cognitive behavioral training that is focused on skills specifically related to ToM skills such as "recognition and assessment of feelings of others; assessment of the context in which particular information can be provided or not; assessment of how others think about oneself; recognition and understanding of the motives and intentions underlying the behaviour of others and understanding of deception and humour" (Steerneman et al., 1996, p. 253). A foundational skill that is needed to develop other ToM skills is recognizing cognitive activities such as desires and beliefs that underly intentional behavior (Wellman, 1990). There are both "first-order" and "second-order" dimensions to belief. First-order belief refers to recognizing that an individual knows something because they observed that it happened, which typically develops around age 4. Second-order belief refers to an individual's capacity to think about thinking, which typically develops around age 6.

The understanding of false beliefs also develops around the age of 4, which has the central feature of deception (Steerneman et al., 1996). In a false belief situation, one individual has access to specific information that another individual does not, the person having being "deceived." This results in the "deceived" person having an inaccurate view of the situation that is different than the person having all of the needed information. In the early 1980s, "false belief" tests were developed where a child was given a hypothetical scenario and was asked to explain the behavior of an ignorant story character (Wellman et al., 2001). An example is the Sally/Anne false belief task (Baron-Cohen et al., 1985), a scenario in which a character named Sally puts her ball in a box and then leaves the room. While she is away and can't see, another character, Anne, moves the ball from the box to a basket. The child is asked where Sally will look for her ball when she returns. Most children with ASD with a mental age in other measures greater than 4 fail this test while comparison groups of the same age with Down's syndrome, general developmental delay, or specific language delays pass them (Perner et al., 1989). These were later adapted to include more complex scenarios that required the learner to use second order beliefs to reason about mental states such as what one person thinks about another person's thoughts (White et al., 2009).

As demonstrated by false belief tests and other measures of ToM skills, individuals with ASD have difficulty understanding mental states and their effects on behavior (Baron-Cohen, 1995; Baron-Cohen et al., 1985). There has been a variety of teaching procedures used to teach ToM skills researched with the ASD population such as picture-in-the-head teaching (Swettenham, 1996), thought-bubble training (Wellman et al., 2002), social cognition training (Gevers et al., 2006; Steerneman et al., 1996; Turner-Brown et al., 2008), and mind reading (Golan & Baron-Cohen, 2006). What constitutes something as a ToM intervention is that it focuses the student "on the internal, subjective mental representations of themselves and those around them" (Begeer et al., 2011, p. 998).

Brief Overview of the Literature

The term ToM was first used by Premack and Woodruff (1978) to refer to the ability to ascribe thoughts, feeling, ideas, and intentions to others and to use this knowledge to predict their behavior. In the 1990s, Steerneman and colleagues developed a social cognitive training program that attempted to teach ToM skills to learners with ASD and pervasive developmental disorder from ages 4 to 12 as an alternative to behaviorally based social skills programs that often had positive short-term effects but lacked evidence of long-term benefits (Steerneman et al., 1996). Initial activities in the program focused on perception and imitation skills such as describing yourself and getting to know others. This was followed by recognizing emotions and finally ToM skills such as recognizing the difference between fantasy and reality, assessing social situations, recognizing intentions in others, developing self-related ideas, pretense, understanding the thoughts and feelings of others, the use of imagination, and understanding humor. Activities include, but are not limited to, things such as drawing something that cannot be seen as described by another person, describing what another person or character in a scenario sees from their perspective, role-playing, videotaping, using puppets, or telling stories that describe misleading situations. Several other studies that used some version of this program were conducted and published throughout the next two decades (Begeer et al., 2011, 2015; de Veld et al., 2017; Gevers et al., 2006).

Swettenham (1996) and McGregor et al. (1998) published studies where beliefs were likened to "pictures-in-the-head," and "thought-bubbles" were used to represent these mental states and found that this strategy increased false belief understanding in learners with mental ages of 4 or older. In 2002, Wellman et al. built on these findings in their study, which showed generalization of false belief understanding over time and scenarios. Fisher and Happe (2005) conducted a randomized controlled study on an adaptation of "pictures in the head" and found that the intervention improved performance on ToM tasks, which maintained for up to 3 months but did not affect daily applied use of these skills.

Other studies used group-based training targeting conversational skills only (Chin & Bernard-Opitz, 2000), a combination of conversational and ToM skills (Feng et al., 2008; Ozonoff & Miller, 1995), and videotapes of social interaction vignettes to train reading facial expressions, desires, and beliefs (Bell & Kirby, 2002). A study using the manualized program I Can Problem Solve (ICPS) showed marginal effectiveness in developing ToM skills in preschoolers with ASD (Szumski et al., 2017).

Core Reviews

The NAC used the term ToM Training and gave it a rating of Emerging in 2009 based on four articles (Bell & Kirby, 2002; Fisher & Happe, 2005; Gevers et al., 2006; Wellman et al., 2002) and also included an article targeting ToM skills under Language Training Production and Understanding (Chin & Bernard-Opitz, 2000) and under Social Skills Package (Ozonoff & Miller, 1995). The number of citations of articles reviewed in 2015 was not provided but the intervention again received a rating of Emerging. The NPDC (Wong et al., 2014) gave the intervention a rating of Insufficient Evidence in 2014 based on one article (Begeer et al., 2011) and included three articles targeting ToM skills (Chin & Bernard-Opitz, 2000; Feng et al., 2008; Ozonoff & Miller, 1995) under Social Skills Treatment. In 2020, the NCAEP (Steinbrenner et al., 2020) recategorized it as a Social Skills Treatment, which was considered an EBP and included six articles targeting ToM skills (Begeer et al., 2011, 2015; de Veld et al., 2017; Feng et al., 2008; Ozonoff & Miller, 1995; Szumski et al., 2017).

Age and Diagnostic Considerations/ Prerequisite Skills and Abilities

There are large gaps in the research on ToM interventions but what does exist supports the use with all school-age individuals with ASD with average and above measured intelligence that have deficits in social or the pragmatic use of language.

Reported Outcomes

The research on ToM Interventions consistently has indicated that they can result in improvements in imitation, conversational skills, emotion recognition and regulation, perception taking, recognizing the difference between fantasy and reality, assessing social situations, recognizing intentions in others, developing self-related ideas, pretense, understanding the thoughts and feelings of others, the use of imagination, and understanding humor when directly taught in one-on-one or small-group formats but fail to significantly generalize to real-life situations.

Qualifications Needed

No formal training is required to implement ToM Interventions. However, individuals who use these practices should consider training in its application through consultation with an experienced implementer or other training formats.

How, Where, and When Typically Implemented

Considerable overlap exists between ToM Interventions and other interventions included in this section such as VM, Cartooning, Social Problem-Solving Interventions, Social Thinking®, and Social Narratives/Story-Based Interventions. ToM Interventions are often included in daily "social skills" instruction by teachers in schools and community-based groups. ToM Interventions have also been implemented by parents with positive results (de Veld et al., 2017).

Potential Risks

There are no documented or obvious risks associated with ToM Interventions.

Costs

ToM Interventions are cost-effective in terms of time and other resources. There are no costs associated with training and no additional teaching time is required or materials need to be purchased other than those typically found in natural educational settings.

Rating

   Promising/Emerging Practice

Resources and Suggested Readings

Cherry, K. (2021). *How the theory of mind helps us understand others.* https://www.verywell mind.com/theory-of-mind-4176826

Social Decision-Making Strategies

Description

Social Decision-Making Strategies assist the learner in identifying problems, generating alternatives, understanding consequences, and determining how to correct situations (Myles & Simpson, 2003). Many individuals with ASD struggle to understand social situations, which can lead to behavior that impacts their social relationships and overall quality of life. We have included three interventions under this category: (1) Stop, Observe, Deliberate, Act (SODA) (2) Social Autopsies, and (3) Situations-Options-Consequences-Choices-Strategies (SOCCSS).

Stop, Observe, Deliberate, Act (SODA)

SODA (Bock, 2001, 2007) is a social behavioral learning strategy designed to assist learners in determining how they will act and converse with others in new social environments and has four steps:

1. Stop: Observe the room arrangement, activities, and routines in the new environment and choose a place to observe further.

2. Observe: What are the people doing and saying? What is the length of conversation and what do they do after the conversation ends?

3. Deliberate: What would I like to do and say? How will I know when others will like to visit longer or when they would like the conversation to end?

4. Act: Approach the person I would like to visit, greet them appropriately, listen to them, and ask a related question. Look for cues that the person would like to visit longer or end the conversation and respond accordingly.

Social Autopsies

Social Autopsies are intended to help students understand the cause-and-effect relationship between social behaviors and the reactions of others and correct social mistakes by using four steps: (1) identify the error, (2) determine who was harmed, (3) decide how to correct the error, and (4) develop a plan so that the error does not occur again. Social Autopsies were originally developed by Rick Lavoie, who is a special education teacher, administrator, consultant, and public speaker and the author of many books, some of which have been made into videos, on topics related to learning disabilities. Social autopsies were included in his book and video titled *Last One Picked . . . First One Picked On: Learning Disabilities and Social Skills With Rick Lavoie* (Bieber, 1994). According to Lavoie, the success of the strategy lies in its structure of practice, immediate feedback, and positive reinforcement—all components of Behavioral Skills Training, which is also described in this section. To date, there have been no empirical studies specifically conducted on Social Autopsies.

Situations-Options-Consequences-Choices-Strategies (SOCCSS)

SOCCSS (Roosa, 1995) has six sequential steps:

1. Situation: Identify who was involved, what happened, when it happened, where it happened, and why it happened.

2. Options: Brainstorm and record several options of choices that could have been made without evaluating them.

3. Consequences: List potential consequence(s) for each option.

4. Choices: Prioritize options and consequences and select the option the student thinks they will be able to do and what will lead to the best outcome based on what they want.

5. Strategies: Develop a plan to carry out the chosen option.

6. Simulation: Practice the chosen option in contrived situations.

Brief Overview of the Literature

There are two peer-reviewed articles published on the strategy SODA (Bock, 2001, 2007). Leaf et al. (2020) categorized Social Autopsies as a Social Narrative.

Core Reviews

Simpson et al. (2005) is the only core review that uses the term Social Decision-Making Interventions and included Social Autopsies, SOCCSS, and SODA under this category. They did not review any articles and gave the category the rating of Promising Practice. Although the other core reviews did not review the term Social Decision-Making Interventions, they all included an article on SODA (Bock, 2007)— the NAC under Story-Based Intervention Package in 2009 and the NPDC (Wong et al., 2014) and NCAEP (Steinbrenner et al., 2020) under Social Narratives—which were all given the ratings of Evidence-Based or Established Practices.

Age and Diagnostic Considerations/ Prerequisite Skills and Abilities

The subjects in the Bock study in 2007 were four subjects with Asperger's in the fourth and fifth grades. The similarities to other CBIS would support their use with all school-age individuals with ASD with average and above measured intelligence that have deficits in social or the pragmatic use of communication and/or executive functioning skills.

Reported Outcomes

The Bock study reported increases in cooperative learning, playing organized sport games, and visiting during lunches, which were maintained for one month and were similar to levels of these skills in neurotypical peers.

Qualifications Needed

No formal training is required to implement any of the Social Decision-Making Strategies described above. However, individuals who use these practices should consider training in its application through consultation with an experienced implementer or other training formats.

How, Where, and When Typically Implemented

In addition to receiving explicit instruction in a small-group format, every educator with whom the student has regular contact (e.g., parents, bus drivers, teachers, custodians, cafeteria workers) should know how to do various Social Decision-Making Strategies, and ideally the skills should be reviewed and practiced immediately before situation in which they needed to be applied to foster generalization and maintenance.

Costs

Social Decision-Making Strategies are cost-effective in terms of time and other resources. There are no costs associated with training, no additional teaching time is required, and no materials need to be purchased other than those typically found in natural educational settings.

Potential Risks

There are no documented or obvious risks associated with Social Decision-Making Strategies.

Rating

At this time we are not giving Social Decision-Making Strategies a rating based on the fact that there are three different strategies included in this category. Each strategy has various levels of research support with only one (SODAS) being included in the core reviews under Social Narratives. We recommend that each strategy be researched separately. Researching these and other interventions targeting social problem-solving and other pragmatic language skills should be a priority as they are currently overlooked skills in the existing research literature.

Resourced and Suggested Readings

Last One Picked, First One Picked On. https://www.youtube.com/watch?v=TyaHlOYtkI4.
The Ohio Center for Autism and Low Incidence (OCALI) has free resources on both Social Autopsies and SOCCS. https://www.ocali.org/project/resource_gallery_of_interventions/page/social_autopsy.

Cartooning

Description

An important early stage of Cognitive Behavioral-Based Interventions involved education about the links between thoughts, emotions, and behavior (Anderson & Morris, 2006). Cartooning uses illustrations and visual symbols to help explain these links attempting to make abstract concepts that can be difficult for some learners to comprehend more concrete so that they can be understood and reflected on (Hagiwara & Myles, 1999; Kuttler et al., 1998). Cartooning can further be used to attempt to understand how these links impact various social situations and identify what behaviors the learner should engage in to increase the likelihood of desired outcomes (Coogle et al., 2017). Comic Strip Conversations is the most common Cartooning Intervention. It uses a set of eight symbols and specific colors to denote basic conversational concepts such as what people say, think, and feel in a comic strip format (Rogers & Myles, 2001).

Brief Overview of the Literature

In the early 1990s, several studies found that individuals with ASD had a much easier time understanding "false drawings" (Charman & Baron-Cohen, 1992) or "false photographs" (Leekam & Perner, 1991; Leslie & Thaiss, 1992) than "false beliefs" while typically developing peers found them equally difficult. This suggests that visual representations help individuals with ASD understand mental concepts. McGregor et al. (1998) found that people with ASD did better on false belief tasks if they utilized a "picture-in-the-head" procedure, which put a photograph of the original location of an object into a doll's head creating a tangible image of the doll's beliefs. Parsons and Mitchell (1999) conducted two studies on the use of "thought bubbles" and found that individuals with ASD were able to understand them as representing someone's thoughts. In the early 2000s, there were several studies done on using Comic Strip Conversations™ in combination with Social Stories™, another intervention also developed by Carol Gray, and found that they had a positive effect on the social behaviors of individuals with ASD ages 4 to 12 (Hutchins & Prelock, 2006, 2012), in developing ToM in skills in a 5-year-old boy with ASD (Hutchins & Prelock, 2008) and helping an adolescent with Asperger syndrome interpret social situations (Rogers & Myles, 2001).

Core Reviews

Only Simpson et al. (2005) included Cartooning as a reviewed intervention giving it a rating of Limited Supporting Information for Practice based on two articles (Parsons & Mitchell, 1999; Rogers & Myles, 2001). Comic Strip Conversations (Gray, 1994), Mind Reading (Howlin et al., 1999), and Pragmatism (Arwood & Brown, 1999) were identified as example Cartooning programs.

Other Systematic Reviews/Meta-Analyses

In 2020, Leaf classified Cartooning as a Social Narrative and reviewed six articles (Ahmed-Husain & Dunsmuir, 2014; Hutchins & Prelock, 2006, 2008, 2012; Pierson & Glaeser, 2005, 2007) concluding that none of them had convincing evidence.

Age and Diagnostic Considerations/ Prerequisite Skills and Abilities

The existing research uses Cartooning with learners ages four to adolescence.

Reported Outcomes

Cartooning could be considered a type of visual support that helps explain social events (Hagiwara & Myles, 1999; Swaggart et al., 1995). Empirical evidence supports the use of the Visually Based Interventions as an effective medium for teaching social and academic skills to this population of individuals (Dettmer et al., 2000; MacDuff et al., 1993). However, more empirical research is needed.

Qualifications Needed

Cartooning can be implemented by educators, parents, paraprofessionals, and others who have a rapport with a student with ASD, knows the student well enough to understand their likely interpretation of a social event, understands the concept of cartooning, and can draw cartoons as little or no training is required. Gray (1994) offers guidelines for Cartooning that may be helpful to potential cartoon users, although they have not been empirically validated.

How, Where, and When Typically Implemented

Cartooning usually occurs in a one-on-one setting as it is very individualized based on the learner but could be expanded for use in various small-group and even large-group settings to illustrate cognitive concepts more broadly. It can be implemented in school, clinical, home, and community settings. Cartooning is more likely to be effective when used within a more evidence-based Behavioral Skills Training structure that minimally includes direct instruction, modeling, rehearsal, and feedback and could include the Teaching Interaction Procedure components of providing rationale and consideration of examples and non-examples.

Costs

Although this strategy is typically used in a one-on-one setting, it incurs no costs other than personnel and time. Training in using this technique is available through Gray (1994) and is often a standard part of university-course content related to ASD or through a school-based, in-service workshop, so costs associated would vary based on professional development fees of the providing individuals.

Potential Risks

There are no documented or obvious risks associated with Cartooning.

Rating

 Limited Supporting Information for Practice

Resources and Suggested Readings

Arwood, E., & Kaulitz, C. (2007). *Learning with a visual brain in an auditory world: Visual language strategies for individuals with autism spectrum disorders*. APC.

Gray, C. (1994). *Comic strip conversations: Colorful, illustrated interactions with students with autism and related disorders*. Jenison Public Schools.

Self-Management Interventions (SMI)

Description

Practically speaking, self-management is synonymous with self-regulation or self-control and refers to the efforts one exerts to change or control their behavior (Baumeister et al., 1994). Self-management encompasses a variety of thinking processes and behaviors, which include but are not limited to the following:

- Controlling emotional responses
- Attending to relevant information
- Planning future behavior
- Remaining flexible through unexpected setbacks
- Completing tasks independently
- Acting in goal-directed ways

Importantly, students who develop self-management skills are less dependent on others to incentivize and direct their behaviors (Blair & Diamond, 2008; Shapiro & Cole, 1994). SMI are specific student-directed interventions that include some direct way of scaffolding self-management processes (e.g., goal-setting, self-monitoring, self-evaluation) to improve targeted outcomes (e.g., attention, productivity) (Crutchfield & Wood, 2018). Common SMI for students with autism includes goal-setting, self-monitoring, self-evaluation, self-instruction, positive self-talk, self-reinforcement, and other meta-cognitive approaches (Quinn et al., 1994).

Self-Monitoring

Self-Monitoring represents the most utilized and scientifically supported SMI (Lee et al., 2007). Self-management involves the collecting and recording of data over time by the target student (Mace & Kratochwill, 1988). Self-management approaches have seen application in various fields, including education, health and wellness, athletics, and chronic illness. For students with autism, self-management has been used to reduce stereotypic behaviors (Crutchfield et al., 2015), improve social outcomes (Parker & Kamps, 2011), increase attention and productivity (Bouck et al., 2014), and decrease disruptive/antisocial behaviors (Wills et al., 2019). Current self-management research explores ways to deliver self-management interventions using portable technology (e.g., smartphones, wearables, tablets, and personal computers) (Chia et al., 2018).

Brief Overview of the Literature

An SMI was first used to address stereotypic behavior in young children with autism in 1990 (Koegel & Koegel, 1990). Since that time, over 50 studies have examined the effectiveness of SMI for students with autism across a wide variety of outcomes. Similarly, since 2007, researchers have compiled three systematic reviews of SMI for students with autism (Aljadeff-Abergel et al., 2015; Chia et al., 2018) and completed four meta-analyses of single-case research examining SMI for school-age children with autism (Carr, 2016; Carr et al., 2014; Davis et al., 2016; Lee et al., 2007).

Core Reviews

All of the peer-reviewed articles in the Cognitive Behavioral Interventions category reviewed by Simpson et al. (2005) are on Self-Monitoring or self-management, which are rated as Promising Practices. The NAC, the NPDC (Wong et al., 2014), and the NCAEP (Steinbrenner et al., 2020) all used the term self-management. The NAC gave the rating of Established in both of its reports, and the NPDC and NCAEP gave the rating of Evidenced Based Practice in both of their reports.

Age and Diagnostic Considerations/ Prerequisite Skills and Abilities

Research supports the use of SMI and, in particular, self-management for all school-age children with autism. However, most of the research is currently focused on students in elementary schools (see Davis et al., 2016; Lee et al., 2007). Research supports the use of SMI for students who meet criteria for Level I, Level II, and Level III autism (Davis, et al., 2016; Lee et al., 2007). It is important to note that Self-Monitoring, in particular, has broad support in the literature to justify its adoption for all students with autism, even students who have limited language capabilities and co-occurring ID (Ganz, 2008). Keep in mind that practitioners may need to scaffold specific components (e.g., monitoring prompts, picture cues, technology delivery) of Self-Monitoring Interventions to ensure individual students can access the intervention (Crutchfield, & Wood, 2018).

Reported Outcomes

A broad research base supports the use of SMI and self-management to address a wide variety of skill areas including social-communication, adaptive skill, classroom routines, and repetitive and restrictive behaviors.

Qualifications Needed

No formal training is required to implement SMI and self-management.

How, Where, and When Typically Implemented

These interventions are typically administered in school settings, including broad support for use in general education (Davis et al., 2016). Further, self-management should be at the core of any SMI treatment package. In their 2014 meta-analysis on SMI and outcomes for students with autism, Carr et al. identified 29 studies that met their narrow inclusion criteria. Each of these 29 studies included self-management as a core component of the SMI. Researchers used other procedures; for example, self-reinforcement was present in 57 percent of the studies, and self-goal setting was present in 9 percent of the studies. However, it is clear from this evidence, and supported by similar reviews and meta-analysis (e.g., Lee et al., 2007; Southall & Gast, 2011) that self-management is the main component of SMI represented in the literature. Also, it is important to note, SMI are generally packaged treatments that typically include teacher-led instruction or training around the behaviors of interest (Carr et al., 2014; Davis et al., 2016; Lee et al., 2007). This training usually involves discrimination training to support students in distinguishing between occurrences and non-occurrences of the targeted behavior. Finally, SMI are frequently packaged with reinforcement contingencies that feature student-selected reinforcement.

Costs

SMI are cost-effective approaches as they take little time and materials to develop and once developed have the potential to increase teacher capacity, by empowering students to self-direct at least a component of their own behavior management.

Potential Risks

There are no documented or obvious risks associated with SMI.

Rating

     Evidence-Based Practice

Resources and Suggested Readings

AFIRM modules through UNC Chapel Hill offers a free online course on self-management. https://afirm.fpg.unc.edu/node/1319

Crutchfield, S. A., & Wood, L. (2018) *How to use cognitive behavioral interventions and self-management interventions*. ProEd.

Kansas Technical Assistance System Network (TASN) offers a free online report on self-management. https://www.ksdetasn.org/resources/1196

Neitzel, J., & Busick, M. (2009). *Overview of self-management*. National Professional Development Center on Autism Spectrum Disorders, Frank Porter Graham Child Development Institute, The University of North Carolina.

The Coping Cat Program

Description

The Coping Cat Program is a CBIS initially designed to address anxiety disorders such as generalized anxiety disorder (GAD), social phobia (SP), and separation anxiety disorder (SAD) in typically developing children, ages 7 to 13 (Kendall, 1994; Kendall et al., 1997). The goal of The Coping Cat Program is to teach children to recognize their signs of anxiety and then use a pretaught coping strategy to help manage these feelings (McNally Keehn et al., 2013). This program typically consists of child sessions, parent sessions, and homework. The C.A.T. Project, a version of The Coping Cat Program specially designed for adolescents, ages 14 to 17, is also available. The Coping Cat Program consists of 16 weeks of intervention that utilize the following strategies (Sulkowski et al., 2012):

1. Modeling

2. Relaxation Techniques

3. Exposure Tasks

4. Contingency Management

5. Problem-Solving

6. Self-Evaluation

The program is divided into two parts. In its first eight sessions, the program teaches children and their families about anxiety and provides them with a variety of cognitive-behavioral strategies to cope with the anxiety. The second eight sessions allow children to practice previously taught skills and strategies through exposure to anxiety-provoking situations (Beidas et al., 2010). The Coping Cat Program uses the mnemonic F.E.A.R. to guide children through the exposure situations. F.E.A.R. stands for four steps: The *F*–Feeling Frightened? step focuses on somatic reactions (e.g., physical reactions such as pain, fatigue, weakness). The *E*–Expecting Bad Things to Happen? step helps youth identify anxious cognitions (e.g., thoughts, expectations, interpretations) surrounding the situation. The *A*–Attitudes and Actions that Can Help step prompts children to use pretaught coping skills (e.g., coping thoughts, problem-solving, relaxation techniques). Finally, the *R*–Results and Rewards step urges children to evaluate their performance and effort and provides an opportunity to be rewarded for facing their fears (Beidas et al., 2010; Ferris, 2017). The acronym is important to helping students remember the steps and become more fluent in using the strategies during times of anxiety.

Brief Overview of the Literature

The research on The Coping Cat Program and its effectiveness for children and youth with ASD is slowly emerging. The first empirical study evaluating The Coping Cat Program for children with ASD was completed by McNally Keehn et al. (2013). This study included 22 children, ages 3 to 14, with a diagnosis of ASD and at least one primary anxiety disorder of GAD, SP, or SAD. In a random assignment, 12 children received training on The Coping Cat Program, while 10 others were randomly assigned to the waitlist. Nine modifications, determined not to impact fidelity (Kendall & Hedtke, 2006), were made to accommodate the learning style of youth with ASD and increase treatment success (McNally Keehn et al., 2013). Some of the modifications included extra time reviewing content and homework with parents, increased session length, using written and visual materials, simplified language, integration of child-specific interests and preoccupations, and enhanced and individualized reinforcement strategies. Results of this pilot study provided preliminary results indicating that the modified version of the program may be effective in reducing anxiety levels in students with ASD.

In another study, Weiss et al. (2015) assessed whether parenting stress was associated with changes in anxiety following participation in a modified version of The Coping Cat Program. Results indicated that children who were provided with the modified Coping Cat Program demonstrated reductions in anxiety according to measures of parent report with 50 percent of participants exhibiting clinically meaningful improvements using a conservative index. "Children themselves, however, did not report significant change in anxiety from pre- to post-treatment, nor had they reported scores in the clinical range prior to treatment" (p. 161). Finally, significant correlations were found between change in parenting stress and change in child anxiety from pre- to post-treatment.

Finally, Ferris (2017) examined the impact of the Brief Coping Cat Program (Kendall et al., 2013) as a school-based intervention for reducing anxiety in children with ASD. The Brief Coping Cat Program consisted of eight sessions that included the same information and objectives as described in the 16-session program. Basic accommodations and modifications such as decreasing session lengths, use of visual supports, scheduled sensory breaks, and frequent positive reinforcement were implemented to meet individual student needs. Results indicated a positive effect for decreasing student and teacher perceived levels of anxiety for all three elementary-age participants.

Core Reviews

In the core reviews, Coping Cat was referenced in the Cognitive Behavioral Intervention Package (CBIP) category by the NAC in 2015, which was given the rating of Established. The NCAEP (Steinbrenner et al., 2020) referenced Coping Cat in the CBIS category in 2020, which was given the rating of EBP.

Other Peer Reviewed Research

Two additional experimental peer-reviewed studies were identified by the author of this text and are summarized here.

AUTHOR(S)	N	SETTING	AGE/ GENDER	DIAGNOSES	FINDINGS
Ferris (2017)	3	School	7 to 11 yrs. 2 males 1 female	ASD and co-occurring anxiety	Decreases in perceived levels of anxiety
Weiss et al. (2015)	18		8 to 12 yrs. 15 males 3 females	ASD and co-occurring anxiety	Reductions in anxiety according to measures of parent report with 50% of participants exhibiting clinically meaningful improvements using a conservative index. "Children themselves, however, did not report significant change in anxiety from pre- to post-treatment, nor had they reported scores in the clinical range prior to treatment" (p. 161).

Age and Diagnostic Considerations/ Prerequisite Skills and Abilities

The modified Coping Cat Program was developed for individuals with ASD and co-occurring anxiety, ages 7 to 13, and the C.A.T. Project can be used with individuals ages 14 to 17. Prerequisite skills could include self-awareness, the ability to understand and recognize one's feelings, sustained attention, problem-solving, abstract, higher-order thinking, and the ability to select and use appropriate coping strategies. Many of these required skills can be addressed by modifications in the program (Walters et al., 2016).

Reported Outcomes

Preliminary results indicate the modified Coping Cat Program can decrease anxiety levels in individuals with ASD and a co-occurring anxiety disorder such as GAD, SP, or SAD.

Qualifications Needed

The Coping Cat Program should be implemented by a professional with training and experience in providing cognitive behavioral training/therapy and in working with individuals with ASD.

How, Where, and When Typically Implemented

The Coping Cat Program can be implemented in a variety of settings including schools, homes, and communities either in a one-on-one format or with small groups.

Costs

The cost of accessing The Coping Cat Program will depend on the setting in which the services are provided. If services are provided in a school setting, no cost should be incurred. If the program is provided by a private therapist, social worker, or psychologist, the cost will align with their fee schedule. There is a Coping Cat Program manual for the implementer ($24 on Amazon), a workbook for students ($26.95) on Amazon) and a companion for parents ($19 on Amazon).

Potential Risks

There are no documented or obvious risks associated with The Coping Cat Program.

Rating

   Promising/Emerging Practice

Resources and Suggested Readings

Kendall, P. C., & Hedtke, K. A. (2006). *Coping cat workbook* (2nd ed.). Workbook Publishing.

Mindfulness-Based Interventions

Description

Mindfulness involves developing qualities of attention and awareness through the direct practice of present moment awareness (Kabat-Zinn, 2002). Mindfulness-Based Interventions have demonstrated mixed results in reducing symptoms of specific psychiatric disorders, though they do hold promise for certain subgroups including depression, pain conditions, smoking cessation, and addictive disorders (Goldberg et al., 2018). Mindfulness may also reduce general and situational anxiety for many individuals, though evidence is still emerging (Blanck et al., 2018). It is well documented that students with autism report higher levels of anxiety than same-age controls, and many have argued that students with autism would benefit from Mindfulness-Based Therapies (Hartley et al., 2019). The primary Mindfulness-Based Interventions include Mindfulness-Based Stress Reduction (MBSR; Kabat-Zinn, 2003a, 2003b) and Mindfulness-Based Cognitive Therapy (MBCT; Segal et al., 2018). The primary purpose of these approaches is to support students with autism in reducing rumination and preventing negative thought patterns through nonjudgmental present moment awareness (Hartley et al., 2019). Parents, caregivers, and families of individuals with autism also report higher levels of stress and anxiety and may benefit from ongoing Mindfulness programs.

Brief Overview of the Literature

Singh et al. (2011) documented a functional relationship between a Mindfulness approach ("Soles of the Feet Meditations"; Singh et al., 2003) and reductions in aggressive behavior for three youth with autism. Since then, several experimental and quasi-experimental research studies have examined the effects of Mindfulness-Based Interventions on different aspects of well-being for individuals with autism and their families.

Core Reviews

Mindfulness was not included in any of the core reviews. It was included in this resource because it is increasingly being used by many professionals in the educational setting including general and special educators, OTs, SLPs, school psychologists, and counselors.

Other Peer Reviewed Research

The peer-reviewed studies that the author of this text was able to identify are summarized here.

AUTHORS	N	PARTICIPANTS	SETTING	FINDINGS
Conner & White (2018)	9	Adults; Clinical diagnosis of ASD; IQ of 80 and above	Individual sessions; Therapist led	Improvements in impulse control, emotional regulation, and emotional acceptance
de Bruin et al. (2015)	23	Adolescents; Clinical diagnosis of ASD; Caregivers	Group; Therapist led	Improvements in quality of life for both adolescents and caregivers and rumination for adolescents

(Continued)

(Continued)

AUTHORS	N	PARTICIPANTS	SETTING	FINDINGS
Hwang et al. (2015)	6	Children; ASD clinical diagnosis; Caregivers	Home; Delivered by parents	Improvements in quality of life and stressors for caregivers; Reductions in problem behaviors for ASD participants
Ridderinkhof et al. (2018)	43	Youth (8 to 18); ASD diagnosis; IQ of 80 and above	Group; Therapist led	Improvements in social communication
Singh et al. (2011)	3	Adolescents Clinical diagnosis of ASD	Home; Delivered by parents	Reductions in aggression for each participant
Spek et al. (2013)	41	Adults with ASD; IQ of 85 and above	Group; Therapist led with individual practice	Improvements in depression, anxiety, rumination, and positive affect

Age and Diagnostic Considerations/ Prerequisite Skills and Abilities

Currently the literature supports the use of Mindfulness-Based Interventions for students with autism who do not have co-occurring ID. The research also supports these approaches for adolescents or adults with autism.

Reported Outcomes

The current research literature supports the use of Mindfulness for broad improvements in overall well-being, but little research supports their usage to improve the core symptoms of autism.

Qualifications Needed

These interventions are generally implemented by therapists and Mindfulness practitioners who have undergone training and extensive practice in Mindfulness techniques. When parents facilitated the Mindfulness-Based Interventions Therapies for their child, they too underwent extensive training.

How, Where, and When Typically Implemented

To date no research has implemented Mindfulness techniques in school settings so it is unclear how these approaches would translate to a school environment.

Costs

Mindfulness-Based Interventions often have costs associated with them to either train the parent or caregiver in the meditation techniques or to pay the Mindfulness practitioner. For example, an 8-week MBSR course for a layperson generally costs between $300 and $500.

Potential Risks

While no adverse effects were reported in the research on autism and Mindfulness, other researchers have pointed out that intense meditation may result in psychotic episodes and/or prolonged depression in certain individuals, though these experiences remain isolated.

Practitioner Testimonial(s)

Mindfulness is a tool you can use in any classroom, at any age and with any ability level. Teaching your students to correctly breathe in order to calm their mind and body is the most powerful tool they have. We teach Mindfulness in our cross-categorical classroom with elementary and middle school-age students. They learn how to recognize their emotions and the sensations that their bodies have during those emotions. Mindfulness is not a tool that anyone ever "masters." It is an ongoing skill that strengthens over time and with practice. Finding a short time each day to practice Mindfulness through meditation, yoga, and tapping techniques can be a great intervention for your classrooms. We recommend using quick 3- to 5-minute meditations to get started and always modeling Mindfulness with your students when they are first learning. You can build up to longer meditations as your students become more comfortable and confident with their abilities.

—Kristen McKearney and Stephanie Kopecky
K–8 Essentials—Nebraska Educational Service Unit #3
Just 5 Teachers

Rating

☺ Promising/Emerging Practice

This rating is based on the six peer-reviewed studies summarized above.

Resources and Suggested Reading

Kabat-Zinn, J. (2012). *Mindfulness for beginners: Reclaiming the present moment—and your life*. Sounds True.

Kansas Technical Assistance System Network (TASN) offers several free online webinars related to Mindfulness. They can be accessed at ksdetasn.org by searching Mindfulness in their resource library.

Social Thinking™

Description

Through problem-solving, perspective-taking, and the development of reciprocal conversation skills, Social Thinking teaches social communication and executive function skills across a range of ages. The fundamental social cognitive processes that result in the outwardly visible social "skills" are taught using specific Social Thinking terminology and procedures. Social Thinking as a therapeutic methodology was developed by Michele Garcia Winner in the late 1990s and early 2000s (Winner, 2005, 2007a). She has continued to work and collaborate with different colleagues, specifically Pamela Crooke, to expand the curriculum to include all ages and to incorporate EBPs such as visual supports, role-playing, modeling, and reinforcement.

Social Thinking is a cognitive behavior intervention strategy (CBIS), is used with people with mental health difficulties as well as people with disabilities. CBIS is founded on a number of fundamental ideas: (1) part of psychological issues stem from flawed or harmful ways of thinking; (2) a portion of psychological issues can be attributed to learned undesirable behavioral patterns; and (3) people with psychological issues can develop stronger coping mechanisms, which will help them manage their symptoms and improve their effectiveness. The goal of CBIS is to assist people in developing coping skills so they can learn to alter their own thinking, problematic emotions, and behavior through activities done both during and outside of sessions. Many CBIS-based social "skills" interventions have been evaluated for children with ASD (Bauminger, 2002, 2007a, 2007b; Crooke et al., 2008; Laugeson et al., 2012; Lopata et al., 2006; Wood et al., 2009) which address the influence on behavior of teaching emotion recognition and interpretation and social problem-solving and its the relationship to later social adjustment (Koning et al., 2013).

Social Thinking principles, strategies, and practices are clearly outlined in several sets and series of books and materials that parents and professionals can purchase and receive training in. It is crucial to understand that this intervention is not a static intervention method with prescribed practices, even though it is based on a prescribed curriculum from (Winner, 2000, 2005). On the Social Thinking website, within the Methodology section, a brief outline of the Social Thinking process is described:

1. "Social thinking is our meaning maker. We observe and listen to interpret the perspective of others.

2. When seeking to engage or simply share space with others, we use social thinking to adapt our social behavior (social skills) effectively as a means to meet our social goals.

3. Our social thinking and social skills directly impact how others feel about us. This impacts how we are treated, how we feel about others, and ultimately—how we feel about ourselves." (Methodology: Social Thinking's Three-Part Process of Social Thinking, nd).

Through different social cognitive activities, this process and the curriculum is intended to promote fundamental concepts (e.g., engaging in "expected" and decreasing "unexpected" behavior, perspective-taking, listening with yours eyes), but these concepts must remain flexible in response to interactions within each therapy session and with others in generalized settings (Winner, 2000, 2005).

Social Thinking, as is true of CBIS overall, is more than teaching "skills" because it focuses on the meta-cognitive processes of the thinking and problem-solving (Bauminger, 2002; Koning et al., 2013) about why and how we interact with others in different situations and that we need to be paying attention to other people's behavior and adjust our behavior based on their behavior, while also thinking about how others' feelings are affected by our behavior. The emphasis on making abstract concepts more concrete by breaking them down into manageable portions, followed by interpretation of the meaning of each component, and finally reintegration of all relevant sources of information into a meaningful entity is a crucial factor contributing to the success of *social thinking* and Social Thinking for individuals with ASD (Winner, 2007a, 2007b, 2008, 2013).

Brief Overview of the Literature

While Social Thinking is a CBIS intervention method, a field which is supported by a great deal of empirical research, it has not been until about the last 10 years that research studies have been implemented to specifically study Social Thinking and its unique strategies and procedures. In particular, Lee et al. (2016) discovered that when Social Thinking was used as an intervention, students showed significantly increased skill levels. Crooke et al. (2008) discovered that social communication strategies from the Social Thinking curriculum significantly improved the use of "expected" social behaviors and decreased the use of "unexpected" behaviors of kids and teens with ASD in casual and informal conversations.

Leaf et al. (2016) published an article that described Social Thinking as a pseudoscience with no empirical evidence to support its implementation with individuals with ASD, as well as being an intervention that can inhibit the use of the evidence-based intervention of ABA. These authors are all behavior analysts and are professionals who provide interventions for individuals with ASD based on ABA. This article and the approach these authors took to discount Social Thinking brought about much controversy and discussion among behavioral and non-behavioral interventionists who work with individuals with ASD. Crooke and Winner (2016) published a response to this article in which they refuted the claims and corrected the meaning of quotes taken out of context about Social Thinking as a methodology and *social thinking* as a cognitive ability. It is helpful for practitioners working with individuals with ASD to read these short articles and utilize critical thinking regarding evidence-based interventions to determine if Social Thinking as a methodology is appropriate to utilize in their own classroom therapy sessions based on the individual needs of their students.

Core Reviews

The NAC (2015) is the only core review that included Social Thinking as a reviewed intervention and classified it as an Unestablished Intervention based on an unspecified number of studies. According to the NAC (2015), "Unestablished Interventions" are those for which there is little or no evidence in the scientific literature that allows us to draw firm conclusions about their effectiveness or ineffectiveness with individuals with ASD. It should be noted that only research studies or articles published prior to 2012 were listed as being reviewed as part of the decision process for making this rating determination.

Other Peer Reviewed Research

Five studies (not an exhaustive list) that have been conducted and published in peer-reviewed journals are outlined below along with the reported outcomes.

AUTHOR(S)	N	SETTING	AGE/ GENDER	DIAGNOSES	RESEARCH DESIGN	OUTCOMES/ FINDINGS	COMMENTS
Baker-Ericzén et al. (2018)	8	Small group	18- to 29-year-olds	Asperger's syndrome	Pilot Study with pre- and post-intervention assessment	Employment rates more than doubled post-intervention, with an increase from 22% to 56% of participants employed. Intervention has promise as a supported employment intervention program for individuals with ASD.	Intervention was called SUCCESS and was a supported employment intervention to improve executive functions and social communication skills. San Diego, CA
Clavenna-Deane et al. (2020)	4	School and employment settings	High school students (3 boys, 1 girl; ages 18 to 20)	ASD	Random assignment to multiple baseline design across participants, with generalization probes	Social Thinking combined with peer modeling and self-evaluation was effective in the school setting at increasing social communication skills for 3 of the 4 participants.	Generalization of the intervention to the employment setting yielded promising results for the use of supportive comments with two of the four participants. Kansas
Crooke et al. (2008)	6	Whole-group teaching sessions	Male: Ages 9 to 11 years	HFA and Asperger's syndrome	Pre- and post-treatment measures (part of a larger multiple baseline with generalization probes research project)	All subjects demonstrated significant increase in "expected" behavior (verbal utterances/ behavior), initiation, and listening with eyes. A decrease (but not statistically significant) was found in "unexpected" (verbal utterances/ behavior and non-verbal behavior) behaviors.	Warrants further research. Group instruction can be effective in improving behaviors. Further research on whether more 1:1 is needed for significant decrease in inappropriate behaviors.

AUTHOR(S)	N	SETTING	AGE/ GENDER	DIAGNOSES	RESEARCH DESIGN	OUTCOMES/ FINDINGS	COMMENTS
Lee et al. (2016)	39	Small group (2 to 4 students); 90-minute sessions after school	12- to 15-year-olds	33 with ASD; 6 with no diagnosis (30 males and 9 females) 14 middle schools	Pre- and post-intervention assessment (Rating Scale)	Mean total score for the students increased from a pre-training rating of 2.74 to a post-training rating of 3.14 across the subscales of the Social Thinking ILAUGH Scale. Five out of 6 subscales showed significant improvement.	People from home setting and school setting were trained in the rating scales for pre- and post-intervention and both settings of ratings were consistent among raters for all participants across both settings. China
Nowell et al. (2019)	17	Community-based within employment setting	6- to 7-year-olds (1st and 2nd grade)	ASD	Randomized delayed treatment control group design with pre- and post-intervention assessments of both parents and children	Combined with Structured TEACCHing. Intervention group demonstrated increase in social communication and self-regulation knowledge	Intervention was called Growing, Learning and Living with Autism University of North Carolina, Chapel Hill

Age and Diagnostic Considerations/ Prerequisite Skills and Abilities

The Social Thinking strategies and curriculum can be used with individuals ages 3 through adulthood. There is specific curriculum developed for different age groups, and the Social Thinking website indicates the age ranges for the different curriculum and products.

Reported Outcomes

In the few pilot and single-subject design studies that have been conducted with individuals with ASD, the interventions utilized in Social Thinking have proven effective in improving social relationships with peers and parents (e.g., initiation, perspective-taking, humor, attending to speaker) and in the workplace (e.g., obtaining employment and increasing hours of paid work within one's job) (Baker-Ericzén et al., 2018; Clavenna-Deane et al., 2020; Lee et al., 2016). It was also found to be effective in improving "expected" (appropriate) behaviors, decreasing "unexpected" (inappropriate or challenging) behaviors, and increasing social communication and self-regulation skills (Baker-Ericzén et al., 2018; Crooke et al., 2008; Nowell et al., 2019).

Qualifications Needed

A parent or professional needs to receive initial training from an individual experienced with utilizing Social Thinking vocabulary, curriculum, and teaching procedures. Online training modules by Winner and Crooke for different Social Thinking procedures and strategies are available on the Social Thinking website.

How, Where, and When Typically Implemented

In order for individuals to understand the underlying concepts and learn how to utilize new social cognitive skills that are being taught, Social Thinking is most effective when teaching individuals in small groups and 1:1 settings.

Costs

The associated costs specific to using Social Thinking procedures are minimal and come from paying the costs for training, materials, and curriculum that are needed to implement the intervention.

Potential Risks

There are no potential risks associated with using Social Thinking procedures.

Rating

    Promising/Emerging Practice

Resources and Suggested Readings

The Social Thinking website contains articles, training videos, curriculum, resources and products, and a schedule of in-person or live video trainings that can accessed at www .socialthinking.com

The Zones of Regulation™

Description

The Zones of Regulation is a cognitive-behavioral based resource designed by OT Leah Kuypers (2011) with the intent to help teach children emotional awareness and identification, integration of physical and emotional experiences, and self-regulation. Students use the Zones of Regulation to identify where their feelings are coming from based on what their body is "telling them" and to understand their unique physical and emotional experiences. The Zones of Regulation explain emotions through the context of affect, regulation/dysregulation, and physical observations. There are four zones: Green, Yellow, Blue, and Red. Each zone is based on the physical experience of the student and contains a subset of emotions often linked to those physical experiences.

The Green Zone is what is considered the optimal zone for learning. In this zone, students are content if not happy, able to focus and attend to task, and are regulated. Some feelings often associated with the Green Zone are happy, calm, focused, and proud.

The Yellow Zone is the zone associated with mild dysregulation and tension building. This zone is the first sign that a student may be starting to become dysregulated. Students may appear agitated, be unable to focus, or start to increase physical or communicative activity. Some feelings often associated with the Yellow Zone are frustration, worry, excitement, silliness, and annoyance. Not all of the emotions in the Yellow Zone are what may typically be considered negative emotional states. Students can also become dysregulated from excitement or silliness.

The Blue Zone is what may come to mind when we hear that someone is feeling "blue." The Blue Zone is a low-energy zone where an individual may feel sluggish, tired, or bored. A student who is in the Blue Zone may appear less talkative, have a flat affect, show signs of sadness, not participate in activities, or move slower than usual. Feelings often associated with this zone are sadness, sickness, boredom, exhaustion, withdrawal, and fear.

When someone is in the Red Zone, they are experiencing feelings and a degree of dysregulation that may cause them to act out. Students in the Red Zone may hit or exhibit other physically aggressive behaviors, engage in SIB, yell or shout, cry, and/or destroy property. Some feelings that are commonly associated with the Red Zone are anger, terror, devastation, panic, elation, and overstimulation.

Students with ASD may struggle with identifying and regulating their emotions and may have impacted self-regulation or executive function skills. As such, it can be helpful to teach students with ASD to identify their emotions and how they feel in their body. Students can learn about their "triggers" or what causes them to be in a certain zone, experience a certain feeling, or escalate their dysregulation. Once students are familiar with their experience of different feelings and where they fall in the Zones of Regulation, they can think about tools that they can use and make plans for how to work through certain feelings and/or levels of dysregulation.

The Zones of Regulation have some central tenants intended to help educators implement it effectively.

▶ It is important to validate individual experiences and remember that there are no "bad" zones. In the same way that we all get angry or sad sometimes, we all experience differing levels of dysregulation. Students should be encourage to share the zone they are in and why they feel that way.

▶ Prompt students using the language of the Zones of Regulation when in real-life situations. This may look like "You said you did not want to do math, and your body is getting a little fast. You may be in the Yellow Zone right now. What tools can you use?"

▶ The Zones of Regulation curriculum involves students in creating a "toolbox" with strategies that can help them when they feel dysregulated in different ways. Students should be encouraged to think through what helps them and to have that list of tools available.

Brief Overview of the Literature

The research that creator Leah Kuypers has identified is discussed on the Zones of Regulation website and can be accessed at https://www.zonesofregulation.com/research--evidence-base.html

Core Reviews

The Zones of Regulation was not included in any of the core reviews. It was included in this resource because it is used by many professionals in the educational setting including general and special educators, OTs, SLPs, school psychologists, and counselors.

Other Peer Reviewed Research

Although there are some anecdotal articles (Valkanos et al., 2016) and several dissertations listed in the Research and Scholarly Articles section on the Zones of Regulation website, there are few peer-reviewed studies. Those that the author of this text was able to locate are summarized here.

AUTHORS	N	SETTING	AGE/ GENDER	DIAGNOSES	RESEARCH DESIGN	FINDINGS
Anderson et al. (2017)	6	After School Club	Ages 8 to 11	Fetal Alcohol Syndrome	Pre-test/ post-test	Children were able to identify zones, place feelings in the correct zones, utilize self-regulation strategies, and 4 of 6 showed clinical improvement on BRIEF.
Conklin & Jairam (2021)	97	School	Ages 7 and 8 2nd Grade	None given At-risk social, academic and/ or emotional behavior on universal screener (SAEBERS)	Quasi-experimental Pre-test/ Post-test	No significant difference in social emotional competencies between Zones of Regulation and control groups
Ochocki et al. (2020)	63	School	2nd and 3rd Grades	None identified Disruptive behavior 22.2% Special Education Eligible	RCT	Increase in self-regulation skills with a small effect size. No significant difference between experimental group and control group

Age and Diagnostic Considerations/ Prerequisite Skills and Abilities

According to the authors, the Zones of Regulation is designed for children ages 4 years through adulthood. The Zones of Regulation has been used with a wide variety of students—both neurotypical and neurodivergent—and it comes with a variety of lesson plans and resources for a range of age groups and developmental levels. The Zones of Regulation framework is designed to be language-rich so in order to best access the curriculum, students should have receptive communication skills that allow them to understand the language used as well as verbal expressive communication skills. Therefore, the creators recommend it for students with Level 1 or Level 2 autism with mild to moderate support needs for behavior, daily living skills, and in the domain of verbal and nonverbal communication. However, the Zones of Regulation curriculum has been successfully adapted for students with ASD who are minimally verbal communicators and many of the materials are picture supported. Learners would benefit from skills in recognizing and identifying colors, as well as words or pictures to assist with identifying the zones.

Reported Outcomes

Reported outcomes are mixed. Some studies report reductions in problem behavior and increases in on-task behaviors and emotional awareness. Some studies report mixed or no effects.

Qualifications Needed

No formal training is required to implement the Zones of Regulation.

How, Where, and When Typically Implemented

The Zones of Regulation is designed to be implemented by a variety of professionals who work with children and can be implemented across educational environments and therapeutic settings. Some schools have adopted it as part of their schoolwide positive behavior intervention system (PBIS). Educators may choose to implement the lesson plans for the Zones of Regulation during time that is dedicated to social-emotional learning or social skills development, and individual teachers may consider using it as a check-in to start the day, before or after a transition or activity, or as a reminder in the moment if a learner appears to show signs of dysregulation. The framework can be adapted for implementation in the home settings by parents and other caregivers.

Costs

The complete Zones of Regulation guide and curriculum is $59.99, and the 7-hour complete online training webinar for one person is $190.00. Discounted group rates are offered for groups larger than 13. In addition to the required book and training, the makers of the Zones of Regulation offer a variety of additional tools such as posters, activity cards, and games. These range from $24.99 plus tax to $64.99 plus tax and are designed to be used in conjunction with the curriculum guide.

Potential Risks

There are no documented or obvious risks associated with the Zones of Regulation. However, use of time and financial resources may prohibit the implementation of other interventions with a stronger evidence base.

Practitioner Testimonials(s)

Teaching the Zones of Regulation to students has proven time and time again to be beneficial. I have used this with kids as young as preschool and as old as late high school. Kids learn to label and understand emotions in themselves as well as others. They learn that ALL the zones are OK and that the key is for your emotions to match the situation. This leads to learning expected and unexpected behaviors. This program teaches students to manage their emotions by building their "toolbox" that allows them to move through the different zones. Kids learn to rate the size of the problem, which helps them take control of their emotions. While this is different for every student, they learn to scale their emotions and reactions and learn strategies to keep them in the appropriate zone at the right time. I enjoy hearing kids discuss their emotions and offer support based on their observations. "Oh, that kid is in the blue zone. I'm going to see if they want to play Legos with me." Or "That kid is in the red zone. I was in the red zone last night with my brother when he took my toys. Maybe they want a coloring page." The lessons are planned out, but you can easily scale the lessons to meet your students where they are. There are so many handouts so it is easy to get this program started!

—Amy Schulte

I have used Zones of Regulation with a wide range of students throughout the years. I like the way it teaches children to identify their emotions through observation of themselves and others. My favorite part though is that it teaches children how to regulate their emotions. I had a student who felt big emotions and had a hard time remaining in control when he felt these emotions. Through the Zones of Regulation, he learned how to identify what emotion he was feeling and come up with a resolution. He would say, "I am in the green zone! I am having fun" or "I am in the red zone. I need to take some breaths." With practice across settings and people, he was able to generalize this skill and carry it with him. Although this student is no longer in my classroom, I am able to keep touch with him and his family. When visiting with the student recently, he was telling me a story about fireworks on the 4th of July. He told me that when the fireworks were too close to him, it put him in the yellow zone, but when they were far away, he was in the green zone. He was able to enjoy the fireworks at a distance with his mother because he was able to identify his emotion and a way to get back into the green zone!

—Brooke Bailey

Rating

🙂 Promising/Emerging Practice

This rating is based on the existence of significant gray literature (see more information on gray literature in the Evidence-Based Practice chapter), teacher testimonials, widespread use by experienced educators, and potential implementation to improve overlooked skill deficits across the entire ASD spectrum. The Zones of Regulation and/or similar programs that attempt to make abstract concepts more concrete through visuals should be researched further with students with ASD specifically combined with other EBPs.

Resources and Suggested Readings

The complete research base is available at https://www.zonesofregulation.com/research--evidence-base.html#:~:text=The%20Zones%20of%20Regulation%20is,%2C%20and%20social%2Demotional%20theories

Free downloadable handouts are available at https://www.zonesofregulation.com/free-downloadable-handouts.html

The official website for the Zones of Regulation is https://zonesofregulation.com/index.html

The official Zones of Regulation curriculum guide is available at https://www.zonesofregulation.com/book.html

The Zones of Regulation app from Selossoft, Inc., ($5.99) is available at https://apps.apple.com/us/app/the-zones-of-regulation/id610272864

The Incredible 5-Point Scale

Description

The Incredible 5-Point Scale was designed by two teachers with experience working with students with ASD, Kari Buron, MS, and Mitzi Curtis, MEd, in 2003. It was originally developed to teach "social understanding" to students with ASD. In general, a scale is developed for a specific social skill or situation (e.g., volume levels, flirting, sportsmanship) and examples are provided based on level of appropriateness. For example, in the library, an appropriate voice level may be a 1 (whisper), whereas when you are in danger and need help, a 5 (shouting) may be most appropriate. Or for a more complex social skill, flirting, Buron and Curtis provide the example of 1 (or most appropriate) as "sitting next to a girl in class and introducing yourself" whereas a 5 (or most inappropriate) would be "telling a girl she has a good body" (Buron & Curtis, 2012, p. 3). To increase effectiveness of the scale, they recommend creating the scale with input from the individual who will be using it. It is important to note that when this scale is used, it is typically paired with teaching strategies such as video modeling, social narratives, and/or behavioral rehearsal.

Brief Overview of the Literature

The author of this text found only one experimental study evaluating the practice, a dissertation written by McBride Pinheiro in 2019, in which the researcher evaluated the Incredible 5-Point Scale with a 4-year-old preschool student with a developmental delay. She found that the scale was effective in decreasing the student's target behavior of inappropriate play with peers, defined as being physically (e.g., hitting, spitting, kicking) or emotionally (e.g., taking toys, taunting) aggressive towards peers. Gray literature such as unpublished dissertations have not been peer reviewed and they are not considered to be the same level of evidence as peer-reviewed studies, but for interventions that have very little peer-reviewed evidence they should be considered as they do provide at least some level of evidence.

The premise of the Incredible 5-Point Scale is based on Baron-Cohen's (2009) empathizing-systemizing theory, in which he hypothesized individuals with ASD exhibit a desire to analyze cause and effects and to organize information systematically. While the Incredible 5-Point Scale itself has not been evaluated, it does incorporate other EBPs presented in this book, including visual supports, social narratives/Social Stories(™), and behavioral rehearsal and role-play.

Core Reviews

The Incredible 5-Point Scale was not included in any of the core reviews. It was included in this resource because it is increasingly being used by many professionals in the educational setting, including general and special educators, OTs, SLPs, school psychologists, and counselors.

Age and Diagnostic Considerations/ Prerequisite Skills and Abilities

This scale has only been experimentally evaluated with a 4-year-old preschool student with developmental delay (McBride Pinheiro, 2019). However, the developers of the scale recommend its use to be effective for a variety of other students such as those with emotional disorders, OCD, Tourette syndrome, anxiety, or other significant behavioral support needs. The Incredible 5-Point Scale can be used for young children (ages 3 to 5) through school-age students in grades K–12. The authors state skills such as verbal communication and reading are not necessary prerequisite skills.

Reported Outcomes

According to multiple anecdotal reports, the Incredible 5 Point Scale has supported students in better navigating social situations in which the student needs to adjust their behavior according to different situations. Therefore, the targeted reported outcomes typically relate to social and communication skills, as well as behavior outcomes.

Qualifications Needed

Buron and Curtis (2012) do not specify any qualifications needed by the implementer. However, the Incredible 5-Point Scale is typically implemented by a school professional who has experience working with the student with ASD.

How, Where, and When Typically Implemented

The scale itself is typically paired with other social skill teaching strategies such as social narratives, VM, and behavioral rehearsal. In their anecdotal vignettes, the authors suggest the scale can be used in school settings, including alternative behavioral support settings, as well as in vocational training and in leisure scenarios such as summer camp.

Costs

There are no associated costs with using the Incredible 5-Point Scale, as free resources are available on the developers' website. The most recent version of the developers' book is available for purchase on Amazon for approximately $25 (see Resources and Suggested Readings section).

Potential Risks

There are no documented or obvious risks associated with the Incredible Five-Point Scale.

Practitioner Testimonial(s)

The Five-Point Scale has become my go-to proactive behavior strategy. The form that I use the most includes the faces that show what the behavior or emotion looks like. The second part describes how the behavior or emotion feels or what the body is doing during the behavior or emotion. The third part provides choices that can be used when the behavior or emotion is happening. I typically have the student draw the faces and label each one with an emotion. I have them describe how it feels. For the third part, we discuss options that are available to do during the behavior or emotion. I scribe all of the written parts for them using their own words. The student uses their Five-Point Scale during check-in times throughout the school day to assess regulation and to encourage self-awareness and self-regulation.

—Teri Berkgren

Rating

    Promising/Emerging Practice

This rating is based on teacher testimonials, widespread use by experienced educators, and the potential to improve overlooked skill deficits across the entire ASD spectrum. The 5-Point Scale and/or similar programs that attempt to make abstract concepts more concrete through visuals should be researched further with students with ASD specifically combined with other EBPs.

Resources and Suggested Readings

Buron, K. D. (2022). *The incredible 5-point scale.* 5 Point Scale Publishing. https://www.5points cale.com/

Buron, K. D., & Curtis, M. (2021). *The incredible 5-point scale: Assisting students in understanding social interactions and managing their emotional responses* (2nd ed., rev.). 5 Point Scale Publishing.

The developers of the Incredible 5-Point Scale published a revised version of their text titled *The Incredible 5-Point Scale: Assisting students in understanding social interactions and managing their emotional responses* in 2022. It is available for purchase through Amazon for $24.99. The book was originally published through AAPC Publishing, but is now self-published by Kari Dunn Buron through her company, 5 Point Scale Publishing.

The developers have also published a website in which users can access free downloadables as well as affiliate links to their books on Amazon. It appears the website is maintained by Kari Buron alone and can be accessed at, https://www.5pointscale.com/

The Nebraska Autism Spectrum Disorders Network offers a free online webinar on The Incredible Five-Point Scale that can be accessed athttps://www.unl.edu/asdnetwork/webinars?combine=scale&tid=All

The Ohio Center for Autism and Low Incidence (OCALI) offers a free online course on the Incredible 5-Point Scale. After creating an account, it can be accessed at https://autisminternetmodules.org/search?qtitle=scale

Social Narratives/Story-Based Interventions

Description

Social Narratives are short descriptions of social situations that "highlight relevant features of a target behavior or skill and offer examples of appropriate responding. Social Narratives are aimed at helping learners adjust to changes in routine, adapt their behaviors based on the social and physical cues of a situation, or to teach specific social skills or behaviors. Social Narratives are individualized according to learner needs and typically are quite short, often told in a story format, and often include pictures or other visual aids. Usually written in first person from the perspective of the learner, they include sentences that detail the situation, provide suggestions for appropriate learner responses, and describe the thoughts and feelings of other people involved in the situation" (NCAEP, Steinbrenner et al., 2020, p. 121). The NAC used the term Story-Based Interventions, most recently defined as interventions that "identify a target behavior and involve a written description of the situations under which specific behaviors are expected to occur. Most stories aim to increase perspective taking skills and are written from an 'I' or 'some people' perspective" (NAC, 2015, p. 69).

Carol Gray's Social Stories

The most well-known example of a Social Narrative/Story-Based Intervention identified by both the NCAEP and the NAC is Social Stories, which was developed and trademarked by Carol Gray in the early 1990s. Zimmerman and Ledford (2017) use the term Social Narrative and Social Stories™ synonymously. Social Stories are written in positive language from either a first- or third-person perspective. Social Stories are made up of six types of sentences that answered who, what, when, where, and why questions about the social situation being described:

- Descriptive sentences provide information about the setting, subjects, and actions.

- Directive sentences suggest appropriate behavioral responses.

- Perspective sentences describe the feelings and reactions of others in the situation.

- Control sentences provide analogies with related actions and responses.

- Cooperative sentences help to identify what others in the situation could do to help.

- Affirmative sentences are used to stress important points.

A Social Story always contains descriptive sentences while the other types are not required. If the other types of sentences are used, there must be more descriptive sentences at a ratio of 4 to 1. In 2004, Gray specified 10 defining characteristics in Social Stories 10.0, which was updated with more detail in 2010 in Social Stories 10.1 and again in Social Stories 10.2 in 2014 (Gray, n.d.).

Brief Overview of the Literature

The seminal article on Social Stories was published in 1993 (Gray & Garand, 1993). There has been a great deal of debate and confusion since that time surrounding the definition of a "social story" and the level of evidence that supports this intervention. Many studies on "social stories" do not follow the defining characteristics provided by Carol Gray. In a systematic review conducted by Styles in 2011 of 51 studies on "social stories," he found that "A number of the earlier studies did not follow Gray's (1998, 2004) Social Story ration/formula but this appears to have been more consistently adhered to in more recent studies with most researchers reporting that their Social Stories conformed to Gray's various guidelines. However, the true extent to which they have been adhered to by researchers is unclear; five studies were explicit about not doing so while a further 12 made no reference to them" (p. 421). Eighteen of the 21 studies included under Social Narratives by the NCAEP (2020) had the term Social Stories in the title. However, only five of them included the trademark symbol. The latest systematic review on social stories (Milne et al., 2020) included studies on "story-based interventions that do not follow the guidelines provided by Gray but were still classified as social stories by the authors" (p. 265). Several other systematic reviews that not were included in the 2011 Styles review (Karal & Wolfe, 2018; Kokina & Kern, 2010; Leaf et al., 2015; Reynhout & Carter, 2006; Rhodes, 2014) acknowledged Gray's trademarked definition in their introduction but did not include it in their inclusion criteria of the studies reviewed.

Core Reviews

Simpson et al. (2005) used the term Social Stories and gave the intervention a rating of Promising Practice. The NAC used the term Story-Intervention Package in 2009 and Story-Based Interventions in 2015. It stated that Social Stories was the most well-known Story-Based Intervention and rated the intervention as Established in both of its reports. The NPDC (Wong et al., 2014) and NCAEP (Steinbrenner et al., 2020) both used the term Social Narratives, gave the rating of EBP, and listed Social Stories as a manualized intervention meeting criteria (MIMC) and rated the intervention as an EBP based on a total of 21 studies.

Other Systematic Reviews/Meta-Analyses

There is one systematic review of Social Stories published after 2017 and therefore not included in the latest core review (Qi et al., 2018) that included peer-review studies published between 1998 and 2012 that had at least one participant with diagnosed autism, Asperger Syndrome, or PDD-NOS and followed Gray's guidelines. The authors identified 22 articles and concluded that 32 percent of the studies showed moderate to strong evidence of effectiveness based on visual analysis following the Work Works Clearinghouse (WWC) standards and 52 to 90 percent could be considered effective based on calculations scored on four nonoverlap indices to evaluate intervention, maintenance, and generalization effects.

Age and Diagnostic Considerations/ Prerequisite Skills and Abilities

The available research that follow's Gray's guidelines supports the use of Social Stories with learners with ASD from early childhood through adolescence.

Reported Outcomes

The lack of precision in definition makes it very difficult for a practitioner to determine the actual evidence base supporting or not supporting Social Narratives/Story-Based Interventions. The most recent systematic review on Social Stories concluded that the intervention has been shown to be effective in decreasing inappropriate behavior. Mixed results were found when Social Stories were used to increase social communication skills as well as other appropriate behaviors.

Qualifications Needed

No formal training is required to implement. However, individuals who use these practices should consider training in its application through consultation with an experienced implementer or other training formats.

How, Where, and When Typically Implemented

Used according to Carol Gray's guidelines as part of an Evidence-Based Social Skills Training structure, Social Stories can potentially be a helpful tool to provide rationale for the skill, perspectives of others involved in the situation, and consistency of language across implementers. Social Narratives/Story-Based Interventions should be used with interventions with a stronger evidence base such as Modeling, Prompting, video modeling, or Reinforcement.

Costs

Social Narratives/Story-Based Interventions are cost-effective in terms of time and other resources. There are no costs associated with training, no additional teaching time is required, and no materials need to be purchased other than those typically found in natural settings.

Potential Risks

There are no documented or obvious risks associated with Social Narratives/Story-Based Interventions.

Practitioner Testimonial(s)

Social Narratives have been a staple in my classroom! I use them for a variety of skills or situations that my students are struggling with. When a student struggles with transitioning to new activities such as an upcoming field trip, a school concert, or assembly, a Social Narrative has worked wonderfully with these students. It helps them become familiar with what is going to happen during these events and helps them feel more comfortable and confident when they know what is going on. I have also used them to help describe what appropriate behaviors and social skills look like and do not look like. Social Narratives help my students learn those appropriate skills and increase their success in my classroom and in our school!

—Tracie Betz

(Continued)

(Continued)

I have used Story-Based Interventions throughout my career. One of my favorite experiences with Story-Based Interventions was when I was working with a preschool student with significant anxiety and autism. The student behaved in a very repetitive way each time he would get anxious. When he first became anxious, he would begin to flap his hands, then if the anxiety continued, he would begin to rock or pace, and if not supported he would rock to the point of banging his head or pace till he would hit a wall or run out of the room. After noticing that these behaviors occurred in a pattern, we created a social narrative for him with tools to self-regulate from the start of the anxiety. It went something like this: "Sometimes I get mad, angry, or nervous. When this happens, I start to flap my hands. When I flap my hands, I know my body is at a 2 and I need to use my tools. I can spin my fidget spinner, ask for a break in the rocking chair, or get a drink of water. When I do these things my body goes back to a 1 and I can become calm. I can learn and play with my friends." The first time I read the story with the student, I could see his anxiety go down immediately. He asked to take the story home, and then carried it around for weeks. It became a comforting reminder of what to do when he was getting upset. I am happy to stay this young man is now in high school with the tools and strategies he needs to self-regulate and participate with peers in a meaningful and productive way.

—Lindy McDaniel

Rating

   Promising/Emerging Practice

Resources and Suggested Readings

Carol Gray Social Stories. https://carolgraysocialstories.com/

Collet-Klingenberg, L., & Franzone, E. (2008). *Overview of social narratives.* University of Wisconsin, Waisman Center, The National Professional Development Center on Autism Spectrum Disorders.

Suhrheinrich, J., Chan, J., Melgarejo, M., Reith, S., Stahmer, A., & AFIRM Team. (2018). *Social narratives.* National Professional Development Center on Autism Spectrum Disorder, FPG Child Development Center, University of North Carolina. https://afirm.fpg.unc.edu/social-narratives

Wong, C. (2013). *Social narratives (SN) fact sheet.* The University of North Carolina, Frank Porter Graham Child Development Institute, The National Professional Development Center on Autism Spectrum Disorders.

FaceSay™

Description

FaceSay is a computer-based social skills program that uses realistic avatar assistants within repetitious computer games to increase the social interactions of learners with ASD. FaceSay consists of three different games that provide learners with simulated practice in a variety of skills such as eye contact and joint attention (Amazing Gaze), facial processing and recognition (Band Aid Clinic), and emotion recognition (Follow the Leader), with the ultimate goal of increasing learners' social competence in the natural environment (Hopkins et al., 2011; Rice et al., 2015). The games assist learners in identifying facial features that are associated with different emotions.

Brief Overview of the Literature

In a study completed by Hopkins et al. (2011), an randomized control trial (RCT) was used to evaluate the effectiveness of the FaceSay program for students with ASD who were categorized as "low-functioning autism" (LFA) or "high-functioning autism" (HFA) according to their score on the Kaufman Brief Intelligence Test, second edition (KBIT II; Kaufman, 1990). Results indicated that students in the LFA intervention group demonstrated improvements in 2 of the 3 target areas, including emotion recognition and social interactions, when compared to the LFA control group. Students in the LFA group also increased their ability to recognize and label feelings when depicted in photographs and demonstrated some generalization to the natural environment. Participants in the HFA intervention group demonstrated improvements in all three target skills including facial recognition, emotion recognition, and social interactions as compared to the HFA control group. These participants recognized and labeled feelings depicted in photographs and drawings that generalized the skills to the natural environment and maintained their emotional recognition abilities after the intervention.

In a second study, Rice et al. (2015) used scores on standardized assessments and teacher ratings to investigate improvements in affect recognition, mentalizing (i.e., Theory of Mind [ToM]), and social skills in school-age children with ASD after using FaceSay. Results showed significant differences between experimental and control groups in the areas of affect recognition and ToM, as well as decreases in teacher ratings on a teacher observation assessment. No significant differences were noted between the experimental and control groups in the number of positive or negative social skills observed, and the newly learned skills did not generalize to interactions with their peers (Kouo & Egel, 2016; Rice et al., 2015).

Core Reviews

The only core review that references FaceSay is the NCAEP (Steinbrenner et al., 2020) in 2020. It cited one article (Hopkins et al., 2011) and included it under the category of Technology-Aided Instruction, which was given the rating of EBP. It also listed it as an MIMC.

Age and Diagnostic Considerations/ Prerequisite Skills and Abilities

According to the company website, FaceSay works best for learners 4 to 12 years of age (Symbionica, LLC, n.d.). No prerequisite skills or abilities emerged from the research as all participants demonstrated gains in the targeted social skills. However, participants who were considered to have HFA appeared to gain more skills and maintain the skills after the study was completed.

Reported Outcomes

According to Hopkins et al. (2011) and Rice et al. (2015), FaceSay appears to be a promising tool for increasing social skills for students with ASD. The research demonstrated increases in facial recognition, emotion regulation, social interactions, and ToM. Decreases in teacher ratings were also noted.

Qualifications Needed

No qualifications or training requirements were mentioned in the research or on the product website.

How, Where, and When Typically Implemented

According to the company website, FaceSay can be run without an internet connection. A sound card with speakers or headphones are required, and a touch screen is optional, but if used, it will allow learners to physically participate in interactions that require gestures and other movements (Symbionica, LLC, n.d.). FaceSay can be implemented in school, clinical, home, and community settings.

Costs

FaceSay offers a free trial. The cost depends on the setting and number of students. Currently, it appears that the cost ranges from $79 (USD) for the Home Edition for two children to $749 (USD) for the Unlimited Student License on 1 PC. Volume discounts are available (Symbionica, LLC, n.d.).

Potential Risks

There are no documented or obvious risks associated with FaceSay.

Rating

   Promising/Emerging Practice

This rating is based on the inclusion of the intervention under the EBP of Technology-Aided Instruction by the NCAEP in 2020.

Resources and Suggested Readings

FaceSay™ can be accessed at http://www.facesay.com/

Hopkins, I. M., Gower, M. W., Perez, T. A., Smith, D. S., Amthor, F. R., Wimsatt, C. F., & Biasini, F. J. (2011). Avatar assistant: Improving social skills in students with autism spectrum disorder through a computer-based intervention. *Journal of Autism and Developmental Disorders, 41*, 1543–1555.

Rice, L. M., Wall, C. A., Fogel, A., & Shic, F. (2015). Computer-assisted face processing instruction improves emotion recognition, mentalizing, and social skills in students with ASD. *Journal of Autism and Developmental Disorders, 45*(7), 2176–2186.

Mind Reading: The Interactive Guide to Emotions

Description

Mind Reading: The Interaction Guide to Emotions is an interactive computer program that uses faces, voices, and other related stimuli to assist users in learning to recognize complex emotions (Baron-Cohen et al., 2004; LaCava et al., 2007). According to the program manual, Mind Reading consists of three main applications: the Emotions Library, Learning Center, and Game Zone. The Emotions Library provides video clips, audio clips, definitions, and stories for 412 emotions and mental states. The 412 emotions are divided into 24 emotion groups and six developmental levels ranging from 4 years to adulthood. The Learning Center provides opportunities for users to practice and improve their emotion recognition using systematic lessons and quizzes. Users can earn rewards by successfully completing tasks. The rewards can be used by participants to "unlock" items of interest. The final application, the Games Zone, consists of five educational games that allow learners to practice and continue to learn about the targeted emotions (Baron-Cohen et al., 2004; Thomeer et al., 2011). Mind Reading can be purchased as a DVD-ROM and a CD-ROM. A sound card and speakers are required.

Brief Overview of the Literature

Several studies have examined the impact of the Mind Reading software on the emotion recognition and social skills of individuals with ASD. Golan and Baron-Cohen (2006a, 2006b) conducted two of the earliest studies on the Mind Reading software. Both investigations examined the impact of 10 to 15 weeks of in-home use of the Mind Reading software for adults with Asperger's syndrome and mild autism in comparison to control groups. Results indicated that the intervention improved participants' ability to recognize emotions and mental states using faces and voices. Although adults did not generalize these skills, the children performed well when applied to new environments and stimuli (Golan & Baron-Cohen, 2006a, 2006b; LaCava et al., 2007).

Researchers LaCava et al. (2007, 2010) found comparable results to Golan and Baron-Cohen (2006a, 2006b). In LaCava et al. (2010)'s first study, participants significantly improved their ability to identify basic and complex emotions. In addition, the participants generalized these abilities to faces and voices not included in the software. The second study (LaCava et al., 2010) added a tutor as an independent variable. The tutors sat next to the participants, assisted them with accessing the software and ensured the participants were using the correct program. The tutors also initiated informal conversations regarding real-world situations in which an emotion may be important and mimed the emotions to provide more practice. Likewise, the results of the second study showed higher scores on pre- and post-tests indicating an increase in the ability to identify basic and complex emotions, with most of the participants generalizing these abilities to black and white and color photos and drawings not included in the software. Although not statistically significant in either study, the intervention led to changes in the percentage of intervals during which participants engaged in positive social interactions as recorded by a trained observer.

In addition to the tutor (LaCava et al., 2010), Mind Reading has been paired with other independent variables such as *in vivo* rehearsal (Thomeer et al., 2011), comprehensive psychosocial treatment (Lopata et al., 2016), and comprehensive school-based intervention (CSBI, Lopata et al., 2019) including skill instruction groups, therapeutic activities, repeated practice, etc. Lopata et al. (2016, 2019) used random control trials to examine the impact of the Mind Reading software as a component of a summer program involving a comprehensive psychosocial treatment and of a CSBI. Results from the summer program indicated that participants who received the Mind Reading intervention paired with the comprehensive psychosocial treatment demonstrated more significant improvements in facial emotion recognition skills than the participants who received the comprehensive psychosocial treatment only. These improvements, however, were primarily demonstrated on the assessment measure that is directly aligned with the Mind Reading program.

The second study completed by Lopata et al. (2019), which examined the impact of the Mind Reading program as a component of a CSBI, resulted in significant improvements on the test of emotion recognition skills for the CSBI group in comparison to the same-as-usual (SAU) control group. Improvements were also evident on parent and teacher ratings of ASD symptoms and social and social-communication skills. No differences between groups were detected for recess social interactions or academic skills.

In a final study, Thomeer et al. (2015) used a random control trial to evaluate the impact of the Mind Reading software and in vivo rehearsal on the emotion recognition, autism symptoms, and social skills of children with HFA. An in vivo rehearsal consisted of staff displaying a newly acquired emotion, then the child identifying that emotion. In some instances, the children were asked to display an emotion requested by staff. Data analysis indicated significant increases in emotion recognition for the treatment group on 3 of the 4 measures of emotion recognition with results maintaining at the 5-week follow-up. Results also indicated significant lower scores on instruments that measure ASD symptoms at post-test and follow-up.

Core Reviews

Of the core reviews, only the NCAEP (Steinbrenner et al., 2020) included Mind Reading as a reviewed intervention in 2020. It cited one article (Golan & Baron-Cohen, 2006a) and included it under the category of Technology-Aided Instruction which was given the rating of EBP. It also listed it as a manualized intervention meeting criteria (MIMC).

Other Peer Reviewed Research

The author of this text identified five peer-reviewed studies not included in the core reviews and they are summarized here.

AUTHOR(S)	N	SETTING	AGE/ GENDER	DIAGNOSES	FINDINGS
LaCava et al. (2010)	4	Public elementary school	4 males 7 to 10 yrs.	PDD-NOS or autism	Each participant increased their ER scores on computer and picture task, however the increased ability to recognize emotions did not appear to impact participants' social interactions.
Lopata et al. (2016)	36 18 (treatment group 1) 18 (treatment group 2)		34 males 2 females 7 to 12 yrs.	HFASD	Participants who received the Mind Reading intervention in addition to the comprehensive psychosocial treatment demonstrated more significant improvements in facial emotional recognition skills on one of the assessments than the participants who received the comprehensive psychosocial treatment only. However, the same results were not evident with other assessment measures.
Lopata et al. (2019)	103 52 (treatment group) 51 (1 dropped out) (Services-as-usual)		6 to 12 yrs. 94 males 8 females	ASD	Students in the CSBI group increased their scores on tests measuring emotion recognition skills, on parent–teacher ratings of ASD symptoms, and social and social-communication skills as compared to students in the SAU group. Differences between groups were not detected for recess social interactions or academic skills.
Thomeer et al. (2011)	11	Clinic	7 to 12 yrs.	HFASD	The ability of subjects to display emotion improved significantly. ASD-associated symptoms decreased significantly according to a standardized rating scale given to parents. There were high levels of treatment fidelity and parent and child reported satisfaction.
Thomeer et al. (2015)	43 22 Treatment 21 Control	Computer lab on college campus	Treatment 19 males 3 females Control 19 males 2 females 7 to 12 yrs.	HFASD	Participants demonstrated significant increases in emotion recognition for the treatment group on 3 of the 4 measures of emotion recognition with results maintaining at the 5-week follow-up. Results also indicated significant lower scores on instruments that measure ASD symptoms at posttest and follow-up.

Age and Diagnostic Considerations/ Prerequisite Skills and Abilities

Most study participants were between the ages of 6 and 12 years with IQ scores greater than 70, Verbal Comprehension Index or Perceptual Reasoning Index greater than 80, expressive or receptive language scores greater than or equal to 80, and a diagnosis that is commensurate with HFA or Asperger's syndrome.

Reported Outcomes

All studies reported significant increases in emotion recognition skills, especially on the Cambridge Mindreading Face-Voice Batter for Children (CAM-C) that is aligned with the Mind Reading software. Some studies reported changes in secondary measures such as autism symptoms. Younger participants were better able to generalize the learned skills than adults.

Qualifications Needed/ How, Where, and When Typically Implemented

No qualifications or training requirements were mentioned in the research or on the product website.

Costs

According to the website, http://www.silverliningmm.com/mindreading.htm, both the Mind Reading DVD and the Mind Reading CD-ROM set can be purchased for $129.95. Demos are available on this website.

Potential Risks

There are no documented or obvious risks associated with Mind Reading.

Rating

  Promising/Emerging Practice

Resources and Suggested Readings

Baron-Cohen, S., Golan, O., Wheelwright, S., & Hill, J. J. (2004). *Mind reading: The interactive guide to emotions*. Jessica Kingsley Publishers.

The social skills software *Mind Reading* can be accessed at http://www.silverliningmm.com/mindreading.htm

Naturalistic Developmental Behavioral Interventions (NDBI)

Introduction

Naturalistic Developmental Behavioral Interventions (NDBI) "are implemented in natural settings, involve shared control between child and therapist, utilize natural contingencies, and use a variety of behavioral strategies to teach developmentally appropriate, and prerequisite skills" (Schreibman et al., 2015, p. 1). These interventions combine principles from both behavioral and developmental science. The teacher focuses on functional learning targets across all areas of development and plans for and always promotes generalization. Teaching sessions happen throughout the learner's day in their home, school, and community within socially meaningful and reinforcing interactions with others. Priority learning targets are those that are the precursors to many other essential skills, two examples being imitation and joint attention. Interactions are primarily child directed and incorporate their interests building more complex skills over time. Reinforcing consequences are used that are naturally found in the environment and are related to the interaction such as food at lunchtime and access to preferred toys during play time.

Core Reviews

Simpson et al. (2005) did not review Naturalistic Intervention or Teaching Strategies as a broad intervention category but did review Incidental Teaching, pivotal response training (PRT), and Joint Action Routines (JARS) as individual interventions, which are included in this section. The NAC used the term *Naturalistic Teaching Strategies* and included 32 articles in 2009 and three articles in 2015, resulting in the rating of Established. The NPDC (Wong et al., 2014) and the NCAEP (Steinbrenner et al., 2020) used the term *Naturalistic Intervention* and gave a rating of EBP based on a total of 75 studies. The 2015 Schreibman et al. article included Incidental Teaching and PRT as NDBI and repeatedly referenced joint attention interventions. Therefore, those interventions were included in this section.

Interventions Included in This Section

- Incidental Teaching
- Imitation-Based Interventions
- Milieu Teaching—includes Enhanced Milieu Training (MMC)
- Joint Attention Interventions—includes Joint Attention Symbolic Play and Emotion Regulation (JASPER) (MIMC)
- Pivotal Response Interventions—includes Pivotal Response Treatment/Training (MIMC and CTM)

Resources and Suggested Readings

Franzone, E. (2020). *Naturalistic intervention.* Autism Internet Module. Ohio Center for Autism and Low Incidence Disabilities (OCALI). This site can be accessed at https://autisminternetmodules.org/search?qtitle=naturalistic

Suhrheinrich, J., Chan, J., Melgarejo, M. Reith, S., Stahmer, A., & AFIRM Team. (2018). *Naturalistic intervention.* National Professional Development Center on Autism Spectrum Disorder, FPG Child Development Center, University of North Carolina. This site can be accessed at https://afirm.fpg.unc.edu/naturalistic-intervention

Wong, C. (2013). *Naturalistic intervention (NI) fact sheet.* The University of North Carolina, Frank Porter Graham Child Development Institute, The National Professional Development Center on Autism Spectrum Disorders. This fact sheet can be accessed at https://autismpdc.fpg.unc.edu/sites/autismpdc.fpg.unc.edu/files/Naturalistic_factsheet.pdf

Incidental Teaching

Description

Incidental Teaching involves providing instruction based on student interests and motivation by using a variety of behavior analytic strategies such as time delay, modeling, prompting, errorless learning, and reinforcement within typical daily activities. Incidental Teaching begins when the teacher organizes the learning environment around the interests of the child, keeping in mind preplanned learning objectives (e.g., labeling common nouns, identifying prepositions, or labeling colors). Organization of the environment begins when the teacher takes note of the items and activities the child enjoys and then puts those items out of reach but where they are still visible. Once items are out of reach, the teacher then waits for teachable moments, all of which are initiated by the child when they reach for, gesture toward, or verbally request a desired item or event. Once a child initiates, the teacher then prompts an elaborated response. For example, if the child says "ball" to ask for a ball, before providing the ball the adult says "red ball." Once the child emits the elaborated response, the teacher delivers praise and access to the ball.

Brief Overview of the Literature

Incidental Teaching was first researched by Hart and Risley (1975, 1978, 1980) and is considered one of the first naturalistic teaching strategies used in ABA. Single-case research since that time has confirmed that Incidental Teaching can be as, or more, effective than adult-directed, ABA-based teaching methods such as discrete trial teaching (DTT) in teaching language production that generalizes to other communication partners and environments (Charlop-Christy & Carpenter, 2000; Farmer-Dougan, 1994; Hsieh et al., 2011; McGee & Daly, 2007; McGee et al., 1983, 1985, 1986, 1992, 1994; 1999; Miranda-Linné & Medlin, 1992).

Core Reviews

Only Simpson et al. (2005) included the specific term Incidental Teaching as a reviewed intervention and rated it as a Promising Practice based on eight studies. The others considered Incidental Teaching to be a part of other interventions such as Naturalistic Interventions/Teaching Strategies, Parent Implemented Interventions, Comprehensive Behavior Treatment of Young Children, and Behavior Packages, which were all rated as Established or EBP.

Age and Diagnostic Considerations/ Prerequisite Skills and Abilities

Incidental Teaching has been researched primarily with preschool- and elementary-age children with ASD and older individuals who were not functionally verbal or had significant ID.

Reported Outcomes

Incidental Teaching has been shown to be effective primarily in increasing and enhancing generalization of communication skills. However, it has also been used to improve academic and social skills.

Qualifications Needed

No formal training in Incidental Teaching as a stand-alone intervention is required. Nonetheless, individuals who use this method must be familiar with and trained in its application through consultation with an experienced implementer or other training formats.

How, Where, and When Typically Implemented

Incidental Teaching takes place during typical activities while other teaching objectives are being taught. Parents and teachers may easily integrate Incidental Teaching into adaptive skill routines and play sessions and peers can be taught to facilitate Incidental Teaching sessions.

Costs

Incidental Teaching is cost-effective in terms of time and other resources. There are no costs associated with training and no additional teaching time is required. No materials need to be purchased other than those typically found in natural settings.

Potential Risks

There are no documented or obvious risks associated with Incidental Teaching.

Rating

 Evidence-Based Practice

Resources and Suggested Readings

Charlop-Christy, M. H. (2008). *How to do incidental teaching*. ProEd.

Florida Atlantic University. (n.d.). *Fact sheet-incidental teaching*. This fact sheet can be accessed at https://www.fau.edu/education/centersandprograms/card/documents/incidentalteaching

Kansas Technical Assistance System Network (TASN). (2022). *Incidental teaching procedures*. This site can be accessed at https://www.ksdetasn.org/resources/2041.g.pdf

Knapp Center for Childhood Development. (n.d.). *What is incidental teaching?* This site can be accessed at http://knappcenter.org/wp-content/uploads/2017/05/Topic-3_Incidental-Teaching-Guide.pdf

Imitation-Based Interventions

Description

Imitation is a mechanism through which new skills are learned throughout a person's lifetime. Babies begin imitating in early infancy when they imitate caregivers' facial expressions and vocalizations. Caregivers respond by performing the facial expression or vocalization again, thereby creating a reciprocal exchange that provides the foundation for developing various skills. The development of imitation continues throughout early childhood within the natural environment. During Imitation-Based Interventions, the teacher attempts to develop the learner's imitation skills by repeating their actions and vocalizations during play. Specifically, in Reciprocal Imitation Training (RIT) the teacher follows the learner's lead and engages with the same toys and materials. The teacher then imitates the learner's verbal and nonverbal behavior and describes their actions using simple language, a process called linguistic mapping. Once the learner notices the teacher imitating them, the teacher models actions the learner has done previously with those play materials and then prompts the learner to imitate them in return. Once the learner begins imitating these familiar actions using those same play materials, novel actions are modeled. Finally, the teacher can add in meaningful gestures and vocalizations related to the play activity to promote novelty, surprise, and repeated imitation.

Brief Overview of the Literature

Research on Imitation-Based Interventions with children with ASD started in the early 2000s (Field et al., 2001; Ross & Greer, 2003) and continued for the next two decades (Heimann et al., 2006; Ingersoll et al., 2007; Ingersoll & Lalonde, 2010; Ishizuka & Yamamoto, 2016; Tsiouri & Greer, 2007). Several studies have found a significant relationship between the ability to imitate and other social behaviors often delayed in individuals with ASD such as joint attention, social reciprocity, and language development (McDuffie et al., 2007; Rogers, 1999; Stone et al., 1997; Young et al., 1994). Research has also shown that Imitation Training during play in the natural environment leads to higher rates of imitation in children with ASD as opposed to Imitation Training that takes place during adult-directed activities such as Discrete Trial Teaching. According to Ingersoll (2008), Discrete Trial Teaching results in poor spontaneous use of skills and poor generalization. She and her colleagues developed RIT with the goal of teaching individuals with autism to imitate others during play and generalize imitation to other environments (Ingersoll, 2010, 2012; Ingersoll & Schreibman, 2006).

Core Reviews

Simpson et al. (2005) did not include any Imitation-Based Interventions. The NAC used the term Imitation-Based Intervention and gave a rating of Emerging in 2009 based on six articles and again in 2015 based on an unspecified number of articles. The NPDC (Wong et al., 2014) used the term Reciprocal Imitation Training in 2014 and gave the rating of Some but Insufficient Support based on four articles. In 2020, the NCAEP (Steinbrenner et al., 2020) recategorized RIT under the broader category of Naturalistic Behavior Intervention, which was rated as an EBP.

Age and Diagnostic Considerations/ Prerequisite Skills and Abilities

Imitation-Based Interventions are used with young children with ASD, specifically those who are nonverbal or have severe language delays. There have been a few studies done using RIT with adolescents with significant ID (Ingersoll et al., 2013, 2016) with promising results.

Reported Outcomes

Imitation-Based Interventions have been reported to improve the pivotal skill of joint attention and various language, social and play skills, as well as decreasing challenging and self-stimulatory behavior.

Qualifications Needed

No formal training is required to implement Imitation-Based Interventions. Nonetheless, individuals who use this method must be familiar with and trained in its application through consultation with an experienced implementer or other training formats.

How, Where, and When Typically Implemented

Interventions targeting imitation skills can be scheduled during the school day and implemented by teachers and paraprofessionals. In addition, parents have been successfully trained to implement Imitation-Based Interventions in the home environment (Ingersoll & Gergans, 2007). Imitation-Based Interventions have been paired with VM in both the school and home settings (Cardon, 2012; Kleeberger & Mirenda, 2010; McDowell et al., 2015).

Costs

Imitation-Based Interventions are cost-effective in terms of time and other resources. There are no costs associated with training and no additional teaching time is required. No materials need to be purchased other than those typically found in natural settings.

Potential Risks

There are no documented or obvious risks associated with Imitation-Based Interventions.

Rating

  Promising/Emerging Practice

Resources and Suggested Readings

The Hanen Center. (n.d.). *Do this doesn't cut it: Helping children with autism learn to imitate.* This site can be accessed at https://www.hanen.org/MyHanen/Articles/Research/ -Do-This--Doesn-t-Cut-It--Helping-children-with-au.aspx

McRory Pediatric Services, Inc. (2021). *Which approach should you use?* This site can be accessed at https://www.mcrorypediatrics.com/post/which-approach-should-you-use

QC Balance Autism. (2020). *Reciprocal Imitation Training.* This site can be accessed at https://www.youtube.com/watch?v=m0ncwlRrxZA

Milieu Teaching

Description

Milieu Teaching is a package of behaviorally based teaching strategies that includes Modeling, Mand-Modeling, Time Delay, and Incidental Teaching as methods for developing language. When teaching begins, the implementer determines the child's interests by watching their gaze and following their lead. When the child reaches toward an item they want, the implementer provides a model that serves to prompt the child to respond. For example, the learner may be looking at or reaching for a block. In response, the implementer might say, "Block." If the learner responds by saying "Block," the implementer provides reinforcement in the form of verbal praise such as, "You want the block!" along with access to the block. If the learner does not respond correctly, the same model is provided a second time and the learner is given a second opportunity to respond. If the learner fails to respond again, the implementer provides the model again and then immediately delivers the item.

During the Mand-Model procedure, the child is playing with the same toy but is not immediately given the model. Instead, the implementer presents a verbal mand such as "What do you want?" and if the child responds correctly, verbal praise and access to the item is delivered. If the child responds incorrectly, but their motivation for the item remains high, the Mand-Model is presented again (e.g., "What do you want?"). If their motivation for the items has started to wane, a model (e.g., "Block") is given instead so that teaching can still occur before the child loses interest in the item entirely. If the child responds incorrectly again, or does not respond at all, corrective feedback is given along with access to the item.

Once the child has begun to successfully ask for the item, a Time Delay procedure is then used to support generalization and independence. For example, when the child reaches for the item, instead of immediately providing a Model or a Mand-Model, the implementer might pause for a few seconds in order to see if the child will emit the response independently. If successful, the implementer delivers praise and immediate access to the item. An incorrect response, or failure to respond, results in a Model or Mand-Model, followed by delivery of the item.

Finally, the use of Incidental Teaching ensures the child has multiple opportunities throughout their day to respond and use language. For example, if the teacher is familiar with the child's interests, they may incorporate those items into multiple activities so that frequent responding can occur. Likewise, the teacher should use the Model, Mand-Model, and Time Delay procedures throughout the child's day to ensure generalization and use of language skills across multiple items, activities, and settings.

Enhanced Milieu Teaching (EMT) uses the same teaching procedures as Milieu Teaching, but it also includes responsive interaction strategies that serve to model new language and build verbal social interactions while also considering environmental arrangement so as to promote higher levels of engagement. During EMT, the implementer follows the learner's lead and joins them in their self-directed play while avoiding directions and questions. During play, the implementer notices each time the learner attempts communication and responds by talking about what the learner is doing. If the learner stops communicating, the implementer imitates and describes the learner's nonverbal behaviors. For example, if the learner is stacking blocks, the implementer also stacks blocks and says "Stack blocks." The implementer can model different actions with the same toy (e.g., tap blocks) or the same actions with different toys (e.g., stack cups). Predictably sequenced routines that have a beginning, middle, and end are used so the learner can predict what actions and words will come next (e.g., stack blocks, tap blocks, spin blocks). In addition, language is simplified to match the learner's so it is easier to imitate and understand. Any communication from the learner is expanded upon by the implementer by immediately imitating it and adding more words. The goal of EMT is to connect existing communication with new language so the learner develops new vocabulary and more complex phrases. Finally, environmental arrangement strategies to support communication include offering choices, pausing within a routine, and waiting for the learner to initiate a response, waiting with a cue, providing inadequate amounts of items or toys, and providing assistance.

Brief Overview of the Literature

The term *Milieu Teaching* was first used by Hart and Rogers-Warren (1978). In the 1990s, Kaiser and colleagues developed EMT (Hemmeter & Kaiser, 1994; Kaiser et al., 1997; Kaiser & Hester, 1994) and trained parents and other implementers to use this intervention (Alpert & Kaiser, 1992; Hancock & Kaiser, 2002; Kaiser et al., 2000; Kaiser & Roberts, 2013).

Core Reviews

None of the core reviews included the specific term *Milieu Teaching* in their reviews. The NAC referred to Prelinguistic Milieu Teaching under Naturalistic Teaching Strategies in both 2009 and 2015 and also referred to Milieu Teaching under the same category in 2015. In 2014, the NPDC (Wong et al., 2014) included two articles on Milieu Teaching (Hancock & Kaiser, 2002; Olive et al., 2007) under Naturalistic Intervention and one (Kaiser et al., 2000) under Parent-Implemented Intervention. In 2020 the NCAEP (Steinbrenner et al., 2020) listed Milieu Teaching (Kaiser & Roberts, 2013) as an MIMC and also referenced Enhanced and Prelinguistic Milieu Teaching under Naturalistic Intervention, which was given the rating of EBP.

Other Peer Reviewed Research

One additional peer-reviewed study was identified by the author of this text and is summarized here.

AUTHORS	N	SETTING	AGE/ GENDER	DIAGNOSIS	RESEARCH DESIGN	FINDINGS
Christensen-Sandfort and Whinnery (2013)	3	Early Childhood classroom	4 yrs./ Male 5 yrs./ Female 5 yrs./ Male	ASD	Multiple baseline across participants	Increased spontaneous language production in all three participants

Age and Diagnostic Considerations/ Prerequisite Skills and Abilities

Milieu Teaching has primarily been researched with young children with ASD. One study involved an adolescent who used a communication book (Hamilton & Snell, 1993) indicating that Milieu Teaching may be effective for use with older students who are not functionally verbal.

Reported Outcomes

Milieu Teaching is reported to increase the frequency of language production, which includes the use of Augmentative Communication Devices and Picture Exchange Systems (Christensen-Sandfort & Whinnery, 2013; Hamilton & Snell, 1993; Ogletree et al., 2012; Olive et al., 2007).

Qualifications Needed

No formal training is required to implement Milieu Teaching. Nonetheless, individuals who use this method must be familiar with and trained in its application through consultation with an experienced implementer or other training formats. Teachers and other implementers can learn Milieu Teaching strategies, integrate into adaptive skill and play sessions, and generalize them to home interactions with parents. Much of the research literature focused on training parents to implement Milieu Teaching.

How, Where, and When Typically Implemented

Milieu Teaching can be implemented both in a child's home and in classrooms and is typically carried out during play. Because it is play based in nature and follows the child's leads and interests to develop language, Milieu Teaching is most often implemented in early childhood classrooms.

Costs

Milieu Teaching is cost-effective in terms of time and other resources. There are no costs associated with training and no additional teaching time is required, nor are there materials that need to be purchased other than those typically found in natural classroom settings.

Potential Risks

There are no documented or obvious risks associated with Milieu Teaching.

Rating

  Evidence-Based Practice

Resources and Suggested Readings

Kaiser, A. P. (2011). *Kidtalk: Naturalistic communication intervention strategies for parents and teachers of young children.* This site can be accessed at https://www.aucd.org/docs/SIG%20Docs/EIEC/Kaiser_Webinar_2_22_11.pd

Joint Attention Interventions

Description

Joint attention happens when two people intentionally pay attention to the same thing during a social interaction and starts developing at about 1 year of age. It is a pivotal learning target in that it is essential for developing other language and communication skills. Examples of early joint attention are following another person's eye gaze, pointing to objects to direct another person's attention, and showing someone an item. Many children with ASD are delayed in understanding the purpose of communication and its reciprocal nature. Joint attention interventions build these foundational skills through arranging the learner's environment in a way that supports and increases the opportunities and motivation for the learner to use language in meaningful ways.

Joint Attention Routines (JARs) are communication routines based on the learner's interests that happen between the learner and an adult or peer partner. Simpson et al. (2005) identify three types of JARs: (1) *preparation or fabrication of a specific end product* such as snack preparation, art, and product assembly; (2) *story or central plot line*, including pretend play and community living skills; and (3) *cooperative turn-taking games*, which may occur during activities such as morning circle routine, group music therapy, and recreational therapy sessions. The structure of the routines provide a scaffold that allows the learner to respond appropriately within a particular context even though they have a limited response skill set.

Joint Attention Symbolic Play and Emotion Regulation (JASPER) was developed by Dr. Connie Kasari at the University of California in Los Angeles and was identified as an MIMC by the NCAEP in 2020. It is a targeted modular intervention that targets joint attention, symbolic play, engagement, and regulation, which are the foundations of social communication.

Brief Overview of the Literature

Joint Attention Interventions were first introduced in the research literature in 1984 by Snyder-McLean et al., who built on the work of Bruner and colleagues in the mid-1970s that stressed the importance of JARs as a framework within which communication and ultimately language is acquired (Bruner, 1975, Bruner & Sherwood, 1976, Ratner & Bruner, 1978). Research on Joint Attention Interventions at that time involved learners with ID. The use of JARS with learners with autism started with the work of Koegel and Koegel (Koegel et al., 1987) as an alternative to traditional Discrete Trial Training. Many others expanded this body of research (Chang et al, 2016; Goods et al., 2013; Gulsrud et al., 2007; Harrop et al., 2017; Kaale et al., 2012; Kasari et al., 2006, 2008, 2014; Krstovska-Guerrero & Jones, 2013; Prizant et al., 2000; Shire et al., 2020; Whalen & Schreibman, 2003), which is based on the natural language paradigm that deemed these interventions to be appropriate for children with autism because they lack understanding of the function of communicative behavior and that communication is a reciprocal event (Koegel & Koegel, 1995).

Core Reviews

Simpson et al. (2005) included JARs and gave the rating of Promising Practice based on one study that did not include a subject with ASD (Snyder-McLean et al., 1984) and one book (Snyder-McLean et al., 1988). The NAC used the term Joint Attention Interventions in 2009 and reviewed five articles giving the intervention an

Established rating. In 2015, it did not include any interventions involving joint attention but did reference Joint Attention Interventions in the Behavioral Intervention, Parent Training Package, and Social Skills Package sections, which were all given an Established rating. The NPDC used the term Joint Attention-Symbolic Play Instruction in 2014 and reviewed three articles (Gulsrud et al., 2007; Kasari et al., 2006, 2008) giving the intervention a rating of Some Support. In 2020, the NCAEP (Steinbrenner et al., 2020) did not include any interventions involving joint attention in the name, but did list JASPER as an MIMC.

Age and Diagnostic Considerations/ Prerequisite Skills and Abilities

JARs have primarily been researched with young children with ASD who do not have functional verbal skills.

Reported Outcomes

JARs are reported to improve joint attention, play skills, and self-regulation in addition to increasing engagement and communication with others.

Qualifications Needed

No formal training is required to implement Joint Attention Interventions. Nonetheless, individuals who use this method must be familiar with and trained in its application through consultation with an experienced implementer or other training formats.

How, Where, and When Typically Implemented

Teachers and their assistants can learn to implement Joint Attention Interventions, integrate into adaptive skill and play sessions, and generalize them to home interactions with parents. There are formal trainings leading to various levels of certification in JASPER described in the costs section below.

Costs

Joint Attention Interventions are cost-effective in terms of time and other resources. Teachers could learn about Joint Attention Interventions themselves through the courses and suggested readings below at no cost. No additional teaching time is required or materials need to be purchased other than those typically found in natural settings.

There is a manual associated with JASPER available in paperback and e-book for $65, hardcover for $125, and a print/e-book combination for $71.50 with a limited duplication license for use at your place of employment. There is also a free companion website and reproducible supplementary materials. JASPER offers a Level 1: Introductory JASPER Training for those providing direct one-on-one service in both in person and virtual formats for a minimum cost of $3,600. There is also a Level 2: Advanced Training for both coaching caregivers and training practitioners for those with a graduate degree in a related field and 5 years of experience working with young children with special needs who have completed and maintained certification in the

Level 1 training. The advanced training involves a 5-day in-person workshop and follow-up submission of at least three videos to ensure implementation fidelity with the price for everything starting at $3,450.

Potential Risks

There are no documented or obvious risks associated with joint attention interventions.

Rating

 Evidence-Based Practice

Resources and Suggested Readings

Ben-Arieh, J. (2008). *How to use joint action routines*. ProEd.

The JASPER website can be accessed at https://www.jaspertraining.org/about

Kansas Technical Assistance System Network (TASN). *Are they looking? Joint attention and the young child with ASD*. This site can be accessed at https://www.ksdetasn.org/resources/1221

Kasari, C., Gulsrud, A. C., Shire, S. Y., & Strawbridge, C. (2021). *The JASPER model for children with autism: Promoting joint attention, symbolic play, engagement and regulation*. Guilford Press.

Pivotal Response Interventions

Description

Pivotal Response Interventions use the principles of ABA in a manner that excludes negative interactions, reduces dependence on artificial prompts, and takes place in the natural environment targeting foundational skills such as self-initiation, choice making, responding to multiple cues, and self-management that are likely to result in substantial collateral gains in other important areas of development. The focus is on increasing the motivation of the learner to in turn decrease disruptive avoidance and escape behavior through strategies such as giving the learner choices, mixing previously mastered learning targets with novel tasks, varying tasks, reinforcing attempts, and using reinforcement that exists naturally in the environment. There is a large focus on training those who commonly interact with the learner, such as parents and teachers, to use these interventions in a variety of natural settings.

Pivotal Response Training (PRT) was first developed by Drs. Robert and Lynn Koegel, who are currently the clinical directors of the Koegel Autism Center in California. They have trademarked the terms Pivotal Response Treatment®, Pivotal Response Training®, and Pivotal Response Teaching® and have done extensive research and trainings on PRT around the world. Odom et al. (2010) included PRT (Koegel & Koegel, 2006) as a comprehensive treatment model.

Brief Overview of the Literature

A seminal research study that examined Pivotal Response Interventions used the term Natural Language Paradigm as the focus of the intervention involved was on improving language skills (Koegel et al., 1987). Many other studies followed that explored the effect Pivotal Response Interventions had on other behaviors and used the terms pivotal social skills (Hupp & Reitman, 2000; Koegel & Frea, 1993), Pivotal Response Intervention (Koegel et al., 1999a; Koegel et al., 1999b), PRT (Brock et al., 2017; Kuhn et al., 2008; Pierce & Schreibman, 1997; Stahmer, 1995, 1999) and Pivotal Response Treatment (Hardan et al., 2015; Mohammadzaheri et al., 2015; Nefdt et al., 2010; Robinson, 2011).

Core Reviews

Simpson et al. (2005) used the term Pivotal Response Training and gave a rating of Scientifically Based Practice based on four studies (Hupp & Reitman, 2000; Koegel et al., 1999a, 1999b; & Pierce & Schreibmann, 1997). In 2009, the NAC used the term Pivotal Response Treatment and in 2015 added Pivotal Response Training, Pivotal Response Teaching and Natural Language Paradigm, reviewed six articles, and gave the intervention category a rating of Established Intervention. The NPDC (Wong et al., 2014) used the term Pivotal Response Training in 2014 reviewing 14 articles and giving the intervention a rating of EBP. In 2020, the NCAEP (Steinbrenner et al., 2020) classified PRT under the broader category of Naturalistic Intervention which was given the rating of EBP and included PRT (Koegel & Koegel, 2006) as an MIMC.

Age and Diagnostic Considerations/ Prerequisite Skills and Abilities

Pivotal Response Interventions are designed for use with learners from early childhood through adolescence with developmental delays in pivotal behaviors. The potential learner should show curiosity in manipulating objects, minimally attend to the environment, and demonstrate preliminary imitation skills.

Reported Outcomes

Pivotal Response Interventions have been demonstrated to improve verbal communication, social interactions, joint attention, and learning readiness skills and decrease stereotypic behaviors in learners with ASD.

Qualifications Needed

Since Pivotal Response Interventions are a subset of ABA, a BCBA or professional in a related field trained in ABA principles (e.g. psychologist, SLP, special education teacher) may be a helpful resource for training and implementation information. As of the writing of this manuscript, according to the list provided on the website of The Koegel Autism Center, there are over 130 certified professionals in Pivotal Response Treatment in 18 countries around the world.

How, Where, and When Typically Implemented

Pivotal Response Interventions involve individuals with whom the learner interacts most often, such as family members and teachers, with guidance from a trained facilitator, and take place in inclusive natural settings such as general education classrooms, homes, and various community locations.

Costs

Pivotal Response Interventions are meant to decrease the number of hours facilitators highly trained and skilled in their methodologies are needed for implementation so they are potentially cost, time, and manpower efficient (Koegel, et al., 1999a). The goal is to systematically facilitate learning within the context of the natural environment, leading to independence and self-education throughout the entire day, not just during more formal training sessions. As the learner's skills improve in pivotal areas, family members and teachers provide more natural ongoing support. The Koegel Autism Center provides virtual consultation in English, Spanish, Greek, Dutch, French, and German to parents and professionals starting at $160 which includes analysis of provided video clips of the learner and a 45-minute session with a Pivotal Response Treatment–certified provider. It also offers onsite trainings ranging from 2 to 5 days for $2,500 per day plus travel costs. There are a variety of resources available to learn more about Pivotal Response Interventions at a range of prices.

Potential Risks

There are no documented or obvious risks associated with the use of pivotal response interventions.

Rating

 Evidence-Based Practice

Resources and Suggested Readings

Koegel Autism: Pivotal Response Treatment (PRT)® Training and Services can be accessed at https://www.autismprthelp.com/

Koegel, R. L., & Koegel, L. K. (2012). *The PRT pocket guide: Pivotal Response Treatment for autism spectrum disorders*. Paul H. Brookes. (Approximately $24 new on Amazon.com; used copies are available.)

Koegel, R. L., & Koegel, L. K. (2018). *Pivotal Response Treatment Part 1*. University of Nebraska, Nebraska Autism Spectrum Disorders Network. This site can be accessed at https://www.unl.edu/asdnetwork/pivotal-response-treatment-part-1

Koegel, R. L., & Koegel, L. K. (2018). *Pivotal Response Treatment Part 2*. University of Nebraska, Nebraska Autism Spectrum Disorders Network. This site can be accessed at https://www.unl.edu/asdnetwork/pivotal-response-treatment-part-2

The Ohio Center for Autism and Low Incidence Disabilities (OCALI) (n.d.). *Pivotal Response Training (PRT)*. This site can be accessed at https://autisminternetmodules.org/m/492

Suhrheinrich, J., Chan, J., Melgarejo, M., Reith, S., Stahmer, A., & AFIRM Team. (2018). *Pivotal response training*. National Professional Development Center on Autism Spectrum Disorder, FPG Child Development Center, University of North Carolina. This site can be accessed at https://afirm.fpg.unc.edu/pivotal-response-training

Wong, C. (2013). *Pivotal response training (PRT) fact sheet*. The University of North Carolina, Frank Porter Graham Child Development Institute, The National Professional Development Center on Autism Spectrum Disorders. This fact sheet can be accessed at https://autismpdc.fpg.unc.edu/sites/autismpdc.fpg.unc.edu/files/PRT_factsheet.pdf

Vismara, L. A., & Bogin, J. (2009). *Overview of pivotal response training*. University of California at Davis School of Medicine, M.I.N.D. Institute, The National Professional Development Center on Autism Spectrum Disorders.

Developmental Relationship-Based Interventions (DRBI)

Introduction

DRBI are based on developmental theory focusing on the importance of building social relationships, specifically affection, attachment, bonding, and a sense of relatedness. Hobson (1990) observed that early profound disruption in an individual's interpersonal relationships could result in deficits in the capacity to symbolize, which could account for cognitive, language, and social deficits and explain restricted patterns of interests and abilities. This perspective argues for a social-affective interpretation of ASD and the need for individuals impacted by the condition to express their attachments to others in socially appropriate ways. Mahoney and Perales (2003) use the term Relationship-Focused Interventions and defined them as those that encourages caregivers, specifically parents, to use strategies that are designed to help them interact more responsively with children by using strategies such as "take one turn and wait," "follow the child's lead," or "imitate your child" (p. 77). These types of strategies closely mirror those that are used in naturalistic developmental behavioral interventions (NDBI) such as time delay, joining self-directed play, and imitation, which are described in detail in the NDBI section of this resource.

Core Reviews

Simpson et al. (2005) used the term Interpersonal Relationship Interventions and Treatments and included DIRFloor Time and Relationship Development Intervention (RDI) in this category. The NAC used the term Developmental Relationship-Based Treatment in both 2009 and 2015 and rated these interventions as Emerging. They did not specify which interventions fell into this category. The NPDC (Wong et al., 2014) and the NCAEP (Steinbrenner et al., 2020) did not include any of the interventions included in this section.

Interventions Included in This Section

- Responsive Teaching (RT)
- Developmental, Individual-Different, Relationship-Based Model (DIR/Floor Time®) *(CTM)*
- Relationship Development Intervention (RDI) *(CTM)*

Responsive Teaching (RT)

Description

RT is a curriculum designed to be implemented by caregivers through daily routines to increase their responsiveness or child orientation during their interactions with the child to help develop pivotal behavior such as initiation, joint attention, and social play. Responsiveness requires that the signals of the child are monitored, perceived accurately, and responded to appropriately in a way that results in the child being effectively engaged in the interaction.

There are five dimensions of responsiveness: (1) reciprocity, (2) contingency, (3) shared control, (4) affect, and (5) match. Reciprocity means that the caregiver and child pay attention to each other engaging in balanced, back-and-forth exchanges within shared, cooperative activities that promote more frequent joint activity routines. Contingency refers to a direct relationship between the behaviors of the caregiver and the child in terms of time and interests. Caregiver behaviors should happen as immediate as possible after the child's behavior and should be related to their interests. Shared control means that caregivers should respond to the child more than directing them and that any directions should be used to facilitate the actions and communication that the child initiates. Affect should be expressive, animated, warm, and communicate enjoyment and acceptance of whatever the child is doing both verbally and nonverbally. Match refers to the caregiver making it easier for the child to understand what is happening by adjusting their responses to be similar or slightly more complex than the child's responses, to be related to the child's interests, and to mimic their behaviors in terms of speed, voice volume, and body movements. Matching means being flexible and having expectations that are compatible with and supportive of the child's natural tendencies.

The Responsive Teaching curriculum provides a structure for intervention planning and implementation, which includes seven steps: (1) Identify caregiver concerns and classify them into one or more developmental domains, (2) target social play as the first pivotal behavior, (3) select the pivotal behavior most relevant to the child's developmental needs, (4) assess progress on pivotal behaviors, (5) select discussion points and strategies for intervention session, (6) complete the intervention session plans, and (7) record intervention session activities. The curriculum also has a section on developing family action plans of one to three follow-through activities to increase proficiency of the caregivers and infuse responsiveness into daily life.

Brief Overview of the Literature

Relationship-focused interventions that provide the foundation of RT were first researched in the 1980s by Mahoney and his colleagues and continued through the early 2000s primarily with individuals who were diagnosed with Down syndrome (Mahoney et al., 1985; Mahoney, 1988a, 1988b; Mahoney et al., 2006). Mahoney and Perales (2003, 2005) conducted several studies on the use of relationship-focused interventions with subjects with pervasive developmental disorder and ASD with positive outcomes. In 2007, Mahoney and MacDonald published *Autism and Developmental Delays in Young Children: The Responsive Teaching Curriculum for Parents and Professionals*. RT is based on research on the caregiver characteristic of responsiveness or child orientation which is "the degree to which parents support and encourage activities and behaviors their child is involved with" (Mahoney & MacDonald, 2007, p. 31) and has been identified as the primary caregiver characteristic that influences the development of communication (Bornstein et al., 1999; Hoff-Ginsberg & Shatz, 1982; Nelson, 1973) and social-emotional well-being (Birigen & Robinson, 1991; Kochanska et al., 1999; van den Boom, 1995; Vereijken et al., 1997) even when the child has developmental delays (Brooks-Gunn & Lewis, 1984; Mahoney et al., 1985, Mahoney, 1988a, 1988b; Siller & Sigman, 2002). RT is considered a comprehensive treatment model (Odom et al., 2010).

Core Reviews

None of the core reviews includes RT as reviewed intervention. In 2009, the NAC references "response education" under Naturalistic Teaching Strategies which was rated as Established and RT under Developmental Relationship-Based Treatment which was given the rating of Emerging.

Age and Diagnostic Considerations/ Prerequisite Skills and Abilities

RT has primarily been used with learners under the age of 6 with delays in pivotal behaviors with and without ID. The potential learner should show curiosity in manipulating objects, minimally attend to the environment, and demonstrate preliminary imitation skills.

Reported Outcomes

RT has been demonstrated to improve social emotional functioning, communication, and cognitive skills.

Qualifications Needed

No formal training in RT is required. Nonetheless, individuals who use this method would greatly benefit from training in its application through consultation with an experienced implementer or other training formats.

How, Where, and When Typically Implemented

Parents and teachers may easily integrate RT into typical daily activities.

Costs

RT is cost-effective in terms of time and other resources. There are minimal to no costs associated with training, no additional teaching time is required, and no materials need to be purchased other than those typically found in natural settings.

Potential Risks

There are no documented or obvious risks associated with RT.

Rating

☺ Limited Supporting Information for Practice

Resources and Readings

Autism Spectrum Disorder Fact Sheet can be accessed at http://www.autism-help.org/intervention -responsive-teaching.htm

Welcome to Responsive Teaching. This site can be accessed at https://www.responsiveteaching .org

Developmental, Individual-Difference, Relationship-Based Model (DIRFLOORTIME®)

Description

The DIRFloortime Model is a developmental, interactive, play-based intervention approach that simultaneously emphasizes functional developmental milestones, individual strengths and differences, relationships, and environments needed to support skill development. DIRFloortime is based on a theory developed by Stanley Greenspan that "examines the functional developmental capacities of children in the context of their unique biologically based processing profile and their family relationships and interactive patterns" (Wieder & Greenspan, 2003, p. 425). Social-emotional development starting at birth is considered the foundation for all other skill development. The model describes development as a process unique to and guided by each individual and fueled by relationships with others. The International Council of Development and Learning (ICDL) is a not-for-profit organization that is the official home to DIRFloortime. It provides a variety of resources for parents and professionals, including live and virtual trainings, mentoring services, and several YouTube videos that describe the intervention. DIRFloortime is considered a CTM (Odom et al., 2010).

Brief Overview of the Literature

Greenspan's theory first appeared in the peer-reviewed literature in the late 1990s (Greenspan & Wieder, 1997a, 1997b). The Play and Language for Autistic Youngsters (PLAY) Project, a parent-mediated, developmental approach focused on social reciprocity, was later developed based on the DIR theoretical framework (Solomon et al., 2007, 2014). Much of the research on interventions using principles of the DIRFloortime Model in the last decade has been published in occupational therapy (Dionne & Martini, 2011; Liao et al., 2014; Reis et al., 2018) and medical (Pajareya & Nopmaneejumruslers, 2012; Praphatthanakunwong et al., 2018; Solomon et al., 2014) journals.

Core Reviews

Simpson et al. (2005) reviewed DIRFloortime and gave it the rating of Limited Supporting Information for Practice based on one article (Greenspan & Wieder, 1997b). Although it did not include it as a reviewed intervention in 2009, the NAC referenced one article (Solomon et al., 2007) on the Play Project and listed it as an Unestablished intervention in 2015. The NPDC (Wong et al., 2014) and the NCAEP (Steinbrenner et al., 2020) did not include the DIRFloortime Model as a reviewed intervention.

Other Systematic Reviews/Meta-Analyses

Boshoff et al. (2020) conducted a systematic review of the peer-reviewed research literature published between 2007 and 2018. All participants had a reported diagnosis of ASD, Asperger's syndrome, or other PDD-NOS. They identified four articles (Liao et al., 2014; Pajareya & Nopmaneejumruslers, 2011, 2012; Praphatthanakunwong et al., 2018) that used the DIRFloortime Model and five studies (Casenhiser et al.,

2011; Dionne & Martini, 2011; Reis et al., 2018; Solomon et al., 2007, 2014) that used interventions based on its principles. One of the studies (Reis et al., 2018) also incorporated speech and occupational therapy. All of the studies took place in the home with intervention done by the subject's parents with guidance from a trained professional (e.g., OT, SLP, rehabilitative medical professional). All of the studies mostly used outcome measures in the emotional and social developmental area and all showed positive results in skills such as joint attention, initiation, involvement in social interactions, and reciprocal communication.

Age and Diagnostic Considerations/ Prerequisite Skills and Abilities

The research conducted on DIRFloortime included subjects from ages 2 to 12 with diagnoses of autism, Asperger's syndrome, or other PDD-NOS with the severity of symptoms ranging from mild to severe.

Reported Outcomes

The research on DIRFloortime reported improvements in joint attention, initiation, involvement in social interactions, and reciprocal communication.

Qualifications Needed

Caregivers can implement DIRFloortime with training and oversight of a professional trained in interventions based on the principles of the DIRFloortime Model.

How, Where, and When Typically Implemented

DIRFloortime occurs primarily in the home environment with the consultation of a professional trained in interventions based on the principles of the DIRFloortime Model.

Costs

According to Scheibel et al. (2022), who conducted an evaluation of the time and financial resources needed to implement DIRFloortime, the total cost with a single student is "$9,976 for the 1st year and $7,448 annually" (p. 8).

Potential Risks

There are no documented or obvious risks associated with DIRFloortime. It should be noted that this intervention cannot be implemented alongside the behavioral interventions as it is based on different theories and methodologies. In addition, the use of time and financial resources may prohibit the implementation of interventions with a stronger evidence base.

Rating

   Limited Supporting Information for Practice.

Resources and Suggested Readings

The DIR® and DIRFloortime® Training Program can be accessed at https://www.floortime.org
DIRFloortime (International Council on Development and Learning, Inc.) can be accessed at
https://www.icdl.com/research

Relationship Development Intervention (RDI)

Description

RDI is a cognitive-developmental approach based on experience sharing in which primary caregivers learn how to perceive and scaffold opportunities for the learner "to respond in more flexible, thoughtful ways to novel, challenging and increasingly unpredictable settings and problems" (Gutstein et al., 2007, p. 399). The goal is that through these shared experiences and daily opportunities the learner is guided to develop authentic reciprocal relationships and improve other skills often delayed in individuals with ASD, such as communication, emotional regulation, executive functioning, and problem-solving. RDI is considered a comprehensive treatment model (Gutstein, 2009; Odom et al., 2010).

Brief Overview of the Literature

RDI was created by psychologist Steven Gutstein and was first described in the book *Solving the Relationship Puzzle* published in 2001, followed by *Relationship Development Intervention with Young Children: Social and Emotional Development Activities for Asperger Syndrome, Autism, and PDD and NLD* and *Relationship Development Intervention with Children, Adolescents and Adults* in 2002. Gutstein co-authored an article in 2002 published in *Focus on Autism and Other Developmental Disabilities* describing the critical components of experiencing sharing, how they relate to the social deficits of individuals specifically with Asperger's syndrome, and the proposed relationship development program (Gutstein & Whitney, 2002). Gutstein was the lead author on an article with the purpose of evaluating the RDI program in 2007 published in the journal *Autism* (Gutstein et al., 2007) followed by the most recently published book *The RDI Book: Forging New Pathways for Autism, Asperger's and PDD with the Relationship Development Intervention® Program* in 2009 published by Gutstein's publishing company, Connections Center Publishing.

Core Reviews

Only Simpson et al. (2005) included RDI as a reviewed intervention. They included one article (Gutstein & Whitney, 2002) and three books with Gutstein as the lead author (Gutstein, 2001; Gutstein & Sheely, 2022a, 2022b) and gave the intervention a rating of Limited Supporting Information for Practice. The NAC included one article (Gutstein et al., 2007) under Developmental-Relationship Based Treatment which was given the rating of Emerging.

Age and Diagnostic Considerations/ Prerequisite Skills and Abilities

In their books published in 2001, Gutstein and Sheely regard RDI as suitable for individuals from 2 years of age across the entire autism spectrum.

Reported Outcomes

In the 2007 article, Gutstein reports that as a result of RDI, individuals are more social related, engage in more reciprocal communication, function in school settings with less adult participation, and are more flexible and adaptive.

Qualifications Needed

To be able to implement RDI, caregivers need to attend 6 days of intensive workshops followed by weekly or biweekly consultation with a certified RDI consultant. Consultants have a variety of background including but not limited to social workers, OTs, speech pathologists, psychologists, and teachers. Becoming a consultant involves two professional training courses providing a combination of online and in-person formats and the completion of 14 projects under the supervision of an RDI training supervisor. The entire process takes approximately a year.

How, Where, and When Typically Implemented

The primary agents of change in RDI are the learner's primary caregivers, who are trained to integrate RDI opportunities into daily routines.

Costs

Costs of the RDI program are those associated with the training and follow-up consultation required for both the primary caregivers and consultants. The price is not specified on the official RDI website.

Potential Risks

There are no documented or obvious risks associated with RDI. However, use of time and financial resources may prohibit the implementation of other interventions with a stronger evidence base.

Rating

  Limited Supporting Information for Practice

Resources and Suggested Readings

RDIConnect™ official website can be accessed at www.rdiconnect.com

Relational Frame Theory (RFT)-Based Interventions

SECTION 7

Introduction

In behavioral psychology and education, there has been a recent resurgence of interest in the study of novel, emergent, or derived behaviors that cannot be explained by a history of direct training (Barnes-Holmes et al., 2004; Niklas et al., 2010). This emergent responding research has focused on relational responding (Hayes et al., 2001), a viable and alternative method to traditional means of educational training. Relational Frame Theory (RFT), an instructional framework, focuses on the explicit teaching of a few specific skills and the emergence of novel responding (Hayes et al., 2001). There is a growing body of literature describing instructional strategies based on fundamental and applied research on derived relational responding that can inform professionals working with individuals with developmental disabilities, including ASD (Rehfeldt & Barnes-Holmes, 2009). Researchers have demonstrated that the ability to derive relations amongst stimuli correlates with cognitive and verbal skills; teaching relational framing may mitigate these deficits in students with ASD (Gross & Fox, 2009; O'Hora et al., 2005; Thirus et al., 2016). RFT attempts to explain how human language and cognition develop by relating concepts to each other through three properties (Cooper et al., 2020):

1) Mutual entailment: The feature in which a unidirectional relation from stimulus A to stimulus B entails a second unidirectional relation from B to A

   Example: If a child is shown two coins, told that coin A is worth more than coin B, and they derive that coin B is less than coin A.

2) Combinatorial entailment: The feature whereby two stimulus relations can be combined to derive a third relation

   Example: If you show the same child in the example above three coins and tell them that coin A is worth more than coin B and coin B is worth more than coin C, they derive that A is worth more than C and C is worth less than A.

3) Transformation of stimulus functions means that when stimuli are involved in a relational frame, any function attached to one of those stimuli transfers through the frame to any or all of the other stimuli involved.

   Example: A child derives an equivalence relation consisting of the spoken word "stop," a stop sign, and a red stoplight. They derive that when the crossing guard says "stop," it is time to stop. Subsequently, a stop sign and the crossing guard saying "stop" evoke similar behavior (Dymond & Rehfeldt, 2000; Gross & Fox, 2009; Smyth et al., 2006).

The idea behind RFT is that the language and cognitive skill deficits of individuals with ASD are because they cannot make derived relations and that teaching derived relations as early as possible is crucial for improving these skill areas. Educational technologies inspired by these findings demonstrate no dimensions of learning that cannot be trained. Practitioners inspired by relational learning have shown that establishing a history of reinforced relational responding in individuals is an effective and efficient educational practice (Barnes-Holmes et al., 2016; Rehfeldt & Barnes-Holmes, 2009).

Patterns of relational responding are referred to as relational frames. Some examples of relational frames include (Niklas et al., 2010) the following:

- Sameness or coordination
  - Example: A = B
- Comparison
  - Example: Elephants are bigger than cats.
- Opposition
  - Example: Black is the opposite of white.
- Distinction
  - Example: Boys are not the same as girls.
- Hierarchy
  - Example: A carrot is a type of vegetable.
- Analogy
  - Example: A is to B as C is to D.
- Deixis or deictic
  - Example: I am tall, and you are short.
- Temporality
  - Example: 10 a.m. comes before 10.

Core Reviews

RFT has yet to be included in core reviews of EBPs for individuals with ASD. Several articles have been published in peer-reviewed journals to demonstrate the effectiveness of RFT in teaching academic skills to students with ASD. It is included in this book due to growing support in teaching individuals with ASD in clinical and school settings.

Interventions Included in This Section

- Stimulus Equivalence Instruction (SEI)
- Matrix Training
- PEAK: Promoting Emergence of Advanced Knowledge
- Acceptance and Commitment Therapy/Training (ACT)

Resources and Suggested Readings

Fox, E. J. (n.d.). *An introduction to relational frame theory.* FoxyLearning. This site can be accessed at https://foxylearning.com/product/introduction-to-relational-frame-theory/

Niklas, T., Barnes-Holmes, D., & Hayes, S. C. (2010). *Learning RFT: An introduction to relational frame theory and its clinical applications.* Context Press.

PEAK Relational Training. (n.d.). This site can be accessed at https://www.peak2aba.com/

Rehfeldt, R. A., & Barnes-Holmes, Y. (2009). *Derived relational responding applications for learners with autism and other developmental disabilities: A progressive guide to change.* Context Press.

Stimulus Equivalence Instruction (SEI)

Description

SEI may provide a viable and alternative method to traditional means of teaching. SEI is an instructional framework that focuses on the direct teaching of a few specific skills and the emergence of novel responses. In the match-to-sample (MTS) teaching arrangement, the learner is taught to select the stimulus (sample stimuli) to the stimulus it matches (comparison stimuli) (Blair et al., 2019; Sidman & Tailby, 1982) often in an array of nonmatching comparison stimuli (Cooper et al., 2020). Typical MTS stimulus equivalence programs involve training and testing that rely on selection-based responding (Albright et al., 2016).

Stimulus Equivalence is an example of a type of relational frame—specifically, the frame of coordination (Barnes-Holmes et al., 2016; Blair et al., 2018). Cooper et al. (2020) define *Stimulus Equivalence* as the emergence of accurate responses to untrained stimulus–stimulus relations following the training of responses to some stimulus–stimulus relations. To meet the definition of an equivalence class, one must be able to demonstrate reflexivity, symmetry, and transitivity (Cooper et al., 2020).

▶ Reflexivity or generalized identity matching is when a stimulus is matched to itself without training or reinforcement (represented by the mathematical statement A = A).

Example: A student is taught that the word "dog" is the same as "dog." The student then tells his mother that the word "dog" is the same as the word "dog."

▶ Symmetry is achieved when the reversibility of a sample stimulus with a comparable stimulus is demonstrated (represented by the mathematical statement if A = B, then B = A).

Example: A student is taught that the word "dog" is the same as the word "perro." The next day in class they tell their teacher that the word "perro" means "dog."

▶ Transitivity is the final and critical test of stimulus equivalence. Transitivity is when untrained, nonreinforced stimulus–stimulus relations emerge as a product of training two or more different stimulus–stimulus relations. (represented by the mathematical statement if A = B, and B = C, then A = C).

Example: A student is taught that the word "dog" is the same as the word "perro," and that the word "dog" also means "chien." Without any training, they tell their sibling that "perro" means "chien."

Figure   Schematic representation of trained and tested conditional relations. Solid arrows indicate trained relations, and dashed arrows indicate tested relations. Members of the response class are notated as (A) word "Dog," (B) word "Perro," and (C) word "Chien."

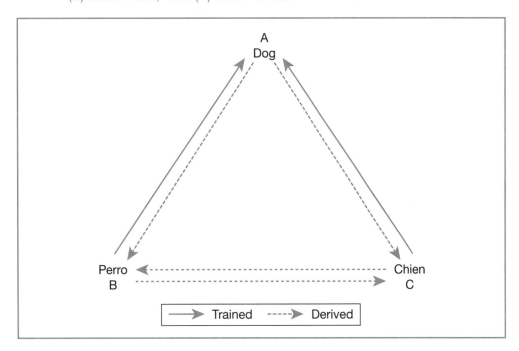

When transitivity is achieved, the learner makes untrained accurate connections between stimuli, deriving accurate relations "for free" (Stewart et al., 2013). Behavior analysts and educators can use stimulus equivalence to their advantage when designing programs that establish more than directly trained stimulus–response relationships (Wetherby, 1978). SEI may be used as a stand-alone teaching technology, when traditional approaches fail, or as a supplement to curriculum-based classroom instruction (Stromer et al., 1992). The application of derived stimulus relations methodologies to promote emergent learning by directly teaching a few specific skills, or relations will cause other, untaught skills or relations to emerge; thus, in the long run, more learning benefits will occur per educational unit of time (Critchfield et al., 2018).

Brief Overview of the Literature

In 1971, Murray Sidman described the emergence of novel stimulus–stimulus relations, or "equivalences," by a boy with an ID while teaching reading skills (Sidman, 1971). In an unplanned experiment, the researchers identified that the boy was able to select printed words in the presence of corresponding pictures despite never having being directly taught the relations among these stimuli (Rehfeldt & Barnes-Holmes, 2009).

Since the stimuli were physically dissimilar, the untrained selection responses could not be explained by stimulus generalization. Sidman labeled this effect of this training "stimulus equivalence" because the result was the interchangeability or equivalence of the stimuli (Brodsky & Fienup, 2018; Critchfield et al., 2018). This research is regarded as a landmark in the analysis of language and cognition; the ability to form relational classes is a uniquely human ability (Dickens & Dickens, 2001).

Instruction focusing on stimulus relations emphasizes aspects of generative learning through relations that are generative, the conditions of which systematically train specific relations to create "free" or emergent learning (Critchfield et al., 2018; Dickens & Dickens, 2001). This has strong implications for the efficiency of teaching and learning (Sidman, 2009).

Much research has been conducted on the use of SEI MTS procedures to teach academically relevant concepts (Brodsky & Fienup, 2018) to students. Academic skills taught through the emergent learning paradigm include reading comprehension and written expression (Brooks Newsome et al., 2014; Joyce & Wolking, 1989; Sidman, 1971), categorization, geography skills (Dixon et al., 2017), piano skills (Hill et al., 2020), and fractal-decimal delations (Hammond et al., 2012) among others.

Core Reviews

SEI has yet to be included in core reviews of EBPs for individuals with autism. SEI is included here as there is growing support for its use with individuals with ASD in clinical as well as school settings (Barnes-Holmes et al., 2016).

Other Systematic Reviews/Meta-Analyses

In a literature review on the formation of equivalence classes in individuals with ASD by Gibbs and Tullis (2021), the authors provided a summary of research into the emergence of equivalence relations in individuals with ASD.

AUTHOR(S)/ YEAR	N	AGE/ GENDER	DIAGNOSIS	SETTING	RESEARCH DESIGN	EMERGENT SKILLS TESTED	TEACHING PROCEDURES	OUTCOMES/ FINDINGS
Arntzen et al. (2014)	1	17 yrs. Male	ASD	School	Pretest/ posttest	Botanical skills	Match-to-sample	Positive
Daar et al. (2015)	3	10 to 11 yrs. 1 Male 2 Females	ASD	School	Multiple probe across participants	Various nouns	Match-to-sample	Positive
DiCola & Clayton (2017)	5	4 to 7 yrs. 4 Males 1 Female	ASD	University center	Multiple baseline across participants	Say-do correspondence	Match-to-sample & correspondence training	Variable
Dixon et al. (2016a)	2	13 to 15 yrs. Males	ASD	School	Multiple baseline across participants	Geometry	Match-to-sample	Positive
Dixon et al. (2016b)	2	10 to 11 yrs. Males	ASD, cognitive delay	School	Multiple baseline across participants	Derived rule following	Rule statements	Positive
Dixon et al. (2017a)	3	10 to 11 yrs. Males	ASD, cognitive delay	School	Multiple baseline across skills	Gustatory– visual–auditory relations	Match-to- sample, Training Trial Blocks	Variable

AUTHOR(S)/ YEAR	N	AGE/ GENDER	DIAGNOSIS	SETTING	RESEARCH DESIGN	EMERGENT SKILLS TESTED	TEACHING PROCEDURES	OUTCOMES/ FINDINGS
Dixon et al. (2017b)	2	9 to 12 yrs. 1 Male 1 Female	ASD	School	Multiple probe across participants	Geography	Training Trial Blocks, Listener Training	Positive
Kenny et al. (2014)	6	5 to 7 yrs. 4 Males 2 Females	ASD	School	A-B-A Reversal	Arbitrary Symbols	Match-to-sample	Variable
McLay et al. (2016)	10	4 to 11 yrs. 9 Males 1 Female	ASD	School Home	Pretest/ posttest	Numeracy	Discrete Trial Training	Variable
Monteiro & Barros (2016)	4	5 to 7 yrs. 3 Males 1 Female	ASD	University center	Pretest/ posttest	Country names, maps, and flags	Match-to-sample	Variable
Mullen et al. (2017)	2	4 to 5 yrs. Males	ASD	School	Nonconcurrent multiple baseline across participants	Auditory– tactile–visual relations with arbitrary words and symbols	Discrete Trial Training	Positive
Santos et al. (2017)	2	8 to 10 yrs. Males	ASD	University center	Pretest/ posttest	Arbitrary visual stimuli	Match-to-sample	Positive
Silva & Debert (2017)	2	10 yrs. Males	ASD	School	Nonconcurrent multiple baseline across participants	Arbitrary visual stimuli	Go/go-go procedure	Variable
Sprinkle & Miguel (2013)	2	8 to 9 yrs. Females	ASD	Home	Multiple baseline across participants with pretest/ posttest	Activity schedule	Superimposition and fading, conditional discrimination training	Positive
Stanley et al. (2018)	3	13 to 18 yrs. Males	ASD	School	Nonconcurrent multiple baseline across participants with embedded multiple probe	Academics (chemistry, unit conversion, history)	Match-to-sample	Positive
Varella & de Souza (2014)	4	7 to 15 yrs. 3 Males 1 Female	ASD	School	Pretest/ posttest	Arbitrary visual and auditory stimuli	Match-to-sample	Variable
Varella & de Souza (2015)	1	3 yrs.	ASD	Home	Multiple probe across stimulus sets	Images and dictated names of upper case and lowercase letters	Match-to-sample	Positive

Age and Diagnostic Considerations/ Prerequisite Skills and Abilities

SEI has demonstrated the ability to teach a variety of skills from preschool through higher education and beyond. Although much literature is dedicated to the use of SEI to teach individuals with disabilities, this methodology is also effective for neurotypical children and adults (Cassidy et al., 2016). Prior to implementing SEI, the student must have learning readiness skills. Learning readiness skills include sitting in a chair, orienting toward and attending to the instructor, and learning materials

(Higbee, 2009). Additional prerequisite skills include generalized imitation, joint attention (Barnes-Holmes et al., 2016), and the ability to MTS. Instructors should identify reinforcing stimuli prior to delivery of instruction, in order to maximize positive learning outcomes.

Reported Outcomes

SEI is reported to improve academic skills in addition to complex language, social, and executive functioning skills.

Qualifications Needed

No formal training is required to implement SEI. Nonetheless, individuals who use this method must be familiar with the literature and trained in MTS conditional discrimination procedures (Cooper et al., 2020; Rehfeldt et al., 2009; Sidman, 2009).

How, Where, and When Typically Implemented

Teachers and their assistants can learn to implement SEI, integrate it into natural environment training sessions, and generalize them to home instructions with parents.

Costs

SEI interventions are cost-effective in terms of time and other resources. Teachers could learn about SEI interventions themselves through the suggested readings below at no cost. No additional teaching time is required, and no materials need to be purchased other than those typically found in natural settings.

Potential Risks

There are no documented risks associated with the use of SEI.

Rating

   Promising/Emerging Practice

Resources and Suggested Readings

Caldwell, T. (2019, December 2). *Stimulus equivalence and equivalence-based instruction*. LinkedIn. This site can be accessed at https://www.linkedin.com/pulse/stimulus-equivalence-equivalence-based-instruction-tim-caldwell/

Maguire, R. W., & Allen, R. F. (2022). *Stimulus equivalence for students with developmental disabilities*. Routledge.

Parry-Cruwys, R. (2021, January 18). *Episode 143—Stimulus equivalence*. ABA Inside Track. This episode can be accessed at https://www.abainsidetrack.com/home/2020/10/14/episode-143-stimulus-equivalence

Pilgrim, C. (n.d.). *An introduction to stimulus equivalence: What is it and why does it matter?* BehaviorLive. This site can be accessed at https://behaviorlive.com/courses/course-an-introduction-to-stimulus-equivalence-what-is-it-and-why-does-it-matter

Matrix Training

Description

Matrix Training is a teaching approach "that facilitates generalization of taught information to related but untaught information through the arrangement of components of desired skills along the horizontal and vertical axes of a rectangle, then systematically teaching combinations of components across the resulting matrix" (NCAEP 2020). It is a way of organizing learning targets that include two or more component elements that can be combined. Some combinations are directly taught and some are probed to see if the student learns them without being directly taught (Curiel et al., 2020). The purpose of matrix training is to facilitate generative learning repertoire by featuring systematic use of instructions (Jimenez-Gomez et al., 2019; Pauwels et al., 2015; Stokes & Baer, 1977). Recombinative generalization is demonstrated when students emit untrained response recombinations when novel untrained stimulus combinations are presented (Goldstein, 1983; Mayer et al., 2019). The acquisition of untaught targets may be conceptualized through the perspective of derived stimulus relations and RFT. The history of reinforcement for trained exemplars establishes generalized response units, called relational frames (Barnes-Holmes et al., 2018; Jimenez-Gomes et al., 2019).

The tables below provides an example of matrix training to teach cold/shape combinations. In this technique, a learner is directly taught to label a "red circle" and "yellow triangle." If the individual is then able to label "yellow circle" or "red triangle" without being directly taught, recombinative generalization has occurred. There are two common training layouts: 1) diagonal training and 2) overlap or stepwise training. In diagonal training, the cells are along the diagonal providing exposure to all stimuli encountered in generalization probes (Axe & Sainato, 2010). After the diagonal cells are taught, the remaining cells are probed to assess for their occurrence without direct teaching. Diagonal training is typically used when all the words are known individually but not together. Overlap training is typically used when all of the words are unknown and the teacher is attempting to teach both the words and the word order (Goldstein, 1983).

Diagonal Training

Shaded cells are directly taught and white cells are probed.

	CIRCLE	TRIANGLE	SQUARE	RECTANGLE	STAR	DIAMOND
Red	Red Circle	Red Triangle	Red Square	Red Rectangle	Red Star	Red Diamond
Yellow	Yellow Circle	Yellow Triangle	Yellow Square	Yellow Rectangle	Yellow Star	Yellow Diamond
Purple	Purple Circle	Purple Triangle	Purple Square	Purple Rectangle	Purple Star	Purple Diamond
Green	Green Circle	Green Triangle	Green Square	Green Rectangle	Green Star	Green Diamond
Blue	Blue Circle	Blue Triangle	Blue Square	Blue Rectangle	Blue Star	Blue Diamond
Orange	Orange Circle	Orange Triangle	Orange Square	Orange Rectangle	Orange Star	Orange Diamond

Overlap or Stepwise Training

Shaded cells are directly taught and white cells are probed.

	CIRCLE	TRIANGLE	SQUARE	RECTANGLE	STAR	DIAMOND
Red	Red Circle	Red Triangle	Red Square	Red Rectangle	Red Star	Red Diamond
Yellow	Yellow Circle	Yellow Triangle	Yellow Square	Yellow Rectangle	Yellow Star	Yellow Diamond
Purple	Purple Circle	Purple Triangle	Purple Square	Purple Rectangle	Purple Star	Purple Diamond
Green	Green Circle	Green Triangle	Green Square	Green Rectangle	Green Star	Green Diamond
Blue	Blue Circle	Blue Triangle	Blue Square	Blue Rectangle	Blue Star	Blue Diamond
Orange	Orange Circle	Orange Triangle	Orange Square	Orange Rectangle	Orange Star	Orange Diamond

Brief Overview of the Literature

The first research study on matrix training was published is 1925 by Esper. Children with ASD often display significant deficits in acquiring language skills, such as tacting objects and these deficits can interfere with the acquisition of academic skills (Yoder et al., 2015). Research on matrix training mostly has focused on language acquisition (e.g., Axe & Sainato, 2010; Curiel et al., 2016; Ezell & Goldstein, 1989; Goldstein, 1984; Goldstein et al., 1987; Goldstein & Mousetis, 1989; Mineo & Goldstein, 1990; Naoi et al., 2006; Romski & Ruder, 1984) and social and play skills (Dauphin et al., 2004; MacManus et al., 2015; Wilson et al., 2017). A foremost goal of matrix training is to increase instructional efficiency by eliminating the need to explicitly teach some responses and eliminating the need to teach the same response across multiple antecedent conditions (Pauwels et al., 2015). The National Clearinghouse on Autism Evidence and Practice Review Team (NCAEP, 2020) report on EBPs for Children, Youth, and Young Adults with Autism Spectrum Disorder (2020) included matrix training as an EBP with some evidence. Evidence to support the efficacy of this intervention is emerging, but further research is needed to meet the criteria of an EBP.

Core Reviews

Only the NCAEP (Steinbrenner et al., 2020) reviewed Matrix Training and gave it a rating of Some but Insufficient Evidence-based on two articles (Frampton et al., 2016; MacManus et al., 2015).

Other Systematic Reviews/Meta-Analyses

REVIEW	YEARS	NUMBER OF ARTICLES	CONCLUSIONS
Curiel et al., 2020	1999–2017	12	Produced an average of 69% of learning without direct teaching across the areas of language, play, sentence construction, and spelling

Curiel et al. (2020) reviewed twelve articles published between 1999 and 2017 on Matrix Training with individuals with ASD. Findings suggest that matrix training produced an average of 69% of learning targets without direct teaching across the areas of language, play, sentence construction, and spelling.

Age and Diagnostic Considerations/ Prerequisite Skills and Abilities

Delays in language development is a defining characteristic of individuals with ASD and language acquisition is particularly delayed in individuals who are not functionally verbal-making matrix training particularly useful with learners with those characteristics. The intervention has mostly been used with students ages four to twelve years.

Reported Outcomes

Students diagnosed with ASD often require explicit instruction that can be labor-and time-intensive; a focus on generalization of learned skills should be programmed to facilitate effective instructional techniques (Pauwels et al., 2015). Matrix Training addresses these considerations by providing a distinct framework for systematic selection of targets to be taught so that instructional gains are maximized (Weissman-Young, 2019). Emerging evidence attests that matrix training is effective and efficient for increasing participants' ability to generalize new combinations of trained stimuli, a technology that can be used to teach language and other academic skills in the classroom (Weissman-Young, 2019). This is desired because true learning of concepts occurs more quickly and valuable instructional time can be used more efficiently (Axe & Sainato, 2010).

Qualifications Needed

Matrix Training can be used by anyone adequately trained in how to do it. Individuals with the knowledge to adequately train an implementer would mostly likely be a BCBA or special education teacher.

How, Where, and When Typically Implemented?

The teaching procedure used in matrix training is most often a form of discrete trial teaching, but it also has been trained through computer programming and video modeling.

Costs

Matrix Training is cost-effective in terms of time and other resources. Teachers could learn about matrix training interventions themselves through the suggested readings below at no cost. There are minimal to no costs associated with purchasing materials other than those typically found in natural settings. Additional costs must be considered when using computerized programs or video modeling.

Potential Risks

There are no documented or obvious risks associated with Matrix Training.

Rating

   Promising/Emerging Practice

Resources and Suggested Readings

Episode 49 – Matrix Training with Cormac MacManus. ABA Inside Track. (n.d.). https://www.abainsidetrack.com/get-ceus/episode-49-matrix-training

YouTube. (2020, January 5). *Matrix training & applied behavior analysis.* YouTube. https://www.youtube.com/watch?v=QvYHFaimbw0

PEAK: Promoting the Emergence of Advanced Knowledge Relational Training System

Description

The PEAK Relational Training System is an assessment and curriculum guide for teaching basic and advanced language skills from a behavior analytic approach. The PEAK system teaches prerequisite skills for equivalence and relational learning that allows for the development of derived responding. Derived responding, or learning through relations between stimuli without needing to be directly taught, is a process that is at the heart of human language and responsible for our ability to readily make relations between concepts in language. The use of PEAK to establish flexible skills in individuals with disabilities has been peer reviewed in scientific research studies demonstrating its potential as a valid assessment and learning program (Belisle & Dixon, 2018b; Dixon et al., 2016; McKeel et al., 2015).

PEAK contains four separate learning modules to address four individual dimensions of language:

1. Direct Training—basic foundational learning abilities

2. Generalization—emphasis on using skills in novel ways, heavily aligned to common core standards

3. Equivalence—designed to teach concept formation and perceptual behavior

4. Transformation—created to produce awareness of the abstract concepts of relational frames

Each module includes a direct preassessment, full-itemized skill assessment, and a 184-item curriculum that increases in complexity with a program sheet for each goal and description for each of the 184 goals.

PEAK Comprehensive Assessment (PCA)

The PCA is a standardized assessment that correlates to each of the four PEAK modules. The PCA was created to provide standardization and improve upon the slight variations that could occur with the administration of previous assessments. In addition to providing standardization of delivery, the PCA also helps reduce assessment time while maintaining correlation with the prior PEAK assessment tools. The PCA requires approximately 1 to 1.5 hours to complete, and the results include scores for each module, and each factor within them. The PCA provides additional comparison stimuli for receptive test items to reduce the probability of a chance-correct response that may occur when selecting from too small of an array. Items that may have been culturally narrow were removed and replaced with items that are more universal across cultures. The transformation subtest provides a broader range of relational frames, and correct, incorrect, and query responses are provided along with cut-off scores to eliminate subjectivity in scoring (Belisle & Dixon, 2018a).

PEAK-Direct Training

The PEAK-Direct Training's four factors are listed and described below along with a table that provides the typical age scores across each factor, allowing for a quantitative comparison to a typical developing peer group and determination of the degree of difference from such peers.

 ▶ Foundational Learning Skills measure basic instruction following, modeled responding, and attention to the environment.

 ▶ Perceptual Learning Skills measure basic cognitive abilities such as matching, finding objects from an array, naming or signing items, and completing basic "Wh-" questions.

 ▶ Verbal Comprehension Skills measure more complex verbal abilities such as multiple-step instruction following, multiword vocal or signing utterances, beginning concept formations, and social exchanges.

 ▶ Verbal Reasoning, Memory, and Mathematic Skills measure basic logic processes, advanced cognitive abilities needed for effective social behavior, complex language, and beginning mathematical computation skills.

PEAK DIRECT TRAINING FACTOR	YEARS OF AGE				
	1–2	3–4	5–6	7–8	9–10
Foundational Learning	2	30	34	34	34
Perceptual Learning Skills	0	18	21	22	22
Verbal Comprehension	0	19	80	94	100
Verbal Reasoning, Memory, and Math Skills	0	0	10	22	28
Total Score	2	67	145	172	184

PEAK-Generalization

PEAK-Generalization's four factors are listed and described below along with a table that provides the typical age scores across each factor, allowing for a quantitative comparison to a typical developing peer group and determination of the degree of difference from such peers.

Foundational Learning and Basic Social Skills measure basic instruction following, gross and fine motor imitation, basic receptive and expressive identification skills, making requests, and basic social skills such as sharing and identifying basic emotions.

Basic Verbal Comprehension, Memory, and Advanced Social Skills measure more advanced abilities such as creativity in responding, basic perspective taking, complex verbal interactions, generalized direction following, "Wh-" questions, basic reading and writing skills, responding after a delay, and basic math skills.

Advanced Verbal Comprehension, Reading and Writing, and Basic Problem-Solving Skills measure even more complex skills such as detecting lies, detecting patterns, punctuation transcription, basic reading and writing skills, early counting, measuring weights and quantities, and early problem-solving skills.

Verbal Reasoning, Problem-Solving, Logic, and Mathematical Skills measure application of math skills to problem-solving, time-telling, and spending money, problem-solving including varied responding and applying logic, and advanced verbal skills such as identifying sarcasm, rhyming, and guessing.

PEAK GENERALIZATION FACTOR	YEARS OF AGE							
	1–2	3–4	5–6	7–8	9–10	11–12	13–14	15–16
Foundational Learning & Basic Social Skills	1	20	25	26	28	29	33	33
Basic Verbal Comprehension, Memory, & Advanced Skills	1	15	24	36	55	57	58	59
Advanced Verbal Comprehension, Basic Problem-Solving, & Advanced Math Skills	2	4	9	13	50	53	61	63
Verbal Reasoning, Advanced Problem-Solving, & Advanced Reading & Writing Skills	0	0	0	0	16	20	26	29
Total Score	4	39	58	75	149	159	178	184

PEAK-Equivalence

The PEAK Equivalence subtest assesses an individual's ability in establishing the language skills that underlie symbolic behavior and true language. The individual's capacity to gain new knowledge or behavior without the behavior being directly reinforced; or, to make inferences from events that occur in the environment. Individuals are first taught to match identical objects through each of the sense modes (e.g., sight, smell, touch). Then, individuals are taught to interpret new information in terms of previously learned information across categories of Reflexivity, Symmetry, Transitivity, and Equivalence.

PEAK-Transformation

The Transformation subtest assessment targets an individual's ability in early skills that underlie complex cognition, reasoning, and problem-solving. It measures skills in identifying events and objects across the frames of Coordination, Comparison, Opposition, Distinction, Hierarchical, and Deictic in both receptive, expressive, and combined modes.

Figure   Graphical display of the progression of skills targeted in and across each of the PEAK Relational Training System Modules. PEAK-DT and PEAK-G skill groups were taken from the component analysis for reach module. PEAK-E and PEAK-T skill groups were taken directly from the complexity conceptualizations found in each of the modules

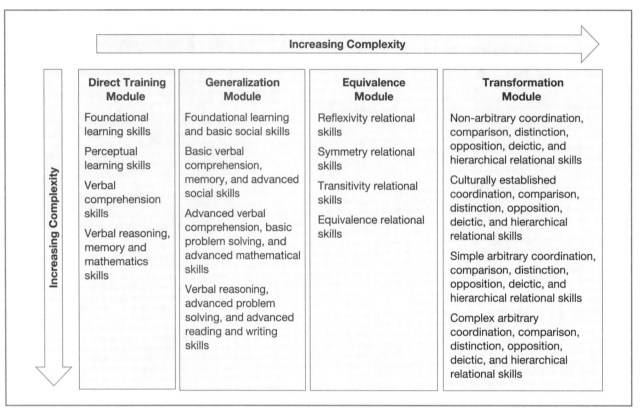

Image from Dixon et al. (2017)

Core Reviews

Since the publication of the PEAK modules is fairly recent and peer-reviewed research articles started being published in 2014, it is logical that they would not be well known at the time of the core reviews and therefore are not included. However, there are many publications with results indicating successful outcomes of the PEAK curriculum, and they are highlighted below in the Reported Outcomes section.

Age and Diagnostic Considerations/ Prerequisite Skills and Abilities

The PEAK assessment and curriculum require individuals to have prerequisite skills of scanning and making a selection, matching to a sample, and receptively responding to instructions. The PEAK assessment and curriculum can be used as early as 18 months through adulthood for neurotypically developing and developmentally disabled (all) individuals.

Reported Outcomes

The PEAK curriculum is reported to result in significant gains in complex VB (Dixon et al., 2018; McKeel et al., 2015), gains on intelligence tests (Dixon et al., 2019; May & St. Cyr, 2021), improved skills of answering wh-questions (Daar et al., 2015), academic skills (Stanley et al., 2018), and identifying emotions (O'Connor et al., 2020).

Qualifications Needed

The PEAK assessment and curriculum can be delivered by an educator or behavior specialist without requiring specialized training, but additional trainings are provided through the peak2aba.com website across varying levels and intensities.

How, Where, and When Typically Implemented

Applications of PEAK can be seen in school, clinical, and home therapies as part of a comprehensive educational or behavioral program.

Costs

PEAK assessment and curriculum packages start at $390.

PEAK trainings:

PEAK Level 1-Foundational $385, web-based, self-paced training

PEAK Level 2: Experiential, live, virtual training

PEAK Comprehensive Assessment (PCA) #100, web-based, self-paced training

Potential Risks

There are no documented or obvious risks associated with the PEAK Relational Training System.

Rating

 Promising/Emerging Practice

Resources and Suggested Readings

Dixon, M. R. (2014). *The PEAK relational training system: Direct training module*. Shawnee Scientific Press.

Dixon, M. R. (2014). *The PEAK relational training system: Generalization module*. Shawnee Scientific Press.

Dixon, M. R. (2015). *The PEAK relational training system: Equivalence module*. Shawnee Scientific Press.

Dixon, M. R. (2016). *The PEAK relational training system: Transformation module*. Shawnee Scientific Press.

Fox, E. J. (n.d.). *An introduction to relational frame theory*. FoxyLearning. The site can be accessed at https://foxylearning.com/product/introduction-to-relational-frame-theory/

The Nebraska Autism Spectrum Disorders Network offers several free online webinars on PEAK that can be accessed at https://www.unl.edu/asdnetwork/webinars?combine=PEAK

PEAK Relational Training. (n.d.). This site can be accessed at https://www.peak2aba.com/

Rehfeldt, R. A., & Barnes-Holmes, Y. (Eds.). (2009). *Derived relational responding applications for learners with autism and other developmental disabilities: A progressive guide to change*. Context Press.

Acceptance and Commitment Therapy/Training (ACT)

Description

ACT is based on an experimental analysis of human language and cognition, (Hayes, 2004). ACT is considered a "third wave" Cognitive Behavior Therapy (CBT) therapy that moves beyond the more traditional cognitive therapies; its underlying philosophies are more contextualistic (Dimidjian et al., 2016). ACT uses acceptance and mindfulness practices to develop actions guided by the person's core values (Hayes et al., 1999). An underpinning of ACT is that human suffering is common to everyone, not just those with clinically significant or diagnosable mental health conditions. For this reason, evidence-based applications of ACT improve psychological wellbeing across a wide range of areas (Hooper & Larsson, 2015). Ultimately, ACT aims to improve psychological flexibility to maximize human potential for a rich and meaningful life, while handling the inevitable pain (Harris, 2019). ACT consists of six core therapeutic processes:

▶ Contacting the present moment—Be here now
▶ Defusion—Watch your thinking
▶ Acceptance—Open up
▶ Self-as-Context—The noticing self
▶ Values—Know what matters
▶ Committed Action—Do what it takes

These processes are organized into the Hexaflex diagram below:

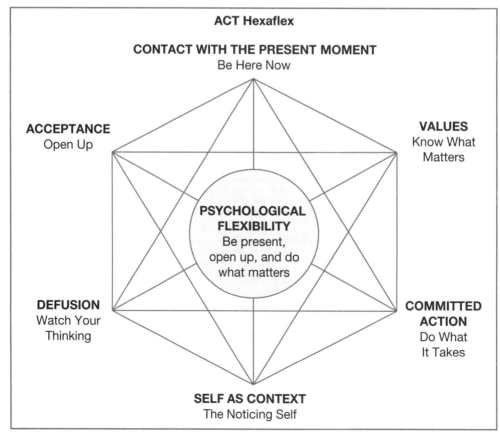

Harris, 2019.

Additionally, a core concept of ACT is toward and away moves. Essentially, toward moves are the things that an individual wants to start or do more of that moves them toward their values and the person they want to be (Harris, 2019). Conversely, away moves are things an individual does that are unlike the person they want to be, not in line with their values, and makes them feel worse over time (Harris, 2019). Using this framework, an individual can identify behaviors or moves that move them toward their personal values and the person they would like to be.

Brief Overview of the Literature

Few articles have been published in peer-reviewed journals to demonstrate the effectiveness of ACT with individuals in school settings and even fewer with individuals with autism in schools. General evidence exists to support the use of ACT with children and adolescents to address problem areas such as chronic pain, OCD, challenging behavior, anxiety, autism, tic-related disorders, depression, sexualized behavior, stress, attention-deficit hyperactivity disorder, and posttraumatic stress disorder (Swain et al., 2015). While the methods vary among existing evidence, overall findings were encouraging for the utility of the ACT model when applied to children and adolescents.

Core Reviews

ACT has yet to be included in core reviews of EBPs for individuals with ASD. ACT is included here as there is growing support for its use with individuals with ASD in clinical as well as school settings.

Other Peer Reviewed Research

The experimental peer-reviewed studies that the author of this text was able to locate are summarized here. Although only one includes a subject with ASD, the findings indicate that ACT may have positive effects on common co-morbid conditions/symptoms and skill deficits. In addition, all of the studies were conducted in schools so they provide valuable information for those working in this environment.

AUTHOR(S)	N	SETTING	AGE/ GENDER	DIAGNOSES	FINDINGS
Aydin and Aydin (2020)	6	Public high school	17 to 19 yrs. Female	None	Perceptions about exams improved, increased present moment awareness
Burckhardt et al. (2016)	267	Independent Episcopalian high school	15 to 18 yrs. Male and Female	None	Reduction in depression scores, stress scores, and DASS-Total scores. Improvement in symptom scores
Burckhardt et al. (2017)	48	Private high school	14 to 16 yrs. Male and Female	None	Stress scores had greater improvement than anxiety over time.

(Continued)

(Continued)

AUTHOR(S)	N	SETTING	AGE/ GENDER	DIAGNOSES	FINDINGS
Livheim et al. (2015) *Includes two studies*	51 32	Public high school	12.5 to 17.75 yrs. Male and Female 14 to 15 yrs. Male and Female	None	Significant intervention effects for depressive symptoms Significant intervention effects for stress symptoms
Murrell et al. (2015)	7	Urban charter school	11 to 15 yrs. Male and Female	LD and/or disruptive behavior problems and ADHD	Significant changes for 2 participants; 86% endorsed improvements, 85% indicated attitude toward home or school improved
Pahnke et al. (2014)	28	Special school serving students with ASD	13 to 21 yrs.	ASD	Levels of stress, hyperactivity, and emotional distress were reduced.
Takahashi et al. (2020)	270	Public junior high school	14 to 15 yrs.	None	Reduced avoidance and hyperactivity/inattention
Theodore-Oklota et al. (2015)	210	Public middle school	11 to 13 yrs. Male and Female	None	Program group engaged in more problem-solving coping compared to the waitlist group

Age and Diagnostic Considerations/ Prerequisite Skills and Abilities

ACT is designed for use with individuals with average to above average cognitive and language abilities with any accompanying diagnosis including ASD. Available research on the use of ACT-based interventions in schools includes adolescent or young adult participants in various countries and types of school settings. ACT has been used with individuals with diagnoses such as learning disabilities, attention-deficit/hyperactivity disorder and autism with favorable results in attitudes toward home and school (Murrell et al., 2015) as well as reduced stress hyperactivity and emotional distress (Pahnke et al., 2014).

Reported Outcomes

Emerging research indicates that ACT is effective in the treatment of children across various presenting problems and may be a viable treatment option.

Qualifications Needed

No formal training is required to implement ACT processes and practices. Individuals who use these practices should consider training in its application through consultation with an experienced implementer or other training formats.

How, Where, and When Typically Implemented

ACT takes place during typical individual or group learning or counseling sessions. Additionally, there are a few commercially produced ACT curriculums for use with individuals with ASD and/or emotional challenges that require no formal training and can be used immediately upon purchase.

Costs

ACT is cost-effective in terms of time and other resources. Training costs vary with readily available training for any budget. Additionally, curriculum and other tangible resources are reasonably priced for implementation.

Potential Risks

There are no documented or obvious risks associated with ACT.

Rating

 Promising/Emerging Practice

Resources and Suggested Readings

Dimidjian, S., Arch, J. J., Schneider, R. L., Desormeau, P., Felder, J. N., & Segal, Z. V. (2016). Considering meta-analysis, meaning, and metaphor: A systematic review and critical examination of "third wave" cognitive and behavioral therapies. *Behavior Therapy, 47*(6), 886–905.

Dixon, M. R. (2014). *ACT for children with autism and emotional challenges.* Shawnee Scientific Press.

Dixon, M. R., Paliliunas, D., & Critchfield, T. S. (2018). *AIM: A behavior analytic curriculum for social-emotional development in children.* Shawnee Scientific Press.

Harris, R. (2019). *ACT made simple: An easy-to-read primer on acceptance and commitment therapy* (2nd ed.). New Harbinger.

Transition

Introduction

Students with ASD go through many transitions during their lifetime, and these transitions are often challenging for both students and families. Accordingly, school professionals must effectively support students to successfully transition to different life phases. Examples of such transitions include attending school for the first time and progressing through different school levels (e.g., primary school to secondary school). Adolescents with ASD also experience a major life transition when they graduate from the K–12 public school system and move into adulthood.

School professionals can help adolescents with ASD prepare for adulthood by implementing high-quality transitioning planning. IDEA (2004) mandates that transition planning begin by age 16 or earlier if the IEP team determines it appropriate or according to the state where the student lives. Some states mandate that transition planning begin by age 14. As described in person-centered planning (PCP; further described below), the student should be the central person and focus of transition planning. In particular, the student's strengths, preferences, and interests should be emphasized during the transition planning process. The transition component of the IEP will include the student's postsecondary goals in the areas of employment, education or training, and independent living (if appropriate). Students must be invited to their IEP meeting if transition planning is a focus (IDEA, 2004). In addition, students can take a leadership role in preparing for their lives after high school, including leading their own IEP meetings.

The majority of intervention research has been conducted on school-age students with ASD rather than adolescents and young adults. However, there is still a considerable amount of research relevant to improving outcomes for adolescents and young adults with ASD.

Core Reviews

The Steinbrenner et al. (2020) report organized the identified EBPs according to age ranges and outcome areas. The following EBPs have empirical evidence supporting their use for high school students ages 15 to 18 or young adults ages 19 to 22:

EBPS FOR HIGH SCHOOL STUDENTS AGES 15 TO 18	EBPS FOR YOUNG ADULTS AGES 19 TO 22
• Antecedent-based interventions	• Antecedent-based interventions
• Augmentative and alternative communication	• Cognitive behavioral instructional strategies
• Behavioral momentum intervention	• Differential reinforcement of alternative, incompatible, or other behavior
• Cognitive behavioral instructional strategies	• Discrete trial training
• Differential reinforcement of alternative, incompatible, or other behavior	• Functional behavioral assessment
• Direct instruction	• Modeling
• Discrete trial training	• Naturalistic intervention
• Exercise and movement	• Prompting
• Extinction	• Reinforcement
• Functional behavioral assessment	• Response interruption/redirection
• Functional communication training	• Self-management
• Modeling	• Social skills training
• Naturalistic intervention	• Task analysis
• Parent-implemented intervention	• Technology-aided instruction and intervention
• Peer-based instruction and intervention	• Time delay
• Prompting	• Video modeling
• Reinforcement	• Visual supports
• Response interruption/redirection	
• Self-management	
• Social narratives	
• Social skills training	
• Task analysis	
• Technology-aided instruction and intervention	
• Time delay	
• Video modeling	
• Visual supports	

Source. NCAEP, Steinbrenner et al. (2020).

Implementing EBPs with empirical support for adolescents and young adults with ASD can support their adult outcomes. Unfortunately, young adults with ASD are vulnerable to experiencing a lack of success in the postschool outcome areas recognized by IDEA (2004): competitive employment, education or training, and independent living. Young adults with ASD are less likely to experience positive competitive employment outcomes compared to individuals without disabilities (Lipscomb et al., 2017; Newman et al., 2011; Roux et al., 2015). Many young adults with ASD desire to attend college (Cai & Richdale, 2016). However, they are attending college at lower rates compared to individuals with other types of disabilities (Roux et al., 2015) and will likely need specialized support to successfully navigate the college environment and demands. In addition, the majority of young adults with ASD continue to live at home and report challenges with independent living during the transition to adulthood (Sosnowy et al., 2018). Accordingly, school professionals must support transition-age students with ASD to achieve their personal goals in these important postschool outcome areas.

Interventions Included in This Section

In this section, we will review the following interventions to students with ASD during different life transitions:

- Systemic Transition in Education Programme for Autism Spectrum Disorder (STEP-ASD)

- Self-Determined Learning Model of Instruction (SDLMI)

- Person-Centered Planning (PCP)

Systemic Transition in Education Programme for Autism Spectrum Disorder (STEP-ASD)

Description

The STEP-ASD is a standardized and manualized program to support the transition from primary to secondary school for students with ASD. Mandy et al. (2016) developed this intervention based on clinical experiences and focus groups with parents to reduce emotional and behavioral problems of students with ASD as they transition to secondary school. One of the key components of the STEP-ASD intervention is to modify the school environment rather than focus on modifying the individual. School professionals and families work together to help the student with ASD successfully transition to secondary education. The STEP-ASD intervention includes the following steps:

1. A bridge meeting is held during the summer prior to the student transitioning to secondary school. School professionals and the family identify the student's needs and strategies to best support the student during the transition.

2. School professionals and the family develop an individualized "transition management plan" and "pupil profile."

3. School professionals share the transition management plan and pupil profile with the secondary school professionals prior to the student transitioning there.

4. When the student begins attending the secondary school, all strategies discussed are implemented.

5. Primary school professionals make scripted telephone calls to secondary school professionals during the first two semesters of secondary school to ensure the transition management plan is being implemented.

Brief Overview of the Literature

There is only one known study conducted to examine the effectiveness of the STEP-ASD intervention. Mandy et al. (2016) conducted a nonrandomized controlled trial experiment in which they measured outcomes before and after the transition to secondary school. Participants were divided into two groups: those who received the STEP-ASD intervention ($n = 17$) and the control group who did not receive the intervention ($n = 20$). The primary outcome was reduction of emotional and behavioral problems as measured by the *Strengths and Difficulties Questionnaire* (Goodman, 2001). This questionnaire consists of 25 items and measures internalizing and externalizing challenges. Students who received the STEP-ASD program showed larger reductions in their emotional and behavioral challenges whereas the control group showed no improvement. Related to feasibility of the STEP-ASD program, the majority of students in the STEP-ASD group reported the bridge meeting to be helpful. Similarly, the majority of school staff found the transition pack to be helpful and would recommend the STEP-ASD program to other professionals.

Mandy et al. (2016) acknowledged their study is a "pilot study" (p. 588) and encouraged additional research to further evaluate the efficacy of STEP-ASD. As described, it is important to note the STEP-ASD program is to support students' transition from primary to secondary school (not the transition to adulthood). In addition, there are several components of the STEP-ASD program that are similar to other interventions or programs to support the transition of students with ASD, such as PCP and effective collaboration among families and school professionals.

The NCAEP Review Team (2020) is the only review that included the STEP-ASD program and rated it as insufficient evidence.

Core Reviews

The only core review that included STEP-ASD as a reviewed intervention was the NCAEP (Steinbrenner et al., 2020) in 2020, which gave a rating of Insufficient Evidence-based on one study (Mandy et al., 2016).

Age and Diagnostic Considerations/ Prerequisite Skills and Abilities

The STEP-ASD program is for students who are transitioning from primary to secondary school. The average age of students included in the Mandy et al. (2016) study was 11 years. There are no prerequisite skills or abilities needed of the students. Rather, the focus is on students who are transitioning to secondary school.

Reported Outcomes

The STEP-ASD program can potentially reduce emotional and behavioral problems of students with ASD as they transition to secondary school.

Qualifications Needed

There is no specific training to implement the STEP-ASD program. School professionals at both the primary and secondary schools must collaborate to best support the student and their family during the transition. Similar to other collaborative approaches, the school professionals must have knowledge of the student and their strengths, weaknesses, and areas of need.

How, Where, and When Typically Implemented

The STEP-ASD program is not an intervention or teaching strategy but, rather, a collaborative approach to support students during their transition to secondary school. The STEP-ASD program is implemented when students are moving from primary to secondary school. Activities related to the STEP-ASD program will occur in school settings.

Costs

There are no costs associated with the STEP-ASD program.

Potential Risks

There are no documented or obvious risks associated with the STEP-ASD program.

Rating

😐 Limited Supporting Information for Practice

Resources and Suggested Readings

There are no additional resources or suggested readings beyond the Mandy et al. (2016) article.

Self-Determined Learning Model of Instruction (SDLMI)

Description

The SDLMI is an instructional intervention which supports young people to take action on their self-reported goals and is based on the component elements of self-determination, self-regulated problem-solving, and research on student-directed learning (Mithaug et al., 1998; Shogren et al., 2019; Wehmeyer et al., 2000; Wehmeyer & Shogren, 2008). This EBP (NTACT, 2016) supports students with and without disabilities (Lee et al., 2015) and is intended to be used by teachers and other school professionals across a variety of academic and non-academic areas. Students decide on a goal, whether short or long term, and work through three phases: (1) Set a Goal; (2) Take Action; and (3) Adjust Goal or Plan. Throughout each phase, the teacher provides support by asking guiding questions and using explicit instruction in the components of self-determination (Shogren et al., 2019). Teachers provide multiple opportunities for students to participate in goal-directed activities (Burke et al., 2019). Instruction and practice are provided in choice-making, decision-making, problem-solving, goal-setting, planning, goal attainment, self-management, self-advocacy, self-awareness, and self-knowledge.

Brief Overview of the Literature

SDLMI has been researched in single-study, quasi-experimental, and RCTs across 900 students (Burke et al., 2019; National Technical Assistance Center on Transition [NTACT], 2016). SDLMI increases student self-determination, access to the general education curriculum, and academic and transition goal attainment, which therefore improves student outcomes after high school (Lee et al., 2015; Wehmeyer & Shogren, 2008).

Core Reviews

SDMLI was not included in any of the core reviews. It was included in this resource because it is increasingly being used by many professionals.

Age and Diagnostic Considerations/ Prerequisite Skills and Abilities

SDLMI can be implemented with elementary through transition-age students with and without disabilities (Lee et al., 2015; Palmer & Wehmeyer, 2003). SDLMI may be used with students with varying levels of support needs, including students with complex communication needs (Burke et al., 2020).

Reported Outcomes

Shogren et al. (2019) reported, "Students set and achieved academic-related goals with the SDLMI over 16 weeks in an inclusive, general education classroom including students with and without disabilities" (p. 4). Other reported outcomes of SDLMI implementation include high level of goal attainment, increased access to general education curriculum, more positive employment outcomes and community participation, and increased self-determination (Shogren et al., 2019).

Qualifications Needed

To implement the SDLMI, the implementer is typically a teacher or other school professional who is working with school-age students who are working on improving their self-determination skills. The implementer should have a positive rapport with the student and be knowledgeable about the SDLMI procedures and materials.

How, Where, and When Typically Implemented

SDLMI can be implemented in any setting that is related to the student's goals, including school, home, community, or place of employment. Materials are designed so that teachers can use it with the whole class for 15 minutes, twice a week on skills related to SDLMI. Teachers could also target goals in 15-to-30-minute sessions for students who require more support or attention to these goals. SDLMI is highly individualized and can be modified or extended depending upon the support needs of the student (Shogren et al., 2019).

Costs

SDLMI teacher guide and supplemental materials are provided at no cost through the Kansas University Center on Developmental Disabilities (selfdetermination.ku.edu). The materials are intended to be used as a supplement to expert-led training offered through KUCDD. Contact information is available at www.selfdetermination.ku.edu/homepage/contact-page/

Potential Risks

There are no documented or obvious risks associated with SDLMI.

Rating

     Evidence-Based Practice

Resources and Suggested Readings

Beach Center on Disability at the University of Kansas: https://beachcenter.lsi.ku.edu/beach-self-determination

Kansas University Center on Developmental Disabilities (KUCDD): https://selfdetermination.ku.edu/

National Technical Assistance Center on Transition (NTACT): https://transitioncoalition.org/topics/secondary-education/self-determination/

Person-Centered Planning (PCP)

Description

Individuals with Disabilities Education Act (IDEA) (2004) mandates that a student's preferences and interests be accounted for in transition planning and IEP development (IDEA, 2004). PCP is one framework for addressing this requirement. PCP is a team approach to transition planning in which the student (i.e., the learner served under IDEA) leads other team members in the identification and acquisition of supports and services to facilitate their community life and involvement upon leaving school (NCAEP, 2019). Research studies dating back to the 1990s include implementation of PCP activities, such as self-identification of strengths and assets and community mapping (Miner & Bates, 1997), as well as "whole life planning" led by the student (Whitney-Thomas et al., 1998).

Mount and Zwernik (1989) first introduced PCP as a new method of transition planning and emphasized the importance of prioritizing the student's own vision of their future. Additionally, these authors state that the student's team members must be supportive and willing to assist the student in making necessary connections to successfully participate in the community. The intention of PCP is to support students in pursuing their own hopes for careers, recreation, and community involvement rather than guiding them toward predetermined or convenient outcomes.

PCP has commonly been used as a component of high-quality transition planning over the past several decades. In addition, there are several curricula developed to incorporate PCP in transition planning, such as the Self-Directed IEP model (Martin et al., 1996), self-advocacy strategy (Van Reusen et al., 2007), and Take Charge for the Future (Kohler & Field, 2003).

Brief Overview of the Literature

Several early studies (Miner & Bates, 1997; Mount & Zwernick, 1998; Whitney-Thomas et al., 1998) laid the groundwork for the current version of the PCP framework. However, according to the NCAEP in 2020, there is only one study (Hagner et al., 2012) that currently contributes to the evidence base for PCP as a practice. PCP currently has the rating of Some but Insufficient Evidence through NCAEP's ratings system.

Hagner et al. (2012) conducted a group design study in which 49 high school students with ASD were randomly assigned to either participate in PCP practices within transition planning or go about business as usual. High school students who participated in PCP scored higher on measures of future expectations, self-determination, and career decision-making ability than students who did not participate in PCP (Hagner et al., 2012). In addition, the parents of students who participated in PCP scored higher on measures of expectations for their child's future than parents of students who did not participate in PCP.

Although only one study comprises PCP's current evidence base, this study is important. Teachers may consider leadership opportunities in which students can benefit from during the transition planning process.

Core Reviews

Only the NCAEP (Steinbrenner et al., 2020) included PCP in its 2020 review giving the rating of Some but Insufficient Evidence-based on one study (Hagner et al., 2012).

Age and Diagnostic Considerations/ Prerequisite Skills and Abilities

Though PCP is mentioned in the academic literature most commonly for high school students and young adults, there is no age limit or requirement for prioritizing student preferences and needs across the lifespan. PCP is commonly incorporated into transition planning, which is required to begin at age 16 but may start earlier according to the state where the student lives and if the IEP team determines it appropriate to do so (IDEIA, 2004).

In order to participate in PCP, the student must have a communication method that permits them to indicate personal preferences. The student may communicate verbally, through the use of AAC, gesturally, or otherwise.

Traditionally, PCP involves the student serving as the team lead in planning efforts. For example, they might facilitate meetings or discussions with transition planning team members (NCAEP, 2019). Students may present their strengths and interests and describe how they will meet their postsecondary goals.

Previous research in the area of PCP has included students with intellectual and developmental disabilities, including those with ASD. It is worth noting that the PCP framework and mindset can be used with a wide range of students, including those without disabilities.

Reported Outcomes

Potential benefits to implementing or using the PCP framework with a transition-age youth with ASD include potentially developing higher levels of leadership, self-confidence, self-awareness, and self-determination skills.

Qualifications Needed

Qualifications needed by the implementer of PCP are similar to transition planning broadly. That is, the teacher should know the student and their strengths, preferences, and interests, as well as their postsecondary goals. Tondora et al. (2020) described five competency domains for teachers and other related professionals to implement PCP, such as focusing on the student's strengths and being culturally informed.

How, Where, and When Typically Implemented

PCP is a framework for transition planning, and IDEA (2004) mandates that a transition plan be implemented for students with disabilities no later than age 16. Therefore, PCP is most commonly used with transition-age youth with disabilities including ASD. However, as noted above, transition planning using PCP can begin earlier. Likewise, emphasis on student preference and the student as integral to their educational planning can be incorporated earlier in life as well. There are no universally agreed upon standards for how to implement PCP (Tondora et al., 2020).

Costs

There are no upfront costs affiliated with implementing PCP. If one elects to use a PCP-based curriculum to guide transition planning procedures, they may be required to purchase the necessary materials. Examples of PCP curricula available at a price or for free include:

- *Self-Advocacy Strategy: Enhancing Student Motivation and Self-Determination* (Van Resuen et al., 2007): $20 per book copy

- *Self-Directed IEP Model* (Martin et al., 1996). Free to download from the University of Oklahoma's Zarrow Institute website: https://www.ou.edu/education/centers-and-partnerships/zarrow/choicemaker-curriculum/choicemaker-self-determination-materials

- *Whose Future Is It* Anyway? (Wehmeyer et al., 2004). Free to download from the University of Oklahoma's Zarrow Institute website: https://www.ou.edu/education/centers-and-partnerships/zarrow/transition-education-materials/whos-future-is-it-anyway

Potential Risks

Risks involved with PCP practices are minimal and are no greater than risks associated with daily school activities for the student.

Rating

 Limited Supporting Information for Practice

Resources and Suggested Readings

Five competency domains for staff who facilitate person-centered planning. National Center on Advancing Person-Centered Practices and Systems (NCAPPS): https://ncapps.acl.gov/docs/NCAPPS_StaffCompetencyDomains_201028_final.pdf

Person centered planning: Resource guide from the Administration for Community Living (ACL). U.S. Department of Health and Human Services: https://acl.gov/programs/consumer-control/person-centered-planning

Miscellaneous Non-Educational Interventions

Introduction

Miscellaneous Interventions are any interventions included or referenced in one or more of the core reviews but did not fit in any of the other sections.

Interventions Included in This Section

- Peer-Mediated Instruction and Intervention
- Parent-Implemented Interventions
- Music-Mediated Interventions (MMI)
- Music Intensity
- Animal-Assisted Intervention
- Art Therapy
- Outdoor Adventure
- Toilet Training
- Social Emotional Neuroscience Endocrinology (SENSE) Theatre
- Exercise and Movement (EXM) Interventions
- Gentle Teaching
- Sensory Integration (SI) Interventions

Peer-Mediated Instruction and Intervention (PMI)

Description

Peer-Mediated Instruction and Intervention is a type of intervention in which peers without disabilities support the social interactions or other learning goals of students with ASD. Teachers or other related professionals commonly organize the context for peers without disabilities and students with ASD to interact with one another. Examples of such contexts include play groups, social network groups, recess, as well as academic learning time. Teachers provide necessary supports, such as prompts and reinforcement, to the peers and students with ASD to engage in directed tasks (NCAEP, Steinbrenner et al., 2020).

Brief Overview of the Literature

Peer-related social competence is defined as the ability to engage in reciprocal interactions and form relationships with peers (Stichter & Conroy, 2006). Researchers report that children with ASD typically display low rates of appropriate social behavior with their peers (Zhang & Wheeler, 2011) and, consequently, form few friendships (Carter et al., 2005). PMI can be used to support the social competence of students with ASD. An examination of the literature emphasizes that the following strategies are examples of common Peer-Mediated Interventions: Peer networks, circle of friends, buddy skills packages, peer initiation training, and peer-mediated social interaction training, structured play groups, and cooperative learning groups (NAC, 2015). *Structured play groups* are defined as small group activities characterized by their occurrences in a defined area and with a defined activity. Typically developing peers and students with ASD in structured play groups participate in a shared learning activity (NCAEP, 2014). Adults are often needed to lead, prompt, and scaffold such activities to support all students. *Cooperative learning groups* are defined as academic learning tasks organized around joint activities and goals (NCAEP, 2014). Research indicates that specifically designed Peer-Mediated Instructional arrangement strategies within the classroom facilitate maintenance and generalization of learned skills in half of the reviewed studies (Bene et al., 2014).

Core Reviews

Both the NPDC (Wong et al., 2014) and NCAEP (Steinbrenner et al., 2020) used the terms Peer-Based Instruction and Intervention (PBII) as a reviewed intervention and gave the ratings of Evidenced Based Practice based on a total of 44 studies.

Other Systematic Reviews/Meta-Analyses

Chan et al. (2009) reviewed 42 articles focused on Peer-Mediated Intervention and established it as an Evidence-Based Practice for individuals with ASD. Between 2014 and 2016, several researchers (Bene et al., 2014; Chang & Locke, 2016; Watkins et al., 2015) each examined 5 to 14 studies of Peer-Mediated Instruction and found that Peer-Mediated Instruction was a promising intervention for promoting social interaction between students with ASD and their peers in inclusive settings and has a strong impact on academic and communication skills.

Zagona and Mastergeorge (2018) reviewed 17 articles and found that participants demonstrated increases in social-communication skills when peer training occurred. Finally, O'Donoghue et al. (2021) reviewed 25 articles and found that Peer-Mediated Instruction can increase social interaction for children with autism who are minimally verbal.

Age and Diagnostic Considerations/ Prerequisite Skills and Abilities

According to the Steinbrenner et al. (2020) report, Peer-Mediated Instruction and Intervention is effective for students with ASD ages 3 to 18 including preschoolers and elementary school, middle school, and high school students. Peer-Mediated Instruction may be implemented with teens or young adults with ASD involved in social settings in which peers or other individuals are a part of a social context.

Reported Outcomes

Peer-Mediated Instruction is a versatile and potentially effective intervention for use with individuals with ASD (Chan et al., 2009). Reported outcomes can include but are not limited to communication, social, joint attention, cognitive, school readiness, academic, challenging behavior, and mental health outcomes (Streinbrenner et al., 2020).

Qualifications Needed

An important consideration is the necessity of a peer or peers in the social situation in which the individual with ASD is learning a new skill. This social context needs to be natural and allow the individual with ASD to learn from a peer(s) in order to develop the necessary targeted skill(s). Training provided to peers and parents, teachers, and others within the social context is necessary in order to properly engage, prompt, and reinforce the individual with ASD.

How, Where, and When Typically Implemented

It is best if Peer-Mediated Interventions occur in natural environments in which the individual with ASD already engages. This intervention is typically implemented throughout the day on an ongoing basis in naturally occurring situations. Peer-Mediated Instruction often used with infants, toddlers, and youth with ASD. Peer-Mediated Instruction may also be implemented with teens or young adults with autism involved in social settings in which peers or other individuals are a part of a social context. Although not as commonly researched, Peer-Mediated Intervention may also be implemented with adults with ASD in home or community settings.

Costs

There are no direct costs for Peer-Mediated Interventions or Instruction. The cost of training by a practitioner (e.g., teacher, therapist) might occur. However, the intervention is implemented by peers in natural settings and there is no cost associated with this particular strategy or instruction.

Potential Risks

There are no demonstrated risks associated with Peer-Mediated Interventions or Instruction. Some teachers may be concerned regarding potential missed learning opportunities for the peer without ASD but research indicates there are actually benefits associated with serving as a peer mentor (Travers & Carter, 2022).

Rating

     Evidence-Based Practice

Resources and Suggested Readings

Collins, T. A., & Hawkins, R. O. (Eds.). (2020). *Peers as change agents: A guide to implementing peer-mediated interventions in schools.* Oxford University Press.

Hall, T., & Stegila, A. (2003). *Peer mediated instruction and intervention.* National Center on Accessing the General Curriculum. This site can be accessed at https://guide.swiftschools.org/sites/default/files/documents/PeerMedInstrucNov3.pdf

The Nebraska Autism Spectrum Disorders Network offers a free online webinar on Peer-Mediated Interventions. It can be accessed at https://www.unl.edu/asdnetwork/peer-mediated-interventions

The Ohio Center for Autism and Low Incidence (OCALI) offers a free online course on Peer Mediated Instruction and Intervention. It can be accessed at https://autisminternetmodules.org/search?qtitle=peer

Sam, A., & AFIRM Team. (2015). *Peer-mediated instruction and intervention.* National Professional Development Center on Autism Spectrum Disorder, FPG Child Development Center, University of North Carolina. This site can be accessed at http://afirm.fpg.unc.edu/Peer-mediated-instruction-and- intervention

Parent-Implemented Interventions

Description

Parent-Implemented Interventions are interventions implemented by a parent with their child that promotes an increase in the child's social, communication, or developmental skills, while also promoting a decrease in their challenging behavior (NCAEP, Steinbrenner et al., 2020). Before the intervention, parents receive training to implement various evidenced-based strategies. Parents may choose to implement interventions individually or as a part of a group. Parent-Implemented Interventions can focus on functional or academic skills, or both, within the natural context of the home or community setting. Parents directly use individualized intervention practices with their child to increase positive learning opportunities and acquisition of important skills (Koegel et al., 2002). A positive and trusting relationship between parents and practitioners strongly supports the effectiveness of Parent-Implemented Interventions and positive outcomes for individuals with ASD.

Brief Overview of the Literature

Several seminal research articles support the use of Parent-Implemented Interventions. Koegel et al. (1982) first began researching the effectiveness of Parent-Implemented Interventions, which were the cost and time-effective as they are implemented directly in the child's home and community settings rather than a clinic or school setting. Research has shown that parents can learn how to implement behavioral and developmental intervention strategies with their child and do so with fidelity to increase social communication skills and decrease negative behaviors (Chan et al., 2009; McConachie et al., 2007; Patterson et al., 2012; Roberts et al., 2007; Steiner et al., 2012). Overall, Parent-Implemented Interventions can also improve the broader family function, reducing stress, and providing opportunities for positive family interactions (Coolican et al., 2010). Research supports that Parent-Implemented Interventions are a best practice for treatment of infants and toddlers at suspected risk for ASD (Zwaigenbaum et al., 2015). An expansion of this work includes Project ImPACT (Improving Parents as Communication Teachers), as a specific Parent-Mediated Intervention created for young children with communication delays, including those with autism (Ingersoll & Wainer, 2013). The Stepping Stones-Triple P (Positive Parenting Program) is also a parent- and family-support strategy that has been created in response to the need for positive Parent-Based Interventions for young children with developmental disabilities (Mazzucchelli & Sanders, 2012).

Core Reviews

In 2015 the NAC used the term Parent Training Package and gave the rating of Established based on 11 studies. The NPDC (Wong et al., 2014) and NCAEP (Steinbrenner et al., 2020) used the term Parent-Implemented Intervention and gave the rating of EBP based on a total of 55 studies. The NCAEP also included The Collaborative Model for Promoting Competence and Success (COMPASS) (Ruble et al., 2012) and gave the rating of Some Evidence. COMPASS was previously called Collaborative Coaching, which is systematic consultation between parent and teacher and ongoing coaching across the school year to help the team promote achievement of IEP goals utilizing EBPs (NCAEP, Steinbrenner et al., 2020).

Other Systematic Reviews/Meta-Analyses

This is further supported by literature reviews, such as Barton and Fettig (2013), in which 24 studies were examined, utilizing 16 different interventions within the home and community setting with parents. After training was provided, parents implemented a variety of interventions across natural settings with their children with ASD, each proving to be successful. The National Clearing House on Autism Evidence and Practice (2020) also identified 42 interventions in total that were implemented by parents between 2012 and 2017, including both Stepping Stones Triple P and Project IMPACT within their literature review, which were both identified as an MIMC by the NCAEP in 2020. All interventions that were parent-implemented focused on children ages 0 to 5 across all domains.

Age and Diagnostic Considerations/ Prerequisite Skills and Abilities

Based on core studies, Parent-Implemented Interventions may occur at any age. However, parent-implemented interventions are frequently implemented at a young age, such as between the ages of 2 and 9, when foundational skills are forming in the areas mentioned above (e.g., communication, behavior). Effective Parent-Implemented Interventions include multiple steps that occur prior to implementing an intervention strategy (Hendricks, 2009). First, identify the needs of the family using family questionnaires or other methods. Second, select the desired goals for the individual as a part of the Individual Family Service Plan (IFSP) or the IEP. Third, families and practitioners should agree upon an intervention, including the following components: parent training, location, format, data collection method, assessment, and more. After an intervention plan is developed, parents are taught how to implement the intervention through a structured parent training program (Johnson et al., 2007). Once training is completed, practitioners and families should collaborate to establish a plan for implementation of the intervention.

Reported Outcomes

Research supports the effectiveness of Parent-Implemented Intervention designed to increase communication in children with ASD and reduce interfering behavior. These interventions have been used to increase social communication skills, conversation skills, spontaneous language, use of Augmentative and Alternative Communication, joint attention, academic skills, and interactions in play. Lastly, they have been used to improve compliance, increase eating, and to reduce aggression and disruptive behaviors. In the given studies, parents have implemented specific interventions with their child with fidelity across multiple domains in multiple environments. In addition, parents reported increased feelings of control and reduced family stress.

Qualifications Needed

There are no specifications for who can implement Parent-Implemented Interventions. However, parents do need to know how to implement the selected interventions. Therefore, some type of training may be necessary for the parent depending on the intervention, teaching strategy, or behavior program. Parents are urged to implement with fidelity (according to the intervention and training provided) and implement on a consistent basis.

How, Where, and When Typically Implemented

Interventions are typically implemented in the home or natural community settings. After determining the needs of the family and child with autism, Parent-Implemented Interventions may be implemented on an ongoing basis. Examples may include behavioral training, communication training, or academic intervention training, all implemented in the home or natural community settings.

Costs

Parent-Implemented Interventions often involve training by a practitioner. This may be a related service provider, such as an OT or speech therapist, special education teacher, or provider working with the family directly. Costs associated with consultations and services may vary but are sometimes covered. Once trained on how to implement the specific intervention at home, there is no cost to the family outside of checking in with the practitioner to make modifications. Parent-Implemented Interventions can be a cost-effective and relatively straightforward approach to implementing effective interventions in a family-friendly manner. Parents may incur the costs of any required intervention materials, such as assistive technology devices, if not provided by support providers.

Potential Risks

*There are no documented or obvious risks associated with Parent-Implemented Interventions.

Rating

   Evidence-Based Practice

Resources and Suggested Readings

Amsbary, J., & AFIRM Team. (2017). *Parent implemented intervention*. National Professional Development Center on Autism Spectrum Disorders, FPG Child Development Center, University of North Carolina. This site can be accessed at http://afirm.fpg.unc.edu/parent-implementedintervention

The Ohio Center for Autism and Low Incidence (OCALI) offers a free online course on Parent Implemented Intervention. It can be accessed at https://autisminternetmodules.org/search?qtitle=parent

Parent-Implemented Intervention. *The Center on Secondary Education for Students with Autism Spectrum Disorder*. This site can be accessed at https://csesa.fpg.unc.edu/resources/ebp-briefs/parent-implemented-intervention

Siller, M., & Morgan, L. (2018). *Handbook of parent-implemented interventions for very young children with autism*. Springer International.

Music-Mediated Interventions (MMI)

Description

MMI are those that incorporate the combination and isolation of music characteristics to support new skills, behaviors, and learning. The NCAEP defines MMI as "intervention that incorporates songs, melodic intonation, and/or rhythm to support learning or performance of skills/behaviors. It includes music therapy, as well as other interventions that incorporate music to address target skills" (NCAEP, Steinbrenner et al., 2020, p. 28). Music's characteristics such as rhythm, melody, and tempo are malleable so they can be individualized to meet the various needs of learners with ASD.

Brief Overview of the Literature

Music has a long history of functions within cultures and communities (Merriam, 1964). The scientific phenomenon of music and the brain has been established by researchers to influence cognition including memory, attention, executive functioning, language and communication, socialization, and motor planning.

Core Reviews

Simpson et al. (2005) used the term Music Therapy and gave it the rating of Limiting Supporting Information for Practice based on 17 articles. The NAC used the term Music Therapy and gave it a rating of Emerging in both 2009 and 2015 based on six and seven articles respectively. The NPDC (Wong et al., 2014) used the term Music Therapy in 2014 and gave it the rating of Some Support, and the NCAEP (Steinbrenner et al., 2020) used the term MMI in 2020 and gave it a rating of EBP based on nine articles.

Other Systematic Reviews/Meta-Analyses

A systematic review conducted in 2021 examined all publications on music used in intervention with the *DSM5* definition of neurodevelopmental disorders (NDDs) including ASD between January 1970 and September 2020 resulting in 22 eligible studies (Meyer-Benarous et al., 2021). Meyer-Benarous et al. (2021) define the music interventions in two categories: (1) educational music therapy and (2) improvisational music therapy. Of the 22 studies reviewed, 10 presented educational music therapy on communication, social engagement, cognition, and motor coordination. Improvisational music therapy accounted for nine studies.

A systematic review of scientific studies on the effects of music in people with or at risk for ASD was also conducted by Applewhite et al. and published in 2022. The purpose of this review was to address the benefits and potential side effects of MMI with these populations and the overall effects on neurological functioning and impacts on cognitive, motor, emotional, social, sensory, and learning skills. The authors emphasize the difference of music perception by those with ASD from their neurotypical peers and therefore the importance of collecting the opinions of music preference and individual music sensitivities from ASD participants before beginning any intervention.

Age and Diagnostic Considerations/ Prerequisite Skills and Abilities

No prerequisites or music abilities are necessary in order to be a candidate for MMI. However, consideration of the learners music abilities will dictate the complexity of the stimulus. Evidence in the NCAEP 2020 report supports the implementation of MMI for the following needs and age range: adaptive/self-help (0 to 5), challenging/interfering behaviors (0 to 14), communication (0 to 14), motor (0 to 14), play (0 to 5), school readiness (0 to 14), and social (0 to 14). The systematic reviews (Applewhite et al., 2002; Meyer-Benarous et al., 2001) pose considerations when implementing MMI to include cognitive function, complexity of music stimulus, sound sensitivities, and intention. Results of the systematic reviews suggest that individuals with ASD and intellectual developmental disabilities (IDD) respond better to some MMIs than other populations. Cognitive level of the individual has presented a relationship to the complexity of music stimulus and outcome. A more significant cognitive impairment responds best to simple musical stimulus, and higher cognitive function responds best to more complex music stimulus.

Reported Outcomes

Music therapy was reported to have positive effects on selective and sustained attention, coordination and synchrony, echoic response, interacting, requesting, imitation, verbal initiation, verbal and nonverbal communication, social awareness and engagement, and emotional understanding (Meyer-Benarous et al., 2021). Positive effects for improvisational music therapy included cooperation, self-control, eye contact, turn-taking, communication, and social engagement (Meyer-Benarous et al., 2021).

Qualifications Needed

MMI are best implemented by a board-certified music therapist who is equipped with education and training to assess and design the treatment plan relative to the MMI. Once the treatment plan is established, some MMIs can be facilitated by the educator if a protocol is established, documented, trained, coached, and supervised. Please note that a music educator is not trained in this area as their primary focus is on teaching music skills. Per the definitions above, MMIs are utilized to influence non-music goals. As discussed in the systematic reviews (Applewhite et al., 2022; Meyer-Benarous et al., 2021), there are multiple MMI passive or active on the part of the individual, and in some cases, a mix of the two. When referring to music therapy as a service, multiple philosophical orientations and philosophies add to the complexity of the delivery and require the board-certified music therapist for ethical facilitation of standardized techniques and strategies as well as real-time decision-making established in the clinical setting.

How, Where, and When Typically Implemented

MMIs can be delivered in group or individual settings dependent upon the individual's goals. The rate of services is determined by the team and professionals relative to the assessment and literature supporting the specific MMI. For example, the delivery of improvisational music therapy experiences for exercising executive functioning can occur for 5 to 15 minutes a session with multiple sessions in a day for consecutive days whereas a 30-minute music-mediated social competence group would be best delivered weekly.

Costs

The cost of MMI are dependent on (a) availability and contract with board-certified music therapists, (b) materials and resources necessary to support the MMI, and (c) ongoing professional development to stay current with best practice. Investment in computer applications for auditory integration is not advised given lack of evidence and aforementioned risks. Other prerecorded music and even goal-based music experiences are available digitally to supplement live MMI delivery by qualified professionals.

Potential Risks

Although music has many positive qualities, its potential for harm is respected and accounted for in the music therapy profession (Silverman et al., 2020). Some potential risks of implementing MMI include unpredictable emotional responses due to uni-dentified trauma, physiological responses to vibrotactile stimulation unfamiliar to the individual causing concern and undue stress, sound sensitivity without the ability to mediate the stimulus physically or communicate such, or prompt dependency. This is by no means an exhaustive list, but it represents a rationale for implementing with care by doing due diligence before delivery and exercising observation skills during facilitation to know if the intervention should be ceased and re-evaluated.

Rating

   Promising/Emerging Practice

*This rating is given with the caveat that the critical features and differences between MMI and "Music Therapy" need to be more clearly defined in future research.

Resources and Suggested Readings

American Music Therapy Association. (n.d.). *About music therapy & AMTA*. This site can be accessed at https://www.musictherapy.org/about/

American Music Therapy Association. (n.d.). *Fact sheet: Music therapy and autism spectrum disorders (ASD)*. This site can be accessed at https://www.musictherapy.org/assets/1/7/Fact_Sheet_ASD_and_MT__8-26-15.pdf

American Music Therapy Association. (2010). *Autism spectrum disorders: Music therapy research and evidence-based practice support*. This site can be accessed at https://www.musictherapy.org/assets/1/7/bib_autism10.pdf

Nowell, S., Sam, A., Waters, V., Dees, R., & AFIRM Team. (2022). Music-Mediated Intervention. The University of North Carolina at Chapel Hill, Frank Porter Graham Child Development Institute, Autism Focused Intervention Modules and Resources. This site can be accessed at https://afirm.fpg.unc.edu/music-mediated-intervention

Ohio Center for Autism and Low Incidence Disabilities (OCALI). (n.d.). *Music mediated interventions (MMI)*. This site can be accessed at https://autisminternetmodules.org/

Music Intensity

Description

The use of music in the treatment of children with autism has been documented since the 1940s (Reschke-Hernandez, 2011). The investigation of background music and its effect on the vocalizations of children with autism have also brought upon interest in the music therapy and educational professions (Preis et al., 2016). The manipulation of the volume (measured in decibels, dB) of recorded music is referred in the literature as *Music Intensity* and has presented some evidence to decreasing immediate levels of vocal stereotypy in children with autism (Lanovaz et al., 2014; Lanovaz et al., 2013; Lanovaz et al., 2011; Lanovaz et al., 2009; Saylor et al., 2012).

Brief Overview of the Literature

The majority of the literature investigating the effect of Music Intensity and noncontingent music on individuals with autism is conducted by Lanovaz and colleagues between 2009 and 2014 relating to vocal stereotypy (Lanovaz et al., 2014; Saylor et al., 2012; Lanovaz et al., 2013; Lanovaz et al., 2009; Lanovaz et al., 2011;). The "music" applied in these students include the Carnival of the Animals by Camilie Saint-Saëns (classical), television tunes, and other preferred melodies. Studies did not indicate if any of the modified music included sung lyrics. Researchers have generally assessed the effects of noncontingent music during 5-to-10-minute brief sessions (e.g., Saylor et al., 2012) with volume of music intensity averaging 70 dB (similar to a vacuum) and 50 dB (similar to a speaking voice) as reported by Lanovaz, Sladeczek et al. (2011). Lanovaz, Rapp et al. (2014) expanded on these results by investigating the application of Music Intensity within a "sequential intervention model" that involved differential reinforcement and simple prompts progressively. Recent literature suggests more combined methods such as Gibbs et al.'s (2018) investigation of noncontingent music as the "matched stimulation" and response interruption and redirection in "suppressing" vocal stereotypy and increasing on-task behavior (p. 899).

Core Reviews

Simpson et al., and the NAC did not include Music Intensity as a reviewed intervention. The NPDC (Wong et al., 2014) gave Music Intensity the rating of Insufficient Evidence-based on one study (Lanovaz, Sladeczek, & Rapp, 2011) and the NCAEP (Steinbrenner et al., 2020) recategorized Music Intensity as an Antecedent-Based Intervention (ABI) which was given the rating of Evidence-Based Practice.

Age and Diagnostic Considerations/ Prerequisite Skills and Abilities

Music Intensity as a practice extends across the lifespan and abilities from school-age children with ASD addressing stereotypy to the motivation and physical output of adults during exercise. A prerequisite involves considering the musical preferences of the learner and potentially functional analysis to determine what is reinforcing the stereotypy as Music Intensity is more likely to be successful as an intervention if it is automatically reinforced.

Reported Outcomes

Music Intensity has some evidence that it could reduce immediate levels of vocal stereotypy in children with ASD or produce effects on future occurrences of the vocal stereotypy. Results indicate reduction in immediate and subsequent levels of stereotypy as well as increases and maintenance in appropriate behaviors with no "collateral behaviors" manifesting in the absence of the vocal stereotypy. However, these results have yet to be replicated.

Qualifications Needed

Implementation of music intensity can be designed and implemented by a licensed educator or an appropriately trained implementer. A benefit of music intensity is that it does not require undivided attention on the part of the implementer (Lanovaz et al., 2014).

How, Where, and When Typically Implemented

The literature presented music intensity in alternating 5-minute intervals for a total of 15-minute conditions three to five times a week (Lanovaz et al., 2011). Type of music and exact implementation procedures would need to be based on an individualized assessment (Lanovaz et al., 2012).

Costs

The cost of Music Intensity is limited to the music source. However, consultation with a credentialed music therapist is encouraged and cost would be based on their fee schedule and vary by region.

Potential Risks

Although music has many positive qualities, its potential for harm is respected and accounted for in the music therapy profession. Some potential risks of implementing Music Intensity include increasing inappropriate behaviors (Buckley & Newchok, 2006). Educators would need to implement with care by doing due diligence before delivery and closely observing during facilitation to know if the intervention should be ceased and reevaluated.

Rating

  Limited Supporting Information for Practice

Resources and Suggested Readings

Speaking of autism... An autistic person speaks about living with autism. (n.d.). *Understanding auditory sensitivities in autistic-people: It's not just about volume.* This site can be accessed at https://speakingofautismcom.wordpress.com/2019/03/25/understanding-auditory-sensitivities-in-autistic-people-its-not-just-about-volume/

Wong, C., Odom, S. L., Hume, K. Cox, A. W., Fettig, A., Kucharczyk, S., Brock, M. E., Plavnick, J. B., Fleury, V. P., & Schultz, T. R. (2014). *Evidence-based practices for children, youth, and young adults with autism spectrum disorder.* The University of North Carolina, Frank Porter Graham Child Development Institute, Autism Evidence-Based Practice Review Group.

Animal-Assisted Intervention (AAI)

Description

AAI includes animal-assisted therapy and animal-assisted activities (Griffin et al., 2011; Kruger & Serpell, 2010). The practice of using animals as part of a therapeutic intervention for individuals with autism employs multiple species, which includes horses, dogs, guinea pigs, llamas, and dolphins. Individuals with autism struggle with social interaction skills, which is one of the hallmark areas of concerns for those on the spectrum. It has been suggested that individuals with autism may not experience the same type of social aversions toward animals that impact their ability to interact with humans.

Brief Overview of the Literature

In a meta-analysis of 49 studies of AAI for a range of populations, Nimer and Lundahl (2007) found four key areas of improvement from AAI, which included autism symptoms, medical difficulties, behavioral problems, and emotional well-being. While they concluded that AAI may be a promising addition to other established interventions for individuals with ASD, only 4 of the 49 studies reviewed included individuals with ASD. This is common methodological weakness in AAI research leading to a reliance on anecdotal evidence (Griffin et al., 2011).

The purpose of O'Haire's review in 2013 was to move, beyond anecdotal accounts by looking at a comprehensive overview of empirical research on AAI for ASD. The aims were to (a) describe the characteristics of AAI for ASD, (b) evaluate the state of the evidence base, and (c) summarize the reported outcomes. The final sample included 14 articles (1.16% of the total initial pool) published between 1989 and 2012 that met the inclusion criteria with 11 of the 14 studies published from 2008 to 2012 (O'Haire, 2013). Treatment settings varied as did the number of interventionists as well as the length and type of training provided for the interventionists and the length of time and duration of the intervention.

Core Reviews

Simpson et al. (2005) included Pet/Animal Therapy and reviewed three articles all on dolphin-assisted therapy giving the rating of Limited Supporting Information for Practice. The NAC included Animal-Assisted Therapy as an Unestablished Intervention in 2015. The NCAEP (Steinbrenner et al., 2020) included AAI in 2020 and gave it a rating of Some but Insufficient Evidence based on one study (Becker et al., 2017).

Other Systematic Reviews/Meta-Analyses

O'Haire (2017) published a systematic literature review to synthesize all research on AAI for autism published from 2012 to 2015. At that time 28 studies revealed that AAI programs generally included one animal per participant with a total contact time of approximately 10 hours over the course of 8 to 12 weeks (O'Haire, 2017). The most reported outcome was increased social interaction found to be significant in 22 of the 28 studies. While the number of studies of AAI for autism increased each year, with four in 2012 and 10 in 2015, there remained small numbers of studies with most (55%) focusing on horses, and still little information was provided regarding trainer/handler certification or training, and dose of AAI programs ranged from 1 to 52 weeks with most lasting between 8 to 12 weeks. Many of the studies had small sample sizes and no studies included adults. Most studies used a survey or interview techniques. Most used and at least one standardized assessment tool. The findings should be interpreted as preliminary in most cases. The most assessed outcome was social interaction (n = 22) with all reporting positive effects. Language and communication were evaluated in 12 of the studies with 75 percent (n = 9) reporting significant improvements.

The results of this literature review indicate that the most researched species in AAI is the horse, and the most researched species as a companion or service animal is the dog. The qualifications of the handler and the animal were still only reported in about half of the studies. There was also high variability of dosing/duration of programs. The large variability of AAI characteristics indicates that the practice is not yet standardized (O'Haire, 2017). There has been improvement in research methodology that has increased the rigor of the evidence-base on AAI for autism, but there are still many areas that need attention and improvement. O'Haire concluded that ongoing study should focus on technique refinement, evidence-based procedures, and the effects of individual differences.

Age and Diagnostic Considerations/ Prerequisite Skills and Abilities

Some sort of AAI would be appropriate for every age and severity level of ASD. The type of animal used and the type of activity would dictate prerequisite skills and abilities.

Reported Outcomes

There is a considerable amount of anecdotal evidence that indicates AAI can support individuals with ASD to develop sensory and social skills, manage problem behaviors, and improve quality of life (O'Haire, 2013). A systematic literature review of AAI for ASD published in 2012 indicated that interacting with animals can enhance psychosocial well-being (O'Haire, 2010) with documented benefits including reduced stress, lowered heart rate and blood pressure, reduced loneliness and isolation, increased social interaction and connection, and increased socioemotional functioning (Friedman & Son, 2009; Wells, 2009).

The most common outcome of AAI for ASD was increased social interaction, which was reported in 9 of the 14 studies with greater social interaction in the presence of an animal, and two studies reported concurrent decreases in social isolation and self-absorption (Silva et al., 2011). A small number of studies collected data on language and communication that suggested children with ASD may demonstrate increased language and communication during and immediately following AAI (O'Haire, 2013). Two studies demonstrated significant decreases in ASD severity, three studies decreased in problem behaviors, one study reported significantly fewer instances of physical and verbal aggression in the presence of an animal versus no animal (Silva et al., 2011), and two studies described enhanced quality of life because of AAI (O'Haire, 2013).

Qualifications Needed

Since the type of animal (e.g., guinea pig, dog, horse, dolphin) and the actual intervention used in AAI (e.g., caring for a pet, dog-assisted social skills groups, therapeutic riding, dolphin therapy) vary, the qualifications of the implementers needed would also greatly vary.

How, Where, and When Typically Implemented

Because of the species utilized during the intervention process it can occur in various settings for varying amounts of time as well as varying durations. Current practices should be viewed as potentially promising enrichment interventions, rather than stand alone or complementary EBP.

Costs

Costs of AAI will vary greatly depending on the type of animal used.

Potential Risks

The use of time and financial resources involved with AAI may prohibit the implementation of other interventions with a stronger evidence base. The risks of AAI depends on the type of animal, the environment, and the quality of supervision.

Practitioner Testimonial(s)

I have been working in the field of autism for 30 years and provided consultative services for most of that time. When my lab/golden retriever, Zoey, was a puppy, the vet told me that I should train her to be a service dog. At that time, for many reasons, there was really no way for me to devote the time and energy into her training. That was 12 years ago. In May of 2021, my 17-year-old Lab/Newfoundland passed away leaving just Zoey. In June, I made the decision to begin training Zoey as a therapy/service dog. Many in the training community were hesitant to support this project given her age due to concerns as to how she might react with unexpected touch or pain from someone stepping on her or some other unforeseen event. She is a remarkable dog and has picked up so many things so quickly, it is amazing! She goes everywhere with me, and her presence has enriched the lives of so many children and adults! She gravitates to those who are stressed and anxious and will not leave them until she "feels" they are calm. She has the softest ears and head, and people just love to pet her and de-stress. She loves everyone, and is so patient, especially with students with autism and emotional or behavioral issues. I have truly seen the increased social interaction and communication in children with autism. She allows them to load their stuffed animals on top of her and they bring her grilled cheese and lemonade from the kitchen area during free play. They count her toes and talk to her. I have observed children with autism who were fearful of dogs not only lose their fear of dogs, but they become so excited to see Zoey back in the building and run to see her. I have been in various places in the community and children with autism seem to seek her out, and she them. Honestly, I cannot tell you why she is so good with people and children who struggle in some way, but she is. I cannot tie it to any specific training she has had or a specific amount of interaction/dosing she has had with children that led/leads to various improvements for some individuals. There may be just too many variables to be able to conduct standardized research that will let us know what qualities must be present in the animal, what training a handler must have, and what needs an individual with autism must exhibit to be able to move AAI to an evidence-based practice. I see evidence every day that lets me know these individuals are benefitting from their experiences with Zoey, and I know that I am truly benefitting from watching these amazing interactions and growth daily.

—Lisa Robbins

Rating

At this time we are not giving AAI a rating due to the wide range of animals, costs, activities, and amount of time involved in the existing research literature. Future research should focus on specific types of animals and clearly define the critical features of each intervention and details regarding implementation.

Art Therapy

Description

Art Therapy involves a process of using clinical interventions to develop art activities with the goal of analyzing behaviors, psychological attributes, and challenges in order to form a treatment plan based on the individual learner's strengths and needs (Alter-Muri, 2017). The process is more important than the product. Art Therapy has been suggested as being useful for individuals with ASD because it requires little or no verbal interaction and can build on those individuals' preference for visual information as well as being tailored to their behavior and sensory sensitivities (Round et al., 2017). The goal of therapy sessions is to work with students with ASD to regulate their over- or understimulated processing experiences to improve a variety of skills by allowing unconscious images to emerge and be contained, creating a tool to process hidden thoughts and feelings (Alter-Muri, 2017; Martin, 2009).

Brief Overview of the Literature

Two of the first peer-reviewed studies using Art Therapy with learners with ASD were conducted in the late 1980s/early 1990s. Steinberger (1987) conducted a case study implementing Art Therapy in an outpatient clinic. The goal of Art Therapy was to assist the participant, "Bobby," in forming and maintaining relationships with other individuals. Before Bobby arrived for sessions, art materials were placed on the table. In later sessions, Bobby was allowed to choose his materials and store them upon completion. Researchers observed that Bobby found felt markers most satisfying since they were precise and quickly produced an effective result. In contrast, paint made Bobby anxious because of the messiness. Findings indicate that Bobby had a decrease in agitation, anger, arm flapping, and strange vocalizations and increased academic achievement and social awareness. Nine months after the conclusion of this study and implementation of Art Therapy, Bobby was able to attend many general education classes in junior high school, although clearly a causal relationship with the Art Therapy he experienced was not established. In Kornreich and Schimmel (1991), the researcher worked with three students one on one in a private workshop studio school. Each participant participated in roughly 10 sessions that occurred once a week. Results indicated an increase in self-esteem, sense of identity, improved communication, greater self-control, as well as more pleasure in daily activities (Kornreich & Schimmel, 1991)

Core Reviews

Simpson et al. (2005) was the only core review that included any studies on Art Therapy and gave it a rating of Limited Supporting Information for Practice based on the two studies previously described.

Other Systematic Reviews/Meta-Analyses

In 2014 with the goal of providing a structure for evaluating Art Therapy in a consistent way, Schweizer et al. developed a framework to establish the critical components organizing them in four areas: (1) art therapeutic means and forms of expression; (2) behavior of therapists in terms of interaction with clients as well as handling of materials; (3) context, setting, reason for referral, duration, and other treatment methods; and (4) short- and long-term outcomes. She and her colleagues conducted a review of 18 clinical case descriptions published between the years of 1985 to 2012.

The ages of students varied, and reported outcomes included increased relaxation and flexibility and improved self-image, social, communication, and learning skills.

Age and Diagnostic Considerations/ Prerequisite Skills and Abilities

Art Therapy has been used with students with ASD from preschool to adulthood with mild support needs to more severe forms of autism.

Reported Outcomes

Limited research indicates that students with ASD who participate in Art Therapy may have improvements in academics, communication, social, emotional, and behavioral skills.

Qualifications Needed

Art therapists are health-care professionals who hold a master's degree or above in Art Therapy or a similar field. They are trained in both nondirected and directed Art Therapy activities developed based on the unique needs of each individual.

How, Where, and When Typically Implemented

Art therapists work in K–12 schools, hospitals, clinics, or other health institutions with the goal to address health and overall well-being of individuals using a variety of tools (Martin, 2009). In schools, Art Therapy sessions typically involve one-on-one sessions or small groups so that the therapist can focus on individualizing goals for each student (Ullmann, 2012).

Costs

The cost of Art Therapy will depend on the setting in which the services are provided. If services are provided in a school setting, no cost should be incurred. If the program is provided by a private art therapist, the cost will align with their fee schedule.

Potential Risks

There are no documented or obvious risks associated with Art Therapy. However, use of time and financial resources, especially if a private art therapist is being considered, may prohibit the implementation of other interventions with a stronger evidence base.

Rating

   Limited Supporting Information for Practice

Resources and Suggested Readings

Blossom Children's Center. (2020). *Benefits of art therapy for children with autism*. This site can be accessed at https://blossomchildrenscenter.com/2020/02/27/benefits-of-art-therapy-for-children-with-autism/

Outdoor Adventure Interventions

Description

Outdoor Adventure Interventions are "group camp-style activities that incorporate songs, rope courses, and debriefs focusing on teamwork, trust, communication, facing fears, and self-determination" (NCAEP, Steinbrenner et al., 2020, p. 31). Outdoor programs rely heavily on social and communication skills, two areas that are difficult for many individuals with ASD.

Brief Overview of the Literature

The only study identified examining Outdoor Adventure Interventions with individuals with ASD was conducted by Zachor et al. (2017) and included in the NCAEP 2020 review. This study focused on how the program impacted individual's self-image, adaptive skills, and severity of typical autism symptoms as well as the instructor's perception of the individual's future capabilities. There were 51 participants with 40 of the participants being male with ages ranging from 3 to 7 years. The study took place over 13 weekly sessions, which began with a song and then involved activities that encouraged communication between the instructor and other participants, including a two-way climbing rope ladder, rope elevator, rope bridge, and a rope swing. Following each session, the participants were asked various questions about the session in a closing meeting (e.g., What activities did you enjoy doing?).

Core Reviews

The only core review that included Outdoor Adventure was the NCAEP (Steinbrenner et al., 2020) in 2020, which gave it a rating of Some but Insufficient Evidence based on one study described above.

Age and Diagnostic Considerations/ Prerequisite Skills and Abilities

The study identified by the core reviews involved Outdoor Adventure Programs with individuals ages 3 to 7. However, this intervention could potentially benefit individuals with ASD of all ages.

Reported Outcomes

Outdoor Adventure Interventions could possibly have a positive impact on the severity of social impairment symptoms of individuals with ASD. However, there are an insufficient number of studies that have examined the effects of these interventions for this population.

Qualifications Needed

Outdoor Adventure Therapy is implemented by trained educators and there should also be a health-focused professional involved as well as experts in behavioral health.

How, Where, and When Typically Implemented

Outdoor Adventure Activities are implemented on campgrounds that have the appropriate equipment and where oversight is available.

Costs

Personnel and supplies needed for the Outdoor Adventure Intervention Therapy are the main expenses and will vary greatly depending on the particulars of the organization providing the intervention.

Potential Risks

Potential risks of Outdoor Adventure Therapy depend on the setting, adult supervision, and safety training policies. The use of time and financial resources on Outdoor Adventure Therapy may prohibit the implementation of other interventions with a stronger evidence base.

Practitioner Testimonial(s)

I have been involved with Camp Encourage for 6 years and seen so much growth throughout the years in many campers. As an overnight camp for children 8 to 18 on the autism spectrum, we combine a variety of activities to address campers' self-esteem, social skills, independence, acceptance, and recreational skills. Common activities that campers participate in include swimming, zip lining, low ropes courses, archery, arts and crafts, board games, karaoke, musical improv, laser tag, social skills group classes, and many more. Through our social skills group time, we are able to address self-appreciation by teaching campers to notice the good in themselves and others through specific group and individual programming. Our goal is that by the end of a camp session, each camper has increased self-esteem and can name at least one positive thing about themselves. Through outdoor activities like zip lining and archery, we are able to address independence and reactional skills. Additionally, these skills work on self-esteem by teaching campers a new skill. All activities at camp can help generate social skills by counselors modeling turn taking, conversational skills, and connecting based on common interests. At meals, we provide social scripts as needed to start conversations and connection. After each camp session, parents of campers and volunteers fill out surveys to share memories, suggestions, and provide us with some data about the success of our programming. Data from the 2021 feedback survey showed that 100% of parents reported that their child's self-esteem was increased at Camp Encourage and 100% of parents reported that Camp Encourage provided increased social opportunities and growth.

—Brooke Bailey

Rating

   Limited Supporting Information for Practice

Resources and Suggested Readings

Camp Encourage can be accessed at https://www.campencourage.org
Operation Shine Camp can be accessed at http://www.kidsanddreams.org

Toilet Training

Description

An individual is toilet trained when they can recognize when they need to use the toilet, eliminate in the toilet, and have few or no accidents (Kurniawan et al., 2018). Blum et al. (2004) defined effective daytime toilet training as when a child has fewer than four wetting accidents per week. Competent toileting is a critical life skill that individuals with autism often experience challenges in acquiring at the same age as typical developing peers, which is by approximately the age of 5 (Dalrymple & Ruble 1992). This would indicate a need for effective training strategies that can easily be shared with caregivers and educators.

Brief Overview of the Literature

Azrin and Foxx (1971) established an intensive toilet-training protocol for nine adult individuals with ID in a residential setting since referred to as Rapid Toilet Training (RTT). Since the development of the RTT protocol, there have been numerous studies that replicate their efficacy in educational and outpatient settings, but the training process occurred over long periods of time. Many researchers have adapted minor components while maintaining the major elements (i.e., positive reinforcement, hydration where the subject is provided increased access to fluids, scheduled sittings) with the removal of urine alarms (Cicero & Pfadt, 2002; Post & Kirkpatrick, 2004) and the removal of the required practice to clean soiled items and repeatedly practice walking from the site of the accident (Cicero & Pfadt, 2002). Saral and Ulke-Kurkcuoglu (2020) conducted a comprehensive review of the literature on toilet-training individuals with developmental delays of all ages by evaluating these areas of focus in 23 studies published from 2009 to 2019. All of the toilet-training programs in the studies are derivatives and modified versions of the original Azrin and Foxx study. They concluded that no standardized toileting programs of fixed components for individuals with developmental disabilities have existed ever since the Azrin and Foxx study, so there is still no agreement on a common toileting program for individuals with ASD or other developmental disabilities in the literature.

There are few studies that deal directly with the issue of toilet training in school settings. Cocchiola et al. (2012) conducted a study that evaluated a public school–based toilet-training procedure implemented by paraprofessional staff. The procedure consisted of multiple components that included the removal of diapers during school hours, a scheduled time interval for bathroom visits, a maximum of 3 minutes sitting on the toilet at each visit, positive reinforcement for urination in the toilet, and gradually increasing time intervals for bathroom visits as each student progressed through training. Additional research focusing on the procedures in other schools to determine generality was suggested along with the importance of detecting self-initiations.

Core Reviews

In 2009, the NAC included five articles (Bainbridge & Myles, 1999; Cicero & Pfadt, 2002; Keen et al., 2007; Post & Kirkpatrick, 2004; Taylor et al., 1994) that addressed toileting in some manner under the Behavioral Package intervention category, which was rated as an Established Treatment. The NPDC 2015 review was the only core review to include the specific term of Toilet Training as a reviewed intervention. It included one article (LeBlanc, 2005) and it was given the rating of Some but Insufficient Evidence. In 2020, the NCAEP (Steinbrenner et al., 2020) recategorized Toilet Training as an Antecedent-Based Intervention, a category that was given the rating of EBP, and it also included an article on Toilet Training (Post & Kirkpatrick, 2004) under the Prompting category, which was also given the rating of EBP.

Age and Diagnostic Considerations/ Prerequisite Skills and Abilities

Since typical peers become toilet trained between the ages of 2 and 5, attempting toilet training with individuals with ASD should ideally also occur when the learner is in this mental age range as long as the individual is able to sit on the toilet being used for approximately 5 minutes, has shown indications that they are starting to recognize when they need to use the toilet, have some control over their facilities, and have no contraindicated medical conditions.

Qualifications Needed

No formal training is required to implement toilet training.

How, Where, and When Typically Implemented

Caregivers and educators can implement a toilet-training protocol in both home and school settings. The most common behavioral intervention used in toilet-training protocols is positive reinforcement (Saral & Ulke-Kurkcuoglu, 2020). There have been several studies that have used VM in conjunction with versions of the Azrin and Foxx protocol (Drysdale et al., 2015; Lee et al., 2014; McLay et al., 2015).

Costs

Caregivers could implement a toilet-training protocol in natural settings at no cost.

Potential Risks

Common complications that can occur while toilet training include toileting refusal, withholding, constipation, night wetting (encopresis), and hiding to defecate. If any of these happens, trainers should be calm and supportive and see professional advice from a qualified professional (Baird et al., 2019).

Practitioner Testimonial(s)

I have been working in the field of autism for 30 years and have provided consultative services for most of that time. I have been asked to "potty train" so many children with autism over the years that my nickname has become "the pee pee whisperer." Each time I successfully train another child, people encourage me to "write it up" and share my experience and expertise with others. This is by no means an attempt at providing any type of "gold standard" research on the task of toilet training individuals with autism but is rather my anecdotal account of what my many experiences have taught me over the years with the hope that they may be useful to someone else in their quest to toilet train a child with ASD.

I have lost count of the number of children I have successfully potty trained with autism. There are too many to remember. I have trained individuals of various age levels and abilities in both school and home settings. I have been able to successfully have the child urinate in the toilet on the first day of training with 100% success! I have trained children in a school setting where they were completely and totally potty trained in the school setting but would not become trained at home for several more years.

Foundational Concepts

- Toilet training is not simply a task that can be accomplished using the principles of traditional ABA such as reinforcement. There is a physiological component that plays a significant part in their ability to understand what those who are doing the training are wanting.

- Change is often difficult for individuals with autism. They become set in their ways and when they learn how to do something one way and in one setting, it is often difficult for them to make a change and understand why the change is needed. What we know about behavior is that the longer someone has been exhibiting a behavior, the longer it will take to change that behavior. By the time the toilet-training process is age appropriate, the child has been completing this process in a diaper for years. Now adults want them to complete this process in a strange, cold, loud porcelain "baby pool." They have no idea why we want to change what's been working pretty well so far from their perspective.

- The initial component skill of toilet training is sitting on the toilet for approximately 5 minutes. If a child has not reached that point of tolerance, wait to begin the additional steps of toilet training until that has been accomplished.

- The child needs to not only understand what we are wanting them to do on the toilet but also to physically feel the sensation of having to urinate while they are at the toilet. Getting those two things to happen at the same time is key!

My Toilet Training Protocol

- If I am training in the home, I'm there first thing in the morning. If I'm training at school, I'm there as soon as the child arrives.

- Caregivers have been communicated with so they are aware I will be working with their child, and I have asked for the child's favorite things to drink to be on hand in an amount so that I will not run out during our session, which could be the entire day. I will go with whatever the child prefers to drink and I've asked to save this drink for only our session that day.

- Our day revolves around toilet training. That means typical routines will not be followed and we will spend the majority of our day in an area that is close to a toilet. That can be a classroom, someone's office that contains a private bathroom, etc. Our activities and work for the day should be a variety of things the child enjoys working on or playing with.

- If a child arrives at school wearing a diaper or a pull-up, it comes off and underwear goes on. I usually ask the caregivers to send extra pairs of underwear that day just to have on hand in case they are needed. As part of this process, we include sitting on the toilet. Since I am fairly confident nothing is going to occur, we just sit for a minute or two, get up, pull up/put on underwear and pants, wash/dry hands, and return to our work area.

- Upon returning, the child drinks 8 to 10 sips of their preferred drink by sucking a straw for easy counting. I set a timer for 15 minutes and the child goes about the next activity.

- When the timer goes off, we stop the activity and begin the bathroom routine. I often use a visual timer and prime the child that the timer will be going off soon and it will be time to use the potty.

- This process is continued every 15 minutes for about an hour and a half. Then I set the timer for 10-minute intervals. I can often observe signs that the child's bladder is getting full and they are becoming a bit uncomfortable such acts as squirming around while on the toilet or avoidance behavior. I verbally validate that I know this is hard for them and that it is okay to "let it go" and "pee pee goes in the potty." I always provide positive reinforcement for the steps in the process in the form of praise and possibly tangibles.

- Sometimes it's helpful to push a bit on the tummy when things start to fill up to release some of the muscles that are tensing up because the child isn't exactly sure what they are supposed to do. Usually when they feel like this, they have a diaper or pull-up on, which is familiar and they know what to do. This new situation is confusing to them so I explain it to them in terms they understand.

- The process is repeated until success is reached. There is nothing more rewarding than watching the relief and understanding on the face of a child who has just figured out what this is all about and what adults are wanting them to do!

- This can take a couple of hours or more, but I've never had it not work! This is one of the most rewarding experiences for me, the child, and his family as this is definitely a life skill that will make their life and their parents' lives easier on many levels!

—Lisa Robbins

Rating

At this time we are not giving Toilet Training a rating based on the mixed categorizations and ratings by the core reviews. Different protocols exist and the critical features of each need to be defined and the protocols researched individually.

Resources and Suggested Readings

Nebraska Autism Spectrum Disorders Network. (2019). *Toilet training for children with autism spectrum disorders.* This site can be accessed at https://www.unl.edu/asdnetwork/webinars?tid=All&combine=toilet

SENSE Theatre®

Description

SENSE Theatre incorporates theatrical games and role-playing exercises to potentially improve social skills. Individuals with ASD are paired with typically developing, trained peers who are models for adaptive social interaction (Corbett, 2016; Corbett et al., 2017). The goal of SENSE Theatre as an intervention is to combine art and science to create a sense of community and an environment that is supportive and enjoyable.

Brief Overview of the Literature

There are few empirical-based studies demonstrating the effects of the SENSE Theatre intervention. Dr. Blythe Corbett—Director of the Social Emotional NeuroScience Endocrinology (SENSE) lab at Vanderbilt University Medical Center—and her colleagues combined their background in writing and acting with their knowledge of clinical research. In 2016 Corbett conducted a randomized experimental design study to determine the effects of a peer-mediated theatre-based intervention for students with ASD. Researchers studied neural, cognitive, and behavioral functioning while including a social competence framework. Participants were high functioning and had a previous diagnosis of autism and their ages ranged from 8 to 14. The intervention was delivered over the course of 10 sessions, which was similar to a summer camp. There were three components of the intervention: typically developing peer actors, SENSE Theatre sessions, and homework that included practicing with video models. The video modeling component was monitored by checking log-in stamps. There were many significant findings within this study. Engagement in exercises such as role play and improvisational games increased the awareness of social cues in students with ASD. It is hypothesized that this type of intervention contributes to mindfulness of nonverbal cues through understanding body language. Lastly, reliable parent reports suggested that gains were made in the area of social communication, which improved interaction in home and community environments (Corbett, 2016).

Corbett et al. (2017) extended their research testing the effects of the SENSE Theatre intervention focusing on stress and anxiety. Individuals partaking in the treatment participated in 10-week, 4-hour sessions. Components of the intervention included peers acting, SENSE Theatre sessions, and homework using video modeling. Findings were indicative of significant effects, which resulted in the reduction of anxiety.

Core Reviews

The NAC included SENSE Theatre Intervention as a reviewed intervention in 2015 and gave it the rating of Unestablished. The NPDC (Wong et al., 2014) and NCAEP (Steinbrenner et al., 2020) did not review it as an individual intervention but the NCAEP did include two articles on interventions involving theatre in 2020 under PBII (Corbett, 2016; Corbett et al., 2017) and Social Skills Training (Corbett et al., 2017), which were both rated as an EBP.

Age and Diagnostic Considerations/ Prerequisite Skills and Abilities

Studies on SENSE Theatre included subjects ranging in age from 8 to 14.

Reported Outcomes

Research indicates that SENSE Theatre reduces stress and anxiety for students with ASD. This intervention has also helped students with ASD become aware of verbal and nonverbal cues while also understanding body language.

Qualifications Needed

SENSE Theatre is ideally administered by an individual trained with an acting background.

How, Where, and When Typically Implemented

SENSE Theatre and other theater-based programs are community-based programs and their availability will vary. It has been administered at a satellite school at a university. Similar programs could potentially be implemented in other school settings.

Costs

The cost of SENSE Theatre is not given on their website.

Potential Risks

There are no documented or obvious risks associated with SENSE Theatre. However, use of time and financial resources, may prohibit the implementation of other interventions with a stronger evidence base.

Rating

   Limited Supporting Information for Practice

Resources and Suggested Readings

SENSE Theatre can be accessed at https://sensetheatre.com/

Exercise and Movement (EXM) Interventions

Description

EXM interventions "use physical exertion, specific motor skills/techniques, or mindful movement to target a variety of skills and behaviors" (NCAEP, Steinbrenner et al., 2020, p. 28). It is based on the theory that physiological responses to exercise may cause sedation and relaxation in psychological and behavioral responses (Thompson & Blanton, 1987), which may have a positive impact on behavior, and specifically automatically maintained stereotypical behavior (Lang et al., 2010; Neely et al., 2015).

Brief Overview of the Literature

The earliest study on using EXM with learners with ASD was conducted by Schleien et al. (1988) to teach appropriate play skills followed by three studies in the 1990s addressing self-stimulatory behaviors (Celiberti et al., 1997; Levinson & Reid, 1993; Rosenthal-Malek & Mitchell, 1997). It has been reported by several studies since that time not included in the core reviews that physical activity intervention improves behavioral (Elliott et al., 1994) and social (Sowa & Meulenbroek, 2012) outcomes for learners with ASD.

Core Reviews

The NAC used the term Exercise and gave it a rating of Emerging in both 2009 based on four studies and 2015 based on an unspecified number of studies. In 2014, the NPDC (Wong et al., 2014) used the term Exercise and gave it a rating of EBP based on six studies. In 2020, the NCAEP (Steinbrenner et al., 2020) used the term EXM and again gave it a rating of EBP based on 11 additional studies.

Other Systematic Reviews/Meta-Analyses

The most recent meta-analysis by Park et al. (2021) examined EXM in 14 peer-reviewed articles from 2001 to 2018 and found a moderate to large positive effect on behaviors of individuals with ASD. The smallest effect was on engagement and the largest on problem behavior.

Age and Diagnostic Considerations/ Prerequisite Skills and Abilities

The literature found positive outcomes in individuals with ASD ranging in age from 6 to 22. Initial health assessments are encouraged by trained medical professionals before implementing.

Reported Outcomes

Reported positive outcomes in the literature included improvements in language production, memory, self-control, on-task behavior, social skills, academic engagement, and play skills. The most common intervention in the literature was the use of EXM to reduce problem behavior such as self-stimulatory behaviors, vocal and physical stereotypy, repetitive behaviors, and others that prevent access to academic and social environments. Sports-related skills had a higher rate of effectiveness than just exercise as they have functional and social application maximizing generalization and automatic reinforcement within the natural environment.

Qualifications Needed

EXM interventions implemented by "professional practitioners with clinical experience" (Park et al., 2021, p. 363), with two examples in the literature being a gym teacher or riding instructor but could also include sports coaches, have proven to be more effective than when implemented by educators or researchers. These professionals can provide training and implementation support to practitioners working in settings where physical activities are common.

How, Where, and When Typically Implemented

EXM is most often used in the school setting but can take place in a home and community setting. It is often with prompting, modeling, reinforcement, and visual supports. The frequency and duration of sessions ranged from one to 10 times a week for 3 to 60 minutes.

Costs

The cost of EXM will vary based on access to resources, equipment, and professionals.

Potential Risks

Consultation with medical professionals for those with existing health needs is recommended. Risks associated with general exercise should be expected and controlled for with quality equipment, safe environment, and trained professionals.

Rating

   Evidence-Based Practice

Resources and Suggested Readings

Cox, A. W. (2013). *Exercise (ECE) fact sheet*. The University of North Carolina, Frank Porter Graham Child Development Institute, The National Professional Development Center on Autism Spectrum Disorders. This fact sheet can be accessed at https://autismpdc.fpg.unc .edu/sites/autismpdc.fpg.unc.edu/files/Exercise_factsheet.pdf

Griffin, W., & AFIRM Team. (2015). *Exercise*. National Professional Development Center on Autism Spectrum Disorder, FPG Child Development Center, University of North Carolina. This site can be accessed at http://afirm.fpg.unc.edu/exercise

Gentle Teaching

Description

Gentle Teaching is a philosophical approach that emphasizes safe and caring relationships between caregivers and individuals with ASD. It was originally designed as a non-aversive method for reducing challenging behaviors and improving the quality of life for people who exhibited maladaptive behaviors. By focusing on environmental and interpersonal factors, the goal of Gentle Teaching is to create bonded relationships between individuals with disabilities and their caregivers, and the interpersonal bond that results from this intervention forms the foundation for making positive changes. Gentle Teaching is made up of four basic assumptions (McGee, 1990):

1. Frequent and unconditional value giving is central to interactional exchange.

2. Everyone has an inherent longing for affection and warmth.

3. Dominating actions, such as the use of restraint and punishment, need to be decreased and replaced with value-centered behaviors.

4. Change in both the caregiver and the person exhibiting maladaptive behaviors is critical.

The idea is that these bonded relationships will result in positive behavioral changes to remove barriers to inclusive education, community participation, and peer interactions rather than simple behavioral control by using various techniques including errorless teaching strategies, task analysis, environmental management, precise and conservative prompting, joint participation in activities, identification of precursors to target behaviors, reduction of verbal instruction, reduction of verbal and/or physical demands, choice-making, fading assistance, integration of other caregivers and peers into relationships, and use of dialogue as an expression of unconditional valuing (McGee, 1990, 1992). Caregivers can use these in various combinations based on their own judgment of the moment-to-moment changes in the learner's behavior (Jones & McCaughey, 1992; McGee, 1985).

Brief Overview of the Literature

Gentle Teaching first appears in the literature in 1985 (McGee, 1985). Jones and McCaughey (1992) conducted a critical review of Gentle Teaching and concluded that there were similarities between Gentle Teaching and many procedures used in ABA and identified that additional research and analyses of objective data were needed. Mudford (1995) did an additional review of nine peer reviewed studies independently evaluating Gentle Teaching and found that two had clinically significant reductions in problem behaviors, two increased SIB, and five had no clinically significant changes in levels of behaviors. A study by Cullen and Mappin (1998) on the effects of Gentle Teaching on people with complex learning and behavior challenges indicated that its use may result in some positive changes in interactions between staff and clients but did not find any effects on changing the levels of challenging behavior. There has not been any published peer-reviewed studies on Gentle Teaching since.

Core Reviews

Only Simpson et al. (2005) included Gentle Teaching as a reviewed intervention, reviewing five studies and giving the rating of Limited Supporting Information for Practice.

Age and Diagnostic Considerations/ Prerequisite Skills and Abilities

Gentle Teaching is widely applicable and can be used for all school-age learners with ASD with mild to severe support needs.

Reported Outcomes

The main developer of Gentle Teaching (McGee, 1985) reported that the challenging behavior of more than 600 individuals was decreased using this approach but there were significant methodological limitations to the research conducted. The ABA procedures included as part of Gentle Teaching such as errorless teaching strategies, task analysis, environmental management, precise and conservative prompting, joint participation in activities, identification of precursors to target behaviors, reduction of verbal instruction, reduction of verbal and/or physical demands, choice-making, and fading assistance have had positive effects on a variety of skills. See the Behavioral Interventions section of this resource for additional information.

Qualifications Needed

Anyone who has been appropriately trained and who works with individuals with disabilities can potentially use Gentle Teaching in a variety of environments.

How, Where, and When Typically Implemented

Gentle Teaching can be implemented in school, clinical, home, and community settings.

Costs

Implementing Gentle Teaching requires only the financial resources needed to train caregivers in its philosophy and techniques. The Gentle Teaching website has a link to register for training but no information is given about cost.

Potential Risks

There are no documented or obvious risks associated with Gentle Teaching. However, use of time and financial resources may prohibit the implementation of other interventions with a stronger evidence base.

Rating

    Limited Supporting Information for Practice

Resources and Suggested Readings

Gentle Teaching Unconditional Relationship: The Center of Education and Caregiving can be accessed at https://www.gentleteaching.nl/gentle/en/

Sensory Integration (SI) Interventions

Description

SI Interventions "target a person's ability to integrate sensory information (visual, auditory, tactile, proprioceptive, and vestibular) from their body and environment in order to respond using organized and adaptive behavior" (NCAEP, Steinbrenner et al., 2020, p. 29). SI theory states that some children suffer from a neural dysfunction that causes the nervous system to insufficiently receive and process incoming information (Ayres, 2005). Individuals with ASD are believed to be especially vulnerable to SI dysfunction. For these persons, the sensory areas are thought to have difficulty receiving the appropriate information or adequate information from the processing areas of the brain: the thalamus and brainstem. As a result, behaviors and responses are impaired. Individuals with SI dysfunction may not respond to the environment, may be oversensitive to the environment, or may seek out more sensory input. Indicators of SI dysfunction include oversensitivity or underreaction to stimuli; unusually high or low level of activity; coordination problems; delays in speech, language, or motor skills; behavior problems; and poor self-concept.

Students with SI dysfunction may be hyper- or hyposensitive to sensory input. Those who are hypersensitive receive too much information in the sensory areas of the brain. Thus, they are overloaded, which can result in two primary behaviors: (1) no motor response because the brain is unable to make sense of the information, or (2) a fleeing response, because the brain finds the sensation aversive. Being hyperloaded results in emotional states of agitation and frustration or avoidance and anxiety. Brains of students who are hyposensitive are believed to receive insufficient information. Resulting behaviors may include (1) no response to sensory stimuli or (2) excess motor activity (e.g., self-stimulation, hyperactivity) because the brain wants more information. Emotional states that result are also thought to involve lethargy or hyperactivity and inattention.

Of the seven sensory systems (see table that follows), three are the main focus of SI interventions: (1) proprioceptive (i.e., muscles and joints); (2) vestibular (i.e., gravity and movement); and (3) tactile (i.e., touch) (Ayres, 2005). These three systems are believed to be central to all other abilities because they are the largest sensory systems, the most interconnected with other sensory systems, and the most utilized. Activities designed to address these sensory needs include riding scooter boards, using swings, jumping on trampolines, and wrapping students in fabric. Therapy frequently appears to be child-directed play, due to the theory that students seek out sensory input to fulfill their needs.

SYSTEM	LOCATION	FUNCTION
Tactile (touch)	Skin—density of cell distribution varies throughout the body. Areas of greatest density include mouth, hands, and genitals.	Provides information about the environment and object qualities (touch, pressure, texture, hard, soft, sharp, dull, heat, cold, pain)

SYSTEM	LOCATION	FUNCTION
Vestibular (balance)	Inner ear—Stimulated by head movements and input from other senses, especially visual	Provides information about where our body is in space and whether or not we or our surroundings are moving Tells about speed and direction of movement
Proprioception (body awareness)	Muscles and joints—Activated by muscle contractions and movement	Provides information about where a certain body part is and how it is moving
Visual (sight)	Retina of the eye—Stimulated by light	Provides information about objects and persons Helps us define boundaries as we move through time and space
Auditory (hearing)	Inner ear—Stimulated by air and sound waves.	Provides information about sound in the environment (loud, soft, high, low, near, far)
Gustatory (taste)	Chemical receptors in the tongue—Closely entwined with the olfactory (smell) system	Provides information about different types of taste (sweet, sour, bitter, salty, spicy)
Olfactory (smell)	Chemical receptors in the nasal structure—Closely associated with the gustatory system	Provides information about different types of smell (musty, acrid, putrid, flowery, pungent)

Core Reviews

Simpson et al. (2005) used the term and gave it a rating of Promising Practice based on their review of seven articles. In 2009 and 2015, the NAC used the term SI Package and gave it the rating of Unestablished based on seven articles and an unspecified number of articles respectively. In 2014, the NPDC (Wong et al., 2014) used the term SI and Fine Motor Intervention and gave the rating of Some but Insufficient Evidence-based on one article (Pfeiffer et al., 2011). In 2020, the NCAEP (Steinbrenner et al., 2020) only included the version of SI® trademarked by Ayres (2005) and not "a variety of unsupported interventions that address sensory issues (Barton et al., 2015; Case-Smith et al., 2015; Watling & Hauer, 2015)" (Steinbrenner et al., 2020, p. 41), giving the Ayres model the rating of EBP based on three articles (Kashefimehr et al., 2018; Pfeiffer et al., 2011; Schaaf et al., 2014).

Age and Diagnostic Considerations/ Prerequisite Skills and Abilities

SI is potentially widely applicable and can be used for all school-age learners with ASD with mild to severe support needs.

Reported Outcomes

Proponents of SI indicate such benefits as improvement in mental processing and organization of sensations, resulting in adaptive responses and increased satisfaction (Myles et al., 2000). However, there is no objective way to measure improved neurological function because problems with Sensory Integration are not specifically associated with localized areas of the brain.

Qualifications Needed

Appropriate implementation of SI requires extensive training and understanding of how neural and physiological systems work. It is also essential for a trained OT with knowledge in the area of sensory dysfunction to evaluate the child prior to implementing any form of SI.

How, Where, and When Typically Implemented

SI is implemented by OT primarily in clinical settings but it can occur in any environment, including home, school, and the community under consultation and guidance of an appropriately trained OT. In addition, some sensory techniques prescribed by an OT may be used by the child without the assistance of another person.

Costs

SI techniques are most often provided by OTs so costs would depend on their fee schedule and the cost of any equipment (e.g. swings) needed. For school-age students with identified educational disabilities, these services are often offered as part of the child's individualized education plan (IEP), if deemed necessary by a team. In these situations, there is no cost to the family.

Potential Risks

Risks may result from implementation of SI by unqualified and inadequately trained individuals. Because the three targeted sensory systems (i.e., proprioceptive, vestibular, and tactile) are closely connected to the autonomic nervous system (which is responsible for breathing, digestions, heart rate, and so on), unregulated sensory stimulation may result in adverse effects (e.g., vomiting, malaise, irregular heart rhythms). In addition, individuals with seizure disorders must be closely monitored related to the use of this method. Furthermore, supplies needed for SI can be costly and the use of time and financial resources may prohibit the implementation of other interventions with a stronger evidence base.

Rating

   Limited Supporting Information for Practice

Resources and Suggested Readings

About Ayres Sensory Integration. This site can be accessed at https://www.theottool box.com/ayres-sensory-integration/

Biomedical and Nutritional Treatments

Introduction

Autism is a complex neurological phenomenon with uncertain etiology (Simpson, & Myles, 2016). The most common and most scientifically validated treatments for autism are behavioral-based approaches to teaching and learning (National Autism Center, 2015). However, for decades parents, medical professionals, and individuals with autism have been interested in biomedical and nutritional supports that might alleviate some of the symptoms of autism or at least improve associated comorbidities (e.g., insomnia, gastrointestinal distress [GID], nutrient deficiencies; Golnik, & Ireland, 2009). These approaches are not well understood scientifically and range from relatively benign and possibly useful interventions (e.g., probiotics) to dangerous medical interventions (e.g., chelation) that can have disastrous consequences.

Core Reviews

No core reviews list any biomedical or nutritional treatments as evidenced-based or as emerging or promising practices. One review, the National Autism Center lists gluten-casein free diets as an unestablished intervention. However, despite this lack of evidence, many of these approaches are widely adopted as surveys of prevalence indicate that as many as 52–95% of youth with ASD are accessing at least one alternative therapy (Golnik, & Ireland, 2009).

Purpose of This Section

The purpose of this section is to outline the state of the evidence related to these biomedical and nutritional approaches as they directly relate to ASD and to identify approaches that may be particularly harmful or useful for individuals with ASD. It can help educators to be aware what choices parents and families may be making and discussing as treatments for their child outside the educational setting. It is important to understand that while the medical field may have evidence that a specific treatment may help some individuals, we are only reviewing and reporting on the research and practice that have specifically been implemented with individuals with ASD and how that treatment specifically addresses the manifestation of ASD within an individual. For example, just because there is evidence that antibiotics kill bacterial infections in a person, this does not mean that using antibiotics improves a person's ability to speak, and could in fact be misused and harm a person if a person were consistently given large doses of antibiotics in order to try to make them speak (this is a fictitious scenario but is a similar example of what has occurred and is occurring with many medical or nutritional treatments being used with individuals with ASD). No ratings are provided for the treatments that are reviewed because they are not utilized within an educational setting and are not ones that an educator would make any decisions about whether to use or not.

Treatments Included in This Section

- Hyperbaric Oxygen Therapy (HBOT)
- Specialized Diets
- Microbiome Therapies
- Vitamin and Mineral Supplementation
- Cannabis
- Chelation

Resources and Suggested Readings

Karhu, E., Zukerman, R., Eshraghi, R. S., Mittal, J., Deth, R. C., Castejon, A. M., Trivedi, M., Mittal, R., & Eshraghi, A. A. (2020). Nutritional interventions for autism spectrum disorder. *Nutrition Reviews*, *78*(7), 515–531.

Hyperbaric Oxygen Therapy (HBOT)

Description

In HBOT, individuals are exposed to high oxygen concentrations inside a pressurized chamber (Xiong et al., 2016). This produces an artificial state of excess oxygen supply in tissue and organs known as hyperoxia (Podgórska-Bednarz & Perenc, 2021). HBOT has demonstrated some efficacy in advanced wound care, radiation injury, and certain types of decompression injuries and associated embolisms, by delivering excess oxygen to the blood, tissue, organs, and neurological system of patients (Podgórska-Bednarz & Perenc, 2021). Some individuals with autism may have increased neuro-inflammation, decreased blood flow to certain parts of the brain, and increased markers of inflammation (Xiong et al., 2016). Currently, it is unclear what role these differences play in ASD etiology and severity. The hypothesis for HBOT is that exposure to high concentrations of oxygen may decrease inflammation and increase blood flow to the brain, thereby improving ASD symptoms. There is also some speculation that HBOT may improve other inflammatory symptoms associated with ASD (e.g., GID).

Brief Overview of the Literature

Three recent systematic reviews (Podgórska-Bednarz & Perenc, 2021; Sakulchit et al., 2017; Xiong et al., 2016) have summarized the existing literature on HBOT and autism. All three reviews came to the same conclusion: There is no evidence to support the use of HBOT for the core symptoms with autism. Since 2015, four separate intervention studies have focused on the effects of HBOT on autism symptomology. Only one study (Lasheen et al., 2019) produced promising results, and this only on the auditory processing of a small sample ($n = 20$) of students with autism (Podgórska-Bednarz & Perenc, 2021). The three other studies produced no effects for HBOT or had serious methodological flaws (e.g., no control group) (Podgórska-Bednarz & Perenc, 2021).

Core Reviews

None of the Core Reviews included HBOT in their reviews of interventions for individual with ASD.

Reported Outcomes

The current state of the literature does not support HBOT for any outcome relevant to ASD.

Qualifications Needed/How, Where, and When Typically Implemented

As a medical intervention, HBOT is usually conducted under the supervision of medical professionals.

Costs

Home HBOT chambers can cost as much as $8,000 to $15,000 depending on the size of the unit. Outpatient therapies can cost between $250 to $450 per session.

Potential Risks

HBOT is not without risks; in fact it has a side-effect profile that is greater than those of control treatments (Sampanthavivat et al., 2012). Possible side effects include pressure related ear injuries, fatigue, headaches, and psychological symptoms associated with being confined to a closed space (Podgórska-Bednarz & Perenc, 2021). **THIS TREATMENT CAN CAUSE HARM TO INDIVIDUALS.**

Specialized Diets

Description

Individuals with autism report gastrointestinal distress (e.g., abdominal pain, constipation, diarrhea) at a higher rate than individuals without autism (Gogou & Kolios, 2018). Similarly, many individuals with autism have selective eating habits, specific nutrient deficiencies, and altered gastrointestinal microbiota (GIM; Whiteley et al., 2013). Though some of these characteristics are well described (e.g., gastrointestinal distress; selective eating), it is not clear how these characteristics affect the core symptoms of autism (Elder et al., 2015). Specific hypotheses, such as intestinal permeability (Navarro et al., 2015), GIM imbalances (Afzal et al., 2003), and yeast/fungal overgrowths (Emam et al., 2012), have not demonstrated consistent research findings (Elder et al., 2006).

Despite this lack of clarity, parents, practitioners, and individuals with autism have been using specialized diets to treat many of the symptoms of autism (Elder et al., 2006). Some reports indicate that 80 percent of parents of a child with autism have tried at least one nutritional intervention (Gogou & Kolios, 2018; Karhu et al., 2020). While there are numerous dietary and other nutritional interventions (e.g., vitamin and mineral supplementation), the primary dietary treatments include the Gut and Psychology Syndrome (GAPS) Diet, the Gluten-Free Casein-Free (GFCF) Diet, the Ketogenic Diet (KD), and the Candida Diet (CD). Below is a brief overview of these diets and their hypothesized effect on autism.

GAPS: The GAPS diet is a low carbohydrate diet, featuring high consumption of animal proteins and fats and restricted consumption of processed foods. GAPS has been reported to improve several health and certain functional gastrointestinal disorders and specific psychological conditions, including autism and schizophrenia (Campbell-McBride, 2008). Proponents of the GAPS diet point to a complex interaction between intestinal permeability, nutrient malabsorption, and dysbiotic or unbalanced GIM as the primary drivers of systemic illness, including autism (Campbell-McBride, 2008). These phenomena are not well understood scientifically, and limited research supports this hypothesis of autism (Mulloy et al., 2010).

GFCF: One of the more durable nutritional treatments of autism is the GFCF diet (Mulloy et al., 2010). Gluten is a protein found in wheat and other grains, while casein is a protein found in mammalian dairy products (Dosman et al., 2013). Proponents of this treatment believe these proteins are not successfully converted to amino acids by the gastrointestinal tracks of individuals with autism. As such, these proteins pass through the intestinal walls (a phenomenon called "leaky gut") and can attach to neuroreceptors creating the symptoms of autism (Mulloy et al., 2010).

Therefore, the GFCF diet is an elimination diet that restricts the user from consuming gluten- and casein-containing foods (Elder et al., 2006). Researchers and practitioners have hypothesized that this restriction will reduce the ability of proteins released from gluten and casein to enter the bloodstream, impacting common autism symptoms (Keller et al., 2021). Unfortunately, this hypothesis is based on unreliable and, at best, correlational research. For example, some research suggests that individuals with autism have highly permeable intestinal walls (Horvath & Perman, 2002), while other researchers have found no differences in the intestinal permeability of youth with autism compared to same-age samples (Robertson et al., 2008).

KD: The KD restricts carbohydrates, allows for the minimum amount of protein, and requires high-fat intake (Castro et al., 2015), thus requiring the body to use fat as the primary source of energy (Napoli et al., 2014). The KD has demonstrated efficacy for treating specific metabolic disorders and epilepsy in some patients (Napoli et al., 2014). Proponents of this approach argue that since autism has been associated with some metabolic dysfunction and increases seizure activity, KD has the potential to improve some autism-associated symptoms (Napoli et al., 2014; Li et al., 2021).

CD: Certain types of fungus and bacteria live symbiotically with human hosts. Candida is a yeast-like fungus that lives in the mucous membranes of the human host, whose immune system regulates the overall populations of these organisms (Emam et al., 2012). In some cases, an imbalance can develop between the host and the fungal or bacterial communities that reside in the host. This can lead to overgrowths of bacterial and fungal communities, causing symptoms in the host (Emam et al., 2012; Fugelsang & Edwards, 2010). One hypothesis of autism is that the symptoms of autism result from extreme fungal overgrowths and fungal infections (Emam et al., 2012). The CD is generally a low-carbohydrate, low-sugar diet that can limit the growth of fungal communities. Similarly, broad antifungals may be used to eliminate fungal overgrowths. The research supporting this hypothesis is contradictory and relatively low-quality (Herman & Herman, 2022).

Brief Overview of the Literature

The scientific literature surrounding dietary treatments of autism is mainly descriptive, with few experimental analyses of specific diets on the core symptoms of autism. The exception to this has been the GFCF diet. To date, researchers have conducted six randomized control trials, including 143 participants with autism, and numerous quasi-experimental and single-case studies. The results of these studies indicate that the GFCF; is not significantly associated with improvements in the core symptoms of autism (Gonzalez-Domenech et al., 2020; Keller et al., 2021). In fact, the four systematic reviews of experimental and quasi-experimental research have come to the same conclusion: There is limited evidence to support the use of GFCF diets for individuals with autism, and the research that does indicate positive results is of poor quality (see Keller et al., 2021; Mari-Bausat et al., 2014; Mulloy et al., 2010; Reissmann et al., 2020).

Similarly, the GFCF trial has failed at least one challenge trial. In this important study, individuals with autism were kept on a strict GFCF diet and presented with gluten and casein randomly without their knowledge. Researchers then monitored participant behavior, communication, and other symptoms of autism for changes after the challenge, and no changes were detected when consuming gluten or casein (Hyman et al., 2016).

Core Reviews

Simpson et al. (2005) included GFCF and Candida in their reviews. They rated both as Limited Supporting Information for Practice. The NAC included GFCF in both its 2009 and 2015 reviews. They rated it as an Unestablished Treatment while also discussing the possibility of harmful effects (Arnold et al., 2003; Heiger et al., 2008).

Age and Diagnostic Considerations/ Prerequisite Skills and Abilities

Theoretically all students with autism could benefit from dietary management, though current research has failed to demonstrate durable effects. To date the only recommendation from research is that students with autism who may be celiac, or lactose intolerant, may benefit from specific elimination diets (Mari-Bauset et al., 2014).

Reported Outcomes

There is conflicting information on dietary treatments of autism; there are many anecdotal claims of effectiveness but limited scientific demonstration of improvements on the core symptoms of autism.

Qualifications Needed

While no direct training is required, some of these diets can be very restrictive, and those considering such a drastic way of eating may benefit from consulting with a dietician or nutritionist to ensure participants are receiving appropriate levels of macro- and micronutrients.

Costs

GFCF and other specialty diets may also be much more expensive. For example, the cost of gluten-free products is 240 percent more expensive than the same type of product containing gluten (Baspinar & Yardimci, 2020).

Potential Risks

Paradoxically some researchers have documented increased GID when implementing a GFCF diet (Keller et al., 2021). Other researchers have documented nutrient deficiencies for individuals with autism following long-term elimination diets (Arnold et al., 2003; Heiger et al., 2008). Finally, eating in a restrictive way may lead to more social isolation and limit opportunities for students with autism to share a meal with others or attend parties and other activities with food (Cornish, 2002).

Microbiome Therapies

Description

The human gastrointestinal microbiome (GIM) includes vast microorganisms (e.g., bacteria, fungi) that inhabit the colon and, to a lesser degree, the small bowel (Tan et al., 2021). While each human's GIM is remarkably unique, a healthy GIM contains mostly organisms from four primary phyla in various proportions (Firmicutes, Bacteroidetes, Actinobacteria, and Proteobacteria). A diverse, plentiful, and resilient GIM is ideal for the gastrointestinal tract's healthy functioning and the individual's overall health (Das & Nair, 2019). Emerging research also indicates that specific imbalances in these communities lead to GIM dysbiosis, including a loss of bacterial diversity and resilience (Das & Nair, 2019). GIM dysbiosis is indicated in many chronic health conditions, including diabetes, obesity, inflammatory bowel disease, and certain psychiatric disorders (e.g., depression, schizophrenia; Herd et al., 2018).

Many individuals with autism have gastrointestinal distress at higher rates than individuals without autism (Fowlie et al., 2018). These symptoms are characterized by frequent abdominal pain, diarrhea, or constipation (Chaidez et al., 2014). Some researchers have theorized that these symptoms may increase frustration, anger, and anxiety in individuals with autism and thereby explain some of the behavioral difficulties associated with autism (Ferguson et al., 2019; Mazefsky et al., 2014). Though this theory has limited scientific support, gastrointestinal distress can cause troubling symptoms that decrease the overall quality of life (Leader et al., 2021). Several studies have also indicated that individuals with autism have altered GIM compared to age-controlled peers without autism (De Angelis et al., 2013; Finegold et al., 2010) and higher rates of GIM dysbiosis, though specific patterns of GIM dysbiosis in autism have yet to be identified (Fattorusso et al., 2019). This research has inconsistent findings, as some researchers have failed to demonstrate a difference in the GIM of individuals with and without autism (see Son et al., 2015). Further, some research has suggested that GIM dysbiosis in autism may result from the overselective eating habits of individuals with autism (Berding & Donovan, 2020; Yap et al., 2021). However, some researchers and practitioners have posited that GIM dysbiosis may play a more active role in autism symptomology and that by improving the diversity and health of the GIM, one might improve the behavioral symptoms of autism (Li et al., 2017; Tan et al., 2021). To date, researchers have primarily focused on manipulating the GIM through diets (see Speciality and Elimination Diets in this volume), antibiotics, probiotics, and fecal microbiota transplants (FMT).

Antibiotics/Antifungals Antibiotics and antifungal medications target bacterial and fungal organisms. Some targeted antibiotics have improved irritable bowel syndrome (IBS) and other functional gastrointestinal disorders (Ford et al., 2018). The hypothesized benefit for autism is that severe GIM dysbiosis may allow for the overgrowth of specific bacterial or fungal communities. These overgrowths may produce neurotoxins that cause or exacerbate some of the symptoms of autism (Sandler et al., 2000). Treating with antibiotics or antifungal medication may reduce the bacterial communities causing these symptoms (Sandler et al., 2000).

Probiotics Generally speaking, probiotics are living microorganisms that the individual intentionally ingests in the hopes that they will support existing microbiome communities or establish new microbiome communities and thereby attempt to balance the larger GIM (Liu et al., 2019). Probiotics have been used successfully to improve irritable bowel syndrome (IBS) symptoms and other functional gastrointestinal disorders (Liu et al., 2019). The hypothesized benefit for autism is that they may support regulation of the GIM and thereby improve symptoms of autism or gastrointestinal distress often associated with autism (Arnold et al., 2019).

Fecal Microbiota Transplantation (FMT) The FMT process involves administering human fecal matter from a healthy donor into the intestinal tract of the recipient (Tan et al., 2021). The purpose of this procedure is to introduce microorganisms from healthy donors in high numbers to create durable improvements in the GIM (Gupta et al., 2021). FMT has shown some inconsistent improvements in IBS but has become a standard of care for advanced or recurrent bacterial infection by clostridiodes difficile (c. diff), an opportunistic bacterium that can cause severe inflammation and damage to the colon (Drekonja et al., 2015). The hypothesized benefit for autism is that it can help balance the GIM and thereby improve gastrointestinal distress and the behavioral symptoms of autism (Tan et al., 2021).

Brief Overview of the Literature

None of these treatments are present in existing summaries on evidenced-based practice for autism. However, similar to specialty and elimination diets, these approaches (especially probiotics) are a popular treatment option amongst parents and caregivers (Liu et al., 2019). Unfortunately, the existing research on these treatments lacks efficacious findings and rigorous methodology (Tan et al., 2021). Though there is some suggestive evidence that these approaches might lead to some improvements in certain behavioral aspects of autism, there is still a lack of conclusive evidence about the efficacy of these approaches (Yang et al., 2020).

To date, two studies have investigated the effects of targeted antibiotics (Sandler et al., 2000; Xiong et al., 2016), and one non-experimental case study (Baker & Shaw, 2020) has reported on the effects of antifungal medications in autism. *Currently, the scientific evidence for the use of antibiotics and antifungal medications is considerably lacking.* In contrast to the other approaches discussed in this chapter, there is considerable research on probiotics with 13 completed studies, including four double-blind randomized control trials. However, the findings are not particularly promising, with none of the randomized control trials demonstrating significant differences in behavioral symptoms between prebiotics and placebo groups (Tan et al., 2021). Additional quasi-experimental studies on probiotics have shown encouraging findings. *However, it remains difficult to accept probiotics as a feasible treatment of autism, given the current state of the literature.* Finally, there have been two trials of FMT for students with autism. These trials were largely successful in demonstrating a proof of concept as the intervention was well tolerated and improvements over baseline autism symptoms were noted (even at lengthy follow-up). However, neither of these studies demonstrated experimental control and as such are sufficiently lacking in their ability to determine any certain treatment effect. *FMT remains largely unsupported by scientific evidence as a treatment for autism.*

Researchers have also investigated the effects of these microbiome therapies on the gastrointestinal distress experienced by many individuals with autism. The research on probiotics does support some improvements in gastrointestinal distress for individuals with autism, though more research is needed (Tan et al., 2021). Similarly, individuals participating in the FMT interventions registered drastic improvements in gastrointestinal distress compared to baseline, but these studies lacked a control group (Tan et al., 2021).

Core Reviews

None of the Core Reviews included Microbiome Therapies in their review of interventions for individuals with ASD.

Age and Diagnostic Considerations/ Prerequisite Skills and Abilities

Research has yet to demonstrate clear treatment protocols for these approaches. Students with autism and gastrointestinal distress may benefit the most from probiotic usage, though there is still some uncertainty (Shaaban et al., 2019).

Reported Outcomes

The current state of the literature does not support the use of microbiome therapies to improve the larger behavioral symptoms of autism. There may be some benefits to the gastrointestinal distress exhibited by many individuals with autism, though this too needs further investigation.

Qualifications Needed

While probiotics have decent safety profile and are widely available over the counter, there may be some concern about worsening symptoms of gastrointestinal distress (Shaaban et al., 2018). Antibiotics and antifungal medication must be prescribed and used under the supervision of medical professionals.

How, Where, and When Typically Implemented

FMT is a serious medical procedure that should only be conducted under the care of a medical team (see risks).

Costs

The costs of antibiotics, antifungals, and probiotics are relatively inexpensive. The cost of FMT is not widely available as it is currently not FDA approved for broad clinical use. Costs for FMT for *c diff* infection were approximately $5,500 (Luo et al., 2020) in 2020.

Potential Risks

Antibiotic and antifungal medications are widely prescribed and used around the world with acceptable safety profiles, but certain antibiotics can have side effects including disruptions to the GIM and increases in gastrointestinal distress. Probiotics are generally considered safe and are widely used as health supplements. However, some reports of increased gastrointestinal distress are common with probiotic usage.

Finally, FMT is a serious medical procedure and extreme care should be taken, especially concerning donor screening. It is possible to introduce pathogenic bacteria into the host through FMT, and a few resulting deaths are described in the literature (Gupta et al., 2021). The FDA has not approved FMT for anything other than recurrent *c diff* infections (Kelly & Tebas, 2018). **FMT TREATMENT CAN CAUSE HARM AND/OR DEATH IN INDIVIDUALS.**

Vitamin and Mineral Supplementation

Description

Several studies have demonstrated nutrient deficiencies in individuals with autism, including low levels of vitamin A (Sweetman et al., 2019), zinc (Sweetman et al., 2019), iron (Bener et al., 2017), vitamin D (Kittana et al., 2021), B vitamins (Barnhill et al., 2018), and omega-3 fatty acids (Cheng et al., 2017), among other nutrients. Researchers have theorized that selective eating habits (Cornish, 1998) and nutrient malabsorption via gastrointestinal impairment (Dosman et al., 2007) account for these deficiencies. Researchers have also theorized that certain nutrient deficiencies (especially folate and vitamin D) early in life may be an environmental risk factor for developing autism, though these claims remain largely theoretical (Mazahery et al., 2016). Nonetheless treating autism with vitamin and mineral supplements are commonplace; in fact, supplementation is likely the most utilized medical treatment for autism (Adams et al., 2011; Bjørklund et al., 2019). While supporting the lack of nutrition often encountered in the selective diets of people with autism seems uncontroversial, though perhaps excessive (Stewart et al., 2015), using vitamin supplements to treat the larger symptoms of autism remains unsupported by scientific investigation (Travers et al., 2016). Common nutritional supplements for autism include vitamin D, vitamin C, B vitamins, magnesium, and omega-3 fatty acids.

Brief Overview of the Literature

Vitamin and mineral supplementation are not included in the current reviews of evidenced-based practice. However, they are widely adopted with an estimated 49 percent of medical providers recommending youth with autism use vitamin and mineral supplementation (Adams et al., 2011), and 56 percent of children with autism using multivitamin or mineral supplementation (Stewart et al., 2015). Two recent systematic reviews summarized nine randomized control trials (Sathe et al., 2017) and 18 randomized control trials (Li et al., 2018) and both came to similar conclusions about the quality of the evidence surrounding vitamin and mineral supplementation. Namely, there is little evidence that these approaches can reliably improve the core symptoms of autism, but they may be able to return blood serum levels of vitamins and minerals to appropriate levels. They also both noted that the considerable heterogeneity of the literature, particularly the differences in supplement types, dosages, and durations of treatment across studies, makes interpretation particularly challenging.

Core Reviews

Simpson et al. (2005) included a review on Megavitamin Therapy and rated it Limited Supporting Information for Practice. The NAC (2009, 2015) and the NPDC (Wong et al., 2014) and NCAEP (Steinbrenner et al., 2020) did not include any reviews on vitamins as intervention or treatments for individuals with ASD.

Age and Diagnostic Considerations/ Prerequisite Skills and Abilities

As with many of the other alternative therapies, there is little scientific information guiding implementation protocols. This is particularly problematic for vitamin and mineral supplementation as there are virtually no scientifically supported recommendations for dosage and duration of treatment, which could lead to additional risks.

Reported Outcomes

Some studies have reported improvements in irritability and behavioral outcomes, though these findings lack replication and consistency. Studies have reported increases in measured levels of vitamins and minerals after supplementation.

Qualifications Needed/
How, Where, and When Typically Implemented

These treatments should only be considered under the guidance of medical professionals.

Costs

Vitamin and mineral supplements are relatively inexpensive with costs depending on specific nutrients and dosage.

Potential Risks

As there are no clear benefits of using vitamin and mineral supplementation and no clear guidelines to follow on dosage and length of treatment, practitioners and families should exercise caution when using the supplements as some risks are involved. For example, excessive use of vitamin D supplementation can lead to skin rashes, diarrhea, hyperactivity, and reduced sleep (Kittana et al., 2021). Excessive omega-3 supplementation can lead to skin abnormalities, altered taste, kidney dysfunction, liver damage, acute bleeding, and gastrointestinal discomfort (Chang & Su, 2020). In a review of the nutrient intake of young children with autism, Stewart et al. (2015) concluded that relatively few children with autism even need the micronutrients in the supplements they are taking, which leads to excessive intake of certain vitamins and minerals.

Cannabis

Description

Cannabidiol (CBD) and tetrahydrocannabinol (THC) are the principal cannabinoids of the cannabis plant (Aran et al., 2021). THC is a psychoactive compound that can have intoxicating effects, while CBD is a nonpsychoactive compound that may have some anti-inflammatory properties (Agarwal et al., 2019). Research on the potential medical benefits of cannabis (both CBD and THC in different ratios) is currently at an all-time high, with substantial evidence for its positive effects on chronic pain and peripheral neuropathy and moderate evidence for its positive effects on multiple sclerosis (MS) and some seizure disorders (Karst, 2018). The FDA does not currently approve cannabis to treat any medical condition. Similarly, there is substantial research interest in the effects of CBD on various health conditions, with broad anecdotal evidence of its benefits. Similar to the research on cannabis, the research on CBD is inconclusive, though it has shown promising results in reducing certain seizure activity (Sholler et al., 2020).

Endogenous cannabinoids or endocannabinoids (eCBs) are molecules produced in the human body that act on the same neuroreceptors as THC. These molecules represent the body's cannabinoids (similar to endorphins being the body's own morphine) and are thought to influence stress response, anxiety, and rumination (Hill et al., 2010). To date, two studies have demonstrated that people with autism have lower levels of specific eCBs than people without autism, which may contribute to some of the behavioral and communication phenomena surrounding autism (Aran et al., 2019; Karhson et al., 2018). While the exact mechanism for cannabis's effect on autism is still uncertain, it is thought that the supplementation of eCBs by the cannabinoids (CBD and THC) found in the cannabis plant may have some neuromodulation benefits (Agarwal et al., 2019; Aran et al., 2021). This hypothesis is currently based on limited and unreplicated research.

Brief Overview of the Literature

The current literature on cannabis and autism is limited and inconclusive (Fletcher et al., 2022). However, two RCTs indicate that cannabis (especially high CBD low THC strains) may be beneficial at improving some behavioral outcomes for students with autism (Aran et al., 2019; Aran et al., 2021). Unfortunately, the research on cannabis is plagued with high discontinuation rates, with up to 27 percent of participants discontinuing treatment for a variety of reasons including low efficacy, adverse side effects, and difficulty administering the medication (Fletcher et al., 2022). This high attrition rate may be inflating the efficacy of these reports, which had relatively small sample sizes to begin with.

Core Reviews

None of the Core Reviews included Cannabis in their review of interventions for individuals with ASD.

Age and Diagnostic Considerations/ Prerequisite Skills and Abilities

One of the current barriers (besides lack of efficacy data) to using cannabis as a potential treatment for autism is the lack of specific protocols (Fletcher et al., 2022). It is likely that some individuals with autism will respond differently to different strains of cannabis and certainly some students may be more prone to adverse events than others. Similarly, dosage and specific types of cannabinoids most beneficial to specific individuals is currently unknown.

Reported Outcomes

While quite limited, early research suggests that cannabis products may be most beneficial for behavioral and emotional challenges often associated with autism (e.g., aggression, problem behaviors, anger; Aran et al., 2021).

Qualifications Needed

Anecdotal reports indicate that parents and families are turning to cannabis in response to failed behavioral and pharmacological treatments, and there are broad claims of its effectiveness on social and traditional media (Fletcher et al., 2022; Bar-Lev Schleider et al., 2019). However, cannabis (especially high THC strains) can have adverse effects, and research on recreational cannabis is clear that cannabis can be potentially damaging to developing brains (Rieder, 2016).

How, Where, and When Typically Implemented

It is illegal to provide young children with THC containing substances in most states, though some states allow for its use with children under physician prescription (Duvall et al., 2019).

Costs

Due to legalization in many states, THC-containing cannabis is relatively inexpensive. CBD products (especially high-quality, minimally processed supplements) can be quite expensive, with single doses as high as $3.00 to $6.00; with some protocols calling for multiple doses a day, it can be easy to spend upward of $200 to $300 a month on CBD supplements.

Potential Risks

CBD appears to have a good safety profile, though not completely risk free, as there may be a risk of liver damage at high, sustained doses (Bilge & Ekici, 2021). In the research on autism and cannabis (using products with a high CDB to TCH ratio), the most common adverse events were drowsiness (occurring in 7.5% of participants), decreased appetite (5.1%), and gastrointestinal symptoms (4.7%). THC-containing products are more likely to cause adverse events, especially at high doses and for young children (Fletcher et al., 2022). In the autism research, 2 participants (<1%) had serious psychotic or behavioral episodes and were removed from the studies immediately (Fletcher et al., 2022). *Due to the potential for serious adverse events, the American Academy of Pediatrics does not support the use of medicinal cannabis for children due to insufficient evidence and the high risk of harm* (American Academy of Pediatrics, 2015). **THIS TREATMENT CAN CAUSE HARM TO INDIVIDUALS.**

Chelation

Description

One hypothesis for autism severity and etiology is that heavy metals (e.g., mercury, lead) exist in higher concentrations in the systems of individuals with ASD compared to same-age peers without ASD. The increased levels of these heavy metals in turn create or enhance the symptoms of ASD (James et al., 2015). This hypothesis is not supported scientifically, and there is even conflicting evidence as to whether individuals with autism even have higher-than-expected levels of heavy metals in blood or urine samples (Hertz-Picciotto et al., 2010). Chelation is a specialized medical intervention that is a standard medical procedure for acute lead or mercury poisoning and generally takes place at a hospital under the care of a medical team (James et al., 2015). Chelation removes heavy metals from a patient's system through the oral or subdermal administration of chelating agents that bind the heavy metals and allow them to be passed in the patient's urine (Crisponi et al., 2015). This is a delicate process requiring ongoing medical supervision and testing, as certain metals and minerals are required for the body's systems to function appropriately (Brown et al., 2006). Over-chelating can lead to heart failure, kidney problems, and death in extreme cases (Brown et al., 2006). Chelation as an alternative therapy for ASD is surprisingly prevalent with approximately 7 percent of families seeking out this type of treatment (Davis et al., 2013).

Brief Overview of the Literature

Two systematic reviews (Davis et al., 2013; James et al., 2015) have summarized the evidence supporting chelation and come to the same conclusion: There is no evidence that this approach produces positive outcomes for students with autism, and there is a real risk of adverse effects.

Core Reviews

Simpson et al. (2005) discussed chelation as a medical intervention in their chapter "Mercury: Vaccinations and Autism." They rated the intervention as Limited Supporting Information for Practice. The NAC, NPDC (Wong et al., 2014), and NCAEP (Steinbrenner et al., 2020) did not include Chelation as an intervention within their reviews.

Reported Outcomes

The current state of the literature does not support chelation therapy for any outcome relevant to ASD.

Qualifications Needed/
How, Where, and When Typically Implemented

This approach should only be considered for those individuals with acute heavy metal poisoning under the direct supervision of a qualified medical team.

Potential Risks

This approach has led to at least three deaths of young children with autism by cardiac arrest (Brown et al., 2006). **THIS TREATMENT CAN CAUSE HARM AND/OR DEATH.**

Other Interventions With Potential for Causing Significant Harm

Introduction

Interventions that have the potential for causing significant physical or psychological harm should not be used by educators. This section is also structured differently in that it does not summarize the core reviews. The purpose of the section is to give educators a summary of the research that is available regarding these interventions and important information to share with others who may be considering them.

Interventions Included in This Section

- Rapid Prompting Method (RPM™)
- Holding Therapy
- Contingent Electric Skin Shock (CESS)

Rapid Prompting Method (RPM™)

Description

Developed and trademarked by Soma Mukhopadhyay, RPM is described as a "brain-based" instructional, therapeutic, and communication practice designed to teach and assist students with autism in communication by pointing, writing, and typing letters (Mukhopadhyay, 2008). Individuals with autism who use RPM to communicate do so by touching letters on a letterboard or typing letters on a keyboard to make phrases and sentences; a communication support person generally holds the letterboard or the keyboard at least initially (Travers et al., 2016). Anecdotal evidence has produced astonishing claims of RMP effectiveness, with RPM users writing books, completing speaking tours, and attending colleges and universities, despite demonstrating limited language capabilities before using RPM (Travers et al., 2016). Despite these claims, little evidence supports the use of RPM to increase expressive language (or any other outcomes) for individuals with autism (Schlosser et al., 2019). Further, no research has confirmed authorship authenticity, and therefore the communications generated via RPM may not originate from the individual using RPM but rather from the communication support person (Schlosser et al., 2019). Given these exaggerated claims without evidence and concerns about communication authenticity, RPM is justifiably compared to the discredited communication technique of facilitated communication (FC), and indeed the similarities are striking (Travers et al., 2014).

Brief Overview of the Literature

In their 2019 systematic review of RPM, Schlosser and colleagues identified zero experimental studies demonstrating the effectiveness of RPM. They identified six studies that included some mention of RPM, but these were largely descriptive studies without participant or research design details (Schlosser et al., 2019). As such, RPM is not evidenced based, and given the unanswered questions about communication, authenticity practitioners should avoid using this approach for students with autism.

Reported Outcomes

The current state of the literature does not support the use of RPM for core symptoms of autism or other associated target behaviors.

Qualifications Needed/
How, Where, and When Typically Implemented

Soma Mukhopadhyay recommends training camps and workshops through an affiliated nonprofit, Helping Autism through Learning and Outreach (HALO).

Costs

HALO training camps and courses range from $850 to $1,000.

Potential Risks

Considerable risk is associated with communication modalities that cannot isolate author authenticity. Reports have documented the dangers of these approaches including the highly publicized case of Anna Stubblefield, a Rutgers professor who was convicted of repeated sexual assault. Dr. Stubblefield used facilitated communication (FC) to obtain consent for sexual contact with an adult with cognitive impairments. The jury ruled that the young man was unable to offer consent and was therefore sexually exploited (see Sherry, 2016 for a review of the case). FC and its adjacent practices (i.e., RPM, supported typing) are dangerous and have no place in evidenced-based programs for students with autism.

Rating

 Potential for Causing Significant Harm

Holding Therapy (HT)

Description

Holding Therapy, sometimes called Attachment Therapy (AT), is a discredited therapy that was used rather extensively in Europe and parts of the United States, primarily in the 1970s and 1980s (Mercer, 2014). Holding Therapy, as the name implies, features the physical holding of a child by a caregiver or therapist (Mercer, 2014). It is hypothesized by proponents of the treatment that this type of physical restraint has a therapeutic benefit, especially for individuals who have childhood mental illness or attachment-related disorders (Mercer, 2014). Alarmingly, some therapists even advocated for provoking states of agitation or denying access to toileting and food or drink during Holding Therapy/AT (Howlin, 2005). It was hypothesized that Holding Therapy would treat autism and other developmental disorders by repairing attachment deficiencies between the mother and child (Medavarapu et al., 2019).

Brief Overview of the Literature

Holding Therapy/AT has no known benefits. There is no research connecting Holding Therapy/AT to positive outcomes for students with autism, or any children for that matter (Mercer, 2014; Pignotti, & Mercer, 2007). It is based on the faulty assumption that autism is caused by a lack of attachment between children with autism and their caregivers, a notion that has been scientifically rejected for almost 50 years (Rimland, 1964). Recent systematic reviews have focused on the international concerns and overall disapproval of Holding Therapy (Mercer, 2014). Most mentions of Holding Therapy in recent reviews have been to remind readers of the dangers associated with the discredited intervention (Medavarapu et al., 2019). A review regarding international concerns about Holding Therapy reports cases of Holding Therapy in Britain, the Czech Republic, and Russia (Mercer, 2014). Along with the association of child deaths due to Holding Therapy, there has been no significant evidence to support the treatment, leading Holding Therapy to be labeled as "unproven" (Mercer, 2013).

Reported Outcomes

The current state of the literature does not support Holding Therapy for any outcome relevant to ASD.

Qualifications Needed/
How, Where, and When Typically Implemented

Holding Therapy has been conducted by caregivers at home and practitioners in a clinical setting.

Costs

Costs associated with training materials are dependent on the parents' decision to practice themselves or look to a therapist; however, it is critical to note that these resources are not evidence-based. The ultimate cost of Holding Therapy is potential death during sessions.

Potential Risks

Holding Therapy is not without risks, as it comes with ethical and safety concerns (Howlin, 2005). In 2000, a 10-year-old girl died during an Holding Therapy session, one of many deaths reported because of Holding Therapy (Mercer, 2014). Holding Therapy has been rejected by the American Psychological Association, the National Association of Social Workers, and other groups nationwide due to ethical and safety concerns (Mercer, 2014; Pignotti & Mercer, 2007).

Rating

 Potential for Causing Significant Harm

Contingent Electric Skin Shock (CESS)

Description

Autism has long been one of the most serious and difficult-to-treat developmental disorders, due in part to the increased levels of challenging behavior, including self-injurious behavior (SIB), often associated with autism (Matson & LoVullo, 2008). SIB refers to acts of physical aggression that an individual directs at themselves that result in or have the potential to result in injury or harm (Steenfeldt-Kristensen et al., 2020). Unfortunately, self-injurious behavior (SIB), is quite prevalent in autism, occurring in an estimate of 42 percent of cases. These behaviors range in severity from self-hitting or self-biting to more serious forms of self-injury that can result in serious tissue damage and even in rare cases of death (Matson & LuVullo, 2008; Steenfeldt-Kristensen et al., 2020). To date, an extensive body of literature supports the use of a variety of behavioral-based treatments for reducing self-injury including functional analysis or functional behavior assessment, antecedent interventions, reinforcement procedures, extinction, and punishment procedures (Chezan et al., 2017). Successful treatments of SIB are most likely to include a functional analysis or functional behavior assessment and a multicomponent behavioral package featuring many of the procedures listed above (Chezan et al., 2017).

CESS is the application of a painful, but ultimately noninjurious, electrical stimulus delivered to the limbs or back for a brief duration, immediately following the SIB (Favell et al., 1982). Historically aversive stimuli were used to reduce the severe behaviors of individuals with autism. Indeed, one of the first treatment models of behavioral-based therapy for young children with autism, the UCLA Young Autism Project (YAP), incorporated spanks and slaps and other forms of physical punishment procedures (Leaf et al., 2022). Similarly, Lovaas and other pioneers of applied behavioral analysis (ABA; e.g., Favell et al., 1982) used contingent electric skin shock to reduce treatment-resistant aggressive and SIB in youth with autism. Fortunately, in 1990 the field of ABA and special education pivoted away from aversive stimuli and embraced the technology of "non-aversive" behavioral support (see Horner et al., 1990). Some researchers and institutions continued to research and use CESS procedures for cases of serious SIB, but these procedures were largely rejected by most of the ABA community (Leaf et al., 2022). To quote from the Hoerner and colleagues paper in 1990 that re-oriented the field to positive supports, ". . . positive programming is the expected technology. The routine use of procedures that deliver pain (shock, pinching, slaps), procedures that result in harm (bruises, cuts, broken bones), and procedures that are disrespectful or dehumanizing (facial sprays, shaving cream in mouth, foul smells) are no longer acceptable" (Horner et al., 1990, p. 8).

Brief Overview of the Literature

The literature on CESS and other aversive stimuli is mostly dated, though some researchers continue to publish research on CESS and advocate for its careful use (see Israel et al., 2010; Yadollahikhales et al., 2021). The published literature often demonstrates a positive treatment effect for CESS, and indeed it does appear moderately effective at reducing SIB and other severe behavioral challenges (Favell et al., 1982). However, the published data on CESS has some noticeable flaws, namely, demonstrated difficulties in fading the procedure (Israel et al., 2010; Linscheid et al., 1990), the prevalence of stimuli satiation (i.e., the need for increasingly painful stimuli; Yadollahikhales et al., 2021), and the lack of generalization and transfer of results (Zarcone et al., 2020). Further, there are some broad methodological concerns about the CESS research. Early treatment studies existed before the adoption of single-case research methodology guidelines (see Kratochwill et al., 2010); as such, some general concerns about overall quality persist (e.g., lack of inter-rate reliability). Current research on CESS (e.g., Israel et al., 2008, 2010) similarly lacks quality indicators, including problems with experimental control, inter-rater reliability, and procedural integrity (Zarcone et al., 2020). Even without considering the ethical questions, the proponents of these treatments have done a poor job convincing the scientific community that these approaches are necessary and superior to nonaversive approaches.

The ethical concerns of inflicting pain to change behavior are obvious, and contrary to the code of ethics for behavior analysts (see Behavior Analyst Certification Board, 2020). Proponents of these treatments indicate that CESS is necessary because less intrusive, nonaversive approaches have failed to change serious behaviors. Yet published papers on CESS rarely produce data on these failed trials and even use CESS for nonserious behaviors (e.g., noncompliance, yelling; Zarcone et al., 2020). Further examination of the potential harms of CESS have produced clear evidence of the adverse events of CESS including fear, burns, depression, increases in other negative behaviors, and obvious pain. Given the overall effectiveness of positive behavioral treatments for SIB (see Chezan et al., 2017), CESS seems uniquely unnecessary and cruel. Particularly since the population of students most likely to endure CESS are students with cognitive and language impairments who have limited abilities to self-advocate.

Age and Diagnostic Considerations/ Prerequisite Skills and Abilities

The connected fields of ABA and special education have generally moved beyond aversive treatment of problem behaviors. Practitioners and families looking to reduce challenging, and SIB should investigate the sections of this guide dealing with functional analysis or functional behavior assessment, positive behavioral supports, antecedent interventions, and reinforcement procedures.

Reported Outcomes

Though published research demonstrates some effectiveness for CESS in reducing SIB and other severe behaviors, the ethical concerns, lack of long-term effectiveness, and general methodology concerns of the literature base result in this treatment being classified as unrecommended (Zarcone et al., 2020).

Qualifications Needed/ How, Where, and When Typically Implemented

This procedure is currently used and advocated for a small number of private centers focused on supporting adults with autism and serious behaviors.

Costs

The costs of CESS are unclear, as this procedure remains on the fringe of ABA.

Potential Risks

Due to the risk of adverse events, including emotional distress, fear, burns and tissue damage, depression, and the development of other negative avoidance behaviors, the practice was banned by the FDA in 2020; however, a court ruling in 2021 overturned this ban (Diament, 2020; Zarcone et al., 2020). In response to this court decision,

Congress passed a bill in early June of 2022 banning the practice; the bill has yet to be approved by the U.S. Senate (Diament, 2020). CESS is still being used and advocated for by one small center in Massachusetts (Judge Rothberg Center). The leading behavior analysis professional organization, Applied Behavior Analysis International (ABAI), has launched a working group to deliver a position paper on the practice, though local chapters of ABAI have already denounced it (Putnam et al., 2021). Other autism advocacy groups (e.g., Autism Speaks, Autism Society of America) have similarly denounced the practice.

Rating

  Potential for Causing Significant Harm

References

Core Reviews

National Autism Center (NAC). (2009). *Findings and conclusions: National standards report.* Randolph, MA: Author.

National Autism Center (NAC). (2015). *Findings and conclusions: National standards project, phase 2.* Randolph, MA: Author.

(NCAEP) Steinbrenner, J. R., Hume, K., Odom, S. L., Morin, K. L., Nowell, S. W., Tomaszewski, B., Szendrey, S., McIntyre, N. S., Yücesoy-Özkan, S., & Savage, M. N. (2020). *Evidence-based practices for children, youth, and young adults with Autism.* The University of North Carolina at Chapel Hill, Frank Porter Graham Child Development Institute, National Clearinghouse on Autism Evidence and Practice Review Team.

(NPDC) Wong, C., Odom, S. L., Hume, K., Cox, A. W., Fettig, A., Kucharczyk, S., & Schultz, T. R. (2014). *Evidence based practices for children, youth, and young adults with autism spectrum disorder.* Chapel Hill: The University of North Carolina, Frank Porter Graham Child Development Institute, Autism Evidence-Based Practice Review Group.

Simpson, R., deBoer-Ott, S., Griswold, D., Myles, B., Byrd, S., Ganz, J., Cook, K., Otten, K., Ben-Arieh, J., Kline, S. A., Adams, L. (2005). *Autism spectrum disorders: Interventions and treatments for children and youth.* Thousand Oaks, CA: Corwin Press.

Front Matter

Preface

Heflin, J. L., & Simpson, R. L. (1998a). Interventions for children and youth with autism: Prudent choices in a world of exaggerated claims and empty promises. Part I: Intervention and treatment option review. *Focus on Autism and Other Developmental Disabilities, 13*(4), 194–211.

Heflin, J. L., & Simpson, R. (1998b). Interventions for children and youth with autism: Prudent choices in a world of exaggerated claims and empty promises. Part II: Legal/policy analysis and recommendations for selecting interventions and treatments. *Focus on Autism and Other Developmental Disabilities, 13*(4), 212–220.

Simpson, R. L. (2005). Evidence-based practices and students with autism spectrum disorders. *Focus on Autism and Other Developmental Disabilities, 20*(3), 140–149.

Person-First Language Versus Identity-First Language

Abel, S., Machin, T., & Brownlow, C. (2019). Support, socialize and advocate: An exploration of the stated purposes of Facebook autism groups. *Research in Autism Spectrum Disorders, 61,* 10–21.

American Psychiatric Association. (2013). *Diagnostic and statistical manual of mental disorders: DSM-V-TR* (5th ed.). Author.

American Psychological Association. (2020). *Publication manual of the American Psychological Association* (7th ed.). Author.

Bradshaw, P., Pickett, C., van Driel, M. L., Brooker, K., & Urbanowicz, A. (2021). "Autistic" or "with autism"?: Why the way general practitioners view and talk about autism matters. *Australian Journal of General Practice, 50*(3), 104–108.

Draper, E. A. (2018). Navigating the labels: Appropriate terminology for students with disabilities. *General Music Today, 32*(1), 30–32.

Dunn, D. S., & Andrews, E. E. (2015). Person-first and identity-first language: Developing psychologists' cultural competence using disability language. *American Psychologist, 70*(3), 255–264.

An Overview of Autism Spectrum Disorder

Adams, C., & Gaile, J. (2020). Evaluation of a parent preference-based outcome measure after intensive communication intervention for children with social (pragmatic) communication disorder and high-functioning autism spectrum disorder. *Research in Developmental Disabilities, 105,* 103752.

Allred, S. (2009). Reframing Asperger syndrome: Lessons from other challenges to the *Diagnostic and Statistical Manual* and ICIDH approaches. *Disability & Society, 24*(3), 343–355.

Altman, K., Haavik, S., & Cook, J. W. (1978). Punishment of self-injurious behavior in natural settings using contingent aromatic ammonia. *Behaviour Research and Therapy, 16*(2), 85–96.

American Psychiatric Association. (2000). *Diagnostic and statistical manual of mental disorders* (4th ed.). American Psychiatric Publishing.

American Speech-Language-Hearing Association. (n.d.). *Social communication disorder* [Practice portal]. www.asha.org/Practice-Portal/Clinical-Topics/Social-Communication-Disorder/

Arias, V. D., Gomez, L. E., Moran, M. L., Alcedo, M. A., Monsalve, A., & Fontanil, Y. (2018). Does quality of life differ for children with autism spectrum disorder and intellectual disability compared to peers without autism? *Journal of Autism and Developmental Disorders, 48*(1), 123–136.

Association for Professional Behavior Analysts (APBA). (2017/2022). *Identifying applied behavior analysis guidelines* (White Paper). https://www.apbahome.net/page/practiceguidelines

Association for Professional Behavior Analysts (APBA). (2019). *Clarifications: ASD Guidelines.* https://www.apbahome.net/page/practiceguidelines

Baer, D. M., Wolf, M. M., & Risley, T. R. (1968). Some current dimensions of applied behavior analysis. *Journal of Applied Behavior Analysis, 1*(1), 91–97.

Bailey, S. L, Pokrzywinski, J., & Bryant, L. E. (1983). Using water mist to reduce self-injurious and stereotypic behavior. *Applied Research in Mental Retardation, 4*(3), 229–241.

Baker, B. L., & Blacher, J. (2021). Behavior disorders and social skills in adolescents with intellectual disability: Does co-morbid autism matter? *Journal of Mental Health Research in Intellectual Disabilities, 14*(2), 174–188.

Barrett, R. P., Matson, J. L., Shapiro, E. S., & Ollendick, T. H. (1981). A comparison of punishment and DRO procedures for treating stereotypic behavior of mentally retarded children. *Applied Research in Mental Retardation, 2*(3), 247–256.

Barton, L. E., Brulle, A. R., & Allen C. (1983). Aversive techniques and the doctrine of least restrictive alternative. *Exceptional Education Quarterly, 3*(4), 1–8.

Behavior Analyst Certification Board (BACB). (2019). *The history of ethics at the BACB.* https://www.bacb.com/the-history-of-ethics-at-the-bacb/

Behavior Analyst Certification Board. (2020). *Ethics code for behavior analysts.* https://bacb.com/wp-content/ethics-code-for-behavior-analysts/

Behavior Analyst Certification Board (BACB). (2022a). *About the BACB.* https://www.bacb.com/about/

Behavior Analyst Certification Board (BACB). (2022b). *BACB certificant data.* https://www.bacb.com/bacb-certificant-data/

Berkell Zager, D. (1999). *Autism: Identification, education, and treatment.* Erlbaum.

Bölte, S., Girdler, S., & Marschik, P. B. (2019). The contribution of environmental exposure to the etiology of autism spectrum disorder. *Cellular and Molecular Life Sciences: CMLS, 76*(7), 1275–1297.

Brukner-Wertman, Y., Laor, L., & Golan, O. (2016). Social (pragmatic) communication disorder and its relation to the autism spectrum: Dilemmas arising from the *DSM-5* Classification. *Journal of Autism and Developmental Disorders, 46*(8), 2821–2829.

Burack, J. A., & Volkmar, F. R. (1992). Development of low- and high-functioning autistic children. *Journal of Child Psychology and Psychiatry, 33*(3), 607–616.

Capal, J. K., Macklin, E. A., Lu, F., & Barnes, G. (2020). Factors associated with seizure onset in children with autism spectrum disorder. *Pediatrics, 145*(Suppl 1), S117–S125.

Carmack, H. (2014). Social and tertiary health identities as argument in the *DSM-V* Asperger's/autism debate. *Western Journal of Communication, 78*(4), 462–479.

Castellani, C. A., & Arking, D. A. (2020). High-risk, high-reward genetics in ASD. *Neuron, 105*(3), 407–410.

Chambers, B., Murray, C. M., Boden, Z. V., & Kelly, M. P. (2020). "Sometimes labels need to exist": Exploring how young adults with Asperger's syndrome perceive its removal from the *Diagnostic and Statistical Manual of Mental Disorders* fifth edition. *Disability & Society, 35*(4), 589–608.

Chawarska, K., Klin, A., Volmar, F.R. (2008). *Autism spectrum disorders in infants and toddlers: Diagnosis, assessment and treatment.* Guilford Press.

Chou, W. J., Wang, P. W., Hsiao, R. C., Hu, H. F., & Yen, C. F. (2020). Role of school bullying involvement in depression, anxiety, suicidality, and low self-esteem among adolescents with high-functioning autism spectrum disorder. *Frontiers in Psychiatry, 11*, 9.

Constantino, J. N. (2012). The *Social Responsiveness Scale—Second Edition* (SRS-2). WPS. https://www.wpspublish.com/srs-2-social-responsiveness-scale-second-edition

Corte, H. E., Wolf, B. J., & Locke, A. (1971). Comparison of procedures for eliminating self-injurious behavior of retarded adolescents. *Journal of Applied Behavior Analysis, 4*(3), 201–213.

The Council of Autism Service Providers (CASP). (2020). *Applied behavior analysis treatment of autism spectrum disorder: Practice guidelines for healthcare funders and managers* (2nd ed.). https://casproviders.org/asd-guidelines/

de Boer, S. R. (2018). *Pro-Ed series on autism spectrum disorders: Discrete trial training* (2nd ed). ProEd.

DeFilippis, M. (2018). Depression in children and adolescents with autism spectrum disorder. *Children, 5*(9), 112.

Dolata, J. K., Suarez, S., Calamé, B., & Fombonne, E. (2022). Pragmatic language markers of autism diagnosis and severity *Research in Autism Spectrum Disorders, 94*, 1–10.

Duker, P. (1975). Intra-subject controlled time-out (Social Isolation) in the modification of self-injurious behaviour. *Journal of Intellectual Disability Research, 19*(2), 107–112.

The Editors of *The Lancet.* (2010). Retraction—ileal-lymphoid-nodular hyperplasia, non-specific colitis, and pervasive developmental disorder in children. *The Lancet, 375*(9713), 445.

El Achkar, C. M., & Spence, S. J. (2015). Clinical characteristics of children and young adults with co-occurring autism spectrum disorder and epilepsy. *Epilepsy & Behavior, 47*, 183–190.

Estes, A., Munson, J., Rogers, S. J., Greenson, J., Winter, J., & Dawson, G. (2015). Long-term outcomes of early intervention in 6-year-old children with autism spectrum disorder. *Journal of the American Academy of Child & Adolescent Psychiatry, 54*(7), 580–587.

Fine, H. J. (1979). Cues and clues to differential diagnosis in childhood autism. *Psychotherapy: Theory, Research and Practice, 16*(4), 452–459.

Fombonne, E. (2009). Epidemiology of pervasive developmental disorders. *Pediatric Research, 65*(6), 591–598.

Frankel, F., Moss, D., Schofield, S., & Simmons, J. Q. (1976). Case study: Use of differential reinforcement to suppress self-injurious and aggressive behavior psychological reports. *Psychological Reports, 39*(3, Pt. 1), 843–849.

Gamlin, C. (2017). When Asperger's disorder came out. *Psychiatria Danubina, 29*(Suppl. 3), 214–218.

Gaugler, T., Klei, L. Sanders, S. J., Bodea, C. A., Goldberg, A. P., Lee, A. B., Mahajan, M., Manaa, D., Pawitan, Y., Reichert, J., Ripke, S., Sandin, S., Sklar, P., Svantesson, O., Reichenberg, A., Hultman, C. M., Devlin, B., Roeder, K., & Buxbaum, J. D. (2014). Most genetic risk for autism resides with common variation. *Nature Genetics, 46*(8). 881–885

Geschwind, D. H. (2011). Genetics of autism spectrum disorders. *Trends in Cognitive Sciences, 15*(9), 409–416.

Giles, D. C. (2014). "*DSM-V* is taking away our identity": The reaction of the online community to the proposed changes in the diagnosis of Asperger's disorder. *Health, 18*(2), 179–195.

Gioia, G., Isquith, P. K., Guy, S. C., & Kenworthy, L. (2017). *The Behavior Rating Inventory of Executive Functions—second edition* (BRIEF-2) and *preschool version* (BRIEF-P). PAR, Inc. https://www.parinc.com/Products/Pkey/24

Hallett, V., Ronald, A., Rijsdijk, F., & Happé, F. (2010). Association of autistic-like and internalizing traits during childhood: A longitudinal twin study. *American Journal of Psychiatry, 167*(7), 809–817.

Harris, S. L., & Romanczyk, R. G. (1976). Treating self-injurious behavior of a retarded child by overcorrection. *Behavior Therapy, 7*(2), 235–239.

Harrison, P., & Oakland, T. (2015). *The Adaptive Behavior Assessment System–Third Edition* (ABAS-3). Pearson Assessments. https://www.pearsonassessments.com/store/usassessments/en/Store/Professional-Assessments/Behavior/Brief/Adaptive-Behavior-Assessment-System-%7C-Third-Edition/p/100001262.html

Hollocks, M. J., Lerh, J. W., Magiati, I., Meiser-Stedman, R., & Brugha, T. S. (2019). Anxiety and depression in adults with autism spectrum disorder: A systematic review and meta-analysis. *Psychological Medicine, 49*(4), 559–572.

Homer, A. L., & Peterson, L. (1980). Differential reinforcement of other behavior: A preferred response elimination procedure. *Behavior Therapy, 11*(4), 449–471.

Howard, J. S., Sparkman, C. R., Cohen, H. G., Green, G., & Stanislaw, H. (2005). A comparison of intensive behavior analytic and eclectic treatments for young children with autism. *Research in Developmental Disabilities, 26*, 359–383.

Hudson, C. C., Hall, L., & Harkness, K. L. (2019). Prevalence of depressive disorders in individuals with autism spectrum disorder: A meta-analysis. *Journal of Abnormal Child Psychology, 47*, 165–175.

Individuals with Disabilities Education Improvement Act (2004). Public Law 108-446.

Jones, F. H., Simmons, J. Q., & Frankel, F. (1974). An extinction procedure for eliminating self-destructive behavior in a 9-year-old autistic girl. *Journal of Autism and Childhood Schizophrenia, 4*, 241–250.

Kanner, L. (1943). Autistic disturbances of affective contact. *Nervous Child: Journal of Psychopathology, Psychotherapy, Mental Hygiene, and Guidance of the Child, 2*, 217–50.

Kazdin, A. E. (1975). The impact of applied behavior analysis on diverse areas of research. *Journal of Applied Behavior Analysis, 8*(2), 213–229.

Kim, J. A., Szatmari, P., Bryson, S. E., Streiner, D. L., & Wilson, F. J. (2000). The prevalence of anxiety and mood problems among children with autism and Asperger syndrome. *Autism, 4*, 117–132.

Kircher, A. S., Joseph, J., Pear, J. J., Garry, L., & Martin, G. L. (1971). Shock as punishment in a picture-naming task with retarded children. *Journal of Applied Behavior Analysis,4*(3), 227–233.

Klinger, L. G., Cook, M. L., & Dudley, K. M. (2021). Predictors and moderators of treatment efficacy in children and adolescents with autism spectrum disorder. *Journal of Clinical Child & Adolescent Psychology, 50*(4), 517–524.

Korkman, M., Kirk, U., & Kemp, S. (2007). The *Developmental Neuropsychological Assessment—second edition* (NEPSY-II). Pearson Assessments. https://www.pearsonassessments.com/store/usassessments/en/Store/Professional-Assessments/Academic-Learning/Brief/NEPSY-%7C-Second-Edition/p/100000584.html

Lichstein, K. L., & Schreibman, L. (1976). Employing electric shock with autistic children. *Journal of Autism and Childhood Schizophrenia, 6*(2), 163–173.

Lord, C., & Bishop, S. L. (2015). Recent advances in autism research as reflected in DSM-5 criteria for autism spectrum disorder. *Annual review of clinical psychology, 11*, 53–70.

Lord, C., Luyster, R. J., Gotham, K., & Whitney Guthrie, W. (Toddler Module). (2012a). The *Autism Diagnostic Observation Schedule—second edition* (ADOS-2). WPS https://www.wpspublish.com/ados-2-autism-diagnostic-observation-schedule-second-edition

Lord, C., Rutter, M., Dilavore, P. C., Risi, S., Gotham, K., & Bishop, S. L. (Modules 1–4). (2012b). *The Autism Diagnostic Observation Schedule—second edition* (ADOS-2). WPS. https://www.wpspublish.com/ados-2-autism-diagnostic-observation-schedule-second-edition

Lovaas, O. I. (1987). Behavioral treatment and normal educational and intellectual functioning in young autistic children. *Journal of Consulting and Clinical Psychology, 55*(1), 3.

Lovaas, O. I., Schaeffer, B., & Simmons, J. O. (1965). Building social behavior in autistic children by use of electric shock. *Journal of Experimental Research in Personality 1*(2), 99–100.

Lovaas, O. I., & Simmons, J. Q. (1969). Manipulation of self-destruction in three retarded children. *Journal of Applied Behavior Analysis, 2*(3), 143–157.

Maenner, M. J., Shaw, K. A., Bakian, A. V., Bilder, D. A., Durkin, M. S., Esler, A., Furnier, S. M., Hallas, L., Hall-Lande, J., Hudson, A., Hughes, M., Patrick, M., Pierce, K., Poynter, J. N., Salinas, A., Shenouda, J., Vehorn, A., Warren, A., . . . & Cogswell, M. E. (2021). *Prevalence and characteristics of autism spectrum disorder among children aged 8 years—Autism and Developmental Disabilities Monitoring Network, 11 sites, United States, MMWR surveillance summary 2021.* Center for Surveillance, Epidemiology, and Laboratory Services, Centers for Disease Control and Prevention (CDC), U.S. Department of Health and Human Services.

Mandy, W., Wang, A., Lee, I., & Skuse, D. (2017). Evaluating social (pragmatic) communication disorder. *Journal of Child Psychology and Psychiatry, 58*(10), 1166–1175.

Mannion, A., & Leader, G. (2013). Comorbidity in autism spectrum disorder: A literature review. *Research in Autism Spectrum Disorders, 7*(12), 1595–1616.

Matson, J. L., & Shoemaker, M. (2009). Intellectual disability and its relationship to autism spectrum disorders. *Research in Developmental Disabilities, 30*(6), 1107–1114.

Mauk, J., Reber, M., & Batshaw, M. (1997). Autism and other developmental disorders. In M. Batshaw (Ed.), *Children with developmental disabilities* (pp. 425–447). Brookes.

Mayo Clinic Staff. (2021, October). *Explaining epilepsy.* Mayo Clinic. https://www.mayoclinic.org/diseases-conditions/epilepsy/symptoms-causes/syc-20350093

Mazurek, M. O., Kanne, S. M., & Miles, J. H. (2012). Predicting improvement in social–communication symptoms of autism spectrum disorders using retrospective treatment data. *Research in Autism Spectrum Disorders 6*, 535–545.

McEachin, J. J., Smith, T., & Lovaas, O. I. (1993). Long-term outcome for children with autism who received early intensive behavioral treatment. *American Journal on Mental Retardation, 97*, 359–372.

McGinnis, E., Scott-Miller, D., Neel, R., & Smith, C. (1985). Aversives in special education programs for behaviorally disordered students: A debate. *Behavioral Disorders, 10*(4), 295–304.

Measel, C. J., & Alfieri P. A. (1976). Treatment of self-injurious behavior by a combination of reinforcement for incompatible behavior and overcorrection. *American Journal of Mental Deficiency, 81*(2), 147–153.

Miller, L., & Reynolds, J. (2009). Autism and vaccination—the current evidence. *Journal for Specialists in Pediatric Nursing, 14*(3), 166–172.

Min Liew, S. M., Thevaraja, N., Hong, R. Y., & Magiati, I. (2015). The relationship between autistic traits and social anxiety, worry, obsessive–compulsive, and depressive symptoms: specific and non-specific mediators in a student sample. *Journal of Autism and Developmental Disorders, 45*(3), 858–872.

Molloy, H., & Vasil, L. (2002). The social construction of Asperger syndrome: The pathologising of difference? *Disability & Society, 17*(6), 659–669.

Moloney, P. (2010). "How can a chord be weird if it expresses your soul?" Some critical reflections on the diagnosis of Asperger's syndrome. *Disability & Society, 25*(2), 135–148.

Myers, D. V. (1975). Extinction, DRO, and response—Cost procedures for eliminating self-injurious behavior: A case study. *Behaviour Research and Therapy, 13*(2–3), 189–191.

Myles, B. S., & Simpson, R. L. (2003). *Asperger syndrome: A guide for parents and educators.* ProEd.

Naglieri, J., & Goldstein, S. (2017). *The Comprehensive Executive Function Inventory* (CEFI). WPS. https://www.wpspublish.com/cefi-comprehensive-executive-function-inventory

National Institutes of Health (NIH). (2017, January 31). *What causes autism?* U.S. Department of Health and Human Services. https://www.nichd.nih.gov/health/topics/autism/conditioninfo/causes

National Research Council. (2001). *Educating Children with Autism.* Washington, DC: The National Academies Press.

Newborg, J. (2020). *Battelle Developmental Inventory—third edition* (BDI-3). Riverside Insights at riversideinsights.com/battelle_3e

Norbury, C. F. (2014). Practitioner Review: Social (pragmatic) communication disorder conceptualization, evidence and clinical implications. *Journal of Child Psychology and Psychiatry, 55*(3), 204–216.

Parsloe, S. M., & Babrow, A. S. (2016). Removal of Asperger's syndrome from the DSM V: Community response to uncertainty. *Health Communication, 31*, 485–494.

Pezzimenti, F., Han, G. T., Vasa, R. A., & Gotham, K. (2019). Depression in youth with autism spectrum disorder. *Child and Adolescent Psychiatric Clinics, 28*(3), 397–409.

Pringle, B. A., Colpe L. J., Blumberg, S. J., Avila, R. M., & Kogan, M. D. (2012). *Diagnostic history and treatment of school-aged children with autism spectrum disorder and special health care needs* (NCHS data brief, No 97). National Center for Health Statistics. https://www-cdc-gov.ezproxy.library.tufts.edu/nchs/products/databriefs/db97.htm

Reichow, B. (2012). Overview of meta-analyses on early intensive behavioral intervention for young children with autism spectrum disorders. *Journal of Autism and Developmental Disorders, 42*(4), 512–520.

Reynolds, C. R., & Kamphaus, R. W. (2015). *The Behavior Assessment System for Children—third edition (BASC-3).* Pearson Assessments. https://www.pearsonassessments.com/store/usassessments/en/Store/Professional-Assessments/Behavior/Comprehensive/Behavior-Assessment-System-for-Children-%7C-Third-Edition-/p/100001402.html

Rincover, A., & Devaney, J. (1982). The application of sensory extinction principles to self-injury in developmentally disabled children. *Analysis and Intervention in Developmental Disabilities, 2,* 67–86.

Risley, T. R. (1968). The effects and side effects of punishing the autistic behaviors of a deviant child. *Journal of Applied Behavior Analysis, 1*(1), 21–34.

Roane, H. S., Wayne, W. Fisher, W. W., James, E., & Carr, J. E. (2016). Applied behavior analysis as treatment for autism spectrum disorder. *The Journal of Pediatrics, 175,* 27–32.

Robins, D. L., Fein, D., & Barton, M. (2009). *Modified checklist for autism in toddlers, revised, with follow -up (M-CHAT-R/F) TM. LineageN.*

Rutter, M., Bailey, A., & Lord, C. (2003a). *The Social Communication Questionnaire* (SCQ). WPS. https://www.wpspublish.com/scq-social-communication -questionnaire

Rutter, M., LeCouteur, A., & Lord, C. (2003b). The *Autism Diagnostic Interview-Revised* (ADI-R). WPS. https://www.wpspublish.com/adi-r-autism-diagnostic -interviewrevised

Sajwaj, T., Libet, J., & Agras, S. (1974). Lemon-juice therapy: The control of life-threatening rumination in a six-month-old infant. *Journal of Applied Behavior Analysis, 7*(4), 557–563.

Satterstrom, F. K., Kosmicki, J. A., Wang, J., Breen, M. S., De Rubeis, S., An, J. Y., Peng, M., Collins, R., Grove, J., Klei, L., Stevens, C., Reichert, J., Mulhern, M. S., Artomov, M., Gerges, S., Sheppard, B., Xu, X., Bhaduri, A., Norman, U., . . . Dias, C. (2020). Large-scale exome sequencing study implicates both developmental and functional changes in the neurobiology of autism. *Cell, 180*(3), 568–584.

Schofield, D., Zeppel, M. J. B., Tanton, R., Veerman J. L., Kelly, S. J., Passey, M. E., & Shrestha, R. N. (2019). Intellectual disability and autism: Socioeconomic impacts of informal caring, projected to 2030. *The British Journal of Psychiatry, 215,* 654–660.

Smith, O., & Jones, S. C. (2020). "Coming out" with autism: Identity in people with an Asperger's diagnosis after DSM-5. *Journal of Autism and Developmental Disorders, 50*(2), 592–602.

Soffer, M., & Argaman-Danos, S. (2021). Self-labeling, perceived stigma toward autism spectrum disorder, and self-esteem and the change in autism nosology. *Disability and Health Journal, 14*(4), 101162.

Sparrow, S. S., Cicchetti, D. C., & Saulnier, C. A. (2016). *The Vineland Adaptive Behavior Scales* (3rd ed.). Pearson Assessments. https://www.pearsonassessments.com/store/usassessments/en/Store/Professional -Assessments/Behavior/Adaptive/Vineland-Adaptive-Behavior-Scales-%7c-Third-Edition/p/100001622.html

Squires, J., & Bricker, D. (2009). *Ages & Stages Questionnaires—third edition* (ASQ-3). Brookes. https://products.brookespublishing.com/Ages-Stages-Questionnaires-Third-Edition-ASQ-3-P569.aspx

Squires, J., Bricker, D., & Twombly, E. (2015). *The Ages & Stages Questionnaires: Social-Emotional—Second Edition* (ASQ:SE-2). Brookes. https://products.brookespublishing.com/Ages-Stages-Questionnaires-Social-Emotional-Second-Edition-ASQSE-2-P849.aspx

Stokes, T. F., & Baer, D. M. (1977). An implicit technology of generalization. *Journal of Applied Behavior Analysis, 10*(2), 349–367.

Strasser, L., Downes, M., Kung, J., Cross, J. H., & De Haan, M. (2018). Prevalence and risk factors for autism spectrum disorder in epilepsy: A systematic review and meta-analysis. *Developmental Medicine & Child Neurology, 60*(1), 19–29.

Tanner, M., & Zeiler, T. M. (1975). Punishment of self-injurious behavior using aromatic ammonia as the aversive stimulus. *Journal of Applied Behavior Analysis, 8*(1), 53–57.

Tarpley, H. D., & Schroeder, S. R. (1979). Comparison of DRO and DRI on rate of suppression of self-injurious behavior. *American Journal of Mental Deficiency, 84*(2), 188–194.

Taylor, L. J., Andrew, J. O., & Whitehouse. (2016). Autism spectrum disorder, language disorder, and social (Pragmatic) Communication Disorder: Overlaps, distinguishing features, and clinical implications. *Australian Psychologist, 51*(4), 287–295.

Turk, J., Bax, M., Williams, C., Amin, P., Eriksson, M., & Gillberg, C. (2009). Autism spectrum disorder in children with and without epilepsy: Impact on social functioning and communication. *Acta Paediatrica, 98*(4), 675–681.

Ung, D., Wood, J. J., Ehrenreich-May, J., Arnold, E. B., Fuji, C., Renno, P., Murphy, T., K., Lewin, A. B., Mutch, P. J., & Storch, E. A. (2013). Clinical characteristics of high-functioning youth with autism spectrum disorder and anxiety. *Neuropsychiatry, 3*(2), 147–157.

U.S. Department of Education. (March 2022). *A history of the Individuals with Disabilities Education Act.* https://sites.ed.gov/idea/IDEA-History#1975

van der Linden, S. L., Clarke, C. E., & Maibach, E. W. (2015). Highlighting consensus among medical scientists increases public support for vaccines: Evidence from a randomized experiment. *BMC Public Health, 15,* 1207.

Van Houten, R., Axelrod, S., Bailey, J. S., Favell, J. E., Foxx, R. M., Brian, A., Iwata, B. A., & Lovaas, O. I. (1988). The right to effective behavioral treatment. *The Behavior Analyst, 21*(4), 381–384.

VanMeter, L., Fein, D., & Morris, R. (1997). Delay versus deviance in autistic social behavior. *Journal of Autism and Developmental Disorders, 27,* 557–569.

Van Steensel, F. J., Bögels, S. M., & Perrin, S. (2011). Anxiety disorders in children and adolescents with autistic spectrum disorders: A meta-analysis. *Clinical Child and Family Psychology Review, 14*(3), 302–317.

Vasa, R. A., & Mazurek, M. O. (2015). An update on anxiety in youth with autism spectrum disorders. *Current Opinion in Psychiatry, 28*(2), 83.

Viscidi, E. W., Johnson, A. L., Spence, S. J., Buka, S. L., Morrow, E. M., & Triche, E. W. (2014). The association between epilepsy and autism symptoms and maladaptive behaviors in children with autism spectrum disorder. *Autism, 18*(8), 996–1006.

Volkmar, F., Siegel, M., Woodbury-Smith, M., King, B., McCracken, J., & State, M. (2014). Practice parameter for the assessment and treatment of children and adolescents with autism spectrum disorder. *Journal of the American Academy of Child & Adolescent Psychiatry, 53*(2), 237–257.

Wakefield, J. (1998). Autism, inflammatory bowel disease, and MMR vaccine. *The Lancet, 351*(9112), 1355.

Wechsler. (2014). *Wechsler Intelligence Scale for Children—fifth edition (WISC-V)*. Pearson.

Weismer, S. E., Rubenstein, E., Wiggins, L., & Durkin, M. S. (2021). A preliminary epidemiologic study of social (pragmatic) communication disorder relative to autism spectrum disorder and developmental disability without social communication deficits. *Journal of Autism and Developmental Disorders, 51*(8), 2686–2696.

Zabel, R. H., Peterson, R., Zabel, R., McGinnis, E., Scott-Miller, D., Neel, R., & Smith, C. (1985). Aversives in special education programs for behaviorally disordered students: A debate. *Behavioral Disorders, 10*(4), 295–304.

Zwaigenbaum, L., Bryson, S. E., Brian, J., Smith, I. M., Sacrey, L., Armstrong, V., Roberts, W., Szatmari, P., Garon, N., Vaillancourt, T., & Roncadin, C. (2021, May/June). Assessment of autism symptoms from 6 to 18 months of age using the Autism Observation Scale for infants in a prospective high-risk cohort. *Child Development, 92*(3), 1187–1198.

Evidence-Based Practice (EBP)

Advancing the EBP Movement

Barnhill, G., Hagiwara, T., Myles, B. S., & Simpson, R. L. (2000). Asperger syndrome: A study of the cognitive profiles of 37 children and adolescents. *Focus on Autism and Other Developmental Disabilities, 15*(3), 146–153.

Boynton, J. (2012). Facilitated communication—What harm it can do: Confessions of a former facilitator. *Evidence-Based Communication Assessment and Intervention, 6*, 3–13.

Carnine, D. (1997). Bridging the research-to-practice gap. *Exceptional Children, 63*(4), 513–521.

Centers for Medicare and Medicaid Services [CMMS]. (2010). *Report on state services to individuals with autism spectrum disorders (ASD)*. Abt Associates.

Cook, B. G. (2014). A call for examining replication and bias in special education research. *Remedial and Special Education, 35*, 233–261.

Cook, B. G., Collins, L. W., Cook, S. C., & Cook, L. (2020). Evidence-based reviews: How evidence-based practices are systematically identified. *Learning Disabilities Research & Practice, 35*(1), 6–13.

Cook, B. G., Lloyd, J. W., Mellor, D., Nosek, B. A., & Therrien, W. J. (2018). Promoting open science to increase the trustworthiness of evidence in special education. *Exceptional Children, 85*(1), 104–118.

Cook, B. G., & Odom, S. L. (2013). Evidence-Based practices and implementation science in special education. *Exceptional Children, 79*, 135–144.

Detrich, R. (2020). Cost effectiveness analysis: A component of evidence-based education. *School Psychology Review, 49*(4), 423–430.

Dingfelder, H. E., & Mandell, D. S. (2011). Bridging the research-to-practice gap in autism intervention: An application of diffusion of innovation theory. *Journal of Autism and Developmental Disorders, 41*(5), 597–609.

Dolata, J. K., Suarez, S., Calamé, B., & Fombonne, E. (2022). Pragmatic language markers of autism diagnosis and severity. *Research in Autism Spectrum Disorders, 94*, 101970.

Endrew F. v. Douglas County School District RE–1, 580 U.S. (2017).

Every Student Succeeds Act of 2015, P.L. 114-95, 20 U.S.C.6301 (2016).

Fixsen, D., Blase, K., Metz, A., & Van Dyke, M. (2013). Statewide implementation of evidence-based programs. *Exceptional Children, 79*(2), 213–230.

Franco, A., Malhotra, N., & Simonovits, G. (2014). Publication bias in the social sciences: Unlocking the file drawer. *Science, 345*, 1502–1505.

Gage, N. A., Cook, B. G., & Reichow, B. (2017). Publication bias in special education meta-analyses. *Exceptional Children, 83*(4), 428–445.

Georgiades, S., Szatmari, P., & Boyle, M. (2013). Importance of studying heterogeneity in autism. *Neuropsychiatry, 3*, 123–125.

Green, L. (2008). Making research relevant: If it is an evidence-based practice, where's the practice-based evidence? *Family Practice, 25*, 120–124.

Griswold, D. E., Barnhill, G. P., Myles, B. S., Hagiwara, T., & Simpson, R. (2002). Asperger syndrome and academic achievement. *Focus on Autism and Other Developmental Disabilities, 17*(2), 94–102.

Gwynette, M. F. (2013). Heterogeneity in autism spectrum disorder(s). *Journal of American Academy of Child and Adolescent Psychiatry, 52*, 1095–1096.

Heflin, J., & Simpson, R. (1998). Interventions for children and youth with autism: Prudent choices in a world of exaggerated claims and empty promises. Part II: Legal policy analysis and recommendations for selecting interventions and treatments. *Focus on Autism and Other Developmental Disabilities, 13*(4), 212–220.

Individuals with Disabilities Education Improvement Act of 2004. P.L. 108-446, 20 U.S.C. § 1400 (2005).

Klein, R. A., Ratliff, K. A., Vianello, M., Adams, R. B., Bahník, Š., Bernstein, M. J., Bocian, K., Brandt, M. J., Brooks, B., Brumbaugh, C. C., Cemalcilar, Z., Chandler, J., Cheong, W., Davis, W. E., Devos, T., Eisner, M., Frankowska, N., Furrow, D., Galliani, E. M., . . . Nosek, B. A. (2014) Investigating variation in replicability. *Social Psychology, 45*, 142–152.

Knight, V. F., Huber, H. B., Kuntz, E. M., Carter, E. W., & Juarez, A. P. (2019). Instructional practices, priorities and preparedness for educating students with autism and intellectual disability. *Focus on Autism and Other Developmental Disabilities, 34*(1), 3–14.

LaCava, P. G. (2018, November). *How to choose, use and evaluate evidence-based practices for students with autism spectrum disorders*. Presentation at the OCALICON Annual Conference, Columbus, OH.

LaCava, P. G., Jackson, C., Soares, S., & Grattan, A. (May, 2021). *Autism and evidence-based practices: Surveying educators' knowledge, training and use*. Poster presentation at the International Society of Autism Research annual meeting (online).

Lang, R., Tostanoski, A. H., Travers, J., & Todd, J. (2014). The only study investigating the rapid prompting method has serious methodological flaws but data suggest the most likely outcome is prompt dependency. *Evidence-Based Communication Assessment and Intervention, 8*, 40–48.

Landrum, T. J., Cook, B. G., Tankersley, M. K., & Fitzgerald, S. (2007). Teacher perceptions of the useability of intervention information from personal versus data-based sources. *Education and Treatment of Children, 30*(4), 1–16.

Leko, M. M., Roberts, C., Peyton, D., & Pua, D. (2019). Selecting evidence-based practices: What works for me. *Intervention in School and Clinic, 54*(5), 286–294.

Levin, H. M., McEwan, P. J., Belfield, C., Bowden, A. B., & Shand, R. (2018). *Economic evaluation in education: Cost effectiveness and benefit-cost analysis.* SAGE.

Makel, M. C., & Plucker, J. A. (2014). Facts are more important than novelty: Replication in the education sciences. *Educational Researcher, 43*, 304–316.

Malott, R. W. (1992). Should we train applied behavior analysts to be researchers? *Journal of Applied Behavioral Analysis, 25*(1), 83–88.

Mandy, W., Wang A., Lee I., & Skuse, D. (2017). Evaluating social (pragmatic) communication disorder. *Journal of Child Psychology and Psychiatry, 58*(10), 1166–1175.

Myles, B. S., Barnhill, G., Barnhill, G., Hagiwara, T., Griswold, D. E., & Simpson, R. L. (2001). A synthesis of studies on the intellectual, academic, social/emotional and sensory characteristics of children and youth with Asperger Syndrome. *Education and Training in Mental Retardation and Developmental Disabilities, 36*(3), 304–311.

Myles, B. S., Constant, J. A., Simpson, R. L., & Carlson, J. K. (1989). Educational assessment of students with higher-functioning autistic disorder. *Focus on Autistic Behavior, 4*(1), 1–15.

Myles, B. S., Hilgenfeld, T. D., Barnhill, G., Griswold, D., Hagiwara, T., & Simpson, R. L. (2002). Analysis of reading skills in individuals with Asperger syndrome. *Focus on Autism and Other Developmental Disabilities, 17*(1), 44–47.

Myles, B. S., & Simpson, R. L. (1994). Reflections on "An Analysis of Characteristics of Students Diagnosed as Having Higher-Functioning Autistic Disorder." *Exceptionality, 5*(1), 49–53.

Myles, B., & Simpson, R. L. (2001a). Effective practices for students with Asperger syndrome. *Focus on Exceptional Children, 34*(3), 1–14.

Myles, B., & Simpson, R. L. (2001b). Understanding the hidden curriculum: An essential social skill for children and youth with Asperger syndrome. *Intervention in School and Clinic, 36*(5), 279–286.

Myles, B., & Simpson, R. L. (2002a). The complexities of Asperger syndrome: What we know and what we have yet to learn. *Educational Horizons, 81*(1), 38–44.

Myles, B., & Simpson, R. L. (2002b). Asperger syndrome: An overview of characteristics. *Focus on Autism and Other Developmental Disabilities, 17*(3), 132–137.

Myles, B., & Simpson, R. L. (2002c). Students with Asperger syndrome: Implications for counselors. *Counseling and Human Development, 34*(7), 1–14.

Myles, B., Simpson, R. L., & Becker, J. (1994). An analysis of characteristics of students diagnosed as having higher-functioning autistic disorder. *Exceptionality, 5*(1), 19–30.

Myles, B., Simpson, R. L., & Johnson, S. (1995). Students with higher functioning autistic disorder: Do we know who they are. *Focus on Autistic Behavior, 9*(6), 11–15.

National Research Council. (2001). *Educating children with autism.* Committee on Educational Interventions for Children with Autism, Division of Behavioral and Social Sciences and Education. National Academy Press.

Norbury, C. F. (2014). Practitioner review: Social (pragmatic) communication disorder conceptualization, evidence and clinical implications. *Journal of Child Psychology and Psychiatry, 55*(3), 204–216.

Odom, S. L., Collet-Klingenberg, L., Rogers, S. J., & Hatton, D. D. (2010). Evidence-based practices in interventions for children and youth with autism spectrum disorders. *Preventing School Failure, 54*(4), 275–282.

Open Science Collaboration. (2015). Estimating the reproducibility of psychological science. *Science, 349*(6251), aac4716.

Polanin, J. R., Tanner-Smith, E. E., & Hennessy, E. A. (2016). Estimating the difference between published and unpublished effect sizes a meta-review. *Review of Educational Research, 86*, 207–236.

Prizant, B. M. (2011). The use and misuse of evidence-based practice: Implications for persons with ASD. *Autism Spectrum Quarterly, Fall, 43*, 46–49.

Reichow, B., Doehring, P., Cicchetti, D. V., & Volkmar, F. R. (Eds.). (2011). *Evidence-based practices and treatments for children with autism.* Springer.

Sackett, D. I., Straus, S. E., Richardson, W. S., Rosenberg, W., Haynes, R. B. (2000). *Evidence-Based Medicine: How to practice and teach EBM*, 2nd edition. Churchill Livingstone.

Sam, A. M., Cox, A. W., Savage, M. N., Waters, V., & Odom, S. L. (2020). Disseminating information on evidence-based practices for children and youth with autism spectrum disorder: AFIRM. *Journal of Autism and Developmental Disorders, 50*, 1931–1940.

Sam, A. M., & Hume, K. (2019). Learning supports for students on the autism spectrum. In R. Jordan, J. M. Roberts, & K. Hume (Eds.), *The SAGE handbook of autism and education.* SAGE

Scheibel, G., Zane, T. L., & Zimmerman, K. N. (2022). An economic evaluation of emerging and ineffective interventions: Examining the role of cost when translating research into practice. *Exceptional Children, 88*(2), 1–18.

Shadish, W. R., Zelinsky, N. A., Vevea, J. L., & Kratochwill, T. R. (2016). A survey of publication practices of single-case design researchers when treatments have small or large effects. *Journal of Applied Behavior Analysis, 49*, 656–673.

Simpson, R. L. (2005). Evidence-based practices and students with autism spectrum disorders. *Focus on Autism and Other Developmental Disabilities, 20*(3), 140–149.

Simpson, R. L., Myles, B., & Ganz, J. (2000). Tailoring our response: Asperger syndrome and problems of aggression and violence. *Reaching Today's Youth, 5*(1), 12–17.

Slocum, T. A., Detrich, R., Wilczynski, S. M., Spencer, T. D., Lewis, T., & Wolfe, K. (2014). The evidence-based practice of applied behavior analysis. *The Behavior Analyst, 37*(1), 41–56.

Todd, J. (2016). Old horses in new stables: Rapid prompting, facilitated communication, science, ethics, and the history of magic. In R. M. Foxx & J. A. Mulick (Eds.) *Controversial therapies for autism and intellectual disabilities* (2nd ed., pp. 372–409). Routledge.

Tostanoski, A., Lang, R., Raulston, T., Carnett, A., & Davis, T. (2014). Voices from the past: Comparing the rapid prompting method and facilitated communication. *Developmental Neurorehabilitation, 17,* 219–223.

Travers, J. C., Cook, B. G., Therrien, W. J., & Coyne, M. D. (2016). Replication research and special education. *Remedial and Special Education, 37,* 195–204.

Zients, J. D. (2012). *M-12-14. Memorandum to the heads of executive departs. From: Jeffrey D. Zients, Acting Director. Subject: Use of evidence and evaluation in the 2014 Budget.*

Structure of This Resource

Cook, B. G., Collins, L. W., Cook, S. C., & Cook, L. (2020). Evidence-based reviews: How evidence-based practices are systematically identified. *Learning Disabilities Research & Practice, 35*(1), 6–13.

Frost, L., & Bondy, A. (2002). *The picture exchange communication system training manual* (2nd ed.). Pyramid Educational Products.

Golan, O., & Baron-Cohen, S. (2006). Systemizing empathy: Teaching adults with Asperger syndrome or high-functioning autism to recognize complex emotions using interactive multimedia. *Development and Psychopathology, 18*(2), 591.

Gray, C. (2000). *The new social story book.* Future Horizons.

Gutstein, S. E., Burgess, A. F., & Montfort, K. (2007). Evaluation of the Relationship Development Intervention. *Autism, 11,* 397–411.

Hopkins, I. M., Gower, M. W., Perez, T. A., Smith, D. S., Amthor, F. R., Wimsatt, F. C., & Biasini, F. J. (2011). Avatar assistant: Improving social skills in students with an ASD through a computer-based intervention. *Journal of Autism and Developmental Disorders, 41*(11), 1543–1555.

Hoyson, M., Jamieson, B., & Strain, P. S. (1984). Individualized group instruction of normally developing and autistic-like children: The LEAP curriculum model. *Journal of the Division for Early Childhood, 8,* 157–172.

Ingersoll, B., & Dvortcsak, A. (2019). *The Project ImPACT manual for parents.* Guilford Press.

Kaiser, A. P., & Roberts, M. Y. (2013). Parent-implemented enhanced milieu teaching with preschool children who have intellectual disabilities. *Journal of Speech, Language, and Hearing Research, 56*(1), 295–309.

Kasari, C., Kaiser, A., Goods, K., Nietfeld, J., Mathy, P., Landa, R., Murphy, S., & Almirall, D. (2014). Communication interventions for minimally verbal children with autism: A sequential multiple assignment randomized trial. *Journal of the American Academy of Child & Adolescent Psychiatry, 53*(6), 635–646.

Kaufman, B. (1981). *A miracle to believe in.* Fawcett Crest.

Knight, V. F., Huber, H. B., Kuntz, E. M., Carter, E. W., & Juarez, A. P. (2019). Instructional practices, priorities and preparedness for educating students with autism and intellectual disability. *Focus on Autism and Other Developmental Disabilities, 34*(1), 3–14.

Koegel, R., & Koegel, L. (2006). *Pivotal response treatments for autism.* Paul H. Brookes.

Landrum, T. J., Cook, B. G., Tankersley, M. K., & Fitzgerald, S. (2007). Teacher perceptions of the useability of intervention information from personal versus data-based sources. *Education and Treatment of Children, 30*(4), 1–16.

Laugeson, E. A., & Frankel, F. (2010). *Social skills for teenagers with developmental and autism spectrum disorders: The PEERS treatment manual.* Routledge.

LeClerc, S., & Easley, D. (2015). Pharmacological therapies for autism spectrum disorder: A review. *Pharmacy and Therapeutics, 40*(6), 389–397.

Mahoney, G., & Perales, F. (2005). Relationship-focused early intervention with children with pervasive developmental disorders and other disabilities: A comparative study. *Journal of Developmental and Behavioral Pediatrics, 26*(2), 77–85.

Odom, S. L., Boyd, B. A., Hall, L. J., & Hume, K. (2010). Evaluation of comprehensive treatment models for individuals with autism spectrum disorders. *Journal of Autism and Developmental Disorders, 40*(4), 425–436.

Panerai, S., Ferrante, L., & Zingale, M. (2002). Benefits of the treatment and education of autistic and communication handicapped children (TEACCH) program as compared with a non-specific approach. *Journal of Intellectual Disability Research, 46,* 318–327.

Rogers, S. J., Hayden, D., Hepburn, S., Charlifue-Smith, R., Hall, T., & Hayes, A. (2006). Teaching young nonverbal children with autism useful speech: A pilot study of the Denver model and PROMPT interventions. *Journal of Autism and Developmental Disorders, 36,* 1007–1024.

Scheibel, G., Zane, T. L., & Zimmerman, K. N. (2022). An economic evaluation of emerging and ineffective interventions: Examining the role of cost when translating research into practice. *Exceptional Children, 88*(3), 245–262.

Solomon, R., Necheles, J., Ferch, C., & Bruckman, D. (2007). Pilot study of a parent training program for young children with autism. *Autism, 11,* 205–224.

Turner, K. M., Markie-Dadds, C., & Sanders, M. R. (2010). *Practitioner's manual for primary care triple P.* Triple P International Pty.

Section 1: Behavioral Interventions

Introduction

Cooper, J. O., Heron, T. E., & Heward, W. L. (2007). *Applied behavior analysis* (2nd ed.). Pearson Education.

Dixon, D. R., Linstead, E., Granpeesheh, D., Novack, M. N., French, R., Stevens, E., Stevens, L., & Powell, A. (2016). An evaluation of the impact of supervision intensity, supervisor qualifications, and caseload on outcomes in the treatment of autism spectrum disorder. *Behavior Analysis in Practice, 9*(4), 339–348.

Estes, A., Munson, J., Rogers, S. J., Greenson, J., Winter, J., & Dawson, G. (2015). Long-term outcomes of early intervention in 6-year-old children with autism spectrum disorder. *Journal of the American Academy of Child & Adolescent Psychiatry, 54*(7), 580–587.

Leaf, J. B., Cihon, J. H., Ferguson, J. L., Milne, C. M., Leaf, R., & McEachin, J. (2021). Advances in our understanding of behavioral intervention: 1980 to 2020 for individuals diagnosed with autism spectrum disorder. *Journal of Autism and Developmental Disorders, 51*(12), 4395–4410.

Leaf, J. B., Leaf, R., McEachin, J., Taubman, M., Ala'i-Rosales, S., Ross, R. K., Smith, T., & Weiss, M. J. (2016). Applied behavior analysis is a science and, therefore, progressive. *Journal of Autism and Developmental Disorders, 46*(2), 720–731.

Matson, J. L., & Jang, J. (2013). Autism spectrum disorders: Methodological considerations for early intensive behavioral interventions. *Research in Autism Spectrum Disorders, 7*(7), 809–814.

National Research Council (U.S.) (Ed.). (2001). *Educating children with autism*. National Academy Press.

Reichow, B. (2012). Overview of meta-analyses on early intensive behavioral intervention for young children with autism spectrum disorders. *Journal of Autism and Developmental Disorders, 42*(4), 512–520.

Simpson, R. L. (2004). Finding effective intervention and personnel preparation practices for students with autism spectrum disorders. *Exceptional Children, 70*(2), 135–144.

Smith, T. (2001). Discrete trial training in the treatment of autism. *Focus on Autism and Other Developmental Disabilities, 16*(2), 86–92.

Antecedent-Based Interventions (ABI)

Alberto, P. A., & Troutman, A. C. (2008). *Applied behavior analysis for teachers* (8th ed.). Prentice Hall.

Conroy, M. A., Asmus, J. M., Sellers, J. A., & Ladwig, C. N. (2005). The use of an antecedent-based intervention to decrease stereotypic behavior in a general education classroom: A case study. *Focus on Autism and Other Developmental Disabilities, 20*(4), 223–230.

Conroy, M. A., & Stichter, J. P. (2003). The application of antecedents in the functional assessment process. *Journal of Special Education, 37*(1), 15.

Kern, L., Choutka, C. M., & Sokol, N. G. (2002). Assessment-based antecedent interventions used in natural settings to reduce challenging behaviors: An analysis of the literature. *Education & Treatment of Children, 25*, 113–130.

Pokorski, E. A., Barton, E. E., Ledford, J. R., Taylor, A. L., Johnson, E., & Winters, H. K. (2019). Comparison of antecedent activities for increasing engagement in a preschool child with ASD during a small group activity.

Education and Training in Autism and Developmental Disabilities, 54(1), 94–103.

Wong, C., Odom, S., Hume, K., Cox, A., Fettig, A., Kucharczyk, S., Brock, M., Plavnick, J., Fleury, V., & Schultz, T. (2015). Evidence-based practices for children, youth, and young adults with autism spectrum disorder: A comprehensive review. *Journal of Autism & Developmental Disorders, 45*(7), 1951–1966.

Discrete Trial Teaching (DTT)

Downs, A., Conley-Downs, R., Fossum, M., & Rau, K. (2008). Effectiveness of discrete trial teaching with preschool students with developmental disabilities. *Education and Training in Developmental Disabilities, 43*, 443–453.

Fingerhut, J., & Moeyaert, M. (2022). Training individuals to implement discrete trials with fidelity: A meta-analysis. *Focus on Autism and Other Developmental Disabilities*, 1–12.

Howard, J. S., Sparkman, C. R., Cohen, H. G., Green, G., & Stanislaw, H. (2005). A comparison of intensive behavior analytic and eclectic treatments for young children with autism. *Research in Developmental Disabilities, 26*(4), 359–383.

Leaf, J. B., & Cihon, J. H. (2016). A progressive approach to discrete trial teaching: Some current guidelines. *International Electronic Journal of Elementary Education, 9*(2), 361–372.

Lovaas, O. I. (1981). *Teaching developmentally disabled children: The ME book*. Pro-Ed.

Lovaas, O. I. (1987). Behavioral treatment and normal educational and intellectual functioning in young autistic children. *Journal of Consulting and Clinical Psychology, 55*(1), 3–9.

Matson, J. L., Turygin, N. C., Beighley, J., Rieske, R., Tureck, K., & Matson, M. L. (2012). Applied behavior analysis in autism spectrum disorders: Recent developments, strengths, and pitfalls. *Research in Autism Spectrum Disorders, 6*(1), 144–150.

McEachin, J. J., Smith, T., & Lovaas, O. I. (1993). Long-term outcome for children with autism who received early intensive behavioral treatment. *American Journal on Mental Retardation, 97*(4), 359–372.

Errorless Learning

Braga-Kenyon, P., Guilhardi, P., Lionello-Denolf, K. M., & Dube, W. V. (2017). Teaching visual conditional discriminations using errorless learning: The role of prompts requiring simple and conditional discriminative control. *European Journal of Behavior Analysis, 18*(2), 180–194.

Flora, S., Rach, J., & Brown, K. (2020, June). "Errorless" toilet training: "The potty party." *International Electronic Journal of Elementary Education, 12*(5), 453–457.

Foran-Conn, D., Hoerger, M., Kelly, E., Cross, R. R., Jones, S., Walley, H., & Firth, L. (2021). A comparison of most to least prompting, no-no prompting and responsive prompt delay procedures. *Behavioral Interventions, 36*, 1024–1041.

Gerencser, K. R., Higbee, T. S., Contreras, B. P., Pellegrino, A. J., & Gunn, S. J. (2018). Evaluation of interactive computerized training to teach paraprofessionals to implement errorless discrete trial instruction. *Journal of Behavioral Education, 27*, 461–487.

Leaf, J. B., Cihon, J. H., Ferguson, J. L., Milne, C. M., Leaf, R., & McEachin, J. (2020). Comparing error correction to errorless learning: A randomized clinical trial. *The Analysis of Verbal Behavior, 36*, 1–20.

Mueller, M. M., Palkovic, C. M., & Maynard, C. S. (2007). Errorless learning: Review and practical application for teaching children with pervasive developmental disorders. *Psychology in the Schools, 44*(7), 691–700.

Severtson, J. M., & Carr, J. E. (2017). Training novice instructors to implement errorless discrete-trial teaching: A sequential analysis. *Behavior Analysis in Practice, 5*(2), 13–23.

Wilkinson, K. M. (Commentary Author). (2008). Errorless techniques show some advantages over error-correction techniques for teaching photograph–object relationships to children with autism. *Evidence-based Communication Assessment and Intervention, 2*(2), 103–105.

Task Analysis

Allinder, R. M., Bolling, R. M., Oats, R. G., & Gagnon, W. A. (2000). Effects of teacher self-monitoring on implementation of curriculum-based measurement and mathematics computation achievement of students with disabilities. *Remedial and Special Education, 21*, 219–226.

Browder, D. M., Trela, K., & Jimenez, B. (2007). Training teachers to follow a task analysis to engage middle school students with moderate and severe developmental disabilities in grade-appropriate literature. *Focus on Autism and Other Developmental Disorders, 22*(4), 206–219.

Moats, L., & Lyon, G. R. (1996). Wanted: Teachers with knowledge of language. *Topics in Language Disorders, 16*, 73–81.

Szidon, K., & Franzone, E. (2009). *Task analysis.* National Professional Development Center on Autism Spectrum Disorders, Waisman Center, University of Wisconsin.

Prompting and Fading

Leaf, J. B., Sheldon, J. B., & Sherman, J. A. (2010). Comparison of simultaneous prompting and no-no prompting in two-choice discrimination learning with children with autism. *Journal of Applied Behavior Analysis, 43*, 215–228.

Libby, M. E., Weiss, J. S., Bancroft, S., & Ahearn, W. H. (2008). A comparison of most-to-least and least-to-most prompting on acquisition of solitary play skills. *Behavior Analysis in Practice, 1*, 37–43.

MacDuff, G. S., Krantz, P. J., & McClannahan, L. E. (2001). Prompts and prompt-fading strategies for people with autism. In G. Maurice, G. Green, & R. Foxx (Eds.), *Making a difference: Behavioral intervention for autism* (pp. 37–50). Pro-Ed.

Soluaga, D., Leaf, J. B., Taubman, M., McEachin, J., & Leaf, R. (2008). A comparison of flexible prompt fading and constant time delay for five children with autism. *Research in Autism Spectrum Disorders, 2*, 753–765.

Walker, G. (2008). Constant and progressive time delay procedures for teaching children with autism: A literature review. *Journal of Autism and Developmental Disorders, 38*, 261–275.

Time Delay

Alison, C., Root, J. R., Browder, D. M., & Wood, L. (2017). Technology-based shared story reading for students with autism who are English-language learners. *Journal of Special Education Technology, 32*(2), 91–101.

Browder, D. M., Ahlgrim-Delzell, L., Spooner, F., Mims, P. J., & Baker, J. N. (2009). Using time delay to teach literacy to students with severe developmental disabilities. *Exceptional Children, 75*(3), 343–364.

Browder, D. M., Root, J. R., Wood, L., & Allison, C. (2017). Effects of a story-mapping procedure using the iPad on the comprehension of narrative texts by students with autism spectrum disorder. *Focus on Autism and Other Developmental Disabilities, 32*(4), 243–255.

Browder, D. M., Spooner, F., & Courtade, G. R. (2020). *Teaching students with moderate and severe disabilities* (2nd ed.). Guilford Press.

Browder, D. M., Wood, L. A., Thompson, J. L., & Ribuffo, C. (2014). *Evidence-based practices for students with severe disabilities.* (Document NO. IC-3). CEEDAR Center.

Carlile, K. A., Reeve, S. A., Reeve, K. F., & DeBar, R. M. (2013). Using activity schedules on the iPod touch to teach leisure skills to children with autism. *Education & Treatment of Children, 36*(2), 33–57.

Coleman, M. B., Hurley, K. J., & Cihak, D. F. (2012). Comparing teacher-directed and computer-assisted constant time delay for teaching functional sight words to students with moderate intellectual disability. *Education and Training in Autism and Developmental Disabilities, 47*(3), 280–292.

Collins, B. C. (2022). *Systematic instruction for students with moderate and severe disabilities* (2nd ed.). Brookes Publishing.

Cooper, J. O., Heron, T. E., & Heward, W. L. (2020). *Applied behavior analysis* (3rd ed.). Pearson.

Courtade, G. R., Test, D. W., & Cook, B. G. (2014). Evidence-based practices for learners with severe intellectual disability. *Research and Practice for Persons with Severe Disabilities, 39*(4), 305–318.

DiGennaro Reed, F. D., Blackman, A. L., Erath, T. G., Brand, D., & Novak, M. D. (2018). Guidelines for using behavioral skills training to provide teacher support. *Teaching Exceptional Children, 50*(6), 373–380.

Horn, A. L., Gable, R. A., Bobzien, J. L., Tonelson, S. W., & Rock, M. L. (2020). Teaching young adults job skills using a constant time delay and eCoaching intervention package. *Career Development and Transition for Exceptional Individuals, 43*(1), 29–39.

Jimenez, B. A., & Kemmery, M. (2013). Building the early numeracy skills of students with moderate intellectual disability. *Education and Training in Autism and Developmental Disabilities, 48*(4), 479–490.

Knight, V. F., Spooner, F., Browder, D. M., Smith, B. R., & Wood, C. L. (2013). Using systematic instruction and graphic organizers to teach science concepts to students with autism spectrum disorders and intellectual disability. *Focus on Autism and Other Developmental Disabilities, 28*(2), 115–126.

Root, J. R., & Browder, D. M. (2019). Algebraic problem solving for middle school students with autism and intellectual disability. *Exceptionality, 27*(2), 118–132.

Shepley, C., Lane, J. D., & Ault, M. J. (2019). A review and critical examination of the system of least prompts. *Remedial and Special Education, 40*(5), 313–327.

Shepley, C., Lane, J. D., & Gast, D. L. (2016a). Using SMART board technology to teach young students with disabilities and limited group learning experience to read environmental text. *Education and Training on Autism and Developmental Disabilities, 51*(4), 404–420.

Shepley, C., Lane, J. D., & Shepley, S. B. (2016b). Teaching young children with social-communication delays to label actions using videos and language expansion models. *Focus on Autism and Other Developmental Disabilities, 31*(4), 243–253.

Smith, K. A., Ayres, K. A., Alexander, J., Ledford, J. R., Shepley, C., & Shepley, S. B. (2016). Initiation and generalization of self-instructional skills in adolescents with autism and intellectual disability. *Journal of Autism and Developmental Disorders, 46*(4), 1196–1209.

Snell, M. E., & Gast, D. L. (1981). Applying time delay procedure to the instruction of the severely handicapped. *Journal of the Association for the Severely Handicapped, 6*(3), 3–14.

Spooner, F., Kemp-Inman, A., Ahlgrim-Delzell, L., Wood, L., & Ley Davis, L. (2015). Generalization of literacy skills through portable technology for students with severe disabilities. *Research and Practice for Persons with Severe Disabilities, 40*(1), 52–70.

Swain, R., Lane, J. D., & Gast, D. L. (2015). Comparison of constant time delay and simultaneous prompting procedures: Teaching functional sight words to students with intellectual disabilities and autism spectrum disorder. *Journal of Behavioral Education, 24*(2), 210–229.

Touchette, P. E. (1971). Transfer of stimulus control: Measuring the moment of transfer. *Journal of the Experimental Analysis of Behavior, 15*(3), 347–354.

Winstead, O., Lane, J. D., Spriggs, A. D., & Allday, R. A. (2019). Providing small group instruction to children with disabilities and same-age peers. *Journal of Early Intervention, 41*(3), 202–219.

Wolery, M., Ault, M. J., & Doyle, P. (1992). *Teaching students with moderate to severe disabilities: Use of response prompting strategies.* Longman.

Behavioral Momentum

Cowan, R. L., Abel, L., & Candel, L. (2017). A meta-analysis of single-subject research on behavioral momentum to enhance success in students with autism. *Journal of Autism and Developmental Disorders, 47*, 1464–1477.

Fisher, W. W., Greer, B. D., Fuhrman, A. M., Saini, V., & Simmons, C. A. (2018). Minimizing resurgence of destructive behavior using behavioral momentum theory. *Journal of Applied Behavior Analysis, 51*(4), 831–853.

Nevin, J. A., Mandell, C., & Atak, J. A. (1983). The analysis of behavioral momentum. *Journal of the Experimental Analysis of Behavior, 39*(1), 49–59.

Nevin, J. A., & Shahan, T. A. (2011). Behavioral momentum theory: Equations and applications. *Journal of Applied Behavior Analysis, 44*(4), 877–855.

Rosales, M. K., Wilder, D. A., Montalvo, M., & Fagan, B. (2021). Evaluation of the high-probability instructional sequence to increase compliance with multiple low-probability instructions among children with autism. *Journal of Applied Behavior Analysis, 54*(2), 760–769.

Response Interruption and Redirection (RIR)

Ahearn, W. H., Clark, K. M., MacDonald, R. P. F., & Chung, B. I. (2007). Assessing and treating vocal stereotypy in children with autism. *Journal for Applied Behavior Analysis, 40*, 263–275.

Aherns, E. N., Lerman, D. C., Kodak, T., Worsdell, A. S., & Keegan, C. (2011). Further evaluation of response interruption and redirection as treatment for stereotypy. *Journal of Applied Behavior Analysis, 44*(1), 95–108.

Athens, E. S., Vollmer, T. R., Sloman, K. N., & St. Peter Pipkin, C. (2008). An analysis of vocal stereotypy and therapist fading. *Journal of Applied Behavior Analysis, 41*, 291–297.

Ollendick, T. H., Matson, J. L., & Martin, J. E. (1978). Effectiveness of hand overcorrection for topographically similar and dissimilar self stimulatory behavior. *Journal of Experimental Child Psychology, 25*, 396–403.

Reinforcement

Campanaro, A. M., Vladescu, J. C., Kodak, T., Debar, R. M., & Nippes, K. C. (2020). Comparing skill acquisition under varying onsets of differential reinforcement: A preliminary analysis. *Journal of Applied Behavior Analysis, 53*(2), 690–706.

Cividini-Motta, C., & Ahearn, W. H. (2013). Effects of two variations of differential reinforcement on prompt dependency. *Journal of Applied Behavior Analysis, 46*, 640–650.

Delmolino, L., LaRue, R. H., & Sloman, K. N. (2014). The effects of magnitude-based differential reinforcement on the skill acquisition of children with autism. *Journal of Behavioral Education, 23*, 470–487.

Fiske, K. E., Isenhower, R. W., Bamond, M. J., & Lauderdale-Litti, S. (2019). An analysis of the value of token reinforcement using a multiple schedule assessment. *Journal of Applied Behavior Analysis, 53*(1), 563–571.

Nevin, J. A. (1988). Behavioral momentum and the partial reinforcement effect. *Psychological Bulletin, 103*(1), 44–56.

Rey, C. N., Betz, A. M., Sleiman, A. A., Toshikazu Kuroda, T., & Podlesnik, C. A. (2020). The role of adventitious reinforcement during differential reinforcement of other behavior: A systematic replication. *Journal of Applied Behavior Analysis (Fall), 53*(4), 2440–2449.

Richman, D. M., Barnard-Brak, L., Grubb, L., Bosch, A., & Abby, L. (2015). Meta-analysis of noncontingent reinforcement effects on problem behaviour. *Journal of Applied Behavior Analysis, 48*(1), 131–152.

Slocum, S. K., & Vollmer, T. R. (2015). A comparison of positive and negative reinforcement for compliance to treat problem behavior maintained by escape. *Journal of Applied Behavior Analysis, 48*(3), 563–574.

Weston, R., Hodges, A., & Davis, T. N. (2018). Differential reinforcement of other behaviors to treat challenging behaviors among children with autism: A systematic and quality review. *Behavior Modification, 42*(4), 584–609.

Whitaker, S. (1996). A review of DRO: The influence of the degree of intellectual disability and the frequency of the target behaviour. *Journal of Applied Research in Intellectual Disabilities, 9*(1), 61–79.

Differential Reinforcement

Cividini-Motta, C., & Ahearn, W. H. (2013). Effects of two variations of differential reinforcement on prompt dependency. *Journal of Applied Behavior Analysis, 46*, 640–650.

Cooper, J. O., Heron, T. E., & Heward, W. L. (2007). *Applied behavior analysis*. (2nd ed). Pearson Education.

Homer, A. L., & Peterson, L. (1980). Differential reinforcement of other behavior: A preferred response elimination procedure. *Behavior Therapy, 11*, 449–471.

Jessel, J., & Ingvarsson, E. T. (2016). Recent advances in applied research on DRO procedures. *Journal of Applied Behavior Analysis, 49*, 991–995.

Poling, A., & Ryan, C. (1982). Differential reinforcement of other behavior schedules: Therapeutic applications. *Behavior Modification, 6*, 3–21.

Weston, R., Hodges, A., & Davis, T. N. (2018). Differential reinforcement of other behaviors to treat challenging behaviors among children with autism: A systematic and quality review. *Behavior Modification, 42*(4), 584–609.

Whitaker, S. (1996). A review of DRO: The influence of the degree of intellectual disability and the frequency of the target behaviour. *Journal of Applied Research in Intellectual Disabilities, 9*(1), 61–79.

Modeling

Bandura, A., Ross, D., & Ross, S. A. (1961). Transmission of aggression through imitation of aggressive models. *Journal of Abnormal and Social Psychology, 63*, 575–582.

Bandura, A., Ross, D., & Ross, S. A. (1963). Vicarious reinforcement and imitative learning. *Journal of Abnormal and Social Psychology, 67*(6), 601–607.

Charlop-Christy, M. H., Le, L., & Freeman, K. A. (2000). A comparison of video modeling with in vivo modeling for teaching children with autism. *Journal of Autism and Developmental Disorders, 30*(6), 537–552.

DeQuinzio, J. A., & Taylor, B. A. (2015). Teaching children with autism to discriminate the reinforced and nonreinforced responses of others: Implications for observational learning. *Journal of Applied Behavior Analysis, 48*(1), 38–51.

Matson, J. L., Matson, M. L., & Rivet, T. T. (2007). Social-skills treatments for children with autism spectrum disorders: An overview. *Behavior Modification, 31*(5), 682–707.

McDowell, L. S., Gutierrez Jr., A., & Bennett, K. D. (2015). Analysis of live modeling plus prompting and video modeling for teaching imitation to children with autism. *Behavioral Interventions, 30*(4), 333–351.

Plavnick, J. B., & Hume, K. A. (2014). Observational learning by individuals with autism: A review of teaching strategies. *Autism, 18*(4), 458–466.

Rigsby-Eldredge, M., & McLaughlin, T. F. (1992). The effects of modeling and praise on self-initiated behavior across settings with two adolescent students with autism. *Journal of Developmental and Physical Disabilities, 4*(3), 205–218.

Taylor, B. A., & DeQuinzio, J. A. (2012). Observational learning and children with autism. *Behavior Modification, 36*(3), 341–360.

Townley-Cochran, D., Leaf, J. B., Taubman, M., Leaf, R., & McEachin, J. (2015). Observational learning for students diagnosed with autism: A review paper. *Review Journal of Autism and Developmental Disorders, 2*(3), 262–272.

Functional Behavioral Assessment (FBA)

Alter, P. J., Conroy, M. A., Mancil, G. R., & Haydon, T. (2008). A comparison of functional behavior assessment methodologies with young children: Descriptive methods and functional analysis. *Journal of Behavioral Education, 17*(2), 200–219.

Beavers, G. A., Iwata, B. A., & Lerman, D. C. (2013). Thirty years of research on the functional analysis of problem behavior: Thirty years of functional analysis. *Journal of Applied Behavior Analysis, 46*(1), 1–21.

Campbell, J. M. (2003). Efficacy of behavioral interventions for reducing problem behavior in persons with autism: A quantitative synthesis of single-subject research. *Research in Developmental Disabilities, 24*(2), 120–138.

Edwards, W. H., Magee, S. K., & Ellis, J. (2002). Identifying the effects of idiosyncratic variables on functional analysis outcomes: A case study. *Education and Treatment of Children, 25*(3), 317–330.

Filter, K. J., & Horner, R. H. (2009). Function-based academic interventions for problem behavior. *Education and Treatment of Children, 32*(1), 1–19.

Hanley, G. P. (2011). Prevention and treatment of severe problem behavior. In E. A. Mayville & J. A. Mulick (Eds.), *Behavioral foundations of effective autism treatment*. Sloan.

Ingram, K., Lewis-Palmer, T., & Sugai, G. (2005). Function-based intervention planning: Comparing the effectiveness of FBA function-based and non-function-based intervention plans. *Journal of Positive Behavior Interventions, 7*(4), 224–236.

McIntosh, K., Brown, J. A., & Borgmeier, C. J. (2008). Validity of functional behavior assessment within a response to intervention framework: Evidence, recommended practice, and future directions. *Assessment for Effective Intervention, 34*(1), 6–14.

Nelson, J. R., Roberts, M. L., Mathur, S. R., & Rutherford, R. B. (1999). Has public policy exceeded our knowledge base? A review of the functional behavioral assessment literature. *Behavioral Disorders, 24*(2), 169–179.

Office of Special Education Programs. (2004). Section 1415 (k) (1). *Individuals with Disabilities Education Act.*

Functional Communication Training (FCT)

Carr, E. G., & Durand, V. (1985). Reducing behavior problems through functional communication training. *Journal of Applied Behavior Analysis, 18*, 111–126.

Durand, V. M., & Carr E. G. (1987). Social influences on "self-stimulatory" behavior: Analysis and treatment application. *Journal of Applied Behavior Analysis, 20*(2), 119–132.

Ghaemmaghami, M., Hanley, G. P., & Jessel, J. (2021). Functional communication training: From efficacy to effectiveness. *Journal of Applied Behavior Analysis, 54*(1), 122–143.

Gregori, E., Wendt, O., Gerow, S., Peltier, C., Genc-Tosun, D., Lory, C., & Gold, Z. S. (2020). Functional communication training for adults with autism spectrum disorder: A systematic review and quality appraisal. *Journal of Behavioral Education, 29*, 42–63.

Heath, A. K., Ganz, J. B., Parker, R., Burke, M., & Ninci, J. (2015). A meta-analytic review of functional communication training across mode of communication, age, and disability *Journal of Autism and Developmental Disorders, 2*, 155–166.

Lambert, J. M., Bloom, S. E., & Irvin, J. (2012). Trial-based functional analysis and functional communication training in an early childhood setting. *Journal of Applied Behavior Analysis, 45*(3), 579–584.

Landa, R. K., Hanley, G. P., Gover, H. C., Rajaraman, A., & Ruppel, K. W. (2022). Understanding the effects of prompting immediately after problem behavior occurs during functional communication training. *Journal of Applied Behavior Analysis, 55*(1), 121–137.

Lindgren, S., Wacker, D., Schieltz, K. Suess, A., Pelzel, K., Kopelman, T., Lee, J., Romani, P., & O'Brien, M. (2020). A randomized controlled trial of functional communication training via telehealth for young children with autism spectrum disorder. *Journal of Autism and Developmental Disorders, 50*(12), 4449–4462.

Mancil, G. R., & Boman, R. (2010). Functional communication training in the classroom: A guide for success. *Preventing School Failure, 54*(4), 238–246.

Mancil, G. R., Conroy, M. A., Nakeo, T., & Alter, P. J. (2006). Functional communication training in the natural environment: A pilot investigation with a young child with autism spectrum disorder. *Education and Treatment of Children, 29*(4),615–633.

O'Neill, R. E., & Sweetland-Baker, M. (2001). Brief report: An assessment of stimulus generalization and contingency effects in functional communication training with two students with autism. *Journal of Autism and Developmental Disorders, 31*(2), 235–40.

Reichle, J., & Wacker, D. (2017). *Functional communication training for problem behavior.* Guilford Press.

Tiger, J. H., Hanley, G. P., & Bruzek, J. (2008). Functional communication training: A review and practical guide. *Behavior Analysis in Practice, 1*, 16–23.

Wacker, D. P., Steege, M. W., Northup, J., Sasso, G., Berg, W., Reimers, T., Cooper, L., Cigrand, K., & Donn, L. (1990). A component analysis of functional communication training across three topographies of severe behavior problems. *Journal of Applied Behavior Analysis, 23*(4), 417–429.

Extinction

Cooper, J. O., Heron, T. E., & Heward, W. L. (2020). *Applied behavior analysis* (3rd ed.). Pearson Education.

Cuvo, A. J., Godard, A., Huckfeldt, R., & DeMattei, R. (2010). Training children with autism spectrum disorders to be compliant with an oral assessment. *Research in Autism Spectrum Disorders, 4*(4), 681–696.

Devlin, S., Healy, O., Leader, G., & Hughes, B. M. (2011). Comparison of behavioral intervention and sensory-integration therapy in the treatment of challenging behavior. *Journal of Autism and Developmental Disorders, 41*(10), 1303–1320.

Kahng, S., Iwata, B. A., & Lewin A. B. (2002). Behavioral treatment of self-injury, 1964–2000. *American Journal on Mental Retardation, 107*, 212–221.

Kelley, M. E., Lerman, D. C., & Van Camp, C. M. (2002). The effects of competing reinforcement schedules on the acquisition of functional communication. *Journal of Applied Behavior Analysis, 35*(1), 59–63.

MacNaul, H. L., & Neely, L. C. (2018). Systematic review of differential reinforcement of alternative behavior without extinction for individuals with autism. *Behavior Modification, 42*(3), 398–421.

Matson, J. L., & Lovullo, S. (2008). A review of behavioral treatments for self-injurious behaviors of persons with autism spectrum disorders. *Behavior Modification, 32*(1), 61–76.

O'Reilly, M, Edrisinha, C., Sigafoos, J., Lancioni, G., Cannella, H., Machalicek, W., Langthorne, P. (2007). Manipulating the evocative and abative effects of an establishing operation: Influences on challenging behavior during classroom instruction. *Behavioral Interventions 22*, 137–145

Sullivan, L., & Bogin, J. (2010). *Overview of extinction.* National Professional Development Center on Autism Spectrum Disorders, M.I.N.D. Institute, University of California at Davis Medical School.

Waters, M. B., Lerman, D. C., & Hovanetz, A. N. (2009). Separate and combined effects of visual schedules and extinction plus differential reinforcement on problem behavior occasioned by transitions. *Journal of Applied Behavior Analysis, 42*(2), 309–313.

Punishment Procedures

Behavior Analyst Certification Board. (2020). *Ethics code for behavior analysts. Section 2: Responsibility in practice.*

Cooper, J. O., Heron, T. E., & Heward, W. L. (2007). *Applied behavior analysis* (2nd ed.). Pearson Education.

Favell, J. E., & Lovaas, O. I. (1987). Protection for clients undergoing aversive/restrictive interventions. *Education and Treatment of Children, 10*(4), 311–325.

Hanley, G. P., Piazza, C. C., Fisher, W. W., & Maglieri, K. A. (2005). On the effectiveness of and preference for punishment and extinction components of function-based interventions. *Journal of Applied Behavior Analysis, 38*, 51–65.

Leaf, J. B., Townley-Cochran, D., Cihon J. H., Mitchell, E., Leaf, R., Taubman M., & McEachin J. (2019). Descriptive analysis of the use of punishment-based techniques with children diagnosed with autism spectrum disorder. *Education and Training in Autism and Developmental Disabilities, 54*(2), 107–118.

Lerman, D. C., & Vorndran, C. M. (2002). On the status of knowledge for using punishment: Implications for treating behavior disorders. *Journal of Applied Behavior Analysis, 35*, 431–464.

Regalado, M., Sareen, H., Inkelas, M., Wissow, L. S., & Halfon, N. (2004). Parents' discipline of young children: Results from the National Survey of Early Childhood Health. *Pediatrics, 113*(Suppl. 5), 1952–1958.

Tanner, B. A., & Zeiler, M. (1975). Punishment of self-injurious behavior using aromatic ammonia as the aversive stimulus. *Journal of Applied Behavior Analysis, 8*(1), 53–57.

Van Houten, R., Axelrod, S., Bailey, J. S., Favell, J. E., Foxx, R. M., Iawata, B. A., & Lovaas, O. I., (1988). The right to effective behavioral treatment. *Journal of Applied Behavior Analysis, 1*(21), 89–95.

Vittrup, B., Holden, G. W., & Buck, J. (2006). Attitudes predict the use of physical punishment: A prospective study of the emergence of disciplinary practices. *Pediatrics, 117*(6), 2055–2064.

Westling, D. L. (2010). Teachers and challenging behavior: Knowledge, views, and practices. *Remedial and Special Education, 31*(1), 48–63.

The Ziggurat Model and Comprehensive Autism Planning System (CAPS)

Aspy, R., & Grossman, B. G. (2007). *The Ziggurat Model: A framework for designing comprehensive intervention for individuals with high-functioning autism and Asperger syndrome.* AAPC Publishing.

Henry, S. A., & Myles, B. S. (2007). *The Comprehensive Autism Planning System (CAPS) for individuals with Asperger syndrome, autism, and related disabilities: Integrating best practices throughout the student's day.* AAPC Publishing.

Myles, B. S., Grossman, B. G., Aspy, R., & Henry, S. A. (2009). Planning a comprehensive program for young children with autism spectrum disorders. *International Journal of Early Childhood Special Education, 1*(2), 164–180.

Myles, B. S., Grossman, B. G., Aspy, R., Henry, S. A., & Coffin, A. B. (2007). Planning a comprehensive program for students with autism spectrum disorders using evidence-based practices. *Education and Training in Developmental Disabilities, 42*(4), 398–409.

Smith, S. M., Smith Myles, B., Aspy, R., Grossman, B. G., & Henry, S. A. (2010). Sustainable change in quality of life for individuals with ASD: Using a comprehensive planning process. *Focus on Exceptional Children, 43*(3), 1–24.

Webster, A., Cumming, J., & Rowland, S. (2017). Empowering parents to create a vision for their children with autism spectrum disorder. In A. Webster, J. Cumming, & S. Rowland, *Empowering parents of children with autism spectrum disorder* (pp. 93–109). Springer, Singapore.

Early Intensive Behavioral Interventions

UCLA Young Autism Project

Cohen, H., Amerine-Dickens, M., & Smith, T. (2006). Early intensive behavioral treatment: Replication of the UCLA model in a community setting. *Journal of Developmental and Behavioral Pediatrics, 27*, S145–S155.

Eikeseth, S., Smith, T., Jahr, E., & Eldevik, S. (2007). Outcome for children with autism who began intensive behavioral treatment between ages 4 and 7: A comparison study. *Behavior Modification, 31*, 264–278.

Lovaas, O. I. (1987). Behavioral treatment and normal educational and intellectual functioning in young autistic children. *Journal of Consulting and Clinical Psychology, 55*, 3–9.

Lovaas, O. I. (1993). The development of a treatment-research project for developmentally disabled and autistic children. *Journal of Applied Behavior Analysis, 26*, 617–630.

Nicolosi, M., & Dillenburger, K. (2022). The University of California at Los Angeles-Young Autism Project: A systematic review of replication studies. *Behavioral Interventions, 37*(2), 415–464.

Reichow, B., & Wolery, M. (2009). Comprehensive synthesis of early intensive behavioral interventions for young children with autism based on the UCLA young autism project model. *Journal of Autism and Developmental Disorders, 39*(1), 23–41.

Sheinkopf, S. J., & Siegel, B. (1998). Home-based behavioral treatment of young children with autism. *Journal of Autism and Developmental Disorders, 28*, 15–23.

Early Start Denver Model

Cidav, Z., Munson, J., Estes, A., Dawson, G., Rogers, S., & Mandell, D. (2017). Cost offset associated with early start Denver model for children with autism. *Journal of*

American Academy of Child & Adolescent Psychiatry, 56(9), 777–783.

Dawson, G., Rogers, S. J., Munson, J., Smith, M., Winter, J., Greenson, J., Donaldson, A., & Varley, J. (2010). Randomized, controlled trial of an intervention for toddlers with autism: The early start Denver model. *Pediatrics, 125,* 17–23.

Mahler, M. S., Pine, F., & Bergman, A. (1975). *The psychological birth of the human infant.* Basic Books.

Odom, S. L., Boyd, B., Hall, L., & Hume, K. (2010). Evaluation of comprehensive treatment models for individuals with autism spectrum disorders. *Journal of Autism and Developmental Disorders, 40,* 425–436.

Piaget, J. (1954). *Construction of reality in the child.* Ballantine Books.

Piaget, J. (1962). *Play, dreams, and imitation in childhood.* Norton.

Piaget, J. (1966). *Psychology of intelligence.* Littlefield, Adams.

Rogers, S. J., & Dawson, G. (2010). *Early start Denver model for young children with autism: Promoting language, learning, and engagement.* Guilford Press.

Rogers, S. J., Hall, T., Osaki, D., Reaven, J., & Herbison, J. (2000). The Denver model: A comprehensive, integrated educational approach to young children with autism and their families. In J. Handleman & S. Harris (Eds.), *Preschool education programs for children with autism* (2nd ed., pp. 215–232). Pro-Ed.

Rogers, S. J., Hayden, D., Hepburn, S., Charlifue-Smith, R., Hall, T., & Hayes, A. (2006). Teaching young nonverbal children with autism useful speech: A pilot study of the Denver model and PROMPT interventions. *Journal of Autism and Developmental Disorders, 36,* 1007–1024.

Rogers, S. J., Herbison, J., Lewis, H., Pantone, J., & Reis, K. (1986). An approach for enhancing the symbolic, communicative, and interpersonal functioning of young children with autism and severe emotional handicaps. *Journal of the Division for Early Childhood, 10,* 135–148.

Rogers, S. J., & Lewis, H. (1989). An effective day treatment model for young children with pervasive developmental disorders. *Journal of the American Academy of Child and Adolescent Psychiatry, 28,* 207–214.

Rogers, S. J., Lewis, H. C., & Reis, K. (1987). An effective procedure for training early special education teams to implement a model program. *Journal of the Division for Early Childhood, 11,* 180–188.

Weiss, R. (1981). INREAL intervention for language handicapped and bilingual children. *Journal of the Division for Early Childhood, 4,* 40–51.

Learning Experiences: An Alternative Program for Preschoolers and Parents (LEAP)

Dodge, D. T., Colker, L. J., & Heroman, C. (2002). *The creative curriculum for preschool* (4th ed.). Teaching Strategies.

Hoyson, M., Jamieson, B., & Strain, P. S. (1984). Individualized group instruction of normally developing and autistic-like children: The LEAP curriculum model. *Journal of the Division for Early Childhood, 8*(2), 157–172.

Kohler, F. W., & Strain, P. S. (1999). Maximizing peer-mediated resources in integrated preschool classrooms. *Topics in Early Childhood Special Education, 19*(2), 92–102.

Odom, S. L., Boyd, B., Hall, L., & Hume, K. (2010). Evaluation of comprehensive treatment models for individuals with autism spectrum disorders. *Journal of Autism and Developmental Disorders, 40,* 425–436.

Schopler, E., Reichler, R. J., & Renner, B. R. (1998). *Childhood Autism Rating Scale.* Western Psychological Resources.

Strain, P. S., & Bovey, E. H. (2011). Randomized, controlled trial of the LEAP model of early intervention for young children with autism spectrum disorders. *Topics in Early Childhood Special Education, 31*(3), 133–154.

Strain, P. S., & Cordisco, L. (1993). The LEAP preschool model: Description and outcomes. In S. Harris & J. Handleman (Eds.), *Preschool education programs for children with autism* (pp. 224–244). Pro-Ed.

Strain, P. S., & Hoyson, M. (2000). The need for longitudinal, intensive social skill intervention: LEAP follow-up outcomes for children with autism. *Topics in Early Childhood Special Education, 20*(2), 116–122.

Strain, P. S., & Kohler, F. W. (1998). Peer-mediated social intervention for young children with autism. *Seminars in Speech and Language, 19,* 391–405.

Section 2: Visual Supports

Schedules

Arntzen, E., Gilde, K., & Pedersen, E. (1998). Generalized schedule following in a youth with autism. *Scandinavian Journal of Behaviour Therapy, 27*(3), 135–141.

Brodhead, M. T., Courtney, W. T., & Thaxton, J. R. (2018). Using activity schedules to promote varied application use in children with autism. *Journal of Applied Behavior Analysis, 51*(1), 80–86.

Bryan, L. C., & Gast, D. L. (2000). Teaching on-task and on-schedule behaviors to high-functioning children with autism via picture activity schedules. *Journal of Autism and Developmental Disorders, 30*(6), 553–567.

Cihak, D. F. (2011). Comparing pictorial and video modeling activity schedules during transitions for students with autism spectrum disorders. *Research in Autism Spectrum Disorders, 5*(1), 433–441.

Dettmer, S., Simpson, R. L., Myles, B. S., & Ganz, J. B. (2000). The use of visual supports to facilitate transitions of students with autism. *Focus on Autism and Other Developmental Disabilities, 15*(3), 163–169.

Giles, A., & Markham, V. (2017). Comparing book-and tablet-based picture activity schedules: Acquisition and preference. *Behavior Modification, 41*(5), 647–664.

Hall, L. J., McClannahan, L. E., & Krantz, P. J. (1995). Promoting independence in integrated classrooms by teaching aides to use activity schedules and decreased prompts. *Education & Training in Mental Retardation & Developmental Disabilities, 30*(3), 208–217.

Krantz, P. J., MacDuff, M. T., & McClannahan, L. E. (1993). Programming participation in family activities for children with autism: Parents' use of photographic activity schedules. *Journal of Applied Behavior Analysis, 26*(1), 137–138.

Lequia, J., Machalicek, W., & Rispoli, M. J. (2012). Effects of activity schedules on challenging behavior exhibited in children with autism spectrum disorders: A systematic review. *Research in Autism Spectrum Disorders, 6*(1), 480–492.

MacDuff, G. S., Krantz, P. J., & McClannahan, L. E. (1993). Teaching children with autism to use photographic activity schedules: Maintenance and generalization of complex response chains. *Journal of Applied Behavior Analysis, 26*(1), 89–97.

Massey, N., & Wheeler, J. J. (2000). Acquisition and generalization of activity schedules and their effects on task engagement in a young child with autism in an inclusive pre-school classroom. *Education & Training in Mental Retardation & Developmental Disabilities, 35*(3), 326–335.

Morrison, R. S., Sainato, D. M., Benchaaban, D., & Endo, S. (2002). Increasing play skills of children with autism using activity schedules and correspondence training. *Journal of Early Intervention, 25*(1), 58–72.

O'Reilly, M., Sigafoos, J., Lancioni, G., Edrisinha, C., & Andrews, A. (2005). An examination of the effects of a classroom activity schedule on levels of self-injury and engagement for a child with severe autism. *Journal of Autism and Developmental Disorders, 35*, 305–311.

Schmit, J., Alper, S., Raschke, D., & Ryndak, D. (2000). Effects of using a photographic cueing package during routine school transitions with a child who has autism. *Mental Retardation, 38*(2), 131–137.

Independent Work Systems

Hume, K., & Odom, S. (2007). Effects of an individual work system on the independent functioning of students with autism. *Journal of Autism and Developmental Disabilities, 37*, 1166–1180.

Hume, K., & Reynolds, B. (2010). Implementing work systems across the school day: Increasing engagement in students with autism spectrum disorders. *Preventing School Failure: Alternative Education for Children and Youth, 54*(4), 228–237.

Odom, S. L., Boyd, B., Hall, L., & Hume, K. (2010). Evaluation of comprehensive treatment models for individuals with autism spectrum disorders. *Journal of Autism and Developmental Disorders, 40*, 425–436.

O'Hara, M., & Hall, L. J. (2014). Increasing engagement of students with autism at recess through structured work systems. *Education and Training in Autism and Developmental Disabilities, 49*(4), 568–575.

Panerai, S., Ferrante, L., & Zingale, M. (2002). Benefits of the treatment and education of autistic and communication handicapped children (TEACCH) programme [sic] as compared with a non-specific approach. *Journal of Intellectual Disability Research, 46*, 318–327.

Panerai, S., Zingale, M., Trubia, G., Finocchiaro, M., Zuccarello, R., Ferri, R., & Elia, M. (2009). Special education versus inclusive education: The role of the TEACCH program. *Journal of Autism and Developmental Disorders, 39*(6), 874–882.

Schopler, E. (1994). A statewide program for the treatment and education of autistic and related communication handicapped children (TEACCH). *Child and Adolescent Psychiatric Clinics, 3*(1), 91–103.

Virues-Ortega, J., Julio, F. M., & Pastor-Barriuso, R. (2013). The TEACCH program for children and adults with autism: A meta-analysis of intervention studies. *Clinical Psychology Review, 33*(8), 940–953.

Scripting

Akers, J. S., Pyle, N., Higbee, T. S., Pyle, D., & Gerencser, K. R. (2016). A synthesis of script fading effects with individuals with autism spectrum disorder: A 20-year review. *Review Journal of Autism and Developmental Disorders, 3*(1), 1–17.

Brown, J. L., Krantz, P. J., McClannahan, L. E., & Poulson, C. L. (2008). Using script fading to promote natural environment stimulus control of verbal interactions among youths with autism. *Research in Autism Spectrum Disorders, 2*(3), 480–497.

Charlop-Christy, M. H., & Kelso, S. E. (2003). Teaching children with autism conversational speech using a cue card/written script program. *Education & Treatment of Children, 26*(2), 108–127.

Ganz, J. B., Kaylor, M., Bourgeois, B., & Hadden, K. (2008). The impact of social scripts and visual cues on verbal communication in three children with autism spectrum disorders. *Focus on Autism and Other Developmental Disabilities, 23*(2), 79–94.

Goldstein, H., Kaczmarek, L., Pennington, R., & Shafer, K. (1992). Peer-mediated intervention: Attending to, commenting on, and acknowledging the behavior of preschoolers with autism. *Journal of Applied Behavior Analysis, 25*(2), 289–305.

Hundert, J., Rowe, S., & Harrison, E. (2014). The combined effects of social script training and peer buddies on generalized peer interaction of children with ASD in inclusive classrooms. *Focus on Autism and Other Developmental Disabilities, 29*(4), 206–215.

Krantz, P. J., & McClannahan, L. E. (1993). Teaching children with autism to initiate to peers: Effects of a script-fading procedure. *Journal of Applied Behavior Analysis, 26*(1), 121–132.

Krantz, P. J., & McClannahan, L. E. (1998). Social interaction skills for children with autism: A script-fading procedure for beginning readers. *Journal of Applied Behavior Analysis, 31*(2), 191–202.

Leaf, J. B., Ferguson, J. L., Cihon, J. H., Milne, C. M., Leaf, R., & McEachin, J. (2020). A critical review of social narratives. *Journal of Developmental and Physical Disabilities, 32*(2), 241–256.

Ledbetter-Cho, K., Lang, R., Davenport, K., Moore, M., Lee, A., Howell, A., Drew, C., Dawson, D., Charlop, M. H., Falcomata, T., & O'Reilly, M. (2015). Effects of script training on the peer-to-peer communication of children with autism spectrum disorder. *Journal of Applied Behavior Analysis, 48*(4), 785–799.

Loveland, K. A., & Tunali, B. (1991). Social scripts for conversational interactions in autism and Down syndrome. *Journal of Autism and Developmental Disorders, 21*(2), 177–186.

Parker, D., & Kamps, D. (2011). Effects of task analysis and self-monitoring for children with autism in multiple social settings. *Focus on Autism and Other Developmental Disorders, 26*(3), 131–142.

Sarokoff, R. A., Taylor, B. A., & Poulson, C. L. (2001). Teaching children with autism to engage in conversational exchanges: Script fading with embedded textual stimuli. *Journal of Applied Behavior Analysis, 34*(1), 81–84.

Stevenson, C. L., Krantz, P. J., & McClannahan, L. E. (2000). Social interaction skills for children with autism: A script-fading procedure for nonreaders. *Behavioral Interventions, 15*(1), 1–20.

Wichnick-Gillis, A. M., Vener, S. M., & Poulson, C. L. (2016). The effect of a script-fading procedure on social interactions among young children with autism. *Research in Autism Spectrum Disorders, 26*, 1–9.

Power Cards

Angell, M. E., Nicholson, J. K., Watts, E. H., & Blum, C. (2011). Using a multicomponent adapted power card strategy to decrease latency during interactivity transitions for three children with developmental disabilities. *Focus on Autism and Other Developmental Disabilities, 26*(4), 206–217.

Baker, M., Koegel, R., & Koegel, L. K. (1998). Increasing the social behavior of young children with autism using their obsessive behaviors. *Journal of the Association for Persons With Severe Handicaps, 23*(4), 300–308.

Campbell, A., & Tincani, M. (2011). The power card strategy: Strength-based intervention to increase direction following of children with autism spectrum disorder. *Journal of Positive Behavior Interventions, 13*(4), 240–249.

Charlop-Christy, M., & Haymes, L. (1998). Using objects of obsession as token reinforcers for children with autism. *Journal of Autism and Developmental Disorders, 28*(3), 189–197.

Daubert, A., Hornstein, S., & Tincani, M. (2015). Effects of a modified power card strategy on turn taking and social commenting of children with autism spectrum disorder playing board games. *Journal of Developmental and Physical Disabilities, 27*(1), 93–110.

Davis, K. M., Boon, R. T., Cihak, D. F., & Fore, C. (2010). Power cards to improve conversational skills in adolescents with Asperger syndrome. *Focus on Autism and Other Developmental Disabilities, 25*(1), 12–22.

Dettmer, S., Simpson, R., Myles, B. S., & Ganz, J. (2000). The use of visual supports to facilitate transitions of students with autism. *Focus on Autism and Other Developmental Disabilities, 15*(3), 163–169.

Gagnon, E. (2001). *Power cards: Using special interests to motivate children and youth with Asperger syndrome and autism.* AAPC Publishing.

Hinton, M., & Kern, L. (1999). Increasing homework completion by incorporating student interests. *Journal of Positive Behavior Interventions, 1*(4), 231–234, 241.

Keeling, K., Myles, B. S., Gagnon, E., & Simpson, R. L. (2003). Using the power card strategy to teach sportsmanship skills to a child with autism. *Focus on Autism and Other Developmental Disabilities, 18*(2), 105–111.

Kuttler, S., Myles, B. S., & Carlson. (1998). The use of social stories to reduce precursors to tantrum behavior in a student with autism. *Focus on Autism and Other Developmental Disabilities, 13*(3), 176–182.

Leaf, J. B., Ferguson, J. L., Cihon, J. H., Milne, C. M., Leaf, R., & McEachin, J. (2020). A critical review of social narratives. *Journal of Developmental and Physical Disabilities, 32*(2), 241–256.

Quill, K. (1992). Instructional considerations for young children with autism: The rationale for visually cued instruction. *Journal of Autism and Developmental Disorders, 27*(6), 697–714.

Quill, K. (1995). Visually cued instruction for children with autism and pervasive developmental disorders. *Focus on Autistic Behavior, 10*(3), 10–20.

Section 3: Language Training
Introduction

Grow, L., & LeBlanc, L. (2013). Teaching receptive language skills: Recommendations for instructors. *Behavior Analysis in Practice, 6*(1), 56–75.

Verbal Behavior-Based Intervention

DeSouza, A. A., Akers, J. S., & Fisher, W. W. (2017). Empirical application of Skinner's verbal behavior to interventions for children with autism: A review. *The Analysis of Verbal Behavior, 33*(2), 229–259.

Dipuglia, A., & Miklos, M. (2014). *Instructing functional verbal behavior in public schools: Recent outcomes from the PATTAN Autism initiative.* Symposium presented at the 40th Annual Convention of the Association for Behavior Analysis, Chicago, IL.

Dixon, M. R. (2014). *PEAK relational training system: Direct training module.* Shawnee Scientific Press.

Dymond, S., O'Hora, D., Whelan, R., & O'Donovan, A. (2006). Citation analysis of Skinner's verbal behavior: 1984–2004. *The Behavior Analyst, 29*(1), 75–88.

Eshleman, J. W. (1991). Quantified trends in the history of verbal behavior research. *The Analysis of Verbal Behavior, 9*(1), 61–80.

Guess, D., Sailor, W., & Baer, D. M. (1976). *Functional speech and language training for the severely handicapped: (Steps 43–60) Size, relation and location.* H & H Enterprises.

Mason, L. L., & Andrews, A. (2019). The verbal behavior stimulus control ratio equation: A quantification of language. *Perspectives on Behavior Science, 42*(2), 323–343.

Partington, J. (2006). *Assessment of Basic Language and Learning Skills-Revised (The ABLLS-R).* Behavior Analysts.

Petursdottir, A. I. (2018). The current status of the experimental analysis of verbal behavior. *Behavior Analysis: Research and Practice, 18*(2), 151.

Petursdottir, A. I., & Devine, B. (2017). The impact of Verbal Behavior on the scholarly literature from 2005 to 2016. *The Analysis of Verbal Behavior, 33*, 212–228.

Skinner, B. F. (1957). *Verbal behavior.* Appleton-Century-Crofts.

Sundberg, M. L. (2008). *VB-MAPP Verbal Behavior Milestones Assessment and Placement Program:Aa language and social skills assessment program for children with autism or other developmental disabilities: guide.* Mark Sundberg.

Williams, G., & Greer, R. D. (1993). A comparison of verbal-behavior and linguistic-communication curricula for training developmentally delayed adolescents to acquire and maintain vocal speech. *Behaviorology, 1*(1), 31–46.

Augmentative and Alternative Communication (AAC)

Aydin, O., & Diken, I. (2020). Studies comparing augmentative and alternative communication systems (AAC) applications for individuals with autism spectrum disorder: A systematic review and meta-analysis. *Education and Training in Autism and Developmental Disabilities, 55*(2), 119–141.

Biggs, E. E., Carter, E. W., & Gilson, C. B. (2018). Systematic review of interventions involving aided AAC modeling for children with complex communication needs. *American Journal on Intellectual and Developmental Disabilities, 123*(5), 443–473.

Bridges, S. J. (2004). Multicultural issues in augmentative and alternative communication and language. *Topics in Language Disorders, 24*(1), 62–75.

Bryen, D. N., & Joyce, D. G. (1986). Sign language and the severely handicapped. *Journal of Special Education, 20*(2), 183–194.

Crowe, B., Machalicek, W., Wei, Q., Drew, C., & Ganz, J. (2021). Augmentative and alternative communication for children with intellectual and developmental disability: A mega-review of the literature. *Journal of Developmental and Physical Disabilities, 34*(1), 1–42.

Feeley, K., & Jones, E. (2012). Instructional strategies. In S. S. Johnston, J. Reichle, K. M. Feeley, & E. A. Jones, *AAC strategies for individuals with moderate to severe disabilities* (pp. 119–154). Brookes.

Ganz, J. B., Earles-Vollrath, T. L., Heath, A. K., Parker, R. I., Rispoli, M. J., & Duran, J. B. (2011). A meta-analysis of single case research studies on aided augmentative and alternative communication systems with individuals with autism spectrum disorders. *Journal of Autism and Developmental Disorders, 42*(1), 60–74.

Ganz, J. B., Pustejovsky, J. E., Reichle, J., Vannest, K., Foster, M., Fuller, M. C., Pierson, L. M., Wattanawongwan, S., Bernal, A., Chen, M., Haas, A., Skov, R., Smith, S. D., & Yllades, V. (in press[a]). Selecting communicative interventions targets for school-aged participants with ASD and ID: A single-case experimental design meta-analysis. *Review Journal of Autism and Developmental Disorders.*

Ganz, J. B., Pustejovsky, J. E., Reichle, J., Vannest, K., Foster, M., Haas, A., Pierson, L. M., Wattanawongwan, S., Bernal, A., Chen, M., Skov, R., & Smith, S. D. (2022). Considering instructional contexts in AAC interventions for people with ASD and/or IDD experiencing complex communicative needs: A single case design meta-analysis. *Review Journal of Autism and Developmental Disorders.*

Ganz, J. B., Pustejovsky, J. E., Reichle, J., Vannest, K., Foster, M., Pierson, L. M., Wattanawongwan, S., Bernal, A., Chen, M., Haas, A., Sallese, M. R., Skov, R., & Smith, S. D. (in press[b]). Participant characteristics predicting communication outcomes in AAC implementation for individuals with ASD and IDD: A systematic review and meta-analysis. *Augmentative and Alternative Communication.*

Ganz, J. B., & Simpson, R. L. (2018). *Interventions for individuals with autism disorder and complex communication needs.* Brookes.

Gevarter, C., & Zamora, C. (2018). Naturalistic speech-generating device interventions for children with complex communication needs: A systematic review of single-subject studies. *American Journal of Speech-Language Pathology, 27*(3), 1073–1090.

Holyfield, C., Drager, K. D. R., Kremkow, J. M. D., & Light, J. (2017). Systematic review of AAC intervention research for adolescents and adults with autism spectrum disorder. *Augmentative and Alternative Communication, 33*(4), 201–212.

Huer, M. B., Parette, H. P., JR, & Saenz, T. I. (2001). Conversations with Mexican Americans regarding children with disabilities and augmentative and alternative communication. *Communication Disorders Quarterly, 22*(4), 197–206.

Hume, K., Steinbrenner, J. R., Odom, S. L., Morin, K. L., Nowell, S. W., Tomaszewski, B., Szendrey, S., McIntyre, N. S., Yücesoy-Özkan, S., & Savage, M. N. (2021). Evidence-based practices for children, youth, and young adults with autism: Third generation review. *Journal of Autism and Developmental Disorders, 51*(11), 4013–4032.

Johnston, S. S., Blue, C., Gevarter, C., Ivy, S., & Stegenga, S. (2020). Opportunity barriers and promising practices for supporting individuals with complex communication needs. *Current Developmental Disorders Reports, 7*, 100–108.

Kulkarni, S. S., & Parmar, J. (2017). Culturally and linguistically diverse student and family perspectives of AAC. *Augmentative and Alternative Communication, 33*(3), 170–180.

Logan, K., Iacono, T., & Trembath, D. (2016). A systematic review of research into aided AAC to increase social-communication functions in children with autism spectrum disorder. *Augmentative and Alternative Communication, 33*(1), 51–64.

Lorah, E. R., Holyfield, C., Miller, J., Griffen, B., & Lindbloom, C. (2022). A systematic review of research comparing mobile technology speech-generating devices to other AAC modes with individuals with autism spectrum disorder. *Journal of Developmental and Physical Disabilities, 34*(2), 187–210.

Morin, K. L., Ganz, J. B., Gregori, E. V., Foster, M. J., Gerow, S. L., Genç-Tosun, D., & Hong, E. R. (2018). A systematic quality review of high-tech AAC interventions as an evidence-based practice. *Augmentative and Alternative Communication, 34*(2), 104–117.

Pennington, R. (2019). *Applied behavior analysis for everyone: Principles and practices explained by applied researchers who use them.* AAPC Publishing.

White, E. N., Ayres, K. M., Snyder, S. K., Cagliani, R. R., & Ledford, J. R. (2021). Augmentative and alternative communication and speech production for individuals with ASD: A systematic review. *Journal of Autism and Developmental Disorders, 51*(11), 4199–4212.

Aided Language Modeling

Biggs, E. E. (2017). *Embedding peer implemented AAC modeling within a peer network intervention for students with complex communication needs* (No. 10753368) [Doctoral dissertations, Vanderbilt University]. ProQuest Dissertation and Theses database.

Cafiero, J. (2001). The effect of an augmentative communication intervention on the communication, behavior, and academic program of an adolescent with autism. *Focus on Autism and Other Developmental Disabilities, 16*, 179–193.

Chipinka, M. (2016). *The effects of augmented input on receptive and expressive language for native augmentative and alternative communication (AAC) users during shared storybook readings* (Publication No. 10196441) [Doctoral dissertation, California State University, Long Beach]. ProQuest Dissertation and Theses database.

Dorney, K. E., & Erickson, K. (2019). Transactions within a classroom-based AAC intervention with preschool students with autism spectrum disorders: A mixed-methods investigation. *Exceptionality Education International, 29*(2), 42–58.

Drager, K. D., Postal, V. J., Carrolus, L., Castellano, M., Gagliano, C., & Glynn, J. (2006). The effect of aided language modeling on symbol comprehension and production in 2 preschoolers with autism. *American Journal of Speech-Language Pathology, 15*(2), 112.

Hall, A. R. (2014). *Semantically-based therapeutic approach through aided language stimulation in a child with autism spectrum disorder* (No. 1563349) [Doctoral dissertation, Duquesne]. ProQuest Dissertation and Theses database.

Novak, J. A. (2016). *The effects of an aided modeling intervention on adolescents with autism who use AAC* (No. 10247399) [Doctoral Dissertation, Nova Southeastern University]. ProQuest Dissertation and Theses database.

Assistive Technology (AT)

Bernard-Opitz, V., Siriam, N., & Nakhoda-Sapuan, S. (2001). Enhancing social problem solving in children with autism and normal children through computer-assisted instruction. *Journal of Autism and Developmental Disorders, 31*(4), 377–384.

Chen, S. H. A., & Bernard-Opitz, V. (1993). Comparison of personal and computer-assisted instruction for children with autism. *Mental Retardation, 31*(6), 368–376.

David, D. O., Costescu, C. A., Matu, S., Szentagotai, A., & Dobrean, A. (2020). Effects of a robot-enhanced intervention for children with ASD on teaching turn-taking skills. *Journal of Educational Computing Research, 58*(1), 29–62.

Dyches, T. T. (1998). Effects of switch training on the communication of children with autism and severe disabilities. *Focus on Autism and Other Developmental Disabilities, 13*(3), 151–162.

Ennis-Cole, D., & Smith, D. (2011). Assistive technology and autism: Expanding the technology role of the school librarian. *School Libraries Worldwide, 17*(2), 86–98.

Fagea, C., Conseld, C., Etechegoyhenb, K., Amestoyb, A., Bouyard, M., Mazone, C., & Sauzeone, H. (2019). An emotion regulation app for school inclusion of children with ASD: Design principles and evaluation. *Computers & Education, 131*, 1–21.

Fletcher-Watson, S. (2014). A targeted review of computer-assisted learning for people with autism spectrum disorders: Towards a consistent methodology. *Review Journal of Autism Developmental Disorder, 1*, 87–100.

Flores, M., Hill, D. A., Faciane, L. B., Edwards, M. A., Tapley, S. C., & Dowling, S. J. (2014). The Apple iPad assistive technology for story-based interventions. *Journal of Special Education Technology, 29*(2), 27–37.

Ganz, J. B., Boles, M. B., Goodwyn, F. D., & Flores, M. M. (2014). Efficacy of handheld electron visual supports to enhance vocabulary in children with ASD. *Focus on Autism and Other Developmental Disabilities, 29*(1), 3–12.

Gentry, T., Kriner, R., Sima, A., McDonough, J., & Wehman, P. (2015). Reducing the need for personal supports among workers with autism using an iPod Touch as an assistive technology: Delayed randomized control trial. *Journal of Autism and Developmental Disorders, 45*, 669–684.

Hagiwara, T., & Myles, B. S. (1999). A multimedia social story intervention: Teaching skills to children with autism. *Focus on Autism and Other Developmental Disabilities, 14*(2), 82–95.

Hopkins, I. M., Gower, M. W., Perez, T. A., Smith, D. S., Amthor, F. R., Wimsatt, F. C., & Biasini, F. J. (2011). Avatar assistant: Improving social skills in students with an ASD through computer-based instruction. *Journal of Autism and Developmental Disabilities, 41*, 1543–1555.

Individuals with Disabilities Education Act, 20 U.S.C. § 300.105 (2004).

Lee, G. T., Ju, X., & Jin, N. (2021). Brief report: Using computer-assisted multiple exemplar instruction to facilitate the development of bidirectional naming for children with autism spectrum disorders. *Journal of Autism and Developmental Disorders, 51*, 417–4722.

McKissick, B. R., Davis, L. L., Spooner, F., Fisher, L. B., & Graves, C. (2018). Using computer-assisted instruction to teach science vocabulary to students with autism spectrum disorders and intellectual disabilities. *Rural Special Education Quarterly, 37*(4), 207–218.

Odom, S. L., Thompson, J. L., Hedges, S., Boyd, B. A., Dykstra, J. R., Duda, M. A., Szidon, K. L., Smith, L. E., & Bord, A. (2015). Technology-aided interventions for adolescents with autism spectrum disorder. *Journal of Autism and Developmental Disorders, 45*, 3805–3819.

Pellecchia, M., Marcus, S. C., Spaulding, C., Seidman, M., Xie, M., Rump, K., Reisinger, E. M., & Mandel, D. S. (2020). Randomized trial of a computer-assisted intervention for children with autism in schools. *Journal of Academy of Child and Adolescent Psychiatry, 59*(3), 373–380.

Pellegrino, A. J., Higbee, T. S., Becerra, L. A., & Gerencser, K. R. (2020). Comparing stimuli delivered table versus flashcards on receptive labeling in children with autism spectrum disorder. *Journal of Behavioral Education, 29*, 606–618.

Saadatzi, M. N., Pennington, R. C., Welch, K. C., & Graham, J. H. (2018). Effects of a robot peer on the acquisition and observational learning of sight words in young adults with autism spectrum disorders. *Journal of Special Education Technology, 33*(4), 284–296.

Sandgreen, H., Frederiksen, L. H., & Bilenberg, N. (2021). Digital interventions for autism spectrum disorder: A meta-analysis. *Journal of Autism and Developmental Disorders, 51*, 3138–3152.

Schlosser, R. W., Blischak, D. M., Belfiore, P. J., Bartley, C., & Barnett, N. (1998). Effects of synthetic speech output and orthographic feedback on spelling in a student with autism: A preliminary study. *Journal of Autism and Developmental Disorders, 28*(4), 309–319.

Tjus, T., Heinmann, M., & Nelson, K. E. (2001). Interaction patterns between children and their teachers when using a specific multi-media and communication strategy: Observations from children with autism and mixed intellectual disabilities. *Autism: The International Journal of Research and Practice, 5*(2), 175–187.

Van Laarhoven, T., Carreon, A., Bonneau, W., & Largerhausen, A. (2018). Comparing mobile technologies for teaching vocational skills to individuals with autism spectrum disorders and/or intellectual disabilities using universally-designed prompting systems. *Journal of Autism and Developmental Disorders, 48*, 2516–2529.

Whalen, C., Moss, D., Ilan, A. B., Vaupel, M., Fielding, P., MacDonald, K., Cernich, S. & Symon, J. (2010). Efficacy of TeachTown: Basics computer-assisted intervention for the Intensive Comprehensive Autism Program in Los Angeles Unified School District. *Autism, 14*(3), 179–197.

Picture Exchange Communication System (PECS®)

Bondy, A. S., & Frost, L. A. (1993). Mands across the water: A report on the application of the picture-exchange communication system in Peru. *The Behavior Analyst, 16*(1), 123–128.

Bondy, A. S., & Frost, L. A. (1994). The picture exchange communication system. *Focus on Autistic Behavior, 9*(3), 1–19.

Carr, D., & Felce, J. (2007). The effects of PECS teaching to phase III on the communicative interactions between children with autism and their teachers. *Journal of Autism and Developmental Disorders, 37*(4), 724–737.

Charlop-Christy, M. H., Carpenter, M., Le, L., LeBlanc, L. A., & Kellet, K. (2002). Using the Picture Exchange Communication System (PECS) with children with autism: Assessment of PECS acquisition, speech, social-communicative behavior, and problem behavior. *Journal of Applied Behavior Analysis, 35*(3), 213–231.

Dogoe, M. S., Banda, D. R., & Lock, R. H. (2010). Acquisition and generalization of the picture exchange communication system behaviors across settings, persons, and stimulus classes with three students with autism. *Education and Training in Autism and Developmental Disabilities, 45*(2), 216–229.

Ganz, J. B., Simpson, R. L., & Corbin-Newsome, J. (2008). The impact of the Picture Exchange Communication System on requesting and speech development in preschoolers with autism spectrum disorders and similar characteristics. *Research in Autism Spectrum Disorders, 2*(1), 157–169.

Greenberg, A. L., Tomaino, M. A. E., & Charlop, M. H. (2012). Assessing generalization of the Picture Exchange Communication System in children with autism. *Journal of Developmental and Physical Disabilities, 24*(6), 539–558.

Hu, X., & Lee, G. (2019). Effects of PECS on the emergence of vocal mands and the reduction of aggressive behavior across settings for a child with autism. *Behavioral Disorders, 44*(4), 215–226.

Lerna, A., Esposito, D., Conson, M., Russo, L., & Massagli, A. (2012). Social-communicative effects of the Picture Exchange Communication System (PECS) in Autism Spectrum Disorders: Social-communicative effects of PECS in ASD. *International Journal of Language & Communication Disorders, 47*(5), 609–617.

McCoy, A., & McNaughton, D. (2018). Training education professionals to use the Picture exchange communication system: A review of the literature. *Behavior Analysis in Practice, 12*(3), 667–676.

Sulzer-Azaroff, B., Hoffman, A. O., Horton, C. B., Bondy, A., & Frost, L. (2009). The Picture Exchange Communication System (PECS): What do the data say? *Focus on Autism and Other Developmental Disabilities, 24*(2), 89–103.

Section 4: Social, Emotional, and Behavioral Skills Training

Introduction

Aldred, C., Green, J., & Adams, C. (2004). A new social communication intervention for children with autism: Pilot randomized controlled treatment study suggesting effectiveness. *Journal of Child Psychology and Psychiatry, 45*(8), 1420–1430.

Bauminger, N. (2002). The facilitation of social-emotional understanding and social interaction in high-functioning children with autism: Intervention outcomes. *Journal of Autism and Developmental Disorders, 32*(4), 283–298.

Bauminger, N. (2007a). Brief report: Group social-multimodal intervention for HFASD. *Journal of Autism and Developmental Disorders, 37,* 1605–1615.

Bauminger, N. (2007b). Brief report: Individual social-multi-modal intervention for HFASD *Journal of Autism and Developmental Disorders, 37,* 1593–1604.

Crooke, P. J., Hendrix R. E., & Rachman, J. Y. (2008). Brief report: Measuring the effectiveness of teaching social thinking to children with Asperger syndrome (AS) and high functioning autism (HFA). *Journal of Autism and Developmental Disorders 38,* 581–591.

Faherty, C. (2000). *Asperger's? What does it mean?* Future Horizons.

Ingersoll, B., Dvortcsak, A., Whalen, C., & Sikora, D. (2005). The effects of a developmental, social-pragmatic language intervention on rate of expressive language production in young children with autistic spectrum disorders. *Focus on Autism and Other Developmental Disabilities, 20*(4), 213–222.

Keen, D., Rodger, S., Doussin, K., & Braithwaite, M. (2007). A pilot study of the effects of a social-pragmatic intervention on the communication and symbolic play of children with autism. *Autism, 11*(1), 63–71.

Koning, C., Magill-Evans, J. M., Volden, J., & Dick, B., (2011). Efficacy of cognitive behavior therapy-based social skills intervention for school-aged boys with autism spectrum disorders. *Research in Autism Spectrum Disorders 7,* 1282–1290.

Laugeson, E. A., Frankel, F., Mogil, A., Dillon, A. R., & Mogil C. (2012). Evidence-based social skills training for adolescents with autism spectrum disorders: The UCLA PEERS program. *Journal of Autism and Developmental Disorders 42,* 1025–1036.

Loncola, J. A., & Craig-Unkefer, L. (2005). Teaching social communication skills to young urban children with autism. *Education and Training in Developmental Disabilities, 40*(3), 243–263.

Lopata, C., Donnelly, J. P., Thomeer, M. L., Rodgers, J. D., Lodi-Smith, J., Booth, A. J., & Volker, M. A. (2020). Moderators of school intervention outcomes for children with autism spectrum disorder. *Journal of Abnormal Child Psychology 48,* 1105–1114.

Lopata, C., Thomeer, M. L., Volker, M. A., & Nida, R. E. (2006). Effectiveness of a cognitive-behavioral treatment on the social behaviors of children with Asperger disorder. *Focus on Autism and Other Developmental Disabilities 21*(4), 237–244.

McAfee, J. (2002). *Navigating the social world.* Future Horizons.

Moore, S. T. (2002). *Asperger Syndrome and the elementary school experience: Practical solution for academic and social difficulties.* Autism Asperger.

Myles, B. S., & Adreon, D. (2001). *Asperger Syndrome and adolescence: Practical solutions for school success.* Autism Asperger.

Myles, B. S., & Simpson, R. L. (2003). *Asperger syndrome: A guide for educators and parents.* Pro-Ed.

Myles, B. S., & Southwick, J. (1999). *Asperger Syndrome and difficult moments: Practical solutions for tantrums, rage, and meltdowns.* Autism Asperger.

Reaven, J., Blakeley-Smith, A., Culhane-Shelburne, K., & Hepburn, S. (2012). Group cognitive behavior therapy for children with high-functioning autism spectrum disorders and anxiety: A randomized trial. *Journal of Child Psychology and Psychiatry, 53*(4), 410–419.

Rodgers, J. D., Thomeer, M. L., Lopata, C., Volker, M. A., Lee, G. K., McDonald, C. A., Smith, R. A., Biscotto, A. A. (2015). RCT of a psychosocial treatment for children with high-functioning ASD: Supplemental analyses of treatment effects on facial emotion encoding. *Journal of Developmental and Physical Disabilities, 27*(2), 207–221.

Salt, J., Shemilt, J., Sellars, V., Boyd, S., Coulson, T., & McCool, S. (2002). The Scottish Centre for autism preschool treatment programme. II: The results of a controlled treatment outcome study. *Autism: The International Journal of Research and Practice, 6*(1), 33–46.

Sofronoff, K., Attwood, T., & Hinton, S. (2005). A randomised controlled trial of a CBT intervention for anxiety in children with Asperger syndrome. *Journal of Child Psychology and Psychiatry, 46*(11), 1152–1160.

Sofronoff, K., Attwood, T., Hinton, S., & Levin, I. (2007). A randomized controlled trial of a cognitive behavioural intervention for anger management in children diagnosed with Asperger syndrome. *Journal of Autism and Developmental Disorders, 37*(7), 1203–1214.

Winner, M. G. (2000). *Inside out: What makes the person with social-cognitive deficits tick?* Author.

Wood, J. J., Drahota, A., Sze, K., Har, K., Chiu, A., & Langer, D. A., (2009). Cognitive behavioral therapy for anxiety in children with autism spectrum disorders: A randomized, controlled trial. *Journal of Child Psychology and Psychiatry 50*(3), 224–234.

Behavioral Skills Training (BST)

Bornstein, M. R., Bellack, A. S., & Hersen, M. (1977). Social skills training for unassertive children: A multiple baseline analysis. *Journal of Applied Behavior Analysis, 10,* 183–195.

Brady, J. P. (1984). Social skills training for psychiatric patients, II: Clinical outcome studies. *The American Journal of Psychiatry, 141,* 491–498.

Breidenbach, D. C. (1984). Behavioral skills training for students: A preventive program. *Children and Schools, 6,* 231–240.

Burke, R. V., Andersen, M. N., Bowen, S. L., Howard, M. R., & Allen, K. D. (2010). Evaluation of two instruction methods to increase employment options for young adults with autism spectrum disorders. *Research in Developmental Disabilities, 31*(6), 1223–1233.

Gianoumis, S., Seiverling, L., & Sturmey, P. (2012). The effects of behavior skills training on correct teacher implementation of natural language paradigm teaching skills and child behavior. *Behavioral Interventions, 27*(2), 57–74.

Gunby, K. V., Carr, J. E., & Leblanc, L. A. (2010). Teaching abduction prevention skills to children with autism. *Journal of Applied Behavior Analysis, 43*(1), 107–112.

Kornacki, L. T., Ringdahl, J. E., Sjostrom, A., & Nuernberger, J. E. (2013). A component analysis of a behavioral skills training package used to teach conversational skills to young adults with autism spectrum and other developmental disorders. *Research in Autism Spectrum Disorders, 7*, 1370–1376.

Leaf, J. B., Townley-Cocran, D., Taubman, M., Cihon, J. H., Oppenheim-Leaf, M., Kassardjian, A., Leaf, R., McEachin, J., & Pentz, T. G. (2015). The teaching interaction procedure and behavioral skills training for individuals diagnosed with autism spectrum disorder: A review and commentary. *Review Journal of Autism and Developmental Disorders, 2*, 402–413.

Ledbetter-Cho, K., Lang, R., Davenport, K., Moore, M., Lee, A., O'Reilly, M., Watkins, L., & Falcomata, T. (2016). Behavioral skills training to improve the abduction-prevention skills of children with autism. *Behavior Analysis in Practice, 9*(3), 266–270.

Miltenberger, R. G. (2012). *Behavioral skills training procedures* (*Behavior modification: Principles and procedures*, pp. 251–269). Cengage Learning.

Nuernberger, J. E., Ringdahl, J. E., Vargo, K. K., Crumpecker, A. C., & Gunnarsson, K. F. (2013). Using a behavioral skills training package to teach conversation skills to young adults with autism spectrum disorders. *Research in Autism Spectrum Disorders, 7*(2), 411–417.

Palmen, A., & Didden, R. (2012). Task engagement in young adults with high-functioning autism spectrum disorders: Generalization effects of behavioral skills training. *Research in Autism Spectrum Disorders, 6*(4), 1377–1388.

Ryan, G., Brady, S., Holloway, J., & Lydon, H. (2017). Increasing appropriate conversation skills using a behavioral skills training package for adults with intellectual disability and autism spectrum disorder. *Journal of Intellectual and Developmental Disabilities, 23*(4), 567–580.

Seiverling, L., Pantelides, M., Ruiz, H. H., & Sturmey, P. (2010). The effect of behavioral skills training with general-case training on staff chaining of child vocalizations within natural language paradigm. *Behavioral Interventions, 25*(1), 53–75.

Seiverling, L., Williams, K., Sturmey, P., & Hart, S. (2012). Effects of behavioral skills training on parental treatment of children's food selectivity. *Journal of Applied Behavior Analysis, 45*(1), 197–203.

Taras, M. E., Matson, J. L., & Leary, C. (1988). Training social interpersonal skills in two autistic children. *Journal of Behavioral Therapy and Experimental Psychiatry, 19*, 275–280.

Turner, S. M., Hersen, M., & Bellack, A. S. (1978). Social skills training to teach prosocial behaviors in an organically impaired and retarded patient. *Journal of Behavior Therapy and Experimental Psychiatry, 9*, 253–258.

Whitehill, M. B., Hersen, M., & Bellack, A. S. (1980). Conversation skills training for socially isolated children. *Behaviour Research and Therapy, 18*, 217–225.

The Teaching Interaction Procedure (TIP)

Dotson, W. H., Leaf, J. B., Sheldon, J. B., & Sherman, J. A. (2010). Group teaching of conversational skills to adolescents on the autism spectrum. *Research in Autism Spectrum Disorders, 4*, 199–209.

Dotson, W. H., Richman, D. M., Abby, L., Thompson, S., & Plotner, A. (2013). Teaching skills related to self-employment to adults with developmental disabilities: An analog analysis. *Research in Developmental Disabilities, 34*, 2336–2350.

Ferguson, B. R., Gillis, J. M., & Sevlever, M. (2013). A brief group intervention using video games to teach sportsmanship skills to children with autism spectrum disorders. *Child and Family Behavior Therapy, 35*, 293–306.

Hui Shyuan, N. A., Schulze, K., Rudrud, E., & Leaf, J. B. (2016). Using the teaching interactions procedure to teach social skills to children with autism and intellectual disability. *American Journal on Intellectual and Developmental Disabilities, 121*(6), 501–519.

Kassardjian, A., Leaf, J. B., Ravid, D., Leaf, J. A., Alcalay, A., Dale, S., Tsuji, K., Taubman, M., Leaf, R., McEachin, J., & Oppenheim-Leaf, M. L. (2014). Comparing the teaching interaction procedure to social stories: A replication study. *Journal of Autism and Developmental Disorders, 44*(9), 2329–2340.

Kassardjian, A., Taubman, M., Rudrud, E., Leaf, J. B., Edwards, A., McEachin, J., Leaf, R., & Schulze, K. (2013). Utilizing teaching interactions to facilitate social skills in the natural environment. *Education and Training in Autism and Developmental Disabilities, 48*, 245–257.

Leaf, J. B., Dotson, W. H., Oppenheim, M. L., Sheldon, J. B., & Sherman, J. A. (2010). The effectiveness of a group teaching interaction procedure for teaching social skills to young children with a pervasive developmental disorder. *Research in Autism Spectrum Disorders, 4*, 186–198.

Leaf, J. B., Oppenheim-Leaf, M. L., Call, N. A., Sheldon, J. B., Sherman, J. A., Taubman, M., McEachin, J., Dayharsh, J., & Leaf, R. (2012). Comparing the teaching interaction procedure to social stories for people with autism. *Journal of Applied Behavior Analysis, 45*(2), 281–298.

Leaf, J. B., Taubman, M., Bloomfield, S., Palos-Rafues, L., Leaf, R., McEachin, J., & Oppenheim, M. L. (2009). Increasing social skills and pro-social behavior for three children diagnosed with autism through the use of a teaching package. *Research in Autism Spectrum Disorders, 3*, 275–289.

Leaf, J. B., Townley-Cocran, D., Taubman, M., Cihon, J. H., Oppenheim-Leaf, M., Kassardjian, A., Leaf, R., McEachin, J., & Pentz, T. G. (2015). The teaching interaction procedure and behavioral skills training for individuals diagnosed with autism spectrum disorder: A review and commentary. *Review Journal of Autism and Developmental Disorders, 2*, 402–413.

Leaf, J. B., Tsuji, K. H., Griggs, B., Edwards, A., Taubman, M., McEachin, J., Leaf, R., & Oppenheim-Leaf, M. L. (2012). Teaching social skills to children with autism using the cool versus not cool procedure. *Education and Training in Autism and Developmental Disabilities, 47*, 165–175.

Oppenheim-Leaf, M. L., Leaf, J. B., & Call, N. A. (2012a). Teaching board games to two children with an autism spectrum disorder. *Journal of Developmental and Physical Disabilities, 24*, 347–358.

Oppenheim-Leaf, M. L., Leaf, J. B., Dozier, C., Sheldon, J. B., & Sherman, J. A. (2012b). Teaching typically developing children to promote social play with their siblings. *Research in Autism Spectrum Disorders, 6*, 777–791.

Peters, B., Tullis, C. A., & Gallagher, P. A. (2016). Effects of a group teaching interaction procedure on the social skills of students with autism spectrum disorders. *Education and Training in Autism and Developmental Disabilities, 51*(4), 421–433.

Video Modeling

Bandura, A. (1969). Social-learning theory of identificatory processes. In D. A. Goslin (Ed.), *Handbook of socialization theory and research* (2nd ed., pp. 213–262). Guilford Press.

Fragale, C. L. (2014). Video modeling interventions to improve play skills of children with autism spectrum disorders: A systematic literature review. *Review Journal of Autism and Developmental Disorders, 1*(3), 165–178.

Ledoux Galligan, M. R., Suhrheinrich, J., & Kraemer, R. K. (2022). Video modeling for high school students with autism spectrum disorder. *Journal of Special Education Technology, 37*(1), 126–134.

Qi, C. H., Barton, E. E., Collier, M., & Lin, Y. L. (2018). A systematic review of single-case research studies on using video modeling interventions to improve social communication skills for individuals with autism spectrum disorder. *Focus on Autism and Other Developmental Disabilities, 33*(4), 249–257.

Rayner, C., Denholm, C., & Sigafoos, J. (2009). Video-based intervention for individuals with autism: Key questions that remain unanswered. *Research in Autism Spectrum Disorders, 3*(2), 291–303.

Yakubova, G., Hughes, E. M., & Shinaberry, M. (2016). Learning with technology: Video modeling with concrete–representational–abstract sequencing for students with autism spectrum disorder, *Journal of Autism and Developmental Disorders, 46*, 2349–2362.

Cool Versus Not Cool

Au, A., Mountjoy, T. Leaf, J. B., Leaf, R., Taubman, M., McEachin, J., & Tsuji, K. (2016). Teaching social behaviour to individuals diagnosed with autism spectrum disorder using the cool versus not cool procedure in a small group instructional format. *Journal of Intellectual and Developmental Disability, 41*(2), 115–124.

Cihon, J. H., Ferguson, J. L., Lee, M., Leaf, J. B., Leaf, R., & McEachin, J. (2021). Evaluating the cool versus cool procedure via telehealth. *Behavior Analysis in Practice, 15*, 260–268.

Leaf, J. A., Leaf, J. B., Milne, C., Townley-Cochran, D., Oppenheim-Leaf, M. L., Cihon, J. H., Taubman, M., McEachin, J., & Leaf, R. (2016). The effects of the cool versus not cool procedure to teach social game play to individuals diagnosed with autism spectrum disorder. *Behavior Analysis in Practice, 9*, 34–49.

Leaf, J. B., Taubman, M., Leaf, J., Dale, S., Tsuji, K., Kassardjian, A., Alcalay, A., Milne, C., Mitchell, E., Townley-Cochran, D., Leaf, R., & McEachin, J. (2015). Teaching social interaction skills using cool versus not cool. *Child & Family Behavior Therapy, 37*(4), 321–334.

Leaf, J. B., Taubman, M., Milne, C., Dale, S., Leaf, J., Townley-Cochran, D., Tsuju, L., Kassardjian, A., Alcalay, A., Leaf, R., & McEachin, J. (2016). Teaching social communication skills using a cool versus not cool procedure plus role-playing and a social skills taxonomy. *Education and Treatment of Children, 39*(1), 44–63.

Leaf, J. B., Tsuji, K. H., Griggs, B., Edwards, A., Taubman, M., McEachin, J., Leaf, R., & Oppenheim-Leaf, M. L. (2012). Teaching social skills to children with autism using the cool versus not cool procedure. *Education and Training in Autism and Developmental Disabilities, 47*(2), 165–175.

The Program for the Education and Enrichment of Relationship Skills (PEERS®)

Hill, T. L., Gray, S. A. O., Baker, C. N., Boggs, K., Carey, E., Johnson, C., Kamps, J. L., & Varela, R. E. (2017). A pilot study examining the effects of PEERS Program on social skills and anxiety in adolescents with autism spectrum disorders. *Journal of Developmental & Physical Disabilities, 29*(5), 797–808.

Laugeson, E. A., Ellingsen, R., Sanderson, J., Tucci, L., & Bates, S. (2014). The ABC's of teaching social skills to adolescents with autism spectrum disorder in the classroom: The UCLA PEERS© program. *Journal of Autism and Developmental Disorders, 44*(9), 2244–2256.

Laugeson, E. A., & Frankel, F. (2010). *Social skills for teenagers with developmental and autism spectrum disorders: The PEERS treatment manual.* Routledge.

Laugeson, E. A., Frankel, F., Mogil, C., & Dillon, A.R. (2009). Parent-assisted social skills training to improve friendships in teens with autism spectrum disorders. *Journal on Autism and Other Developmental Disorders, 39*, 596–606.

McVey, A. J., Dolan, B. K., Willar, K. S., Pleiss, S., Karst, J. S., Casnar, C. L., Caiozzo, C., Voght, E. M., Gordon, N. S., & Van Hecke, A. V. (2016). A replication and extension of the PEERS® for young adults social skills intervention: Examining effects on social skills and social anxiety in young adults with autism spectrum disorder. *Journal of Autism and Developmental Disorders, 46*(12), 3739–3754.

Schiltz, H. K., McVey, A. J., Dolan, B. K., Willar, K. S., Pleiss, Sheryl, K., Jeffrey, S., Carson, A. M., Caiozzo, C., Vogt, E. M., Yund, B. D., & Hecke, A. V. (2017). Changes in depressive symptoms among adolescents with ASD completing the PEERS® social skills intervention. *Journal of Autism and Developmental Disorders, 48*(3), 834–843.

Schohl, K. A., Van Hecke, A. V., Carson, A. M., Dolan, B., Karst, J., & Stevens, S. (2014). A replication and extension of the PEERS intervention: Examining effects on social skills and social anxiety in adolescents with autism spectrum disorders. *Journal of Autism and Developmental Disorders, 44*(3), 532–545.

Tripathi, I., Estabillo, J. A., Moody, C. T., & Laugeson, E. A. (2022). Long-term treatment outcomes of PEERS® for preschoolers: A parent-mediated social skills training program for children with autism spectrum disorder. *Journal of Autism and Developmental Disorders, 52*, 2610–2626.

Yoo, H. J., Bahn, G., Cho, I. H., Kim, E. K., Kim, J. H., Min, J. W., Lee, W. H., Seo, J. S., Jun, S. S., Bong, G., Cho, S., Shin, M. S., Kim, B. N., Kim, J. W., Park, S., & Laugeson, E. A. (2014). A randomized controlled trial of the Korean version of the PEERS parent-assisted social skills training program for teens with ASD. *Autism Research, 7*(1), 145–61.

Theory of Mind Interventions

Baron-Cohen, S. (1995) *Mindblindness: An essay on autism and theory of mind.* MIT Press/Bradford.

Baron-Cohen, S. Leslie, A. M., & Frith, U. (1985). Does the autistic child have a "theory of mind?" *Cognition, 21*, 37–46.

Begeer, S., Gevers, C., Clifford, P., Verhoeve, M., Kat, K., Hoddenbach, E., & Boer, F. (2011). Theory of mind training in children with autism: A randomized controlled trial. *Journal of Autism and Developmental Disorders, 41*(8), 997–1006.

Begeer, S., Howlin, P., Hoddenbach, E., Clauser, C., Lindauer, R., Clifford, P., Gevers, C., Boer, F., & Koot, H. M. (2015). Effects and moderators of a short theory of mind intervention for children with autism spectrum disorder: A randomized controlled trial. *Autism Research, 8*(6), 738–748.

Bell, K. S., & Kirby, J. R. (2002). Teaching emotion and belief as mindreading instruction for children with autism. *Developmental Disabilities Bulletin, 30*(1), 16–50.

Chin, H. Y., & Bernard-Opitz, V. (2000). Teaching conversational skills to children with autism: Effect on the development of a theory of mind. *Journal of Autism and Developmental Disorders, 30*(6), 569–583.

de Veld, D. M. J., Howlin, P., Hoddenbach, E., Mulder, F., Wolf, I., Koot, H. M., Lindauer, R., & Begeer, S. (2017). Moderating effects of parental characteristics on the effectiveness of a theory of mind training for children with autism: A randomized controlled trial. *Journal of Autism and Developmental Disorders, 47*(7), 1987–1997.

Feng, H., Lo, Y. Y., Tsai, S., & Cartledge, G. (2008). The effects of theory-of-mind and social skill training on the social competence of a sixth-grade student with autism. *Journal of Positive Behavior Interventions, 10*(4), 228–242.

Fisher, N., & Happe, F. (2005). A training study of theory of mind and executive function in children with autistic spectrum disorders. *Journal of Autism and Developmental Disorders, 35*(6), 757–771.

Gevers, C., Clifford, P., Mager, M., & Boer, F. (2006). Brief report: A theory-of-mind-based social-cognition training program for school-aged children with pervasive developmental disorders: An open study of its effectiveness. *Journal of Autism and Developmental Disorders, 36*(4), 567–571.

Golan, O., & Baron-Cohen, S. (2006). Systemizing empathy: Teaching adults with Asperger syndrome or high-functioning autism to recognize complex emotions using interactive multimedia. *Development and Psychopathology, 18*, 591–617.

McGregor, E., Whiten, A. & Blackburn, P. (1998). Transfer of the picture-in-the-head analogy to natural contexts to aid false belief understanding in autism. *Autism, 2*, 367–387.

Ozonoff, S., & Miller, J. N. (1995). Teaching theory of mind: A new approach to social skills training for individuals with autism. *Journal of Autism and Developmental Disorders, 25*(4), 415–433.

Perner, J., Frith, U., Leslie, A. M., & Leekam, S. R. (1989). Exploration of the autistic child's theory of mind: Knowledge, belief, and communication. *Child Development, 60*, 689–700.

Premack, D., & Woodruff, G. (1978). Does the chimpanzee have a theory of mind? *Behavioural and Brain Sciences, 4*, 515–526.

Steerneman, P., Jackson, S., Pelzer, H., & Muris, P. (1996). Children with social handicaps: An intervention programme using a theory of mind approach. *Clinical Child Psychology and Psychiatry, 1*, 251–263.

Swettenham, J. (1996). Can children with autism be taught to understand false belief using computers? *Journal of Child Psychology and Psychiatry and Allied Disciplines, 37*, 157–165.

Szumski, G., Smogorzewska, J., Grygiel, P., & Orlando, A. M. (2017). Examining the effectiveness of naturalistic social skills training in developing social skills and theory of mind in preschoolers with ASD. *Journal of Autism and Developmental Disorders, 49*(7), 2822–2837.

Turner-Brown, L. M., Perry, T. D., Dichter, G. S., Bodfish, J. W., & Penn, D. L. (2008). Brief report: Feasibility of social cognition and interaction training for adults with high functioning autism. *Research in Autism Spectrum Disorders, 3*, 1014–1022.

Wellman, H. M. (1990). *The child's theory of mind.* MIT Press.

Wellman, H. M., Baron-Cohen, S., Caswell, R., Gomez, J. C., Swettenham, J., Toye, E., & Lagattuta, K. (2002). Thought-bubbles help children with autism acquire an alternative to a theory of mind. *Autism, 6*(4), 343–363.

Wellman, H. M., Cross, D., & Watson, J. (2001). Meta-analysis of theory-of-mind development: The truth about false belief. *Child Development, 72*, 655–684.

White, S., Hill, E., Happe, F., & Frith, U. (2009). Revisiting the strange stories: Revealing mentalizing impairments in autism. *Child Development, 80*, 1097–1117.

Social Decision-Making Strategies

Bieber, J. (1994). *Learning disabilities and social skills with Richard LaVoie: Last one picked . . . First one picked on.* Public Broadcasting Service.

Bock, M. A. (2001). SODA strategy: Enhancing the social interaction skills of youngsters with Asperger Syndrome. *Intervention in School and Clinic, 36*(5), 272–278.

Bock, M. A. (2007). The impact of social-behavioral learning strategy training on the social interaction skills of four students with Asperger syndrome. *Focus on Autism and Other Developmental Disabilities, 22*(2), 88–95.

Leaf, J. B., Ferguson, J. L., Cihon, J. H., Milne, C. M., Leaf, R., & McEachin, J. (2020). A critical review of social narratives. *Journal of Developmental and Physical Disabilities, 32*(2), 241–256.

Myles, B. S., & Simpson, R. L. (2003). *Asperger syndrome: A guide for educators and parents.* ProEd.

Roosa, J. B. (1995). *Men on the move: Competence and cooperation: Conflict resolution and beyond.* Author.

Cartooning

Ahmed-Husain, S., & Dunsmuir, S. (2014). An evaluation of the effectiveness of comic strip conversations in promoting the inclusion of young people with autism spectrum disorder in secondary schools. *International Journal of Developmental Disabilities, 60*(2), 89–108.

Anderson, S., & Morris, J. (2006). Cognitive behavior therapy for people with Asperger syndrome. *Behavioral and Cognitive Psychotherapy, 34*, 293–303.

Arwood, E., & Brown, M. M. (1999). *A guide to cartooning and flowcharting: See the ideas.* Apricot.

Charman, T., & Baron-Cohen, S. (1992). Understanding drawings and beliefs: A further test of the metarepresentation theory of autism. *Journal of Child Psychology and Psychiatry, 33*, 1105–1112.

Coogle, C. G., Ahmed, S., Aljaffal, M. A., Alsheef, M. Y., & Hamdi, H. A. (2017). Social narrative strategies to support children with autism spectrum disorder. *Early Childhood Education Journal, 46*, 445–450.

Dettmer, S., Simpson, R. L., Myles, B. S., & Ganz, J. B. (2000). The use of visual supports to facilitate transitions of students with autism. *Focus on Autism and Other Developmental Disabilities, 14*(3), 163–169.

Gray, C. (1994). *Comic strip conversations: Colorful, illustrated interactions with students with autism and related disorders.* Jenison Public Schools.

Hagiwara, T., & Myles, B. S. (1999). A multimedia social story intervention: Teaching skills to children with autism. *Focus on Autism and Other Developmental Disabilities, 14*(2), 82–95.

Howlin, P., Baron-Cohen, S., & Hadwin, J. (1999). *Teaching children with autism to mind-read: A practical guide.* Wiley.

Hutchins, T. L., & Prelock, P. A. (2006). Using social stories and comic strip conversations to promote socially valid outcomes for children with autism. *Seminars in Speech and Language, 27*(1), 47–59.

Hutchins, T. L., & Prelock, P. A. (2008). Supporting theory of mind development: Considerations and recommendations for professionals providing services to individuals with autism spectrum disorder. *Topics in Language Disorders, 28*(4), 340–364.

Hutchins, T. L., & Prelock, P. A. (2012). Parents' perspective of their children's social behavior: The social validity of Social Stories™ and comic strip conversations. *Journal of Positive Behavior Interventions, 15*(3), 156–168.

Kuttler, S., Myles, B. S., & Carlson, J. K. (1998). The use of social stories to reduce precursors of tantrum behavior in a student with autism. *Focus on Autism and Other Developmental Disabilities, 13*(3), 176–182.

Leaf, J. B., Ferguson, J. L., Cihon, J. H., Milne, C. M., Leaf, R., & McEachin, J. (2020). A critical review of social narratives. *Journal of Developmental and Physical Disabilities, 32*, 241–256.

Leekam, S. R., & Perner, J. (1991). Does the autistic child have a metarepresentational deficit? *Cognition, 40*, 203–218.

Leslie, A. M., & Thaiss, L. (1992). Domain specificity in conceptual development: Neuropsychological evidence from autism. *Cognition, 43*, 225–251.

MacDuff, G. S., Krantz, P. J., & McClannahan, L. E. (1993). Teaching children with autism to use photographic activity schedules: Maintenance and generalization of complex response chains. *Journal of Applied Behavior Analysis, 26*(1), 89–97.

McGregor, E., Whiten, A., & Blackburn, P. (1998). Teaching theory of mind by highlighting intention and illustrating thoughts: A comparison of their effectiveness with three-year-olds and autistic subjects. *British Journal of Developmental Psychology, 16*, 281–300.

Parsons, S., & Mitchell, P. (1999). What children with autism understand about thoughts and thought bubbles. *Autism, 3*(1), 17–38.

Pierson, M. R., & Glaeser, B. C. (2005). Extension of research on social skills training using comic strip conversations to students without autism. *Education and Training in Developmental Disabilities, 40*(3), 279–284.

Pierson, M. R., & Glaeser, B. C. (2007). Using comic strip conversations to increase social satisfaction and decrease loneliness in students with autism spectrum disorder. *Education and Training in Developmental Disabilities, 42*(4), 460–466.

Rogers, M. F., & Myles, S. B. (2001). Using social stories and comic strip conversations to interpret social situations for an adolescent with Asperger syndrome. *Intervention in School and Clinic, 36*(5), 310–313.

Swaggart, B. L., Gagnon, E., Bock, S. J., Earles, T. L., Quinn, C., Myles, B. S., & Simpson, R. L. (1995). Using social stories to teach social and behavioral skills to children with autism. *Focus on Autistic Behavior, 10*(1), 116.

Self-Management Interventions

Aljadeff-Abergel, E., Schenk, Y., Walmsley, C., Peterson, S. M., Frieder, J. E., & Acker, N. (2015). The effectiveness of self-management interventions for children with autism—A literature review. *Research in Autism Spectrum Disorders, 18*, 34–50.

Baumeister, R. F., Heatherton, T. F., & Tice, D. M. (1994). *Losing control: How and why people fail at self-regulation.* Academic Press.

Blair, C., & Diamond, A. (2008). Biological processes in prevention and intervention: The promotion of self-regulation as a means of preventing school failure. *Development and psychopathology, 20*(3), 899–911.

Bouck, E. C., Savage, M., Meyer, N. K., Taber-Doughty, T., & Hunley, M. (2014). High-tech or low-tech? Comparing self-monitoring systems to increase task independence for students with autism. *Focus on Autism and Other Developmental Disabilities, 29*(3), 156–167.

Carr, M. E. (2016). Self-management of challenging behaviors associated with autism spectrum disorder: A meta-analysis. *Australian Psychologist, 51*(4), 316–333.

Carr, M. E., Moore, D. W., & Anderson, A. (2014). Self-management interventions on students with autism: A meta-analysis of single-subject research. *Exceptional Children, 81*(1), 28–44.

Chia, G. L. C., Anderson, A., & McLean, L. A. (2018). Use of technology to support self-management in individuals with autism: Systematic review. *Review Journal of Autism and Developmental Disorders, 5*(2), 142–155.

Crutchfield, S. A., Mason, R. A., Chambers, A., Wills, H. P., & Mason, B. A. (2015). Use of a self-monitoring application to reduce stereotypic behavior in adolescents with autism: A preliminary investigation of I-Connect. *Journal of Autism and Developmental Disorders, 45*(5), 1146–1155.

Crutchfield, S. A., & Wood, L. (2018). *How to use cognitive behavioral interventions and self-management interventions.* ProEd.

Davis, J. L., Mason, B. A., Davis, H. S., Mason, R. A., & Crutchfield, S. A. (2016). Self-monitoring interventions for students with ASD: A meta-analysis of school-based research. *Review Journal of Autism and Developmental Disorders, 3*(3), 196–208.

Ganz, J. B. (2008). Self-monitoring across age and ability levels: Teaching students to implement their own positive behavioral interventions. *Preventing School Failure: Alternative Education for Children and Youth, 53*(1), 39–48.

Koegel, R. L., & Koegel, L. K. (1990). Extended reductions in stereotypic behavior of students with autism through a self-management treatment package. *Journal of Applied Behavior Analysis, 23*(1), 119–127.

Lee, S. H., Simpson, R. L., & Shogren, K. A. (2007). Effects and implications of self-management for students with autism: A meta-analysis. *Focus on Autism and Other Developmental Disabilities, 22*(1), 2–13.

Mace, F. C., & Kratochwill, T. R. (1988). Self-monitoring. In J. C. Witt, S. N. Elliott, & F. M. Gresham (Eds.), *Handbook of behavior therapy in education* (pp. 489–522). Springer.

Parker, D., & Kamps, D. (2011). Effects of task analysis and self-monitoring for children with autism in multiple social settings. *Focus on Autism and Other Developmental Disabilities, 26*(3), 131–142.

Quinn, C., Swaggart, B. L., & Myles, B. S. (1994). Implementing cognitive behavior management programs for persons with autism: Guidelines for practitioners. *Focus on Autistic Behavior, 9*(4), 1–13.

Shapiro, E. S., & Cole, C. L. (1994). *Behavior change in the classroom: Self-management interventions.* Guilford Press.

Southall C. M., Gast D. L. (2011). Self-management procedures: A comparison across the autism spectrum. *Education and Training in Autism and Developmental Disabilities, 46,* 155–171.

Wills, H. P., Mason, R., Huffman, J. M., & Heitzman-Powell, L. (2019). Implementing self-monitoring to reduce inappropriate vocalizations of an adult with autism in the workplace. *Research in Autism Spectrum Disorders, 58,* 9–18.

The Coping Cat Program

Beidas, R. S., Benjamin, C. L., Puleo, C. M., Edmunds, J. M., & Kendall, P. C. (2010). Flexible applications of the coping cat program for anxious youth. *Cognitive and Behavioral Practice, 17*(2), 142–153.

Ferris, C. A. (2017). *School-based application of the brief coping cat program for children with autism spectrum disorder and co-occurring anxiety* [Electronic thesis or dissertation, University of Dayton]. OhioLINK Electronic Theses and Dissertations Center.

Kendall, P. C. (1994). Treating anxiety disorders in children: Results of a randomized clinical trial. *Journal of Consulting and Clinical Psychology, 62*(1), 100–110.

Kendall, P. C., Crawley, S. A., Benjamin C. L., & Mauro, C. F. (2013). *The brief coping cat: Therapist manual for the 8-session workbook.* Workbook Publishing.

Kendall, P. C., Flannery-Schroeder, E., Panichelli-Mindel, S., Southam-Gerow, M., Henin, A., & Warman, M. (1997). Therapy for youths with anxiety disorders: A second randomized clinical trial. *Journal of Consulting and Clinical Psychology, 65,* 366–380.

Kendall, P. C., & Hedtke, K. A. (2006). *Cognitive-behavioral therapy for anxious youth: Therapist manual* (3rd ed.). Workbook Publishing.

McNally Keehn, R. H., Lincoln, A. J., Brown, M. Z., & Chavira, D. A. (2013). The coping cat program for children with autism spectrum disorder: A pilot randomized controlled trial. *Journal of Autism and Developmental Disorders, 43,* 57–67.

Sulkowski, M. L., Joyce, D. K., & Storch, E. A. (2012). Treating childhood anxiety in schools: Service delivery in a response to intervention paradigm. *Journal of Child and Family Studies, 21,* 938–947.

Walters, S., Loades, M., & Russell, A. (2016). A systematic review of effective modifications to cognitive behavioural therapy for young people with autism spectrum disorders. *Review Journal of Autism and Developmental Disorders, 3,* 137–153.

Weiss, J. A., Viecili, M. A., & Bohr, Y. (2015). Parenting stress as a correlate of cognitive behavior therapy responsiveness in children with autism spectrum disorders and anxiety. *Focus on Autism and Other Developmental Disabilities, 30*(3), 154–164.

Mindfulness-Based Interventions

Blanck, P., Perleth, S., Heidenreich, T., Kröger, P., Ditzen, B., Bents, H., & Mander, J. (2018). Effects of mindfulness exercises as stand-alone intervention on symptoms of anxiety and depression: Systematic review and meta-analysis. *Behaviour Research and Therapy, 102*, 25–35.

Conner, C. M., & White, S. W. (2018). Brief report: Feasibility and preliminary efficacy of individual mindfulness therapy for adults with autism spectrum disorder. *Journal of Autism and Developmental Disorders, 48*(1), 290–300.

de Bruin, E. I., Blom, R., Smit, F. M., van Steensel, F. J., & Bögels, S. M. (2015). MYmind: Mindfulness training for youngsters with autism spectrum disorders and their parents. *Autism, 19*(8), 906–914.

Goldberg, S. B., Tucker, R. P., Greene, P. A., Davidson, R. J., Wampold, B. E., Kearney, D. J., & Simpson, T. L. (2018). Mindfulness-based interventions for psychiatric disorders: A systematic review and meta-analysis *Clinical Psychology Review, 59*, 52–60.

Hartley, M., Dorstyn, D., & Due, C. (2019). Mindfulness for children and adults with autism spectrum disorder and their caregivers: A meta-analysis. *Journal of Autism and Developmental Disorders, 49*(10), 4306–4319.

Hwang, Y. S., Kearney, P., Klieve, H., Lang, W., & Roberts, J. (2015). Cultivating mind: Mindfulness interventions for children with autism spectrum disorder and problem behaviours, and their mothers. *Journal of Child and Family Studies, 24*(10), 3093–3106.

Kabat-Zinn, J. (2002). Commentary on Majumdar et al: Mindfulness meditation for health. *Journal of Alternative and Complementary Medicine, (8)*6, 731–735.

Kabat-Zinn, J. (2003a). Mindfulness-based interventions in context: Past, present, and future. *Clinical Psychology: Science and Practice, 10*(2), 144–156.

Kabat-Zinn, J. (2003b). Mindfulness-based stress reduction (MBSR). *Constructivism in the Human Sciences, 8*(2), 73.

Ridderinkhof, A., de Bruin, E. I., Blom, R., & Bögels, S. M. (2018). Mindfulness-based program for children with autism spectrum disorder and their parents: Direct and long-term improvements. *Mindfulness, 9*(3), 773–791.

Segal, Z. V., Williams, M., & Teasdale, J. (2018). *Mindfulness-based cognitive therapy for depression.* Guilford Press.

Singh, N. N., Lancioni, G. E., Manikam, R., Winton, A. S., Singh, A. N., Singh, J., & Singh, A. D. (2011). A mindfulness-based strategy for self-management of aggressive behavior in adolescents with autism. *Research in Autism Spectrum Disorders, 5*(3), 1153–1158.

Singh, N. N., Wahler, R. G., Adkins, A. D., Myers, R. E., & Mindfulness Research Group. (2003). Soles of the feet: A mindfulness-based self-control intervention for aggression by an individual with mild mental retardation and mental illness. *Research in Developmental Disabilities, 24*(3), 158–169.

Spek, A. A., Van Ham, N. C., & Nyklíček, I. (2013). Mindfulness-based therapy in adults with an autism spectrum disorder: A randomized controlled trial. *Research in Developmental Disabilities, 34*(1), 246–253.

Social Thinking™

Baker-Ericzén, M. J., Fitch, M. A., Kinnear, M., Jenkins, M. M., Twamley, E. W., Smith, L., Montano, G., Feder, J., Crooke, P. J., Winner, M. G., & Leon, J. (2018). Development of the supported employment, comprehensive cognitive enhancement, and social skills program for adults on the autism spectrum: Results of initial study. *Autism, 22*(1), 6–19.

Bauminger, N. (2002). The facilitation of social-emotional understanding and social interaction in high-functioning children with autism: Intervention outcomes. *Journal of Autism and Developmental Disorders, 32*(4), 283–298.

Bauminger, N. (2007a). Brief report: Group social-multimodal intervention for HFASD. *Journal of Autism Developmental Disorders, 37*, 1605–1615.

Bauminger, N. (2007b). Brief report: Individual social-multi-modal intervention for HFASD. *Journal of Autism Developmental Disorders, 37*, 1593–1604.

Clavenna-Deane, B., Pearson, M., & Hansen, B. (2020). The impact of social communication on employment success for adolescents with autism spectrum disorders. *Journal of the American Academy of Special Education Professionals*, 68–85.

Crooke, P. J., Hendrix, R. E., & Rachman, J. Y. (2008). Brief report: Measuring the effectiveness of teaching social thinking to children with Asperger syndrome (AS) and high functioning autism (HFA). *Journal of Autism and Developmental Disorders, 38*(3), 581–591.

Crooke, P. J., & Winner, M. G. (2016). Social Thinking® methodology: Evidence-based or empirically supported? A response to Leaf et al. (2016). *Behavior Analysis in Practice, 9*(4), 403–408.

Koning, C., Magill-Evans, J. M., Volden, J., & Dick, B. (2013). Efficacy of cognitive behavior therapy-based social skills intervention for school-aged boys with autism spectrum disorders. *Research in Autism Spectrum Disorders, 7*, 1282–1290.

Laugeson, E. A., Frankel, F., Gantman, A., Dillon, A. R., & Mogil, C. (2012). Evidence-based social skills training for adolescents with autism spectrum disorders: The UCLA PEERS program. *Journal of Autism Developmental Disorders, 42*, 1025–1036.

Leaf, J. B., Kassardjian, A., Oppenheim-Leaf, M. L., Cihon, J. H., Taubman, M., Leaf, R., & McEachin, J. (2016). Social Thinking®: Science, pseudoscience, or anti-science? *Behavior Analytic Practice, 9*(2), 152–157.

Lee, K. Y. S., Crooke, P. J., Lui, A. L. Y., Kan, P. P. K., Mark, Y., van Hasselt, C. A., & Tong, M. C. F. (2016). The outcome of a social cognitive training for mainstream adolescents with social communication deficits in a Chinese community. *International Journal of Disability, Development and Education, 63*(2), 201–223.

Lopata, C., Thomeer, M. L., Volker, M. A., & Nida, R. E. (2006). Effectiveness of a cognitive-behavioral treatment on the social behaviors of children with Asperger disorder. *Focus on Autism and Other Developmental Disabilities, 21*(4), 237–244.

Methodology: Social Thinking's Three-Part Process of Social Thinking. (n.d.) https://www.socialthinking.com/social-thinking-methodology

Nowell, S. W., Watson, L. R., Boyd, B., & Klinger, L. G. (2019). Efficacy study of a social communication and self-regulation intervention for school-age children with autism spectrum disorder: A randomized controlled trial. *Language Speech and Hearing Serving Schools, 50*(3), 416–433.

Winner, M. G. (2000). *Inside out: What makes the person with social cognitive deficits tick?* Think Social Publishing.

Winner, M. G. (2005). *Think social! A Social Thinking® curriculum for school-age students.* Think Social Publishing.

Winner, M. G. (2007a). *Thinking about you thinking about me* (2nd ed.). Think Social Publishing.

Winner, M. G. (2007b). *Social behavior mapping© connecting behavior, emotions, and consequences across the day.* Think Social Publishing.

Winner, M. G. (2008). *A politically incorrect look at evidence-based practices and teaching social skills: A literature review and discussion.* Think Social Publishing.

Winner, M. G. (2013). *Why teach Social Thinking®?* Think Social Publishing.

Wood, J. J., Drahota, A., Sze, K., Har, K., Chiu, A., & Langer, D. A. (2009). Cognitive behavioral therapy for anxiety in children with autism spectrum disorders: A randomized, controlled trial. *Journal of Child Psychology and Psychiatry, 50*(3), 224–234.

The Zones of Regulation™

Anderson, S., Bartholow, B., Snow, J., Stratiner, M., Nash, J., & Jirikowic, T. (2017). Developing self-regulation in children with FASD using the Zones of Regulation. *SIS Quarterly Practice Connections, 2*(4), 5–7.

Conklin, M., & Jairam, D. (2021). The effects of co-teaching Zones of Regulation on elementary students' social, emotional, and academic risk behaviors. *Advanced Journal of Social Science, 8*(1), 171–192.

Kuypers, L. (2011). *The Zones of Regulation: A curriculum designed to foster self-regulation and emotional control.* Social Thinking Publishing.

Ochocki, S., Frey, A. J., Patterson, D. A., Herron, F., Beck, N., & Dupper, D. R. (2020). Evaluating the Zones of Regulation® intervention to improve the self-control of elementary students. *International Journal of School Social Work, 5*(2).

Valkanos, C., Huber-Lee, C., & Cahill, S. M. (2016). Blue–yellow–red–green: Teaching self-regulation skills to first graders. *OT Practice, 21*(12), 7–11.

The Incredible 5-Point Scale

Baron-Cohen, S. (2009). Autism: The empathizing-systemizing (E-S) theory. *Annals of the New York Academy of Sciences, 1156*(1), 68–80.

Buron, K. D., & Curtis, M. (2003). *The incredible 5-point scale: Assisting students with autism spectrum disorders in understanding social interactions and controlling their emotional responses.* AAPC Publishing.

Buron, K. D., & Curtis, M. (2012). *The incredible 5-point scale: The significantly improved and expanded second edition.* AAPC Publishing.

McBride Pinheiro, B. A. (2019). *Exploring the incredible 5-point scale: Impact on target behaviors in preschool.* [Doctoral dissertation, University of Rhode Island]. Open Access Dissertations.

Social Narratives/Story-Based Interventions

Gray, C. (n.d.). *Comparison of social stories TM 10.0 – 10.2 Criteria.* Author.

Gray, C. A. (1998). Social stories and comic strip conversations with students with Asperger syndrome and high-functioning autism. In E. Schopler & G. B. Mesibov (Eds.), Asperger syndrome or high functioning autism?. New York: Plenum.

Gray, C. (2000). *The new social story book.* Future Horizons.

Gray, C. A. (2004). Social Stories™ 10.0: The new defining criteria & guidelines. *Jenison Autism Journal, 15,* 2–21.

Gray, C. A., & Garand, J. D. (1993). Social stories: Improving responses of students with autism with accurate social information. *Focus on Autistic Behavior, 8*(1), 1–10.

Karal, M. A., & Wolfe, P. S. (2018). Social story effectiveness on social interaction for students with autism. *Education and Training in Autism and Developmental Disabilities, 53*(1), 44–58.

Kokina, A., & Kern, L. (2010). Social story™ interventions for students with autism disorders: A meta-analysis. *Journal of Autism and Developmental Disabilities, 40*(7), 812–826.

Leaf, J. B., Oppenheim-Leaf, M. L., Leaf, R. B., Taubman, M., McEachin, J., Parker, T., Waks, A. B., & Mountjoy, T. (2015). What is the proof? A methodological review of studies that have utilized social stories. *Education and Training in Autism and Developmental Disabilities, 50*(2), 127–141.

Milne, C. M., Leaf, J. B., Cihon, J. H., Ferguson, J. L. McEachin, R. L., & Ferguson, J. L. (2020). What is the proof now? An updated methodological review of research on social stories. *Education and Training in Autism and Developmental Disabilities, 55*(3), 264–276.

Qi, C. H., Baron, E. E., Collier, M., Ling Lin, Y., & Montoya, C. (2018). A systematic review of effects of social stories interventions for individuals with autism spectrum disorder. *Focus on Autism and Other Developmental Disabilities, 33*(1), 25–34.

Reynhout, G., & Carter, M. (2006). Social stories for children with disabilities. *Journal of Autism and Developmental Disorders, 36,* 445–469.

Rhodes, C. (2014). Do social stories help to decrease disruptive behaviour in children with autistic spectrum disorders? A review of the published literature. *Journal of Intellectual Disabilities, 18,* 35–50.

Styles, A. (2011). Social StoriesTM: does the research evidence support the popularity?. *Educational Psychology in Practice, 27*(4), 415–436.

Zimmerman, K. N., & Ledford, J. R. (2017). Beyond ASD: Evidence for the effectiveness of social narratives. *Journal of Early Intervention, 39*(3), 199–217.

FaceSay™

Hopkins, I. M., Gower, M. W., Perez, T. A., Smith, D. S., Amthor, F. R., Wimsatt, C. F., & Biasini, F. J. (2011). Avatar assistant: Improving social skills in students with autism spectrum disorder through a computer-based intervention. *Journal of Autism and Developmental Disorders, 41*, 1543–1555.

Kaufman, A. S. (1990). *Kaufman brief intelligence test, second edition: KBIT-II*. Circle Pines, MN: AGS, American Guidance Service.

Kouo, J. L., & Egel, A. L. (2016). The effectiveness of interventions in teaching emotion recognition to children with autism spectrum disorders. *Revised Journal of Autism Developmental Disorders, 3*, 254–265.

Rice, L. M., Wall, C. A., Fogel, A., & Shic, F. (2015). Computer-assisted face processing instruction improves emotion recognition, mentalizing, and social skills in students with ASD. *Journal of Autism and Developmental Disorders, 45*(7), 2176–2186.

Symbionica, LLC. (n.d.). *FaceSay™*. http://www.facesay.com/

Mind Reading: The Interactive Guide to Emotions

Baron-Cohen, S., Golan, O., Wheelwright, S., & Hill, J. J. (2004). *Mind reading: The interactive guide to emotions*. Jessica Kingsley Publishers.

Golan, O., & Baron-Cohen, S. (2006a). Systemizing empathy: Teaching adults with Asperger Syndrome or high-functioning autism to recognize complex emotions using interactive multimedia. *Development and Psychopathology, 18*, 591–617.

Golan, O., & Baron-Cohen, S. (2006b). *Systemizing empathy: Teaching emotion recognition to people with autism using interactive multimedia*. Doctoral dissertation, University of Cambridge.

LaCava, P. G., Golan, O., Baron-Cohen, S., & Myles, B. S. (2007). Using assistive technology to teach emotion recognition to students with Asperger syndrome: A pilot study. *Remedial and Special Education, 28*(3), 174–181.

LaCava, P. G., Rankin, A., Mahlios, E., Cook, K., & Simpson, R. L. (2010). A single case design evaluation of a software and tutor intervention addressing emotion recognition and social interaction in four boys with ASD. *Autism, 14*, 161–178.

Lopata, C., Thomeer, M. L., Rodgers, D. J., Donnelly, J. P., & McDonald, C. A. (2016). RCT of mind reading as a component of a psychosocial treatment for high-functioning children with ASD. *Research in Autism Spectrum Disorders, 21*, 25–36.

Lopata, C., Thomeer, M. L., Rodgers, D. J., Donnelly, J. P., McDonald, C. A., Volker, M. A., Smith, T. H., & Wang, H.

(2019). Cluster randomized trial of a school intervention for children with autism spectrum disorder. *Journal of Clinical Child & Adolescent Psychology, 48*(6), 922–933.

Thomeer, T. L., Rodgers, J. D., Lopata, C., McDonald, C. A., Volker, M. A., Toomey, J. A., Smith, R. A., & Gullo, G. (2011). Open-trial pilot of mind reading and in vivo rehearsal for children with HFASD. *Focus on Autism and Other Developmental Disabilities, 26*(3), 153–161.

Thomeer, M. L., Smith, R. A., Lopata, C., Volker, M. A., Lipinski, A. M., Rodgers, J. D., McDonald, C. A. & Lee, G. K. (2015). Randomized controlled trial of mind reading and in vivo rehearsal for high-functioning children with ASD. *Journal of Autism and Developmental disorders, 45*, 2115–2127.

Section 5: Natural Developmental Behavioral Interventions (NDBI)

Introduction

Schreibman, L., Dawson, G., Stahmer, A. C., Landa, R., Rogers, S. J., McGee, G. G., Kasari, C., Ingersoll, B., Kaiser, A. P., Bruinsma, Y., McNerney, E., Wetherby, A., & Halladay, A. (2015). Naturalistic developmental behavioral interventions: Empirically validated treatments for autism spectrum disorder. *Journal of Autism and Developmental Disorders, 45*(8), 2411–2428.

Incidental Teaching

Charlop-Christy, M. H., & Carpenter, M. H. (2000). Modified incidental teaching sessions: A procedure for parents to increase spontaneous speech in their children with autism. *Journal of Positive Behavior Interventions, 2*(2), 98–112.

Farmer-Dougan, V. (1994). Increasing requesting by adults with developmental disabilities using incidental teaching with peers. *Journal of Applied Behavior Analysis, 27*(3), 533–544.

Hart, B. M., & Risley, T. R. (1975). Incidental teaching of language in the preschool. *Journal of Applied Behavior Analysis, 8*, 411–420.

Hart, B. M., & Risley, T. R. (1978). Promoting productive language through incidental teaching. *Education and Urban Society, 10*(4), 407–429.

Hart, B. M., & Risley, T. R. (1980). In vivo language intervention: Unanticipated general effects. *Journal of Applied Behavior Analysis, 13*(3), 407–432.

Hsieh, H. H., Wilder, D. A., & Abellon, O. E. (2011). The effects of training on caregiver implementation of incidental teaching. *Journal of Applied Behavior Analysis, 44*(1), 199–203.

McGee, G. G., Almeida, C., Sulzer-Azaroff, B., & Feldman, R. S. (1992). Promoting reciprocal interactions via peer incidental teaching. *Journal of Applied Behavior Analysis, 25*(1), 117–126.

McGee, G. G., & Daly, T. (2007). Incidental teaching of age-appropriate social phrases to children with autism. *Research and Practice for Persons with Severe Disabilities, 32*(2), 112–123.

McGee, G. G., Daly, T., & Jacobs, H. A. (1994). The Walden preschool. In S. L. Harris & J. S. Handleman (Eds.), *Preschool education programs for children with autism* (pp. 127–162). Pro-Ed.

McGee, G. G., Krantz, P. J., Mason, D., & McClannahan, L. E. (1983). A modified incidental teaching procedure for autistic youth: Acquisition and generalization of receptive object labels. *Journal of Applied Behavior Analysis, 16*(3), 329–338.

McGee, G. G., Krantz, P. J., & McClannahan, L. E. (1985). The facilitative effects of incidental teaching on preposition use by autistic children. *Journal of Applied Behavior Analysis, 18*(1), 17–31.

McGee, G. G., Krantz, P. J., & McClannahan, L. E. (1986). An extension of incidental teaching procedures to reading instruction for autistic children. *Journal of Applied Behavior Analysis, 19*(2), 147–157.

McGee, G. G., Morrier, M. J., & Daly, T. (1999). An incidental teaching approach to early intervention for toddlers with autism. *Journal of the Association for Persons With Severe Handicaps, 24*(3), 133–146.

Miranda-Linné, F., & Medlin, L. (1992). Acquisition, generalization, and spontaneous use of color adjectives: A comparison of incidental teaching and traditional discrete-trial procedures for children with autism. *Research in Developmental Disabilities, 13*(3), 191–210.

Imitation-Based Interventions

Cardon, T. A. (2012). Teaching caregivers to implement video modeling imitation training via iPad for their children with autism. *Research in Autism Spectrum Disorders, 6*(4), 1389–1400.

Field, T., Field, T., Sanders, C., & Nadel, J. (2001). Children with autism display more social behaviors after repeated imitation sessions. *Autism: The International Journal of Research and Practice, 5*(3), 317–323.

Heimann, M., Laberg, K. E., & Nordoen, B. (2006). Imitative interaction increases social interest and elicited imitation in non-verbal children with autism. *Infant and Child Development, 15*(3), 297–309.

Ingersoll, B. (2008). The Social Role of Imitation in Autism: Implications for the Treatment of Imitation Deficits. *Infants & Young Children, 21*(2), 107–119.

Ingersoll, B. (2010). Brief report: Pilot randomized controlled trial of reciprocal imitation training for teaching elicited and spontaneous imitation to children with autism. *Journal of Autism and Developmental Disorders, 40*(9), 1154–1160.

Ingersoll, B. (2012). Brief report: Effect of a focused imitation intervention on social functioning in children with autism. *Journal of Autism and Developmental Disorders, 42*(8), 1768–1773.

Ingersoll, B., Berger, N., Carlsen, D., & Hamlin, T. (2016). Improving social functioning and challenging behaviors in adolescents with ASD and significant ID: A randomized pilot feasibility trial of reciprocal imitation training in a residential setting. *Developmental Neurorehabilitation, 20*(4), 236–246.

Ingersoll, B., & Gergans, S. (2007). The effect of a parent-implemented imitation intervention on spontaneous imitation skills in young children with autism. *Research in Developmental Disabilities, 28*(2), 163–175.

Ingersoll, B., & Lalonde, K. (2010). The impact of object and gesture imitation training on language use in children with autism spectrum disorder. *Journal of Speech, Language and Hearing Research, 53*(4), 1040–1051.

Ingersoll, B., Lewis, E., & Kroman, E. (2007). Teaching the imitation and spontaneous use of descriptive gestures in young children with autism using a naturalistic behavioral intervention. *Journal of Autism and Developmental Disorders, 37*(8), 1446–1456.

Ingersoll, B., & Schreibman, L. (2006). Teaching reciprocal imitation skills to young children with autism using a naturalistic behavioral approach: Effects on language, pretend play, and joint attention. *Journal of Autism and Developmental Disorders, 36*(4), 487–505.

Ingersoll, B., Walton, K., Carlsen, D., & Hamlin, T. (2013). Social intervention for adolescents with autism and significant intellectual disability: Initial efficacy of reciprocal imitation training. *American Journal on Intellectual and Developmental Disabilities, 118*(4), 247–261.

Ishizuka, Y., & Yamamoto, J. I. (2016). Contingent imitation increases verbal interaction in children with autism spectrum disorders. *Autism, 20*(8), 1011–1020.

Kleeberger, V., & Mirenda, P. (2010). Teaching generalized imitation skills to a preschooler with autism using video modeling. *Journal of Positive Behavior Interventions, 12*(2), 116–127.

McDowell, L. S., Gutierrez, A., & Bennett, K. D. (2015). Analysis of live modeling plus prompting and video modeling for teaching imitation to children with autism. *Behavioral Interventions, 30*(4), 333–351.

McDuffie, A. Turner, L. Stone, W. Yoder, P. Wolery, M. & Ulman, T. (2007). Developmental correlates of different types of motor imitation in young children with autism spectrum disorders. *Journal of Autism and Developmental Disorders, 37*(3), 401–412.

Rogers, S. J. (1999). An examination of the imitation deficit in autism. In J. Nadel & G. Butterworth (Ed.), *Imitation in infancy* (pp. 254–279). Cambridge University Press.

Ross, D. E., & Greer, R. D. (2003). Generalized imitation and the mand: Inducing first instances of speech in young children with autism. *Research in Developmental Disabilities, 24*(1), 58–74.

Stone, W., Ousley, O., & Littleford, C. (1997). Motor imitation in young children with autism: What's the object? *Journal of Abnormal Child Psychology, 25*, 475–485.

Tsiouri, I., & Greer, R. D. (2007). The role of different social reinforcement contingencies in inducing echoic tacts through motor imitation responding in children with severe language delays. *Journal of Early and Intensive Behavior Intervention, 4*(4), 629–647.

Young, J. M., Krantz, P. J., McClannahan, L. E., & Poulson, C. L. (1994). Generalized imitation and response-class formation in children with autism. *Journal of Applied Behavior Analysis, 27*(4), 685–697.

Milieu Teaching

Alpert, C. L., & Kaiser, A. P. (1992). Training parents as milieu language teachers. *Journal of Early Intervention, 16*, 31–52.

Christensen-Sandfort, R. J., & Whinnery, S. B. (2013). Impact of milieu teaching on communication skills of young children with autism spectrum disorder. *Topics in Early Childhood Special Education, 32*(4), 211–222.

Hamilton, B. L., & Snell, M. E. (1993). Using the milieu approach to increase spontaneous communication book use across environments by an adolescent with autism. *AAC: Augmentative and Alternative Communication, 9*(4), 259–272.

Hancock, T. B., & Kaiser, A. P. (2002). The effects of trainer-implemented enhanced milieu teaching on the social communication of children with autism. *Topics in Early Childhood Special Education, 22*(1), 39–54.

Hart, B. M., & Rogers-Warren, A. K. (1978). A milieu approach to teaching language. In R. L. Schiefelbusch (Ed.), *Language intervention strategies* (Vol. 2, pp. 192–235). University Park Press.

Hemmeter, M. L., & Kaiser, A. P. (1994). Enhanced milieu teaching: An analysis of parent-implemented language intervention. *Journal of Early Intervention, 18*(3), 269–289.

Kaiser, A. P., Hancock, T. B., & Hester, P. P. (1997). *A comparison of parent and therapist implemented enhanced milieu teaching.* Paper presented at the annual meeting of the American Association on Mental Retardation, New York.

Kaiser, A. P., Hancock, T. B., & Nietfeld, J. P. (2000). The effects of parent-implemented enhanced milieu teaching on the social communication of children who have autism. *Early Education and Development, 11*(4), 423–446.

Kaiser, A. P., & Hester, P. P. (1994). Generalized effects of enhanced milieu teaching. *Journal of Speech, Language, and Hearing Research, 37*, 1320–1340.

Kaiser, A. P., & Roberts, M. Y. (2013). Parent-implemented enhanced milieu teaching with preschool children who have intellectual disabilities. *Journal of Speech, Language, and Hearing Research, 56*(1), 295–309.

Ogletree, B. T., Davis, P., Hambrecht, G., & Phillips, E. W. (2012). Using milieu training to promote photograph exchange for a young child with autism. *Focus on Autism and Other Developmental Disabilities, 27*(2), 93–101.

Olive, M. L., De la Cruz, B., Davis, T. N., Chan, J. M., Lang, R. B., O'Reilly, M. F., & Dickson, S. M. (2007). The effects of enhanced milieu teaching and a voice output communication aid on the requesting of three children with autism. *Journal of Autism and Developmental Disorders, 37*, 1505–1513.

Joint Attention Interventions

Bruner, J. S. (1975). The ontogenesis of speech act. *Journal of Child Language, 2*(1), 1–19.

Bruner, J. S., & Sherwood, V. (1976). Early rule structure: The case of peekaboo. In J. S. Bruner, A. Jolly, & K. Sylva (Eds.), *Play: Its rule in evolution and development.* Penguin.

Chang, Y. C., Shire, S. Y., Shih, W., Gelfand, C., & Kasari, C. (2016). Preschool deployment of evidence-based social communication intervention: JASPER in the classroom. *Journal of Autism and Developmental Disorders, 46*(6), 2211–2223.

Goods, K. S., Ishijima, E., Chang, Y. C., & Kasari, C. (2013). Preschool based JASPER intervention in minimally verbal children with autism: Pilot RCT. *Journal of Autism and Developmental Disorders, 43*(5), 1050–1056.

Gulsrud, A. C., Kasari, C., Freeman, S., & Paparella, T. (2007). Children with autism's response to novel stimuli while participating in interventions targeting joint attention or symbolic play skills. *Autism, 11*(6), 535–546.

Harrop, C., Gulsrud, A., Shih, W., Hovsepyan, L., & Kasari, C. (2017). The impact of caregiver-mediated JASPER on child restricted and repetitive behaviors and caregiver responses. *Autism Research, 10*(5), 983–992.

Kaale, A., Smith, L., & Sponheim, E. (2012). A randomized controlled trial of preschool-based joint attention intervention for children with autism. *Journal of Child Psychology and Psychiatry, 53*(1), 97–105.

Kasari, C., Freeman, S., & Paparella, T. (2006). Joint attention and symbolic play in young children with autism: A randomized controlled intervention study. *Journal of Child Psychology and Psychiatry, 47*(6), 611–620.

Kasari, C., Kaiser, A., Goods, K., Nietfeld, J., Mathy, P., Landa, R., Murphy, S., & Almirall, D. (2014). Communication interventions for minimally verbal children with autism: A sequential multiple assignment randomized trial. *Journal of the American Academy of Child & Adolescent Psychiatry, 53*(6), 635–646.

Kasari, C., Paparella, T, Freeman, S. N., & Jahromi, L. (2008). Language outcome in autism: Randomized comparison of joint attention and play interventions. *Journal of Consulting and Clinical Psychology, 76*, 125–137.

Koegel, R. L., & Koegel, L. K. (Eds.). (1995). *Teaching children with autism: Strategies for initiating positive interactions and improving learning opportunities.* Paul H. Brookes.

Koegel, R., O'Dell, M. C., & Koegel, L. K. (1987). A natural language paradigm for teaching nonverbal autistic children. *Journal of Autism and Developmental Disorders, 17*(2), 187–200.

Krstovska-Guerrero, I., & Jones, E. A. (2013). Joint attention in autism: Teaching smiling coordinated with gaze to respond to joint attention bids. *Research in Autism Spectrum Disorders, 7*(1), 93–108.

Prizant, B. M., Wetherby, A. M., & Rydell, P. J. (2000). Communication intervention issues for children with autism spectrum disorders. In A. M. Wetherby & B. M. Prizant (Eds.), *Autism spectrum disorders—A transactional developmental perspective* (pp. 193–224). Paul H. Brookes.

Ratner, N., & Bruner, J. (1978). Games, social exchange, and the acquisition of language. *Journal of Child Language, 5*, 391–401.

Shire, S. Y., Baker Worthman, L., Shih, W., & Kasari, C. (2020). Comparison of face-to-face and remote support for interventionists learning to deliver JASPER intervention with children who have autism. *Journal of Behavioral Education, 29*(2), 317–33.

Snyder-McLean, L. K, Cripe, J., & McNay, V. J. (1988). *Using joint action routines in an early intervention program* (1988 experimental edition). Bureau of Child Research, University of Kansas, and Parsons Research Center, Parsons, Kansas.

Snyder-McLean, L. K., Solomonson, B., McLean, J. E., & Sack, S. (1984). Structuring joint action routines: A strategy for facilitating communication and language development in the classroom. *Seminars in Speech and Language 5*(3), 213–228.

Whalen, C., & Schreibman, L. (2003). Joint attention training for children with autism using behavior modification procedures. *Journal of Child Psychology and Psychiatry, 44*(3), 456–468.

Pivotal Response Interventions

Brock, M. E., Dueker, S. A., & Barczak, M. A. (2017). Brief report: Improving social outcomes for students with autism at recess through peer-mediated pivotal response training. *Journal of Autism and Developmental Disorders, 48*(6), 2224–2230.

Hardan, A. Y., Gengoux, G. W., Berquist, K. L., Libove, R. A., Ardel, C. M., Phillips, J., Frazier, T. W., & Minjarez, M. B. (2015). A randomized controlled trial of pivotal response treatment group for parents of children with autism. *Journal of Child Psychology and Psychiatry and Allied Disciplines, 56*(8), 884–892.

Hupp, S. D. A., & Reitman, D. (2000). Parent-assisted modification of pivotal social skills for a child diagnosed with PDD: A clinical replication. *Journal of Positive Behavior Interventions, 2*(3), 183–187.

Koegel, R. L., & Frea, W. D. (1993). Treatment of social behavior in autism through the modification of pivotal social skills. *Journal of Applied Behavior Analysis, 26*(3), 369–377.

Koegel, R. L., & Koegel, L. K. (2006) *Pivotal Response Treatments for autism: Communication, social, and academic development.* Paul H. Brookes.

Koegel, L. K., Koegel, R. L., Harrower, J. K., & Carter, C. M. (1999a). Pivotal Response Intervention I: Overview of approach. *Journal of the Association for Persons With Severe Handicaps, 24*(3), 174–185.

Koegel, L. K., Koegel, R. L., Shoshan, Y., & McNerney, E. (1999b). Pivotal Response Intervention II: Preliminary long-term outcome data. *Journal of the Association for Persons With Severe Handicaps, 24*(3), 186–198.

Koegel, R. L., O'Dell, M. C., & Koegel, L. K. (1987). A natural language teaching paradigm for nonverbal autistic children. *Journal of Autism and Developmental Disorders, 17*(2), 187–200.

Kuhn, L. R., Bodkin, A. E., Devlin, S. D., & Doggett, R. A. (2008). Using Pivotal Response Training with peers in special education to facilitate play in two children with autism. *Education and Training in Developmental Disabilities, 43*(1), 37–45.

Mohammadzaheri, F., Koegel, L. K., Rezaei, M., & Bakhshi, E. (2015). A randomized clinical trial comparison between Pivotal Response Treatment (PRT) and adult-driven applied behavior analysis (ABA) intervention on disruptive behaviors in public school children with autism. *Journal of Autism and Developmental Disorders, 45*(9), 2899–2907.

Nefdt, N., Koegel, R., Singer, G., & Gerber, M. (2010). The use of a self-directed learning program to provide introductory training in Pivotal Response Treatment to parents of children with autism. *Journal of Positive Behavior Interventions, 12*(1), 23–32.

Odom, S. L., Boyd, B. A., Hall, L. J., & Hume, K. (2010). Evaluation of comprehensive treatment models for individuals with autism spectrum disorders. *Journal of Autism and Developmental Disorders, 40*(4), 425–436.

Pierce, K., & Schreibman, L. (1997). Multiple peer use of Pivotal Response Training to increase social behaviors of classmates with autism: Results from trained and untrained peers. *Journal of Applied Behavior Analysis, 30*(1), 157–160.

Robinson, S. E. (2011). Teaching paraprofessionals of students with autism to implement Pivotal Response Treatment in inclusive school settings using a brief video feedback training package. *Focus on Autism and Other Developmental Disabilities, 26*, 105–118.

Stahmer, A. C. (1995). Teaching symbolic play to children with autism using Pivotal Response Training. *Journal of Autism and Developmental Disorders, 25*(2), 123–141.

Stahmer, A. C. (1999). Using Pivotal Response Training to facilitate appropriate play in children with autistic spectrum disorders. *Child Language Teaching and Therapy, 15*(1), 29–40.

Section 6: Developmental Relationship-Based Interventions (DRBI)

Introduction

Hobson, R. P. (1990). On psychoanalytical approaches to autism. *American Journal of Orthopsychiatry, 60*, 324–336.

Mahoney, G., & Perales, F. (2003). Using relationship-focused intervention to enhance the social-emotional functioning of young children with autism spectrum disorder. *Topics in Early Childhood Special Education, 23*(2), 77–89.

Responsive Teaching (RT)

Biringen, Z., & Robinson, J. (1991) Emotional availability in mother-child interactions: A reconceptualization for research. *American Journal of Orthopsychiatry, 61*(2), 258–271.

Bornstein, M. H., Tamis-LeMonda, C. S., & Haynes, O. M. (1999). First words in the second year: Continuity, stability, and models of concurrent and predictive correspondence in vocabulary and verbal responsiveness across age and context. *Infant Behavior and Development, 22*(1), 65–85.

Brooks-Gunn, J., & Lewis, M. (1984). Maternal responsivity in interactions with handicapper infants. *Child Development, 55*, 782–793.

Hoff-Ginsberg, E., & Shatz, M. (1982). Linguistic input and the child's acquisition of language. *Psychological Bulletin, 92*, 3–26.

Kochanska, G., Forman, D. R., & Coy, K. C. (1999). Implications of the mother-child relationship in infancy for socialization in the second year of life. *Infant Behavior and Development, 22*(2), 249–265.

Mahoney, G. J. (1988a). Maternal communication style with mentally retarded children. *American Journal of Mental Retardation, 93*, 352–359.

Mahoney, G. J. (1988b). Communication patterns between mothers and developmentally delayed infants. *First Language, 8*, 157–172.

Mahoney, G. J., Finger, I., & Powell, A. (1985). The relationship between maternal behavioral style to the developmental status of mentally retarded infants. *American Journal of Mental Deficiency, 90*, 296–302.

Mahoney, G., & MacDonald, J. (2007). *Autism and developmental delays in young children: The responsive teaching curriculum for parents and professionals*. ProEd.

Mahoney, G., & Perales, F. (2003). Using relationship-focused intervention to enhance the social-emotional functioning of young children with autism spectrum disorders. *Topics in Early Childhood Special Education , 23*(2), 77–89.

Mahoney, G., & Perales, F. (2005). A comparison of the impact of relationship-focused intervention on young children with pervasive developmental disorders and other disabilities. *Journal of Developmental and Behavioral Pediatrics, 26*(2), 77–85.

Mahoney, G., Perales, F., Wiggers, B., & Herman, B. (2006). Responsive teaching: Early intervention for children with Down syndrome and other disabilities. *Down Syndrome: Research & Practice, 11*(1), 18–28.

Nelson, K. (1973). Structure and strategy in learning to talk. *Monographs of the Society for Research in Child Development, 38*, 1–135.

Odom, S. L., Boyd, B., Hall, L., & Hume, K. (2010). Evaluation of comprehensive treatment models for individuals with autism spectrum disorders. *Journal of Autism and Developmental Disorders, 40*, 425–436.

Siller, M., & Sigman, M. (2002). The behaviors of parents of children with autism predict the subsequent development of their children's communication. *Journal of Autism and Developmental Disorders, 32*(2), 77–89.

van den Boom, D. C. (1995). Do first-year intervention effects endure? Follow-up during toddlerhood of a sample of Dutch irritable infants. *Child Development, 66*(6), 1798–1816.

Vereijken, C. M. J. L., Riksen-Walraven, M., & Kondo-Ikemura, K. (1997). Maternal sensitivity and infant attachment security in Japan: A longitudinal study. *International Society for the Study of Behavioural Development, 21*(1), 35–49.

Developmental, Individual-Difference, Relationship-Based Model (DIRFloor Time®)

Boshoff, K., Bowen, H., Paton, H., Cameron-Smith, S., Graetz, S., Young, A., & Lane, K. (2020). Child development outcomes of DIR/Floortime™-based programs: A systematic review. *Canadian Journal of Occupational Therapy, 87*(2), 153–164.

Casenhiser, D., Shanker, S., & Stieben, J. (2011). Learning through interaction in children with autism: Preliminary data from a social communication-based intervention. *Autism, 17*(2), 220–241.

Dionne, M., & Martini, R. (2011). Floortime play with a child with autism: A single-subject study. *Canadian Journal of Occupational Therapy, 78*, 196–203.

Greenspan, S. I., & Wieder, S. (1997a). An integrated developmental approach to interventions for young children with severe difficulties in relating and communicating. *Zero to Three, 17*, 5–18.

Greenspan, S. I., & Wieder, S. (1997b). Developmental patterns and outcomes in infants and children with disorders in relating and communicating: A chart review of 200 cases of children with autistic spectrum diagnoses. *Journal of Developmental and Learning Disorders, 1*, 87–141.

Liao, S., Hwang, Y., Chen, Y., Lee, P., Chen, S., & Lin, L. (2014). Home-based DIR/Floortime™ intervention program for preschool children with autism spectrum disorders: Preliminary findings. *Physical & Occupational Therapy in Paediatrics, 34*(4), 56–367.

Odom, S. L., Boyd, B., Hall, L., & Hume, K. (2010). Evaluation of comprehensive treatment models for individuals with autism spectrum disorders. *Journal of Autism and Developmental Disorders, 40*, 425–436.

Pajareya, K., & Nopmaneejumruslers, K. (2011). A pilot randomized controlled trial of DIR/Floortime™ Parent Training Intervention for pre-school children with autistic spectrum disorders. *Autism, 5*(5), 563–577.

Pajareya, K., & Nopmaneejumruslers, K. (2012). A one-year prospective follow-up study of a DIR/Floortime™ Parent Training Intervention for pre-school children with autistic spectrum disorders. *Journal of the Medical Association of Thailand, 95*(9), 1184–1193.

Praphatthanakunwong, N., Kiatrungrit, K., Hongsanguansri, S., & Nopmaneejumruslers, K. (2018). Factors associated with parent engagement in DIR/Floortime for treatment of children with autism spectrum disorder. *General Psychiatry, 31*(2), e000009.

Reis, H. I., Pereira, A. P., & Almeida, L. S. (2018). Intervention effects on communication skills and sensory regulation on children with ASD. *Journal of Occupational Therapy, Schools, & Early Intervention, 11*(3), 346–359.

Scheibel, G., Zane, T. L., & Zimmerman, K. N. (2022). Emerging and ineffective interventions: Examining the role of cost when translating research into practice. *Exceptional Children, 88*(3), 1–18.

Solomon, R., Egeren, L. A. V., Mahoney, G., Huber, M. S. Q., & Zimmerman, P. (2014). PLAY project home consultation intervention program for young children with autism spectrum disorders: A randomized controlled trial. *Journal of Developmental and Behavioral Pediatrics, 35*(8), 475–485.

Solomon, R., Necheles, J., Ferch, C., & Bruckman, D. (2007). Pilot study of a parent training program for young children with autism: The play project home consultation program. *Autism, 11*(3), 205–224.

Wieder, S., & Greenspan, S. I. (2003). Climbing the symbolic ladder in the DIR model through floor time/interactive plan. *Autism, 7*(4), 425–435.

Relationship-Development Intervention (RDI)

Gutstein, S. E. (2001). *Solving the relationship puzzle.* Future Horizons.

Gutstein, S. E. (2009). *The RDI book: Forging new pathways for autism, Asperger's and PDD with the Relationship Development Intervention® Program.* Connections Center.

Gutstein, S. E., Burgess, A. F., & Montfort, K. (2007). Evaluation of the relationship development intervention program. *Autism, 11*, 397–411.

Gutstein, S. E., & Sheely, R. K. (2002a). *Relationship development intervention with young children: Social and emotional development activities for Asperger syndrome, autism, and PDD and NLD.* Jessica Kingsley.

Gutstein, S. E., & Sheely, R. K. (2002b). *Relationship development intervention with children, adolescents and adults.* Jessica Kingsley.

Gutstein, S. E., & Whitney, T. (2002). Asperger syndrome and the development of social competence. *Focus on Autism and Other Developmental Disabilities, 17*(3), 161–171.

Odom, S. L., Boyd, B., Hall, L., & Hume, K. (2010). Evaluation of comprehensive treatment models for individuals with autism spectrum disorders. *Journal of Autism and Developmental Disorders, 40*, 425–436.

Section 7: Relational Frame Theory (RFT)-Based Interventions

Introduction

Barnes-Holmes, D., Barnes-Holmes, Y., Smeets, P. M., Cullinan, V., & Leader, G. (2004). Relational frame theory and stimulus equivalence: Conceptual and procedural issues. *International Journal of Psychology & Psychological Therapy, 4*(2), 181–214.

Barnes-Holmes, Y., Kavanagh, D., & Murphy, C. (2016). Relational frame theory: Implications for education and developmental disabilities. In R. D. Zettle, S. C. Hayes, D. Barnes-Holmes, & A. Biglan (Eds.), *The*

Wiley handbook of contextual behavioral science (pp. 227–253). Wiley Blackwell.

Cooper, J. O., Heron, T. E., & Heward, W. L. (2020). *Applied behavior analysis.* Pearson Education Limited.

Dymond, S., & Rehfeldt, R. A. (2000). Understanding complex behavior: The transformation of stimulus functions. *The Behavior Analyst, 23*(2), 239–254.

Gross, A. C., & Fox, E. J. (2009). Relational frame theory: An overview of the controversy. *The Analysis of Verbal Behavior, 25*(1), 87–98.

Hayes, S. C., Barnes-Holmes, D., & Roche, B. (2001). *Relational frame theory: A post-Skinnerian account of human language and cognition.* Klewer/Plenum.

Niklas, T., Barnes-Holmes, D., & Hayes, S. C. (2010). *Learning RFT: An introduction to relational frame theory and its clinical applications.* Context Press.

O'Hora, D., Peláez, M., & Barnes-Holmes, D. (2005). Derived relational responding and performance on verbal subtests of the WAIS-III. *The Psychological Record, 55*, 155–175.

Rehfeldt, R. A., & Barnes-Holmes, Y. (2009). *Derived relational responding applications for learners with autism and other developmental disabilities: A progressive guide to change.* Context Press.

Smyth, S., Barnes-Holmes, D., & Forsyth, J. P. (2006). A derived transfer of simple discrimination and self-reported arousal functions in spider fearful and non-spider fearful participants. *Journal of the Experimental Analysis of Behavior, 85*(2), 223–246.

Thirus, J., Starbrink, M., & Jansson, B. (2016). Relational frame theory, mathematical and logical skills: A multiple exemplar training intervention to enhance intellectual performance. *International Journal of Psychology & Psychological Therapy [Revista Internacional de Psicologia y Terapia Psicologica], 16*, 141–155.

Stimulus Equivalence Instruction (SEI)

Albright, L., Schnell, L., Reeve, K. F., & Sidener, T. M. (2016). Using stimulus equivalence-based instruction to teach graduate students in applied behavior analysis to interpret operant functions of behavior. *Journal of Behavioral Education, 25*, 290–309.

Arntzen, E., Halstadtro, L.-B., Bjerke, E., Wittner, K. J., & Kristiansen, A. (2014). On the sequential and concurrent presentation of trials establishing prerequisites for emergent relations. *The Behavior Analyst Today, 14*(1–2), 1–8.

Barnes-Holmes, Y., Kavanagh, D., & Murphy, C. (2016). Relational frame theory: Implications for education and developmental disabilities. In R. D. Zettle, S. C. Hayes, D. Barnes-Holmes, & A. Biglan (Eds.), *The Wiley handbook of contextual behavioral science* (pp. 227–253). Wiley Blackwell.

Blair, B. J., Tarbox, J., Albright, L., Macdonald, J. M., Shawler, L. A., Russo, S. R., & Dorsey, M. F. (2019). Using equivalence based instruction to teach the visual analysis of graphs. *Behavioral Interventions, 34*(3), 405–418.

Brodsky, J., & Fienup, D. M. (2018). Sidman goes to college: A meta-analysis of equivalence-based instruction in higher education. *Perspectives on Behavior Science, 41*(1), 95–119.

Brooks Newsome, K., Nix Berens, K., Ghezzi, P. M., Aninao, T., & Newsome, W. D. (2014). Training relational language to improve reading comprehension. *European Journal of Behavior Analysis, 15*(2), 165–197.

Cassidy, S., Roche, B., Colbert, D., Stewart, I., & Grey, I. M. (2016). A relational frame skills training intervention to increase general intelligence and scholastic aptitude. *Learning and Individual Differences, 47*, 222–235.

Cooper, J. O., Heron, T. E., & Heward, W. L. (2020). *Applied behavior analysis*. Pearson Education Limited.

Critchfield, T. S. (2018). Efficiency is everything: Promoting efficient practice by harnessing derived stimulus relations. *Behavior Analysis in Practice, 11*(3), 206–210.

Critchfield, T. S., Barnes-Holmes, D., & Dougher, M. J. (2018). Editorial: What Sidman did—historical and contemporary significance of research on derived stimulus relations. *Perspectives on Behavior Science, 41*, 9–32.

Daar, J. H., Negrelli, S., & Dixon, M. R. (2015). Derived emergence of WH question-answers in children with autism. *Research in Autism Spectrum Disorders, 19*, 59–71.

Dickens, T. E., & Dickens, D. W. (2001). Symbols, stimulus equivalence and the origins of language. *Behavior and Philosophy, 29*, 221–244.

DiCola, K., & Clayton, M. (2017). Using arbitrary stimuli to teach say-do correspondence to children with autism. *International Journal of Psychology and Psychological Therapy, 17*, 149–160.

Dixon, M. R., Belisle, J., Stanley, C. R., Daar, J. H., & Williams, L. A. (2016a). Derived equivalence relations of geometry skills in students with autism: An application of the PEAK-E curriculum. *The Analysis of Verbal Behavior, 32*, 38–45.

Dixon, M. R., Speelman, R. C., Rowsey, K. E., & Belisle, J. (2016b). Derived rule-following and transformations of stimulus function in a children's game: An application of PEAK-E with children with developmental disabilities. *Journal of Contextual Behavioral Science, 5*, 186–192.

Dixon, M. R., Belisle, J., Stanley, C. R., Munoz, B. E., & Speelman, R. C. (2017a). Establishing derived coordinated symmetrical and transitive gustatory-visual-auditory relations in children with autism and related intellectual disabilities using the PEAK-E curriculum. *Journal of Contextual Behavior al Science, 6*, 91–95.

Dixon, M. R., Stanley, C., Belisle, J., Galliford, M. E., Alholail, A., & Schmick, A. M. (2017b). Establishing derived equivalence relations of basic geography skills in children with autism. *The Analysis of Verbal Behavior, 33*(2), 290–295.

Gibbs, A. R., & Tullis, C. A. (2021). The emergence of untrained relations in individuals with autism and other intellectual and developmental disabilities: A systematic review of the recent literature. *Review Journal of Autism and Developmental Disorders, 8*, 213–238.

Hammond, J. L., Hirt, M., & Hall, S. S. (2012). *Effects of computerized match-to-sample training on emergent fraction-decimal relations in individuals with Fragile X syndrome*. Research in developmental disabilities.

Higbee, T. S. (2009). Reinforcer identification strategies and teaching learner readiness skills. In R. A. Rehfeldt & Y. Barnes-Holmes, *Derived relational responding applications for learners with autism and other developmental disabilities: A progressive guide to change* (pp. 7–24). New Harbinger.

Hill, K. E., Griffith, K. R., & Miguel, C. F. (2020). Using equivalence-based instruction to teach piano skills to children. *Journal of Applied Behavior Analysis, 53*(1), 188–208.

Joyce, B. G., & Wolking, W. D. (1989). Stimulus equivalence: An approach for teaching beginning reading skills to young children. *Education and Treatment of Children, 12*(2), 109–122.

Kenny, N., Barnes-Holmes, D., Barnes-Holmes, Y., & Stewart, I. (2014). Competing arbitrary and non-arbitrary stimulus relations. *The Psychological Record, 64*(1).

McLay, L., Church, J., & Sutherland, D. (2016). Variables affecting the emergence of untaught equivalence relations in children with and without autism. *Developmental Neurorehabilitation, 19*, 75–87.

Monteiro, P. C. M., & Barros, R. S. (2016). Emergence of auditory-visual relations via equivalence class formation in children diagnosed with autism. *The Psychological Record, 66*, 563–571.

Mullen, S., Dixon, M. R., Belisle, J., & Stanley, C. (2017). Establishing auditory-tactile-visual equivalence classes in children with autism and developmental delays. *The Analysis of Verbal Behavior, 33*, 283–289.

Rehfeldt, R. A., & Barnes-Holmes, Y. (2009). *Derived relational responding: Applications for learners with autism and other developmental disabilities: A progressive guide to change*. New Harbinger.

Rehfeldt, R., Barnes-Holmes, Y., Hayes, S., & Higbee, T. (2009). Reinforcer identification strategies and teaching learner readiness skills. In R. A. Rehfeldt & Y. Barnes-Holmes, *Derived relational responding: Applications for learners with autism and other developmental disabilities: A progressive guide to change* (pp. 7–24). New Harbinger.

Santos, E. A. L., Nogueira, C. B., Queiroz, L. L. D., & Barros, R. D. S. (2017). Equivalence class formation via class-specific consequences in children diagnosed with autism spectrum disorder. *Trends in Psychology, 25*, 831–842.

Sidman, M. (1971). Reading and auditory-visual equivalences. *Journal of Speech and Hearing Research, 14*, 5–13.

Sidman, M. (2009). Equivalence relations and behavior: An introductory tutorial. *The Analysis of Verbal Behavior, 25*(1), 5–17.

Sidman, M., & Tailby, W. (1982). Conditional discrimination vs. matching to sample: An expansion of the testing paradigm. *Journal of the Experimental Analysis of Behavior, 37*(1), 5–22.

Silva, R. A., & Debert, P. (2017). Go/no-go procedure with compound stimuli with children with autism. *Journal of Applied Behavior Analysis, 50*, 750–755.

Sprinkle, E. C., & Miguel, C. F. (2013). Establishing derived textual activity schedules in children with autism. *Behavioral Interventions, 28*, 185–202.

Stanley, C. R., Belisle, J., & Dixon, M. R. (2018). Equivalence-based instruction of academic skills: Application to adolescents with autism. *Journal of Applied Behavior Analysis, 51*, 352–359.

Stewart, I., McElwee, J., & Ming, S. (2013). Language generativity, response generalization, and derived relational responding. *The Analysis of Behavior, 29*(1), 137–155.

Stromer, R., Mackay, H. A., & Stoddard, L. T. (1992). Classroom applications of stimulus equivalence technology. *Journal of Behavioral Education, 2*(3), 225–256.

Varella, A. A. B., & de Souza, D. G. (2014). Emergence of auditory visual relations from a visual-visual baseline with auditory-specific consequences in individuals with autism. *Journal of the Experimental Analysis of Behavior, 102*, 139–149.

Varella, A. A. B., & de Souza, D. G. (2015). Using class-specific compound consequences to teach dictated and printed letter relations to a child with autism. *Journal of Applied Behavior Analysis, 48*, 675–679.

Wetherby, B. (1978). Miniature languages and the functional analysis of verbal behavior. In R. L. Schiefelbusch (Ed.). *Bases of language intervention* (pp. 397–448). University Park Press.

Matrix Training

Axe, J. B., & Sainato, D. M. (2010). Matrix training of preliteracy skills with preschoolers with autism. *Journal of Applied Behavior Analysis, 43*, 635–652.

Barnes-Holmes, D., Finn, M., McEnteggart, C., & Barnes-Holmes, Y. (2018). Derived stimulus relations and their role in a behavior-analytic account of human language and cognition. *Perspectives on Behavioral Science, 41*, 155–173.

Curiel, E. S., Axe, J. B., Sainato, D. M., & Goldstein, H. (2020). Systematic review of matrix training for individuals with autism spectrum disorder. *Focus on Autism and Other Developmental Disabilities, 35*(1), 55–64.

Curiel, E. S. L., Sainato, D. M., & Goldstein, H. (2016). Matrix training of receptive language skills with a toddler with autism spectrum disorder: A case study. *Education and Treatment of Children, 39*, 95–109.

Dauphin, M., Kinney, E. M., & Stromer, R. (2004). Using videoenhanced activity schedules and matrix training to teach sociodramatic play to a child with autism. *Journal of Positive Behavior Interventions, 6*, 238–250.

Esper, E. A. (1925). A technique for the experimental investigation of associative interference in artificial linguistic material. *Language Monographs, 1*, 5–6.

Ezell, H. K., & Goldstein, H. (1989). Effects of imitation on language comprehension and transfer to production in children with mental retardation. *Journal of Speech and Hearing Disorders, 54*, 49–56.

Frampton, S. E., Wymer, S. C., & Hansen, B. (2016). The use of matrix training to promote generative language with children with autism. *Journal of Applied Behavior Analysis, 49*(4), 869–883.

Goldstein, H. (1983). Recombinative generalization: Relationships between environmental conditions and the linguistic repertoires of language learners. *Analysis and Intervention in Developmental Disabilities, 3*, 279–293.

Goldstein, H. (1984). Effects of modeling and corrected practice on generative language learning of preschool children. *Journal of Speech and Hearing Disorders, 49*, 389–398.

Goldstein, H., Angelo, D., & Mousetis, L. (1987). Acquisition and extension of syntactic repertoires by severely mentally retarded youth. *Research in Developmental Disabilities, 8*, 549–574.

Goldstein, H., & Mousetis, L. (1989). Generalized language learning by children with severe mental retardation: Effects of peers' expressive modeling. *Journal of Applied Behavior Analysis, 22*, 245–259.

Jimenez-Gomez, C., Rajagopal, S., Nastri, R., & Chong, I. M. (2019). Matrix training for expanding the communication of toddlers and preschoolers with autism spectrum disorder. *Behavior Analysis in Practice, 12*(2), 375–386.

MacManus, C., MacDonald, R., & Ahearn, W. H. (2015). Teaching and generalizing pretend play in children with autism using video modeling and matrix training. *Behavioral Interventions, 30*(3), 191–218.

Mayer, G. R., Sulzer-Azaroff, B., & Wallace, M. (2019). *Behavior analysis for lasting change.* Sloan.

Mineo, B. A., & Goldstein, H. (1990). Generalized learning of receptive and expressive action-object responses by language-delayed preschoolers. *Journal of Speech and Hearing Research, 55*, 665–678.

Naoi, N., Yokoyama, K., & Yamamoto, J. (2006). Matrix training for expressive and receptive two-word utterances in children with autism. *Japanese Journal of Special Education, 43*, 505–518. National Autism Center.

Pauwels, A. A., Ahearn, W. H., & Cohen, S. J. (2015). Recombinative generalization of tacts through matrix training with individuals with autism spectrum disorder. *The Analysis of Verbal Behavior, 31*, 200–214.

Romski, M. A., & Ruder, K. F. (1984). Effects of speech and speech and sign instruction on oral language learning and generalization of action + object combinations by Down's syndrome children. *Journal of Speech and Hearing Disorders, 49*, 293–302.

Stokes, T. F., & Baer, D. M. (1977). An implicit technology of generalization. *Journal of Applied Behavior Analysis, 10*, 349–367.

Weissman-Young, E. (2019). Effects of matrix training on generative language in young adults with autism. *Capstone Projects and Master's Theses, 636.* https://digitalcommons.csumb.edu/caps_thes_all/636

Wilson, E. R., Wine, B., & Fitterer, K. (2017). An investigation of the matrix training approach to teach social play skills. *Behavioral Interventions, 32*, 278–284.

Yoder, P., Watson, L. R., & Lambert, W. (2015). Value added predictors of expressive and receptive language growth in initially nonverbal preschoolers with autism spectrum disorders. *Journal of Autism and Developmental Disorders, 45*(5), 1254–1270.

PEAK: Promoting the Emergence of Advanced Knowledge Relational Training System

Belisle, J., & Dixon, M. R. (2018a). *PEAK Comprehensive Assessment (PCA)*. Peak2aba.

Belisle, J., & Dixon, M. R. (2018b). *PEAK Relational Training*. Peak2aba.

Daar, J. H., Negrelli, S., & Dixon, M. R. (2015). Derived emergence of WH question–answers in children with autism. *Research in Autism Spectrum Disorders, 19*, 59–71.

Dixon, M. R., Belisle, J., Stanley, C. R., & Rowsey, K. (2018). Student outcomes after 1 year of front line staff implementation of the PEAK curriculum. *Behavioral Interventions, 33*(2), 185–195.

Dixon, M. R., Paliliunas, D., Barron, B. F., Schmick, A. M., & Stanley, C. R. (2019). Randomized controlled trial evaluation of ABA content on IQ gains in children with autism. *Journal of Behavioral Education, 30*(3), 455–477.

Dixon, M. R., Stanley, C. S., Belisle, J., & Rowsey, K. E. (2016). The test-retest and inter-rater reliability of the PEAK-direct training assessment for use with individuals with autism and related disabilities. *Behavior Analytic Research and Practice, 16*, 34–40.

May, B. K., & St. Cyr, J. (2021). The impact of the PEAK curriculum on standardized measures of intelligence: A systems level randomized control trial. *Advances in Neurodevelopmental Disorders, 5*, 245–255.

McKeel, A. N., Dixon, M. R., Daar, J. H., Rowsey, K. E., & Szekely, S. (2015). Evaluating the efficacy of the PEAK relational training system using a randomized controlled trial of children with autism. *Journal of Behavioral Education, 24*(2), 230–241.

O'Connor, M. T., Belisle, J., Stanley, C. R., & Dixon, M. R. (2020). Establishing Multiple-control responding of children with autism to people and emotions in context by utilizing derived stimulus relations. *Behavior Analysis in Practice, 13*(1), 192–196.

Stanley, C. R., Belisle, J., & Dixon, M. R. (2018). Equivalence-based instruction of academic skills: Application to adolescents with autism. *Journal of Applied Behavior Analysis, 51*(2), 352–359.

Acceptance and Commitment Therapy/Training (ACT)

Aydin, Y., & Aydin, G. (2020). Acceptance and commitment therapy based psychoeducation group for test anxiety: A case study of senior high school students. *Pamukkale Üniversitesi Eğitim Fakültesi Dergisi, 50*, 180–200.

Burckhardt, R., Manicavasagar, V., Batterham, P. J., & Hadzi-Pavlovic, D. (2016). A randomized controlled trial of strong minds: A school-based mental health program combining acceptance and commitment therapy and positive psychology. *Journal of School Psychology, 57*, 41–52.

Burckhardt, R., Manicavasagar, V., Batterham, P. J., Hadzi-Pavlovic, D., & Shand, F. (2017). Acceptance and commitment therapy universal prevention program for adolescents: A feasibility study. *Child and Adolescent Psychiatry and Mental Health, 11*(1), 1–10.

Dimidjian, S., Arch, J. J., Schneider, R. L., Desormeau, P., Felder, J. N., & Segal, Z. V. (2016). Considering meta-analysis, meaning, and metaphor: A systematic review and critical examination of "third wave" cognitive and behavioral therapies. *Behavior Therapy, 47*(6), 886–905.

Harris, R. (2019). *ACT made simple: An easy-to-read primer on acceptance and commitment therapy* (2nd ed.). New Harbinger.

Hayes, S. C. (2004). Acceptance and commitment therapy, relational frame theory, and the third wave of behavioral and cognitive therapies. *Behavior Therapy, 35*(4), 639–665.

Hayes, S. C., Strosahl, K. D., & Wilson, K.G. (1999). *Acceptance and commitment therapy: An experiential approach to behavior change*. Guilford Press.

Hooper, N., & Larsson, A. (2015). *The research journey of acceptance and commitment therapy (ACT)*. Palgrave Macmillian.

Livheim, F., Hayes, L., Ghaderi, A., Magnusdottir, T., Högfeldt, A., Rowse, J., & Tengström, A. (2015). The effectiveness of acceptance and commitment therapy for adolescent mental health: Swedish and Australian pilot outcomes. *Journal of Child and Family Studies, 24*(4), 1016–1030.

Murrell, A. R., Steinberg, D. S., Connally, M. L., Hulsey, T., & Hogan, E. (2015). Acting Out to ACTing On: A preliminary investigation in youth with ADHD and comorbid disorders. *Journal of Child and Family Studies, 24*(7), 2174–2181.

Pahnke, J., Lundgren, T., Hursti, T., & Hirvikoski, T. (2014). Outcomes of an acceptance and commitment therapy-based skills training group for students with high-functioning autism spectrum disorder: A quasi-experimental pilot study. *Autism: The International Journal of Research and Practice, 18*(8), 953–964.

Swain, J., Hancock, K., Dixon, A., & Bowman, J. (2015). Acceptance and commitment therapy for children: A systematic review of intervention studies. *Journal of Contextual Behavioral Science, 4*(2), 73–85.

Takahashi, F., Ishizu, K., Matsubara, K., Ohtsuki, T., & Shimoda, Y. (2020). Acceptance and commitment therapy as a school-based group intervention for adolescents: An open-label trial. *Journal of Contextual Behavioral Science, 16*, 71–79.

Theodore-Oklota, C., Orsillo, S. M., Lee, J. K., & Vernig, P. M. (2015). A pilot of an acceptance-based risk reduction program for relational aggression for adolescents. *Journal of Contextual Behavioral Science, 3*(2), 109–116.

Section 8: Transition

Introduction

Cai, R. Y., & Richdale, A. L. (2016). Educational experience and needs of higher education students with autism spectrum disorder. *Journal of Autism and Developmental Disorders, 46*, 31–41.

Goodman, R. (2001). Psychometric properties of the strengths and difficulties questionnaire. *Journal of the American Academy of Child and Adolescent Psychiatry, 40*(11), 1337–1345.

Individuals with Disabilities Education Improvement Act (IDEIA) of 2004, 20 U.S.C. § et. Seq. 1401 (2004). [reauthorization of the Individuals with Disabilities Act of 1990]

Lipscomb, S., Haimson, J., Liu, A. Y., Burghardt, J., Johnson, D. R., & Thurlow, M. L. (2017). *Preparing for life after high school: The characteristics and experiences of youth in special education. Findings from the National Longitudinal Transition Study 2012. Volume 2: Comparisons across disability groups: Full report* (NCEE 2017-4018). U.S. Department of Education, Institute of Education Sciences, National Center for Education Evaluation and Regional Assistance.

Mandy, W., Murin, M., Baykaner, O., Staunton, S., Cobb, R., Hellriegel, J., Anderson, S., & Skuse, D. (2016). Easing the transition to secondary education for children with autism spectrum disorder: An evaluation of the Systemic Transition in Education Programme for Autism Spectrum Disorder (STEP-ASD). *Autism, 20*(5), 580–590.

Newman, L., Wagner, M., Knokey, A. M., Marder, C., Nagle, K., Shaver, D., & Wei, X. (2011). *The post-high school outcomes of young adults with disabilities up to 8 years after high school: A report from the National Longitudinal Transition Study-2* (NLTS-2). National Center for Special Education Research.

Roux, A. M., Shattuck, P. T., Rast, J. E., Rava, J. A., & Anderson, K. A. (2015). *National Autism Indicators Report: Transition into young adulthood.* Life Course Outcomes Research Program, A. J. Drexel Autism Institute, Drexel University.

Sosnowy, C., Silverman, C., & Shattuck, P. (2018). Parents' and young adults' perspectives on transition outcomes for young adults with autism. *Autism, 22*(1), 29–39.

Systemic Transition in Education Programme for Autism Spectrum Disorder (STEP-ASD)

Self-Determined Learning Model of Instruction (SDLMI)

Burke, K. M., Shogren, K. A., Antosh, A. A., LaPlante, T., & Masterson, L. H. (2020). Implementing the SDLMI with students with significant support needs during transition planning. *Career Development and Transition for Exceptional Individuals, 43*(2), 115–121.

Burke, K. M., Shogren, K. A., Raley, S. K., Wehmeyer, M. L., Antosh, A. A., & LaPlante, T. (2019). Implementing evidence-based practices to promote self-determination. *Education and Training in Autism and Developmental Disabilities, 54*(1), 18–29.

Lee, S. H., Wehmeyer, M. L., & Shogren, K. A. (2015). Effect of instruction with the self-determined learning model of instruction on students with disabilities: A

meta-analysis. *Education and Training in Autism and Developmental Disabilities, 50*(2), 237–247.

Mithaug, D., Wehmeyer, M., Agran, M., Martin, J., & Palmer, S. (1998). The self-determined learning model of instruction: Engaging students to solve their learning problems. In M. L. Wehmeyer & D. J. Sands (Eds.), *Making it happen: Student involvement in educational planning, decision-making and instruction* (pp. 299–328). Paul H. Brookes.

National Technical Assistance Center on Transition. (2016). *Evidence-based practices and predictors in secondary transition: What we know and what we still need to know.* Author.

Palmer, S. B., & Wehmeyer, M. L. (2003). Promoting self-determination in early elementary school: Teaching self-regulated problem-solving and goal-setting skills. *Remedial and Special Education, 24*(2), 115–126.

Shogren, K. A., Raley, S. K., Burke, K. M., & Wehmeyer, M. L. (2019). *The self-determined learning model of instruction teacher's guide.* Kansas University Center on Developmental Disabilities.

Wehmeyer, M. L., Palmer, S. B., Agran, M., Mithaug, D. E., & Martin, J. E. (2000). Promoting causal agency: The self-determined learning model of instruction. *Exceptional Children, 66*, 439–453.

Wehmeyer, M. L., & Shogren, K. A. (2008). Self-determination and learners with autism spectrum disorders. In R. L. Simpson & B. S. Myles (Eds.) *Educating children and youth with autism* (2nd ed., pp 433–476). Pro-Ed.

Person-Centered Planning (PCP)

Hagner, D., Kurtz, A., Cloutier, H., Arakelian, C., Brucker, D. L., & May, J. (2012). Outcomes of a family-centered transition process for students with autism spectrum disorders. *Focus on Autism and Other Developmental Disabilities, 27*(1), 42–50.

Individuals with Disabilities Education Improvement Act (IDEIA) of 2004, 20 U.S.C. § et. Seq. 1401 (2004). [reauthorization of the Individuals with Disabilities Act of 1990]

Kohler, P. D., & Field, S. (2003). Transition-focused education: Foundation for the future. *The Journal of Special Education, 37*(3), 174–183.

Martin, J. E., Marshall, L. H., Maxson, L. M., & Jerman, P. L. (1996). *The self-directed IEP.* https://www.ou.edu/education/centers-and-partnerships/zarrow/transition-resources/curriculum/choicemaker

Miner, C. A., & Bates, P. E. (1997). The effect of person centered planning activities on the IEP/transition planning process. *Education and Training in Mental Retardation and Developmental Disabilities, 32*(2), 105–112. http://www.jstor.org/stable/23879030

Mount, B., & Zwernick, K. (1989). *It's never too early it's never too late: A booklet about personal futures planning for persons with developmental disabilities, their families and friends, case managers, service providers and advocates.* Metropolitan Council.

Tondora, J., Croft, B., Kardell, Y., Camacho-Gonsalves, T., & Kwak, M. (2020). *Five competency domains for staff who facilitate person-centered planning*. National Center on Advancing Person-Centered Practices and Systems.

Van Reusen, A. K., Bos, C. S., Schumaker, J. B., & Deshler, D. D. (2007). Self-advocacy strategy: Enhancing student motifcation and self-determination. Edge Enterprises, Inc.

Wehmeyer, M. L., Lawrence, M., Garner, N., Soukup, J., & Palmer, S. (2004). *Whose future is it anyway? A student-directed transition planning process*. https://www.ou.edu/education/centers-and-partnerships/zarrow/transition-resources/curriculum/whose-future

Whitney-Thomas, J., Shaw, D., Honey, K., & Butterworth, J. (1998). Building a future: A study of student participation in person-centered planning. *The Journal of the Association for Persons with Severe Handicaps, 23*(2), 119–133.

Section 9: Miscellaneous Non-Educational Interventions

Peer-Mediated Instruction and Intervention

Bene, K, Banda, D. R., & Brown, D. (2014). A meta-analysis of peer-mediated instructional arrangements and autism. *Review Journal of Autism and Developmental Disorders, 1,* 135–142.

Carter, E. W., Cushing, L. S., Clark, N. M., & Kennedy, C. H. (2005). Effects of peer support interventions on students' access to the general curriculum and social interactions. *Research and practice for persons with severe disabilities, 30*(1), 15-25.

Chan, J. M., Lang, R., Rispoli, M., O'Reilly, M., Sigafoos, J., & Cole, H. (2009). Use of peer-mediated interventions in the treatment of autism spectrum disorders: A systematic review. *Research in Autism Spectrum Disorders, 3*(4), 876–889.

Chang, Y. C., & Locke, J. (2016). A systematic review of peer-mediated interventions for children with autism spectrum disorder. *Research in Autism Spectrum Disorders, 27*, 1–10.

O'Donoghue, M., O'Dea, A., O'Leary, N., Kennedy, N., Forbes, J., & Murphy, C. A. (2021). Systematic review of peer-mediated intervention for children with autism who are minimally verbal. *Review Journal of Autism and Developmental Disorders, 8*, 51–66.

Stichter, J. P., & Conroy, M. A. (2006). How to teach social skills and plan for peer social interactions. Austin, TX: Pro-Ed.

Travers, H. E., & Carter, E. W. (2022). A portrait of peers within peer-mediated interventions: A literature review. *Focus on Autism and Other Developmental Disabilities, 37*(2), 71-82.

Watkins, L., O'Reilly, M., Kuhn, M., Gevarter, C., Lancioni, G. E., Sigafoos, J., & Lang, R. (2015). A review of peer-mediated social interaction interventions for students with autism in inclusive settings. *Journal of Autism and Developmental Disorders, 45*, 1070–1083.

Zagona, A. L., & Mastergeorge, A. M. (2018). An empirical review of peer-mediated interventions: Implications for young children with autism spectrum disorders. *Focus on Autism and Other Developmental Disabilities, 33*(3), 131–141.

Zhang, J., & Wheeler, J. J. (2011). A meta-analysis of peer-mediated interventions for young children with autism spectrum disorders. *Education and Training in Autism and Developmental Disabilities*, 62-77.

Parent-Implemented Interventions

Barton, E. E., & Fettig, A. (2013). Parent-implemented interventions for young children with disabilities: A review of fidelity features. *Journal of Early Intervention, 35*(2), 194–219.

Chan, J. M., Lang, R., Rispoli, M., O'Reilly, M., Sigafoos, J., & Cole, H. (2009). Use of peer-mediated interventions in the treatment of autism spectrum disorders: A systematic review. *Research in Autism Spectrum Disorders, 3*(4), 876–889.

Coolican, J., Smith, I. M., & Bryson, S. E. (2010). Brief parent training in pivotal response treatment for preschoolers with autism. *Journal of Child Psychology and Psychiatry, 51*(12), 1321–1330.

Hendricks, D. R. (2009). *Steps for implementation: Parent-implemented intervention*. The National Professional Development Center on ASD, Frank Porter Graham Child Development Institute, University of North Carolina.

Ingersoll, B., & Wainer, A. (2013). Initial efficacy of Project ImPACT: A parent-mediated social communication intervention for young children with ASD. *Journal of Autism and Developmental Disorders, 43*(12), 2943–2952.

Johnson, C. R., Handen, B. L., Butter, E., Wagner, A., Mulick, J., Sukhodolsky, D. G., Williams, S., Swiezy, N. A., Arnold, L. E., Aman, M. G., Scahill, L., Stigler, K. A., McDougle, C. J., Vitiello, B., & Smith, T. (2007). Development of a parent training program for children with pervasive developmental disorders. *Behavioral Interventions, 22*(3), 201–221.

Koegel, R. L., Symon, J. B., & Kern Koegel, L. (2002). Parent education for families of children with autism living in geographically distant areas. *Journal of Positive Behavior Interventions, 4*(2), 88–103.

Koegel, R. L., & Traphagen, J. (1982). Selection of initial words for speech training with nonverbal children. In R. L. Koegel, A. Rincover, & A. L. Egel (Eds.), *Educating and understanding autistic children*. College-Hill Press.

Mazzucchelli, T. G., & Sanders, M. R. (2012). Stepping stones triple P: A population approach to the promotion of competent parenting of children with disability. *Parenting Research and Practice Monograph, 2*, 1–35.

McConachie, H., & Diggle, T. (2007). Parent implemented early intervention for young children with autism spectrum disorder: A systematic review. *Journal of Evaluation in Clinical Practice, 13*(1), 120–129.

National Clearing House on Autism Evidence and Practice (2021). *Evidence-Based Supports*. NCAEP. https://ncaep.fpg.unc.edu/

Patterson, S. Y., Smith, V., & Mirenda, P. (2012). A systematic review of training programs for parents of children with autism spectrum disorders: Single subject contributions. *Autism, 16*(5), 498–522.

Roberts, J. E., Weisenfeld, L. A. H., Hatton, D. D., Heath, M., & Kaufmann, W. E. (2007). Social approach and autistic behavior in children with fragile X syndrome. *Journal of Autism and Developmental Disorders, 37*(9).

Ruble, L. A., Dalrymple, N. J., & McGrew, J. H. (2012). *Collaborative model for promoting competence and success for students with ASD*. Springer.

Steiner, A. M., Koegel, L. K., Koegel, R. L., & Ence, W. A. (2012). Issues and theoretical constructs regarding parent education for autism spectrum disorders. *Journal of Autism and Developmental Disorders, 42*(6), 1218–1227.

Zwaigenbaum, L., Bauman, M. L., Choueiri, R., Kasari, C., Carter, A., Granpeesheh, D., Zoe Mailloux, Z., Smith Roley, S., Wagner, S., Fein, D., Pierce, K., Buie, T., Davis, P. A., Newschaffer, C., Robins, D., Wetherby, A., Stone, W. L., Yirmiya, N., Estes, A., Hansen, R. L., . . . & Natowicz, M. R. (2015). Early intervention for children with autism spectrum disorder under 3 years of age: Recommendations for practice and research. *Pediatrics, 136*(Supplement 1), S60–S81.

Music-Mediated Interventions (MMI)

Applewhite, B., Cankaya, Z., Heiderscheit, A., & Himmerich, H. (2022). A systematic review of scientific studies on the effects of music in people with or at risk for autism spectrum disorder. *International Journal of Environmental Research and Public Health, 19*, 5150.

Merriam, A. (1964). *The anthropology of music*. Northwestern University Press.

Meyer-Benarous, H., Benarous, X., Vanthron, F., & Cohen, D. (2021). Music therapy for children with autistic spectrum disorder and/or other neurodevelopmental disorders: A systematic review. *Frontiers in Psychiatry, 12*, 643234.

Silverman, M., Gooding, L., & Yinger, O. (2020). It's . . . complicated: A theoretical model of music-induced harm. *Journal of Music Therapy, 57*(3), 251–281.

Music Intensity

Buckley, S. D., & Newchok, D. K. (2006). Analysis and treatment of problem behavior evoked by music. *Journal of Applied Behavior Analysis, 39*(1), 141–144.

Gibbs, A. R., Tullis, C. A., Thomas, R., & Elkins, B. (2018). The effects of noncontingent music and response interruption and redirection on vocal stereotypy. *Journal of Applied Behavior Analysis, 51*(4), 899–914.

Lanovaz, M. J., Fletcher, S. E., & Rapp, J. T. (2009). Identifying stimuli that alter immediate and subsequent levels of vocal stereotypy: A further analysis of functionally matched stimulation. *Behavior Modification, 33*(5), 682–704.

Lanovaz, M. J., Rapp, J. T., & Ferguson, S. (2012). The utility of assessing musical preference before implementation of noncontingent music to reduce vocal stereotypy. *Journal of Applied Behavior Analysis, 45*(4), 845–851.

Lanovaz, M. J., Rapp, J. T., Maciw, I., Prégent-Pelletier, E., Dorion, C., Ferguson, S., & Saade, S. (2014). Effects of multiple interventions for reducing vocal stereotypy: Developing a sequential intervention model. *Research in Autism Spectrum Disorders, 8*, 529–545.

Lanovaz, M. J., Robertson, K. M., Soerono, K., & Watkins, N. (2013). Effects of reducing stereotypy on other behaviors: A systematic review. *Research in Autism Disorders, 7*(10), 1234–1243.

Lanovaz, M. J., Sladeczek, I. E., & Rapp, J. T. (2011). Effects of music on vocal stereotypy in children with autism. *Journal of Applied Behavior Analysis, 44*(3), 647–651.

Preis, J., Amon, R., Robinette, D., & Rozegar, A. (2016). Does music matter? The effects of background music on verbal expression and engagement in children with autism spectrum disorders. *Music Therapy Perspectives, 34*(1), 106–115.

Reschke-Hernandez, A. E. (2011). History of music therapy treatment interventions for children with autism. *Journal of Music Therapy, 48*(2), 169–207.

Saylor, S., Sidener, T. M., Reeve, S. A., Fetherston, A., & Progar, P. R. (2012). Effects of three types of noncontingent auditory stimulation on vocal stereotypy in children with autism. *Journal of Applied Behavior Analysis, 45*(1), 185–190.

Animal-Assisted Intervention (AAI)

Becker, J. L., Rogers, E. C., & Burrows, B. (2017). Animal-assisted social skills training for children with autism spectrum disorders. *Anthrozoös, 30*(2), 307–326.

Friedman, E., & Son, H. (2009). The human-companion animal bond: How humans benefit. *Veterinary Clinics of North America: Small Animal Practice, 39*(2), 293–326.

Griffin, J. A., McCune, S., Maholmes, V., & Hurley, K. (2011). Human-animal interaction research: An introduction to issues and topics. In P. McCardle, S. McCune, J. A. Griffin, & V. Maholmes (Eds.), *How animals affect us: Examining the influence of human-animal interaction on child development and human health* (pp. 3–9). American Psychological Association.

Kruger, K. A., & Serpell, J. A. (2010). Animal-assisted interventions in mental health: Definitions and theoretical foundations. In A. H. Fine (Ed.), *Handbook on animal-assisted therapy: Theoretical foundations and guidelines for practice* (3rd ed., pp. 33–48). Academic Press.

Nimer, J., & Lundahl, B. (2007). Animal-assisted therapy: A meta-analysis. *Anthrozoös, 20*(2), 225–238.

O'Haire, M. E. (2010). Companion animals and human health: Benefits, challenges, and the road ahead. *Journal of Veterinary Behavior: Clinical Applications and Research, 5*(5), 226–234.

O'Haire, M. E. (2013). Animal-assisted intervention for autism spectrum disorder: A systematic literature review. *Journal of Autism & Developmental Disorders, 43*, 1606–1622.

O'Haire, M. E. (2017). Research on animal-assisted intervention and autism spectrum disorder, 2012–2015. *Applied Developmental Science, 21*(3), 200–216.

Silva, K., Correia, R., Lima, M., Magalhaes, A., & de Sousa, L. (2011). Can dogs prime autistic children for therapy? Evidence from a single case study. *The Journal of Alternative and Complimentary Medicine, 17*(7), 1–5.

Wells, D. L. (2009). The effects of animals on human health and well-being. *Journal of Social Issues, 65*(3), 523–543.

Art Therapy

Alter-Muri, S. B. (2017). Art education and art therapy strategies for autism spectrum disorder students. *Art Education, 70*(5), 20–25.

Kornreich, T. Z., & Schimmel, B. F. (1991). The world is attacked by great big snowflakes: Art therapy with an autistic boy. *American Journal of Art Therapy, 29*, 77–84.

Martin, N. (2009). Art therapy and autism: Overview and recommendations. *Art Therapy: Journal of the American Art Therapy Association, 26*(4), 187–190.

Round, A. J., Baker, W., & Rayner, C. (2017). Using visual arts to encourage children with autism spectrum disorder to communicate their feelings and emotions. *Open Journal of Social Sciences, 5*, 90–108.

Schweizer, C., Knorth, E., & Spreen, M. (2014). Art therapy with children with autism spectrum disorders: A review of clinical case descriptions on "what works." *The Arts in Psychotherapy, 41*, 577–593.

Steinberger, E. (1987). Long-term art therapy with an autistic adolescent. *The American Journal of Art Therapy, 26*, 40–47.

Ullmann, P. (2012). *Art therapy and children with autism: Gaining access to their world through creativity.*

Outdoor Adventure Interventions

Zachor, D. A., Vardi, S., Baron-Eitan, S., Brodai-Meir, I., Ginossar, N., & Ben-Itzchak, E. (2017). The effectiveness of an outdoor adventure programme for young children with autism spectrum disorder: A controlled study. *Developmental Medicine and Child Neurology, 59*(5), 550–556.

Toilet Training

Azrin, N. H., & Foxx, R. M. (1971). A rapid method of toilet training the institutionalized retarded. *Journal of Applied Behavior Analysis, 4*, 89–99.

Bainbridge, N., & Myles, B. S. (1999). The use of priming to introduce toilet training to a child with autism. *Focus on Autism and other Developmental Disabilities, 14*(2), 106–109.

Baird, D. C., Bybel, M., & Kowalski, A. W. (2019). Toilet training common questions and answers. *American Family Physician, 100*(8), 468–474.

Blum, N. J., Taubman, B., & Nemeth, N. (2004). Why is toilet training occurring at older ages? A study of factors associated with later training. *Journal of Pediatrics, 145*, 107–111.

Cicero, F. R., & Pfadt, A. (2002). Investigation of a reinforcement-based toilet training procedure for children with autism. *Research in Developmental Disabilities, 23*(5), 319–331.

Cocchiola, M. A., Jr., Martino, G. M., Dwyer, L. J., & Demezzo, K. (2012). Toilet training children with autism and developmental delays: An effective program for school settings. *Behavior Analysis in Practice, 5*(2), 60–64.

Dalrymple, N. J., & Ruble, L. A. (1992). Toilet training and behaviors of people with autism: Parent views. *Journal of Autism and Developmental Disorders, 22*(2), 265–275.

Drysdale, B., Lee, C. Y. Q., Anderson, A., & Moore, D. W. (2015). Using video modeling incorporating animation to teach toileting to two children with autism spectrum disorder. *Journal of Developmental and Physical Disabilities, 27*(2), 149–165.

Keen, D., Brannigan, K. L., & Cuskelly, M. (2007). Toilet training for children with autism: The effects of video modeling. *Journal of Developmental and Physical Disabilities, 19*, 291–303.

Kurniawan, R., Purnamasari, W. M., Rakhmawati, R., & Jalaputra, D. P. E. (2018). Development of game for self-help toilet learning for children with autism. *CommIT (Communication and Information Technology) Journal, 12*(1), 1–12.

LeBlanc, L. A., Carr, J. E., Crossett, S. E., Bennett, C. M., & Detweiler, D. D. (2005). Intensive outpatient behavioral treatment of primary urinary incontinence of children with autism. *Focus on Autism and Other Developmental Disabilities, 20*(2), 98–105.

Lee, C. Y. Q., Anderson, A., & Moore, D. W. (2014). Using video modeling to toilet train a child with autism. *Journal of Developmental and Physical Disabilities, 26*(2), 123–134.

McLay, L., Carnett, A., Van Der Meer, L., & Lang, R. (2015). Using a video modeling-based intervention package to toilet train two children with autism. *Journal of developmental and physical disabilities, 27*(4), 431–451.

Post, A. R., & Kirkpatrick, M. A. (2004). Toilet training for a young boy with pervasive developmental disorder. *Behavioral Interventions, 19*, 45–50.

Saral, D., & Ulke-Kurkcuoglu, G. (2020). Toilet training individuals with developmental delays: A comprehensive review. *International Journal of Early Childhood Special Education, 12*(1), 120–137.

Taylor, S., Cipani, E., & Clardy, A. (1994). A stimulus control technique for improving the efficacy of an established toilet training program. *Journal of Behavior Therapy and Experimental Psychiatry, 25*(2), 155–160.

SENSE Theatre®

Corbett, B. (2016). SENSE theatre intervention for children with autism spectrum disorder (ASD). *SENSE Theatre Research Program, 46*(2), 658–672.

Corbett, B. A., Blain, S. D., Ioannou, S., & Balser, M. (2017). Changes in anxiety following a randomized control trial of a theatre-based intervention for youth with autism spectrum disorder. *Autism, 21*(3), 333–343.

Exercise and Movement (EXM) Interventions

Celiberti, D. A., Bobo, H. E., Kelly, K. S., Harris, S. L., & Handleman, J. S. (1997). The differential and temporal effects of antecedent exercise on the self-stimulatory behavior of a child with autism. *Research in Developmental Disabilities, 18*(2), 139–150.

Elliott, R. O., Dobbin, A. R., Rose, G. D., & Soper, H. V. (1994). Vigorous, aerobic exercise versus general motor training activities: Effects on maladaptive and stereotypic behaviors of adults with both autism and mental retardation. *Journal of Autism and Developmental Disorders, 24*(5), 565–576.

Lang, R., Koegel, L. K., Ashbaugh, K., Regester, A., Ence, W., & Smith, W. (2010). Physical exercise and individuals with autism spectrum disorders: A systematic review. *Research in Autism Spectrum Disorders, 4*(4), 565–576.

Levinson, L. J., & Reid, G. (1993). The effects of exercise intensity on the stereotypic behaviors of individuals with autism. *Adapted Physical Activity Quarterly, 10*(3), 255–268.

Neely, L., Rispoli, M., Gerow, S., & Ninci, J. (2015). Effects of antecedent exercise on academic engagement and stereotypy during instruction. *Behavior Modification, 39*(1), 98–116.

Park, E., Kim, W., & Blair, K. C. (2021). Effectiveness of interventions involving physical activities for individuals with autism spectrum disorder: A meta-analysis. *Education and Training in Autism and Developmental Disabilities, 56*(3), 354–367.

Rosenthal-Malek, A., & Mitchell, S. (1997). Brief report: The effects of exercise on the self-stimulatory behaviors and positive responding of adolescents with autism. *Journal of Autism and Developmental Disorders, 27*(2), 193–202.

Schleien, S. J., Heyne, L. A., & Berken, S. B. (1988). Integrating physical education to teach appropriate play skills to learners with autism: A pilot study. *Adapted Physical Activity Quarterly, 5*(3), 182–192.

Sowa, M., & Meulenbroek, R. (2012). Effects of physical exercise on autism spectrum disorders: A meta-analysis. *Research in Autism Spectrum Disorders, 6*(1), 46–57.

Thompson, J. K., & Blanton, P. (1987). Energy conservation and exercise dependence: A sympathetic arousal hypothesis. *Medicine & Science in Sports & Exercise, 19*(2), 91–99.

Gentle Teaching

Cullen, C., & Mappin, R. (1998). An examination of the effects of gentle teaching on people with complex learning disabilities and challenging behavior *British Journal of Clinical Psychology, 37,* 199–221.

Jones, R. S. P., & McCaughey, R. E. (1992). Gentle teaching and applied behavior analysis: A critical review. *Journal of Applied Behavioral Analysis, 25*(4), 853–867.

McGee, J. J. (1985). Gentle teaching. *Mental Handicap in New Zealand, 9*(3), 13–24.

McGee, J. J. (1990). Gentle teaching: The basic tenet. *Mental Handicap Nursing, 86*(32), 68–72.

McGee, J. J. (1992). Gentle teaching's assumptions and paradigm. *Journal of Applied Behavior Analysis, 25,* 869–872.

Mudford, O. C. (1995). Review of the gentle teaching data. *American Journal on Mental Retardation, 99,* 345–355.

Sensory Integration (SI) Interventions

Ayres, A. J. (2005). *Sensory integration and the child: Understanding hidden sensory challenges.* Western Psychological Services.

Barton, E. E., Reichow, B., Schnitz, A., Smith, I. C., & Sherlock, D. (2015). A systematic review of sensory-based treatments for children with disabilities. *Research in Developmental Disabilities, 37*(1), 64–80.

Case-Smith, J., Weaver, L. L., & Fristad, M. A. (2015). A systematic review of sensory processing interventions for children with autism spectrum disorders. *Autism, 19*(2), 133–148.

Kashefimehr, B., Kayihan, H., & Huri, M. (2018). The effect of sensory integration therapy on occupational performance in children with autism. *OTJR: Occupation, Participation, and Health, 38*(2), 75–83.

Myles, B. S., Cook, K. T., Miller, N. E., Rinner, L., & Robbins, L. A. (2000). *Asperger syndrome and sensory issues.* Autism Asperger.

Pfeiffer, B. A., Koenig, K., Kinnealey, M., Sheppard, M., & Henderson, L. (2011). Effectiveness of sensory integration interventions in children with autism spectrum disorders: A pilot study. *The American Journal of Occupational Therapy, 65*(1), 76–85.

Schaaf, R. C., Benevides, T., Mailloux, Z., Faller, P., Hunt, J., van Hooydonk, E., Freeman, R., Leiby, B., Sendecki, J., & Kelly, D. (2014). An intervention for sensory difficulties in children with autism: A randomized trial. *Journal of Autism and Developmental Disorders, 44*(7), 1493–1506.

Watling, R., & Hauer, S. (2015). Effectiveness of Ayres Sensory Integration® and sensory-based interventions for people with autism spectrum disorder: A systematic review. *American Journal of Occupational Therapy, 69*(5), 6905180030p.1–11.

Section 10: Biomedical and Nutritional Treatments

Introduction

Golnik, A. E., & Ireland, M. (2009). Complementary alternative medicine for children with autism: a physician survey. *Journal of Autism and Developmental Disorders, 39,* 996–1005.

Simpson, R. L., & Myles, B. S. (2016). Educating children and youth with autism: Strategies for *effective practice* (3rd. ed.). ProEd.

Hyperbaric Oxygen Therapy (HBOT)

Lasheen, R. M., Abu-Zaid, M. H., & Tabra, S. A. A. H. (2019). Evaluation of auditory attention and memorys kills in autistic children after hyperbaric O2 treatment. *Egyptian Journal of Ear, Nose, Throat and Allied Sciences, 20*(2), 60–66.

Podgórska-Bednarz, J., & Perenc, L. (2021). Hyperbaric oxygen therapy for children and youth with autism spectrum disorder: A review. *Brain Sciences, 11*(7), 916.

Sakulchit, T., Ladish, C., & Goldman, R. D. (2017). Hyperbaric oxygen therapy for children with autism spectrum disorder. *Canadian Family Physician, 63* (6), 446–448

Sampanthavivat, M., Singkhwa, W., Chaiyakul, T., Karoonyawanich, S., & Ajpru, H. (2012). Hyperbaric oxygen in the treatment of childhood autism: A randomised controlled trial. *Diving and Hyperbaric Medicine, 42*(3), 128–133.

Xiong, T., Chen, H., Luo, R., & Mu, D. (2016). Hyperbaric oxygen therapy for people with autism spectrum disorder (ASD). *Cochrane Database of Systematic Reviews, 10*(10), CD010922.

Specialized Diets

Afzal, N., Murch, S., Thirrupathy, K., Berger, L., Fagbemi, A., & Heuschkel, R. (2003). Constipation with acquired megarectum in children with autism. *Pediatrics, 112*(4), 939–942.

Arnold, G. L., Hyman, S. L., Mooney, R. A., & Kirby, R. S. (2003). Plasma amino acids profiles in children with autism: Potential risk of nutritional deficiencies, *Journal of Autism and Developmental Disabilities, 33*, 449–454.

Baspinar, B., & Yardimci, H. (2020). Gluten-free casein-free diet for autism spectrum disorders: Can it be effective in solving behavioural and gastrointestinal problems? *The Eurasian Journal of Medicine, 52*(3), 292.

Campbell-McBride, N. (2008). Gut and psychology syndrome. *Journal of Orthomolecular Medicine, 23*(2), 90.

Castro, K., Faccioli, L. S., Baronio, D., Gottfried, C., Perry, I. S., & dos Santos Riesgo, R. (2015). Effect of a ketogenic diet on autism spectrum disorder: A systematic review. *Research in Autism Spectrum Disorders, 20*, 31–38.

Cornish, E. (2002). Gluten and casein free diets in autism: A study of the effects on food choice and nutrition. *Journal of Human Nutrition and Dietetics, 15*(4), 261–269.

Dosman, C., Adams, D., Wudel, B., Vogels, L., Turner, J., & Vohra, S. (2013). Complementary, holistic, and integrative medicine: Autism spectrum disorder and gluten- and casein-free diet. *Pediatrics in Review, 34*(10), e36–e41.

Elder, J. H., Kreider, C. M., Schaefer, N. M., & de Laosa, M. B. (2015). A review of gluten- and casein-free diets for treatment of autism: 2005–2015. *Nutrition and Dietary Supplements, 7*, 87.

Elder, J. H., Shankar, M., Shuster, J., Theriaque, D., Burns, S., & Sherrill, L. (2006). The gluten-free, casein-free diet in autism: Results of a preliminary double blind clinical trial. *Journal of Autism and Developmental Disorders, 36*(3), 413–420.

Emam, A. M., Esmat, M. M., & Sadek, A. A. (2012). Candida albicans infection in autism. *Journal of American Science, 8*(12), 739–744.

Fugelsang, K., & Edwards, C. (2010). *Wine microbiology.* Springer Science and Business Media.

Gogou, M., & Kolios, G. (2018). Are therapeutic diets an emerging additional choice in autism spectrum disorder management? *World Journal of Pediatrics, 14*(3), 215–223.

González-Domenech, P. J., Díaz Atienza, F., García Pablos, C., Fernández Soto, M. L., Martínez-Ortega, J. M., & Gutiérrez-Rojas, L. (2020). Influence of a combined gluten-free and casein-free diet on behavior disorders in children and adolescents diagnosed with autism spectrum disorder: A 12-month follow-up clinical trial. *Journal of Autism and Developmental Disorders, 50*(3), 935–948.

Heiger, M. L., England, L. J., Molloy, C. A., Yu, K. F., Manning-Courtney, P., & Mills, J. L. (2008). Reduced bone cortical thickness in boys with autism or autism spectrum disorder. *Journal of Autism and Developmental Disorders, 38*(5), 848–856.

Herman, A., & Herman, A. P. (2022). Could candida overgrowth be involved in the pathophysiology of autism? *Journal of Clinical Medicine, 11*(2), 442.

Horvath, K., & Perman, J. A. (2002). Autism and gastrointestinal symptoms. *Current Gastroenterology Reports, 4*(3), 251–258.

Hyman, S. L., Stewart, P. A., Foley, J., Peck, R., Morris, D. D., Wang, H., & Smith, T. (2016). The gluten-free/casein-free diet: A double-blind challenge trial in children with autism. *Journal of Autism and Developmental Disorders, 46*(1), 205–220.

Karhu, E., Zukerman, R., Eshraghi, R. S., Mittal, J., Deth, R. C., Castejon, A. M., Trivedi, M., Mittal, R., & Eshraghi, A. A. (2020). Nutritional interventions for autism spectrum disorder. *Nutrition Reviews, 78*(7), 515–531.

Keller, A., Rimestad, M. L., Friis Rohde, J., Holm Petersen, B., Bruun Korfitsen, C., Tarp, S., Briciet Lauritsen, M., & Händel, M. N. (2021). The effect of a combined gluten- and casein-free diet on children and adolescents with autism spectrum disorders: A systematic review and meta-analysis. *Nutrients, 13*(2), 470.

Li, Q., Liang, J., Fu, N., Han, Y., & Qin, J. (2021). A ketogenic diet and the treatment of autism spectrum disorder. *Frontiers in Pediatrics, 9*, 650624.

Mari-Bauset, S., Zazpe, I., Mari-Sanchis, A., Llopis-González, A., & Morales-Suarez-Varela, M. (2014). Evidence of the gluten-free and casein-free diet in autism spectrum disorders: A systematic review. *Journal of Child Neurology, 29*(12), 1718–1727.

Mulloy, A., Lang, R., O'Reilly, M., Sigafoos, J., Lancioni, G., & Rispoli, M. (2010). Gluten-free and casein-free diets in the treatment of autism spectrum disorders: A systematic review. *Research in Autism Spectrum Disorders, 4*(3), 328–339.

Napoli, E., Dueñas, N., & Giulivi, C. (2014). Potential therapeutic use of the ketogenic diet in autism spectrum disorders. *Frontiers in Pediatrics, 2*, 69.

Navarro, F., Pearson, D. A., Fatheree, N., Mansour, R., Hashmi, S. S., & Rhoads, J. M. (2015). Are "leaky gut" and behavior associated with gluten and dairy containing diet in children with autism spectrum disorders? *Nutritional Neuroscience, 18*(4), 177–185.

Reissmann, A., Hauser, J., Stollberg, E., Lange, K. W. (2020). Gluten-free and casein-free diets in the management of autism spectrum disorder: A systematic literature review. *Movement and Nutrition in Health and Disease, 4*, 21–38.

Robertson, M. A., Sigalet, D. L., Holst, J. J., Meddings, J. B., Wood, J., & Sharkey, K. A. (2008). Intestinal permeability and glucagon-like peptide-2 in children with autism: A controlled pilot study. *Journal of Autism and Developmental Disorders, 38*(6), 1066–1071.

Whiteley, P., Shattock, P., Knivsberg, A. M., Seim, A., Reichelt, K. L., Todd, L., Carr, K., & Hooper, M. (2013). Gluten- and casein-free dietary intervention for autism spectrum conditions. *Frontiers in Human Neuroscience, 6*, 344.

Microbiome Therapies

Arnold, L. E., Luna, R. A., Williams, K., Chan, J., Parker, R. A., Wu, Q., Hollway, J. A., Jeffs, A., Lu, F., Coury, D. L., Hayes, C., & Savidge, T. (2019). Probiotics for gastrointestinal symptoms and quality of life in autism: A placebo-controlled pilot trial. *Journal of Child and Adolescent Psychopharmacology, 29*(9), 659–669.

Baker, S., & Shaw, W. (2020). Case study: Rapid complete recovery from an autism spectrum disorder after treatment of Aspergillus with the antifungal drugs itraconazole and sporanox. *Integrative Medicine: A Clinician's Journal, 19*(4), 20.

Berding, K., & Donovan, S. M. (2020). Dietary patterns impact temporal dynamics of fecal microbiota composition in children with autism spectrum disorder. *Frontiers in Nutrition, 6*, 193.

Chaidez, V., Hansen, R. L., & Hertz-Picciotto, I. (2014). Gastrointestinal problems in children with autism, developmental delays or typical development. *Journal of Autism and Developmental Disorders, 44*(5), 1117–1127.

Das, B., & Nair, G. B. (2019). Homeostasis and dysbiosis of the gut microbiome in health and disease. *Journal of Biosciences, 44*(5), 1–8.

De Angelis, M., Piccolo, M., Vannini, L., Siragusa, S., De Giacomo, A., Serrazzanetti, D. I., Cristofori, F., Guerzoni, M. E., Gobbetti, M., & Francavilla, R. (2013). Fecal microbiota and metabolome of children with autism and pervasive developmental disorder not otherwise specified. *PloS One, 8*(10), e76993.

Drekonja, D., Reich, J., Gezahegn, S., Greer, N., Shaukat, A., MacDonald, R., Rutks, I., & Wilt, T. J. (2015). Fecal microbiota transplantation for Clostridium difficile infection: A systematic review. *Annals of Internal Medicine, 162*(9), 630–638.

Fattorusso, A., Di Genova, L., Dell'Isola, G. B., Mencaroni, E., & Esposito, S. (2019). Autism spectrum disorders and the gut microbiota. *Nutrients, 11*(3), 521.

Ferguson, B. J., Dovgan, K., Takahashi, N., & Beversdorf, D. Q. (2019). The relationship among gastrointestinal symptoms, problem behaviors, and internalizing symptoms in children and adolescents with autism spectrum disorder. *Frontiers in Psychiatry, 10*, 194.

Finegold, S. M., Dowd, S. E., Gontcharova, V., Liu, C., Henley, K. E., Wolcott, R. D., Youn, E., Summanen, P. H., Granpeesheh, D., Dixon, D., Liu, M., Molitoris, D. R., & Green, J. A., III. (2010). Pyrosequencing study of fecal microflora of autistic and control children. *Anaerobe, 16*(4), 444–453.

Ford, A. C., Harris, L. A., Lacy, B. E., Quigley, E. M., & Moayyedi, P. (2018). Systematic review with meta-analysis: The efficacy of prebiotics, probiotics, synbiotics and antibiotics in irritable bowel syndrome. *Alimentary Pharmacology & Therapeutics, 48*(10), 1044–1060.

Fowlie, G., Cohen, N., & Ming, X. (2018). The perturbance of microbiome and gut-brain axis in autism spectrum disorders. *International Journal of Molecular Sciences, 19*(8), 2251.

Gupta, S., Mullish, B. H., & Allegretti, J. R. (2021). Fecal microbiota transplantation: The evolving risk landscape. *Official Journal of the American College of Gastroenterology|ACG, 116*(4), 647–656.

Herd, P., Palloni, A., Rey, F., & Dowd, J. B. (2018). Social and population health science approaches to understand the human microbiome. *Nature Human Behaviour, 2*(11), 808–815.

Kelly, B. J., & Tebas, P. (2018). Clinical practice and infrastructure review of fecal microbiota transplantation for Clostridium difficile infection. *Chest, 153*(1), 266–277.

Leader, G., Barrett, A., Ferrari, C., Casburn, M., Maher, L., Naughton, K., Arndt, S., & Mannion, A. (2021). Quality of life, gastrointestinal symptoms, sleep problems, social support, and social functioning in adults with autism spectrum disorder. *Research in Developmental Disabilities, 112*, 103915.

Li, Q., Han, Y., Dy, A. B. C., & Hagerman, R. J. (2017). The gut microbiota and autism spectrum disorders. *Frontiers in Cellular Neuroscience, 11*, 120.

Liu, J., Wan, G. B., Huang, M. S., Agyapong, G., Zou, T. L., Zhang, X. Y., Liu, Y. W., Song, Y. Q., Tsai, Y. C., & Kong, X. J. (2019). Probiotic therapy for treating behavioral and gastrointestinal symptoms in autism spectrum disorder: A systematic review of clinical trials. *Current Medical Science, 39*(2), 173–184.

Luo, Y., Lucas, A. L., & Grinspan, A. M. (2020). Fecal transplants by colonoscopy and capsules are cost-effective strategies for treating recurrent Clostridioides difficile infection. *Digestive Diseases and Sciences, 65*(4), 1125–1133.

Mazefsky, C. A., Borue, X., Day, T. N., & Minshew, N. J. (2014). Emotion regulation patterns in adolescents with high-functioning autism spectrum disorder: Comparison to typically developing adolescents and association with psychiatric symptoms. *Autism Research, 7*(3), 344–354.

Sandler, R. H., Finegold, S. M., Bolte, E. R., Buchanan, C. P., Maxwell, A. P., Väisänen, M. L., Nelson, M. N.,

& Wexler, H. M. (2000). Short-term benefit from oral vancomycin treatment of regressive-onset autism. *Journal of Child Neurology, 15*(7), 429–435.

Shaaban, S. Y., El Gendy, Y. G., Mehanna, N. S., El-Senousy, W. M., El-Feki, H. S., Saad, K., & El-Asheer, O. M. (2018). The role of probiotics in children with autism spectrum disorder: A prospective, open-label study. *Nutritional Neuroscience, 21*(9), 676–681.

Son, J. S., Zheng, L. J., Rowehl, L. M., Tian, X., Zhang, Y., Zhu, W., Litcher-Kelly, L., Gadow, K. D., Gathungu, G., Robertson, C. E., Ir, D., Frank, D. N., & Li, E. (2015). Comparison of fecal microbiota in children with autism spectrum disorders and neurotypical siblings in the Simons simplex collection. *PLoS One, 10*(10), e0137725

Tan, Q., Orsso, C. E., Deehan, E. C., Kung, J. Y., Tun, H. M., Wine, E., Madsen, K. L., Zwaigenbaum, L., & Haqq, A. M. (2021). Probiotics, prebiotics, synbiotics, and fecal microbiota transplantation in the treatment of behavioral symptoms of autism spectrum disorder: A systematic review. *Autism Research, 14*(9), 1820–1836.

Xiong, X., Liu, D., Wang, Y., Zeng, T., & Peng, Y. (2016). Urinary 3-(3-hydroxyphenyl)-3-hydroxypropionic acid, 3-hydroxyphenylacetic acid, and 3-hydroxyhippuric acid are elevated in children with autism spectrum disorders. *BioMed Research International, 2016*, 9485412.

Yang, J., Fu, X., Liao, X., & Li, Y. (2020). Effects of gut microbial-based treatments on gut microbiota, behavioral symptoms, and gastrointestinal symptoms in children with autism spectrum disorder: A systematic review. *Psychiatry Research, 293*, 113471.

Yap, C. X., Henders, A. K., Alvares, G. A., Wood, D. L., Krause, L., Tyson, G. W., Restuadi, R., Wallace, L., McLaren, T., Hansell, N. K., Cleary, D., Grove, R., Hafekost, C., Harun, A., Holdsworth, H., Jellett, R., Khan, F., Lawson, L. P., Leslie, J., . . .& Gratten, J. (2021). Autism-related dietary preferences mediate autism-gut microbiome associations. *Cell, 184*(24), 5916–5931.

Vitamin and Mineral Supplementation

Adams, J. B., Audhya, T., McDonough-Means, S., Rubin, R. A., Quig, D., Geis, E., Gehn, E., Loresto, M., Mitchell, J., Atwood, S., Barnhouse, S., & Lee, W. (2011). Effect of a vitamin/mineral supplement on children and adults with autism. *BMC Pediatrics, 11*(1), 1–30.

Barnhill, K., Gutierrez, A., Ghossainy, M., Marediya, Z., Devlin, M., Sachdev, P., Marti, N., & Hewitson, L. (2018). Dietary status and nutrient intake of children with autism spectrum disorder: A case-control study. *Research in Autism Spectrum Disorders, 50*, 51–59.

Bener, A., Khattab, A. O., Bhugra, D., & Hoffmann, G. F. (2017). Iron and vitamin D levels among autism spectrum disorders children. *Annals of African Medicine, 16*(4), 186.

Bjørklund, G., Waly, M. I., Al-Farsi, Y., Saad, K., Dadar, M., Rahman, M., Elhoufey, A., Chirumbolo, S., Jóźwik-Pruska, J., & Kałużna-Czaplińska, J. (2019). The role of vitamins in autism spectrum disorder: What do we know? *Journal of Molecular Neuroscience, 67*(3), 373–387.

Chang, J. P. C., & Su, K. P. (2020). Nutritional neuroscience as mainstream of psychiatry: The evidence-based treatment guidelines for using omega-3 fatty acids as a new treatment for psychiatric disorders in children and adolescents. *Clinical Psychopharmacology and Neuroscience, 18*(4), 469.

Cheng, Y. S., Tseng, P. T., Chen, Y. W., Stubbs, B., Yang, W. C., Chen, T. Y., Wu, C. K., & Lin, P. Y. (2017). Supplementation of omega-3 fatty acids may improve hyperactivity, lethargy, and stereotypy in children with autism spectrum disorders: A meta-analysis of randomized controlled trials. *Neuropsychiatric Disease and Treatment, 13*, 2531.

Cornish, E. (1998). A balanced approach towards healthy eating in autism. *Journal of Human Nutrition and Dietetics, 11*(6), 501–509.

Dosman, C. F., Brian, J. A., Drmic, I. E., Senthilselvan, A., Harford, M. M., Smith, R. W., Sharieff, W., Zlotkin, S. H., Moldofsky, H., & Roberts, S. W. (2007). Children with autism: Effect of iron supplementation on sleep and ferritin. *Pediatric Neurology, 36*(3), 152–158.

Kittana, M., Ahmadani, A., Stojanovska, L., & Attlee, A. (2021). The role of vitamin D supplementation in children with autism spectrum disorder: A narrative review. *Nutrients, 14*(1), 26.

Li, Y. J., Li, Y. M., & Xiang, D. X. (2018). Supplement intervention associated with nutritional deficiencies in autism spectrum disorders: A systematic review. *European Journal of Nutrition, 57*(7), 2571–2582.

Mazahery, H., Camargo, C. A., Jr., Conlon, C., Beck, K. L., Kruger, M. C., & Von Hurst, P. R. (2016). Vitamin D and autism spectrum disorder: A literature review. *Nutrients, 8*(4), 236.

Sathe, N., Andrews, J. C., McPheeters, M. L., & Warren, Z. E. (2017). Nutritional and dietary interventions for autism spectrum disorder: A systematic review. *Pediatrics, 139*(6).

Stewart, P. A., Hyman, S. L., Schmidt, B. L., Macklin, E. A., Reynolds, A., Johnson, C. R., James, S. J., & Manning-Courtney, P. (2015). Dietary supplementation in children with autism spectrum disorders: Common, insufficient, and excessive. *Journal of the Academy of Nutrition and Dietetics, 115*(8), 1237–1248.

Sweetman, D. U., O'Donnell, S. M., Lalor, A., Grant, T., & Greaney, H. (2019). Zinc and vitamin A deficiency in a cohort of children with autism spectrum disorder. *Child: Care, Health and Development, 45*(3), 380–386.

Travers, J. C., Ayers, K., Simpson, R. L., & Crutchfield, S. (2016). Fad, pseudoscientific, and controversial interventions. In R. Lang, T. B. Hancock, & N. N. Singh (Eds.), *Early intervention for young children with autism spectrum disorder* (pp. 257–293). Springer.

Cannabis

Agarwal, R., Burke, S. L., & Maddux, M. (2019). Current state of evidence of cannabis utilization for treatment of autism spectrum disorders. *BMC Psychiatry, 19*(1), 1–10.

American Academy of Pediatrics, & Committee on Substance Abuse. (2015). The impact of marijuana policies on youth: Clinical, research, and legal update. *Pediatrics, 135*(3), 584–587.

Aran, A., Harel, M., Cassuto, H., Polyansky, L., Schnapp, A., Wattad, N., Shmueli, D., Golan, D., & Castellanos, F. X. (2021). Cannabinoid treatment for autism: A proof-of-concept randomized trial. *Molecular Autism, 12*(1), 1–11.

Aran, A., Cassuto, H., Lubotzky, A., Wattad, N., & Hazan, E. (2019). Brief report: Cannabidiol-rich cannabis in children with autism spectrum disorder and severe behavioral problems—a retrospective feasibility study. *Journal of Autism and Developmental Disorders, 49*(3), 1284–1288.

Bar-Lev Schleider, L., Mechoulam, R., Saban, N., Meiri, G., & Novack, V. (2019). Real life experience of medical cannabis treatment in autism: Analysis of safety and efficacy. *Scientific Reports, 9*(1), 1–7.

Bilge, S., & Ekici, B. (2021). CBD-enriched cannabis for autism spectrum disorder: An experience of a single center in Turkey and reviews of the literature. *Journal of Cannabis Research, 3*(1), 1–11.

Duvall, S. W., Lindly, O., Zuckerman, K., Msall, M. E., & Weddle, M. (2019). Ethical implications for providers regarding cannabis use in children with autism spectrum disorders. *Pediatrics, 143*(2).

Fletcher, S., Pawliuk, C., Ip, A., Huh, L., Rassekh, S. R., Oberlander, T. F., & Siden, H. (2022). Medicinal cannabis in children and adolescents with autism spectrum disorder: A scoping review. *Child: Care, Health and Development, 48*(1), 33–44.

Hill, M. N., McLaughlin, R. J., Bingham, B., Shrestha, L., Lee, T. T., Gray, J. M., Hillard, C. J., Gorzalka, B. B., & Viau, V. (2010). Endogenous cannabinoid signaling is essential for stress adaptation. *Proceedings of the National Academy of Sciences, 107*(20), 9406–9411.

Karhson, D. S., Krasinska, K. M., Dallaire, J. A., Libove, R. A., Phillips, J. M., Chien, A. S., Garner, J. P., Hardan, A. Y., & Parker, K. J. (2018). Plasma anandamide concentrations are lower in children with autism spectrum disorder. *Molecular Autism, 9*(1), 1–6.

Karst, A. (2018). Weighing the benefits and risks of medical marijuana use: A brief review. *Pharmacy, 6*(4), 128.

Rieder, M. J., Canadian Pediatric Society, & Drug Therapy and Hazardous Substances Committee. (2016). Is the medical use of cannabis a therapeutic option for children? *Pediatrics & Child Health, 21*(1), 31–34.

Sholler, D. J., Schoene, L., & Spindle, T. R. (2020). Therapeutic efficacy of cannabidiol (CBD): A review of the evidence from clinical trials and human laboratory studies. *Current Addiction Reports, 7*(3), 405–412.

Chelation

Brown, M. J., Willis, T., Omalu, B., & Leiker, R. (2006). Deaths resulting from hypocalcemia after administration of edetate disodium: 2003–2005. *Pediatrics, 118*(2), 786.

Crisponi, G., Nurchi, V. M., Lachowicz, J. I., Crespo-Alonso, M., Zoroddu, M. A., & Peana, M. (2015). Kill or cure: Misuse of chelation therapy for human diseases. *Coordination Chemistry Reviews, 284*, 278–285.

Davis, T. N., O'Reilly, M., Kang, S., Lang, R., Rispoli, M., Sigafoos, J., Lancioni, G., Copeland, D., & Mulloy, A. (2013). Chelation treatment for autism spectrum disorders: A systematic review. *Research in Autism Spectrum Disorders, 7*(1), 49–55.

Hertz-Picciotto, I., Green, P. G., Delwiche, L., Hansen, R., Walker, C., & Pessah, I. N. (2010). Blood mercury concentrations in CHARGE study children with and without autism. *Environmental Health Perspectives, 118*(1), 161–166.

James, S., Stevenson, S. W., Silove, N., & Williams, K. (2015). Chelation for autism spectrum disorder (ASD). *Cochrane Database of Systematic Reviews, 5*, CD010766.

Section 11: Other Interventions With Potential for Causing Significant Harm

Rapid Prompting Method (RPM™)

Mukhopadhyay, S. (2008). *Understanding autism through rapid prompting method.* Outskirts Press.

Schlosser, R. W., Hemsley, B., Shane, H., Todd, J., Lang, R., Lilienfeld, S. O., Trembath, D., Mostert, M., Fong, S., & Odom, S. (2019). Rapid prompting method and autism spectrum disorder: Systematic review exposes lack of evidence. *Review Journal of Autism and Developmental Disorders, 6*(4), 403–412.

Sherry, M. (2016). Facilitated communication, Anna Stubblefield and disability studies. *Disability & Society, 31*(7), 974–982.

Travers, J. C., Ayers, K., Simpson, R. L., & Crutchfield, S. (2016). Fad, pseudoscientific, and controversial interventions. In R. Lang, T. B. Hancock, & N. N. Singh (Eds.), *Early intervention for young children with autism spectrum disorder* (pp. 257–293). Springer.

Travers, J. C., Tincani, M. J., & Lang, R. (2014). Facilitated communication denies people with disabilities their voice. *Research and Practice for Persons with Severe Disabilities, 39*(3), 195–202.

Holding Therapy (HT)

Howlin, P. (2005). The effectiveness of interventions for children with autism. *Journal of Neural Transmission, 69*, 101–119.

Medavarapu, S., Marella, L. L., Sangem, A., & Kairam, R. (2019). Where is the evidence? A narrative literature review of the treatment modalities for autism spectrum disorders. *Cureus, 11*(1), e3901.

Mercer, J. (2013). Holding therapy in Britain: Historical background, recent events, and ethical concerns. *Adoption & Fostering, 37*(2), 144–156.

Mercer, J. (2014). International concerns about holding therapy. *Research on Social Work Practice, 24*(2), 188–191.

Pignotti, M., & Mercer, J. (2007). Holding therapy and dyadic developmental psychotherapy are not supported and acceptable social work interventions: A systematic research synthesis revisited. *Research on Social Work Practice, 17*(4), 513–519.

Rimland, B. (1964). *Infantile autism.* Appleton-Century-Crofts.

Contingent Electric Skin Shock (CESS)

Behavior Analyst Certification Board. (2020). *Ethics code for behavior analysis.* https://bacb.com/wp-content/ethics-code-for-behavior-analysts/

Chezan, L. C., Gable, R. A., McWhorter, G. Z., & White, S. D. (2017). Current perspectives on interventions for self-injurious behavior of children with autism spectrum disorder: A systematic review of the literature. *Journal of Behavioral Education, 26*(3), 293–329.

Diament, M. (2020). *House approves ban on shock devices for those with developmental disabilities.* Disability Scoop. https://www.disabilityscoop.com/2022/06/13/house-approves-ban-on-electric-shock-devices-for-those-with-developmental-disabilities/29894/

Favell, J. E., Azrin, N. H., Baumeister, A. A., Carr, E. G., Dorsey, M. F., Forehand, R., Foxx, R. M., Lovaas, O. I., Rincover, A., Risley, T. R., Romanczyk, R. G., Russo, D. C., Schroeder, S. R., & Solnick, J. V. (1982). The treatment of self-injurious behavior. *Behavior Therapy, 13*(4), 529–554.

Horner, R. H., Dunlap, G., Koegel, R. L., Carr, E. G., Sailor, W., Anderson, J., Albin, R. W., & O'Neill, R. E. (1990). Toward a technology of "nonaversive" behavioral support. *Journal of the Association for Persons with Severe Handicaps, 15*(3), 125–132.

Israel, M. L., Blenkush, N. A., von Heyn, R. E., & Rivera, P. M. (2008). Treatment of aggression with behavioral programming that includes supplementary contingent skin-shock. *The Journal of Behavior Analysis of Offender and Victim Treatment and Prevention, 1*(4), 119.

Israel, M. L., Blenkush, N. A., Von Heyn, R. E., & Sands, C. C. (2010). Seven case studies of individuals expelled from positive-only programs. *The Journal of Behavior Analysis of Offender and Victim Treatment and Prevention, 2*(1), 20.

Kratochwill, T. R., Hitchcock, J., Horner, R. H., Levin, J. R., Odom, S. L., Rindskopf, D. M., & Shadish, W. R. (2010). *Single-case designs technical documentation.* What Works Clearinghouse.

Leaf, J. B., Cihon, J. H., Leaf, R., McEachin, J., Liu, N., Russell, N., Unumb, L., Shapiro, S., & Khosrowshahi, D. (2022). Concerns about ABA-based intervention: An evaluation and recommendations. *Journal of Autism and Developmental Disorders, 52*(6), 2838–2853.

Linscheid, T. R., Iwata, B. A., Ricketts, R. W., Williams, D. E., & Griffin, J. C. (1990). Clinical evaluation of the self-injurious behavior inhibiting system (SIBIS). *Journal of Applied Behavior Analysis, 23*(1), 53–78.

Matson, J. L., & LoVullo, S. V. (2008). A review of behavioral treatments for self-injurious behaviors of persons with autism spectrum disorders. *Behavior Modification, 32*(1), 61–76.

Putnam, R., Miles, B., Liu-Constant, B., Mahoney, P., Ross, R., Ainsleigh, S. A., Vedora, J., Morgan, G., Daly, G., & Guihardi, P. (2021). *Massachusetts Association for Applied Behavior Analysis (MassABA) position statement on the use of electric shock as an intervention in the treatment of individuals with disabilities.* Massachusetts Association for Applied Behavior Analysis.

Steenfeldt-Kristensen, C., Jones, C. A., & Richards, C. (2020). The prevalence of self-injurious behaviour in autism: A meta-analytic study. *Journal of Autism and Developmental Disorders, 50*(11), 3857–3873.

Yadollahikhales, G., Blenkush, N., & Cunningham, M. (2021). Response patterns for individuals receiving contingent skin shock aversion intervention to treat violent self-injurious and assaultive behaviours. *BMJ Case Reports CP, 14*(5), e241204.

Zarcone, J. R., Mullane, M. P., Langdon, P. E., & Brown, I. (2020). Contingent electric shock as a treatment for challenging behavior for people with intellectual and developmental disabilities: Support for the IASSIDD policy statement opposing its use. *Journal of Policy and Practice in Intellectual Disabilities, 17*(4), 291–296.

Index

Solutions YOU WANT | Experts YOU TRUST | Results YOU NEED

INSTITUTES

Corwin Institutes provide regional and virtual events where educators collaborate with peers and learn from industry experts. Prepare to be recharged and motivated!

corwin.com/institutes

ON-SITE PROFESSIONAL LEARNING

Corwin on-site PD is delivered through high-energy keynotes, practical workshops, and custom coaching services designed to support knowledge development and implementation.

www.corwin.com/pd

VIRTUAL PROFESSIONAL LEARNING

Our virtual PD combines live expert facilitation with the flexibility of anytime, anywhere professional learning. See the power of intentionally designed virtual PD.

www.corwin.com/virtualworkshops

CORWIN ONLINE

Online learning designed to engage, inform, challenge, and inspire. Our courses offer practical, classroom-focused instruction that will meet your continuing education needs and enhance your practice.

www.corwinonline.com

PLSN20A8

Visit www.corwin.com

A Sage Company

Helping educators make the greatest impact

CORWIN HAS ONE MISSION: to enhance education through intentional professional learning.

We build long-term relationships with our authors, educators, clients, and associations who partner with us to develop and continuously improve the best evidence-based practices that establish and support lifelong learning.